Marketing Management

CUSTOM EDITION FOR UNIVERSITY OF COLORADO-DENVER
Compiled by Gary R. Schornack

Taken from:
MARKETING MANAGEMENT, ELEVENTH EDITION
Philip Kotler

Philip Kotler

Pearson
Custom
Publishing

Prentice
Hall

Taken from:

Marketing Management, Eleventh Edition
by Philip Kotler
Copyright © 2003, 2000, 1997, 1994, 1991 by Pearson Education, Inc.
Published by Prentice-Hall, Inc.
Upper Saddle River, New Jersey, 07458

This special edition published in cooperation with Pearson Custom Publishing.

Printed in the United States of America

10 9 8 7 6 5 4 3 2 1

Please visit our web site at www.pearsoncustom.com

ISBN 0–536–68064-7

BA 995163

PEARSON CUSTOM PUBLISHING
75 Arlington Street, Suite 300, Boston, MA 02116
A Pearson Education Company

Contents

C H A P T E R

1

defining marketing for the twenty-first century

Kotler on Marketing

The future is not ahead of us. It has already happened. Unfortunately, it is unequally distributed among companies, industries, and nations.

In this chapter we will address the following questions:

- What is the new economy like?
- What are the tasks of marketing?
- What are the major concepts and tools of marketing?
- What orientations do companies exhibit in the marketplace?
- How are companies and marketers responding to the new challenges?

Today it is fashionable to talk about the new economy. We hear that businesses are operating in a globalized economy; that things are moving at a nanosecond pace; that our markets are characterized by hyper-competition; that disruptive technologies are challenging every business; and that business must adapt to the empowered consumer.

The old economy seemed simpler. It was based on the Industrial Revolution and on managing manufacturing industries. Manufacturers applied certain principles and practices for the successful operation of their factories. They standardized products in order to bring down costs. They aimed to continually expand their market size to achieve economies of scale. They tended to replicate their procedures and policies in every *geographic market. The goal was efficiency; and to accomplish this the firm was managed hierar-chically, with a boss on top issuing orders to middle managers, who in turn guided the workers.*

The new economy, in contrast, is based on the Digital Revolution and the management of information. Information has a number of attributes. It can be infinitely differentiated, cus-tomized, and personalized. It can be dispatched to a great number of people who are on a net-work and it can reach them with great speed. To the extent that the information is public and accessible, people will be better informed and able to make better choices.

the new economy

The digital revolution has placed a whole new set of capabilities in the hands of con-sumers and businesses. Consider what consumers have today that they didn't have yesterday:

- *A substantial increase in buying power.* Buyers today are only a click away from comparing competitor prices and product attributes. They can get answers on the Internet in a mat-ter of seconds. They don't need to drive to stores, park, wait on line, and hold discussions with salespeople. On Priceline.com, consumers can even name the price they want to pay for a hotel room, airline ticket, or mortgage, and see if there are any willing suppliers. Business buyers can run a reverse auction where sellers compete during a given time period to capture the buyer's business. Buyers can join with others to aggregate their purchases to achieve deeper volume discounts.
- *A greater variety of available goods and services.* Today a person can order almost anything over the Internet: furniture (Ethan Allen), washing machines (Sears), management con-sulting ("Ernie"), medical advice (cyberdocs). Amazon.com advertises itself as the world's largest bookstore, with over 3 million books; no physical bookstore can match this. Furthermore, buyers can order these goods from anywhere in the world, which helps people living in countries with very limited local offerings to achieve great savings. It also means that buyers in countries with high prices can reduce their costs by ordering in countries with lower prices.
- *A great amount of information about practically anything.* People can read almost any news-paper in any language from anywhere in the world. They can access on-line encyclope-dias, dictionaries, medical information, movie ratings, consumer reports, and countless other information sources.
- *A greater ease in interacting and placing and receiving orders.* Today's buyers can place orders from home, office, or mobile phone 24 hours a day, 7 days a week, and the orders will be delivered to their home or office quickly.
- *An ability to compare notes on products and services.* Today's customers can enter a chat room centered on some area of common interest and exchange information and opinions. Women can visit iVillage to discuss common family problems; movie lovers can visit any number of movie chat rooms to share ideas.

Today's companies also have a new set of capabilities:

- Companies can operate a powerful new information and sales channel with augmented geographical reach to inform and promote their businesses and products. By establishing one or more Web sites, a company can list its products and services, its history, its busi-ness philosophy, its job opportunities, and other information of interest to visitors. Unlike the ads and brochures of the past, the Internet permits them to transmit an almost unlimited amount of information. Companies such as Grainger are putting huge catalogs on their Web sites, making it easy for customers to search for and order products. Each company has the option of turning its Web site into a sales channel as well as an infor-mation channel. Furthermore, since the Internet is worldwide, people from anywhere in the world can learn about the company and place orders.

- Companies can collect fuller and richer information about markets, customers, prospects, and competitors. Not only can companies find abundant information, but they can also conduct fresh marketing research using the Internet. They can arrange for focus groups, send out questionnaires, and gather primary data in several other ways.
- Companies can facilitate and speed up internal communication among their employees. By using the Internet as a private intranet, employees can query one another, seek advice, and download or upload needed information from and to the company's main computer.
- Companies can have two-way communications with customers and prospects, and more efficient transactions. The Internet makes it easy for individuals to send e-mail messages to companies and receive replies, and more companies today are developing extranets with suppliers and distributors for sending and receiving information, placing orders, and making payments more efficiently.
- Companies are now able to send ads, coupons, samples, and information to customers who have requested these items or have given the company permission to send them.
- Companies can customize offerings and services to individual customers. Companies can know the number of visitors to their Web sites and visit frequency. By putting this information into a database and enhancing it with other information, they are in a better position to customize messages, offerings, and services.
- Companies can improve purchasing, recruiting, training, and internal and external communications. All companies are buyers as well as sellers; they can achieve substantial savings in using the Internet to compare sellers' prices, and to purchase materials at auction or by posting their own terms. Companies can recruit new employees through the Internet. Many are also preparing Internet training products that can be downloaded to employees, dealers, and agents so that they can easily be kept up to date.
- Companies can substantially improve logistics and operations for substantial cost savings while improving accuracy and service quality. The Internet provides a more accurate and faster way to send and receive information, orders, transactions, and payments between companies, their business partners, and their customers.

The new capabilities unleashed by the Information Age will lead to substantially new forms of marketing and business. The Industrial Age was characterized by mass-production and mass-consumption, stores overstuffed with inventory, ads everywhere, and rampant discounting. The Information Age promises to lead to more accurate levels of production, more targeted communications, and more relevant pricing.

Here are the views of three leading CEOs on the Internet's impact:

> Every now and then, a technology comes along that is so profound, so universal, that its impact will change everything. It will transform every institution in the world. It will create winners and losers, it will change the way we do business, the way we teach our children, communicate and interact as individuals. —Lou Gerstner, Chairman of IBM.
>
> The Internet ranks as priority No. 1, 2, 3, and 4! . . . Embrace the Internet. Bring me a plan for how you are going to transform your business beyond adding an Internet site. —Jack Welch, former CEO of GE.
>
> Will e-commerce change everything—or just add another small sales channel? The Internet is not just another sales channel. It will transform your business. The future company will operate with a digital nervous system. —Bill Gates, Chairman of Microsoft.

In this book, we want to consider how marketing will change under the impact of these new forces.

Marketing deals with identifying and meeting human and social needs. One of the shortest definitions of marketing is "meeting needs profitably." Whether the marketer is Procter & Gamble, who noticed that people feel overweight and want tasty but less fatty foods, and invented Olestra; or CarMax, who noted that people want more certainty when they buy a used automobile and invented a new system for selling used cars; or IKEA, who noticed that people want good furniture at a substantially lower price and created knock-down furniture—all are motivated to turn a private or social need into a profitable business opportunity. However, marketing is tricky and it has been the Achilles' heel of many formerly prosperous companies. Seemingly invincible businesses such as Sears, Levi's, General Motors, Kodak, and Xerox have confronted newly empowered customers and new competitors, and have had to rethink their business models. Even information-savvy companies such as Cisco Systems, Wal-Mart, Intel, and AOL cannot afford to relax. Jack Welch, GE's brilliant former CEO, repeatedly warned his company: "Change or die."

The companies at greatest risk are those that fail to monitor their customers and competitors and to continuously improve their value offerings. Too many companies have not carefully defined their target market or their value proposition and they compensate by spending an inordinate amount on acquiring new customers, only to lose them. They take a short-term, sales-driven view of their business and ultimately, they fail to satisfy their stockholders, their employees, their suppliers, and their channel partners.

marketing tasks

A recent book entitled *Radical Marketing* praises companies such as Harley-Davidson, Virgin Atlantic Airways, and Boston Beer for succeeding by breaking all the rules of marketing.[1] Instead of commissioning expensive marketing research, spending huge sums on mass advertising, and operating large marketing departments, these companies stretched their limited resources, stayed in close contact with their customers, and created more satisfying solutions to customer needs. They formed buyers' clubs, used creative public relations, and focused on delivering high product quality and winning long-term customer loyalty. (See "Marketing Insight: The Ten Rules of Radical Marketing.")

We can distinguish three stages through which marketing practice might pass:

1. *Entrepreneurial marketing*: Most companies are started by individuals who live by their wits. They visualize an opportunity and knock on every door to gain attention. Jim Koch, founder

marketing **insight**

The Ten Rules of Radical Marketing

In their book *Radical Marketing*, Sam Hill and Glenn Rifkin lay out a set of prescriptive guidelines that can help other companies emulate the radical marketers.

1. *The CEO must own the marketing function.* CEOs of radical marketers never delegate marketing responsibility; they typically act like de facto chief marketing officers.
2. *Make sure the marketing department starts small and flat and stays small and flat.* In order to stay involved with marketing, CEOs must not allow layers of management to grow so numerous that they distance them from the market.
3. *Get face-to-face with the people who matter most—the customers.* For radical marketers, " 'face-to-face' is a mantra." They know the advantages of direct interaction with customers.
4. *Use market research cautiously.* Market research typically tells a marketer what the average customer wants. Radical marketers prefer grassroots techniques.
5. *Hire only passionate missionaries.* Radical marketers "don't have marketers, they have missionaries."
6. *Love and respect your customers.* Radical marketers respect customers as individuals, not as numbers on a spreadsheet.

They recognize that the core customers are responsible for the bulk of their companies' successes.

7. *Create a community of consumers.* Radical marketers "encourage their customers to think of themselves as a community, and of the brand as a unifier of that community."
8. *Rethink the marketing mix.* Radical marketers' marketing techniques often differ dramatically from those used by traditional marketers. For example, traditional marketers seek to reach broad audiences via large-scale advertising, while radical marketers use "surgical strike advertising" characterized by short, targeted ad campaigns.
9. *Celebrate common sense.* Smaller companies with limited resources cannot hope to compete with larger competitors without fresh and different marketing ideas. So radical marketers, for example, limit distribution in order to create loyalty and commitment among their distributors and among their customers.
10. *Be true to the brand.* Radical marketers "are obsessive about brand integrity, and they are fixated on quality."

Source: Sam Hill and Glenn Rifkin, *Radical Marketing* (New York: HarperCollins, 1999), pp. 19–31.

of Boston Beer Company, whose Samuel Adams beer has become a top-selling "craft" beer, started out in 1984 carrying bottles of Samuel Adams from bar to bar to persuade bartenders to carry it. For 10 years he couldn't afford an advertising budget; he sold his beer through direct sales and grassroots public relations. Today his business pulls in $210 million, making it the leader in the craft beer market.

2. *Formulated marketing*: As small companies achieve success, they inevitably move toward more formulated marketing. Boston Beer now spends considerable sums on TV advertising, employs dozens of salespeople, and carries on sophisticated marketing research. It has discovered that continued success requires setting up and managing a capable marketing department.

3. *Intrepreneurial marketing*: Many large companies get stuck in formulated marketing, poring over the latest Nielsen numbers, scanning market research reports, trying to fine-tune dealer relations and advertising messages. These companies lack the creativity and passion of the guerrilla marketers in the entrepreneurial stage.[2] Their brand and product managers need to get out of the office, start living with their customers, and visualize new ways to add value to their customers' lives.

The bottom line is that effective marketing can take many forms. There will be a constant tension between the formulated side of marketing and the creative side. It is easier to learn the formulated side, which will occupy most of our attention in this book; but we will also describe how real creativity and passion operate in many companies.

the scope of marketing

Marketing is typically seen as the task of creating, promoting, and delivering goods and services to consumers and businesses. Marketers are skilled in stimulating demand for a company's products, but this is too limited a view of the tasks marketers perform. Just as production and logistics professionals are responsible for supply management, marketers are responsible for demand management. Marketing managers seek to influence the level, timing, and composition of demand to meet the organization's objectives. Table 1.1 distinguishes eight different states of demand and the corresponding tasks facing marketing managers.

Marketing people are involved in marketing 10 types of entities: goods, services, experiences, events, persons, places, properties, organizations, information, and ideas.

GOODS   Physical goods constitute the bulk of most countries' production and marketing effort. Each year U.S. companies alone market billions of canned and frozen food products, millions of tons of steel, millions of hair dryers, cars, television sets, machines, and various other mainstays of a modern economy. Not only do companies market their goods, but thanks to the Internet, even individuals can market goods.

eBay   Today eBay is the world's largest person-to-person online trading community. It offers efficient one-to-one trading in an auction format on the Web. Individuals can use eBay to sell or buy items in thousands of categories: paintings, stamps, coins, sports memorabilia, toys, dolls. Each day over 400,000 new items are offered, and more than 3.5 million auctions are in progress.

SERVICES   As economies advance, a growing proportion of their activities is focused on the production of services. The U.S. economy today consists of a 70–30 services-to-goods mix. Services include the work of airlines, hotels, car rental firms, barbers and beauticians, maintenance and repair people, dog kennels and dog therapists, as well as professionals working within or for companies, such as accountants, lawyers, engineers, doctors, software programmers, and management consultants. Many market offerings consist of a variable mix of goods and services. At the pure services end would be a psychiatrist listening to a patient or a quartet performing Mozart; at another level would be the telephone call that is supported by a huge investment in plant and equipment; and at a more tangible level would be a fast-food establishment where the customer consumes both a product and a service.

table **1.1**		
Demand States and Marketing Tasks	1. *Negative demand.*	A major part of the market dislikes the product and may even pay a price to avoid it—vaccinations, dental work, vasectomies, and gallbladder operations, for instance. Employers have a negative demand for ex-convicts and alcoholics as employees. The marketing task is to analyze why the market dislikes the product and whether a marketing program consisting of product redesign, lower prices, and more positive promotion can change beliefs and attitudes.
	2. *No demand.*	Target consumers may be unaware of or uninterested in the product. Farmers may not be interested in a new farming method, and college students may not be interested in foreign-language courses. The marketing task is to find ways to connect the benefits of the product with people's natural needs and interests.
	3. *Latent demand.*	Consumers may share a strong need that cannot be satisfied by any existing product. There is a strong latent demand for harmless cigarettes, safer neighborhoods, and more fuel-efficient cars. The marketing task is to measure the size of the potential market and develop goods and services to satisfy the demand.
	4. *Declining demand.*	Every organization, sooner or later, faces declining demand for one or more of its products. Churches have seen membership decline; private colleges have seen applications fall. The marketer must analyze the causes of the decline and determine whether demand can be restimulated by new target markets, by changing product features, or by more effective communication. The marketing task is to reverse declining demand through creative remarketing.
	5. *Irregular demand.*	Many organizations face demand that varies on a seasonal, daily, or even hourly basis. Much mass-transit equipment is idle during off-peak hours and insufficient during peak travel hours. Museums are undervisited on weekdays and overcrowded on weekends. The marketing task, called **synchromarketing,** is to find ways to alter the pattern of demand through flexible pricing, promotion, and other incentives.
	6. *Full demand.*	Organizations face full demand when they are pleased with their volume of business. The marketing task is to maintain the current level of demand in the face of changing consumer preferences and increasing competition. The organization must maintain or improve its quality and continually measure consumer satisfaction.
	7. *Overfull demand.*	Some organizations face a demand level that is higher than they can or want to handle. Yosemite National Park is terribly overcrowded in the summer. The marketing task, called **demarketing,** requires finding ways to reduce demand temporarily or permanently. General demarketing seeks to discourage overall demand and includes such steps as raising prices and reducing promotion and service. Selective demarketing consists of trying to reduce demand from those parts of the market that are less profitable.
	8. *Unwholesome demand.*	Unwholesome products will attract organized efforts to discourage their consumption. Unselling campaigns have been conducted against cigarettes, alcohol, hard drugs, handguns, X-rated movies, and large families. The marketing task is to get people who like something to give it up, using such tools as fear messages, price hikes, and reduced availability.

Sources: See Philip Kotler, "The Major Tasks of Marketing Management," *Journal of Marketing* (October 1973): 42–49; and Philip Kotler and Sidney J. Levy, "Demarketing, Yes, Demarketing," *Harvard Business Review* (November–December 1971): 74–80.

EXPERIENCES   By orchestrating several services and goods, a firm can create, stage, and market experiences. Walt Disney World's Magic Kingdom represents experiential marketing: customers visit a fairy kingdom, a pirate ship, or a haunted house. So does the Hard Rock Café. There is also a market for customized experiences, such as spending a week at a baseball camp playing with some retired baseball greats, paying to conduct the Chicago Symphony Orchestra for five minutes, or climbing Mount Everest.[3]

EVENTS   Marketers promote time-based events, such as the Olympics, company anniversaries, major trade shows, sports events, and artistic performances. There is a whole profession of meeting planners who work out the details of an event and make sure it comes off perfectly.

PERSONS   Celebrity marketing is a major business. Years ago, someone seeking fame would hire a press agent to plant stories in newspapers and magazines. Today every major film star has an agent, a personal manager, and ties to a public relations agency. Artists, musicians, CEOs, physicians, high-profile lawyers and financiers, and other professionals are also getting help from celebrity marketers.[4] People like Madonna and the late Andy Warhol have done a masterful job of marketing themselves. Management consultant Tom Peters, himself a master at self-branding, has advised each person to become a "brand."

PLACES   Places—cities, states, regions, and whole nations—compete actively to attract tourists, factories, company headquarters, and new residents.[5] Stratford, Ontario, in Canada was a fairly run-down city with one asset: its name and a river called Avon. This became the basis for an annual Shakespeare festival that put Stratford on the tourist map. Ireland has been an outstanding place marketer, having attracted more than 500 companies to locate their plants there. It operates the Irish Development Board, the Irish Tourist Board, and the Irish Export Board, responsible for inward investment, tourists, and exports, respectively. Place marketers include economic development specialists, real estate agents, commercial banks, local business associations, and advertising and public relations agencies.

PROPERTIES   Properties are intangible rights of ownership of either real property (real estate) or financial property (stocks and bonds). Properties are bought and sold, and this requires marketing. Real estate agents work for property owners or sellers or buy residential or commercial real estate. Investment companies and banks are involved in marketing securities to both institutional and individual investors.

ORGANIZATIONS   Organizations actively work to build a strong, favorable image in the minds of their target publics. Companies spend money on corporate identity ads. Philips, the Dutch electronics company, puts out ads with the tag line "Let's Make Things Better." The Body Shop and Ben & Jerry's gained attention by promoting social causes. Other companies owe their visibility to a dramatic leader, such as Virgin's Richard Branson or Nike's Phil Knight. Universities, museums, and performing arts organizations all use marketing to boost their public images and to compete for audiences and funds.

INFORMATION   Information can be produced and marketed as a product. This is essentially what schools and universities produce and distribute at a price to parents, students, and communities. Encyclopedias and most nonfiction books market information. Magazines such as *Road and Track* and *Byte* supply information about the car and computer worlds, respectively. We buy software and CDs and we visit the Internet for information. The production, packaging, and distribution of information is one of our society's major industries.[6]

IDEAS   Every market offering includes a basic idea. Charles Revson of Revlon observed: "In the factory, we make cosmetics; in the store we sell hope." Products and services are

Marketing
MEMO

Marketers' Frequently Asked Questions

1. How can we spot and choose the right market segment(s) to serve?
2. How can we differentiate our offering from competitive offerings?
3. How should we respond to customers who press us for a lower price?
4. How can we compete against lower-cost, lower-price competitors from here and abroad?
5. How far can we go in customizing our offering for each customer?
6. What are the major ways in which we can grow our business?
7. How can we build stronger brands?
8. How can we reduce the cost of customer acquisition?
9. How can we keep our customers loyal for a longer period?
10. How can we tell which customers are more important?
11. How can we measure the payback from advertising, sales promotion, and public relations?
12. How can we improve sales force productivity?
13. How can we establish multiple channels and yet manage channel conflict?
14. How can we get the other company departments to be more customer-oriented?

platforms for delivering some idea or benefit. Social marketers are busy promoting such ideas as "Say no to drugs," "Save the rainforest," "Exercise daily," or "Avoid fatty foods."

the decisions marketers make

Marketing managers face a host of decisions, from major ones such as what product features to design into a new product, how many salespeople to hire, or how much to spend on advertising, to minor decisions such as the exact wording or color for new packaging. The "Marketing Memo: Marketers' Frequently Asked Questions" lists many of the questions marketing managers ask, which will be examined in this book.

These questions vary in importance in different marketplaces. Consider the following four markets: consumer, business, global, and nonprofit.

CONSUMER MARKETS   Companies selling mass consumer goods and services such as soft drinks, toothpaste, television sets, and air travel spend a great deal of time trying to establish a superior brand image. This requires getting a clear sense of their target customers and what need(s) their product will meet, and communicating brand positioning forcefully and creatively. Much of a brand's strength depends on developing a superior product and packaging and backing it with promotion and reliable service. Consumer marketers decide on the features, quality level, distribution coverage, and promotion expenditures that will help their brand achieve a number-one or -two position in their target market.

BUSINESS MARKETS   Companies selling business goods and services face well-trained and well-informed professional buyers who are skilled in evaluating competitive offerings. Business buyers buy goods for their utility in enabling them to make or resell a product to others, and they purchase products to make profits. Business marketers must demonstrate how their products will help customers achieve higher revenue or lower costs. Advertising plays a role, but a stronger role is played by sales force, price, and the company's reputation for reliability and quality.

GLOBAL MARKETS   Companies selling goods and services in the global marketplace face additional decisions and challenges. They must decide which countries to enter; how to enter each country (as an exporter, licenser, joint venture partner, contract manufacturer, or solo manufacturer); how to adapt their product and service features to each country; how to price their products in different countries in a narrow enough band to avoid creating a gray market for their goods; and how to adapt their communications to fit the cultural practices of each country. These decisions must be made in the face of a different legal system; different styles of negotiation; different requirements for buying, owning, and disposing of property; a currency that might fluctuate in value; a different language; and conditions of corruption or political favoritism.

NONPROFIT AND GOVERNMENTAL MARKETS   Companies selling their goods to nonprofit organizations such as churches, universities, charitable organizations, or government agencies need to price carefully because these organizations have limited purchasing power. Lower prices affect the features and quality that the seller can build into the offering. Much government purchasing calls for bids, with the lowest bid being favored, in the absence of extenuating factors.

marketing concepts and tools

Marketing boasts a rich array of concepts and tools. We will first define marketing, then describe its major concepts and tools.

defining marketing

We can distinguish between a social and a managerial definition of marketing. A social definition shows the role marketing plays in society. One marketer said that marketing's role is to "deliver a higher standard of living." Here is a social definition that serves our purpose: **Marketing** is a societal process by which individuals and groups obtain what they need and want through creating, offering, and freely exchanging products and services of value with others. For a managerial definition, marketing has often been described as "the art of selling products," but people are surprised when they hear that the most important part of marketing is not selling! Selling is only the tip of the marketing iceberg.

Peter Drucker, a leading management theorist, puts it this way:

> There will always, one can assume, be need for some selling. But the aim of marketing is to make selling superfluous. The aim of marketing is to know and understand the customer so well that the product or service fits him and sells itself. Ideally, marketing should result in a customer who is ready to buy. All that should be needed then is to make the product or service available.[7]

When Sony designed its Walkman, when Nintendo designed a superior video game, and when Toyota introduced its Lexus automobile, these manufacturers were swamped with orders because they had designed the "right" product based on careful marketing homework.

The American Marketing Association offers the following definition: Marketing is the process of planning and executing the conception, pricing, promotion, and distribution of ideas, goods, and services to create exchanges that satisfy individual and organizational goals.[8] Coping with exchange processes calls for a considerable amount of work and skill. Marketing management takes place when at least one party to a potential exchange thinks about the means of achieving desired responses from other parties. We see **marketing management** as the art and science of choosing target markets and getting, keeping, and growing customers through creating, delivering, and communicating superior customer value.

core marketing concepts

Marketing can be further understood by defining several of its core concepts.

TARGET MARKETS AND SEGMENTATION   A marketer can rarely satisfy everyone in a market. Not everyone likes the same soft drink, hotel room, restaurant, automobile, college, and movie. Therefore, marketers start by dividing up the market. They identify and profile distinct groups of buyers who might prefer or require varying product and services mixes. *Market segments* can be identified by examining demographic, psychographic, and behavioral differences among buyers. The marketer then decides which segments present the greatest opportunity—which are its **target markets**. For each chosen target market, the firm develops a *market offering*. The offering is positioned in the minds of the target buyers as delivering some central benefit(s). For example, Volvo develops its cars for buyers to whom automobile safety is a major concern. Volvo, therefore, positions its car as the safest a customer can buy.

Traditionally, a "market" was a physical place where buyers and sellers gathered to buy and sell goods. Economists now describe a market as a collection of buyers and sellers who transact over a particular product or product class (the housing market or grain market); but marketers view the sellers as constituting the industry and the buyers as constituting the market. Figure 1.1 shows the relationship between the industry and the market. Sellers and buyers are connected by four flows. The sellers send goods and services and communications (ads, direct mail) to the market; in return they receive money and information (attitudes, sales data). The inner loop shows an exchange of money for goods and services; the outer loop shows an exchange of information.

MARKETPLACE, MARKETSPACE, AND METAMARKET   Businesspeople often use the term *market* to cover various groupings of customers. They talk about need markets (the diet-seeking market), product markets (the shoe market), demographic markets (the youth market), and geographic markets (the French market); or they extend the concept to cover other markets, such as voter markets, labor markets, and donor markets.

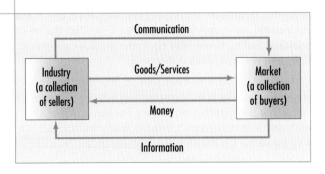

figure **1.1**

A Simple Marketing System

Modern economies abound in markets. Five basic markets and their connecting flows are shown in Figure 1.2. Manufacturers go to resource markets (raw-material markets, labor markets, money markets), buy resources and turn them into goods and services, and then sell finished products to intermediaries, who sell them to consumers. Consumers sell their labor and receive money with which they pay for goods and services. The government collects tax revenues to buy goods from resource, manufacturer, and intermediary markets and uses these goods and services to provide public services. Each nation's economy and the global economy consist of complex interacting sets of markets linked through exchange processes.

Today we can distinguish between a *marketplace* and *marketspace*. The **marketplace** is physical, as when one goes shopping in a store; **marketspace** is digital, as when one goes shopping on the Internet. Many observers believe that an increased amount of purchasing will shift into marketspace.[9]

Mohan Sawhney has proposed the concept of a **metamarket** to describe a cluster of complementary products and services that are closely related in the minds of consumers but are spread across a diverse set of industries. The automobile metamarket consists of automobile manufacturers, new car and used car dealers, financing companies, insurance companies, mechanics, spare parts dealers, service shops, auto magazines, classified auto ads in newspapers, and auto sites on the Internet. In purchasing a car, a buyer

figure **1.2**

Structure of Flows in a Modern Exchange Economy

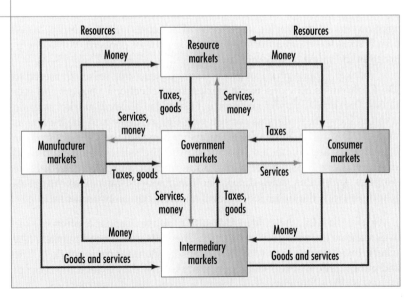

will get involved in many parts of this metamarket, and this has created an opportunity for metamediaries to assist buyers to move seamlessly through these groups, although they are disconnected in physical space. One example is Edmund's (*www.edmunds.com*), a Web site where a car buyer can find the stated features and prices of different automobiles and easily click to other sites to search for the lowest-price dealer, for financing, for car accessories, and for used cars at bargain prices. Metamediaries can also serve other metamarkets such as the home ownership market, the parenting and baby care market, and the wedding market.[10]

MARKETERS AND PROSPECTS   A **marketer** is someone seeking a response (attention, a purchase, a vote, a donation) from another party, called the **prospect**. If two parties are seeking to sell something to each other, we call them both marketers.

NEEDS, WANTS, AND DEMANDS   The marketer must try to understand the target market's needs, wants, and demands. **Needs** are the basic human requirements. People need food, air, water, clothing, and shelter to survive. People also have strong needs for recreation, education, and entertainment. These needs become **wants** when they are directed to specific objects that might satisfy the need. An American needs food but wants a hamburger, French fries, and a soft drink. A person in Mauritius needs food but wants a mango, rice, lentils, and beans. Wants are shaped by one's society. **Demands** are wants for specific products backed by an ability to pay. Many people want a Mercedes; only a few are able and willing to buy one. Companies must measure not only how many people want their product but also how many would actually be willing and able to buy it.

These distinctions shed light on the frequent criticism that "marketers create needs" or "marketers get people to buy things they don't want." Marketers do not create needs: Needs preexist marketers. Marketers, along with other societal factors, influence wants. Marketers might promote the idea that a Mercedes would satisfy a person's need for social status. They do not, however, create the need for social status.

PRODUCT, OFFERING, AND BRAND   Companies address needs by putting forth a **value proposition**, a set of benefits they offer to customers to satisfy their needs. The intangible value proposition is made physical by an **offering**, which can be a combination of products, services, information, and experiences.

A **brand** is an offering from a known source. A brand name such as McDonald's carries many associations in the minds of people: hamburgers, fun, children, fast food, Golden Arches. These associations make up the **brand image**. All companies strive to build brand strength—that is, a strong, favorable brand image.

VALUE AND SATISFACTION   The offering will be successful if it delivers value and satisfaction to the target buyer. The buyer chooses between different offerings on the basis of which is perceived to deliver the most value. Value can be seen as primarily a combination of quality, service, and price (QSP), called the **customer value triad**. Value increases with quality and service and decreases with price.

More specifically, we can define **value** as a ratio between what the customer gets and what he gives. The customer gets benefits and assumes costs. The benefits include functional benefits and emotional benefits. The costs include monetary costs, time costs, energy costs, and psychic costs. Thus value is given by:

$$\text{Value} = \frac{\text{Benefits}}{\text{Costs}} = \frac{\text{Functional benefits} + \text{Emotional benefits}}{\text{Monetary costs} + \text{Time costs} + \text{Energy costs} + \text{Psychic costs}}$$

The marketer can increase the value of the customer offering in several ways:

- Raise benefits
- Reduce costs
- Raise benefits and reduce costs
- Raise benefits by more than the raise in costs
- Lower benefits by less than the reduction in costs

The customer who is choosing between two value offerings, V1 and V2, will examine the ratio V1:V2. She will favor V1 if the ratio is larger than one; she will favor V2 if the ratio is smaller than one; and she will be indifferent if the ratio equals one.

EXCHANGE AND TRANSACTIONS   Exchange is only one of four ways in which a person can obtain a product. One can self-produce the product or service, as when one hunts, fishes, or gathers fruit. One can use force to get a product, as in a holdup or burglary. One can beg, as happens when a homeless person asks for food. Or one can offer a product, a service, or money in exchange for something he or she desires.

Exchange, which is the core concept of marketing, is the process of obtaining a desired product from someone by offering something in return. For exchange potential to exist, five conditions must be satisfied:

1. There are at least two parties.
2. Each party has something that might be of value to the other party.
3. Each party is capable of communication and delivery.
4. Each party is free to accept or reject the exchange offer.
5. Each party believes it is appropriate or desirable to deal with the other party.

Whether exchange actually takes place depends on whether the two parties can agree on terms that will leave them both better off (or at least not worse off) than before. Exchange is a value-creating process because it normally leaves both parties better off.

Two parties are engaged in exchange if they are negotiating—trying to arrive at mutually agreeable terms. When an agreement is reached, we say that a transaction takes place. A **transaction** is a trade of values between two or more parties: A gives X to B and receives Y in return. Smith sells Jones a television set and Jones pays $400 to Smith. This is a classic monetary transaction; but transactions do not require money as one of the traded values. A **barter** transaction involves trading goods or services for other goods or services, as when lawyer Jones writes a will for physician Smith in return for a medical examination.

A transaction involves several dimensions: at least two things of value, agreed-upon conditions, a time of agreement, and a place of agreement. A legal system supports and enforces compliance on the part of the transactors. Without a law of contracts, people would approach transactions with some distrust, and everyone would lose.

A transaction differs from a transfer. In a **transfer**, A gives X to B but does not receive anything tangible in return. Gifts, subsidies, and charitable contributions are all transfers. Transfer behavior can also be understood through the concept of exchange. Typically, the transferer expects to receive something in exchange for his or her gift—for example, gratitude or seeing changed behavior in the recipient. Professional fundraisers provide benefits to donors, such as thank-you notes, donor magazines, and invitations to events. Marketers have broadened the concept of marketing to include the study of transfer behavior as well as transaction behavior.

In the most generic sense, marketers seek to elicit a **behavioral response** from another party. A business firm wants a purchase, a political candidate wants a vote, a church wants an active member, and a social-action group wants the passionate adoption of some cause. Marketing consists of actions undertaken to elicit desired responses from a target audience.

To make successful exchanges, marketers analyze what each party expects from the transaction. Simple exchange situations can be mapped by showing the two actors and the wants and offerings flowing between them. Suppose Caterpillar, the world's largest manufacturer of earth-moving equipment, researches the benefits that a typical construction company wants when it buys earth-moving equipment. These benefits, listed at the top of the exchange map in Figure 1.3, include high-quality equipment, a fair price, on-time delivery, good financing terms, and good parts and service. The items on this want list are not equally important and may vary from buyer to buyer. One of Caterpillar's tasks is to discover the relative importance of these different wants to the buyer.

Caterpillar also has a want list. It wants a good price for the equipment, on-time payment, and good word of mouth. If there is a sufficient match or overlap in the want

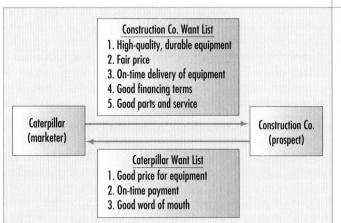

Two–Party Exchange Map Showing Want Lists of Both Parties

lists, a basis for a transaction exists. Caterpillar's task is to formulate an offer that motivates the construction company to buy Caterpillar equipment. The construction company might in turn make a counteroffer. This process of negotiation leads to mutually acceptable terms or a decision not to transact.

RELATIONSHIPS AND NETWORKS   Transaction marketing is part of a larger idea called relationship marketing. **Relationship marketing** has the aim of building mutually satisfying long-term relations with key parties—customers, suppliers, distributors—in order to earn and retain their business.[11] Marketers accomplish this by promising and delivering high-quality products and services at fair prices to the other parties over time. Relationship marketing builds strong economic, technical, and social ties among the parties. It cuts down on transaction costs and time. In the most successful cases, transactions move from being negotiated each time to being a matter of routine.

The ultimate outcome of relationship marketing is the building of a unique company asset called a marketing network. A **marketing network** consists of the company and its supporting stakeholders (customers, employees, suppliers, distributors, retailers, ad agencies, university scientists, and others) with whom it has built mutually profitable business relationships. Increasingly, competition is not between companies but between marketing networks, with the prize going to the company that has built the better network. The operating principle is simple: Build an effective network of relationships with key stakeholders, and profits will follow.[12]

MARKETING CHANNELS   To reach a target market, the marketer uses three kinds of marketing channels. *Communication channels* deliver and receive messages from target buyers, and include newspapers, magazines, radio, television, mail, telephone, billboards, posters, fliers, CDs, audiotapes, and the Internet. Beyond these, communications are conveyed by facial expressions and clothing, the look of retail stores, and many other media. Marketers are increasingly adding dialogue channels (e-mail and toll-free numbers) to counterbalance the more normal monologue channels (such as ads).

The marketer uses *distribution channels* to display, sell, or deliver the physical product or service(s) to the buyer or user. They include distributors, wholesalers, retailers, and agents.

The marketer also uses *service channels* to carry out transactions with potential buyers. Service channels include warehouses, transportation companies, banks, and insurance companies that facilitate transactions. Marketers clearly face a design problem in choosing the best mix of communication, distribution, and service channels for their offerings.

SUPPLY CHAIN   Whereas marketing channels connect the marketer to the target buyers, the **supply chain** describes a longer channel stretching from raw materials to components to final products that are carried to final buyers. The supply chain for women's purses starts with hides, and moves through tanning operations, cutting operations, manufacturing, and the marketing channels bringing products to customers. The supply chain represents a value delivery system. Each company captures only a certain percentage of the total value generated by the supply chain. When a company acquires competitors or moves upstream or downstream, its aim is to capture a higher percentage of supply chain value.

COMPETITION   **Competition** includes all the actual and potential rival offerings and substitutes that a buyer might consider. Suppose an automobile company is planning to buy steel for its cars. Figure 1.4 shows several levels of competitors. The car manufacturer can buy steel from U.S. Steel or other integrated steel mills in the United States or abroad; or buy steel from a minimill such as Nucor at a cost savings; or buy aluminum for certain parts of the car to lighten the cars' weight; or buy engineered plastics for bumpers instead of steel. Clearly, U.S. Steel would be thinking too narrowly of competition if it thought only of other integrated steel companies. In fact, U.S. Steel is more likely to be hurt in the long run by substitute products than by its immediate steel company rivals. It must also consider whether to make substitute materials or stick only to those applications where steel offers superior performance.

We can broaden the picture further by distinguishing four levels of competition, based on the degree of product substitutability:

1. *Brand competition.* A company sees its competitors as other companies offering similar products and services to the same customers at similar prices. Volkswagen might see its major com-

figure **1.4**

U.S. Steel Radar Screen

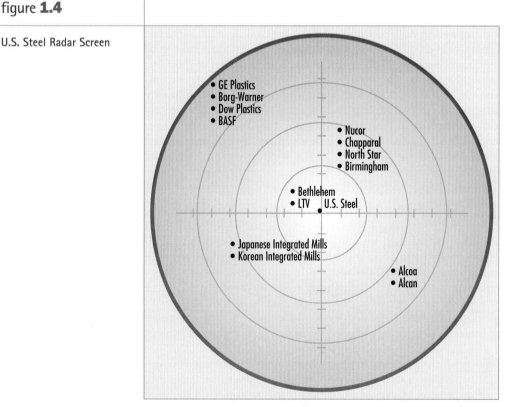

Source: Adrian V. Slywotzky, *Value Migration* (Boston: Harvard Business School Press, 1996), p. 99

petitors as Toyota, Honda, Renault, and other manufacturers of medium-priced automobiles. It would not see itself as competing with Mercedes or with Hyundai.

2. *Industry competition.* A company sees its competitors as all companies making the same product or class of products. Volkswagen would see itself as competing against all other automobile manufacturers.

3. *Form competition.* A company sees its competitors as all companies manufacturing products that supply the same service. Volkswagen would see itself competing against not only other automobile manufacturers, but also against manufacturers of motorcycles, bicycles, and trucks.

4. *Generic competition.* A company sees its competitors as all companies that compete for the same consumer dollars. Volkswagen would see itself competing with companies that sell major consumer durables, foreign vacations, and new homes.

MARKETING ENVIRONMENT   Competition represents only one force in the environment in which the marketer operates. The marketing environment consists of the task environment and the broad environment.

The **task environment** includes the immediate actors involved in producing, distributing, and promoting the offering. The main actors are the company, suppliers, distributors, dealers, and the target customers. Included in the supplier group are material suppliers and service suppliers such as marketing research agencies, advertising agencies, banking and insurance companies, transportation, and telecommunications companies. Included with distributors and dealers are agents, brokers, manufacturer representatives, and others who facilitate finding and selling to customers.

The **broad environment** consists of six components: demographic environment, economic environment, natural environment, technological environment, political-legal environment, and social-cultural environment. These environments contain forces that can have a major impact on the actors in the task environment. Market actors must pay close attention to the trends and developments in these environments and make timely adjustments to their marketing strategies. (See "Marketing for the New Economy: A Snapshot of a Country on the Move.")

MARKETING PROGRAM   The marketer's task is to build a marketing program or plan to achieve the company's desired objectives. The **marketing program** consists of numerous decisions on the mix of marketing tools to use. The **marketing mix** is the set of marketing tools the firm uses to pursue its marketing objectives in the target market.[13]

marketing for the **new economy**

A Snapshot of a Country on the Move

The 2000 U.S. census provides an in-depth look at the population swings, demographic groups, regional migrations, and changing family structure of 281,421,906 people. In addition to its great social and political significance, the census is also an invaluable marketing planning tool. Census marketer Claritas cross-references census figures with consumer surveys and its own grassroots research for clients such as Procter & Gamble Co., Dow Jones & Co., and Ford Motor Co. Partnering with "list houses" that provide customer phone and address information, Claritas can help firms select and purchase mailing lists with specific clusters.

Hyundai relies heavily on census data to develop targeted marketing that maximizes its advertising budget. Working with Claritas software, Hyundai is able to target areas of the country with the most promising customer makeup. For instance, the software enabled Hyundai to determine which zip codes across the country were likely to be interested in a test-drive offer mailing. Within weeks of the mailing, the number of test drives increased, as did sales. More important, the targeted marketing reduced Hyundai's cost per sale by half.

More companies than ever before are turning to the census for clues about consumers. Starbucks uses census data as part of the calculations for site selection for new stores. Blockbuster decides what types of movies and video games to stock in a particular store based on the results of the census. As statistical models and computer algorithms become more sophisticated, the U.S. census is likely to become an indispensable marketing tool.

Source: Amy Merrick, "Counting on the Census," *Wall Street Journal*, February 14, 2001, B1.

figure **1.5**

The Four P Components
of the Marketing Mix

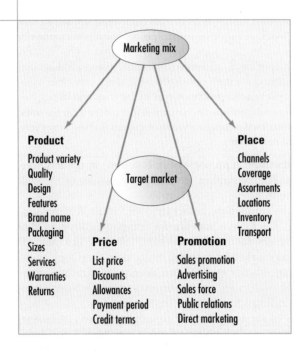

McCarthy classified these tools into four broad groups that he called the four Ps of marketing: product, price, place, and promotion.[14]

The particular marketing variables under each P are shown in Figure 1.5. Marketing-mix decisions must be made for influencing the trade channels as well as the final consumers. Figure 1.6 shows the company preparing an offering mix of products, services, and prices, and utilizing a promotion mix of sales promotion, advertising, sales force, public relations, direct mail, telemarketing, and Internet to reach the trade channels and the target customers.

The firm can change its price, sales force size, and advertising expenditures in the short run. It can develop new products and modify its distribution channels only in the

figure **1.6**

Marketing–Mix Strategy

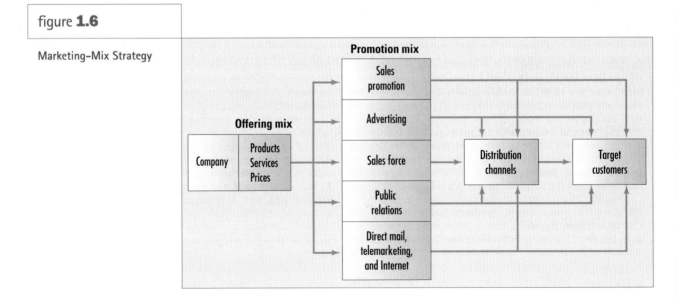

long run. Thus the firm typically makes fewer period-to-period marketing-mix changes in the short run than the number of marketing-mix decision variables might suggest.

Note that the four Ps represent the sellers' view of the marketing tools available for influencing buyers. From a buyer's point of view, each marketing tool is designed to deliver a customer benefit. Robert Lauterborn suggested that the sellers' four Ps correspond to the customers' four Cs.[15]

Four Ps	Four Cs
Product	Customer solution
Price	Customer cost
Place	Convenience
Promotion	Communication

Winning companies will be those that can meet customer needs economically and conveniently and with effective communication.

company orientations toward the marketplace

We have defined *marketing management* as the conscious effort to achieve desired exchange outcomes with target markets, but what philosophy should guide a company's marketing efforts? What relative weights should be given to the interests of the organization, the customers, and society? Very often these interests conflict.

Dexter   One of Dexter Corporation's most popular products was a profitable grade of paper that prevented tea bags from disintegrating in hot water. Unfortunately, the materials used to produce the paper accounted for 98 percent of Dexter's annual hazardous wastes. Dexter assigned an employee task force representing the company's environmental, legal, R&D, and marketing departments to solve the problem. The task force succeeded, and the company increased its market share and virtually eliminated hazardous waste in the process.[16]

Clearly, marketing activities should be carried out under a well-thought-out philosophy of efficiency, effectiveness, and social responsibility. However, there are six competing concepts under which organizations conduct marketing activities: the production concept, product concept, selling concept, marketing concept, customer concept, and societal marketing concept.

the production concept

The production concept is one of the oldest concepts in business. The **production concept** holds that consumers will prefer products that are widely available and inexpensive. Managers of production-oriented businesses concentrate on achieving high production efficiency, low costs, and mass-distribution. They assume that consumers are primarily interested in product availability and low prices. This orientation makes sense in developing countries, where consumers are more interested in obtaining the product than in its features. It is also used when a company wants to expand the market.

Intel   In a 1965 edition of the journal *Electronics*, Intel cofounder Gordon Moore identified Moore's Law, which states that the density of transistors per square inch of a computer microprocessor doubles every 18 months. The more transistors contained by a chip, the more powerful the chip is. For Intel to stay on schedule with the Moore's Law cycle required investment in research and technology, as well as construction of new factories for each successive generation of microprocessor. Over the next 35 years, the company's computer chip production cycles obeyed Moore's Law. Production increased tremendously, prices came down, and Intel generated enormous profits as a result. By the mid-1990s, its processors could be found in more than 80 percent of the world's PCs.[17]

Some service organizations also operate on the production concept. Many medical and dental practices are organized on assembly-line principles, as are some government agencies (such as unemployment offices and license bureaus). Although this management orientation can handle many cases per hour, it is open to charges of impersonal and poor-quality service.

the product concept   *2/c*

Other businesses are guided by the **product concept**, which holds that consumers will favor those products that offer the most quality, performance, or innovative features. Managers in these organizations focus on making superior products and improving them over time. They assume that buyers admire well-made products and can evaluate quality and performance. However, these managers are sometimes caught up in a love affair with their products. Management might commit the "better-mousetrap" fallacy, believing that a better mousetrap will lead people to beat a path to its door. Such was the case when WebTV was launched during Christmas 1996 to disappointing results.

WebTV   It seemed like a couch potato's dream: A TV with a set-top box that allows you to surf the Web and watch TV. Yet, despite a $50-million promotional blitz by WebTV and partners Sony and Philips Electronics, only 50,000 subscribers signed up. Nothing was wrong with the product; the problem was the wrong marketing message. Couch potatoes want to be entertained, whereas computer users want to surf the Web and make use of multimedia, which the underpowered processor in the WebTV box had difficulty handling. A revamped campaign emphasized entertainment over education, and attracted over one million total subscribers by 2000. After the successful debut of digital video recorders that same year, Microsoft, now owner of WebTV, switched to a more interactive strategy. The company offered a new service, called UltimateTV, which combined satellite TV technology and a video recorder unit to provide interactive features for game shows, sports broadcasts, and advertising, as well as e-mail and Internet access.[18]

Product-oriented companies often trust that their engineers can design exceptional products. They get little or no customer input, and very often they will not even examine competitors' products. A General Motors executive said years ago: "How can the public know what kind of car they want until they see what is available?" GM's designers and engineers would design the new car. Then manufacturing would make it. The finance department would price it. Finally, marketing and sales would try to sell it. No wonder the car required such a hard sell! Today GM asks customers what they value in a car and includes marketing people in the very beginning stages of design.

The product concept can lead to what Theodore Levitt called "marketing myopia."[19] He pointed out that customers do not buy drill bits—they buy ways to make holes. Railroad management thought that travelers wanted trains and overlooked the growing competition for transportation from airlines, buses, trucks, and automobiles. Coca-Cola, focused on its soft-drink business, missed seeing the market for coffee bars and fresh-fruit juice bars that eventually impinged on its soft-drink business. McDonald's is in danger of overfocusing on its hamburger business while many diners are turning to sandwiches, pizza, tacos, and other fast foods. These organizations are looking into a mirror when they should be looking out of the window.

the selling concept   *3/c*

The selling concept is another common business orientation. The **selling concept** holds that consumers and businesses, if left alone, will ordinarily not buy enough of the organization's products. The organization must, therefore, undertake an aggressive selling and promotion effort. This concept assumes that consumers typically show buying inertia or resistance and must be coaxed into buying. It also assumes that the company has a whole battery of effective selling and promotion tools to stimulate more buying. The selling concept is epitomized by the thinking of Sergio Zyman, Coca-Cola's former vice president of marketing: The purpose of marketing is to sell more stuff to more people more often for more money in order to make more profit.[21]

The selling concept is practiced most aggressively with unsought goods, goods that buyers normally do not think of buying, such as insurance, encyclopedias, and funeral plots. These industries have perfected various sales techniques to locate prospects and hard sell them on their products' benefits. The selling concept is also practiced in the nonprofit area by fund-raisers, college admissions offices, and political parties.

A political party "sells" its candidate to voters. The candidate moves through voting precincts from early morning to late evening, shaking hands, kissing babies, meeting donors, and making speeches. Countless dollars are spent on radio and television advertising, posters, and mailings. The candidate's flaws are concealed from the public because the aim is to make the sale, not worry about postpurchase satisfaction. After the election, the new official continues to take a sales-oriented view. There is little research into what the public wants and a lot of selling to get the public to accept policies the politician and the party want.[21]

Most firms practice the selling concept when they have overcapacity. Their aim is to sell what they make rather than make what the market wants. In modern industrial economies, productive capacity has been built up to a point where most markets are buyer markets (the buyers are dominant) and sellers have to scramble for customers. Prospects are bombarded with TV commercials, newspaper ads, direct mail, and sales calls. At every turn, someone is trying to sell something. As a result, the public often identifies marketing with hard selling and advertising.

However, marketing based on hard selling carries high risks. It assumes that customers who are coaxed into buying a product will like it; and that if they do not, they will not bad-mouth it or complain to consumer organizations and will forget their disappointment and buy it again. These are indefensible assumptions. One study showed that dissatisfied customers may bad-mouth the product to 10 or more acquaintances; today bad news travels even faster and further with the Internet.[22]

the marketing concept

The marketing concept emerged in the mid-1950s and challenged the preceding concepts.[23] Instead of a product-centered, "make-and-sell" philosophy, we shift to a customer-centered, "sense-and-respond " philosophy. Instead of "hunting," marketing is "gardening." The job is not to find the right customers for your product, but the right products for your customers. As stated by the famed direct marketer Lester Wunderman, "The chant of the Industrial Revolution was that of the manufacturer who said, 'This is what I make, won't you please buy it.' The call of the Information Age is the consumer asking, 'This is what I want, won't you please make it.' "

The **marketing concept** holds that the key to achieving its organizational goals consists of the company being more effective than competitors in creating, delivering, and communicating superior customer value to its chosen target markets. It crystallized in the mid-1950s and has been expressed in many colorful ways:

- "Meeting needs profitably."
- "Find wants and fill them."
- "Love the customer, not the product."
- "Have it your way." (Burger King)
- "You're the boss." (United Airlines)
- "Putting people first." (British Airways)
- "Partners for profit." (Milliken & Company)

figure **1.7**

Contrast Between the Sales Concept and the Marketing Concept

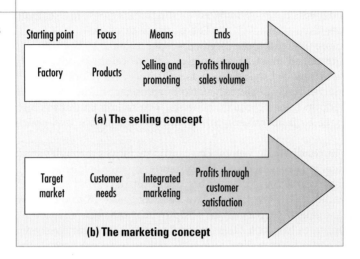

Theodore Levitt of Harvard drew a perceptive contrast between the selling and marketing concepts:

> Selling focuses on the needs of the seller; marketing on the needs of the buyer. Selling is preoccupied with the seller's need to convert his product into cash; marketing with the idea of satisfying the needs of the customer by means of the product and the whole cluster of things associated with creating, delivering and finally consuming it.[24]

The marketing concept rests on four pillars: target market, customer needs, integrated marketing, and profitability. They are illustrated in Figure 1.7, where they are contrasted with a selling orientation. The selling concept takes an inside-out perspective. It starts with the factory, focuses on existing products, and calls for heavy selling and promoting to produce profitable sales. The marketing concept takes an outside-in perspective. It starts with a well-defined market, focuses on customer needs, coordinates all the activities that will affect customers, and produces profits by satisfying customers.

TARGET MARKET   Companies do best when they choose their target market(s) carefully and prepare tailored marketing programs. Terra Lycos is an example.

Terra Lycos   Madrid-based Terra Lycos became a top Internet service provider by aiming at the neglected Hispanic market segment. The company developed tailored marketing programs for the most prosperous one-fifth of Hispanics across eight different markets. As one company executive said: "Our Brazilian product doesn't have anything to do with our Mexican product other than it's under the same brand. Our U.S. product is not targeted to Latin America—it's targeted to the U.S." After a $5-billion merger with Lycos in October 2000, Terra Lycos's stated mission was "to hold the number one or two position in each of the markets in which it operates by delivering services in a highly targeted, localized manner."[25]

CUSTOMER NEEDS   A company can define its target market but fail to correctly understand the customers' needs. Consider the following example:

A major chemical company invented a new substance that hardened into a marble-like material. Looking for an application, the marketing department decided to target the bathtub market. The company created a few model bathtubs and exhibited them at a trade show. It hoped to convince manufacturers to produce bathtubs with the new material. Although bathtub manufacturers thought the tubs were attractive, none signed up. The reason soon became obvious. The bathtub would have to be priced at $2,000, whereas most bathtubs sold in the $500 range. For the higher price, consumers could buy tubs made out of real marble or onyx. In addition, the bathtubs were so heavy that home-owners would have to reinforce their floors.

Understanding customer needs and wants is not always simple. Some customers have needs of which they are not fully conscious, or they cannot articulate these needs, or they use words that require some interpretation. What does it mean when the customer asks for an "inexpensive" car, a "powerful" lawnmower, a "fast" lathe, an "attractive" bathing suit, or a "restful" hotel?

Consider the customer who says he wants an inexpensive car. The marketer must probe further. We can distinguish among five types of needs:

1. Stated needs (the customer wants an inexpensive car)
2. Real needs (the customer wants a car whose operating cost, not its initial price, is low)
3. Unstated needs (the customer expects good service from the dealer)
4. Delight needs (the customer would like the dealer to include an onboard navigation system)
5. Secret needs (the customer wants to be seen by friends as a savvy consumer)

Even the idea of meeting or responding to people's needs is too limited a view of a company's role in the marketplace. Many consumers do not know what they want in a product. Consumers did not know much about cellular phones when they were first introduced. Nokia and Ericsson fought to shape consumer perceptions of cellular phones. Consumers were in a learning mode and companies forged strategies to shape their wants. As stated by Carpenter, "Simply giving customers what they want isn't enough any more—to gain an edge companies must help customers learn what they want."[26]

Responding only to the stated need may shortchange the customer. Consider a woman who enters a hardware store and asks for a sealant to seal glass window panes. This customer is stating a solution, not a need. The salesperson might suggest that tape would provide a better solution. The customer may appreciate that the salesperson met her need, not her stated solution.

A distinction needs to be drawn between responsive marketing, anticipative marketing, and creative marketing. A *responsive* marketer finds a stated need and fills it. An *anticipative* marketer looks ahead into what needs customers may have in the near future. A *creative* marketer discovers and produces solutions customers did not ask for but to which they enthusiastically respond. Hamel and Prahalad believe that companies must go beyond just asking consumers what they want:

> Customers are notoriously lacking in foresight. Ten or 15 years ago, how many of us were asking for cellular telephones, fax machines, and copiers at home, 24-hour discount brokerage accounts, multivalve automobile engines, compact disc players, cars with on-board navigation systems, hand-held global satellite positioning receivers, automated teller machines, MTB, or the Home Shopping Network?[27]

Sony exemplifies creative marketing in its introduction of many successful new products that customers never asked for or even thought were possible: Walkmans, VCRs, videocameras, CDs. Sony is a *market-driving firm,* not just a *market-driven firm.* Akio Morita, its founder, once proclaimed that Sony doesn't serve markets; Sony creates markets.[28] The Walkman is a classic example: In the late 1970s Akio Morita was working on a pet project that would revolutionize the way people listened to music: a portable cassette player he called the Walkman. Engineers at the company insisted there was little demand for such a product, but Morita refused to part with his vision. By the twentieth anniversary of the Walkman, Sony had sold over 250 million in nearly 100 different models.[29]

In the past, "responding to customer needs" meant studying customer needs and making a product that fit these needs on the average, but some of today's companies instead respond to each customer's *individual* need. Dell Computer does not prepare a perfect computer for its target market. Rather, it provides product platforms on which each customer customizes the features he or she desires in the computer. This is a change from a "make-and-sell" philosophy to a philosophy of "sense and respond." Ford too has recently changed its priorities.

Ford   The cover of Ford's 1999 annual report is titled "Connecting with Customers" to reflect the heightened priority that Ford was placing on becoming a customer-driven company. The report noted: "A customer-driven company must be relentless in its focus. It must listen to customers, find ways to fill their needs, and continually seek feedback on how well it is satisfying those needs." Ford expresses its intent as to have customers who "trust our company, love our brands, and delight in our services." To achieve this goal, Ford employs management techniques such as Consumer-Driven Six Sigma. Sigma is the Greek symbol used to represent one standard deviation. The goal of Consumer-Driven Six Sigma is to achieve a value of six sigma, which corresponds to only 3.4 defects per million. Although Ford experienced several setbacks with product recalls and a highly publicized split with long-time tire supplier Firestone in 2001, company management vowed that a strong customer focus would still be the key to turning the company's fortunes around.[30]

Why is it supremely important to satisfy target customers? Because a company's sales each period come from two groups: new customers and repeat customers. One estimate is that attracting a new customer can cost five times as much as pleasing an existing one.[31] Also, it might cost 16 times as much to bring the new customer to the same level of profitability as the lost customer. Customer retention is thus more important than customer attraction.

Although the company must focus on its present customers, it can learn a great deal from its noncustomers in its target market. Why are they buying competitors' products? What is their image of this company? Many new ideas can be garnered in this way.

INTEGRATED MARKETING   When all the company's departments work together to serve the customer's interests, the result is **integrated marketing**. Unfortunately, not all employees are trained and motivated to work for the customer. An engineer once complained that the salespeople are "always protecting the customer and not thinking of the company's interest"! He went on to blast customers for "asking for too much." The following example highlights the coordination problem:

The marketing vice president of a major European airline wants to increase the airline's traffic share. His strategy is to build up customer satisfaction through providing better food, cleaner cabins, better-trained cabin crews, and lower fares; yet he has no authority in these matters. The catering department chooses food that keeps down food costs; the maintenance department uses cleaning services that keep down cleaning costs; the human resources department hires people without regard to whether they are naturally friendly; the finance department sets the fares. Because these departments generally take a cost or production point of view, the vice president of marketing is stymied in creating an integrated marketing mix.

Integrated marketing takes place on two levels. First, the various marketing functions—sales force, advertising, customer service, product management, marketing research—must work together. Too often the sales force thinks product managers set prices or sale quotas "too high"; or the advertising director and a brand manager cannot agree on an advertising campaign. All these marketing functions must be coordinated from the customer's point of view.

figure **1.8**   Traditional Organization Chart Versus Modern Customer–Oriented Company Organization Chart

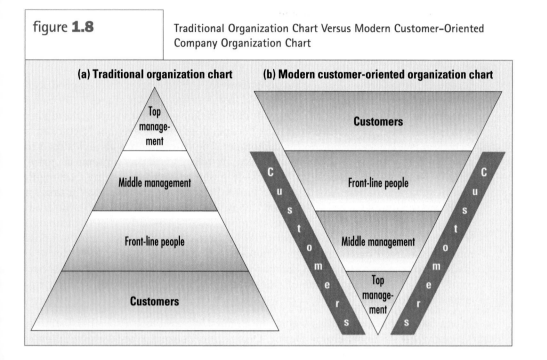

Second, marketing must be embraced by the other departments; they must also "think customer." According to David Packard of Hewlett-Packard: "Marketing is far too important to be left only to the marketing department!" Marketing is not a department so much as a company orientation. Xerox goes so far as to include in every job description an explanation of how that job affects the customer. Xerox factory managers know that visits to the factory can help sell a potential customer if the factory is clean and efficient. Xerox accountants know that customer attitudes are affected by Xerox's billing accuracy and promptness in returning calls.

To foster teamwork among all departments, the company carries out internal marketing as well as external marketing. **External marketing** is marketing directed at people outside the company. **Internal marketing** is the task of hiring, training, and motivating able employees who want to serve customers well. In fact, internal marketing must precede external marketing. It makes no sense to promise excellent service before the company's staff is ready to provide it.

Managers who believe the customer is the company's only true "profit center" consider the traditional organization chart in Figure 1.8(a)—a pyramid with the president at the top, management in the middle, and front-line people and customers at the bottom—obsolete. Master marketing companies invert the chart, as shown in Figure 1.8(b). At the top are the customers; next in importance are the front-line people who meet, serve, and satisfy the customers; under them are the middle managers, whose job is to support the front-line people so they can serve the customers well; and at the base is top management, whose job is to hire and support good middle managers. We have added customers along the sides of Figure 1.8(b) to indicate that all the company's managers must be personally involved in knowing, meeting, and serving customers.

PROFITABILITY   The ultimate purpose of the marketing concept is to help organizations achieve their objectives. In the case of private firms, the major objective is long-run profitability; in the case of nonprofit and public organizations, it is surviving and attracting enough funds to perform useful work. Private firms should not aim for profits as such, but rather to achieve profits as a consequence of creating superior customer value. A company makes money by satisfying customer needs better than its competitors. Consider Frank Perdue's philosophy.

Perdue Chicken Farms   Perdue Farms is America's third largest chicken producer, with margins substantially above the industry average. Market shares in its major markets reach 50 percent, and the product is chicken—a commodity if there ever was one! Yet its colorful founder, Frank Perdue, does not believe that "a chicken is a chicken is a chicken," nor do his customers. The company has always aimed to produce chickens for which discriminating customers will pay a premium price. Perdue raises its chickens on a chemical-free diet to produce quality birds with distinct characteristics. Ads featuring Frank Perdue and the tag line "It takes a tough man to make a tender chicken" were the company's signature line from 1971 until 1995. When Frank Perdue stepped down, a new advertising campaign introduced his son Jim to the country. "After three generations, the Perdues know more about breeding chickens than chickens do," says one of the ads. Under new leadership, the privately held company has continued to prosper. Perdue currently ships 50 million pounds of chicken every week to more than 50 countries across the globe.[32]

Only a handful of companies stand out as master marketers: Procter & Gamble, Kraft, Southwest Airlines, Home Depot, Disney, Nordstrom, Wal-Mart, Milliken & Company, McDonald's, Marriott Hotels, American Airlines, and several Japanese (Sony, Toyota, Canon) and European companies (IKEA, Club Med, Bang & Olufsen, Electrolux, Nokia, ABB, Lego, Tesco). These companies focus on the customer and are organized to respond effectively to changing customer needs. They all have well-staffed marketing departments, and all their other departments—manufacturing, finance, research and development, personnel, purchasing—also accept the concept that the customer is king.

Several scholars have found that companies who embrace the marketing concept achieve superior performance.[33] This was first demonstrated for companies practicing a *reactive market orientation*—understanding and meeting customers' expressed needs; but some critics say this means that companies develop only low-level innovations. Narver and his colleagues argue that high-level innovation is possible if the focus is on customers' latent needs. He calls this a *proactive marketing orientation.*[34] Companies such as 3M, HP, and Motorola have made a practice of researching or imagining latent needs through a "probe-and-learn" process. Companies that practice both a reactive and proactive marketing orientation are implementing a *total market orientation* and are likely to be the most successful.

However, most companies do not embrace the marketing concept until driven to it by circumstances. Various developments prod them to take the marketing concept to heart:

- *Sales decline:* When sales fall, companies panic and look for answers. Today, newspapers are experiencing declining circulation as more people rely on radio, TV, and the Internet for their news. Some publishers now realize that they know little about why people read newspapers. These publishers are commissioning consumer research and attempting to redesign newspapers to be contemporary, relevant, and interesting to readers. They have also set up Web pages.
- *Slow growth:* Slow sales growth leads some companies to search for new markets. They realize they need marketing skills to identify and select new opportunities. Wanting new sources of revenue, Dow Chemical entered consumer markets and invested heavily to acquire consumer marketing expertise to perform well in these markets.
- *Changing buying patterns:* Many companies operate in markets characterized by rapidly changing customer wants. These companies need more marketing know-how if they are to track buyers' changing values.

- *Increasing competition:* Complacent companies may suddenly be attacked by powerful competitors. AT&T was a regulated, marketing-naive telephone company until the 1970s, when the government began allowing other companies to sell telecommunications equipment. AT&T hired the best marketers it could find to help it compete. Companies in deregulated industries all find it necessary to build up marketing expertise.[35]
- *Increasing marketing expenditures:* Companies may find that their expenditures for advertising, sales promotion, marketing research, and customer service are yielding poor results. Management then decides it is time to undertake a serious marketing audit to improve its marketing.[36]

In the course of converting to a marketing orientation, a company faces three hurdles: organized resistance, slow learning, and fast forgetting. Some company departments (often manufacturing, finance, and R&D) believe a stronger marketing function threatens their power in the organization. The nature of the threat is illustrated in Figure 1.9(a) through (e). Initially, the marketing function is seen as one of several equally important functions in a check-and-balance relationship. Lack of demand leads marketers to argue that their function is more important. A few enthusiasts go further and say marketing is the major function of the enterprise, for without customers there would be no company. Enlightened marketers clarify the issue by putting the customer rather than marketing at the center of the company. They argue for a customer orientation in which all functions work together to respond to, serve, and satisfy the customer. Some marketers say that marketing still needs to command a central position if customers' needs are to be correctly interpreted and efficiently satisfied.[37] (See "Marketing Memo: Reasons to Embrace the Marketing Concept.")

Resistance is especially strong in industries where marketing is being introduced for the first time—for instance, in law offices, colleges, deregulated industries, and government agencies; but in spite of resistance, many companies manage to introduce some marketing thinking into their organization. The company president establishes a marketing department; marketing talent is hired; key managers attend marketing seminars; the marketing budget is substantially increased; marketing planning and control systems are introduced. Even with these steps, however, learning comes slowly.

Once marketing has been installed, management must fight a tendency to forget basic principles, especially in the wake of success. For example, look at what happened to Intel.

Intel In June 1994, technicians at Intel discovered a flaw in the newest line of Pentium chips. The problems surfaced only rarely, and Intel management chose to keep knowledge of the flaw from the public. Eventually, the story broke in the national press, and Pentium owners expressed concern. Intel proposed selective replacement to those who had experienced the problem, and the result was a PR nightmare. By December, Intel was offering replacements to all customers who asked for them. Andy Grove referred to the company's handling of the problem as his "biggest mistake"; by not immediately offering replacements, Intel "basically defied [its] consumer population." But despite the negative media attention and the dissatisfied customer responses, Intel managed to avert a major crisis in terms of lost customers and damaged brand image by spending $475 million on replacement chips, issuing a reassuring document to the press explaining the problem, and hiring hundreds of customer service people to handle questions and complaints.

Companies face a particularly difficult task in adapting ad slogans to international markets. Perdue's slogan—"It takes a tough man to make a tender chicken"—was rendered into Spanish as "It takes a sexually excited man to make a chick affectionate." Even when the language is the same, words carry different meanings: Electrolux's British ad line for its vacuum cleaners—"Nothing sucks like an Electrolux"—would certainly not lure customers in the United States![38]

figure **1.9**

Evolving Views of Marketing's Role in the Company

(a) Marketing as an equal function

(b) Marketing as a more important function

(c) Marketing as the major function

(d) The customer as the controlling function

(e) The customer as the controlling function and marketing as the integrative function

the customer concept *5/6*

Today many companies are moving beyond the marketing concept to the customer concept. The **customer concept** is illustrated in Figure 1.10.

Whereas companies practicing the marketing concept work at the level of customer segments, a growing number of today's companies are now shaping separate offers, services, and messages to individual customers. These companies collect information on each customer's past transactions, demographics, psychographics, and media and distribution preferences. They hope to achieve profitable growth through capturing a larger share of each customer's expenditures by building high customer loyalty and focusing on customer lifetime value.

The ability of a company to deal with customers one at a time has become practical as a result of advances in factory customization, computers, the Internet, and database marketing software. Yet the practicing of a one-to-one marketing is not for every company: The required investment in information collection, hardware, and software may exceed the payout. It works best for companies that normally collect a great deal of individual customer information, carry a lot of products that can be cross-sold, carry products that need periodic replacement or upgrading, and sell products of high value.

the societal marketing concept *6/6*

Some have questioned whether the marketing concept is an appropriate philosophy in an age of environmental deterioration, resource shortages, explosive population growth, world hunger and poverty, and neglected social services. Are companies that do an excellent job of satisfying consumer wants necessarily acting in the best long-run interests of consumers and society? The marketing concept sidesteps the potential conflicts among consumer wants, consumer interests, and long-run societal welfare.

Consider the following criticism:

> The fast-food hamburger industry offers tasty but unhealthy food. The hamburgers have a high fat content, and the restaurants promote fries and pies, two products high in starch and fat. The products are wrapped in convenient packaging, which leads to much waste. In satisfying consumer wants, these restaurants may be hurting consumer health and causing environmental problems.

Situations like this one call for a new term that enlarges the marketing concept. Among those suggested are "humanistic marketing" and "ecological marketing." We propose calling it the societal marketing concept. The **societal marketing concept** holds that the organization's task is to determine the needs, wants, and interests of target mar-

figure **1.10**

The Customer Concept

Starting point	Focus	Means	Ends
Individual customer	Customer needs and values	One-to-one marketing integration and value chain	Profitable growth through capturing customer share, loyalty, and lifetime value

kets and to deliver the desired satisfactions more effectively and efficiently than competitors in a way that preserves or enhances the consumer's and the society's well-being.

The societal marketing concept calls upon marketers to build social and ethical considerations into their marketing practices. They must balance and juggle the often conflicting criteria of company profits, consumer want satisfaction, and public interest. Yet a number of companies—including the Body Shop, Ben & Jerry's, and Patagonia—have achieved notable sales and profit gains by adopting and practicing the societal marketing concept. Consider Patagonia.[39]

Patagonia   Patagonia world-class climber Yvon Chouinard founded Patagonia in 1966 by selling rock climbing hardware from the trunk of his car. By the time the company changed its focus to selling soft goods and apparel in the mid-1970s, Patagonia was committed to two main goals: provid[ing] the highest quality gear for outdoor enthusiasts, and "implement[ing] solutions to the environmental crisis." The company gave an "earth tax" of one percent of sales or ten percent of pre-tax profits (whichever is greater) to "activists who take radical and strategic steps to protect habitat, wilderness, and biodiversity." However, as Patagonia expanded, many aspects of its operations contributed to the environmental pollution the company worked so hard to counter. After an internal study in the early 1990s, the company sought to use materials and fabrics that would minimize its impact on the environment, such as Synchilla fleece made from recycled plastic bottles and the 100 percent organic cotton used in every cotton product. The corporate culture avidly supports activism, as evidenced by a company program through which employees receive pay to work up to two months in an environmental organization. Patagonia sent 70 of its 900 employees abroad on such trips in 1999.[40]

Patagonia is practicing a form of the societal marketing concept called **cause-related marketing**. Pringle and Thompson define this as activity by which a company with an image, product, or service to market builds a relationship or partnership with a "cause," or a number of "causes," for mutual benefit."[41]

Companies see cause-related marketing as an opportunity to enhance their corporate reputation, raise brand awareness, increase customer loyalty, build sales, and increase press coverage. They believe that customers will increasingly look for signs of good corporate citizenship that go beyond supplying rational and emotional benefits.

how business and marketing are changing

We can say with some confidence that "the marketplace isn't what it used to be." It is changing radically as a result of major societal forces such as technological advances, globalization, and deregulation. These major forces have created new behaviors and challenges:

- *Customers* increasingly expect higher quality and service and some customization. They perceive fewer real product differences and show less brand loyalty. They can obtain extensive product information from the Internet and other sources, which permits them to shop more intelligently. They are showing greater price sensitivity in their search for value.

- *Brand manufacturers* are facing intense competition from domestic and foreign brands, which is resulting in rising promotion costs and shrinking profit margins. They are being further buffeted by powerful retailers who command limited shelf space and are putting out their own store brands in competition with national brands.

- *Store-based retailers* are suffering. Small retailers are succumbing to the growing power of giant retailers and "category killers." Store-based retailers are facing growing competition from catalog houses; direct-mail firms; newspaper, magazine, and TV direct-to-customer ads; home shopping TV; and e-commerce on the Internet. As a result, they are experiencing shrinking margins. In response, entrepreneurial retailers are building entertainment into stores with coffee bars, lectures, demonstrations, and performances. They are marketing an "experience" rather than a product assortment.

company responses and adjustments

Companies are doing a lot of soul-searching, and many highly respected companies are changing in a number of ways. Here are some current trends:

- *Reengineering:* From focusing on functional departments to reorganizing by key processes, each managed by a multidiscipline team.
- *Outsourcing:* From making everything inside the company to buying more goods and services from outside if they are cheaper and better. More companies are preferring to own brands rather than physical assets; they are decapitalizing. A few companies are moving toward outsourcing everything, making them virtual companies owning very few assets and, therefore, earning extraordinary rates of return.
- *E-commerce:* From attracting customers to stores and having salespeople call on offices to making virtually all products available on the Internet. Consumers can access pictures of products, read the specs, shop among on-line vendors for the best prices and terms, and click to order and pay. Business-to-business purchasing is growing fast on the Internet. Personal selling can increasingly be conducted electronically, with buyer and seller seeing each other on their computer screens in real time.
- *Benchmarking:* From relying on self-improvement to studying "world-class performers" and adopting "best practices."
- *Alliances:* From trying to win alone to forming networks of partner firms.
- *Partner-suppliers:* From using many suppliers to using fewer but more reliable suppliers who work closely in a "partnership" relationship with the company.
- *Market-centered:* From organizing by products to organizing by market segment.
- *Global and local:* From being local to being both global and local, called "glocal."
- *Decentralized:* From being managed from the top to encouraging more initiative and "intrepreneurship" at the local level.

marketer responses and adjustments

Marketers also are rethinking their philosophies, concepts, and tools. Here are the major marketing themes in the new economy:

- *Customer relationship marketing:* From focusing on transactions to building long-term, profitable customer relationships. Companies focus on their most profitable customers, products, and channels.
- *Customer lifetime value:* From making a profit on each sale to making profits by managing lifetime sales. Some companies offer to deliver a constantly needed product on a regular basis at a lower price per unit because they will capture the customer's business for a longer period.
- *Customer share:* From a focus on gaining market share to a focus on building customer share. A bank aims to increase its share of the customer's wallet; the supermarket aims to capture a larger share of the customer's "stomach." Companies build customer share by offering a larger variety of goods to existing customers. They train their employees in cross-selling and up-selling.
- *Target marketing:* From selling to everyone to trying to be the best firm serving well-defined target markets. Target marketing is being facilitated by the proliferation of special-interest magazines, TV channels, and Internet newsgroups.
- *Customization:* From selling the same offer in the same way to everyone in the target market to individualizing and customizing messages and offerings.
- *Customer database:* From collecting sales data to building a rich data warehouse of information about individual customers' purchases, preferences, and demographics, and profitability. Companies can then apply datamining techniques to discover new segments and trends hidden in the data.
- *Integrated marketing communications:* From heavy reliance on one communication tool such as advertising or sales force to blending several tools to deliver a consistent brand image to customers at every brand contact.
- *Channels as partners:* From thinking of intermediaries as customers to treating them as partners in delivering value to final customers.

■ *Every employee a marketer:* From thinking that marketing is done only by marketing, sales, and customer support personnel to recognizing that every employee must be customer-focused.

■ *Model-based decision making:* From basing decisions on intuition or slim data to basing decisions on models and facts on how the marketplace works.

These major themes will be examined throughout this book to help marketers and companies sail safely through the rough but promising waters ahead. Successful companies will be those who can keep their marketing changing with the changes in their marketplace—and marketspace.

summary

1. Businesses today face three major challenges and opportunities: globalization, the effects of advances in technology, and deregulation.

2. Marketing is typically seen as the task of creating, promoting, and delivering goods and services to consumers and businesses. Effective marketing can take many forms: It can be entrepreneurial, formulated, or intrepreneurial; and marketers are involved in marketing many types of entities: goods, services, experiences, events, persons, places, properties, organizations, information, and ideas.

3. Marketers are skilled at managing demand: They seek to influence the level, timing, and composition of demand. To do this, they face a host of decisions, from major ones such as what features a new product should have to minor ones such as the color of packaging. They also operate in four different marketplaces: consumer, business, global, and nonprofit.

4. For each chosen target market, a firm develops a market offering that is positioned in the minds of buyers as delivering some central benefits. Marketers must try to understand the target market's needs, wants, and demands: A product or offering will be successful if it delivers value and satisfaction to the target buyer. The term *markets* covers various groupings of customers. Today there are both physical marketplaces and digital marketspaces, as well as megamarkets.

5. Exchange involves obtaining a desired product from someone by offering something in return. A transaction is a trade of values between two or more parties: It involves at least two things of value, agreed-upon conditions, a time of agreement, and a place of agreement. In the most generic sense, marketers seek to elicit a behavioral response from another party: a purchase, a vote, active membership, adoption of a cause.

6. Relationship marketing has the aim of building long-term, mutually satisfying relations with key parties—customers, suppliers, and distributors—in order to earn and retain their long-term preference and business. The ultimate outcome of relationship marketing is the building of a unique company asset called a marketing network.

7. Marketers reach their markets through various channels—communication, distribution, and selling. Marketers operate in a task environment and a broad environment. They face competition from actual and potential rival offerings and substitutes. The set of tools marketers use to elicit the desired responses from their target markets is called the marketing mix.

8. There are six competing concepts under which organizations can choose to conduct their business: the production concept, product concept, selling concept, marketing concept, customer concept, and societal marketing concept. The first three are of limited use today. The marketing concept holds that the key to achieving organizational goals consists of determining the needs and wants of target markets and delivering the desired satisfactions more effectively and efficiently than competitors. It starts with a well-defined market, focuses on customer needs, coordinates all the activities that will affect customers, and produces profits by satisfying customers. The customer concept addresses the individual needs of specific customers and aims to build customer loyalty and lifetime value.

9. The societal marketing concept holds that the organization's task is to determine the needs, wants, and interests of target markets and to deliver the desired satisfactions more effectively and efficiently than competitors, in a way that preserves or enhances the consumer's and the society's well-being. The concept calls upon marketers to balance three considerations: company profits, consumer want satisfaction, and the public interest.

applications

marketing debate – does marketing create or satisfy needs?

Marketing has often been defined in terms of satisfying customers' needs and wants. Critics, however, maintain that marketing does much more than that and creates needs and wants that did not exist before. According to these critics, marketers encourage consumers to spend more money than they should on goods and services they really do not need.

Take a position: Marketing shapes consumer needs and wants versus Marketing merely reflects the needs and wants of consumers.

marketing and advertising

1. The T. K. Maxx ad shown in Figure 1 stresses the money-saving aspect of shopping for brand-name merchandise at the chain's stores in the United Kingdom. T. K. Maxx in the United States, operated by the same corporate parent, also attracts shoppers by promoting low prices on well-known brands.

   a. How is the combination of brand-name products at low prices likely to affect the customers' perceptions of value at T. K. Maxx?

   b. What else is T. K. Maxx stressing in its advertising to affect customers' perceptions of value?

   c. How might T. K. Maxx use the other aspects of its four Ps (product, place, price, promotion) to enhance customers' perceptions of the value of its total offer?

2. Canada-based Nexen focuses on exploration and production of natural gas and crude oil in locations around the world. Its success depends on a complex network of customers, employees, suppliers, distributors, investors, and other stakeholders. Yet the ad shown in Figure 2 focuses on Nexen's commitment to social responsibility.

   a. Why would Nexen advertise its socially responsible activities in a business magazine?

   b. What effect does the company expect this ad to have on its relationships with various stakeholders?

   c. How can Nexen build on strong stakeholder relationships to compete more effectively in the energy industry?

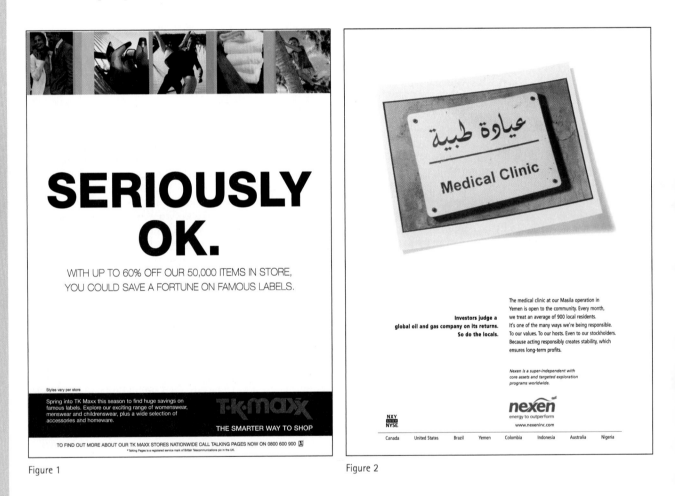

Figure 1

Figure 2

online marketing today

Tesco, the largest supermarket chain in Great Britain, is also the world's most successful online grocery retailer. Tesco rings up $32 billion in annual sales through 900 stores in the United Kingdom, Eastern Europe, and Southeast Asia, and through its profitable Tesco.com Web site *www.tesco.com*, which processes 70,000 orders every week. From appliances to apples, garbage bags to gifts, Tesco.com will deliver whatever its one million customers order, adding a per-order fee of $7. Tesco is now bringing its proven online system to the United States through a partnership with the Safeway chain and Dallas-based GroceryWorks.com.[a] Visit both sites to see what they offer. What benefits might customers perceive in ordering groceries from Texco.com or GroceryWorks.com? What costs might customers perceive? How might the value equation differ for a customer shopping in a local Safeway store?

Source: [a]Gregory Katz, "British Grocer Tesco Tries to Succeed Where Others Have Failed," *Dallas Morning News,* August 2, 2001, *www.dallasnews.com.*

notes

1. Sam Hill and Glenn Rifkin, *Radical Marketing* (New York: HarperBusiness, 1999).

2. Jay Conrad Levinson and Seth Godin, *The Guerrilla Marketing Handbook* (Boston: Houghton Mifflin, 1994).

3. Philip Kotler, "Dream Vacations: The Booming Market for Designed Experiences," *The Futurist* (October 1984): 7–13; B. Joseph Pine II and James Gilmore, *The Experience Economy* (Boston: Harvard Business School Press, 1999); and Bernd Schmitt, *Experience Marketing* (New York: Free Press, 1999).

4. Irving J. Rein, Philip Kotler, and Martin Stoller, *High Visibility* (Chicago: NTC Publishers, 1998).

5. Philip Kotler, Irving J. Rein, and Donald Haider, *Marketing Places: Attracting Investment, Industry, and Tourism to Cities, States, and Nations* (New York: Free Press, 1993); and *Marketing Places Europe* (London: Financial Times Prentice-Hall, 1999).

6. Carl Shapiro and Hal R. Varian, "Versioning: The Smart Way to Sell Information," *Harvard Business Review* (November–December 1998): 106–14.

7. Peter Drucker, *Management: Tasks, Responsibilities, Practices* (New York: Harper and Row, 1973), pp. 64–65.

8. *Dictionary of Marketing Terms*, 2nd ed., ed. Peter D. Bennett (Chicago: American Marketing Association, 1995).

9. Jeffrey Rayport and John Sviokla, "Managing in the Marketspace," *Harvard Business Review* (November–December 1994): 141–50. Also see their "Exploring the Virtual Value Chain," *Harvard Business Review* (November–December 1995): pp. 75–85.

10. Mohan Sawhney, *Seven Steps to Nirvana* (New York: McGraw-Hill, 2001).

11. Evert Gummesson, *Total Relationship Marketing* (Boston: Butterworth-Heinemann, 1999); Regis McKenna, *Relationship Marketing* (Reading, MA: Addison-Wesley, 1991); Martin Christopher, Adrian Payne, and David Ballantyne, *Relationship Marketing: Bringing Quality, Customer Service, and Marketing Together* (Oxford, U.K: Butterworth-Heinemann, 1991).

12. James C. Anderson, Hakan Hakansson, and Jan Johanson, "Dyadic Business Relationships within a Business Network Context," *Journal of Marketing* (October 15, 1994): 1–15.

13. Neil H. Borden, "The Concept of the Marketing Mix," *Journal of Advertising Research* 4 (June): 2–7. For another framework, see George S. Day, "The Capabilities of Market-Driven Organizations," *Journal of Marketing* 58, no. 4 (October 1994): 37–52.

14. E. Jerome McCarthy, *Basic Marketing: A Managerial Approach*, 12th ed. (Homewood, IL: Irwin, 1996). Two alternative classifications are worth noting. Frey proposed that all marketing decision variables could be categorized into two factors: the offering (product, packaging, brand, price, and service) and methods and tools (distribution channels, personal selling, advertising, sales promotion, and publicity). See Albert W. Frey, *Advertising*, 3rd ed. (New York: Ronald Press, 1961), p. 30. Lazer and Kelly proposed a three-factor classification: goods and services mix, distribution mix, and communications mix. See William Lazer and Eugene J. Kelly, *Managerial Marketing: Perspectives and Viewpoints*, rev. ed. (Homewood, IL: Irwin, 1962), p. 413.

15. Robert Lauterborn, "New Marketing Litany: 4P's Passe; C-Words Take Over," *Advertising Age*, October 1, 1990, p. 26.

16. Kathleen Dechant and Barbara Altman, "Environmental Leadership: From Compliance to Competitive Advantage," *Academy of Management Executive* 8, no. 3 (1994): 7–19. Also see Gregory R. Elliott, "The Marketing Concept—Necessary, but Sufficient?: An Environmental View," *European Journal of Marketing* 24, no. 8 (1990): 20–30 see also Ajay Menon and Anil Menon, "Enviropreneurial Marketing Strategy: The Emergence of Corporate Environmentalism as Marketing Strategy," *Journal of Marketing* 61, no. 1 (January 1997): 51–67.

17. David Kirkpatrick, "Intel's Amazing Profit Machine," *Fortune*, February 17, 1997, pp. 60–63.

18. Paul C. Judge, "Are Tech Buyers Different?" *BusinessWeek*, January 26, 1998, pp. 64–65, 68; B. G. Yovovich, "Webbed Feat," *Marketing News*, January 19, 1998, pp. 1, 18.

19. Theodore Levitt's classic article, "Marketing Myopia," *Harvard Business Review* (July–August 1960): 45–56.

20. Sergio Zyman, *The End of Marketing as We Know It* (New York: Harper Business, 1999).

21. Bruce I. Newman, ed., *Handbook of Political Marketing* (Thousand Oaks, CA: Sage Publications, 1999); and Bruce I. Newman, *The Mass Marketing of Politics* (Thousand Oaks, CA: Sage Publications, 1999).

22. Karl Albrecht and Ron Zemke, *Service America!* (Homewood, IL: Dow Jones-Irwin, 1985), pp. 6–7.

23. John B. McKitterick, "What Is the Marketing Management Concept?" In *The Frontiers of Marketing Thought and Action* (Chicago: American Marketing Association, 1957), pp. 71–82; Fred J. Borch, "The Marketing Philosophy as a Way of Business Life," *The Marketing Concept: Its Meaning to Management* (Marketing series, no. 99) (New York: American Management Association, 1957), pp. 3–5; Robert J. Keith, "The Marketing Revolution," *Journal of Marketing* (January 1960): 35–38.

24. Levitt, "Marketing Myopia," p. 50.

25. David J. Lynch, "Net Company Terra Aims for Hispanic Connection," *USA Today*, January 20, 2000, p. B1–2.

26. Private conversation with Carpenter.

27. Gary Hamel and C. K. Prahalad, *Competing for the Future* (Boston: Harvard Business School Press, 1994).

28. Akio Morita, *Made in Japan* (New York: Dutton, 1986), ch. 1.

29. Jonathan Glancey, "The Private World of the Walkman," *The Guardian*, October 11, 1999.

30. Joann Muller, "Ford: Why It's Worse Than You Think," *Business Week,* June 25, 2001; Ford *1999 Annual Report*; Greg Keenan, "Six Degrees of Perfection." *The Globe and Mail*, December 20, 2000.

31. Patricia Sellers, "Getting Customers to Love You," *Fortune,* March 13, 1989, pp. 38–49.

32. Christopher Thorne, "Q&A: Jim Perdue Faces Challenges to Chicken Empire," *AP Newswire*, March 11, 2001.

33. Ajay K. Kohli and Bernard J. Jaworski, "Market Orientation: The Construct, Research Propositions, and Managerial Implications," *Journal of Marketing* (April 1990): pp. 1–18; John C. Narver and Stanley F. Slater, "The Effect of a Market Orientation on Business Profitability," *Journal of Marketing* (October 1990): pp. 20–35; Stanley F. Slater and John C. Narver, "Market Orientation, Customer Value, and Superior Performance," *Business Horizons,* March–April 1994, 22–28; A. Pelham and D. Wilson, "A Longitudinal Study of the Impact of Market Structure, Firm Structure, Strategy and Market Orientation Culture on Dimensions of Business Performance," *Journal of the Academy of Marketing Science* 24, no. 1, (1996): pp. 27–43; Rohit Deshpande and John U. Farley, "Measuring Market Orientation: Generalization and Synthesis," *Journal of Market-Focused Management* 2 (1998): 213–32.

34. John C. Narver, Stanley F. Slater, and Douglas L. MacLachlan, "Total Market Orientation, Business Performance, and Innovation," Working Paper Series, Marketing Science Institute, Report No. 00-116, 2000, pp. 1–34. See also Ken Matsuno and John T. Mentzer. "The Effects of Strategy Type on the Market Orentation—Performance Relationship," *Journal or Marketing* (October 2000): pp. 1–16.

35. Bro Uttal, "Selling Is No Longer Mickey Mouse at AT&T," *Fortune*, July 17, 1978, pp. 98–104.

36. Thomas V. Bonoma and Bruce H. Clark, *Marketing Performance Assessment* (Boston: Harvard Business School Press, 1988); Robert Shaw, *Measuring and Valuing Customer Relationships* (London; Business Intelligence, 1999).

37. Christian Honburg, John P. Workman Jr., and Harley Krohmen, "Marketings Influence Within the Firm," *Journal of Marketing* (January 1999): pp. 1–15.

38. Richard Barnet, *Global Dreams: Imperial Corporations and the New World Order* (New York: Simon & Schuster, 1994), pp. 170-71; Michael R. Czinkota, Ilka A. Ronkainen, and John J. Tarrant, *The Global Marketing Imperative* (Chicago: NTC Business Books, 1995), p. 249.

39. Constance L. Hays, "Getting Serious at Ben & Jerry's," *New York Times*, May 22, pp. D1–2; Anita Roddick, *Business as Unusual* (London: Thomsons, 2001).

40. Roger Rosenblatt, "Heroes for the Planet," *Time,* October 18, 1999; Peter Carlin, "Pure Profit for Small Companies that Stress Social Values as Much as the Bottom Line," *Los Angeles Times Magazine*, February 5, 1995; Natalie Southworth, "Patagonia's Perks Have Workers Turning Green," *The Globe and Mail*, August 23, 2000.

41. Hanish Pringle and Marjorie Thompson, *Brand Soul: How Cause-Related Marketing Builds Brands* (New York: John Wiley & Sons, 1999); Richard Earle, *The Art of Cause Marketing* (Lincolnwood, IL: NTC, 2000).

building customer satisfaction, value, and retention

Kotler on Marketing

It is no longer enough to satisfy customers. You must delight them.

In this chapter, we will address the following questions:

- What are customer value and satisfaction, and how can companies deliver them?
- What makes a high-performance business?
- How can companies both attract and retain customers?
- How can companies improve both customer and company profitability?
- How can companies deliver total quality?

Today's companies are facing their toughest competition ever. We argued in Chapter 1 that companies can outperform the competition if they can move from a product and sales philosophy to a marketing philosophy. John Chambers, CEO of Cisco Systems, put it well: "Make your customer the center of your culture." In Chapter 2, we showed that companies need to move rapidly into the new economy and employ Internet, wireless, and other technologies to achieve a competitive advantage.

In this chapter, we spell out in detail how companies can go about winning customers and outperforming competitors. The answer lies in doing a better job of meeting or exceeding customer expectations. Customer-centered *companies are adept at building customers, not just products; they are skilled in market engi-neering, not just product engineering.*

Too many companies think that it is the marketing or sales department's job to acquire and manage customers, but, in fact, marketing is only one factor in attracting and keeping cus-tomers. The best marketing department in the world cannot sell products that are poorly made or fail to meet a need. The marketing department can be effective only in companies whose employees have implemented a competitively superior customer value-delivery system.

For example, take McDonald's. Every day an average of 45 million people visit its 29,000 restaurants in 121 countries. People do not swarm to McDonald's outlets solely because they love the hamburgers; other restaurants make better-tasting hamburgers. People are flocking to a system, not a hamburger. Throughout the world, this fine-tuned system of suppliers, franchise owners, and employees delivers a high standard of what McDonald's calls QSCV—quality, ser-vice, cleanliness, and value.[1] This chapter describes and illustrates the philosophy of the customer-focused firm and value marketing.[2]

defining customer value and satisfaction

Over 38 years ago, Peter Drucker observed that a company's first task is "to create cus-tomers." However, customers face a vast array of product and brand choices, prices, and suppliers. How do they make their choices?

We believe that customers estimate which offer will deliver the most value. Customers are value-maximizers, within the bounds of search costs and limited knowledge, mobility, and income. They form an expectation of value and act on it. Whether or not the offer lives up to the value expectation affects both satisfaction and repurchase probability.

customer perceived value

Our premise is that customers will buy from the firm that they see as offering the highest perceived value (Figure 3.1): **Customer perceived value (CPV)** is the difference between the prospective customer's evaluation of all the benefits and all the costs of an offering and the perceived alternatives. **Total customer value** is the perceived monetary value of the bundle of economic, functional, and psychological benefits customers expect from a given market offering. **Total customer cost** is the bundle of costs customers expect to incur in evaluating, obtaining, using, and disposing of the given market offering.

An example will help here. Suppose the buyer for a large construction company wants to buy a tractor from Caterpillar or Komatsu. The competing salespeople carefully describe their respective offers. The buyer wants to use the tractor in residential con-struction work. He would like the tractor to deliver certain levels of reliability, durability, performance, and resale value. He evaluates the tractors and decides that Caterpillar has a higher product value based on perceived reliability, durability, performance, and resale value. He also perceives differences in the accompanying services—delivery, training, and maintenance—and decides that Caterpillar provides better service and more knowl-edgeable and responsive personnel. Finally, he places higher value on Caterpillar's cor-porate image. He adds up all the values from these four sources—product, services, per-sonnel, and image—and perceives Caterpillar as delivering greater customer value.

Does he buy the Caterpillar tractor? Not necessarily. He also examines his total cost of transacting with Caterpillar versus Komatsu, which consists of more than the money. As Adam Smith observed over two centuries ago, "The real price of anything is the toil and trouble of acquiring it." Total customer cost includes the buyer's time, energy, and psychic costs. The buyer evaluates these elements together with the monetary cost to form a total customer cost. Then the buyer considers whether Caterpillar's total cus-

figure **3.1**

Determinants of Customer-Delivered Value

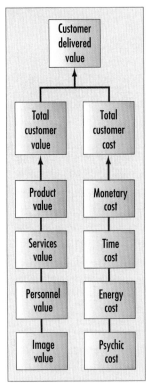

tomer cost is too high in relation to the total customer value Caterpillar delivers. If it is, the buyer might choose the Komatsu tractor. The buyer will buy from whichever source he thinks delivers the highest perceived customer value.

Now let us use this decision-making theory to help Caterpillar succeed in selling to this buyer. Caterpillar can improve its offer in three ways. First, it can increase total customer value by improving product, services, personnel, and/or image benefits. Second, it can reduce the buyer's nonmonetary costs by reducing the time, energy, and psychic costs. Third, it can reduce its product's monetary cost to the buyer.

Suppose Caterpillar concludes that the buyer sees its offer as worth $20,000. Further, suppose Caterpillar's cost of producing the tractor is $14,000. This means that Caterpillar's offer potentially generates $6,000 over the company's cost so Caterpillar needs to charge a price between $14,000 and $20,000. If it charges less than $14,000, it won't cover its costs; if it charges more than $20,000, it will price itself out of the market.

The price Caterpillar charges will determine how much value will be delivered to the buyer and how much will flow to Caterpillar. For example, if Caterpillar charges $19,000, it is creating $1,000 of customer perceived value and keeping $5,000 for itself. The lower Caterpillar sets its price, the higher the customer perceived value and, therefore, the higher the customer's incentive to purchase. To win the sale, Caterpillar must offer more customer perceived value than Komatsu does.[3]

Some marketers might argue that the process we have described is too rational. Suppose the customer chose the Komatsu tractor. How can we explain this choice? Here are three possibilities:

1. The buyer might be under orders to buy at the lowest price. The Caterpillar salesperson's task is to convince the buyer's manager that buying on price alone will result in lower long-term profits.
2. The buyer will retire before the company realizes that the Komatsu tractor is more expensive to operate. The buyer will look good in the short run; he is maximizing personal benefit. The Caterpillar salesperson's task is to convince other people in the customer company that Caterpillar delivers greater customer value.
3. The buyer enjoys a long-term friendship with the Komatsu salesperson. In this case, Caterpillar's salesperson needs to show the buyer that the Komatsu tractor will draw complaints from the tractor operators when they discover its high fuel cost and need for frequent repairs.

The point of these examples is clear: Buyers operate under various constraints and occasionally make choices that give more weight to their personal benefit than to the company's benefit. However, customer perceived value is a useful framework that applies to many situations and yields rich insights. Here are its implications: First, the seller must assess the total customer value and total customer cost associated with each competitor's offer in order to know how his or her offer rates in the buyer's mind. Second, the seller who is at a customer perceived value disadvantage has two alternatives: to increase total customer value or to decrease total customer cost. The former calls for strengthening or augmenting the offer's product, services, personnel, and image benefits. The latter calls for reducing the buyer's costs by reducing the price, simplifying the ordering and delivery process, or absorbing some buyer risk by offering a warranty.[4]

total customer satisfaction

Whether the buyer is satisfied after purchase depends on the offer's performance in relation to the buyer's expectations. In general, **satisfaction** is a person's feelings of pleasure or disappointment resulting from comparing a product's perceived performance (or outcome) in relation to his or her expectations. If the performance falls short of expectations, the customer is dissatisfied. If the performance matches the expectations, the customer is satisfied. If the performance exceeds expectations, the customer is highly satisfied or delighted.[5]

The link between customer satisfaction and customer loyalty is not proportional. Suppose customer satisfaction is rated on a scale from one to five. At a very low level of customer satisfaction (level one), customers are likely to abandon the company and even bad-mouth it. At levels two to four, customers are fairly satisfied but still find it easy to switch when a better offer comes along. At level five, the customer is very likely to repurchase and even spread good word of mouth about the company. High satisfaction or delight creates an emotional bond with the brand or company, not just a rational preference. Xerox's senior management found out that its "completely satisfied" customers are six times more likely to repurchase Xerox products over the following 18 months than its "very satisfied" customers.[6]

CUSTOMER EXPECTATIONS   How do buyers form their expectations? From past buying experience, friends' and associates' advice, and marketers' and competitors' information and promises. If marketers raise expectations too high, the buyer is likely to be disappointed. However, if the company sets expectations too low, it won't attract enough buyers (although it will satisfy those who do buy).[7]

Some of today's most successful companies are raising expectations and delivering performances to match. These companies are aiming for TCS—total customer satisfaction. Xerox, for example, guarantees "total satisfaction" and will replace at its expense any dissatisfied customer's equipment within a period of three years after purchase. Cigna advertises, "We'll never be 100% satisfied until you are, too," and one of Honda's ads says, "One reason our customers are so satisfied is that we aren't." Nissan invites potential Infiniti buyers to drop in for a "guest drive" (not a "test drive"), because the Japanese word for customer is "honored guest." Look at what high satisfaction can do.

Saturn   About a decade ago, Saturn (General Motors' newest car division) changed the whole buyer–seller relationship with a New Deal for car buyers: There would be a fixed price (none of the traditional haggling); a 30-day guarantee or money back; and salespeople on salary, not on commission (none of the traditional hard sell). Once a sale is made, the sales staff surrounds the new owner for a commemorative photo. "The company celebrated its tenth anniversary in 2000 when more than 40,000 Saturn owners visited company headquarters in Spring Hill, Tennessee, to attend the annual Homecoming."[8] Saturn enjoys customer loyalty rates in the 60 percent range, compared with overall industry rates below 40 percent.

A customer's decision to be loyal or to defect is the sum of many small encounters with the company. Consulting firm Forum Corporation says that in order for all these small encounters to add up to customer loyalty, companies need to create a "branded customer experience." Here is how San Francisco's Joie de Vivre chain does this.

Joie de Vivre   Joie de Vivre Hospitality Inc., operates a chain of boutique hotels, restaurants, and resorts in the San Francisco area. Each property's unique décor, quirky amenities, and thematic style are often loosely based on popular magazines. For example, the Hotel del Sol—a converted motel bearing a yellow exterior and surrounded by palm trees wrapped with festive lights—is described as "kind of *Martha Stewart Living* meets *Islands* magazine."[9] Two Silicon Valley hotels offer guests high-speed Internet connections in their rooms and by the pool.[10] The boutique concept enables the hotels to offer personal touches such as vitamins in place of chocolates on pillows. Joie de Vivre now owns the largest number of independent hotel properties in the Bay Area.

DELIVERING HIGH CUSTOMER VALUE   The key to generating high customer loyalty is to deliver high customer value. According to Michael Lanning, in his *Delivering Profitable Value*, a company must design a competitively superior value proposition aimed at a specific market segment, backed by a superior value-delivery system.[11]

The **value proposition** consists of the whole cluster of benefits the company promises to deliver; it is more than the core positioning of the offering. For example, Volvo's core positioning is "safety," but the buyer is promised more than just a safe car; other benefits include a long-lasting car, good service, and a long warranty period. Basically, the value proposition is a statement about the resulting experience customers will gain from the company's market offering and from their relationship with the supplier. The brand must represent a promise about the total experience customers can expect. Whether the promise is kept depends on the company's ability to manage its value-delivery system. The **value-delivery system** includes all the experiences the customer will have on the way to obtaining and using the offering.

A similar theme is emphasized by Simon Knox and Stan Maklan in their *Competing on Value*.[12] Too many companies create a value gap by failing to align brand value with customer value. Brand marketers try to distinguish their brand from others by a slogan ("washes whiter") or a unique selling proposition ("A Mars a day helps you work, rest, and play"), or by augmenting the basic offering with added services ("Our hotel will provide a computer upon request"). Yet, they are less successful in delivering distinctive customer value, primarily because their marketing people focus on brand development. Whether customers will actually receive the promised value proposition will depend on the marketer's ability to influence various core business processes. Knox and Maklan want company marketers to spend as much time influencing the company's core processes as they do designing the brand profile. Here is a company that is a master at delivering customer value.

Superquinn   Superquinn is Ireland's largest supermarket chain and its founder, Feargal Quinn, is Ireland's master marketer. A greeter is posted at the store entrance to welcome and help customers and even offer coffee, to provide umbrellas in case of rain and carryout service to customers' cars. Department managers post themselves in the aisles to interact with customers and answer questions. There is a high-quality salad bar, fresh bread baked every four hours, and indications of when produce arrived, including the farmers' pictures. Superquinn operates a child-care center. It offers a loyalty program that gives points for the amount purchased and also for discovering anything wrong with the store, such as dented cans or bad tomatoes. The loyalty card is recognized by a dozen other firms (a bank, gas station, etc.) who give points for purchasing at their establishments. Because everything is done to exceed normal customer expectations, Superquinn stores enjoy an almost cult following.[13]

In addition to tracking customer value expectations and satisfaction, companies need to monitor their competitors' performance in these areas. One company was pleased to find that 80 percent of its customers said they were satisfied. Then the CEO found out that its leading competitor attained a 90 percent customer satisfaction score. He was further dismayed when he learned that this competitor was aiming for a 95 percent satisfaction score.

Table 3.1 describes four methods companies use to track customer satisfaction.

For customer-centered companies, customer satisfaction is both a goal and a marketing tool. Companies that achieve high customer satisfaction ratings make sure that their target market knows it. The Honda Accord received the number-one rating in customer satisfaction from J. D. Powers for several years, and Honda's advertising of this fact helped it sell more Accords. Dell Computer's meteoric growth in the computer systems industry can be partly attributed to achieving and advertising its number-one rank in customer satisfaction. For more information on how Dell Computer Corporation gets closer to customers, see "Marketing Insight: Customer Configured: How Dell Computer Corporation Clicks with Customers."

MEASURING SATISFACTION   Although the customer-centered firm seeks to create high customer satisfaction, that is not its main goal. If the company increases customer satisfaction by lowering its price or increasing its services, the result may be lower profits.

table **3.1**		
Tools for Tracking and Measuring Customer Satisfaction	*Complaint and suggestion systems:*	A customer-centered organization makes it easy for customers to register suggestions and complaints. Some customer-centered companies—P&G, General Electric, Whirlpool—establish hot lines with toll-free numbers. Companies are also using Web sites and e-mail for quick, two-way communication.
	Customer satisfaction surveys:	Studies show that although customers are dissatisfied with one out of every four purchases, less than 5 percent will complain. Most customers will buy less or switch suppliers. Responsive companies measure customer satisfaction directly by conducting periodic surveys. While collecting customer satisfaction data, it is also useful to ask additional questions to measure repurchase intention and to measure the likelihood or willingness to recommend the company and brand to others.
	Ghost shopping:	Companies can hire people to pose as potential buyers to report on strong and weak points experienced in buying the company's and competitors' products. These mystery shoppers can even test how the company's sales personnel handle various situations. Managers themselves should leave their offices from time to time, enter company and competitor sales situations where they are unknown, and experience firsthand the treatment they receive. A variant of this is for managers to phone their own company with questions and complaints to see how the calls are handled.
	Lost customer analysis:	Companies should contact customers who have stopped buying or who have switched to another supplier to learn why this happened. Not only is it important to conduct exit interviews when customers first stop buying; it is also necessary to monitor the customer loss rate.

The company might be able to increase its profitability by means other than increased satisfaction (for example, by improving manufacturing processes or investing more in R&D). Also, the company has many stakeholders, including employees, dealers, suppliers, and stockholders. Spending more to increase customer satisfaction might divert funds from increasing the satisfaction of other "partners." Ultimately, the company must operate on the philosophy that it is trying to deliver a high level of customer satisfaction subject to delivering acceptable levels of satisfaction to the other stakeholders, given its total resources.

When customers rate their satisfaction with an element of the company's performance—say, delivery—the company needs to recognize that customers vary in how they define good delivery. It could mean early delivery, on-time delivery, order completeness, and so on. Yet if the company had to spell out every element in detail, customers would face a huge survey questionnaire. The company must also realize that two customers can report being "highly satisfied" for different reasons. One may be easily satisfied most of the time and the other might be hard to please but was pleased on this occasion.[14]

Claes Fornell has developed the American Customer Satisfaction Index (ACSI) to measure the perceived satisfaction consumers feel with different firms, industries, economic sectors, and national economies. Some companies and brands with high ACSI scores in 2001 include H. J. Heinz Company (89), Colgate-Palmolive (85), Cadillac (88), and Dell (78).[15]

Companies need to be especially concerned today with their customer satisfaction level because the Internet provides a tool for consumers to spread bad word of mouth—as well as good word of mouth—to the rest of the world.

marketing **insight**

Customer Configured: How Dell Computer Corporation Clicks with Customers

"We have a tremendously clear business model," says Michael Dell, "There's no confusion about what the value proposition is, what the company offers, and why it's great for customers." Dell is now the number one computer systems company.

Dell is extremely responsive. Buyers go on Dell's Web site and design their own computer. They give their payment authorization, which means that Dell receives the money in advance and can use the funds to pay for the supplies needed to build the computer. Because its computers are built-to-order, Dell carries an industry-leading four days of inventory. It takes delivery of components just minutes before they are needed. At its Austin, Texas, factories, a Dell System can in some cases be built, have the software installed, be tested, and be packed in eight hours. Dell's costs are lower, allowing it to price its computers lower than competitors' prices if it wishes.

Yet speed is only one part of the Dell equation. Service is the other. In fact, it was through veering away from its successful business model that Dell discovered the importance of customer service. In 1993, the company began trying to sell to retailers, mainly because everyone else was. Customers were disgruntled because of poor retail service. Dell ultimately abandoned the retail channel.

Most important, Michael Dell decided that "there would be more things we'd have to do besides build a PC." He knew his company had two kinds of customers, corporate and consumer. Whereas the consumer would buy mainly because of price, the corporate buyer needed a carefully developed relationship. Like most successful companies, Dell put the most resources into building relationships with its most profitable customers.

Corporate customers make up about 80 percent of Dell's business, and the company manages its corporate accounts with a top-notch sales team. Dell also installs custom software and keeps track of business customers' inventory for them. Through the use of Premier Dell.com, cus-

tomized customer Web pages at the Dell site, the company has created a 24-hour order-entry system. Big customers can click on the site to see all kinds of information about their preferences and needs. The site can be accessed worldwide by any company subsidiary; and employees, not just purchasing agents, can use the Premier Dell.com to purchase computers according to an automated policy. "It's the ultimate network," Michael Dell says, "and a fabulous way for us to interact with our customers."

The normal practice of companies is to "build to stock." This is a guessing game that companies often lose by building too much or too little. In the auto industry, cars will sit unsold in dealers' lots for 60 days, tying up working capital. Why have auto and other companies not moved from the inefficient "build to stock" model of production to Dell's "build to order" model? Auto manufacturers have invited Michael Dell to speak to them on several occasions. The consensus seems to be that Dell works with 50 main suppliers to put together a $1,000 PC, but a car manufacturer may have to work with 900 suppliers to put together a $20,000 car. In addition to the technical challenge, the auto industry faces dealer and legislative hurdles.

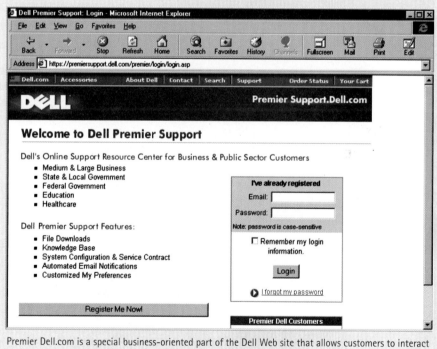

Premier Dell.com is a special business-oriented part of the Dell Web site that allows customers to interact with Dell and customize all phases of doing business with Dell.

Sources: Michele Marchetti, "Dell Computer," *Sales & Marketing Management* (October 1997) 50–53; Evan Ramstad, "Dell Fights PC Wars by Emphasizing Customer Service—Focus Wins Big Clients and Gives IBM and Compaq a Run for Their Money," *Wall Street Journal*, August 15, 1997, p. B4; Saroja Girishankar, "Dell's Site Has Business in Crosshairs," *Internetweek*, April 13, 1998, p. 1; "The *Internetweek* Interview—Michael Dell, Chairman and CEO, Dell Computer," *Internetweek*, April 13, 1998, p. 8; Dale Buss, "Custom Cars Stuck in Gridlock," *The Industry Standard*, October 23, 2000, pp. 90–97; and "A Revolution of One," *The Economist*, April 14, 2001; Betsy Morris, "Can Michael Dell Escape the Box?" *Fortune*, October 16, 2000; Gary McWilliams, "Dell Computer Has a Midlife Crisis," *Wall Street Journal*, August 31, 2000; "Dell Increases Its Market Share as PC Sales Slow," *New York Times*, January 22, 2001; Leah Beth Ward, "Dell Sales Overtake Compaq," *Dallas Morning News*, January 24, 2000.

the nature of high-performance businesses

Some companies navigate all these pitfalls to reach their customer value and satisfaction goals. We call these companies **high-performance businesses**. The consulting firm of Arthur D. Little proposed a model of the characteristics of a high-performance business. It pointed to the four factors shown in Figure 3.2 as keys to success: stakeholders, processes, resources, and organization.[16]

stakeholders

As its first stop on the road to high performance, the business must define its stakeholders and their needs. Traditionally, most businesses focused on their stockholders. Today's businesses are increasingly recognizing that unless they nurture other stakeholders—customers, employees, suppliers, distributors—the business may never earn sufficient profits for the stockholders.

A company can aim to deliver satisfaction levels above the minimum for different stakeholders. For example, it might aim to delight its customers, perform well for its employees, and deliver a threshold level of satisfaction to its suppliers. In setting these levels, a company must be careful not to violate the various stakeholder groups' sense of fairness about the relative treatment they are getting.[17]

There is a dynamic relationship connecting the stakeholder groups. A smart company creates a high level of employee satisfaction, which leads to higher effort, which leads to higher-quality products and services, which creates higher customer satisfaction, which leads to more repeat business, which leads to higher growth and profits, which leads to high stockholder satisfaction, which leads to more investment, and so on. This is the virtuous circle that spells profits and growth.

processes

A company can accomplish its stakeholder goals only by managing and linking work processes. High-performance companies are increasingly focusing on the need to manage core business processes such as new-product development, customer attraction and retention, and order fulfillment. They are reengineering the work flows and building cross-functional teams responsible for each process.[18]

---

figure 3.2

The High Performance Business

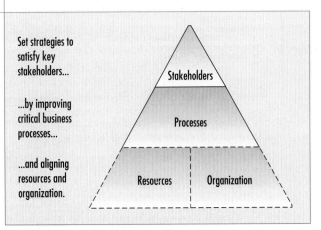

Source: P. Ranganath Nayak, Erica Drazen, and George Kastner, "The High-Performance Business: Accelerating Performance Improvement," *Prism* (First Quarter 1992), p. 6. Reprinted by permission of Arthur D. Little, Inc.

For example, at Xerox a Customer Operations Group links sales, shipping, installation, service, and billing so that these activities flow smoothly into one another. Winning companies will be those that achieve excellent capabilities in managing core business processes through cross-functional teams. A McKinsey & Company study reported:

> High-performing companies emphasize a set of skills notably different from their less successful counterparts. They value cross-functional skills, while other companies pride themselves on their functional strengths. High performers boast, "We've got the best project managers in the world." Low performers say, "We've got the best circuit designers."[19]

AT&T, Polaroid, and Motorola are companies that have reorganized their employees into cross-functional teams; but cross-functional teams are also found in nonprofits and government organizations as well.

San Diego Zoo   As the San Diego Zoo's mission changed from simple exhibition to conservation to education, it changed its organization. The revamped zoo consists of bioclimatic zones, exhibits that immerse zoogoers in an environment of predator and prey and flora and fauna from different parts of the world. Because the zones themselves are more interdependent, the employees who manage them must work together. Gardeners, groundskeepers, and animal care experts are no longer separated by traditional boundaries.[20]

resources

To carry out its business processes, a company needs resources—labor power, materials, machines, information, and energy. Traditionally, companies owned and controlled most of the resources that entered their businesses, but this situation is changing. Some resources under their control are not performing as well as those that they could obtain from outside. Many companies today outsource less critical resources if they can be obtained at better quality or lower cost. Frequently, outsourced resources include cleaning services, landscaping, and auto fleet management. Kodak even turned over the management of its data processing department to IBM. Here are two examples of successful outsourcing.

Palm Computing   According to Donna Dubinsky, president of Palm Computing, her company outsources services whenever they can be done better and more cheaply. This includes outsourcing manufacturing, logistics, services, and customer support systems. Her staff is a group of talented product designers, inventors, and engineers, along with a senior group who manage the outsourced infrastructure organizations.

Topsy-Tail   Tomima Edmark, inventor of the plastic hairstyling piece called Topsy-Tail, grew her company's sales to $80 million in 1993 with only two employees. Instead of hiring 50 or more employees, Edmark and her two employees set up a network of 20 vendors who handled everything from product manufacturing to servicing the retail accounts. Yet Edmark has been careful to follow the first rule of effective outsourcing: She keeps control of new-product development and marketing strategy, the core competencies that make up the heart of her company.[21]

The key, then, is to own and nurture the core resources and competencies that make up the essence of the business. Nike, for example, does not manufacture its own shoes, because certain Asian manufacturers are more competent in this task; but Nike nurtures its superiority in shoe design and shoe merchandising, its two core competencies. We can say that a **core competency** has three characteristics: (1) It is a source of competitive advantage in that it makes a significant contribution to perceived customer benefits, (2) it has a breadth of applications to a wide variety of markets, and (3) it is difficult for competitors to imitate.[22]

Competitive advantage also accrues to companies that possess distinctive capabilities. Whereas core competencies tend to refer to areas of special technical and production expertise, **distinctive capabilities** tend to describe excellence in broader business processes. For example, Wal-Mart has a distinctive capability in product replenishment, based several core competencies including information system design and logistics. George Day sees market-driven organizations as excelling in three distinctive capabilities: market sensing, customer linking, and channel bonding.[23]

Competitive advantage ultimately derives from how well the company has "fitted" its core competencies and distinctive capabilities into tightly interlocking "activity systems." Competitors find it hard to imitate companies such as Southwest Airlines, Dell, or IKEA because they are unable to copy their activity systems.

organization and organizational culture

A company's **organization** consists of its structures, policies, and corporate culture, all of which can become dysfunctional in a rapidly changing business environment. Whereas structures and policies can be changed (with difficulty), the company's culture is very hard to change. Yet changing a corporate culture is often the key to successfully implementing a new strategy.

What exactly is a **corporate culture**? Most businesspeople would be hard-pressed to find words to describe this elusive concept, which some define as "the shared experiences, stories, beliefs, and norms that characterize an organization." Yet, walk into any company and the first thing that strikes you is the corporate culture—the way people are dressed, how they talk to one another, the way they greet customers.

Sometimes corporate culture develops organically and is transmitted directly from the CEO's personality and habits to the company employees. Such is the case with computer giant Microsoft, which began as an entrepreneurial upstart. Even as it has grown to a $23-billion company, Microsoft has not lost the hard-driving culture perpetuated by founder Bill Gates. In fact, most feel that Microsoft's ultracompetitive culture is the biggest key to its success and to its much-criticized dominance in the computing industry.[24]

Microsoft   Do not let the relaxed, low-rise campus buildings, plush lawns, shaded copses, and strictly casual dress code fool you. Microsofties, as Microsoft employees refer to themselves, are fueled with a take-no-prisoners competitive drive that mirrors Gates's own persona. Rivals from Silicon Valley refer to them as "microserfs." Like Gates, who founded the company as a teenager, Microsofties are young; nearly one-third are age 29 or younger, with an average age of 34. Their casual dress code also stems from Gates, who used to fall asleep on the floor of his garage after an all-night code-writing session and go to work in his rumpled clothing the next morning. Although you would not know it to look at the T-shirt-clad employees, many of them are rolling in money from Microsoft stock options. Part of the competitive zeal is due to the drive to sustain a lofty share price, which traded in multiples at or near twice the S&P's 500 until the recent technology stock slide. Insiders own over one-third of the company, and there are more millionaires on staff than in any other firm on earth.

What happens when entrepreneurial companies grow and need to create a tighter structure? What happens when companies with clashing cultures enter a joint venture or merger? In a study by Coopers & Lybrand of 100 companies with failed or troubled mergers, 855 of executives polled said that differences in management style and practices were the major problem.[25] This was the case when Germany's Daimler merged with Chrysler in 1998.

DaimlerChrysler   Daimler-Benz AG and Chrysler Corp. merged in 1998 to form DaimlerChrysler. Executives from both companies thought a host of synergies would enable DaimlerChrysler to swiftly build a global automotive empire. Fundamental differences in the way the two corporations did business, however, contributed to early departures by executives, a stock price slide, management restructuring, and even considerable losses by the American manufacturer. The two companies had contrasting management styles, Daimler preferring to operate a classic bureaucracy and Chrysler traditionally giving decision-making ability to managers lower in the ranks. After restructuring the company in 1999 to give more autonomy to the American division, DaimlerChrysler CEO Jürgen Schrempp angered Chrysler employees anew when he announced that he always intended to make Chrysler a division of Daimler. What began as a highly-touted global "merger of equals" turned into a disaster as the losses piled up at Chrysler and DaimlerChrysler stock languished at more than half off its peak. The company announced 26,000 layoffs in February 2001.[26]

The question of what accounts for the success of long-lasting, high-performance companies was addressed in a six-year study by Collins and Porras called *Built to Last*.[27] The Stanford researchers identified two companies in each of 18 industries, one that they called a "visionary company" and one that they called a "comparison company." The visionary companies were acknowledged as the industry leaders and widely admired; they set ambitious goals, communicated them to their employees, and embraced a high purpose beyond making money. They also outperformed the comparison companies by a wide margin. The visionary companies included General Electric, Hewlett-Packard, and Boeing; the corresponding comparison companies were Westinghouse, Texas Instruments, and McDonnell Douglas.

The authors found three commonalities among the 18 market leaders. First, the visionary companies each held a distinctive set of values from which they did not deviate. Thus, IBM has held to the principles of respect for the individual, customer satisfaction, and continuous quality improvement throughout its history;[28] and Johnson & Johnson holds to the principle that its first responsibility is to its customers, its second to its employees, its third to its community, and its fourth to its stockholders. The second commonality is that visionary companies express their purpose in enlightened terms. Xerox wants to improve "office productivity" and Monsanto wants to "help end hunger in the world." According to Collins and Porras, a company's core purpose should not be confused with specific business goals or strategies and should not be simply a description of a company's product line. (See "Marketing Memo: Why Do You Exist and What Do You Stand For?") The third commonality is that visionary companies have developed a vision of their future and act to implement it. IBM is now working to establish leadership as a "network-centric" company and not simply as the leading computer manufacturer.

Successful companies may need to adopt a new view of how to craft their strategy. The traditional view is that senior management hammers out the strategy and hands it down. Gary Hamel offers the contrasting view that imaginative ideas on strategy exist in many places within a company.[29] Senior management should identify and encourage fresh ideas from three groups who tend to be underrepresented in strategy making: employees with youthful perspectives; employees who are far removed from company headquarters; and employees who are new to the industry. Each group is capable of challenging company orthodoxy and stimulating new ideas.

Strategy must be developed by identifying and selecting among different views of the future. The Royal Dutch/Shell Group has pioneered scenario analysis. A **scenario analysis** consists of developing plausible representations of a firm's possible future that make different assumptions about forces driving the market and include different uncertainties. Managers need to think through each scenario with the question: "What will we do if it happens?" They need to adopt one scenario as the most probable and watch for signposts as time passes that might confirm or disconfirm that scenario.[30]

High-performance companies are set up to create and deliver superior customer value and satisfaction. Let us see how this is done.

delivering customer value and satisfaction

In a hypercompetitive economy with increasingly rational buyers, a company can only win by creating and delivering superior value. This involves the following five capabilities: understanding customer value; creating customer value; delivering customer value; capturing customer value; and sustaining customer value. To succeed, a company needs to use the concepts of a value chain and a value-delivery network.

value chain

Michael Porter of Harvard proposed the **value chain** as a tool for identifying ways to create more customer value (see Figure 3.3).[31] Every firm is a synthesis of activities that are performed to design, produce, market, deliver, and support its product. The value chain identifies nine strategically relevant activities that create value and cost in a specific business. These nine value-creating activities consist of five primary activities and four support activities.

The primary activities represent the sequence of bringing materials into the business (inbound logistics), converting them into final products (operations), shipping out final products (outbound logistics), marketing them (marketing and sales), and servicing them (service). The support activities—procurement, technology development, human resource management, and firm infrastructure—are handled in certain specialized departments, but not only there. For example, several departments may do some procurement and hiring of people. The firm's infrastructure covers the costs of general management, planning, finance, accounting, legal, and government affairs that are borne by all the primary and support activities.

The firm's task is to examine its costs and performance in each value-creating activity and to look for ways to improve it. The firm should estimate its competitors' costs

---

figure 3.3

The Generic Value Chain

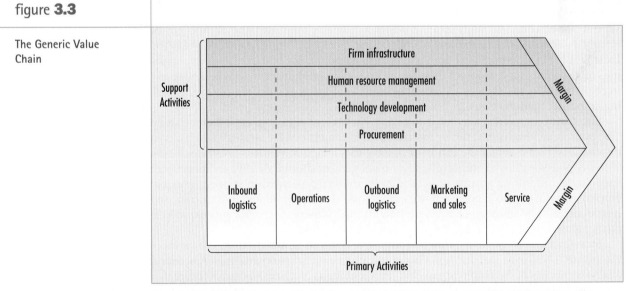

Source: Reprinted with the permission of The Free Press, an imprint of Simon & Schuster, from Michael E. Porter, *Competitive Advantage. Creating and Sustaining Superior Performance.* Copyright 1985 by Michael E. Porter.

and performances as **benchmarks** against which to compare its own costs and performances. It should go further and study the "best of class" practices of the world's best companies.[32]

The firm's success depends not only on how well each department performs its work, but also on how well the various departmental activities are coordinated. Too often, company departments act to maximize their interests. A credit department may take a long time to check a prospective customer's credit so as not to incur bad debts. Meanwhile, the customer waits and the salesperson is frustrated. A traffic department chooses to ship the goods by rail to save money and again the customer waits. Each department has erected walls that slow down the delivery of quality customer service. The solution to this problem is to place more emphasis on the smooth management of core business processes.[33]

These core business processes include:

- *The market sensing process:* All the activities involved in gathering market intelligence, disseminating it within the organization, and acting on the information.
- *The new offering realization process:* All the activities involved in researching, developing, and launching new high-quality offerings quickly and within budget.
- *The customer acquisition process:* All the activities involved in defining target markets and prospecting for new customers.
- *The customer relationship management process:* All the activities involved in building deeper understanding, relationships, and offerings to individual customers.
- *The fulfillment management process:* All the activities involved in receiving and approving orders, shipping the goods on time, and collecting payment.

Strong companies develop superior capabilities in managing their core processes. For example, Wal-Mart has superior strength in its stock replenishment process. As Wal-Mart stores sell their goods, sales information flows via computer not only to Wal-Mart's headquarters, but also to Wal-Mart's suppliers, who ship replacement merchandise to the stores almost at the rate it moves off the shelf.[34] The idea is not to manage stocks of goods, but flows of goods, and Wal-Mart has turned over this responsibility to its leading vendors in a system known as **vendor-managed inventories (VMI).**

the value-delivery network

To be successful a firm also needs to look for competitive advantages beyond its own operations, into the value chains of its suppliers, distributors, and customers. Many companies today have partnered with specific suppliers and distributors to create a superior **value-delivery network** (also called a **supply chain**).[35]

Bailey Controls   An Ohio-headquartered, $300-million-a-year manufacturer of control systems for big factories, Bailey Controls treats some of its suppliers as if they were departments within Bailey. The company recently plugged two of its suppliers directly into its inventory-management system. Every week Bailey electronically sends Montreal-based Future Electronics its latest forecasts of the materials it will need for the next six months. Whenever a bin of parts falls below a designated level, a Bailey employee passes a laser scanner over the bin's bar code, alerting Future to send the parts at once. Although arrangements like this shift inventory costs to the suppliers, the suppliers expect those costs to be more than offset by the gain in volume. It is a win–win partnership.

Betz Laboratories   Betz Laboratories, a Pennsylvania-based maker of industrial water-treatment chemicals, sells chemicals to keep the water in its customers' plants from gunking up pipes or corroding machinery. Today Betz provides its large customers with

figure **3.4**

Levi Strauss's Value–Delivery Network

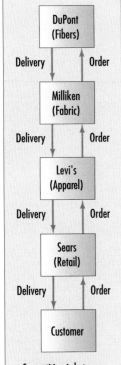

DuPont
(Fibers)

Delivery ↓ ↑ Order

Milliken
(Fabric)

Delivery ↓ ↑ Order

Levi's
(Apparel)

Delivery ↓ ↑ Order

Sears
(Retail)

Delivery ↓ ↑ Order

Customer

Competition is between *networks*, not companies. The winner is the company with the better network.

both goods and expertise. High-level teams composed of Betz's and its customers' engineers and managers examine all the water in the customers' plants. They ask and answer such questions as: Is the water safe for the equipment? Does it meet environmental standards? Is it being used in the most cost-effective way? In less than one year the Betz team in one AlliedSignal plant pinpointed $2.5 million in potential cost savings.

Another excellent example of a value-delivery network is the one that connects Levi Strauss & Company, the famous maker of blue jeans, with its suppliers and distributors (see Figure 3.4). One of Levi's major retailers is Sears. Every night Levi's learns the sizes and styles of its blue jeans sold through Sears and other major outlets. Levi's then electronically orders more fabric for next-day delivery from Milliken & Company, its fabric supplier. Milliken, in turn, relays an order for more fiber to DuPont, its fiber supplier. In this way, the partners in the supply chain use the most current sales information to manufacture what is selling, rather than for a forecast that may not match current demand. In this system, the goods are pulled by demand rather than pushed by supply.

attracting and retaining customers

In addition to working with partners—called **partner relationship management (PRM)**—many companies are intent on developing stronger bonds with their customers—called **customer relationship management (CRM)**. This is the process of managing detailed information about individual customers and carefully managing all the customer "touchpoints" with the aim of maximizing customer loyalty.

attracting customers

Today's customers are becoming harder to please. They are smarter, more price conscious, more demanding, less forgiving, and they are approached by many more competitors with equal or better offers. The challenge, according to Jeffrey Gitomer, is not to produce satisfied customers; several competitors can do this. The challenge is to produce delighted and loyal customers.[36]

Companies seeking to expand their profits and sales have to spend considerable time and resources searching for new customers. To generate leads, the company develops ads and places them in media that will reach new prospects; it sends direct mail and makes phone calls to possible new prospects; its salespeople participate in trade shows where they might find new leads; and so on. All this activity produces a list of suspects. The next task is to identify which suspects are really good prospects, by interviewing them, checking on their financial standing, and so on. Then it is time to send out the salespeople.

computing the cost of lost customers

It is not enough to be skillful in attracting new customers; the company must keep them and increase their business. Too many companies suffer from high **customer churn**—namely, high customer defection. It is like adding water to a leaking bucket. Cellular carriers, for example, are plagued with "spinners," customers who switch carriers at least three times a year looking for the best deal. Many lose 25 percent of their subscribers each year at an estimated cost of $2 billion to $4 billion.

There are steps a company can take to reduce the defection rate. First, the company must define and measure its retention rate. For a magazine, the renewal rate is a good measure of retention. For a college, it could be the first- to second-year retention rate, or the class graduation rate. Second, the company must distinguish the causes of customer attrition and identify those that can be managed better. (See "Marketing Memo: Asking Questions When Customers Leave.") The Forum Corporation analyzed the customers lost by 14 major companies for reasons other than leaving the region or going out of business: 15 percent switched because they found a better product; another 15 percent found a cheaper product; and 70 percent left because of poor or little attention from the supplier. Not much can be done about customers who leave the region or go out of business, but much can be done about those who leave because of poor service, shoddy products, or high prices.[37]

Third, the company needs to estimate how much profit it loses when it loses customers. In the case of an individual customer, the lost profit is equal to the customer's **lifetime value**—that is, the present value of the profit stream that the company would have realized if the customer had not defected prematurely (see the discussion of lifetime value, under "Measuring Customer Lifetime Value"). For a group of lost customers, one major transportation carrier estimated its lost profit as follows:

1. The company had 64,000 accounts.
2. The company lost 5 percent of its accounts this year due to poor service: This was a loss of 3,200 accounts (.05 × 64,000).
3. The average lost account represented a $40,000 loss in revenue. Therefore, the company lost $128,000,000 in revenue (3,200 × $40,000).
4. The company's profit margin is 10 percent. Therefore, the company lost $12,800,000 (.10 × $128,000,000) this year. Because the customers left prematurely, the actual loss over time is much greater.

Fourth, the company needs to figure out how much it would cost to reduce the defection rate. As long as the cost is less than the lost profit, the company should spend the money.

Finally, nothing beats listening to customers. Some companies have created an ongoing mechanism that keeps senior managers permanently plugged in to front-line customer feedback. MBNA, the credit-card giant, asks every executive to listen in on telephone conversations in the customer service area or customer recovery units. Deere & Company, which makes John Deere tractors and has a superb record of customer loyalty—nearly 98 percent annual retention in some product areas—uses retired employees to interview defectors and customers.[38] (See "Marketing for the New Economy: Customer Service Live and Online," for another example.)

the need for customer retention

Unfortunately, most marketing theory and practice centers on the art of attracting new customers rather than on retaining and cultivating existing ones. The emphasis traditionally has been on making sales rather than building relationships; on preselling and selling rather than caring for the customer afterward. A company would be wise to measure customer satisfaction regularly, because the key to customer retention is customer satisfaction.

A highly satisfied customer stays loyal longer, buys more as the company introduces new products and upgrades existing products, talks favorably about the company and its products, pays less attention to competing brands and is less sensitive to price, offers product or service ideas to the company, and costs less to serve than new customers because transactions are routine.

Some companies think they are getting a sense of customer satisfaction by tallying customer complaints, but 96 percent of dissatisfied customers don't complain; many just stop buying.[39] The best thing a company can do is to make it easy for the customer to complain. Suggestion forms and toll-free numbers and e-mail addresses serve this purpose. The 3M Company claims that over two-thirds of its product-improvement ideas come from listening to customer complaints.

Listening is not enough, however. The company must respond quickly and constructively to the complaints:

> Of the customers who register a complaint, between 54 and 70% will do business again with the organization if their complaint is resolved. The figure goes up to a staggering 95% if the customer feels that the complaint was resolved quickly. Customers who have complained to an organization and had their complaints satisfactorily resolved tell an average of five people about the good treatment they received.[40]

marketing for the **new economy**

Customer Service Live and Online

E-commerce companies looking to attract and retain customers are discovering that personalization goes beyond creating customized information. For example, the Lands' End Live Web site offers visitors the opportunity to talk with a customer service representative. Nordstrom takes a similar approach with its Web site to ensure that online buyers are as satisfied with the company's customer service as the in-store visitors; and, with the click of a button, Eddie Bauer's e-commerce site connects shoppers to customer service representatives (CSRs) with a text-based chat feature.

Research from a 1999 survey by Boston Consulting group and Shop.org revealed that 65 percent of online shoppers abandon their purchase before finishing checkout. Worse, only 1.8 percent of visits to online retailers lead to sales, compared with 5 percent of visits to department stores. Analysts attribute this behavior partly to a general absence of interactive customer service in e-commerce. Customers looking for help are often sent to a text help file rather than a live sales representative. This can be frustrating and may prompt a customer to exit the site without buying. Another benefit of providing live sales assistance is the ability to sell additional items. When a representative is involved in the sale, the average amount per order is typically higher.

Not all customer service features involve live personnel. Both Macys.com and gap.com offer prerecorded customer service information. Gap's Web site includes a "zoom" feature, which shoppers can use to get a close look at every detail of a garment, from elastic waistbands to fabric prints. Lands' End Live allows customers to "try on" clothes online using virtual models based on measurements supplied by customers.

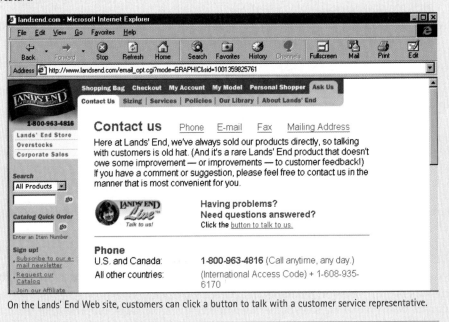

On the Lands' End Web site, customers can click a button to talk with a customer service representative.

Sources: Susan Stellin, "For Many Online Companies, Customer Service Is Hardly a Priority," *New York Times*, February 19, 2001; Michelle Johnson, "Getting Ready for the Onslaught," *Boston Globe*, November 4, 1999.

One company long recognized for its emphasis on customer satisfaction is Maine's L.L. Bean, Inc., which runs a mail-order catalog business in clothing and equipment for rugged living. Bean once refunded the money on a pair of two-year-old shoes because the customer said the pair did not wear as well as expected. L.L. Bean has carefully blended its external and internal marketing programs. To its customers, it offers the following:[41]

100% Guarantee

All of our products are guaranteed to give 100% satisfaction in every way. Return anything purchased from us at any time if it proves otherwise. We will replace it, refund your purchase price or credit your credit card, as you wish. We do not want you to have anything from L.L. Bean that is not completely satisfactory.

To motivate its employees to serve the customers well, it displays the following poster prominently around its offices:[42]

What Is a Customer?

A Customer is the most important person ever in this office . . . in person or by mail.

A Customer is not dependent on us . . . we are dependent on him.

A Customer is not an interruption of our work . . . he is the purpose of it. We are not doing a favor by serving him . . . he is doing us a favor by giving us the opportunity to do so.

A Customer is not someone to argue or match wits with. Nobody ever won an argument with a Customer.

A Customer is a person who brings us his wants. It is our job to handle them profitably to him and to ourselves.

Today, more companies are recognizing the importance of satisfying and retaining customers. Satisfied customers constitute the company's relationship capital. If the company were to be sold, the acquiring company would have to pay not only for the plant and equipment and the brand name, but also for the delivered customer base, namely, the number and value of the customers who would do business with the new firm. Here are some interesting facts bearing on customer retention:[43]

1. Acquiring new customers can cost five times more than the costs involved in satisfying and retaining current customers. It requires a great deal of effort to induce satisfied customers to switch away from their current suppliers.
2. The average company loses 10 percent of its customers each year.
3. A 5 percent reduction in the customer defection rate can increase profits by 25 percent to 85 percent, depending on the industry.
4. The customer profit rate tends to increase over the life of the retained customer.

measuring customer lifetime value

The case for increasing the customer retention rate is captured in the concept of customer lifetime value (CLV). **Customer lifetime value (CLV)** describes the present value of the stream of future profits expected over the customer's lifetime purchases. The company must subtract from the expected revenues the expected costs of attracting, selling, and servicing that customer. Various estimates have been made for different products and services.

- Carl Sewell, in *Customers for Life* (with Paul Brown), estimated that a customer entering his dealership for the first time represents a potential lifetime value of over $300,000.[44] If the customer is satisfied and buys several automobiles from the dealership over his or her buying lifetime, and subtracting the cost of selling and serving the customer, this may be the figure. If the satisfied customer brings in other customers, the figure would be higher.
- Mark Grainer, former chairman of the Technical Assistance Research Programs Institute (TARP), estimated that a loyal supermarket customer is worth $3,800 annually.[45]

Of course, a company needs, in addition to an average customer estimate, a way of estimating CLV for each individual customer. This is because the company must decide on how much to invest in each customer.

We can work out an example of estimating CLV. Suppose a company analyzes its new-customer acquisition cost:

Cost of an average sales call (including salary, commission, benefits, and expenses)	$300
Average number of sales calls to convert an average prospect into a customer	×4
Cost of attracting a new customer	$1,200

This is an underestimate because we are omitting the cost of advertising and promotion, plus the fact that only a fraction of all pursued prospects end up being converted into customers.

Now suppose the company estimates average customer lifetime value as follows:

Annual customer revenue	$5,000
Average number of loyal years	×2
Company profit margin	.10
Customer lifetime value	$1,000

This company is spending more to attract new customers than they are worth. Unless the company can sign up customers with fewer sales calls, spend less per sales call, stimulate higher new-customer annual spending, retain customers longer, or sell them higher-profit products, it is headed for bankruptcy.

There are two ways to strengthen customer retention. One is to erect high switching barriers. Customers are less inclined to switch to another supplier when this would involve high capital costs, high search costs, or the loss of loyal-customer discounts. The better approach is to deliver high customer satisfaction. This makes it harder for competitors to offer just lower prices or switching inducements. The task of creating strong customer loyalty is called customer relationship management.

customer relationship management (crm): the key

The aim of **customer relationship management (CRM)** is to produce high customer equity. **Customer equity** is the total of the discounted lifetime values of all of the firm's customers. Clearly, the more loyal the customers, the higher the customer equity. Rust, Zeithaml, and Lemon distinguish three drivers of customer equity: value equity, brand equity, and relationship equity.[46]

- *Value equity* is the customer's objective assessment of the utility of an offering based on perceptions of its benefits relative to its costs. The subdrivers of value equity are quality, price, and convenience. Each industry has to define the specific factors underlying each subdriver in order to find programs to improve value equity. An airline passenger might define quality as seat width; a hotel guest might define quality as room size. Value equity makes the biggest contribution to customer equity when products are differentiated and when they are more complex and need to be evaluated. Value equity especially drives customer equity in business markets.
- *Brand equity* is the customer's subjective and intangible assessment of the brand, above and beyond its objectively perceived value. The subdrivers of brand equity are customer brand awareness, customer attitude toward the brand, and customer perception of brand ethics. Companies use advertising, public relations, and other communication tools to affect these subdrivers. Brand equity is more important than the other drivers of customer equity where products are less differentiated and have more emotional impact.
- *Relationship equity* is the customer's tendency to stick with the brand, above and beyond objective and subjective assessments of its worth. Subdrivers of relationship equity include loyalty programs, special recognition and treatment programs, community building programs, and knowledge-building programs. Relationship equity is especially important where personal relationships count for a lot and where customers tend to continue with suppliers out of habit or inertia.

This formulation integrates *value management*, *brand management*, and *relationship management* within a customer-centered focus. Companies can decide which driver(s) to strengthen for the best payoff. The researchers believe they can measure and compare the financial return of alternative investments. Companies now have a better framework for choosing strategies and actions based on which would provide the best return on marketing investments.

Figure 3.5 shows the main steps in the process of attracting and keeping customers. The starting point is everyone who might conceivably buy the product or service (suspects). From these the company determines the most likely prospects, which it hopes to convert into first-time customers, and then into repeat customers, and then into clients—people whom the company treats very specially and knowledgeably. The next

figure **3.5**

The Customer–Development Process

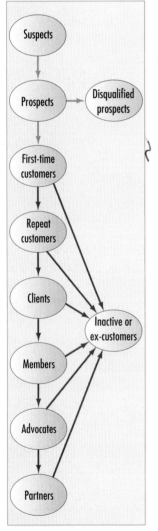

Source: See Jill Griffin, *Customer Loyalty: How to Earn It, How to Keep It* (New York: Lexington Books, 1995), p. 36. Also see Murray Raphel and Neil Raphel, *Up the Loyalty Ladder: Turning Sometime Customers into Full-Time Advocates of Your Business* (New York: HarperBusiness, 1995).

challenge is to turn clients into members by starting a membership program that offers benefits to customers who join, and then into advocates, customers who enthusiastically recommend the company and its products and services to others. The ultimate challenge is to turn advocates into partners.

Some customers inevitably become inactive or drop out. The challenge is to reactivate dissatisfied customers through win-back strategies. It is often easier to reattract ex-customers (because the company knows their names and histories) than to find new ones. The key is to analyze the causes of customer defection through exit interviews and lost customer surveys. The aim is to win back only those customers who have strong profit potential.

How much should a company invest in building loyalty so that the costs do not exceed the gains? We need to distinguish five different levels of investment in customer-relationship building:

1. *Basic marketing:* The salesperson simply sells the product.
2. *Reactive marketing:* The salesperson sells the product and encourages the customer to call if he or she has questions, comments, or complaints.
3. *Accountable marketing:* The salesperson phones the customer to check whether the product is meeting expectations. The salesperson also asks the customer for any product- or service-improvement suggestions and any specific disappointments.
4. *Proactive marketing:* The salesperson contacts the customer from time to time with suggestions about improved product uses or new products.
5. *Partnership marketing:* The company works continuously with its large customers to help improve their performance. (General Electric, for example, has stationed engineers at large utilities to help them produce more power.)

Most companies practice only basic marketing when their markets contain many customers and their unit profit margins are small. Whirlpool is not going to phone each washing machine buyer to express appreciation. At best, it may set up a customer hot line. At the other extreme, in markets with few customers and high profit margins, most sellers will move toward partnership marketing. Boeing, for example, works closely with American Airlines in designing airplanes that fully satisfy American's requirements. As Figure 3.6 shows, the likely level of relationship marketing depends on the number of customers and the profit margin level.

The best relationship marketing going on today is driven by technology. GE Plastics could not target its e-mail effectively to different customers if it were not for advances in database software. Dell Computer could not customize computer ordering for its global corporate customers without advances in Web technology. Companies are using e-mail, Web sites, call centers, databases, and database software to foster continuous contact

figure **3.6**

Levels of Relationship Marketing

	High Margin	Medium Margin	Low Margin
Many customers/ distributors	Accountable	Reactive	Basic or reactive
Medium number of customers/ distributors	Proactive	Accountable	Reactive
Few customers/ distributors	Partnership	Proactive	Accountable

between company and customer. Here is how one company used technology to build customer value:

Ameritrade   The discount brokerage service Ameritrade provides detailed information to its customers, which helps to create strong bonds. It provides customized alerts to the device of the customer's choice, detailing stock movements and analysts' recommendations. The company's Web site permits online trading and provides access to a variety of research tools. Ameritrade developed an investing tutorial called Darwin that it offered free on CD-ROM to its customers. Customers responded to this new focus on their needs: Ameritrade grew from fewer than 100,000 accounts in 1997 to 1.3 million in 2000.[47]

forming strong customer bonds: the basics

Companies that want to form strong customer bonds need to attend to the following basics:

- Get cross-departmental participation in planning and managing the customer satisfaction and retention process.
- Integrate the Voice of the Customer in all business decisions.
- Create superior products, services, and experiences for the target market.
- Organize and make accessible a database of information on individual customer needs, preferences, contacts, purchase frequency, and satisfaction.
- Make it easy for customers to reach appropriate company personnel and express their needs, perceptions, and complaints.
- Run award programs recognizing outstanding employees.

Berry and Parasuraman have gone beyond these basics and identified three retention-building approaches:[48] adding financial benefits, adding social benefits, and adding structural ties.

ADDING FINANCIAL BENEFITS   Two financial benefits that companies can offer are frequency programs and club marketing programs. **Frequency programs (FPs)** are designed to provide rewards to customers who buy frequently and in substantial amounts. Frequency marketing is an acknowledgment of the fact that 20 percent of a company's customers might account for 80 percent of its business.

American Airlines was one of the first companies to pioneer a frequency program in the early 1980s, when it decided to offer free mileage credit to its customers. Hotels next adopted FPs, with Marriott taking the lead with its Honored Guest Program. Shortly thereafter, car rental firms sponsored FPs. Then credit-card companies began to offer points based on card usage level. Sears offers rebates to its Discover cardholders. Today most supermarket chains offer price club cards, which provide member customers with discounts on particular items.

Typically, the first company to introduce an FP gains the most benefit, especially if competitors are slow to respond. After competitors respond, FPs can become a financial burden to all the offering companies, but some companies are more efficient and creative in managing an FP. For example, airlines are running tiered loyalty programs in which they offer different levels of rewards to different travelers. They may offer one frequent-flier mile for every mile flown to occasional travelers and two frequent-flier miles for every mile flown to top customers.

Many companies have created club membership programs to bond customers closer to the company. Club membership can be open to everyone who purchases a product or service, or it can be limited to an affinity group or to those willing to pay a small fee. Although open clubs are good for building a database or snagging customers from competitors, limited membership clubs are more powerful long-term loyalty builders. Fees and membership conditions prevent those with only a fleeting interest in a company's products from joining. These clubs attract and keep those customers who are responsible for the largest portion of business. Some highly successful clubs include the following:

Apple Apple encourages owners of its computers to form local Apple-user groups. By 2001, there were over 600 groups ranging in size from fewer than 25 members to over 1,000 members. The user groups provide Apple owners with opportunities to learn more about their computers, share ideas, get product discounts, and they sponsor special activities and events and perform community service. A visit to Apple's Web site will help a customer find a nearby user group.[49]

Harley-Davidson The world-famous motorcycle company sponsors the Harley Owners Group (H.O.G.), which now numbers 600,000 members in over 1,200 chapters. The first-time buyer of a Harley-Davidson motorcycle gets a free one-year membership. H.O.G. benefits include a magazine called *Hog Tales*, a touring handbook, emergency road service, a specially designed insurance program, theft reward service, discount hotel rates, and a Fly & Ride program enabling members to rent Harleys while on vacation. The company also maintains an extensive Web site devoted to H.O.G., which includes information on club chapters, events, and a special members-only section.[50]

ADDING SOCIAL BENEFITS Company personnel work on increasing social bonds with customers by individualizing and personalizing customer relationships. Table 3.2 contrasts a socially sensitive approach with a socially insensitive approach to customers. In essence, thoughtful companies turn their customers into clients. Donnelly, Berry, and Thompson draw this distinction:

> Customers may be nameless to the institution; clients cannot be nameless. Customers are served as part of the mass or as part of larger segments; clients are served on an individual basis. Customers are served by anyone who happens to be available; clients are served by the professional assigned to them.[51]

The H.O.G. Web site presents the benefits of joining.

table **3.2**	Good Things	Bad Things
Social Actions Affecting Buyer–Seller Relationships	Initiate positive phone calls	Make only callbacks
	Make recommendations	Make justifications
	Candor in language	Accommodative language
	Use phone	Use correspondence
	Show appreciation	Wait for misunderstandings
	Make service suggestions	Wait for service requests
	Use "we" problem-solving language	Use "owe-us" legal language
	Get to problems	Only respond to problems
	Use jargon or shorthand	Use long-winded communications
	Personality problems aired	Personality problems hidden
	Talk of "our future together"	Talk about making good on the past
	Routinize responses	Fire drill and emergency responsiveness
	Accept responsibility	Shift blame
	Plan the future	Rehash the past

Source: Theodore Levitt, *The Marketing Imagination* (New York: Free Press, 1983), p. 119. Reprinted by permission of the *Harvard Business Review.* An exhibit from Theodore Levitt, "After the Sale Is Over," *Harvard Business Review* (September–October 1983): p. 119. Copyright 1983 by the President and Fellows of Harvard College, all rights reserved.

ADDING STRUCTURAL TIES   The company may supply customers with special equipment or computer linkages that help customers manage orders, payroll, and inventory. A good example is McKesson Corporation, a leading pharmaceutical wholesaler, which invested millions of dollars in EDI capabilities to help independent pharmacies manage inventory, order-entry processes, and shelf space. Another example is Milliken & Company, which provides proprietary software programs, marketing research, sales training, and sales leads to loyal customers.

Lester Wunderman, one of the most astute observers of contemporary marketing, thinks talk about "loyalizing" customers misses the point.[52] People can be loyal to their country, family, and beliefs, but less so to their toothpaste, soap, or even beer. The marketer's aim should be to increase the consumer's *proclivity to repurchase* the company's brand.

Here are his suggestions for creating structural ties with the customer:

1. *Create long-term contracts.* A newspaper subscription replaces the need to buy a newspaper each day. A 20-year mortgage replaces the need to re-borrow the money each year. A home heating oil agreement assures continual delivery without renewing the order.
2. *Charge a lower price to consumers who buy larger supplies.* Offer lower prices to people who agree to be supplied regularly with a certain brand of toothpaste, detergent, or beer.
3. *Turn the product into a long-term service.* Daimler-Chrysler is considering selling miles of reliable transportation instead of cars, with the consumer able to order different cars at different times, such as a station wagon for shopping and a convertible for the weekend. Gaines, the dog food company, could offer a Pet Care service that includes kennels, insurance, and veterinary care along with food.

customer profitability, company profitability, and total quality management
measuring profitability

Ultimately, marketing is the art of attracting and keeping profitable customers. According to James V. Putten of American Express, the best customers outspend others by ratios of 16 to 1 in retailing, 13 to 1 in the restaurant business, 12 to 1 in the airline business, and 5 to 1 in the hotel and motel industry.[53] Yet every company loses money on some of its customers. The well-known 20–80 rule says that the top 20 percent of the customers may generate as much as 80 percent of the company's profits. Sherden suggested amending the rule to read 20–80–30, to reflect the idea that the top 20 percent of customers generate 80 percent of the company's profits, half of which are lost serving the bottom 30 percent of unprofitable customers.[54] The implication is that a company could improve its profits by "firing" its worst customers.

Furthermore, it is not necessarily the company's largest customers who yield the most profit. The largest customers demand considerable service and receive the deepest discounts. The smallest customers pay full price and receive minimal service, but the costs of transacting with small customers reduce their profitability. The midsize customers receive good service and pay nearly full price and are often the most profitable. This fact helps explain why many large firms are now invading the middle market. Major air express carriers, for instance, are finding that it does not pay to ignore small and midsize international shippers. Programs geared toward smaller customers provide a network of drop boxes, which allow for substantial discounts over letters and packages picked up at the shipper's place of business. In addition, United Parcel Service (UPS) conducts seminars to instruct exporters in the finer points of shipping overseas.[55]

What makes a customer profitable? A **profitable customer** is a person, household, or company that over time yields a revenue stream that exceeds by an acceptable amount the company's cost stream of attracting, selling, and servicing that customer. Note that the emphasis is on the lifetime stream of revenue and cost, not on the profit from a particular transaction. Here are two illustrations of customer lifetime value.

GM When car buyers look at cars on the lot, they often experience sticker shock. $15,000 may seem like a lot of money to pay for a Cavalier, but that sum is nothing compared to the $276,000 that General Motors estimates its lifetime customers to be worth on average. The six-figure value is a graphic illustration of the importance of keeping the customer satisfied for the life of the automobile to better the chances of a repeat purchase.[56]

Taco Bell When tacos cost less than a dollar each, you would not think Taco Bell would fret over lost customers. However, executives at Taco Bell have determined that a repeat customer is worth as much as $11,000. By sharing such estimates of customer lifetime value with its employees, Taco Bell's managers help employees understand the value of keeping customers satisfied.[57]

Although many companies measure customer satisfaction, most companies fail to measure individual customer profitability. Banks claim that this is a difficult task because a customer uses different banking services and the transactions are logged in different departments. However, banks that have succeeded in linking customer transactions have been appalled by the number of unprofitable customers in their customer base. Some banks report losing money on over 45 percent of their retail customers. There are only two solutions to handling unprofitable customers: raise fees or reduce service support.[58]

figure **3.7**

Customer–Product
Profitability Analysis

		Customers			
		C_1	C_2	C_3	
Products	P_1	+	+	+	Highly profitable product
	P_2	+			Profitable product
	P_3		–	–	Losing product
	P_4	+		–	Mixed-bag product
		High-profit customer	Mixed-bag customer	Losing customer	

A useful type of profitability analysis is shown in Figure 3.7.[59] Customers are arrayed along the columns and products along the rows. Each cell contains a symbol for the profitability of selling that product to that customer. Customer 1 is very profitable; he buys three profit-making products (P1, P2, and P4). Customer 2 yields a picture of mixed profitability; he buys one profitable product and one unprofitable product. Customer 3 is a losing customer because he buys one profitable product and two unprofitable products.

What can the company do about customers 2 and 3? (1) It can raise the price of its less profitable products or eliminate them, or (2) it can try to sell them its profit-making products. Unprofitable customers who defect should not concern the company. In fact, the company should encourage these customers to switch to competitors.

Customer profitability analysis (CPA) is best conducted with the tools of an accounting technique called Activity-Based Costing (ABC). The company estimates all revenue coming from the customer, less all costs. The costs should include not only the cost of making and distributing the products and services, but also such costs as taking phone calls from the customer, traveling to visit the customer, entertainment and gifts—all the company's resources that went into serving that customer. When this is done for each customer, it is possible to classify customers into different profit tiers: platinum customers (most profitable), gold customers (profitable), iron customers (low profitability but desirable), and lead customers (unprofitable and undesirable).

The company's job is to move iron customers into the gold tier and gold customers into the platinum tier, while dropping the lead customers or making them profitable by raising their prices or lowering the cost of serving them. The company's marketing investment ought to be higher in the higher profit tiers (see Figure 3.8).

increasing company profitability

Companies must not only be able to create high absolute value, but also high value relative to competitors at a sufficiently low cost. **Competitive advantage** is a company's ability to perform in one or more ways that competitors cannot or will not match. Michael Porter urged companies to build a sustainable competitive advantage.[60] But few competitive advantages are sustainable. At best, they may be leverageable. A *leverageable advantage* is one that a company can use as a springboard to new advan-

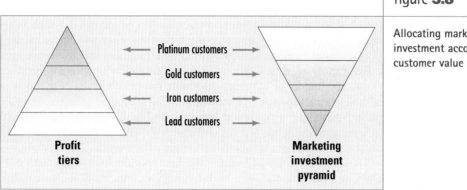

figure 3.8

Allocating marketing
investment according to
customer value

tages, much as Microsoft has leveraged its operating system to Microsoft Office and then to networking applications. In general, a company that hopes to endure must be in the business of continuously inventing new advantages.

Any competitive advantage must be seen by customers as a *customer advantage*. For example, if a company delivers faster than its competitors, this will not be a customer advantage if customers do not value speed. Companies must focus on building customer advantages. Then they will deliver high customer value and satisfaction, which leads to high repeat purchases and ultimately to high company profitability. (For a cogent view of how to measure profitability, see "Marketing Insight: Marketing's Goal: To Increase Shareholder Value.")

marketing **insight**

Marketing's Goal: To Increase Shareholder Value

Companies normally focus on profit maximization rather than on shareholder value maximization. Doyle, in his *Value-Based Marketing*, charges that profit maximization leads to short-term planning and underinvestment in marketing. It leads to a focus on building sales, market share, and current profits. It leads to cost cutting and shedding assets to produce quick improvements in earnings, and erodes a company's long-term competitiveness by neglecting to invest in new market opportunities.

Companies normally measure their profit performance using ROI (return on investment, calculated by dividing profits by investment). This has two problems:

1. Profits are arbitrarily measured and subject to manipulation. Cash flow is more important. As someone observed: "Profits are a matter of opinion; cash is a fact."

2. Investment ignores the real value of the firm. More of a company's value resides in its marketing assets—brands, market knowledge, customer relationships, and partner relationships—than in its balance sheet. These are the drivers of long-term profits.

Doyle argues that marketing will not mature as a profession until it can demonstrate the impact of marketing on **shareholder value**, the market value of a company minus its debt. The market value is the share price times the number of shares outstanding. The share price reflects what investors estimate is the present value of the future lifetime earnings of a company. When management is choosing a marketing strategy, Doyle wants it to apply shareholder value analysis (SVA) to see which alternative course of action will maximize shareholder value.

If Doyle's arguments are accepted, marketing will finally get the attention it deserves in the boardroom. Instead of seeing marketing as a specific function concerned only with increasing sales or market share, senior management will see it as an integral part of the whole management process. It will judge marketing by how much it contributes to shareholder value.

Source: Peter Doyle, *Value-Based Marketing: Marketing Strategies for Corporate Growth and Shareholder Value* (Chichester, England: John Wiley & Sons, 2000).

implementing total quality management

One of the major values customers expect from vendors is high product and service quality. Most will no longer accept or tolerate average quality. If companies want to stay in the race, let alone be profitable, they have no choice but to adopt total quality management (TQM). **Total quality management (TQM)** is an organizationwide approach to continuously improving the quality of all the organization's processes, products, and services.

According to GE's former chairman, John F. Welch Jr., "Quality is our best assurance of customer allegiance, our strongest defense against foreign competition, and the only path to sustained growth and earnings."[61] The drive to produce goods that are superior in world markets has led some countries—and groups of countries—to recognize or award prizes to companies that exemplify the best quality practices.

Japan: In 1951, Japan became the first country to award a national quality prize, the Deming prize (named after W. Edwards Deming, the American statistician who taught the importance and methodology of quality improvement to postwar Japan). Deming's work forms the basis of many TQM practices.

United States: In the mid-1980s, the United States established the Malcolm Baldrige National Quality Award in honor of the late secretary of commerce. The Baldrige award criteria consist of seven measures: customer focus and satisfaction, quality and operational results, management of process quality, human resource development and management, strategic quality planning, information and analysis, and senior executive leadership. Past winners include Xerox, Motorola, Federal Express, IBM, Texas Instruments, and Ritz-Carlton hotels. One of the latest quality awards went to Custom Research, a highly regarded marketing research firm in Minneapolis.

Europe: The European Quality Award was established in 1993. It is awarded to companies that have achieved high grades on certain criteria: leadership, people management, policy and strategy, resources, processes, people satisfaction, customer satisfaction, impact on society, and business results. It established the ISO 9000, which has become a set of generally accepted principles for documenting quality. Earning the ISO 9000 certification involves a quality audit every six months from a registered ISO (International Standards Organization) assessor.[62]

Product and service quality, customer satisfaction, and company profitability are intimately connected. Higher levels of quality result in higher levels of customer satisfaction, which support higher prices and (often) lower costs. The well-known PIMS studies show a high correlation between relative product quality and company profitability.[63]

What exactly is quality? Various experts have defined it as "fitness for use," "conformance to requirements," "freedom from variation," and so on.[64] We will use the American Society for Quality Control's definition: **Quality** is the totality of features and characteristics of a product or service that bear on its ability to satisfy stated or implied needs.[65] This is clearly a customer-centered definition. We can say that the seller has delivered quality whenever the seller's product or service meets or exceeds the customers' expectations. A company that satisfies most of its customers' needs most of the time is called a quality company, but it is important to distinguish between *conformance* quality and *performance* quality (or grade). A Mercedes provides higher performance quality than a Hyundai: The Mercedes rides smoother, goes faster, and lasts longer. Yet both a Mercedes and a Hyundai can be said to deliver the same conformance quality if all the units deliver their respective promised quality.

Total quality is the key to value creation and customer satisfaction. Total quality is everyone's job, just as marketing is everyone's job. This idea was expressed well by Daniel Beckham:

> Marketers who don't learn the language of quality improvement, manufacturing, and operations will become as obsolete as buggy whips. The days of functional marketing are gone. We can no longer afford to think of ourselves as market researchers, advertising people, direct marketers, strategists—we have

to think of ourselves as customer satisfiers—customer advocates focused on whole processes.[66]

Marketing managers have two responsibilities in a quality-centered company. First, they must participate in formulating strategies and policies to help the company win through total quality excellence. Second, they must deliver marketing quality alongside production quality. Each marketing activity—marketing research, sales training, advertising, customer service, and so on—must be performed to high standards.

Marketers play several roles in helping their companies define and deliver high-quality goods and services to target customers. First, they bear the major responsibility for correctly identifying the customers' needs and requirements. Second, they must communicate customer expectations properly to product designers. Third, they must make sure that customers' orders are filled correctly and on time. Fourth, they must check that customers have received proper instructions, training, and technical assistance in the use of the product. Fifth, they must stay in touch with customers after the sale to ensure that they are satisfied and remain satisfied. Sixth, they must gather customer ideas for product and service improvements and convey them to the appropriate departments. When marketers do all this, they are making substantial contributions to total quality management and customer satisfaction, as well as to customer and company profitability.

summary

1. Customers are value-maximizers. They form an expectation of value and act on it. Buyers will buy from the firm that they perceive to offer the highest customer-delivered value, defined as the difference between total customer value and total customer cost.

2. A buyer's satisfaction is a function of the product's perceived performance and the buyer's expectations. Recognizing that high satisfaction leads to high customer loyalty, many companies today are aiming for TCS—total customer satisfaction. For such companies, customer satisfaction is both a goal and a marketing tool.

3. Strong companies develop superior capabilities in managing core business processes such as new-product realization, inventory management, and customer acquisition and retention. Managing these core processes effectively means creating a marketing network in which the company works closely with all parties in the production and distribution chain, from suppliers of raw materials to retail distributors. Companies no longer compete—marketing networks do.

4. Losing profitable customers can dramatically affect a firm's profits. The cost of attracting a new customer is estimated to be five times the cost of keeping a current customer happy. The key to retaining customers is relationship marketing. To keep customers happy, marketers can add financial or social benefits to products, or create structural ties between the company and its customers.

5. Quality is the totality of features and characteristics of a product or service that bear on its ability to satisfy stated or implied needs. Today's companies have no choice but to implement total quality management programs if they are to remain solvent and profitable. Total quality is the key to value creation and customer satisfaction.

6. Marketing managers have two responsibilities in a quality-centered company. First, they must participate in formulating strategies and policies designed to help the company win through total quality excellence. Second, they must deliver marketing quality alongside production quality. Each marketing activity—marketing research, sales training, advertising, customer service, and so on—must be performed to high standards.

applications

marketing debate – online versus off-line privacy?

As more and more firms practice relationship marketing and develop databases of customer information, privacy issues are emerging as an important topic. Consumers and public interest groups are scrutinizing—and sometimes criticizing—the privacy policies of firms. Concerns are also being raised about potential theft of online credit-card information or other potentially sensitive or confidential financial information. Others maintain that the online privacy fears are unfounded and that security issues are every bit as much a concern in the off-line world. They argue that the opportunity to steal information exists virtually everywhere and that it is up to the consumer to protect his or her interests.

Take a position: (1) Privacy is a bigger issue in the online world than the off-line world versus Privacy is no different online than off-line. (2) Consumers on the whole receive more benefit than risk from marketers knowing their personal information.

marketing and advertising

1. Doubletree targets both vacationers and business travelers for its hotels and resort accommodations. The ad in Figure 1 shows how this hotel chain seeks to build relationships with business travelers by adding value in a variety of ways.

   a. What types of benefits are being emphasized in Doubletree's relationship-building efforts with business travelers? Why are these appropriate for the target market?
   b. Which of the customer value and customer cost factors are being addressed in this ad? How do they affect the customer's determination of delivered value?
   c. How else does Doubletree use this ad to stress benefits that appeal to customers as value-maximizers?

2. Blue Martini in Figure 2 makes software that enables people in different locations to move through a Web site at the same time, shopping or chatting as they progress through the pages. By facilitating collaboration between individuals or groups, Blue Martini enhances users' online experience, according to this ad. How does this help customer satisfaction?

   a. If a company using Blue Martini software allowed two sisters to simultaneously browse the same retailing Web site, how would this be likely to affect the sisters' perception of value?
   b. Would Blue Martini be part of the primary or support activities of a business customer's value chain?
   c. What else might Blue Martini do in its advertising to stress the value of its software to its customers' customers?

Figure 1

Figure 2

online marketing today

Any time a company registers a Web site ending in .com or .net, Verisign makes money as the administrator of these U.S. Internet domain names. Verisign also manages electronic payments for Bank of America as well as signature security—allowing legal documents to be signed and exchanged over the Internet—for Ford, Microsoft, and 3,000 other corporations. Quality is therefore very important to the satisfaction of Verisign's business customers, who value both security and accuracy.[a] Visit Verisign's Web site <*www.verisign.com*>, follow the link to its products page, and read about SSL Certificates or Web Site Trust Services. What are the benefits of this bundle of services? Would customers who buy this service be seeking conformance or performance quality? How does this set of services contribute to Verisign's competitive advantage?

[a]Fred Vogelstein, "The Man Who Bought the Internet," *Fortune*, June 25, 2001, pp. 126–127.

notes

1. "Mac Attacks," *USA Today*, March 23, l998, p. B1.

2. See, for example, "Value Marketing: Quality, Service, and Fair Pricing Are the Keys to Selling in the '90s," *BusinessWeek*, November 11, 1991, pp. 132–40.

3. Irwin P. Levin and Richard D. Johnson, "Estimating Price-Quality Tradeoffs Using Comparative Judgments," *Journal of Consumer Research* (June 11, 1984): 593–600. Customer perceived value can be measured as a difference or as a ratio. If total customer value is $20,000 and total customer cost is $16,000, then the customer perceived value is $4,000 (measured as a difference) or 1.25 (measured as a ratio). Ratios that are used to compare offers are often called *value-price ratios.*

4. For more on customer perceived value, see David C. Swaddling and Charles Miller, *Customer Power* (Dublin, OH: The Wellington Press, 2001).

5. For some provocative analysis, see Susan Fournier and David Glenmick, "Rediscovering Satisfaction," *Journal of Marketing*, (October 1999): pp. 5–23.

6. Thomas O. Jones and W. Earl Sasser, Jr., "Why Satisfied Customers Defect," *Harvard Business Review* (November–December 1995): 88–99.

7. For an interesting analysis of the effects of different types of expectations, see William Boulding, Ajay Kalra, and Richard Staelin, "The Quality Double Whammy," *Marketing Service,* 18(4), 1999, pp. 463–484.

8. <www.saturn.com>; "Saturn Illustrates Value of Customer Loyalty," *Louisville Courier-Journal*, September 5, 1999.

9. As quoted in Templin, Neal. "Boutique-Hotel Group Thrives on Quirks," *Wall Street Journal*, March 18, 1999.

10. As quoted in Carlsen, Clifford. "Joie de Vivre Resorts to New Hospitality Strategy," *San Francisco Business Times*, June 18, 1999.

11. Michael J. Lanning, *Delivering Profitable Value* (Oxford, UK: Capstone, 1998).

12. Simon Knox and Stan Maklan, *Competing on Value: Bridging the Gap Between Brand and Customer Value* (London, UK: Financial Times, 1998). See also Richard A. Spreng, Scott B. MacKenzie, and Richard W. Olshawskiy, "A Reexamination of the Determinants of Consumer Satisfaction," *Journal of Marketing,* no. 3 (July 1996): 15–32.

13. Fred Crawford and Ryan Mathews, *The Myth of Excellence: Why Great Companies Never Try to Be the Best of Everything* (New York: Crown Business), pp. 85–100.

14. Companies should also note that managers and salespeople can manipulate customer satisfaction ratings. They can be especially nice to customers just before the survey. They can also try to exclude unhappy customers. Another danger is that if customers know the company will go out of its way to please customers, some may express high dissatisfaction in order to receive more concessions.

15. Claes Fornell, Michael D. Johnson, Eugene W. Anderson, Jaaesung Cha, and Barbara Everitt Bryant, "The American Customer Satisfaction Index: Nature, Purpose, and Findings," *Journal of Marketing,* October 1996, pp. 7–18; and Eugene W. Anderson and Claes Fornell, "Foundations of the American Customer Satisfaction Index," *Total Quality Management,* 11, no. 7, 2000, pp. S869–S882.

16. Tamara J. Erickson and C. Everett Shorey, "Business Strategy: New Thinking for the '90s," *Prism* (Fourth Quarter 1992): 19–35.

17. Robert S. Kaplan and David P. Norton, *The Balanced Scorecard: Translating Strategy into Action* (Boston: Harvard Business School Press, 1996), as a tool for monitoring stakeholder satisfaction.

18. Jon R. Katzenbach and Douglas K. Smith, *The Wisdom of Teams: Creating the High-Performance Organization* (Boston: Harvard Business School Press, 1993); Michael Hammer and James Champy, *Reengineering the Corporation* (New York: HarperBusiness, 1993).

19. T. Michael Nevens, Gregory L. Summe, and Bro Uttal, "Commercializing Technology: What the Best Companies Do," *Harvard Business Review*, (May–June 1990): 162.

20. David Glines, "Do You Work in a Zoo?" *Executive Excellence* 11, no. 10 (October 1994): 12–13.

21. Echo Montgomery Garrett, "Outsourcing to the Max," *Small Business Reports* (August 1994): 9–14. The case for more outsourcing is ably spelled out in James Brian Quinn, *Intelligent Enterprise* (New York: The Free Press, 1992).

22. C. K. Prahalad and Gary Hamel, "The Core Competence of the Corporation," *Harvard Business Review*, (May–June 1990): 79–91.

23. George S. Day, "The Capabilities of Market-Driven Organizations," *Journal of Marketing* (October 1994): 38.

24. "Business: Microsoft's Contradiction," *The Economist* (January 31, 1998): 65–67; Andrew J. Glass, "Microsoft Pushes Forward, Playing to Win the Market," *Atlanta Constitution*, June 24, l998, p. D12.

25. Daniel Howe, "Note to DaimlerChrysler: It's Not a Small World after All," *Detroit News*, May 19, l998, p. B4; Bill Vlasic, "The First Global Car Colossus," *BusinessWeek*, May 18, l998, pp. 40–43; Pamela Harper, "Business 'Cultures' at War," *Electronic News*, August 3, l998, pp. 50, 55.

26. Bill Vlasic, and Bradley Stertz. "Taken for a Ride," *Business Week*, June 5, 2000; Jeffrey Ball, and Scott Miller,. "DaimlerChrysler Isn't Living up to Its Promise," *Wall Street Journal*, July 26, 2000; Eric Reguly, "Daimler, Chrysler Still a Cutture Clash," *The Globe and Mail*, January 30, 2001.

27. James C. Collins and Jerry I. Porras, *Built to Last: Successful Habits of Visionary Companies* (New York: HarperBusiness, 1994).

28. F. G. Rodgers and Robert L. Shook, *The IBM Way: Insights into the World's Most Successful Marketing Organization* (New York: Harper and Row, 1986).

29. Gary Hamel, "Strategy as Revolution," *Harvard Business Review*, (July–August 1996): 69–82.

30. Paul J. H. Shoemaker, "Scenario Plannning: A Tool for Strategic Thinking," *Sloan Management Review*, (Winter 1995): 25–40.

31. Michael E. Porter, *Competitive Advantage: Creating and Sustaining Superior Performance* (New York: The Free Press, 1985).

32. Robert Hiebeler, Thomas B. Kelly, and Charles Ketteman, *Best Practices: Building Your Business with Customer-Focused Solutions* (New York: Simon and Schuster, 1998).

33. Hammer and Champy, *Reengineering the Corporation.*

34. George Stalk, "Competing on Capability: The New Rules of Corporate Strategy," *Harvard Business Review* (March–April 1992): 57–69; Benson P. Shapiro, V. Kasturi Rangan, and John J. Sviokla, "Staple Yourself to an Order," *Harvard Business Review* (July–August 1992): 113–22.

35. Myron Magnet, "The New Golden Rule of Business," *Fortune*, November 28, 1994, pp. 60–64.

36. Jeffrey Gitomer, *Customer Satisfaction Is Worthless: Customer Loyalty Is Priceless: How to Make Customers Love You, Keep Them Coming Back and Tell Everyone They Know* (Austin, TX: Bard Press, l998).

37. Frederick F. Reichheld, "Learning from Customer Defections," *Harvard Business Review* (March–April 1996): 56–69.

38. Ibid.

39. Technical Assistance Research Programs (Tarp), *U.S Office of Consumer Affairs Study on Complaint Handling in America,* 1986.

40. Karl Albrecht and Ron Zemke, *Service America!* (Homewood Il: Dow Jones-Irwin, 1985), pp. 6–7.

41. Courtesy L.L. Bean, Freeport, Maine.

42. Ibid.

43. Frederick F. Reichheld, *The Loyalty Effect* (Boston: Harvard Business School Press, 1996).

44. Carl Sewell and Paul Brown, *Customers for Life* (New York: Pocket Books, 1990), p. 162.

45. Cited in Don Peppers and Martha Rogers, *The One to One Future* (New York: Currency, 1993), pp. 37–38.

46. Roland T. Rust, Valerie A. Zeithaml, and Katherine A. Lemon, *Driving Customer Equity* (New York Free Press 2000).

47. www.ameritrade.com; Rebecca Buckman, "Ameritrade Unveils Index That Tracks Customer Trends," *Wall Street Journal*, December 2, 1999. For a contrast, see Susan Stellin, "For Many Online Companies, Customer Service Is Hardly a Priority," *New York Times*, February 19, 2001.

48. Leonard L. Berry and A. Parasuraman, *Marketing Services: Computing through Quality* (New York: The Free Press, 1991), pp. 136–42. See also Richard Cross and Janet Smith, *Customer Bonding: Pathways to Lasting Customer Loyalty* (Lincolnwood, IL: NTC Business Books, 1995).

49. www.apple.com

50. www.hog.com

51. James H. Donnelly Jr., Leonard L. Berry, and Thomas W. Thompson, *Marketing Financial Services—A Strategic Vision* (Homewood, IL: Dow Jones–Irwin, 1985), p. 113.

52. From a privately circulated paper, Lester Wunderman, "The Most Elusive Word in Marketing," June 2000. Also see Lester Wunderman, *Being Direct* (NewYork: Random House 1996).

53. Quoted in Don Peppers and Martha Rogers, *The One-to-One Future: Building Relationships One Customer at a Time* (New York: Currency Doubleday, 1993), p. 108.

54. William A. Sherden, *Market Ownership: The Art and Science of Becoming #1* (New York: Amacom, 1994), p. 77.

55. Robert J. Bowman, "Good Things, Smaller Packages," *World Trade* 6, no. 9 (October 1993): 106–10.

56. Greg Farrel, "Marketers Put a Price on Your Life." *USA Today*, July 7, 1999.

57. Stephan A. Butscher, "Welcome to the Club: Building Customer Loyalty," *Marketing News*, September 9, 1996, p. 9.

58. Rakesh Niraj, Mahendra Gupta, and Chakravarthi Narasimhan, "Customer Profitability in a Supply Chain," *Journal of Marketing*, July 2001, pp. 1–16.

59. Thomas M. Petro, "Profitability: The Fifth 'P' of Marketing," *Bank Marketing* (September 1990): 48–52; and "Who Are Your Best Customers?" *Bank Marketing* (October 1990): 48–52.

60. Michael E. Porter, *Competitive Strategy: Techniques for Analyzing Industries and Competitors* (New York: Free Press, 1980).

61. "Quality: The U.S. Drives to Catch Up," *Business Week*, November 1982, pp. 66–80. For a more recent assessment of progress, see "Quality Programs Show Shoddy Results," *Wall Street Journal*, May 14, 1992, p. B1. See also Roland R. Rust, Anthony J. Zahorik, and Timothy L. Keiningham, "Return on Quality (ROQ): Making Service Quality Financially Accountable," *Journal of Marketing* 59, no. 2 (April 1995): 58–70.

62. "Quality in Europe," *Work Study* (January–February 1993): 30; Ronald Henkoff, "The Hot New Seal of Quality," *Fortune*, June 28, 1993, pp. 116–20; Amy Zukerman, "One Size Doesn't Fit All," *Industry Week*, January 9, 1995, pp. 37–40; and "The Sleeper Issue of the '90s," *Industry Week*, August 15, 1994, pp. 99–100, 108.

63. Robert D. Buzzell and Bradley T. Gale, *The PIMS Principles: Linking Strategy to Performance* (New York: The Free Press, 1987), ch. 6. (PIMS stands for Profit Impact of Market Strategy.)

64. "The Gurus of Quality: American Companies Are Heading the Quality Gospel Preached by Deming, Juran, Crosby, and Taguchi," *Traffic Management* (July 1990): 35–39.

65. Cyndee Miller, "U.S. Firms Lag in Meeting Global Quality Standards," *Marketing News*, February 15, 1993.

66. J. Daniel Beckham, "Expect the Unexpected in Health Care Marketing Future," *The Academy Bulletin* (July 1992): 3.

5

gathering information and measuring market demand

In this chapter, we will address the following questions:

- What are the components of a modern marketing information system?
- What constitutes good marketing research?
- How can marketing decision support systems help marketing managers make better decisions?
- How can demand be more accurately measured and forecasted?

Kotler on Marketing

Marketing is becoming a battle based more on information than on sales power.

The marketing environment is changing at an accelerating rate, so the need for real-time market information is greater than at any time in the past. The shifts are dramatic: from local to national to global marketing, from buyer needs to buyer wants, from price to non-price competition. As companies expand their geographical market coverage, their managers need more information more quickly. As incomes improve, buyers become more selective in their choices of goods. To predict buyers' responses to different features, styles, and other attributes, sellers must turn to marketing research. As sellers increase their use of branding, product differentiation, advertising, and sales promotion, they require information on the effectiveness of these marketing tools.

Fortunately, the exploding information requirements have given rise to impressive new information technologies: computers, cable television, copy machines, fax machines, scanners, audio and video recorders, videodisc players, CD-ROMs, camcorders, cellular phones, and most impressive of all, the Internet.[1]

the components of a modern marketing information system

Some firms have developed marketing information systems that provide management with rapid and incredible detail about buyer wants, preferences, and behavior. For example, the Coca-Cola Company knows that we put 3.2 ice cubes in a glass, see 69 of its commercials every year, and prefer cans to pop out of vending machines at a temperature of 35 degrees. Kimberly-Clark, which makes Kleenex, has calculated that the average person blows his or her nose 256 times a year. Hoover learned that we spend about 35 minutes each week vacuuming, sucking up about 8 pounds of dust each year and using 6 bags to do so.[2]

Marketers also have extensive information about consumption patterns in other countries. On a per capita basis within Western Europe, for example, the Swiss consume the most chocolate, the Greeks eat the most cheese, the Irish drink the most tea, and the Austrians smoke the most cigarettes.[3]

Nevertheless, many business firms lack information sophistication. Many lack a marketing research department. Others have departments that limit work to routine forecasting, sales analysis, and occasional surveys. In addition, many managers complain about not knowing where critical information is located in the company; getting too much information that they cannot use and too little that they really need; getting important information too late; and doubting the information's accuracy. In today's information-based society, companies with superior information enjoy a competitive advantage. The company can choose its markets better, develop better offerings, and execute better marketing planning.

Every firm must organize and distribute a continuous flow of information to its marketing managers. Companies study their managers' information needs and design marketing information systems (MIS) to meet these needs. A **marketing information system (MIS)** consists of people, equipment, and procedures to gather, sort, analyze, evaluate, and distribute needed, timely, and accurate information to marketing decision makers.

The company's marketing information system should represent a cross between what managers think they need, what managers really need, and what is economically feasible. An internal MIS committee can interview a cross-section of marketing managers to discover their information needs. Some useful questions are:

1. What decisions do you regularly make?
2. What information do you need to make these decisions?
3. What information do you regularly get?
4. What special studies do you periodically request?
5. What information would you want that you are not getting now?
6. What information would you want daily? Weekly? Monthly? Yearly?
7. What magazines and trade reports would you like to see on a regular basis?
8. What topics would you like to be kept informed of?
9. What data analysis programs would you want?
10. What are the four most helpful improvements that could be made in the present marketing information system?

A marketing information system is developed from internal company records, marketing intelligence activities, marketing research, and marketing decision support analysis.

internal records system

Marketing managers rely on internal reports on orders, sales, prices, costs, inventory levels, receivables, payables, and so on. By analyzing this information, they can spot important opportunities and problems.

the order-to-payment cycle

The heart of the internal records system is the order-to-payment cycle. Sales representatives, dealers, and customers dispatch orders to the firm. The sales department prepares invoices and transmits copies to various departments. Out-of-stock items are back ordered. Shipped items are accompanied by shipping and billing documents that are sent to various departments.

Today's companies need to perform these steps quickly and accurately. Customers favor firms that can promise timely delivery. Customers and sales representatives fax or e-mail their orders. Computerized warehouses fill these orders quickly. The billing department sends out invoices as quickly as possible. An increasing number of companies are using the Internet and extranets to improve the speed, accuracy, and efficiency of the order-to-payment cycle. Retail giant Wal-Mart tracks the stock levels of its products daily and its computers send automatic replenishment orders to its vendors.[4]

sales information systems

Marketing managers need timely and accurate reports on current sales. Wal-Mart, for example, knows the sales of each product by store and total each evening. This enables it to transmit nightly orders to suppliers for new shipments of replacement stock. Wal-Mart shares its sales data with its larger suppliers such as P&G and expects P&G to re-supply Wal-Mart stores in a timely manner. Wal-Mart has entrusted P&G with the management of its inventory.

Companies must carefully interpret the sales data so as not to get the wrong signals. Michael Dell gave this illustration: "If you have three yellow Mustangs sitting on a dealer's lot and a customer wants a red one, the salesman is really good at figuring out how to sell the yellow Mustang. So the yellow Mustang gets sold, and a signal gets sent back to the factory that, hey, people want yellow Mustangs."

Here are two companies that are using computer technology to design fast and comprehensive sales reporting systems.

Ascom Timeplex, Inc. Before heading out on a call, sales reps at this telecommunications equipment company use their laptop computers to dial into the company's worldwide data network. They can retrieve the latest price lists, engineering and configuration notes, status reports on previous orders, and e-mail from anywhere in the company; and when deals are struck, the laptop computers record each order, double-check the order for errors, and send it electronically to Timeplex headquarters in Woodcliff Lake, New Jersey.[5]

Montgomery Security In 1996, San Francisco–based Montgomery Security was in a bind. To remain competitive in the financial sector, this NationsBank subsidiary had to find a way for more than 400 finance, research, and sales or trading employees to share information about companies whose stock they were considering taking public. The company solved the problem with Sales Enterprise Software from Siebel Systems. With a common database format, everyone could share information and keep confidential information secure.[6]

databases, data warehouses, and data-mining

Today companies organize their information in databases—customer databases, product databases, salesperson databases, and so forth—and then combine data from the different databases. For example, the customer database will contain every customer's name, address, past transactions, and even demographics and psychographics (activities, interests, and opinions) in some instances. Instead of a company sending a mass "carpet bombing" mailing of a new offer to every customer in its database, it will score the different customers according to their purchase recency, frequency, and monetary value. It will send the offer only to the highest scoring customers. Besides saving on mailing expenses, this will often achieve a double-digit response rate.

Companies warehouse these data and make them easily accessible to decision makers. Furthermore, by hiring analysts skilled in sophisticated statistical methods, they can "mine" the data and garner fresh insights into neglected customer segments, recent customer trends, and other useful information. The customer information can be cross-tabbed with product and salesperson information to yield still deeper insights. (See "Marketing for the New Economy: Companies Turn to Data Warehousing and Data Mining: Exercise Care.")

the marketing intelligence system

Whereas the internal records system supplies results data, the marketing intelligence system supplies happenings data. A **marketing intelligence system** is a set of procedures and sources used by managers to obtain everyday information about developments in the marketing environment. Marketing managers collect marketing intelligence by reading books, newspapers, and trade publications; talking to customers, suppliers, and distributors; and meeting with other company managers. A company can take several steps to improve the quality of its marketing intelligence.

First, it can train and motivate the sales force to spot and report new developments. Sales representatives are positioned to pick up information missed by other means. Yet they are very busy and often fail to pass on that information. The company must "sell" its sales force on their importance as intelligence gatherers. Sales reps should know which types of information to send to which managers. For instance, the Prentice Hall sales reps who sell this textbook let their editors know what is going on in each discipline, who is doing exciting research, and who plans to write cutting-edge textbooks.

Second, the company can motivate distributors, retailers, and other intermediaries to pass along important intelligence. Consider the following example.

Parker Hannifin Corporation   A major fluid-power-products manufacturer, Parker Hannifin requires each of its distributors to forward to Parker's marketing research division a copy of all invoices containing sales of its products. Parker analyzes these invoices to learn about end users, and shares its findings with the distributors.[7]

Many companies hire specialists to gather marketing intelligence. Retailers often send mystery shoppers to their stores to assess how employees treat customers. The city of Dallas hired Feedback Plus, a professional shopper agency, to see how car-pound employees treat citizens picking up their cars. Neiman Marcus employs the same agency to shop at its 26 stores nationwide. "Those stores that consistently score high on the shopping service," says a Neiman Marcus senior VP, "not so coincidentally have the best sales." The stores will tell salespeople that they've "been shopped" and give them copies of the mystery shopper's report. Typical questions on the report are: How long before a sales associate greeted you? Did the sales associate act as if he or she wanted your business? Was the sales associate knowledgeable about products in stock?[8]

marketing for the **new economy**

Companies Turn to Data Warehousing and Data Mining: Exercise Care

Companies are using data mining to extract patterns from large masses of data organized in what is called a data warehouse. Banks and credit-card companies, telephone companies, catalog marketers, and many other companies have a great deal of information about their customers, including not only addresses and phone numbers, but also their transactions and enhanced data on age, family size, income, and other demographic information.

Some observers believe that a proprietary database can provide a company with a significant competitive advantage. It is no wonder that, at its secret location in Phoenix, security guards watch over American Express's 500 billion bytes of data on how its customers have used the company's 35 million green, gold, and platinum charge cards. Amex uses the database to include precisely targeted offers in its monthly mailing of millions of customer bills. MCI Communications Corporation, the long-distance carrier, sifts through 1 trillion bytes of customer phoning data to craft new discount calling plans for different types of customers.

Marriott's Vacation Club International has managed to reduce its volume of mail and yet increase its response rate by developing a model showing which customers in its database are most likely to respond to specific vacation offerings.

Tesco, the British supermarket chain, notifies different groups when there will be a special sale on items they buy. Lands' End can tell which of its 2 million customers should receive special mailings of specific clothing items that would fit their wardrobe needs.

These benefits do not come without heavy cost, not only in collecting the original customer data but also in maintaining them and mining them. Yet when it works, a data warehouse yields more than it costs. A 1996 study by DWI estimated that the average return on investment for a data warehouse over the course of three years is more than 400 percent, but the data have to be in good condition, and the discovered relationships must be valid. British Columbia Telecom wanted to invite 100 of its best customers to a Vancouver Grizzlies basketball game and selected customers who were heavy 900-number users. The invitations were already at the printer when the marketing staff discovered that heavy 900-number users included sex-line enthusiasts. They quickly added other criteria to search for a revised list of guests.

The Marriott Vacation Club International Web site gives interested consumers the opportunity to sell themselves on the Marriott offerings.

Sources: Peter R. Peacock, "Data Mining in Marketing: Part 1," *Marketing Management* (Winter 1998): 9–18, and "Data Mining in Marketing: Part 2," *Marketing Management* (Spring 1998): 15–25; Ginger Conlon, "What the !@#!*?!! Is a Data Warehouse?" *Sales & Marketing Management* (April 1997): 41–48; Skip Press, "Fool's Gold? As Companies Rush to Mine Data, They May Dig Up Real Gems—Or False Trends," *Sales & Marketing Management* (April 1997): 58, 60, 62; John Verity, "A Trillion-Byte Weapon," *BusinessWeek*, July 31, 1995, pp. 80–81.

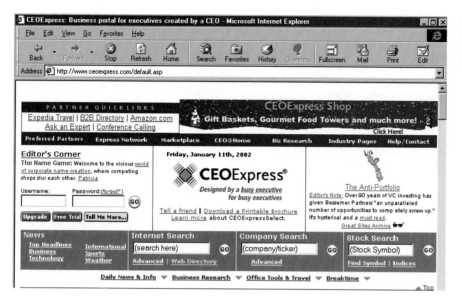

CEOExpress.com is a portal to information: a user clicks on a listing and is then connected to that site.

Third, companies can collect competitive intelligence by purchasing competitors' products; attending open houses and trade shows; reading competitors' published reports; attending stockholders' meetings; talking to employees, dealers, distributors, suppliers, and freight agents; collecting competitors' ads; and looking up news stories about competitors on the Internet.

Ceoexpress.com This site serves as a portal offering the researcher a comprehensive listing of the sites of newspapers, magazines, television stations, government agencies, financial sites, statistical sites, legal sites, and so on. The user simply clicks on any listing and is immediately connected to that site.

Fourth, a company can set up a customer advisory panel made up of representative customers or the company's largest customers or its most outspoken or sophisticated customers. For example, Hitachi Data Systems holds a three-day meeting with its customer panel of 20 members every 9 months. They discuss service issues, new technologies, and customers' strategic requirements. The discussion is free-flowing, and both parties gain: The company gains valuable information about customer needs, and the customers feel more bonded to a company that listens closely to their comments.[9]

Fifth, a company can purchase information from outside suppliers such as the A. C. Nielsen Company and Information Resources, Inc. (see Table 5.1, part D; and "Marketing Memo: Secondary Sources of Data Online" on pages 130–131). These research firms gather consumer-panel data at a much lower cost than the company could manage on its own.

Sixth, some companies circulate marketing intelligence. The staff scans the Internet and major publications, abstracts relevant news, and disseminates a news bulletin to marketing managers. It collects and files relevant information and assists managers in evaluating new information.

table **5.1**	
Secondary–Data Sources	**A. Internal Sources** Company profit-loss statements, balance sheets, sales figures, sales-call reports, invoices, inventory records, and prior research reports. **B. Government Publications** • *Statistical Abstract of the United States* • *County and City Data Book* • *Industrial Outlook* • *Marketing Information Guide* • Other government publications include the *Annual Survey of Manufacturers; Business Statistics;* Census of Manufacturers; Census of Population; Census of Retail Trade, Wholesale Trade, and Selected Service Industries; Census of Transportation; *Federal Reserve Bulletin; Monthly Labor Review; Survey of Current Business;* and *Vital Statistics Report.* **C. Periodicals and Books** • *Business Periodicals Index* • *Standard and Poor's Industry* • *Moody's Manuals* • *Encyclopedia of Associations* • Marketing journals include the *Journal of Marketing, Journal of Marketing Research,* and *Journal of Consumer Research.* • Useful trade magazines include *Advertising Age, Chain Store Age, Progressive Grocer, Sales & Marketing Management,* and *Stores.* • Useful general business magazines include *BusinessWeek, Fortune, Forbes, The Economist,* and *Harvard Business Review.* **D. Commercial Data** • Nielsen Company: Data on products and brands sold through retail outlets (Retail Index Services), supermarket scanner data (Scantrack), data on television audiences (Media Research Services), magazine circulation data (Neodata Services, Inc.), and others. • MRCA Information Services: Data on weekly family purchases of consumer products (National Consumer Panel) and data on home food consumption (National Menu Census). • Information Resources, Inc.: Supermarket scanner data (InfoScan) and data on the impact of supermarket promotions (PromotioScan). • SAMI/Burke: Reports on warehouse withdrawals to food stores in selected market areas (SAMI reports) and supermarket scanner data (Samscam). • Simmons Market Research Bureau (MRB Group): Annual reports covering television markets, sporting goods, and proprietary drugs, with demographic data by sex, income, age, and brand preferences (selective markets and media reaching them). • Other commercial research houses selling data to subscribers include the Audit Bureau of Circulation; Arbitron, Audits and Surveys; Dun & Bradstreet's; National Family Opinion; Standard Rate & Data Service; and Starch.

marketing research system

Marketing managers often commission formal marketing studies of specific problems and opportunities. They may request a market survey, a product-preference test, a sales forecast by region, or an advertising evaluation. It is the job of the marketing researcher to produce customer insight into the problem. We define **marketing research** as the systematic design, collection, analysis, and reporting of data and findings relevant to a specific marketing situation facing the company.

suppliers of marketing research

A company can obtain marketing research in a number of ways. Most large companies have their own marketing research departments.[10]

Procter & Gamble   P&G assigns marketing researchers to each product operating division to conduct research for existing brands. There are two separate in-house research groups, one in charge of overall company advertising research and the other in charge of market testing. Each group's staff consists of marketing research managers, supporting specialists (survey designers, statisticians, behavioral scientists), and in-house field representatives to conduct and supervise interviewing. Brand managers commission annual brand awareness and tracking studies, consumer-use tests, continuous retail audits, and laboratory research studies. Each year, P&G calls or visits over one million people in connection with about 1,000 research projects.

Small companies can hire the services of a marketing research firm or conduct research in creative and affordable ways, such as:

1. Engaging students or professors to design and carry out projects: One Boston University MBA project helped American Express develop a successful advertising campaign geared toward young professionals. The cost: $15,000.
2. Using the Internet: A company can collect considerable information at very little cost by examining competitors' Web sites, monitoring chat rooms, and accessing published data.
3. Checking out rivals: Many small companies routinely visit their competitors. Tom Coohill, a chef who owns two Atlanta restaurants, gives managers a food allowance to dine out and bring back ideas. Atlanta jeweler Frank Maier Jr., who often visits out-of-town rivals, spotted and copied a dramatic way of lighting displays.[11]

Companies normally budget marketing research at one to two percent of company sales. A large percentage is spent on the services of outside firms. Marketing research firms fall into three categories:

1. *Syndicated-service research firms:* These firms gather consumer and trade information, which they sell for a fee. Examples: Nielsen Media Research, SAMI/Burke.
2. *Custom marketing research firms:* These firms are hired to carry out specific projects. They design the study and report the findings.
3. *Specialty-line marketing research firms:* These firms provide specialized research services. The best example is the field-service firm, which sells field interviewing services to other firms.

the marketing research process

Effective marketing research involves the six steps shown in Figure 5.1. We will illustrate these steps with the following situation:

American Airlines (AA) is constantly looking for new ways to serve its passengers; it was one of the first companies to install phone handsets. Now it is reviewing many new ideas, especially to cater to its first-class passengers on

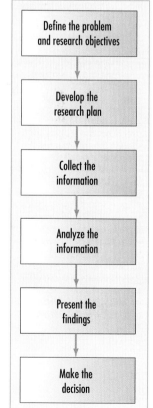

figure **5.1**

The Marketing Research Process

- Define the problem and research objectives
- Develop the research plan
- Collect the information
- Analyze the information
- Present the findings
- Make the decision

continued...

very long flights, many of whom are business people whose high-priced tickets pay most of the freight. Among these ideas are: (1) to supply a power plug in first class so that the business person could work on the computer longer than the two hours normally provided by a battery; (2) to supply an Internet connection with limited access to Web pages and e-mail messaging; (3) to offer 24 channels of satellite cable TV; and (4) to offer a 50-CD audio system that lets each passenger create a customized play list of music and movies to enjoy during the flight. The marketing research manager was assigned to investigate how first-class passengers would rate these services and how much extra they would be willing to pay if a charge was made. He was asked to focus specifically on the Internet connection. One estimate says that airlines might realize revenues of $70 billion over the next decade from in-flight Internet access, if enough first-class passengers would be willing to pay $25 for it. AA could thus recover its costs in a reasonable time. Making the connection available would cost the airline $90,000 per plane.[12]

STEP 1: DEFINE THE PROBLEM, THE DECISION ALTERNATIVES, AND THE RESEARCH OBJECTIVES   Marketing management must be careful not to define the problem too broadly or too narrowly for the marketing researcher. A marketing manager who instructs the marketing researcher to "Find out everything you can about first class air travelers' needs," will collect a lot of unnecessary information. Similarly, a marketing manager who says, "Find out if enough passengers aboard a B747 flying direct between Chicago and Tokyo would be willing to pay $25 for an Internet connection so that American Airlines would break even in one year on the cost of offering this service," is taking too narrow a view of the problem. The marketing researcher might even raise this question: "Why does the Internet connection have to be priced at $25 as opposed to $10, $50, or some other price? Why does American have to break even on the cost of the service, especially if it attracts new users to AA?"

In discussing the problem, American's managers discovered another issue. If the new service were successful, how fast could other airlines copy it? Airline marketing research is replete with examples of new services that have been so quickly copied by competitors that no airline has gained a sustainable competitive advantage. How important is it to be first and how long could the lead be sustained?

The marketing manager and marketing researcher agreed to define the problem as follows: "Will offering an in-flight Internet service create enough incremental preference and profit for American Airlines to justify its cost against other possible investments American might make?" To help think about designing the research, management should first spell out the decisions it might face and then work backward. Suppose management spells out the following decisions: (1) Should American offer an Internet connection? (2) If so, should the service be offered to first-class only, or include business class, and possibly economy class? (3) What price(s) should be charged? (4) On what types of planes and lengths of trips should it be offered?

Now management and marketing researchers are ready to set specific research objectives: (1) What types of first-class passengers would respond most to using an in-flight Internet service? (2) How many first-class passengers are likely to use the Internet service at different price levels? (3) How many extra first-class passengers might choose American because of this new service? (4) How much long-term goodwill will this service add to American Airlines' image? (5) How important is Internet service to first-class passengers relative to providing other services such as a power plug, or enhanced entertainment?

Not all research projects can be this specific. Some research is exploratory—its goal is to shed light on the real nature of the problem and to suggest possible solutions or new ideas. Some research is descriptive—it seeks to ascertain certain magnitudes, such as how many first-class passengers would purchase in-flight Internet service at $25. Some research is causal—its purpose is to test a cause-and-effect relationship.

STEP 2: DEVELOP THE RESEARCH PLAN   The second stage of marketing research calls for developing the most efficient plan for gathering the needed information. The marketing manager needs to know the cost of the research plan before approving it. Suppose the company made a prior estimate that launching the in-flight Internet service would yield a long-term profit of $50,000. The manager believes that doing the research would lead to an improved pricing and promotional plan and a long-term profit of $90,000. In this case, the manager should be willing to spend up to $40,000 on this research. If the research would cost more than $40,000, it is not worth doing.[13] Designing a research plan calls for decisions on the data sources, research approaches, research instruments, sampling plan, and contact methods.

Data Sources   The researcher can gather secondary data, primary data, or both. Secondary data are data that were collected for another purpose and already exist somewhere. Primary data are data freshly gathered for a specific purpose or for a specific research project.

Researchers usually start their investigation by examining secondary data to see whether the problem can be partly or wholly solved without collecting costly primary data. (Table 5.1 on page 128 shows the rich variety of secondary-data sources available in the United States.)[14] Secondary data provide a starting point for research and offer the advantages of low cost and ready availability. See "Marketing Memo: Secondary Sources of Data Online" for a mini-directory of sites where you can conduct free or at least inexpensive market research.

When the needed data do not exist or are dated, inaccurate, incomplete, or unreliable, the researcher will have to collect primary data. Most marketing research projects involve some primary-data collection. The normal procedure is to interview some people individually or in groups, to get a sense of how people feel about the topic in question, and then develop a formal research instrument, debug it, and carry it into the field.

Research Approaches   Primary data can be collected in five ways: through observation, focus groups, surveys, behavioral data, and experiments.

- *Observational research:* Fresh data can be gathered by observing the relevant actors and settings. The American Airlines researchers might meander around first-class lounges to hear how travelers talk about the different carriers and their features. The researchers can fly on competitors' planes to observe their in-flight service. This exploratory research might yield some useful hypotheses about how travelers feel about different air carriers and their services. (For another application of observational research, see "Marketing Insight: Using Observational Research to Study Shopping Behavior.")

- *Focus-group research:* A **focus group** is a gathering of six to ten people who are invited to spend a few hours with a skilled moderator to discuss a product, service, organization, or other marketing entity (see Figure 5.2). The moderator needs to be objective, knowledgeable on the issue, and skilled in group dynamics. Participants are normally paid a small sum for attending. The meeting is typically held in pleasant surroundings and refreshments are served.

    In the American Airlines research, the moderator might start with a broad question, such as "How do you feel about first-class air travel?" Questions then move to how people regard the different airlines, different existing services, different proposed services, and specifically, Internet service. The moderator encourages free and easy discussion, hoping that the group dynamics will reveal deep feelings and thoughts. At the same time, the moderator "focuses" the discussion. The discussion, recorded through note taking or on audiotape or videotape or behind a one-way mirror, is subsequently studied to understand consumer beliefs, attitudes, and behavior.

- Public Register's Annual Report Service—allows searches of 3,200 public companies by company name or industry and offers annual reports via e-mail (*www.prars.com/index.html*).
- Quote.Com—access to a wide range of business wires, companies' directories, and stock quotes (*www.quote.com*).

Government Information:
- Census Bureau (*www.census.gov*).
- FedWorld—a clearinghouse for over 100 federal government agencies (*www.fedworld.gov*).
- Thomas—indexes federal government sites (*thomas.loc.gov*).
- Trade/Exporting/business: Stat-USA (*www.stat-usa.gov*).
- US Business Advisor (*www.business.gov*).

International Information:
- CIA World Factbook—a comprehensive statistical and demographic directory covering 264 countries around the world (*www. odic.gov/cia/publications*).
- The Electronic Embassy (*www.embassy.org*).
- I-Trade—free and fee-based information services for firms wishing to do business internationally (*www.i-trade.com*).
- The United Nations (*www.un.org*).

Sources: Based on information from Robert I. Berkman, *Find It Fast: How to Uncover Expert Information on Any Subject in Print or Online* (New York: HarperCollins, 1997); Christine Galea, "Surf City: The Best Places for Business on the Web," *Sales & Marketing Management*, January 1997, pp. 69–73; David Curle, "Out-of-the-Way Sources of Market Research on the Web," *Online* (January–February 1998): 63–68. See also Jan Davis Tudor, "Brewing Up: A Web Approach to Industry Research," *Online* (July–August 1996): 12.

marketing **insight**

Using Observational Research to Study Shopping Behavior

Paco Underhill runs a firm called Environsell that has been snooping on shoppers for over 20 years. His clients include McDonald's, Starbucks, Estee Lauder, and Blockbuster. His researchers enter different retail settings and use unobtrusive methods to record the movements of shoppers. They use clipboards, track sheets, video equipment, and keen eyes to describe every nuance of shopping behavior, including how people circulate through the store and interact with store personnel. These "retail anthropologists" observe over 70,000 shoppers a year in their "natural habitat"; and they carry out post-shopping exit interviews to confirm their observations. Here are some findings in Underhill's book *Why We Buy: The Science of Shopping*:

- The faster people walk, the narrower their field of vision becomes.
- Shoppers slow down when they see reflective surfaces and speed up when they see blanks.

- Shoppers invariably walk to the right.
- Experiential in-store information has more weight than company advertising.
- Men who take jeans into fitting rooms are more likely to buy than females.
- Women are more likely to avoid narrow aisles than men.
- A Harley-Davidson showroom is filled with three types of shoppers: "well-off male menopause victims looking to recover their virility by buying bikes; blue-collar gear heads who are there for spare parts; and teenage dreamers interested in Harley-logo fashions."

Source: Paco Underhill, *Why We Buy: The Science of Shopping* (New York: Simon & Schuster, 1999).

Focus-group research is a useful exploratory step. Consumer-goods companies have been using focus groups for many years, and an increasing number of newspapers, law firms, hospitals, and public-service organizations are discovering their value. However, researchers must avoid generalizing the reported feelings of the focus-group participants to the whole market, because the sample size is too small and the sample is not drawn randomly.[15]

With the development of the Web, many companies are now conducting online focus groups.[16]

figure **5.2**
Focus–group Research

Cyber dialogue   Janice Gjersten of WPStudio, an online entertainment company, found that online focus-group respondents could be much more honest than those in her traditional, in-person focus groups. Gjersten contacted Cyber Dialogue, which provided focus-group respondents drawn from its 10,000-person database. The focus group was held in a chat room that Gjersten "looked in on" from her office computer. Gjersten could interrupt the moderator at any time with flash e-mails unseen by the respondents. Although the online focus group lacked voice and body cues, the cost was one-third that of a traditional focus group, and a full report came to her in one day, compared to four weeks.

■ *Survey research:* Surveys are best suited for descriptive research. Companies undertake surveys to learn about people's knowledge, beliefs, preferences, and satisfaction, and to measure these magnitudes in the general population. A company such as American Airlines might prepare its own survey instrument to gather the information it needs, or it might add questions to an omnibus survey that carries the questions of several companies at a much lower cost. It can also put the questions to an ongoing consumer panel run by itself or another company or it may do a mall intercept study by approaching people in a shopping mall who might volunteer to answer questions.

■ *Behavioral data:* Customers leave traces of their purchasing behavior in store scanning data, catalog purchases, and customer databases. Much can be learned by analyzing these data. Customers' actual purchases reflect preferences and often are more reliable than statements they offer to market researchers. People may report preferences for popular brands, and yet the data show them actually buying other brands. For example, grocery shopping data show that high-income people do not necessarily buy the more expensive brands, contrary to what they might state in interviews; and many low-income people buy some expensive brands. Clearly, American Airlines can learn many useful things about its passengers by analyzing ticket purchase records.

■ *Experimental research:* The most scientifically valid research is experimental research. The purpose of experimental research is to capture cause-and-effect relationships by eliminating competing explanations of the observed findings. To the extent that the design and execution of the experiment eliminate alternative hypotheses that might explain the results, research and marketing managers can have confidence in the conclusions. It calls for selecting matched groups of subjects, subjecting them to different treatments, controlling extraneous variables, and checking whether observed response differences are statistically significant. To the extent that extraneous factors are eliminated or controlled, the observed effects can be related to the variations in the treatments.

American Airlines might introduce in-flight Internet service on one of its regular flights from Chicago to Tokyo. It might charge $25 one week and charge only $15 the next week. If the plane carried approximately the same number of first-class passengers each week and the particular weeks made no difference, any significant difference in the number of calls made could be related to the different prices charged. The experimental design could be elaborated by trying other prices and including other air routes.

Research Instruments   Marketing researchers have a choice of three main research instruments in collecting primary data: questionnaires, psychological tools, and mechanical devices.

1. *Questionnaires.* A questionnaire consists of a set of questions presented to respondents. Because of its flexibility, the questionnaire is by far the most common instrument used to collect primary data. Questionnaires need to be carefully developed, tested, and debugged before they are administered on a large scale.

   In preparing a questionnaire, the researcher carefully chooses the questions and their form, wording, and sequence. The form of the question asked can influence the response. Marketing researchers distinguish between closed-end and open-end questions. Closed-end questions specify all the possible answers and provide answers that are easier to interpret and tabulate.

Open-end questions allow respondents to answer in their own words and often reveal more about how people think. They are especially useful in exploratory research, where the researcher is looking for insight into how people think rather than measuring how many people think a certain way. Table 5.2 provides examples of both types of questions; and see "Marketing Memo: Questionnaire Dos and Don'ts."

2. *Psychological tools.* Marketing researchers can probe a buyer's deeper beliefs and feelings using psychological tools such as laddering techniques, depth interviews, and Rorschach tests. Laddering involves asking a male consumer, for example, "Why do you want to buy an SUV vehicle? " He may answer, "It is a good-looking car." He is asked a follow-up question: "Why do you want a good-looking car?" Upon receiving his answer, another question is put: "Why is this important to you?" This continues until the researcher arrives at a deeper reason, such as "People will be more impressed with me."

Depth interviewing involves going deeply into the thoughts that an individual may have about a product or service. The late Ernest Dichter was a master of depth interviewing and came out with many surprising findings: People do not like prunes because their wrinkled appearance makes them think of old age; and women do not respond to cake mixes that do not include adding an egg because they see baking as an act of giving birth. Whatever the validity, his findings gave his corporate clients many ideas. Dichter held that qualitative research ("head shrinking") gave far more insight than questionnaire-based, quantitative research ("nose counting").

Zaltman recently introduced a psychological instrument called the Zaltman Metaphoric Elicitation Technique (ZMET), which uses metaphors to access nonverbal images.[17] One study probed what women thought of panty hose. Twenty hose-wearing women were asked to collect pictures that captured their feelings about wearing panty hose. Some of the pictures showed fence posts encased in plastic wrap or steel bands strangling trees, suggesting that panty hose are tight and inconvenient. On the other hand, another picture showed tall flowers in a vase, suggesting that the product made a woman feel thin, tall, and sexy. This technique gets at associations that are less likely to emerge during normal interviewing.

3. *Mechanical devices.* Mechanical devices are occasionally used in marketing research. Galvanometers measure the interest or emotions aroused by exposure to a specific ad or picture. The tachistoscope flashes an ad to a subject with an exposure interval that may range from less than one hundredth of a second to several seconds. After each exposure, the respondent describes everything he or she recalls. Eye cameras study respondents' eye movements to see where their eyes land first, how long they linger on a given item, and so on. An audiometer is attached to television sets in participating homes to record when the set is on and to which channel it is tuned.[18]

4. *Qualitative measures.* Some marketers prefer more qualitative methods for gauging consumer opinion because consumer actions do not always match their answers to survey questions. New tools such as videos, pagers, and informal interviewing will help marketers overcome the limitations of traditional research methods. In 1999, the ad agency Ogilvy & Mather created the Discovery Group, a research unit that creates documentary-style videos by sending researchers with handheld videocameras into consumers' homes. Hours of footage are edited to a 30-minute "highlight reel" which the company uses to analyze consumer behavior for its clients. Other researchers equip consumers with pagers and instruct them to write down what they are doing whenever prompted, or hold more informal interview sessions at a café or bar.

In addition to new qualitative research tools, marketers have developed new methodologies to help them understand target consumers. Two of these are prototyping and articulative interviewing. Customer prototyping attempts to paint a realistic portrait of an individual by describing a specific customer type (e.g., "ideal customer" or "nonuser") in qualitative terms. To arrive at a prototype, marketers strive to answer questions such as "What is important to this person?" and "How does this person want others to view him or her?" The process is repeated until the prototypes begin to overlap. The areas of overlap describe the marketer's target customers. Articulative interviewing is designed to determine what social values interviewees hold dear by having them talk about broad topics such as their various roles in life and their daily activities. The broad format enables the marketer to draw out relevant information; the interviewee is also

table **5.2**		Types of Questions

A. Closed-end Questions

Name	Description	Example
Dichotomous	A question with two possible answers.	In arranging this trip, did you personally phone American? Yes No
Multiple choice	A question with three or more answers.	With whom are you traveling on this flight? ☐ No one ☐ Children only ☐ Spouse ☐ Business associates/friends/relatives ☐ Spouse and children ☐ An organized tour group
Likert scale	A statement with which the respondent shows the amount of agreement/ disagreement.	Small airlines generally give better service than large ones. Strongly disagree / Disagree / Neither agree nor disagree / Agree / Strongly agree 1___ 2___ 3___ 4___ 5___
Semantic differential	A scale connecting two bipolar words. The respondent selects the point that represents his or her opinion.	American Airlines Large ------------------------Small Experienced------------------Inexperienced Modern ------------------------Old-fashioned
Importance scale	A scale that rates the importance of some attribute.	Airline food service to me is Extremely important / Very important / Somewhat important / Not very important / Not at all important 1___ 2___ 3___ 4___ 5___
Rating scale	A scale that rates some attribute from "poor" to "excellent."	American food service is Excellent / Very Good / Good / Fair / Poor 1___ 2___ 3___ 4___ 5___
Intention-to-buy scale	A scale that describes the respondent's intention to buy.	If an in-flight telephone were available on a long flight, I would Definitely buy / Probably buy / Not sure / Probably not buy / Definitely not buy 1___ 2___ 3___ 4___ 5___

B. Open-end Questions

Completely unstructured	A question that respondents can answer in an almost unlimited number of ways.	What is your opinion of American Airlines?
Word association	Words are presented, one at a time, and respondents mention the first word that comes to mind.	What is the first word that comes to your mind when you hear the following? Airline _____ American _____ Travel _____
Sentence completion	An incomplete sentence is presented and respondents complete the sentence.	When I choose an airline, the most important consideration in my decision is _____.
Story completion	An incomplete story is presented, and respondents are asked to complete it.	"I flew American a few days ago. I noticed that the exterior and interior of the plane had very bright colors. This aroused in me the following thoughts and feelings. . . . " Now complete the story.
Picture	A picture of two characters is presented, with one making a statement. Respondents are asked to identify with the other and fill in the empty balloon.	
Thematic Apperception Test (TAT)	A picture is presented and respondents are asked to make up a story about what they think is happening or may happen in the picture.	

Marketing
MEMO

Questionnaire Dos and Don'ts

1. *Ensure that questions are without bias.* Do not lead the respondent into an answer.
2. *Make the questions as simple as possible.* Questions that include multiple ideas or two questions in one will confuse respondents.
3. *Make the questions specific.* Sometimes it is advisable to add memory cues. For example, it is good practice to be specific with time periods.
4. *Avoid jargon or shorthand.* Trade jargon, acronyms, and initials not in everyday use should be avoided.
5. *Steer clear of sophisticated or uncommon words.* Only use words in common speech.
6. *Avoid ambiguous words.* Words such as "usually" or "frequently" have no specific meaning.
7. *Avoid questions with a negative in them.* It is better to say "Do you ever . . . ?" than "Do you never . . . ?"
8. *Avoid hypothetical questions.* It is difficult to answer questions about imaginary situations. Answers cannot necessarily be trusted.
9. *Do not use words that could be misheard.* This is especially important when the interview is administered over the telephone. "What is your opinion of sects?" could yield interesting but not necessarily relevant answers.
10. *Desensitize questions by using response bands.* For questions that ask people their age or companies their turnover, it is best to offer a range of response bands.
11. *Ensure that fixed responses do not overlap.* Categories used in fixed response questions should be sequential and not overlap.
12. *Allow for "others" in fixed response questions.* Pre-coded answers should always allow for a response other than those listed.

Source: Adapted from Paul Hague and Peter Jackson, *Market Research: A Guide to Planning, Methodology, and Evaluation* (London: Kogan Page, 1999). See also Hans Baumgartner and Jan Benedict E. M. Steen Kamp, "Response Styles in Marketing Research: A Cross-National Investigation," May 2001, pp. 143–156.

likely to reveal valuable information regarding core beliefs and other social factors that may influence product decisions.[19]

Sampling Plan   After deciding on the research approach and instruments, the marketing researcher must design a sampling plan. This calls for three decisions:

1. *Sampling unit: Who is to be surveyed?* The marketing researcher must define the target population that will be sampled. In the American Airlines survey, should the sampling unit be only first-class business travelers, first-class vacation travelers, or both? Should travelers under age 18 be interviewed? Should both husbands and wives be interviewed? Once the sampling unit is determined, a sampling frame must be developed so that everyone in the target population has an equal or known chance of being sampled.

The Food & Brand Lab page of Brian Wansink's consumer psychology Web site.

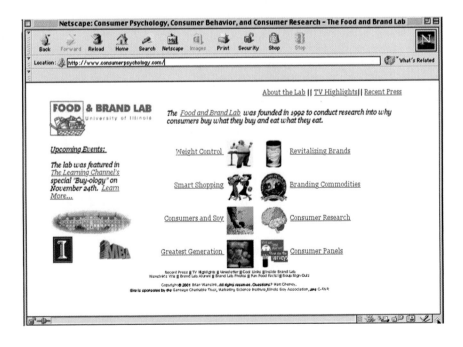

A. Probability Sample	
Simple random sample	Every member of the population has an equal chance of selection
Stratified random sample	The population is divided into mutually exclusive groups (such as age groups), and random samples are drawn from each group
Cluster (area) sample	The population is divided into mutually exclusive groups (such as city blocks), and the researcher draws a sample of the groups to interview
B. Nonprobability Sample	
Convenience sample	The researcher selects the most accessible population members
Judgment sample	The researcher selects population members who are good prospects for accurate information
Quota sample	The researcher finds and interviews a prescribed number of people in each of several categories

Probability and
Nonprobability
Samples

2. *Sample size: How many people should be surveyed?* Large samples give more reliable results than small samples. However, it is not necessary to sample the entire target population or even a substantial portion to achieve reliable results. Samples of less than 1 percent of a population can often provide good reliability, with a credible sampling procedure.

3. *Sampling procedure: How should the respondents be chosen?* To obtain a representative sample, a probability sample of the population should be drawn. Probability sampling allows the calcula-tion of confidence limits for sampling error. Thus, one could conclude after the sample is taken that "the interval 5 to 7 trips per year has 95 chances in 100 of containing the true number of trips taken annually by first-class passengers flying between Chicago and Tokyo." Three types of prob-ability sampling are described in Table 5.3 part A. When the cost or time involved in probability sampling is too high, marketing researchers will take nonprobability samples. Table 5.3, part B describes three types. Some marketing researchers feel that nonprobability samples are very use-ful in many circumstances, even though they do not allow sampling error to be measured.

Contact Methods   Once the sampling plan has been determined, the marketing re-searcher must decide how the subject should be contacted: mail, telephone, personal, or online interview.

The *mail questionnaire* is the best way to reach people who would not give personal interviews or whose responses might be biased or distorted by the interviewers. Mail questionnaires require simple and clearly worded questions. Unfortunately, the response rate is usually low or slow. Telephone interviewing is the best method for gathering information quickly; the interviewer is also able to clarify questions if respon-dents do not understand them. The response rate is typically higher than in the case of mailed questionnaires. The main drawback is that the interviews have to be short and not too personal. Telephone interviewing is getting more difficult because of answering machines and people becoming suspicious of telemarketing.

Personal interviewing is the most versatile method. The interviewer can ask more questions and record additional observations about the respondent, such as dress and body language. Brian Wansink has developed a customer profiling technique based on personal interviews that generates interesting hypotheses which can be further tested or used in communication strategy.[20] At the same time, personal interviewing is the most expensive method and requires more administrative planning and supervision than the other three. It is also subject to interviewer bias or distortion. Personal interviewing takes two forms. In *arranged interviews*, respondents are contacted for an appointment, and often a small payment or incentive is offered. *Intercept interviews* involve stopping people at a shopping mall or busy street corner and requesting an interview. Intercept interviews have the drawback of being nonprobability samples, and the interviews must not require too much time.

There is increased use of *online methods*. Online product testing is expected to grow and provide information faster than traditional marketing research techniques. A company can include a questionnaire on its Web site and offer an incentive to answer the questionnaire; or it can place a banner on some frequently visited site such as Yahoo!, inviting people to answer some questions and possibly win a prize. The company can enter a target chat room and seek volunteers for a survey, or sponsor a chat room and introduce questions from time to time. A company can learn about individuals who visit its site by following how they *clickstream* through the Web site and move to other sites. Computers contain *cookies* that capture this data. By analyzing the clickstreams of different visitors, the company can make inferences about consumer behavior. A company can post different prices, use different headlines, offer different product features on different Web sites or at different times to learn the relative effectiveness of its offerings.

Not everyone is on the Web, however, and online market researchers must find creative ways to reach certain population segments, such as older Americans, the disabled, and Hispanics. One option is to combine off-line sources with the online findings. Providing temporary Internet access at locations such as malls and recreation centers is another strategy. Some research firms use statistical models to fill in the gaps in market research left by off-line consumer segments. Knowledge Networks is an example.

Knowledge Networks   Menlo Park–based Knowledge Networks was founded by two Stanford University professors in 1998. To ensure consistent results, the company distributes WebTV interactive television boxes complete with Internet connections to all respondents. The interactive televisions operate with remote controls in exactly the same fashion as normal TVs, so Internet literacy is not required for participation. It has a network of more than 100,000 Web-ready panelists. Knowledge Networks seeks to become a one-stop marketing research company, performing television- and Internet-usage tracking studies, brand management diagnostics and tracking, product and advertising evaluations, and traditional survey applications. Knowledge Networks calls this a "360-degree view of the consumer."[21]

Many companies are now using *automated telephone surveys* to solicit market research information. One popular approach is to distribute prepaid phone cards as an incentive. A survey is programmed into an interactive call system that not only administers the survey, but also sorts the results virtually any way the client wants them. When the call users place their free calls, a voice prompt asks them if they would like to gain additional minutes by taking a short survey. NBC, Coca-Cola, and Amoco are some of the companies that have used prepaid phone cards to survey their customers.[22]

STEP 3: COLLECT THE INFORMATION   The data collection phase of marketing research is generally the most expensive and the most prone to error. In the case of surveys, four major problems arise. Some respondents will not be at home and must be recontacted or replaced. Other respondents will refuse to cooperate. Still others will give biased or dishonest answers. Finally, some interviewers will be biased or dishonest.

Yet data collection methods are rapidly improving, thanks to computers and telecommunications. Some research firms interview from a centralized location.

Professional interviewers sit in booths and draw telephone numbers at random. When the phone is answered, the interviewer reads a set of questions from a monitor and types the respondents' answers into a computer. This procedure eliminates editing and coding, reduces errors, saves time, and produces all the required statistics. Other research firms have set up interactive terminals in shopping centers. Persons willing to be interviewed sit at a terminal, read the questions from the monitor, and type in their answers. Most respondents enjoy this form of "robot" interviewing.

Several recent technical advances have permitted marketers to research the sales impact of ads and sales promotion. Information Resources, Inc., recruits a panel of supermarkets equipped with scanners and electronic cash registers. Scanners read the universal product code on each product purchased, recording the brand, size, and price for inventory and ordering purposes. Meanwhile, the firm has recruited a panel of store customers who have agreed to charge their purchases with a special Shopper's Hotline ID card, which holds information about household characteristics, lifestyle, and income. These same customers have also agreed to let their television-viewing habits be monitored by a black box. All consumer panelists receive their programs through cable television, and Information Resources controls the advertising messages being sent to their homes. The firm can then capture through store purchases which ads led to more purchasing and by which customers.[23]

STEP 4: ANALYZE THE INFORMATION   The next-to-last step in the marketing research process is to extract findings from the collected data. The researcher tabulates the data and develops frequency distributions. Averages and measures of dispersion are computed for the major variables. The researcher will also apply some advanced statistical techniques and decision models in the hope of discovering additional findings. (Techniques and models are described later in this chapter.)

STEP 5: PRESENT THE FINDINGS   As the last step, the researcher presents the findings. The researcher should present findings that are relevant to the major marketing decisions facing management. The main survey findings for the American Airlines case show that:

1. The chief reasons for using in-flight Internet service are to pass the time surfing, and to send and receive messages from colleagues and family. The charge would be put on passengers' charge accounts and paid by their company.

2. About 5 first-class passengers out of every 10 during a flight would use the Internet service at $25; about 6 would use it at $15. Thus, a charge of $15 would produce less revenue ($90 = 6 × $15) than $25 ($125 = 5 × $25). By charging $25, AA would collect $125 per flight. Assuming that the same flight takes place 365 days a year, AA would annually collect $45,625 (= $125 × 365). Since the investment is $90,000, it will take approximately two years before American Airlines breaks even.

3. Offering in-flight service would strengthen the public's image of American Airlines as an innovative and progressive airline. American would gain some new passengers and customer goodwill.

STEP 6: MAKE THE DECISION   The managers who commissioned the research need to weigh the evidence. They know that the findings could suffer from a variety of errors. If their confidence in the findings is low, they may decide against introducing the in-flight Internet service. If they are predisposed to launching the service, the findings support their inclination. They may even decide to study the issues further and do more research. The decision is theirs, but hopefully the research provided them with insight into the problem. (See Table 5.4)[24]

overcoming barriers to the use of marketing research

In spite of the rapid growth of marketing research, many companies still fail to use it sufficiently or correctly, for several reasons:

table **5.4**		
The Seven Characteristics of Good Marketing Research	1. Scientific method.	Effective marketing research uses the principles of the scientific method: careful observation, formulation of hypotheses, prediction, and testing.
	2. Research creativity.	At its best, marketing research develops innovative ways to solve a problem: a clothing company catering to teenagers gave several young men video cameras, then used the videos for focus groups held in restaurants and other places teens frequent.
	3. Multiple methods.	Marketing researchers shy away from overreliance on any one method. They also recognize the value of using two or three methods to increase confidence in the results.
	4. Interdependence of models and data.	Marketing researchers recognize that data are interpreted from underlying models that guide the type of information sought.
	5. Value and cost of information.	Marketing researchers show concern for estimating the value of information against its cost. Costs are typically easy to determine, but the value of research is harder to quantify. It depends on the reliability and validity of the findings and management's willingness to accept and act on those findings.
	6. Healthy skepticism.	Marketing researchers show a healthy skepticism toward glib assumptions made by managers about how a market works. They are alert to the problems caused by "marketing myths."
	7. Ethical marketing.	Marketing research benefits both the sponsoring company and its customers. The misuse of marketing research can harm or annoy consumers, increasing resentment at what consumers regard as an invasion of their privacy or a disguised sales pitch.

- *A narrow conception of the research:* Many managers see marketing research as a fact-finding operation. They expect the researcher to design a questionnaire, choose a sample, conduct interviews, and report results, often without a careful definition of the problem or of the decisions facing management. When fact-finding fails to be useful, management's idea of the limited usefulness of marketing research is reinforced.
- *Uneven caliber of researchers:* Some managers view marketing research as little more than a clerical activity and treat it as such. Less competent marketing researchers are hired, and their weak training and deficient creativity lead to unimpressive results. The disappointing results reinforce management's prejudice against marketing research. Management continues to pay low salaries to its market researchers, thus perpetuating the basic problem.
- *Poor framing of the problem:* In the famous case where Coca-Cola introduced the New Coke after much research, the failure of the New Coke was largely due to not setting up the research problem correctly from a marketing perspective. The issue is how consumers felt about Coca-Cola as a brand and not necessarily the taste in isolation.
- *Late and occasionally erroneous findings:* Managers want results that are accurate and conclusive. They may want the results tomorrow. Yet good marketing research takes time and money. Managers are disappointed when marketing research costs too much or takes too much time.

- *Personality and presentational differences:* Differences between the styles of line managers and marketing researchers often get in the way of productive relationships. To a manager who wants concreteness, simplicity, and certainty, a marketing researcher's report may seem abstract, complicated, and tentative. Yet in the more progressive companies, marketing researchers are more often being included as members of the product management team, and their influence on marketing strategy is growing.

marketing decision support system

A growing number of organizations are using a marketing decision support system to help their marketing managers make better decisions. John Little defines a **marketing decision support system (MDSS)** as a coordinated collection of data, systems, tools, and techniques with supporting software and hardware by which an organization gathers and interprets relevant information from business and environment and turns it into a basis for marketing action.[25] Table 5.5 describes the major statistical tools, models, and optimization routines that comprise a modern MDSS. Lilien and Rangaswamy recently published *Marketing Engineering: Computer-Assisted Marketing Analysis and Planning*, which includes a disk with widely used modeling software tools.[26]

Once a year, *Marketing News* lists hundreds of current marketing and sales software programs that assist in designing marketing research studies, segmenting markets, setting prices and advertising budgets, analyzing media, and planning sales force activity. Here are examples of decision models that have been used by marketing managers:

BRANDAID: A flexible marketing-mix model focused on consumer packaged goods whose elements are a manufacturer, competitors, retailers, consumers, and the general environment. The model contains submodels for advertising, pricing, and competition. The model is calibrated with a creative blending of judgment, historical analysis, tracking, field experimentation, and adaptive control.[27]

CALLPLAN: A model to help salespeople determine the number of calls to make per period to each prospect and current client. The model takes into account travel time as well as selling time. The model was tested at United Airlines with an experimental group that managed to increase its sales over a matched control group by 8 percentage points.[28]

DETAILER: A model to help salespeople determine which customers to call on and which products to represent on each call. This model was largely developed for pharmaceutical detail people calling on physicians, where they could represent no more than three products on a call. In two applications, the model yielded strong profit improvements.[29]

GEOLINE: A model for designing sales and service territories that satisfies three principles: The territories equalize sales workloads; each territory consists of adjacent areas; and the territories are compact. Several successful applications were reported.[30]

MEDIAC: A model to help an advertiser buy media for a year. The media planning model includes market-segment delineation, sales potential estimation, diminishing marginal returns, forgetting, timing issues, and competitor media schedules.[31]

Some models now claim to duplicate the way expert marketers normally make their decisions. Some recent expert system models include:

PROMOTER evaluates sales promotions by determining baseline sales (what sales would have been without promotion) and measuring the increase over baseline associated with the promotion.[32]

ADCAD recommends the type of ad (humorous, slice of life, and so on) to use given the marketing goals, product characteristics, target market, and competitive situation.[33]

COVERSTORY examines a mass of syndicated sales data and writes an English-language memo reporting the highlights.[34]

table **5.5**	
Quantitative Tools Used in Marketing Decision Support Systems	**Statistical Tools**
	1. Multiple regression: A statistical technique for estimating a "best fitting" equation showing how the value of a dependent variable varies with changing values in a number of independent variables. *Example:* A company can estimate how unit sales are influenced by changes in the level of company advertising expenditures, sales force size, and price.
	2. Discriminant analysis: A statistical technique for classifying an object or persons into two or more categories. *Example:* A large retail chain store can determine the variables that discriminate between successful and unsuccessful store locations.[a]
	3. Factor analysis: A statistical technique used to determine the few underlying dimensions of a larger set of intercorrelated variables. *Example:* A broadcast network can reduce a large set of TV programs down to a small set of basic program types.[b]
	4. Cluster analysis: A statistical technique for separating objects into a specified number of mutually exclusive groups such that the groups are relatively homogeneous. *Example:* A marketing researcher might want to classify a set of cities into four distinct groups.
	5. Conjoint analysis: A statistical technique whereby respondents' ranked preferences for different offers are decomposed to determine the person's inferred utility function for each attribute and the relative importance of each attribute. *Example:* An airline can determine the total utility delivered by different combinations of passenger services.
	6. Multidimensional scaling: A variety of techniques for producing perceptual maps of competitive products or brands. Objects are represented as points in a multidimensional space of attributes where their distance from one another is a measure of dissimilarity. *Example:* A computer manufacturer wants to see where his brand is positioned in relation to competitive brands.
	Models
	1. Markov-process model: This model shows the probability of moving from a current state to any future state. *Example:* A branded packaged-goods manufacturer can determine the period-to-period switching and staying rates for her brand and, if the probabilities are stable, the brand's ultimate brand share.
	2. Queuing model: This model shows the waiting times and queue lengths that can be expected in any system, given the arrival and service times and the number of service channels. *Example:* A supermarket can use the model to predict queue lengths at different times of the day given the number of service channels and service speed.
	3. New-product pretest models: This model involves estimating functional relations between buyer states of awareness, trial, and repurchase based on consumer preferences and actions in a pretest situation of the marketing offer and campaign. Among the well-known models are ASSESSOR, COMP, DEMON, NEWS, and SPRINTER.[c]

4. Sales-response models:	This is a set of models that estimate functional relations between one or more marketing variables—such as sales force size, advertising expenditure, sales-promotion expenditure, and so forth—and the resulting demand level.

Optimization Routines

1. Differential calculus:	This technique allows finding the maximum or minimum value along a well-behaved function.
2. Mathematical programming:	This technique allows finding the values that would optimize some objective function that is subject to a set of constraints.
3. Statistical decision theory:	This technique allows determining the course of action that produces the maximum expected value.
4. Game theory:	This technique allows determining the course of action that will minimize the decision maker's maximum loss in the face of the uncertain behavior of one or more competitors.
5. Heuristics:	This involves using a set of rules of thumb that shorten the time or work required to find a reasonably good solution in a complex system.

[a] S. Sands, "Store Site Selection by Discriminant Analysis," *Journal of the Market Research Society* (1981): 40–51.
[b] V. R. Rao, "Taxonomy of Television Programs Based on Viewing Behavior," *Journal of Marketing Research* (August 1975): 355–58.
[c] See Kevin J. Clancy, Robert Shulman, and Marianne Wolf, *Simulated Test Marketing* (New York: Lexington Books, 1994).

forecasting and demand measurement

One major reason for undertaking marketing research is to identify market opportunities. Once the research is complete, the company must measure and forecast the size, growth, and profit potential of each market opportunity. Sales forecasts are used by finance to raise the needed cash for investment and operations; by the manufacturing department to establish capacity and output levels; by purchasing to acquire the right amount of supplies; and by human resources to hire the needed number of workers. Marketing is responsible for preparing the sales forecasts. If its forecast is far off the mark, the company will be saddled with excess inventory or have inadequate inventory. Sales forecasts are based on estimates of demand. Managers need to define what they mean by market demand. Here is a good example of the importance of defining the market correctly:

Coca-Cola   When Roberto Goizueta became CEO of Coca-Cola, many people thought that Coke's sales were maxed out. Goizueta, however, reframed the view of Coke's market share. He said Coca-Cola accounted for less than 2 ounces of the 64 ounces of fluid that each of the world's 4.4 billion people drank on average every day. "The enemy is coffee, milk, tea, water," he told his people at Coke, and he ushered in a huge period of growth.

---

figure **5.3**

Ninety Types of Demand
Measurement (6 × 5 × 3)

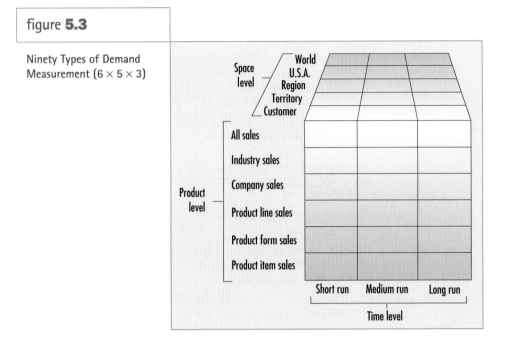

the measures of market demand

Companies can prepare as many as 90 different types of demand estimates (see Figure 5.3). Demand can be measured for six different product levels, five different space levels, and three different time levels.

Each demand measure serves a specific purpose. A company might forecast short-run demand for a particular product for the purpose of ordering raw materials, planning production, and borrowing cash. It might forecast regional demand for its major product line to decide whether to set up regional distribution.

which market to measure?

Marketers talk about potential markets, available markets, served markets, and penetrated markets. Let us start with the definition of market: A **market** is the set of all actual and potential buyers of a market offer. The size of a market hinges on the number of buyers who might exist for a particular market offer. The **potential market** is the set of consumers who profess a sufficient level of interest in a market offer.

However, consumer interest is not enough to define a market. Potential consumers must have enough income and must have access to the product offer. The **available market** is the set of consumers who have interest, income, and access to a particular offer. For some market offers, the company or government may restrict sales to certain groups. For example, a particular state might ban motorcycle sales to anyone under 21 years of age. The eligible adults constitute the *qualified available market*—the set of consumers who have interest, income, access, and qualifications for the particular market offer.

A company can go after the whole available market or concentrate on certain segments. The **target market** (also called the **served market**) is the part of the qualified available market the company decides to pursue. The company, for example, might decide to concentrate its marketing and distribution effort on the East Coast. The company will end up selling to a certain number of buyers in its target market. The **penetrated market** is the set of consumers who are buying the company's product.

These market definitions are a useful tool for market planning. If the company is not satisfied with its current sales, it can take a number of actions. It can try to attract a larger percentage of buyers from its target market. It can lower the qualifications of potential buyers. It can expand its available market by opening distribution elsewhere or lowering its price; or it can reposition itself in the minds of its customers. Consider the case of Target Stores.

Target   Facing stiff competition from top retailers Wal-Mart and Kmart, Target Stores decided to reach more affluent shoppers and woo them away from department stores. The Midwestern discount retailer ran an unusual advertising campaign in some unusual spots: the Sunday magazines of the *New York Times*, the *Los Angeles Times*, and the *San Francisco Examiner*. One ad showed a woman riding a vacuum cleaner through the night sky. The ad simply said "Fashion and Housewares," with the Target logo in the lower right-hand corner. These hip spots gained Target Stores a reputation as the "upstairs" mass retailer, or "Kmart for Yuppies," as one shopper put it. In 2001, Target brought "fashion to food" by adding grocery sections to its retail concept and creating 175,000-square-foot SuperTargets.[35] The company added 14 SuperTarget supercenters in 2000, while revenues for that year rose 12.3 percent to $29.3 billion. Target's success prompted parent company Dayton-Hudson Corporation to change its name to Target Corporation in 2000.

a vocabulary for demand measurement

The major concepts in demand measurement are market demand and company demand. Within each, we distinguish among a demand function, a sales forecast, and a potential.

MARKET DEMAND   As we have seen, the marketer's first step in evaluating marketing opportunities is to estimate total market demand. **Market demand** for a product is the total volume that would be bought by a defined customer group in a defined geographical area in a defined time period in a defined marketing environment under a defined marketing program.

Market demand is not a fixed number, but rather a function of the stated conditions. For this reason, it can be called the *market demand function*. The dependence of total market demand on underlying conditions is illustrated in Figure 5.4(a). The horizontal axis shows different possible levels of industry marketing expenditure in a given time period. The vertical axis shows the resulting demand level. The curve represents the estimated market demand associated with varying levels of industry marketing expenditure.

Some base sales (called the *market minimum*, labeled Q1 in the figure) would take place without any demand-stimulating expenditures. Higher levels of industry marketing expenditures would yield higher levels of demand, first at an increasing rate, then at a decreasing rate. Marketing expenditures beyond a certain level would not stimulate much further demand, thus suggesting an upper limit to market demand called the *market potential* (labeled Q2 in the figure).

The distance between the market minimum and the market potential shows the overall *marketing sensitivity of demand*. We can think of two extreme types of markets, the expansible and the nonexpansible. An *expansible market*, such as the market for racquetball playing, is very much affected in its total size by the level of industry marketing expenditures. In terms of Figure 5.4(a), the distance between Q1 and Q2 is relatively large. A *nonexpansible market*—for example, the market for opera—is not much affected by the level of marketing expenditures; the distance between Q1 and Q2 is relatively small. Organizations selling in a nonexpansible market must accept the market's size (the level of *primary demand* for the product class) and direct their efforts to winning a larger **market share** for their product (the level of selective demand for the company's product).

---

figure **5.4**   Market Demand Functions

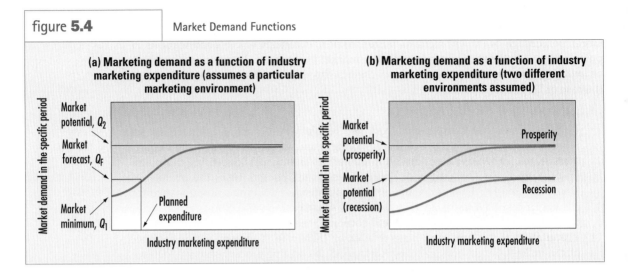

(a) Marketing demand as a function of industry marketing expenditure (assumes a particular marketing environment)

(b) Marketing demand as a function of industry marketing expenditure (two different environments assumed)

It pays to compare the current level of market demand to the potential demand level. The result is called the **market penetration index**. A low market penetration index indicates substantial growth potential for all the firms. A high market penetration index suggests that there will be increased costs in attracting the few remaining prospects. Generally, price competition increases and margins fall when the market penetration index is already high.

A company should also compare its current market share to its potential market share. The result is called the company's **share penetration index**. A low share penetration index indicates that the company can greatly expand its share. The underlying factors holding it back could be many: low brand awareness, low brand availability, benefit deficiencies, too high a price. A firm should calculate the share penetration increases that would occur with investments to remove each deficiency, to see which investments would produce the greatest improvement in share penetration.[36]

It is important to remember that the market demand function is not a picture of market demand over time. Rather, the curve shows alternative current forecasts of market demand associated with alternative possible levels of industry marketing effort in the current period.

MARKET FORECAST   Only one level of industry marketing expenditure will actually occur. The market demand corresponding to this level is called the **market forecast**.

MARKET POTENTIAL   The market forecast shows expected market demand, not maximum market demand. For the latter, we have to visualize the level of market demand resulting from a "very high" level of industry marketing expenditure, where further increases in marketing effort would have little effect in stimulating further demand. **Market potential** is the limit approached by market demand as industry marketing expenditures approach infinity for a given marketing environment.

The phrase "for a given market environment" is crucial. Consider the market potential for automobiles in a period of recession versus a period of prosperity. The market potential is higher during prosperity. The dependence of market potential on the environment is illustrated in Figure 5.4(b). Market analysts distinguish between the position of the market demand function and movement along it. Companies cannot do anything about the position of the market demand function, which is determined by the marketing environment. However, companies influence their particular location on the function when they decide how much to spend on marketing.

Companies interested in market potential have a special interest in the **product penetration percentage**, which is the percentage of ownership or use of a product or service in a population. Here are some U.S. percentages: television (98%), health insurance (84%), car (81%), home ownership (67%), PC (54%), stock ownership (48%), gun ownership (41%), and fax (12%).[37] Companies assume that the lower the product penetration percentage, the higher the market potential, although this assumes that everyone will eventually be in the market for every product.

COMPANY DEMAND   We are now ready to define company demand: **Company demand** is the company's estimated share of market demand at alternative levels of company marketing effort in a given time period. The company's share of market demand depends on how its products, services, prices, communications, and so on are perceived relative to the competitors'. If other things are equal, the company's market share would depend on the size and effectiveness of its market expenditures relative to competitors. Marketing model builders have developed sales-response functions to measure how a company's sales are affected by its marketing expenditure level, marketing mix, and marketing effectiveness.[38]

COMPANY SALES FORECAST   Once marketers have estimated company demand, their next task is to choose a level of marketing effort. The chosen level will produce an expected level of sales. The **company sales forecast** is the expected level of company sales based on a chosen marketing plan and an assumed marketing environment.

The company sales forecast is represented graphically with company sales on the vertical axis and company marketing effort on the horizontal axis, as in Figure 5.4. Too often the sequential relationship between the company forecast and the company marketing plan is confused. One frequently hears that the company should develop its marketing plan on the basis of its sales forecast. This forecast-to-plan sequence is valid if "forecast" means an estimate of national economic activity or if company demand is nonexpansible. The sequence is not valid, however, where market demand is expansible or where "forecast" means an estimate of company sales. The company sales forecast does not establish a basis for deciding what to spend on marketing. On the contrary, the sales forecast is the result of an assumed marketing expenditure plan.

Two other concepts are worth mentioning in relation to the company sales forecast. A **sales quota** is the sales goal set for a product line, company division, or sales representative. It is primarily a managerial device for defining and stimulating sales effort. Management sets sales quotas on the basis of the company sales forecast and the psychology of stimulating its achievement. Generally, sales quotas are set slightly higher than estimated sales to stretch the sales force's effort.

A **sales budget** is a conservative estimate of the expected volume of sales and is used primarily for making current purchasing, production, and cashflow decisions. The sales budget is based on the sales forecast and the need to avoid excessive risk. Sales budgets are generally set slightly lower than the sales forecast.

COMPANY SALES POTENTIAL   **Company sales potential** is the sales limit approached by company demand as company marketing effort increases relative to that of competitors. The absolute limit of company demand is, of course, the market potential. The two would be equal if the company got 100 percent of the market. In most cases, company sales potential is less than the market potential, even when company marketing expenditures increase considerably, relative to competitors'. The reason is that each competitor has a hard core of loyal buyers who are not very responsive to other companies' efforts to woo them.

estimating current demand

We are now ready to examine practical methods for estimating current market demand. Marketing executives want to estimate total market potential, area market potential, and total industry sales and market shares.

TOTAL MARKET POTENTIAL   **Total market potential** is the maximum amount of sales that might be available to all the firms in an industry during a given period, under a given level of industry marketing effort and environmental conditions. A common way to estimate total market potential is as follows: Estimate the potential number of buyers times the average quantity purchased by a buyer times the price.

If 100 million people buy books each year, and the average book buyer buys three books a year, and the average price of a book is $20, then the total market potential for books is $6 billion (100 million $\times$ 6 $\times$ $10). The most difficult component to estimate is the number of buyers for the specific product or market. One can always start with the total population in the nation, say 261 million people. The next step is to eliminate groups that obviously would not buy the product. Let us assume that illiterate people and children under 12 do not buy books, and they constitute 20 percent of the population.

This means that only 80 percent of the population, or approximately 209 million people, would be in the suspect pool. We might do further research and find that people of low income and low education do not read books, and they constitute over 30 percent of the suspect pool. Eliminating them, we arrive at a prospect pool of approximately 146.3 million book buyers. We would use this number of potential buyers to calculate total market potential.

A variation on this method is the *chain-ratio method*. It involves multiplying a base number by several adjusting percentages. Suppose a brewery is interested in estimating the market potential for a new light beer. An estimate can be made by the following calculation:

> Demand for the new light beer = Population X personal discretionary income per capita X average percentage of discretionary income spent on food X average percentage of amount spent on food that is spent on beverages X average percentage of amount spent on beverages that is spent on alcoholic beverages X average percentage of amount spent on alcoholic beverages that is spent on beer X expected percentage of amount spent on beer that will be spent on light beer.

AREA MARKET POTENTIAL   Companies face the problem of selecting the best territories and allocating their marketing budget optimally among these territories. Therefore, they need to estimate the market potential of different cities, states, and nations. Two major methods of assessing area market potential are available: the market-buildup method, which is used primarily by business marketers, and the multiple-factor index method, which is used primarily by consumer marketers.

Market-Buildup Method   The **market-buildup method** calls for identifying all the potential buyers in each market and estimating their potential purchases. This method produces accurate results if we have a list of all potential buyers and a good estimate of what each will buy. Unfortunately, this information is not always easy to gather.

Consider a machine-tool company that wants to estimate the area market potential for its wood lathe in the Boston area. Its first step is to identify all potential buyers of wood lathes in the area. The buyers consist primarily of manufacturing establishments that have to shape or ream wood as part of their operation, so the company could compile a list from a directory of all manufacturing establishments in the Boston area. Then it could estimate the number of lathes each industry might purchase based on the number of lathes per thousand employees or per $1 million of sales in that industry.

An efficient method of estimating area market potentials makes use of the *Standard Industrial Classification (SIC) System* developed by the U.S. Bureau of the Census. The SIC classifies all manufacturing into 20 major industry groups, each with a two-digit code. Thus number 25 is furniture and fixtures. Each major industry group is further subdivided into about 150 groups designated by a three-digit code (number 251 is household furniture, and number 252 is office furniture). Each industry is further subdivided into approximately 450 product categories designated by a four-digit code (number 2521 is wood office furniture, and number 2522 is metal office furniture). For each four-digit SIC number, the Census of Manufacturers provides the number of establishments, subclassified by location, number of employees, annual sales, and net worth.

The SIC System is being changed to the new North American Industry Classification System (NAICS), which was developed by the United States, Canada, and Mexico to provide statistics that are comparable across the three countries. It includes 350 new industries, such as casino hotels, diet and weight reducing centers, HMO medical centers, and software publishers. It uses 20 instead of the SIC's 10 broad sectors of the economy, changes reflecting how the economy has changed. Industries are identified by a six-digit rather than a four-digit code, with the last digit changing depending on the country.

To use the SIC, the lathe manufacturer must first determine the four-digit SIC codes that represent products whose manufacturers are likely to require lathe machines. To get a full picture of all four-digit SIC industries that might use lathes, the company can (1) determine past customers' SIC codes; (2) go through the SIC manual and check off all the four-digit industries that might have an interest in lathes; (3) mail questionnaires to a wide range of companies inquiring about their interest in wood lathes.

The company's next task is to determine an appropriate base for estimating the number of lathes that will be used in each industry. Suppose customer industry sales are the most appropriate base. For example, in SIC number 2511, 10 lathes may be used for every $1 million worth of sales. Once the company estimates the rate of lathe ownership relative to the customer industry's sales, it can compute the market potential.

Table 5.6 shows a hypothetical computation for the Boston area involving two SIC codes. In number 2511 (wood household furniture), there are six establishments with annual sales of $1 million and two establishments with annual sales of $5 million. It is estimated that 10 lathes can be sold in this SIC code for every $1 million in customer sales. The six establishments with annual sales of $1 million account for $6 million in sales, which is a potential of 60 lathes (6310). Altogether, it appears that the Boston area has a market potential for 200 lathes.

The company can use the same method to estimate the market potential for other areas in the country. Suppose the market potentials for all the markets add up to 2,000 lathes. This means that the Boston market contains 10 percent of the total market potential, which might warrant the company's allocating 10 percent of its marketing expenditures to the Boston market. In practice, SIC information is not enough. The lathe manufacturer also needs additional information about each market, such as the extent of market saturation, the number of competitors, the market growth rate, and the average age of existing equipment.

table **5.6**

Market–Buildup Method Using SIC Codes

SIC	(a) Annual Sales in Millions of $	(b) Number of Establishments	(c) Potential Number of Lathe Sales per $1 Million Customer Sales	Market Potential (a × b × c)
2511	1	6	10	60
	5	2	10	100
2521	1	3	5	15
	5	1	5	25
			30	200

If the company decides to sell lathes in Boston, it must know how to identify the best-prospect companies. In the old days, sales reps called on companies door to door; this was called *bird-dogging* or *smokestacking.* Cold calls are far too costly today. The company should get a list of Boston companies and qualify them by direct mail or telemarketing to identify the best prospects. The lathe manufacturer can access Dun's Market Identifiers, which lists 27 key facts for over 9.3 million business locations in the United States and Canada.

Multiple-Factor Index Method   Like business marketers, consumer companies also have to estimate area market potentials, but the customers of consumer companies are too numerous to be listed. Thus the method most commonly used in consumer markets is a straightforward index method. A drug manufacturer, for example, might assume that the market potential for drugs is directly related to population size. If the state of Virginia has 2.28 percent of the U.S. population, the company might assume that Virginia will be a market for 2.28 percent of total drugs sold. A single factor, however, is rarely a complete indicator of sales opportunity. Regional drug sales are also influenced by per capita income and the number of physicians per 10,000 people. Thus it makes sense to develop a multiple-factor index with each factor assigned a specific weight.

The numbers are the weights attached to each variable. For example, suppose Virginia has 2.00 percent of the U.S. disposable personal income, 1.96 percent of U.S. retail sales, and 2.28 percent of U.S. population, and the respective weights are 0.5, 0.3, and 0.2. The buying-power index for Virginia would be

$$0.5(2.00) + 0.3(1.96) + 0.2(2.28) = 2.04$$

Thus 2.04 percent of the nation's drug sales might be expected to take place in Virginia.

The weights used in the buying-power index are somewhat arbitrary. Other weights can be assigned if appropriate. Furthermore, a manufacturer would want to adjust the market potential for additional factors, such as competitors' presence in that market, local promotional costs, seasonal factors, and local market idiosyncrasies.

Many companies compute other area indexes as a guide to allocating marketing resources. Suppose the drug company is reviewing the six cities listed in Table 5.7. The first two columns show its percentage of U.S. brand and category sales in these six cities. Column 3 shows the **brand development index (BDI)**, which is the index of brand sales to category sales. Seattle, for example, has a BDI of 114 because the brand is relatively more developed than the category in Seattle. Portland has a BDI of 65, which means that the brand in Portland is relatively underdeveloped. Normally, the lower the BDI, the higher the market opportunity, in that there is room to grow the brand. However, other marketers would argue the opposite, that marketing funds should go into the brand's strongest markets—where it might be easy to capture more brand share.[39]

table **5.7**				
Calculating the Brand Development Index (BDI)	Territory	**(a)** Percent of U.S. Brand Sales	**(b)** Percent of U.S. Category Sales	BDI (a ÷ b) × 100
	Seattle	3.09	2.71	114
	Portland	6.74	10.41	65
	Boston	3.49	3.85	91
	Toledo	.97	.81	120
	Chicago	1.13	.81	140
	Baltimore	3.12	3.00	104

After the company decides on the city-by-city allocation of its budget, it can refine each city allocation down to census tracts or zip+4 code centers. Census tracts are small, locally defined statistical areas in metropolitan areas and some other counties. They generally have stable boundaries and a population of about 4,000. Zip+4 code centers (which were designed by the U.S. Post Office) are a little larger than neighborhoods. Data on population size, median family income, and other characteristics are available for these geographical units. Marketers have found these data extremely useful for identifying high-potential retail areas within large cities or for buying mailing lists to use in direct-mail campaigns.

INDUSTRY SALES AND MARKET SHARES   Besides estimating total potential and area potential, a company needs to know the actual industry sales taking place in its market. This means identifying its competitors and estimating their sales.

The industry's trade association will often collect and publish total industry sales, although it usually does not list individual company sales separately. Using this information, each company can evaluate its performance against the whole industry. Suppose a company's sales are increasing by 5 percent a year, and industry sales are increasing by 10 percent. This company is actually losing its relative standing in the industry.

Another way to estimate sales is to buy reports from a marketing research firm that audits total sales and brand sales. For example, Nielsen Media Research audits retail sales in various product categories in supermarkets and drugstores and sells this information to interested companies. These audits can give a company valuable information about its total product-category sales as well as brand sales. It can compare its performance to the total industry or any particular competitor to see whether it is gaining or losing share.

Business-goods marketers typically have a harder time estimating industry sales and market shares. Business marketers have no Nielsens to rely on. Distributors typically will not supply information about how much of competitors' products they are selling. Business-goods marketers therefore operate with less knowledge of their market-share results.

estimating future demand

We are now ready to examine methods of estimating future demand. Very few products or services lend themselves to easy forecasting; those that do generally involve a product whose absolute level or trend is fairly constant and where competition is nonexistent (public utilities) or stable (pure oligopolies). In most markets, total demand and company demand are not stable. Good forecasting becomes a key factor in company success. The more unstable the demand, the more critical is forecast accuracy, and the more elaborate is forecasting procedure.

Companies commonly use a three-stage procedure to prepare a sales forecast. They prepare a macroeconomic forecast first, followed by an industry forecast, followed by a company sales forecast. The macroeconomic forecast calls for projecting inflation, unemployment, interest rates, consumer spending, business investment, government expenditures, net exports, and other variables. The end result is a forecast of gross national product, which is then used, along with other environmental indicators, to forecast industry sales. The company derives its sales forecast by assuming that it will win a certain market share.

How do firms develop their forecasts? Firms may do it internally or buy forecasts from outside sources such as marketing research firms, which develop a forecast by interviewing customers, distributors, and other knowledgeable parties; and specialized forecasting firms, which produce long-range forecasts of particular macroenvironmental components, such as population, natural resources, and technology. Some examples are Data Resources, Wharton Econometric Forecasting Associates, Forrester Research, and the Gartner Group. Futurist research firms produce speculative scenarios; two examples are the Hudson Institute and the Futures Group.

All forecasts are built on one of three information bases: what people say, what people do, or what people have done. The first basis—what people say—involves surveying the opinions of buyers or those close to them, such as salespeople or outside experts. It encompasses three methods: surveys of buyer's intentions, composites of sales force opinions, and expert opinion. Building a forecast on what people do involves another method—putting the product into a test market to measure buyer response. The final basis—what people have done—involves analyzing records of past buying behavior or using time-series analysis or statistical demand analysis.

survey of buyers' intentions

Forecasting is the art of anticipating what buyers are likely to do under a given set of conditions. Because buyer behavior is so important, buyers should be surveyed. For major consumer durables (for example, major appliances), several research organizations conduct periodic surveys of consumer buying intentions. These organizations ask questions like the following:

Do you intend to buy an automobile within the next six months?

0.00	0.20	0.40	0.60	0.80	1.00
No chance	Slight possibility	Fair possibility	Good possibility	High possibility	Certain

This is called a **purchase probability scale**. The various surveys also inquire into consumers' present and future personal finances and their expectations about the economy. The various bits of information are then combined into a consumer sentiment measure (Survey Research Center of the University of Michigan) or a consumer confidence measure (Sindlinger and Company). Consumer durable-goods producers subscribe to these indexes in the hope of anticipating major shifts in consumer buying intentions so that they can adjust their production and marketing plans accordingly.

Some surveys measuring purchase probability are geared toward getting feedback on specific new products before they are released in the marketplace.

AcuPOLL's home page shows the range of services it offers.

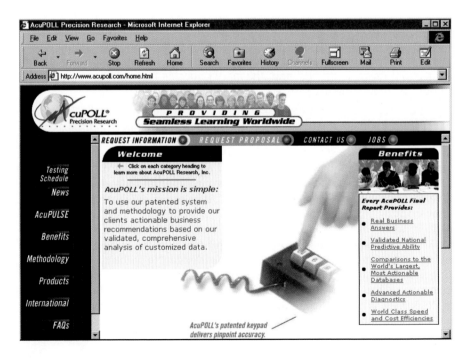

Acupoll Cincinnati-based AcuPOLL® is one of the nation's largest screeners of new products. In 2000 the company sifted through more than 25,000 new products, picking 400 of the most innovative to test on 100 nationally represented primary grocery store shoppers. The consumers see a photo and brief description and are asked (1) whether they would buy the product and (2) whether they think it is new and different. Products deemed both unique and "buys" are dubbed "pure gold." Products that are unique but not desired by customers are dubbed "fool's gold." AcuPOLL's pure gold list for 2000 included StarKist Tuna in a Pouch, Band-Aid Advanced Healing Bandages, and Downy Wrinkle Release wrinkle-removing spray. Fool's gold products included Bisurkey, a meat patty made from bison and turkey meat; IncrEdibles, portable processed foods in a "push-up" style packaging; and Oishii Kaori, a Japanese air freshener offered in coffee or tea scents.[40]

For business buying, various agencies carry out buyer-intention surveys regarding plant, equipment, and materials. The better-known agencies are McGraw-Hill Research and Opinion Research Corporation. Their estimates tend to fall within a 10 percent error band of the actual outcomes. Buyer-intention surveys are particularly useful in estimating demand for industrial products, consumer durables, product purchases where advanced planning is required, and new products. The value of a buyer-intention survey increases to the extent that the cost of reaching buyers is small, the buyers are few, they have clear intentions, they implement their intentions, and they willingly disclose their intentions.

COMPOSITE OF SALES FORCE OPINIONS   Where buyer interviewing is impractical, the company may ask its sales representatives to estimate their future sales. Each sales representative estimates how much each current and prospective customer will buy of each of the company's products.

Few companies use their sales force's estimates without making some adjustments. Sales representatives might be pessimistic or optimistic, or they might go from one extreme to another because of a recent setback or success. Furthermore, they are often unaware of larger economic developments and do not know how their company's marketing plans will influence future sales in their territory. They might deliberately underestimate demand so that the company will set a low sales quota, or they might lack the time to prepare careful estimates or might not consider the effort worthwhile.

To encourage better estimating, the company could supply certain aids or incentives. For example, sales reps might receive a record of their past forecasts compared with their actual sales and also a description of company assumptions on the business outlook, competitor behavior, and marketing plans.

Involving the sales force in forecasting brings a number of benefits. Sales reps might have better insight into developing trends than any other single group. After participating in the forecasting process, sales reps might have greater confidence in their sales quotas and more incentive to achieve them.[41] Also, a "grassroots" forecasting procedure provides very detailed estimates broken down by product, territory, customer, and sales rep.

EXPERT OPINION   Companies can also obtain forecasts from experts, including dealers, distributors, suppliers, marketing consultants, and trade associations. Large appliance companies periodically survey dealers for their forecasts of short-term demand, as do car companies. Dealer estimates are subject to the same strengths and weaknesses as sales force estimates. Many companies buy economic and industry forecasts from well-known economic-forecasting firms. These specialists are able to prepare better economic forecasts than the company because they have more data available and more forecasting expertise.

Occasionally, companies will invite a group of experts to prepare a forecast. The experts exchange views and produce a group estimate (*group-discussion method*); or the experts supply their estimates individually, and an analyst combines them into a single estimate (*pooling of individual estimates*). Alternatively, the experts supply individual estimates and assumptions that are reviewed by the company, then revised. Further rounds of estimating and refining follow (Delphi method).[42]

PAST-SALES ANALYSIS Sales forecasts can be developed on the basis of past sales. *Time-series analysis* consists of breaking down past time series into four components (trend, cycle, seasonal, and erratic) and projecting these components into the future. *Exponential smoothing* consists of projecting the next period's sales by combining an average of past sales and the most recent sales, giving more weight to the latter. *Statistical demand analysis* consists of measuring the impact level of each of a set of causal factors (e.g., income, marketing expenditures, price) on the sales level. Finally, *econometric analysis* consists of building sets of equations that describe a system, and proceeding to fit the parameters statistically.

MARKET-TEST METHOD When buyers do not plan their purchases carefully or experts are not available or reliable, a direct-market test is desirable. A direct-market test is especially desirable in forecasting new-product sales or established product sales in a new distribution channel or territory. (We discuss market testing in detail in Chapter 12.)

summary

1. Three developments make the need for marketing information greater now than at any time in the past: the rise of global marketing, the new emphasis on buyers' wants, and the trend toward nonprice competition.

2. To carry out their analysis, planning, implementation, and control responsibilities, marketing managers need a marketing information system (MIS). The role of the MIS is to assess the managers' information needs, develop the needed information, and distribute that information in a timely manner.

3. An MIS has four components: (a) an internal records system, which includes information on the order-to-payment cycle and sales reporting systems; (b) a marketing intelligence system, a set of procedures and sources used by managers to obtain everyday information about pertinent developments in the marketing environment; (c) a marketing research system that allows for the systematic design, collection, analysis, and reporting of data and findings relevant to a specific marketing situation; and (d) a computerized marketing decision support system that helps managers interpret relevant information and turn it into a basis for marketing action.

4. Companies can conduct their own marketing research or hire other companies to do it for them. Good marketing research is characterized by the scientific method, creativity, multiple research methods, accurate model building, cost-benefit analysis, healthy skepticism, and an ethical focus.

5. The process consists of defining the problem and research objective, developing the research plan, collecting the information, analyzing the information, and presenting the findings to management. In conducting research, firms must decide whether to collect their own data or use data that already exist. They must also decide which research approach (observational, focus-group, survey, behavioral data, or experimental) and which research instrument (questionnaire or mechanical instruments) to use. In addition, they must decide on a sampling plan and contact methods.

6. One major reason for undertaking marketing research is to discover market opportunities. Once the research is complete, the company must carefully evaluate its opportunities and decide which markets to enter. Once in the market, it must prepare sales forecasts based on estimates of demand.

7. There are two types of demand: market demand and company demand. To estimate current demand, companies attempt to determine total market potential, area market potential, industry sales, and market share. To estimate future demand, companies survey buyers' intentions, solicit their sales force's input, gather expert opinions, or engage in market testing. Mathematical models, advanced statistical techniques, and computerized data collection procedures are essential to all types of demand and sales forecasting.

applications

marketing debate – what is the best type of marketing research?

Many market researchers have their favorite research approaches or techniques, although different researchers often have different preferences. For example, some researchers maintain that the only way to really learn about consumers or brands is through in-depth, qualitative research. Others contend that the only legitimate and defensible form of marketing research involves quantitative measures.

Take a position: Marketing research shapes consumer needs and wants versus Marketing research merely reflects the needs and wants of consumers.

marketing and advertising

1. American Beef Producers sponsored the print ad in Figure 1 promoting the nutritional benefits of beef. The ad addresses misconceptions that U.S. consumers have about beef's nutritional value, as revealed in survey research conducted for the National Cattleman's Beef Promotion and Research Board.

   a. When measuring market demand for beef, what space and product levels would the National Cattleman's Beef Promotion and Research Board be most interested in?

   b. Is this ad seeking to increase primary or selective demand for beef? Why?

   c. If the beef producers group needed a relatively accurate measure of market response to this ad, would you recommend that it use a probability or a nonprobability sample?

2. As advertised in Figure 2, Mutual of America wants to help companies of all sizes and types handle their retirement and insurance needs. According to the copy, all business customers "receive the same quality service and care" and "the same freedom of choice" regardless of size.

   a. Which research approaches would be most helpful in identifying any problems that customers might have experienced in working with Mutual of America consultants?

   b. If company marketers decide to collect primary data, would you recommend they use closed-end or open-end questions? Why?

   c. Draft a brief questionnaire that Mutual of America could use to identify additional needs that the company might try to satisfy with new financial services products or services.

Source: Kristin Harmel, "Who Eats Beef? Consumption Depends on Age, Education, UF Study Shows," *ScienceDaily,* September 28, 2000, *www.sciencedaily.com/releases/2000/000914104820.htm*

Figure 1

Figure 2

online marketing today

Research conducted by Purdue University shows that up to 75 percent of consumers fail to complete their online purchases, primarily because of sluggish Web sites, poor site design, and related factors. Seeking to learn what online visitors do and do not do at its Web site, Northwest Airlines has added a new software tool to its online operations. "The success of our online business comes down to our customers and how satisfied they are with our products and services," says Northwest's manager of e-commerce. This new tool, he says, "makes it very easy to determine where we should focus our efforts," by analyzing the online behavior of visitors, finding out which affiliates send the most visitors to the site, and tracking response to online promotions. With this information, the airline will be able to make the site function more efficiently and more effectively to increase sales and customer satisfaction.[43]

Browse Northwest's home page *www.nwa.com* and then follow the link to the "Talk to us" page. Sample several of the links on this page to see how customers can submit questions and feedback. Would such data be included as part of Northwest's marketing information system, marketing intelligence system, or marketing research system? Where would the airline store the primary data about online visitor behavior that its new software tool is collecting? What kind of research approach does this primary data represent? How else might Northwest use its Web site to gather primary data?

you're the marketer: sonic pda marketing plan

Marketing Plan Pro

Marketing information systems, marketing intelligence systems, and marketing research systems are used to gather and analyze data for various parts of the marketing plan. These systems can help marketers examine changes and trends in markets, competition, consumer needs, product usage, and distribution channels, among other areas. They can also turn up evidence of important opportunities and threats that must be addressed.

You are continuing as Jane Melody's assistant at Sonic. She has collected a considerable amount of marketing intelligence about the market and the competitive situation, but you believe Sonic needs more data in preparation for launching the first product. Based on the marketing plan contents discussed in Chapter 4, answer the following questions about how you can use MIS and marketing research to support the development and implementation of Sonic's marketing plan for its new PDA:

- For which sections will you need secondary data? Primary data? Both? Why do you need the information for each section?
- Where can you find suitable secondary data? Identify two non-Internet sources and two Internet sources; describe what you plan to draw from each source, and indicate how you will use the data in your marketing planning.
- What surveys, focus groups, observation, behavioral data, or experiments will Sonic need to support its marketing strategy, including product management, pricing, distribution, and marketing communication? Be specific about the questions or issues that Sonic should seek to resolve using market research data.

Enter your answers about Sonic's use of marketing data and research in the appropriate sections of a written marketing plan or in the Marketing Research, Market Analysis, and Market Trends sections of the *Marketing Plan Pro* software.

notes

1. James C. Anderson and James A. Narus, *Business Market Management: Understanding, Creating and Delivering Value* (Upper Saddle River, NJ: Prentice Hall, 1998), ch. 2.

2. John Koten, "You Aren't Paranoid if You Feel Someone Eyes You Constantly," *Wall Street Journal*, March 29, 1985, pp. 1, 22; "Offbeat Marketing," *Sales & Marketing Management* (January 1990): 35; and Erik Larson, "Attention Shoppers: Don' Look Now but You Are Being Tailed," *Smithsonian Magazine*, January 1993, pp. 70–79.

3. From Consumer Europe 1993, a publication of Euromonitor, pnc. London: Tel 14471 251 8021; U.S. offices: (312) 541-8024.

4. "The dot.com within Ford," *U.S. News & World Report*, February 7, 2000, p. 34.

5. John W. Verity, "Taking a Laptop on a Call," *BusinessWeek*, October 25, 1993, pp. 124–25.

6. Stannie Holt, "Sales-Force Automation Ramps Up," *InfoWorld*, March 23, 1998, pp. 29, 38.

7. James A. Narus and James C. Anderson, "Turn Your Industrial Distributors into Partners," *Harvard Business Review* (March–April 1986): 66–71.

8. Kevin Helliker, "Smile: That Cranky Shopper May Be a Store Spy," *Wall Street Journal*, November 30, 1994, pp. B1, B6. Edward F. McQuarrie, *Customer Visits: Building a Better Market Focus*, 2nd ed. (Newbury Park, CA: Sage Press, 1998).

9. Don Peppers, "How You Can Help Them," *Fast Company* (October–November 1997): 128–36.

10. *1994 Survey of Market Research*, eds. Thomas Kinnear and Ann Root (Chicago: American Marketing Association, 1994).

11. Kevin J. Clancy and Robert S. Shulman, *Marketing Myths That Are Killing Business*, (New York: McGraw-Hill, 1994), p. 58; Phaedra Hise, "Comprehensive CompuServe," *Inc.* (June 1994): 109; "Business Bulletin: Studying the Competition," *Wall Street Journal*, p. A1-5.

12. For some background information on in-flight Internet service, see "In-Flight Dogfight," *Business2.Com*, January 9, 2001, pp. 84–91.

13. For a discussion of the decision-theory approach to the value of research, see Donald R. Lehmann, Sunil Gupta, and Joel Steckel, *Market Research* (Reading, MA: Addison-Wesley, 1997).

14. For an excellent annotated reference to major secondary sources of business and marketing data, see Gilbert A. Churchill Jr., *Marketing Research: Methodological Foundations*, 7th ed. (Fort Worth, TX: Dryden, 1998).

15. Thomas L. Greenbaum, *The Handbook for Focus Group Research* (New York: Lexington Books, 1993).

16. Sarah Schafer, "Communications: Getting a Line on Customers," *Inc. Tech* (1996), p. 102; see also Alexia Parks, "On-Line Focus Groups Reshape Market Research Industry," *Marketing News*, May 12, 1997, p. 28.

17. Kevin Lane Keller, *Strategic Brand Management* (Upper Saddle River, NJ: Prentice Hall, 1998), pp. 317–18; Daniel H. Pink, "Metaphor Marketing," *Fast Company* (April 1998): 214.

18. Roger D. Blackwell, James S. Hensel, Michael B. Phillips, and Brian Sternthal, *Laboratory Equipment for Marketing Research* (Dubuque, IA: Kendall/Hunt, 1970); Wally Wood, "The Race to Replace Memory," *Marketing and Media Decisions* (July

1986): 166–67. See also Gerald Zaltman, "Rethinking Market Research: Putting People Back In," *Journal of Marketing Research* 34, no. 4 (November 1997): 424–37.

9. David Goetzl, "O&M Turns Reality TV into Research Tool," *Advertising Age*, July 10, 2000; Brian Wansink, "New Techniques to Generate Key Marketing Insights," *American Marketing Association: Marketing Research* (Summer 2000).

0. Brian Wansink, "Developing Useful and Accurate Customer Profiles," in *Values, Lifestyles, and Psychographics*, edited by Lynn R. Kahle and Larry Chiagouris (Mahwah, NJ: Lawrence Erlbaum Associates, 1997).

1. <*www.knowledgenetworks.com*>; Peter Sinton, "Polling Using the Internet Seeks to Improve Accuracy," *San Francisco Chronicle*, October 28, 2000.

2. G. K. Sharman, "Sessions Challenge Status Quo," *Marketing News*, November 10, 1997, p. 18; "Prepaid Phone Cards Are Revolutionizing Market Research Techniques," *Direct Marketing* (March 1998): 12.

3. For further reading, see Joanne Lipman, "Single-Source Ad Research Heralds Detailed Look at Household Habits," *Wall Street Journal*, February 16, 1988, p. 39; Joe Schwartz, "Back to the Source," *American Demographics* (January 1989): 22–26; Magid H. Abraham and Leonard M. Lodish, "Getting the Most Out of Advertising and Promotions," *Harvard Business Review*, (May–June 1990): 50–60.

4. Kevin J. Clancy and Peter C. Krieg, *Counterintuitive Marketing: How Great Results Come from Uncommon Sense* (New York: The Free Press, 2000).

5. John D. C. Little, "Decision Support Systems for Marketing Managers," *Journal of Marketing* (Summer 1979): 11. See "Special Issue on Managerial Decision Making," *Marketing Science*, 18(3), 1999 for some contemporary perspectives.

6. Gary L. Lilien and Arvind Rangaswamy, *Marketing Engineering: Computer-Assisted Marketing Analysis and Planning* (Reading, MA: Addison-Wesley, 1998). Also see their *Marketing Management and Strategy: Marketing Engineering Applications* (Reading, MA: Addison-Wesley, 1999).

7. John D. C. Little, "BRANDAID: A Marketing Mix Model, Part I: Structure; Part II: Implementation," *Operations Research* 23 (1975): 628–73.

8. Leonard M. Lodish, "CALLPLAN: An Interactive Salesman's Call Planning System," *Management Science* (December 1971): 25–40.

9. David B. Montgomery, Alvin J. Silk, and C. E. Zaragoza, "A Multiple-Product Sales-Force Allocation Model," *Management Science* (December 1971): 3–24.

30. S. W. Hess and S. A. Samuels, "Experiences with a Sales Districting Model: Criteria and Implementation," *Management Science* (December 1971): 41–54.

31. John D. C. Little and Leonard M. Lodish, "A Media Planning Calculus," *Operations Research* (January–February 1969): 1–35.

32. Magid M. Abraham and Leonard M. Lodish, "PROMOTER: An Automated Promotion Evaluation System," *Marketing Science* (Spring 1987): 101–23.

33. Raymond R. Burke, Arvind Rangaswamy, Jerry Wind, and Jehoshua Eliashberg, "A Knowledge-Based System for Advertising Design," *Marketing Science* 9, no. 3 (1990): 212–29.

34. John D. C. Little, "Cover Story: An Expert System to Find the News in Scanner Data," Sloan School, MIT Working Paper, 1988.

35. *Sources*: "Hitting the Bulls-Eye: Target Sets Its Sights on East Coast Expansion," *Newsweek*, October 11, 1999; Janet Moore and Ann Merrill, "Target Market," *Minneapolis-St. Paul Star Tribune*, July 27, 2001; Clarke Canfield, "Anticipation Builds as Fast-Growing Target Enters Another State," AP Newswire, August 6, 2001.

36. For a good discussion and illustration, see Roger J. Best, *Market-Based Management*, 2nd ed. (Upper Saddle River, NJ: Prentice Hall, 2000), pp. 71–75.

37. "Will the Have-Nots Always Be With Us?" *Fortune*, December 20, 1999, pp. 288–89.

38. For further discussion, see Gary L. Lilien, Philip Kotler, and K. Sridhar Moorthy, *Marketing Models* (Upper Saddle River, NJ: Prentice Hall, 1992).

39. For suggested strategies related to the market area's BDI standing, see Don E. Schultz, Dennis Martin, and William P. Brown, *Strategic Advertising Campaigns* (Chicago: Crain Books, 1984), p. 338.

40. <*www.acupoll.com*>

41. Jacob Gonik, "Tie Salesmen's Bonuses to Their Forecasts," *Harvard Business Review* (May–June 1978): 116–23.

42. Norman Dalkey and Olaf Helmer, "An Experimental Application of the Delphi Method to the Use of Experts," *Management Science* (April 1963): 458–67. Also see Roger J. Best, "An Experiment in Delphi Estimation in Marketing Decision Making," *Journal of Marketing Research* (November 1974): 447–52. For an excellent overview of market forecasting, see Scott Armstrong, ed., *Principles of Forecasting: A Handbook for Researchers and Practitioners* (Norwell, MA: Kluwer Academic Publishers, 2001).

43. Erika Morphy, "Airlines Adopt Intelligence Tool For Online Customer Service," *CRM Daily.com*, August 24, 2001; <*http://www.crmdaily.com/perl/story/13070.html*>; "What Do Consumers Want?" *USA Today Magazine*, May 2001, p. 8.

7

analyzing consumer markets and buyer behavior

In this chapter, we will address the following questions:

- How do the buyer's characteristics—cultural, social, personal, and psychological—influence buying behavior?
- How does the buyer make purchasing decisions?

Kotler On Marketing

The most important thing is to forecast where customers are moving, and to be in front of them.

The aim of marketing is to meet and satisfy target customers' needs and wants. The field of **consumer behavior** studies how individuals, groups, and organizations select, buy, use, and dispose of goods, services, ideas, or experiences to satisfy their needs and desires.

Understanding consumer behavior and "knowing customers" is never simple. Customers may say one thing but do another. They may not be in touch with their deeper motivations. They may respond to influences that change their minds at the last minute. Small companies, such as a corner grocery store, and huge corporations, such as Whirlpool, stand to profit from understanding how and why their customers buy.

Whirlpool Corporation   In the appliance industry, consumer brand loyalties are built up over decades and passed from generation to generation. To shake up entrenched market shares and tap into consumers' often unexpressed needs, appliance giant Whirlpool Corporation hired an anthropologist. The anthropologist went to people's homes, observed how they used their appliances, and talked with all the household members. Whirlpool found that in busy families, women are not the only ones doing the laundry. Armed with this knowledge, company engineers came up with color-coded washer and dryer controls to make it easier for kids and men to pitch in.[1]

Net-Temps   Net-Temps, an online recruiting service for the staffing industry headquartered in Chelmsford, Massachusetts, installed monitoring and tracking tools on its Website to better understand the behavior of its customers. The tools measure the frequency of visits to the Net-Temps site, determine repeat visits, and track advertising. Monitoring software helps the company figure out which temp jobs are in the greatest demand. Net-Temps was recently named the number-one job board for contract professionals in the 2000 Electronic Recruiting Index.[2]

Not understanding your customers' motivations, needs, and preferences can hurt. Consider what happened when Wal-Mart opened its stores in Latin America. Sales have been disappointing, and the question has been raised as to whether Wal-Mart's magic can work in Latin America.

Wal-Mart designed its Latin American stores like those in the United States: narrow aisles crowded with merchandise, huge parking lots, many products with red, white, and blue banners, and so on. However, Latin American shoppers expect wider aisles since they come with larger families; many do not have a car and need door-to-door bus transportation, and the red/white/blue banners seem like Yankee imperialism. Even the Sam's Clubs flopped because the company's huge multipack items were too large for shoppers with small apartments and small disposable incomes. Wal-Mart forgot to study the customer.[3]

Studying customers provides clues for developing new products, product features, prices, channels, messages, and other marketing-mix elements. This chapter explores individual consumers' buying dynamics; the next chapter explores the buying dynamics of business buyers.

influencing buyer behavior

The starting point for understanding buyer behavior is the stimulus-response model shown in Figure 7.1. Marketing and environmental stimuli enter the buyer's consciousness. The buyer's characteristics and decision processes lead to certain purchase decisions. The marketer's task is to understand what happens in the buyer's consciousness between the arrival of outside stimuli and the purchase decisions.

A consumer's buying behavior is influenced by cultural, social, personal, and psychological factors. Cultural factors exert the broadest and deepest influence.

cultural factors

Culture, subculture, and social class are particularly important in buying behavior. **Culture** is the fundamental determinant of a person's wants and behavior. The growing child acquires a set of values, perceptions, preferences, and behaviors through his or her family and other key institutions. A child growing up in the United States is exposed to the following values: achievement and success, activity, efficiency and practicality, progress, material comfort, individualism, freedom, external comfort, humanitarianism, and youthfulness.[4]

Each culture consists of smaller **subcultures** that provide more specific identification and socialization for their members. Subcultures include nationalities, religions, racial groups, and geographic regions. When subcultures grow large and affluent

Model of Buyer Behavior

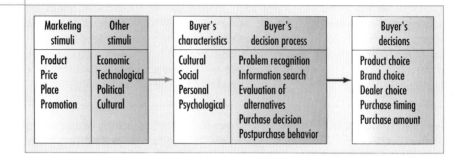

Marketing stimuli	Other stimuli	Buyer's characteristics	Buyer's decision process	Buyer's decisions
Product	Economic	Cultural	Problem recognition	Product choice
Price	Technological	Social	Information search	Brand choice
Place	Political	Personal	Evaluation of	Dealer choice
Promotion	Cultural	Psychological	alternatives	Purchase timing
			Purchase decision	Purchase amount
			Postpurchase behavior	

enough, companies often design specialized marketing programs to serve them. Such programs are known as **diversity marketing**, a practice which was pioneered during the 1980s by large companies like AT&T, Sears Roebuck, and Coca-Cola. Diversity marketing grew out of careful marketing research, which revealed that different ethnic and demographic niches did not always respond favorably to mass-market advertising. (See "Marketing Insight: Marketing to Latinos, African Americans, and Seniors.")

Virtually all human societies exhibit social stratification. Stratification sometimes takes the form of a caste system where the members of different castes are reared for certain roles and cannot change their caste membership. More frequently, it takes the form of **social classes**, relatively homogeneous and enduring divisions in a society, which are hierarchically ordered and whose members share similar values, interests, and behavior.

Social classes reflect not only income, but other indicators such as occupation, education, and area of residence. Social classes differ in dress, speech patterns, recreational preferences, and many other characteristics. Table 7.1 describes the seven U.S. social classes identified by social scientists.

Social classes have several characteristics. First, those within each class tend to behave more alike than persons from two different social classes. Second, persons are perceived as occupying inferior or superior positions according to social class. Third, social class is indicated by a cluster of variables—for example, occupation, income, wealth, education, and value orientation—rather than by any single variable. Fourth, individuals can move up or down the social-class ladder during their lifetimes. The extent of this mobility varies according to how rigid the social stratification is in a given society.

Social classes show distinct product and brand preferences in many areas, including clothing, home furnishings, leisure activities, and automobiles. Social classes differ in media preferences, with upper-class consumers preferring magazines and books and lower-class consumers preferring television. Even within a media category such as TV, upper-class consumers prefer news and drama, and lower-class consumers prefer soap operas and sports programs. There are also language differences among the social classes. Advertising copy and dialogue must ring true to the targeted social class.

social factors

In addition to cultural factors, a consumer's behavior is influenced by such social factors as reference groups, family, and social roles and statuses.

REFERENCE GROUPS   A person's **reference groups** consist of all the groups that have a direct (face-to-face) or indirect influence on the person's attitudes or behavior. Groups having a direct influence on a person are called **membership groups**. Some membership groups are **primary groups**, such as family, friends, neighbors, and co-workers, with whom the person interacts fairly continuously and informally. People also belong

marketing **insight**

Marketing to Latinos, African Americans, and Seniors

Latinos

Expected to account for a quarter of the U.S. population by 2050, Latinos (also called Hispanic Americans) are the fastest growing minority, and soon will be the largest minority in the country. Annual Latino purchasing power is $630 billion on everything from cars to computers. The top five markets for Latinos in the United States are located in Los Angeles, New York City, Miami, Chicago, and San Francisco.

The Latino segment is difficult for marketers. Roughly two dozen nationalities can be classified as "Latino," including Cuban, Mexican, Puerto Rican, Dominican, and other Central and South American groups. The Latino group contains a mix of cultures, physical types, racial backgrounds, and aspirations. Yet despite their differences, Latinos often share strong family values, a need for respect, product loyalty, and a strong interest in product quality. Of course, the main common denominator is language: Marketers that reach out to Latinos with targeted Spanish-language promotions or ads stand to reap big benefits. The best medium for reaching Latinos is Spanish-language TV. Hispanics tend to watch more TV than the average American, and they prefer viewing in their native language.

African Americans

The purchasing power of the country's 34 million African Americans exploded during the prosperous 1990s. African American purchasing power was over $500 billion in 2000. What did African Americans spend their money on? Boys' clothing, athletic footwear, personal care services, and auto rentals. They tend to be strongly motivated by quality and selection, and shop more at neighborhood stores.

Many companies have been successful at tailoring products to meet the needs of African Americans. In 1987, Hallmark Cards, Inc. launched its Afrocentric brand, Mahogany, with only 16 cards; it offers 800 cards today. Other companies offer more inclusive product lines within the same brand. Sara Lee Corporation's L'eggs discontinued its separate line of pantyhose for black women and now offers shades and styles popular among black women as half of the company's general-focus sub-brands. Unfortunately, many marketers think that targeting African Americans simply means serving up images of black superstars and idols such as Michael Jordan, Shacquille O'Neal, and actress Halle Berry. African American media and marketing specialists advise marketers to partner with black-owned media and the black community, and to hire more African Americans.

The 50-Plus Market

The magnitude—and wealth—of the mature market should be important to marketers if they want to profit in the new century. The population of mature consumers, those 50 and older, will swell to 115 million in the next 25 years. With a baby boomer turning 50 every 7 seconds, the size of this group will be even bigger by the time you finish reading this paragraph. The 50-plus market represents a whopping $2 trillion in buying power, and this figure is expected to increase by 29 percent in the next few years.

Not only have youth-obsessed marketers traditionally neglected this huge market, but they have also turned them off with stereotypes of grandmas and grandpas living on fixed incomes. Seniors, particularly boomers-turned-seniors, make buying decisions based on lifestyle, not age, and it is an active lifestyle at that. Pfizer ads feature seniors who now live their lives to the fullest, thanks to Pfizer medications. In one ad, a woman is shown traveling the world; in another, a senior former swimming champion tells how he was able to compete again. A Nike commercial features a senior weight lifter who proudly proclaims, "I'm not strong for my age. I'm strong!"

Yet despite their claims to youth, seniors do have less visual acuity and manual dexterity, and marketers must take this into account when packaging products. Pet packaging peeves for seniors include tiny, condensed type on pharmaceutical labels, heat-sealed inner cereal bags or snack food bags that are difficult to pry open, and shrink wrap that is impossible to remove.

Sources: (Latinos) Leon E. Wynter, "Business & Race: Hispanic Buying Habits Become More Diverse," *Wall Street Journal*, January 8, 1997, p. B1; Lisa A. Yorgey, "Hispanic Americans," *Target Marketing* (February 1998): 67; Carole Radice, "Hispanic Consumers: Understanding a Changing Market," *Progressive Grocer* (February 1997): 109–14. See also Brad Edmondson, "Hispanic Americans in 2001," *American Demographics* (January 1997): 16–17, and "Targeting the Hispanic Market," *Advertising Age*, special section, March 31, 1997, pp. A1–A12. (African-Americans) Valerie Lynn Gray, "Going After Our Dollars," *Black Enterprise* (July 1997): 68–78; David Kiley, "Black Surfing," *Brandweek*, November 17, 1997, p. 36; "L'eggs Joins New Approach in Marketing to African-American Women," *Supermarket Business* (June 1998): 81; Beth Belton, "Black Buying Power Soaring," *USA Today*, July 30, 1998, p. 1B; Dana Canedy, "The Courtship of Black Consumers," *New York Times*, August 11, 1998, p. D1. (50-Plus) Rick Adler, "Stereotypes Won't Work with Seniors Anymore," *Advertising Age*, November 11, 1996, p. 32; Richard Lee, "The Youth Bias in Advertising," *American Demographics* (January 1997): 47–50; Cheryl Russell, "The Ungraying of America," *American Demographics* (July 1997): 12–15; Sharon Fairley, George P. Moschis, Herbert M. Myers, and Arnold Thiesfeldt, "Senior Smarts: The Experts Sound Off," *Brandweek*, August 4, 1997, pp. 24–25; Candace Corlett, "Senior Theses," *Brandweek*, August 4, 1997, pp. 22–23.

table **7.1**		
Characteristics of Major U.S. Social Classes	1. *Upper Uppers* (less than 1%)	The social elite who live on inherited wealth. They give large sums to charity, run the debutante balls, maintain more than one home, and send their children to the finest schools. They are a market for jewelry, antiques, homes, and vacations. They often buy and dress conservatively. Although small as a group, they serve as a reference group to the extent that their consumption decisions are imitated by the other social classes.
	2. *Lower Uppers* (about 2%)	Persons, usually from the middle class, who have earned high income or wealth through exceptional ability in their professions or business. They tend to be active in social and civic affairs and to buy the symbols of status for themselves and their children. They include the nouveau riche, whose pattern of conspicuous consumption is designed to impress those below them.
	3. *Upper Middles* (12%)	These persons possess neither family status nor unusual wealth and are primarily concerned with "career." They are professionals, independent businesspersons, and corporate managers who believe in education and want their children to develop professional or administrative skills. Members of this class are civic-minded and home-oriented. They are the quality market for good homes, clothes, furniture, and appliances.
	4. *Middle Class* (32%)	Average-pay white- and blue-collar workers who live on "the right side of town." Often, they buy popular products to keep up with trends. Twenty-five percent own imported cars, and most are concerned with fashion. The middle class believes in spending more money on "worthwhile experiences" for their children and steering them toward a college education.
	5. *Working Class* (38%)	Average-pay blue-collar workers and those who lead a working-class lifestyle, whatever their income, school background, or job. The working class depends heavily on relatives for economic and emotional support, for tips on job opportunities, for advice, and for assistance. A working-class vacation means staying in town, and "going away" means to a lake or resort no more than two hours away. The working class tends to maintain sharp sex-role divisions and stereotyping.
	6. *Upper Lowers* (9%)	Upper lowers are working, although their living standard is just above poverty. They perform unskilled work and are very poorly paid. Often, upper lowers are educationally deficient.
	7. *Lower Lowers* (7%)	Lower lowers are on welfare, visibly poverty stricken, and usually out of work. Some are not interested in finding a permanent job, and most are dependent on public aid or charity for income.

Sources: Richard P. Coleman, "The Continuing Significance of Social Class to Marketing," *Journal of Consumer Research* (December 1983): 265–80; Richard P. Coleman and Lee P. Rainwater, *Social Standing in America: New Dimension of Class* (New York: Basic Books, 1978).

to **secondary groups**, such as religious, professional, and trade-union groups, which tend to be more formal and require less continuous interaction.

People are significantly influenced by their reference groups in at least three ways. Reference groups expose an individual to new behaviors and lifestyles, and influence attitudes and self-concept; they create pressures for conformity that may affect actual product and brand choices. People are also influenced by groups to which they do not belong. **Aspirational groups** are those a person hopes to join; **dissociative groups** are those whose values or behavior an individual rejects.

Marketers try to identify target customers' reference groups. However, level of reference-group influence varies among products and brands. Reference groups appear to strongly influence both product and brand choice only in the case of automobiles and color televisions; brand choice mainly in such items as furniture and clothing; and product choice mainly in such items as beer and cigarettes.

Manufacturers of products and brands where group influence is strong must determine how to reach and influence opinion leaders in these reference groups. An **opinion leader** is the person in informal, product-related communications who offers advice or information about a specific product or product category, such as which of several brands is best or how a particular product may be used.[5] Marketers try to reach opinion leaders by identifying demographic and psychographic characteristics associated with opinion leadership, identifying the media read by opinion leaders, and directing messages at opinion leaders. The hottest trends in teenage music, language, and fashion start in America's inner cities. Clothing companies like Levi Strauss, that hope to appeal to the fickle and fashion-conscious youth market, have made a concerted effort to monitor urban opinion leaders' style and behavior:

Levi Strauss & Company   Levi Strauss & Co. invented blue jeans 150 years ago. Today, it faces a growing field of competitors. Levi's® SILVERTAB® brand is designed and marketed to reach the 15- to 24-year-old male consumer who is influenced by urban styles. The SILVERTAB® marketing team and creative agency developed integrated marketing programs and brand imagery to appeal this consumer. In 2001 and 2002, this program included the use of hip hop and R & B celebrities Fredro Starr, the Black Eyed Peas, City

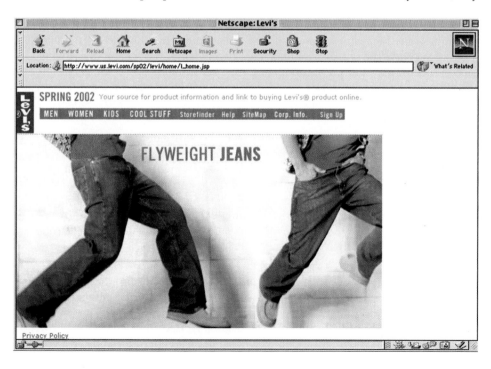

Levi-Strauss's Web site also targets the youth market.

High and Product G & B as models and performers. Additionally, SILVERTAB® used on-line movies, games, sweepstakes and other forms of outreach to drive awareness of the brand, and sales at key retailers. As a reality check, the SILVERTAB® marketing teams literally "check in" with their consumers in focus groups and closet studies. These initiatives have made SILVERTAB® the 5th largest jeanswear brand.[6]

Other clothing companies like Abercrombie and Fitch appeal to a different youth market.

Abercrombie and Fitch   To ensure that its stores reflect the lifestyle of the core customer base, Abercrombie fills its sales staff with college students who look the part. The company recruits 75 percent of its salespeople, or "brand representatives," from college campuses near each store location. The visual appeal of the sales staff is vital to creating the right in-store environment. "We're not interested in salespeople or clerks," said one Abercrombie & Fitch representative. "We're interested in finding people who represent the brand's lifestyle, which is the college lifestyle—leaders who have charisma, who portray the image of the brand."[7]

FAMILY   The family is the most important consumer-buying organization in society, and family members constitute the most influential primary reference group. The family has been researched extensively.[8] We can distinguish between two families in the buyer's life. The **family of orientation** consists of parents and siblings. From parents a person acquires an orientation toward religion, politics, and economics and a sense of personal ambition, self-worth, and love.[9] Even if the buyer no longer interacts very much with his or her parents, their influence on the buyer's behavior can be significant. In countries where parents live with grown children, their influence can be substantial. A more direct influence on everyday buying behavior is the **family of procreation**—namely, one's spouse and children.

Marketers are interested in the roles and relative influence of the husband, wife, and children in the purchase of a large variety of products and services. These roles vary widely in different countries and social classes. Vietnamese Americans, for example, are more likely to adhere to the traditional model in which the man makes the decisions for any large purchase. Similarly, successful ads for Korean Americans usually feature a man in his thirties or forties unless the ad is for a specifically female product, such as jewelry.[10]

In the United States, husband–wife involvement has traditionally varied widely by product category. The wife has traditionally acted as the family's main purchasing agent, especially for food, sundries, and staple-clothing items. In the case of expensive products and services like vacations or housing, husbands and wives have engaged in more joint decision making. Women are rapidly gaining purchasing power in the household. Business guru Tom Peters cites women as the number-one business marketing opportunity, and says:

> The market research is clear: Women make or greatly influence most purchasing decisions. Homes. . . . Medical care. Cars. Vacations. And hammers and nails in the huge DIY (do-it-yourself) industry: One (rare) female DIY-chain exec remarked to me about her male colleagues' amazement that 60% of their customers were women. . . . Women are where the real bucks are. Now close to 8 million women own enterprises in America, up from about 400,000 in 1970. They employ about 18.5 million of us . . . 40% more than old Forbes 500 industrials. About 22% of working wives outearn their hubbies, and women constitute about half the population of those with $500,000 or more in net worth.[11]

Given women's great strides in the workplace, especially in nontraditional jobs, traditional household purchasing patterns are gradually changing. Shifts in social values regarding the division of domestic labor have also weakened such standard conceptions as "women buy all the household goods." Recent research has shown that although traditional buying patterns still hold, baby boomer husbands and wives are more willing to shop jointly for products traditionally thought to be under the separate control of one spouse or the other.[12] Convenience-goods marketers are making a mistake if they think of women as the main or only purchasers of their products. Similarly, marketers of products traditionally purchased by men may need to start thinking of women as possible purchasers.

This is already happening in the car business.

Cadillac   Women now account for 50 percent of the luxury car market, and automakers are paying attention. Male car designers at Cadillac are going about their work with paper clips on their fingers to simulate what it feels like to operate buttons, knobs, and other interior features with longer fingernails. The Cadillac Catera features an air-conditioned glove box to preserve such items as lipstick and film. This greater attention to detail has led to a rise in the number of female Cadillac owners to 28 percent in 2000. For Cadillac's luxury SUV, the Escalade, the percentage of women buyers was 36 percent in 2000.[13]

Another shift in buying patterns is an increase in the amount of dollars spent and the influence wielded by children and teens.[14] The indirect influence on parental spending of kids age 2 to 14 accounted for $300 billion of household purchases in 1997. Indirect influence means that parents know the brands, product choices, and preferences of their children without hints or outright requests. Direct influence describes children's hints, requests, and demands—"I want to go to McDonald's." Direct influence peaked around $290 billion in 2000. Nontraditional marketers are now figuring out that the fastest route to Mom's and Dad's wallets may be through Junior.

Mattel   In 2000, Mattel targeted mothers, instead of young girls, with a print advertising campaign that emphasized Barbie merchandise in new-product categories. The ads were intended to raise awareness among mothers for such Barbie products as apparel and nail polish. "In the case of apparel in particular, mothers are the ones buying the clothes," says Mattel girl's division president Adrienne Fontanella. "When a mother is alone and has to decide between the GAP and Barbie, she's more familiar with the GAP."[15]

General Motors   In the May 1997 issue of *Sports Illustrated for Kids*, a magazine targeted to 8- to 14-year-old boys, the inside cover featured a brightly colored, two-page spread advertising the Chevy Venture minivan. This was GM's first attempt to woo what it calls "backseat consumers." The Venture's brand manager sent the minivan into malls and showed previews of Disney's *Hercules* on a VCR inside it. These days, kids often play a tie-breaking role in deciding what car to buy.[16]

Today companies are more likely to use the Internet to show off their products to children and solicit marketing information from them. Millions of kids under the age of 17 are online. Marketers have jumped online with them, offering freebies in exchange for personal information. Many have come under fire for this practice and for not clearly differentiating ads from games or entertainment. The Direct Marketing Association has taken a strong stand on marketing to children on the Internet. For its guidelines, see "Marketing Memo: What Every Marketer Needs to Know: Internet Ethics for Targeting Kids."

ROLES AND STATUSES   A person participates in many groups—family, clubs, organizations. The person's position in each group can be defined in terms of role and status. A **role** consists of the activities a person is expected to perform. Each role carries a **status**. A Supreme Court justice has more status than a sales manager, and a sales manager has

Marketing
MEMO

What Every Marketer Needs to Know: Internet Ethics for Targeting Kids

The Children's Online Privacy Protection Act, which took effect in April 2000, requires certain Web sites to obtain parental consent before collecting, using, or disclosing personal information from children under 13. In addition to adhering to this act, online marketers should follow the guidelines for ethical marketing to children suggested by the Direct Marketing Association:

1. Promote an online privacy statement.
2. Offer opt-out/opt-in options in which users have a choice of whether to stop or accept unwanted e-mail solicitation.
3. Utilize technology options such as Web site filtering programs like SurfWatch.
4. Take into account the target market's age, knowledge, sophistication, and maturity when making decisions whether to collect data from or communicate with children online.
5. Be sensitive to parents' concerns about the collection of children's data, and support the ability of parents to limit the collection of this data.
6. Limit the use of data collected from children in the course of their online activities to the promotion, sale, or delivery of goods or services; the performance of market research; and other appropriate marketing activities.
7. Explain that the information is being requested for marketing purposes. Implement strict security measures to ensure against unauthorized access, alteration, or dissemination of the data collected from children online.

Source: Adapted from Rob Yoegel, "Reaching Youth on the Web," *Target Marketing* (November 1997): 38–41; "New Rule Will Protect Privacy of Children Online," Press release, www.ftc.gov, October 20, 1999.

more status than an office clerk. People choose products that communicate their role and status in society. Company presidents often drive Mercedes, wear expensive suits, and drink Chivas Regal scotch. Marketers must be aware of the status-symbol potential of products and brands.

personal factors

A buyer's decisions are also influenced by personal characteristics. These include the buyer's age and stage in the life cycle, occupation, economic circumstances, lifestyle, and personality and self-concept.

AGE AND STAGE IN THE LIFE CYCLE   People buy different goods and services over a lifetime. They eat baby food in the early years, most foods in the growing and mature years, and special diets in the later years. Taste in clothes, furniture, and recreation is also age related.

Consumption is shaped by the **family life cycle**. Nine stages of the family life cycle are listed in Table 7.2, along with the financial situation and typical product interests of each group. Marketers often choose life-cycle groups as their target markets. Yet target households are not always family based: There are also single households, gay households, and cohabitor households. In addition, some recent research has identified *psychological* life-cycle stages. Adults experience certain "passages" or "transformations" as they go through life.[17] Marketers pay close attention to changing life circumstances—divorce, widowhood, remarriage—and their effect on consumption.

OCCUPATION AND ECONOMIC CIRCUMSTANCES   Occupation also influences consumption patterns. A blue-collar worker will buy work clothes, work shoes, and lunchboxes. A company president will buy expensive suits, air travel, and country club membership. Marketers try to identify the occupational groups that have above-average interest in their products and services. A company can even tailor its products for certain occupational groups: Computer software companies, for example, design different products for brand managers, engineers, lawyers, and physicians.

Product choice is greatly affected by economic circumstances: spendable income (level, stability, and time pattern), savings and assets (including the percentage that is

table **7.2**

Stages in Family Life
Cycle

1. *Bachelor stage:*	Young, single, not living at home. Few financial burdens. Fashion opinion leaders. Recreation oriented. Buy: basic home equipment, furniture, cars, equipment for the mating game, vacations.
2. *Newly married couples:*	Young, no children. Highest purchase rate and highest average purchase of durables: cars, appliances, furniture, vacations.
3. *Full nest I:*	Youngest child under six. Home purchasing at peak. Liquid assets low. Interested in new products, advertised products. Buy: washers, dryers, TV, baby food, chest rubs and cough medicines, vitamins, dolls, wagons, sleds, skates.
4. *Full nest II:*	Youngest child six or over. Financial position better. Less influenced by advertising. Buy larger-size packages, multiple-unit deals. Buy: many foods, cleaning materials, bicycles, music lessons, pianos.
5. *Full nest III:*	Older married couples with dependent children. Financial position still better. Some children get jobs. Hard to influence with advertising. High average purchase of durables: new, more tasteful furniture, auto travel, unnecessary appliances, boats, dental services, magazines.
6. *Empty nest I:*	Older married couples, no children living with them, head of household in labor force. Home ownership at peak. Most satisfied with financial position and money saved. Interested in travel, recreation, self-education. Make gifts and contributions. Not interested in new products. Buy: vacations, luxuries, home improvements.
7. *Empty nest II:*	Older married. No children living at home, head of household retired. Drastic cut in income. Keep home. Buy: medical appliances, medical-care products.
8. *Solitary survivor:*	In labor force. Income still good but likely to sell home.
9. *Solitary survivor:*	Retired. Same medical and product needs as other retired group; drastic cut in income. Special need for attention, affection, and security.

Sources: William D. Wells and George Gubar, "Life-Cycle Concepts in Marketing Research," *Journal of Marketing Research* (November 1966): 362. Also see Patrick E. Murphy and William A. Staples, "A Modernized Family Life Cycle," *Journal of Consumer Research* (June 1979): 12–22; Frederick W. Derrick and Alane E. Linfield, "The Family Life Cycle: An Alternative Approach," *Journal of Consumer Research* (September 1980): 214–17.

liquid), debts, borrowing power, and attitudes toward spending and saving. Marketers of income-sensitive goods continuously monitor trends in personal income, savings, and interest rates. If economic indicators point to a recession, marketers can take steps to redesign, reposition, and reprice their products so they continue to offer value to target customers.

LIFESTYLE   People from the same subculture, social class, and occupation may lead quite different lifestyles. A **lifestyle** is a person's pattern of living in the world as expressed in activities, interests, and opinions. Lifestyle portrays the "whole person" interacting with his or her environment. Marketers search for relationships between their products and lifestyle groups. For example, a computer manufacturer might find that most computer buyers are achievement-oriented. The marketer may then aim the brand more clearly at the achiever lifestyle.

Psychographics is the science of using psychology and demographics to better understand consumers. One of the most popular commercially available classification systems based on psychographic measurements is SRI Consulting Business Intelligence's (SRIC-BI) VALS™ framework. VALS classifies all U.S. adults into eight primary groups based on psychological attributes and key demographics. The segmentation system is based on responses to a questionnaire featuring 4 demographic and 35 attitudinal questions. The VALS system is continually updated with new data from more then 80,000 surveys per year.[18] (see Figure 7.2).

The major tendencies of the four groups with high resources are:

1. *Actualizers:* Successful, sophisticated, active, "take-charge" people. Purchases often reflect cultivated tastes for relatively upscale, niche-oriented products.
2. *Fulfilleds:* Mature, satisfied, comfortable, reflective. Favor durability, functionality, and value in products.
3. *Achievers:* Successful, career- and work-oriented. Favor established, prestige products that demonstrate success to their peers.
4. *Experiencers:* Young, vital, enthusiastic, impulsive, and rebellious. Spend a comparatively high proportion of income on clothing, fast food, music, movies, and video.

figure **7.2**	
The VALS Segmentation System: An 8-Part Typology	

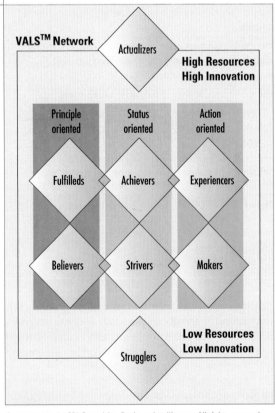

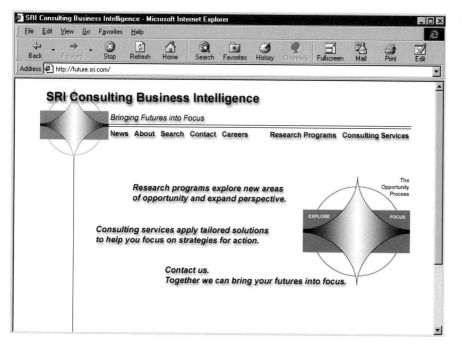

The major tendencies of the four groups with lower resources are:

1. *Believers:* Conservative, conventional, and traditional. Favor familiar products and established brands.
2. *Strivers:* Uncertain, insecure, approval-seeking, resource constrained. Favor stylish products that emulate the purchases of those with greater material wealth.
3. *Makers:* Practical, self-sufficient, traditional, family-oriented. Favor only products with a practical or functional purpose such as tools, utility vehicles, fishing equipment.
4. *Strugglers:* Elderly, resigned, passive, concerned, resource constrained. Cautious consumers who are loyal to favorite brands.

You can find out which VALS type you are by going to SRIC-BI's Web site (www. future.sri.com).

Lifestyle segmentation schemes are by no means universal. McCann-Erickson London, for example, identified the following British lifestyles: Avant-Gardians (interested in change); Pontificators (traditionalists, very British); Chameleons (follow the crowd); and Sleepwalkers (contented underachievers). The advertising agency D'Arcy, Masius, Benton & Bowles published *The Russian Consumer: A New Perspective and a Marketing Approach*, which revealed five categories of Russian consumers: Merchants, Cossacks, Students, Business Executives, and Russian Souls.[19] There are even lifestyle segmentation frameworks for classifying people according to their technology orientation. (See "Marketing for the New Economy: Are You a Mouse Potato or a Techno-Striver?")

PERSONALITY AND SELF-CONCEPT   Each person has personality characteristics that influence his or her buying behavior. By **personality**, we mean a set of distinguishing human psychological traits that lead to relatively consistent and enduring responses to environmental stimuli. Personality is often described in terms of such traits as self-confidence, dominance, autonomy, deference, sociability, defensiveness, and adaptability.[20] Personality can be a useful variable in analyzing consumer brand choices. The idea is that brands also have personalities, and that consumers are likely to choose brands whose personalities match their own. We define **brand personality** as the specific mix of human traits that may be attributed to a particular brand.

marketing for the **new economy**

Are You a Mouse Potato or a Techno-Striver?

Traditional market research may tell you who is buying a computer for the household. It may even tell you the kind of lifestyle she or he has. However, it will not tell you who in the household is using the computer and why. It will not tell you that the wife is using the PC to take a distance-learning course, that the son is using it to download computer games from various Web sites, that the daughter is using it to log on to about a dozen chat groups, or that the husband, a confirmed technophobe, logs on to get stock quotes.

Marketers of technology products can segment consumers based on technology types. Forrester Research, Inc.'s "Technographics" segments consumers into nine categories according to motivation, desire, and ability to invest in technology (see table below).

Both Technographics and the SRI-BI VALS™ systems reinforce the idea of a Consumer resource dimension based on

knowledge as well as income. Some people who are computer-savvy are good prospects for home banking to pay bills, switch money between accounts, and check their balances. VALS points out that not all computer-savvy people are good home-banking prospects—the key is knowing which ones. Non-computer-literate people will still write checks by hand, send payments through "snail mail," and stand in line for a bank teller. The new market research tools also reveal many shades in the spectrum between "the knows" and "the know nots."

Sources: Based on Andy Hines, "Do You Know Your Technology Type?" *The Futurist* (September–October 1997): 10–11; Rebecca Piirto Heath, "The Frontiers of Psychographics," *American Demographics* (July 1996): 38–43; Paul C. Judge, "Are Tech Buyers Different?" *Business Week*, January 26, 1998, pp. 64–65, 68.

	MORE AFFLUENT	LESS AFFLUENT	
	CAREER	FAMILY	ENTERTAINMENT
OPTIMISTS	**Fast Forwards** — These consumers are the biggest spenders, and they are early adopters of new technology for home, office, and personal use.	**New Age Nurturers** — Also big spenders, but focused on technology for home uses, such as a family PC.	**Mouse Potatoes** — They like the online world for entertainment and are willing to spend for the latest in "technotainment."
OPTIMISTS	**Techno-Strivers** — Use technology from cell phones and pagers to online services primarily to gain a career edge.	**Digital Hopefuls** — Families with a limited budget but still interested in new technology. Good candidates for under-$1,000 PC.	**Gadget-Grabbers** — They also favor online entertainment but have less cash to spend on it.
PESSIMISTS	**Hand-Shakers** — Older consumers—typically managers—who do not touch their computers at work. They leave that to younger assistants.	**Traditionalists** — Willing to use technology but slow to upgrade. Not convinced upgrades and other add-ons are worth paying for.	**Media Junkies** — Seek entertainment and cannot find much of it online. Prefer TV and other older media.
	SIDELINED CITIZENS (not interested in technology)		

Source: Paul C. Judge, "Are Tech Buyers Different," *Business Week*, January 26, 1998, p. 65; Data Forrester Research, Inc.

Jennifer Aaker conducted research into brand personalities and identified the following five traits:[21]

1. Sincerity (down-to-earth, honest, wholesome, and cheerful)
2. Excitement (daring, spirited, imaginative, and up-to-date)
3. Competence (reliable, intelligent, and successful)
4. Sophistication (upper-class and charming)
5. Ruggedness (outdoorsy and tough)

She proceeded to analyze some well-known brands and found that a number of them tended to be strong on one particular trait: Levi's with "ruggedness"; MTV with "excitement"; CNN with "competence"; and Campbell's with "sincerity." The implication is that these brands will attract persons who are high on the same personality traits.

Marketers attempt to develop brand personalities that will attract consumers with the same **self-concept**, but self-concept is somewhat slippery. A *person's actual self-concept* (how she views herself) may differ from her *ideal self-concept* (how she would like to view herself) and from her *others-self-concept* (how she thinks others see her). Which self will she try to satisfy in choosing a brand? Self-concept theory has had a mixed record of success in predicting consumer responses to brand images.[22]

psychological factors

A person's buying choices are influenced by four major psychological factors—motivation, perception, learning, and beliefs and attitudes.

MOTIVATION   A person has many needs at any given time. Some needs are *biogenic*; they arise from physiological states of tension such as hunger, thirst, or discomfort. Other needs are *psychogenic*; they arise from psychological states of tension such as the need for recognition, esteem, or belonging. A need becomes a motive when it is aroused to a sufficient level of intensity. A **motive** is a need that is sufficiently pressing to drive the person to act.

Psychologists have developed theories of human motivation, and three of the best known—those of Sigmund Freud, Abraham Maslow, and Frederick Herzberg—carry quite different implications for consumer analysis and marketing strategy.

Freud's Theory   Sigmund Freud assumed that the psychological forces shaping people's behavior are largely unconscious, and that a person cannot fully understand his or her own motivations. A technique called *laddering* can be used to trace a person's motivations from the stated instrumental ones to the more terminal ones. Then the marketer can decide at what level to develop the message and appeal.[23]

When a person examines specific brands, he or she will react not only to their stated capabilities, but also to other, less conscious cues. Shape, size, weight, material, color, and brand name can all trigger certain associations and emotions.

Motivation researchers often collect "in-depth interviews" with a few dozen consumers to uncover deeper motives triggered by a product. They use various *projective techniques* such as word association, sentence completion, picture interpretation, and role playing. Many of these techniques were pioneered by Ernest Dichter, a Viennese psychologist who settled in America. His research produced interesting and occasionally bizarre hypotheses:

- Consumers resist prunes because prunes are wrinkled looking and remind people of old age.
- Men smoke cigars as an adult version of thumb sucking.
- Women prefer vegetable shortening to animal fats because the latter arouse a sense of guilt over killing animals.
- Women don't trust cake mixes unless they require adding an egg, because this helps them feel they are giving "birth."

Today motivational researchers continue the tradition of Freudian interpretation. Jan Callebaut identifies different motives that a product can satisfy. For example, whisky can meet the need for social relaxation, status, or fun. Different whisky brands need to be motivationally positioned in one of these three appeals.[24] Another motivation researcher, Clotaire Rapaille, works on breaking the code behind a lot of product behavior. He claims that the code for coffee in the United States is "home" and therefore coffee advertising must use the home theme. The code for cheese in France is "alive," but when you go to America, cheese is "dead." He advises cheese producers to make cheese "alive."[25]

figure **7.3**

Maslow's Hierarchy of Needs

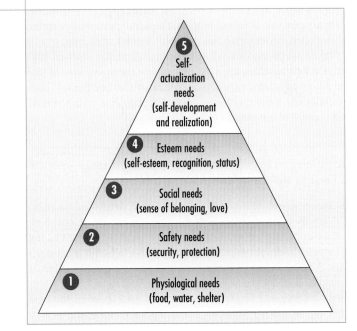

Source: Motivation and Personality, 2nd ed., by A. H. Maslow, 1970. Reprinted by permission of Prentice Hall, Inc., Upper Saddle River, New Jersey.

Maslow's Theory   Abraham Maslow sought to explain why people are driven by particular needs at particular times.[26] Why does one person spend considerable time and energy on personal safety and another on pursuing the high opinion of others? Maslow's answer is that human needs are arranged in a hierarchy, from the most pressing to the least pressing. In order of importance, they are physiological needs, safety needs, social needs, esteem needs, and self-actualization needs (see Figure 7.3). People will try to satisfy their most important needs first. When a person succeeds in satisfying an important need, he or she will then try to satisfy the next-most-important need. For example, a starving man (need 1) will not take an interest in the latest happenings in the art world (need 5), nor in how he is viewed by others (need 3 or 4), nor even in whether he is breathing clean air (need 2); but when he has enough food and water, the next-most-important need will become salient.

Maslow's theory helps marketers understand how various products fit into the plans, goals, and lives of consumers.

Herzberg's Theory   Frederick Herzberg developed a two-factor theory that distinguishes *dissatisfiers* (factors that cause dissatisfaction) and *satisfiers* (factors that cause satisfaction).[27] The absence of dissatisfiers is not enough; satisfiers must be actively present to motivate a purchase. For example, a computer that does not come with a warranty would be a dissatisfier. Yet the presence of a product warranty would not act as a satisfier or motivator of a purchase, because it is not a source of intrinsic satisfaction with the computer. Ease of use would be a satisfier.

Herzberg's theory has two implications. First, sellers should do their best to avoid dissatisfiers (for example, a poor training manual or a poor service policy). Although these things will not sell a product, they might easily unsell it. Second, the manufacturer should identify the major satisfiers or motivators of purchase in the market and then supply them. These satisfiers will make the major difference as to which brand the customer buys.

PERCEPTION   A motivated person is ready to act. How the motivated person actually acts is influenced by his or her perception of the situation. **Perception** is the process by which an individual selects, organizes, and interprets information inputs to create a meaningful picture of the world.[28] Perception depends not only on the physical stimuli, but also on the stimuli's relation to the surrounding field and on conditions within the individual. The key point is that perceptions can vary widely among individuals exposed to the same reality. One person might perceive a fast-talking salesperson as aggressive and insincere; another, as intelligent and helpful. Each will respond differently to the salesperson. In marketing, people's perceptions are more important than the reality.

People can emerge with different perceptions of the same object because of three perceptual processes: selective attention, selective distortion, and selective retention.

Selective Attention   People are exposed to a tremendous amount of daily stimuli: The average person may be exposed to over 1,500 ads a day. Because a person cannot possibly attend to all of these, most stimuli will be screened out—a process called **selective attention**. Selective attention means that marketers have to work hard to attract consumers' notice. The real challenge is to explain which stimuli people will notice. Here are some findings:

1. *People are more likely to notice stimuli that relate to a current need.* A person who is motivated to buy a computer will notice computer ads; he or she will probably not notice DVD ads.
2. *People are more likely to notice stimuli that they anticipate.* You are more likely to notice computers than radios in a computer store because you do not expect the store to carry radios.
3. *People are more likely to notice stimuli whose deviations are large in relation to the normal size of the stimuli.* You are more likely to notice an ad offering $100 off the list price of a computer than one offering $5 off.

Although people screen out much of the surrounding stimuli, they are influenced by unexpected stimuli, such as sudden offers in the mail, over the phone, or from a salesperson. Marketers may attempt to promote their offers intrusively to bypass selective attention filters.

Selective Distortion   Even noticed stimuli do not always come across in the way the senders intended. **Selective distortion** is the tendency to twist information into personal meanings and interpret information in a way that will fit our preconceptions. Unfortunately, there is not much marketers can do about selective distortion.

Selective Retention   People will forget much that they learn but will tend to retain information that supports their attitudes and beliefs. Because of **selective retention**, we are likely to remember good points mentioned about a product we like and forget good points mentioned about competing products. Selective retention explains why marketers use drama and repetition in sending messages to their target market.

LEARNING   When people act, they learn. **Learning** involves changes in an individual's behavior arising from experience. Most human behavior is learned. Learning theorists believe that learning is produced through the interplay of drives, stimuli, cues, responses, and reinforcement.

A **drive** is a strong internal stimulus impelling action. **Cues** are minor stimuli that determine when, where, and how a person responds. Suppose you buy an IBM computer. If your experience is rewarding, your response to computers and IBM will be positively reinforced. Later on, when you want to buy a printer, you may assume that because IBM makes good computers, IBM also makes good printers. In other words, you *generalize* your response to similar stimuli. A countertendency to generalization is discrimination. **Discrimination** means that the person has learned to recognize differences in sets of similar stimuli and can adjust responses accordingly.

Learning theory teaches marketers that they can build up demand for a product by associating it with strong drives, using motivating cues, and providing positive reinforcement. A new company can enter the market by appealing to the same drives that competitors use and by providing similar cue configurations, because buyers are more likely to transfer loyalty to similar brands (generalization); or the company might design its brand to appeal to a different set of drives and offer strong cue inducements to switch (discrimination).

BELIEFS AND ATTITUDES   Through doing and learning, people acquire beliefs and attitudes. These in turn influence buying behavior. A **belief** is a descriptive thought that a person holds about something. People's beliefs about a product or brand influence their buying decisions. A study of the influence of brand beliefs found that consumers were equally split in their preference for Diet Coke versus Diet Pepsi when tasting both on a blind basis.[29] When tasting the branded versions, consumers preferred Diet Coke by 65 percent and Diet Pepsi by only 23 percent (with the remainder seeing no difference). This example highlights the role brand beliefs play in product choice.

Marketers are interested in the beliefs people carry in their heads about their products and brands. Brand beliefs exist in consumers' memory. The associative network memory model posits that memory is a network of nodes and connecting links. The nodes represent stored information (verbal, visual, abstract, or contextual) and the links represent the associations between nodes. Retrieval occurs through a process of *spreading activation*. When a particular node is activated, the information is recalled and further associative information is recalled through the links. Thus a particular brand that is triggered in a node, say, Apple Computer, will activate other nodes carrying such information as "innovative," "user-friendly," "Apple-logo," and "MacIntosh."

Marketers can study the memory networks of different consumers concerning a particular brand and map the main associations that are triggered and their relative strength and frequency. One of these associations can be with a product's country of origin. (See "Marketing Memo: How a Product's Country of Origin Shapes Consumer Brand Beliefs.")

A company has several options when its products are competitively priced but their place of origin turns consumers off. The company can consider co-production with a foreign company that has a better name: South Korea could make a fine leather jacket that it sends to Italy for finishing; or the company can adopt a strategy to achieve world-class quality in the local industry, as is the case with Belgian chocolates, Polish ham, and Colombian coffee. This is what South African wineries are attempting to do.

Marketing
MEMO

How a Product's Country of Origin Shapes Consumer Brand Beliefs

Global marketers know that buyers hold distinct beliefs about brands or products from different countries. Several studies have found the following:

- The impact of country of origin varies with the type of product. Consumers want to know where a car was made but not the lubricating oil.
- Certain countries enjoy a reputation for certain goods: Japan for automobiles and consumer electronics; the United States for high-tech innovations, soft drinks, toys, cigarettes, and jeans; France for wine, perfume, and luxury goods.
- Sometimes country-of-origin perception can encompass an entire country's products. In one study, Chinese consumers in Hong Kong perceived American products as prestigious, Japanese products as innovative, and Chinese products as cheap.
- The more favorable a country's image, the more prominently the "Made in . . . " label should be displayed.
- Attitudes toward country of origin can change over time. Before World War II, Japan had a poor quality image.

Sources: Johnny K. Johansson, "Determinants and Effects of the Use of 'Made In' Labels," *International Marketing Review* (UK) 6, iss. 1 (1989): 47–58; Warren J. Bilkey and Erik Nes, "Country-of-Origin Effects on Product Evaluations," *Journal of International Business Studies* (Spring–Summer 1982): 89–99; P. J. Cattin et al., "A Cross-Cultural Study of 'Made-In' Concepts," *Journal of International Business Studies* (Winter 1982): 131–41; Wai-Sum Siu and Carmen Hau-Ming Chan, "Country-of-Origin Effects on Product Evaluation: The Case of Chinese Consumers in Hong Kong," *Journal of International Marketing and Marketing Research* (October 1997): 115–22; "Old Wine in New Bottles," *The Economist*, February 21, 1998, p. 45; Zeynep Gigrhan-Canli and Durairaj "Cultural Variations in Country of Origin Effects," *Journal of Marketing Research* (August 2000): 309–17.

South African Wineries   South African wines compete for shelf space in European supermarkets, but they are handicapped by the perception that South African vineyards are primitive in comparison to those in Australia and Chile. They are also dogged by South African wine farmers' ugly record of crude labor practices and shady deals. Wine farmers at Nelson's Creek and Fairview have now improved the lives of their workers and given them a stake in the industry. "Wine is such a product of origin that we cannot succeed if South Africa doesn't look good," says Willem Barnard, chief executive of the Ko-operatieve Wijnbouwers Vereniging (KWV), the 80-year-old farmers' co-op that dominates the industry.

Just as important as beliefs are attitudes. An **attitude** is a person's enduring favorable or unfavorable evaluations, emotional feelings, and action tendencies toward some object or idea.[30] People have attitudes toward almost everything: religion, politics, clothes, music, food. Attitudes put them into a frame of mind of liking or disliking an object, moving toward or away from it. Attitudes lead people to behave in a fairly consistent way toward similar objects. People do not have to interpret and react to every object in a fresh way. Because attitudes economize on energy and thought, they are very difficult to change. A person's attitudes settle into a consistent pattern: To change a single attitude may require major adjustments in other attitudes.

Thus a company would be well-advised to fit its product into existing attitudes rather than to try to change people's attitudes. Of course, there are exceptions, where the cost of trying to change attitudes might pay off. Here are two examples of organizations that used ad campaigns to change consumer attitudes, with handsome results:

California Milk Processor Board   After a 20-year decline in milk consumption among Californians, milk processors from across the state formed the California Milk Processor Board (CMPB) in 1993 with one goal in mind: to get people to drink more milk. The ad agency commissioned by the CMPB developed a novel approach to pitching milk's benefits. Research had shown that the majority of consumers already believed milk was good for them. So the campaign would remind consumers of the inconvenience and annoyance of running out of milk, which became known as "milk deprivation." The "Got Milk?" tagline served to remind consumers to make sure they had milk in their refrigerators. Within the first year of the campaign, the number of consumers who reported consuming milk at least "several times a week" jumped from 72 to 78 percent. In 1995, the "Got Milk?" campaign was licensed to the National Dairy Board. In 1998, the National Fluid Milk Processor Education Program, which had been using the "milk mustache" campaign since 1994 to boost sales, bought the rights to the "Got Milk?" tagline. By 1998, "Got Milk?" was being advertised across the country with a combined annual budget of $180 million.[31]

Wood Promotion Network   With a campaign similar in purpose to "Got Milk?", more than 80 wood-products companies joined forces to promote the benefits of wood with a campaign urging consumers to "Be Constructive: Use Wood." Although wood is used by 90 percent of the residential construction market, recent promotional campaigns by steel and concrete manufacturers threatened to erode some of wood's market share. The wood campaign seeks to encourage consumers to choose wood by emphasizing its durability, affordability, and ease of use.[32]

A "Got Milk?" ad from the National Fluid Milk Processor Promotion Board's campaign using mustachioed celebrities—here the cast of the TV sitcom Frasier.

The general populace isn't merely lacking culture, it's lacking calcium. In fact, 60% of men and 90% of women don't get enough. The enlightened among us, however, drink 3 glasses of milk a day. A practice that can prevent a Freudian condition known as "calcium envy."

got milk?

the buying decision process

Marketers have to go beyond the various influences on buyers and develop an understanding of how consumers actually make their buying decisions. Specifically, marketers must identify who makes the buying decision, the types of buying decisions, and the steps in the buying process.

buying roles

It is easy to identify the buyer for many products. In the United States, men normally choose their shaving equipment, and women choose their pantyhose; but even here marketers must be careful in making their targeting decisions, because buying roles change. When ICI, the giant British chemical company, discovered that women made 60 percent of the decisions on the brand of household paint, it decided to advertise its DuLux brand to women.

We can distinguish five roles people play in a buying decision:

- *Initiator:* The person who first suggests the idea of buying the product or service.
- *Influencer:* The person whose view or advice influences the decision.
- *Decider:* The person who decides on any component of a buying decision: whether to buy, what to buy, how to buy, or where to buy.
- *Buyer:* The person who makes the actual purchase.
- *User:* The person who consumes or uses the product or service.

buying behavior

Consumer decision making varies with the type of buying decision. The decisions to buy toothpaste, a tennis racket, a personal computer, and a new car are all very different. Complex and expensive purchases are likely to involve more buyer deliberation

table **7.3**

	High Involvement	Low Involvement
Significant Differences between Brands	Complex buying behavior	Variety-seeking buying behavior
Few Differences between Brands	Dissonance-reducing buying behavior	Habitual buying behavior

Four Types of Buying Behavior

Source: Modified from Henry Assael, *Consumer Behavior and Marketing Action* (Boston: Kent Publishing Co., 1987), p. 87. Copyright 1987 by Wadsworth, Inc. Printed by permission of Kent Publishing Co., a division of Wadsworth, Inc.

and more participants. Henry Assael distinguished four types of consumer buying behavior, based on the degree of buyer involvement and the degree of differences among brands[33] (see Table 7.3).

COMPLEX BUYING BEHAVIOR   Complex buying behavior involves a three-step process. First, the buyer develops beliefs about the product. Second, he or she develops attitudes about the product. Third, he or she makes a thoughtful choice. Consumers engage in complex buying behavior when they are highly involved in a purchase and aware of significant differences among brands. This is usually the case when the product is expensive, bought infrequently, risky, and highly self-expressive, like an automobile.

The marketer of a high-involvement product must understand consumers' information-gathering and evaluation behavior. The marketer needs to develop strategies that assist the buyer in learning about the product's attributes and their relative importance, and which call attention to the high standing of the company's brand on the more important attributes. The marketer needs to differentiate the brand's features, use print media to describe the brand's benefits, and motivate sales personnel and the buyer's acquaintances to influence the final brand choice.

DISSONANCE-REDUCING BUYER BEHAVIOR   Sometimes the consumer is highly involved in a purchase but sees little difference in brands. The high involvement is based on the fact that the purchase is expensive, infrequent, and risky. In this case, the buyer will shop around to learn what is available. If the consumer finds quality differences in the brands, he or she might go for the higher price. If the consumer finds little difference, he or she might simply buy on price or convenience.

After the purchase, the consumer might experience dissonance that stems from noticing certain disquieting features or hearing favorable things about other brands, and will be alert to information that supports his or her decision. In this example, the consumer first acted, then acquired new beliefs, then ended up with a set of attitudes. Marketing communications should supply beliefs and evaluations that help the consumer feel good about his or her brand choice.

HABITUAL BUYING BEHAVIOR   Many products are bought under conditions of low involvement and the absence of significant brand differences. Consider salt. Consumers have little involvement in this product category. They go to the store and reach for the brand. If they keep reaching for the same brand, it is out of habit, not strong brand loyalty. There is good evidence that consumers have low involvement with most low-cost, frequently purchased products.

With these products, consumer behavior does not pass through the normal sequence of belief, attitude, and behavior. Consumers do not search extensively for information, evaluate characteristics, and make a decision. Instead, they are passive recipients of information in television or print ads. Ad repetition creates *brand familiarity* rather than *brand conviction*. After purchase, they may not even evaluate the choice. For low-involvement products, the buying process begins with brand beliefs formed by passive learning and is followed by purchase behavior, which may be followed by evaluation.

Marketers of such products find it effective to use price and sales promotions to stimulate product trial. Television advertising is more effective than print because it is a low-involvement medium that is suitable for passive learning.[34]

Marketers use four techniques to try to convert a low-involvement product into one of higher involvement. First, they can link the product to some involving issue, as when Crest toothpaste is linked to avoiding cavities. Second, they can link the product to some involving personal situation—for instance, by advertising a coffee brand early in the morning when the consumer wants to shake off sleepiness. Third, they might design advertising to trigger strong emotions related to personal values or ego defense. Fourth, they might add an important feature (for example, fortifying a plain drink with vitamins). These strategies at best raise consumer involvement from a low to a moderate level; they do not propel the consumer into highly involved buying behavior. (See "Marketing Memo: How to Derive Fresh Consumer Insights to Differentiate Products and Services.")

VARIETY-SEEKING BUYING BEHAVIOR   Some buying situations are characterized by low involvement but significant brand differences. Here consumers often do a lot of brand switching. Think about cookies. The consumer has some beliefs about cookies, chooses a brand of cookies without much evaluation, and evaluates the product during consumption. Next time, the consumer may reach for another brand out of a wish for a different taste. Brand switching occurs for the sake of variety rather than dissatisfaction.

The market leader and the minor brands in this product category have different marketing strategies. The market leader will try to encourage habitual buying behavior by dominating the shelf space, avoiding out-of-stock conditions, and sponsoring frequent reminder advertising. Challenger firms will encourage variety seeking by offering lower prices, deals, coupons, free samples, and advertising that presents reasons for trying something new.

stages of the buying decision process

Smart companies will immerse themselves in trying to understand the customer's overall experience in learning about a product, making a brand choice, using the product, and even disposing of it. Honda engineers took videos of shoppers loading groceries into car trunks to observe their frustrations and generate possible design solutions. Intuit, the maker of Quicken financial software, watched first-time buyers try to learn Quicken to sense their problems in learning how to use the software. Benson Shapiro and his co-authors urged companies to "staple yourself to an order" to appreciate everything that occurs or might go wrong in the ordering process.[35]

How can marketers learn about the stages in the buying process for their product? They can think about how they themselves would act (*introspective method*). They can interview a small number of recent purchasers, asking them to recall the events leading to their purchase (*retrospective method*). They can locate consumers who plan to buy the product and ask them to think out loud about going through the buying process (*prospective method*); or they can ask consumers to describe the ideal way to buy the product (*prescriptive method*). Each method yields a picture of the steps in the process.

The Edmunds.com home page shows the variety of services this Web company offers those shopping for a car.

Trying to understand the customer's behavior in connection with a product has been called mapping the customer's *consumption system*,[36] *customer activity cycle*,[37] or *customer scenario*.[38] This can be done for such activity clusters as doing laundry, preparing for a wedding, or buying a car. Buying a car, for example, involves a whole cluster of activities, including choosing the car, financing the purchase, buying insurance, buying accessories, and so on. Professor Sawhney views these activities as constituting a **metamarket,** and calls firms that help customers navigate through these activities **metamediaries**.[39] As an example of an online metamediary, consider Edmunds.com:

Edmunds.com   This site provides unbiased, third-party information and advice on buying autos and related services. Here is how it works:

- Auto buyers can read about features, quality, and dealer costs for any automobile on Edmunds' site. They can narrow their search to a few makes and models, and conduct side-by-side comparisons. They can request Edmunds, in collaboration with the manufacturers, to mail them customized brochures with information on selected makes and models.
- They can seek advice by entering the Edmunds Town Hall discussion area to interact with consumers who have bought or owned these autos. They may visit Web sites that present complaints from those who have had negative experiences with a particular seller (see fordsucks.com or bmwlemon.com for examples).
- Soon, buyers will be able to sign up for appointments to test-drive multiple brands and models at a predefined place and time, sponsored by Edmunds and partners like CarMax or AutoNation. They will be able to "kick the tires" for their favorite brands side-by-side, with no sales pressure from dealers and without ever visiting a brand-specific dealer. The appointments will be prearranged, so that buyers will have exactly the models they want to test-drive.
- When buyers decide on a brand and make, they can define the features and options they want, and click on Edmunds' partner Autobytel.com to act as their buying

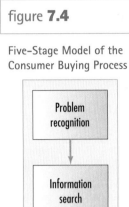

figure 7.4

Five-Stage Model of the Consumer Buying Process

agent. Autobytel informs several local car dealers that there is a "hot" prospect for the particular auto and invites those who have it in stock to bid for the business.
- Buyers can round out the transaction by clicking on other Edmunds business partners. They can prequalify for financing from NationsBank; get extended warranties from Warranty Gold; buy auto insurance from GEICO; and accessorize their auto with items from J. C. Whitney.

Marketing scholars have developed a "stages model" of the buying decision process (see Figure 7.4). The consumer passes through five stages: problem recognition, information search, evaluation of alternatives, purchase decision, and postpurchase behavior. Clearly, the buying process starts long before the actual purchase and has consequences long afterward.[40]

The model in Figure 7.4 implies that consumers pass through all five stages in buying a product, but this is not the case: Consumers may skip or reverse some stages. A woman buying her regular brand of toothpaste goes directly from the need for toothpaste to the purchase decision, skipping information search and evaluation. However, we will use the model in Figure 7.4 because it captures the full range of considerations that arise when a consumer faces a highly involving new purchase.[41]

problem recognition

The buying process starts when the buyer recognizes a problem or need. The need can be triggered by internal or external stimuli. With an internal stimulus, one of the person's normal needs—hunger, thirst, sex—rises to a threshold level and becomes a drive; or a need can be aroused by an external stimulus. A person passes a bakery and sees freshly baked bread that stimulates her hunger; she admires a neighbor's new car; or she sees a television ad for a Hawaiian vacation.

Marketers need to identify the circumstances that trigger a particular need. By gathering information from a number of consumers, marketers can identify the most frequent stimuli that spark an interest in a product category. They can then develop marketing strategies that trigger consumer interest.

information search

An aroused consumer will be inclined to search for more information. We can distinguish between two levels of arousal. The milder search state is called *heightened attention*. At this level a person simply becomes more receptive to information about a product.

At the next level, the person may enter an *active information search*: looking for reading material, phoning friends, and visiting stores to learn about the product. Of key interest to the marketer are the major information sources to which the consumer will turn and the relative influence each will have on the subsequent purchase decision. Consumer information sources fall into four groups:

- *Personal sources:* Family, friends, neighbors, acquaintances
- *Commercial sources:* Advertising, salespersons, dealers, packaging, displays
- *Public sources:* Mass media, consumer-rating organizations
- *Experiential sources:* Handling, examining, using the product

The relative amount and influence of these information sources vary with the product category and the buyer's characteristics. Generally speaking, the consumer receives the most information about a product from commercial sources—that is, marketer-dominated sources. However, the most effective information comes from personal sources. Each information source performs a different function in influencing the buying decision. Commercial information normally performs an informing function, and personal sources perform a legitimizing or evaluation function. For example, physicians often learn of new drugs from commercial sources but turn to other doctors for evaluative information.

- *Alter the importance weights:* The marketer could try to persuade buyers to attach more importance to the attributes in which the brand excels.
- *Call attention to neglected attributes:* The marketer could draw buyers' attention to neglected attributes, such as styling or processing speed.
- *Shift the buyer's ideals:* The marketer could try to persuade buyers to change their ideal levels for one or more attributes.[45]

purchase decision   4)

In the evaluation stage, the consumer forms preferences among the brands in the choice set. The consumer may also form an intention to buy the most preferred brand. However, two factors can intervene between the purchase intention and the purchase decision (Figure 7.6).[46]

The first factor is the *attitudes of others*. The extent to which another person's attitude reduces one's preferred alternative depends on two things: (1) the intensity of the other person's negative attitude toward the consumer's preferred alternative and (2) the consumer's motivation to comply with the other person's wishes.[47] The more intense the other person's negativism and the closer the other person is to the consumer, the more the consumer will adjust his or her purchase intention. The converse is also true: A buyer's preference for a brand will increase if someone he or she respects favors the same brand strongly. The influence of others becomes complex when several people close to the buyer hold contradictory opinions and the buyer would like to please them all.

Related to the attitudes of others is the role played by **infomediaries** who publish their evaluations. Examples include *Consumer Reports*; *Zagats* (which publishes customer reviews of restaurants); professional movie, book, and music reviewers; customer reviews of books and music in Amazon.com; and the increasing number of chat rooms where people discuss products, services, and companies. Consumers are undoubtedly influenced by these evaluations.

The second factor is *unanticipated situational factors* that may erupt to change the purchase intention. Jack Hamilton might lose his job, some other purchase might become more urgent, or a store salesperson may turn him off. Preferences and even purchase intentions are not completely reliable predictors of purchase behavior.

A consumer's decision to modify, postpone, or avoid a purchase decision is heavily influenced by *perceived risk*.[48] The amount of perceived risk varies with the amount of money at stake, the amount of attribute uncertainty, and the amount of consumer self-confidence. Consumers develop routines for reducing risk, such as decision avoidance, information gathering from friends, and preference for national brand names and warranties. Marketers must understand the factors that provoke a feeling of risk in consumers and provide information and support to reduce the perceived risk.

In executing a purchase intention, the consumer may make up to five purchase subdecisions: a *brand decision* (brand A), *vendor decision* (dealer 2), *quantity decision* (one computer), *timing decision* (weekend), and *payment-method decision* (credit card). Purchases of everyday products involve fewer decisions and less deliberation. For example, in buying sugar, a consumer gives little thought to the vendor or payment method.

figure **7.6**

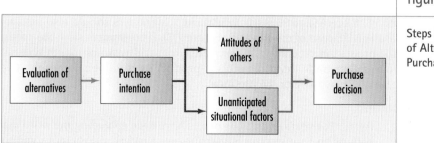

Steps Between Evaluation of Alternatives and a Purchase Decision

5)

postpurchase behavior

After purchasing the product, the consumer will experience some level of satisfaction or dissatisfaction. The marketer's job does not end when the product is bought. Marketers must monitor postpurchase satisfaction, postpurchase actions, and postpurchase product uses.

POSTPURCHASE SATISFACTION   What determines whether the buyer will be highly satisfied, somewhat satisfied, or dissatisfied with a purchase? The buyer's satisfaction is a function of the closeness between the buyer's expectations and the product's perceived performance.[49] If performance falls short of expectations, the customer is *disappointed*; if it meets expectations, the customer is *satisfied*; if it exceeds expectations, the customer is *delighted*. These feelings make a difference in whether the customer buys the product again and talks favorably or unfavorably about it to others.

Consumers form their expectations on the basis of messages received from sellers, friends, and other information sources. The larger the gap between expectations and performance, the greater the consumer's dissatisfaction. Here the consumer's coping style comes into play. Some consumers magnify the gap when the product is not perfect, and they are highly dissatisfied; others minimize the gap and are less dissatisfied.[50]

The importance of postpurchase satisfaction suggests that product claims must truthfully represent the product's likely performance. Some sellers might even understate performance levels so that consumers experience higher-than-expected satisfaction with the product.

POSTPURCHASE ACTIONS   Satisfaction or dissatisfaction with the product will influence a consumer's subsequent behavior. If the consumer is satisfied, he or she will exhibit a higher probability of purchasing the product again. For example, data on automobile brand choice show a high correlation between being highly satisfied with the last brand bought and intention to buy the brand again. One survey showed that 75 percent of Toyota buyers were highly satisfied and about 75 percent intended to buy a Toyota again; 35 percent of Chevrolet buyers were highly satisfied and about 35 percent intended to buy a Chevrolet again. The satisfied customer will also tend to say good things about the brand to others. Marketers say: "Our best advertisement is a satisfied customer."[51]

Dissatisfied consumers may abandon or return the product. They may seek information that confirms its high value. They may take public action by complaining to the company, going to a lawyer, or complaining to other groups (such as business, private, or government agencies). Private actions include making a decision to stop buying the product (*exit option*) or warning friends (*voice option*).[52] In all these cases, the seller has done a poor job of satisfying the customer.[53]

Postpurchase communications to buyers have been shown to result in fewer product returns and order cancellations.[54] Computer companies, for example, can send a letter to new owners congratulating them on having selected a fine computer. They can place ads showing satisfied brand owners. They can solicit customer suggestions for improvements and list the location of available services. They can write intelligible instruction booklets. They can send owners a magazine containing articles describing new computer applications. In addition, they can provide good channels for speedy redress of customer grievances.

POSTPURCHASE USE AND DISPOSAL   Marketers should also monitor how buyers use and dispose of the product (Figure 7.7). If consumers store the product in a closet, the product is probably not very satisfying, and word of mouth will not be strong. If they sell or trade the product, new-product sales will be depressed. Consumers may also find new uses for the product:

Avon   For years Avon's customers have been spreading the word that Skin-So-Soft bath oil and moisturizer is a terrific insect repellent. Whereas some consumers sim-

figure **7.7**

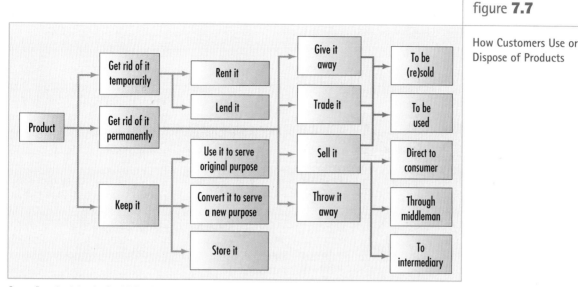

Source: From Jacob Jacoby, Carol K. Berning, and Thomas F. Dietvorst, "What about Disposition?" *Journal of Marketing* (July 1977): 23. Reprinted with permission of the American Marketing Association.

ply bathed in water scented with the fragrant oil, others carried it in their backpacks to mosquito-infested campsites or kept a bottle on the deck of the beach house. After receiving approval by the Environmental Protection Agency, Avon began touting its Skin-So-Soft Moisturizing Suncare Plus as a triple-action product that provided insect repellent and waterproof SPF 15 sun protection, as well as moisturizers. Joey Green, an author of five books on unusual household uses for everyday products, found another use for Skin-So-Soft: removing lime deposits from shower doors.[55]

If consumers throw the product away, the marketer needs to know how they dispose of it, especially if it can hurt the environment (as in the case with beverage containers and disposable diapers). Increased public awareness of recycling and ecological concerns as well as consumer complaints about having to throw away beautiful bottles led French perfume maker Rochas to think about introducing a new refillable fragrance line.

other models of the buying decision process

The five-stage model of the buying decision process shown in Figure 7.4 is one of several models for understanding the buyer's decision process. Here are two other models that marketers have found useful.

HEALTH MODEL   Social marketers in the health field are interested in how patients adopt healthful behaviors, such as stopping smoking or starting a new diet or exercise program. A useful model called Stages of Change distinguishes five stages:[56]

- *Precontemplation:* Not recognizing the problem or the need to change.
- *Contemplation:* Seriously thinking about the problem and the possibility of change.
- *Preparation:* Making a commitment to change and taking steps to prepare for that change.
- *Action:* Successful modification of behavior for a period from 1 day to 6 months.
- *Maintenance:* Continuation of change from 6 months to an indefinite period.

Persons contemplating a change, such as stopping smoking or losing weight, need to pass through these stages. The social marketer's task is to find appeals and tools to help people move from one stage to the next.

figure **7.8**

figure **7.8**

Activity cycle for IBM customers in the global electronic networking capability market space.

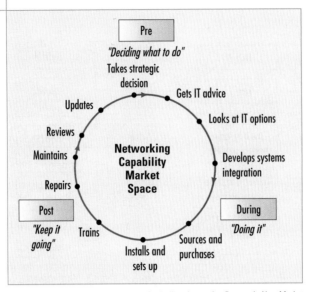

Source: Sandra Vandermerwe, *Customer Capitalism: Increasing Returns in New Market Spaces* (London: Nicholas Brealey, 1999), p. 92, figure 5. Reprinted by permission.

CUSTOMER ACTIVITY CYCLE MODEL   Professor Sandra Vandermerwe focuses on mapping the *pre*, *during*, and *post* phases of a consumer's behavior toward a particular task.[57] The *pre* phase is deciding what to do, the *during* phase is doing it, and the *post* phase is keeping it going. Figure 7.8 shows a *customer activity cycle* for a bank customer contemplating whether to purchase a new software system from IBM or another vendor. IBM's task is to add value at each stage to facilitate the buyer's favoring IBM as the vendor. Figure 7.9

figure **7.9**

Value adds for IBM customers in the global electronic networking capability market space.

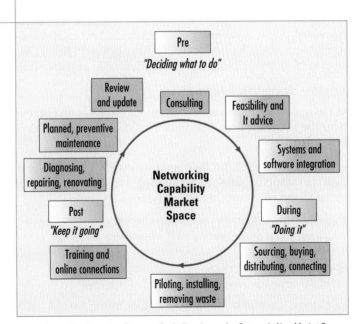

Source: Sandra Vandermerwe, *Customer Capitalism: Increasing Returns in New Market Spaces* (London: Nicholas Brealey, 1999), p. 94, figure 7. Reprinted by permission.

shows the value add-ons that IBM can assemble in order to win the bank's business. Essentially, IBM is putting together a turnkey system to make it easy for the bank to get maximum value. In this way, IBM has created *customer lock-in*. If IBM focused on *product lock-in*, such as only selling the software, customers could have gone elsewhere for the missing services; but with customer lock-in, the bank has little choice but to buy from IBM.

summary

1. Consumer behavior is influenced by four factors: cultural (culture, subculture, and social class); social (reference groups, family, and social roles and statuses); personal (age, stage in the life cycle, occupation, economic circumstances, lifestyle, personality, and self-concept); and psychological (motivation, perception, learning, beliefs, and attitudes). Research into all these factors can provide clues to reach and serve consumers more effectively.

2. To understand how consumers actually make buying decisions, marketers must identify who makes and has input into the buying decision; people can be initiators, influencers, deciders, buyers, or users, and different marketing campaigns might be targeted to each type of person. Marketers must also examine buyers' levels of involvement

and the number of brands available to determine whether consumers are engaging in complex buying behavior, dissonance-reducing buying behavior, habitual buying behavior, or variety-seeking buying behavior.

3. The typical buying process consists of the following sequence of events: problem recognition, information search, evaluation of alternatives, purchase decision, and postpurchase behavior. The marketers' job is to understand the buyer's behavior at each stage. The attitudes of others, unanticipated situational factors, and perceived risk may all affect the decision to buy, as will consumers' levels of postpurchase satisfaction and postpurchase actions on the part of the company.

4. Other models of the buying decision process include the health model and the customer activity cycle model.

applications

marketing debate – is target marketing ever bad?

As marketers increasingly develop marketing programs tailored to certain target market segments, some critics have denounced these efforts as exploitative. For example, the preponderance of billboards advertising cigarettes, alcohol, and other vices in low-income urban areas is seen as taking advantage of a vulnerable market segment. Critics can be especially harsh in evaluating marketing programs that target African Americans and other minority groups, claiming

that they often employ clichéd stereotypes and inappropriate depictions. Others counter with the point of view that targeting and positioning is critical to marketing and that these marketing programs are an attempt to be relevant to a certain consumer group.

> **Take a position:** Targeting minorities is exploitative versus Targeting minorities is a sound business practice.

marketing and advertising

1. This ad in Figure 1 for Quaker Toasted Oatmeal Squares appeals to personal factors that influence consumer buying behavior, including lifestyle and self-concept. It also provides information so that the targeted segment will recognize and understand the bundle of attributes that this cereal product offers to solve the problem of how to eat a "nice, healthy breakfast."

   a. Who is the target audience for this ad, and how does Quaker use the concept of consumer lifestyle to effectively communicate with the target?

   b. Does this ad appeal to the consumer's actual self-concept, ideal self-concept, or others-self-concept? Which is the most appropriate for this product? Explain.

   c. What bundle of attributes does this ad present for the consumer's consideration? What are the benefits associated with each attribute?

2. Businesspeople also have specific needs and buying behavior when they act as consumers. The BlackBerry ad in Figure 2 targets businesspeople who want to avoid losing touch—even momentarily—with colleagues, clients, and other important contacts. Understanding the nuances of this consumer market's buying behavior, BlackBerry presents its wireless device as a convenient solution to the problem of staying connected at all times.

   a. What personal and psychological factors in the buying process have been incorporated into this ad?

   b. What role or roles are being addressed by this ad?

   c. Toward which stage of the consumer buying decision process is this ad most likely geared? Why?

Figure 1

Figure 2

online marketing today

Who would buy pet health insurance—let alone buy it online? Tom Kurtz founded Premier Pet Insurance a few years ago, after his cat needed $2,000 worth of veterinary treatment. Although pet health insurance has long been accepted in Europe, the U.S. market for it remains largely untapped. Fewer than 2 percent of all American cat and dog pets have health insurance, compared with up to 50 percent in Great Britain and Sweden. Now rising costs for sophisticated life-saving procedures such as chemotherapy and kidney transplants are causing more U.S. consumers to consider this type of insurance for their pets. As with other insurance products, many consumers like to shop around and compare policies and rates before making a purchase. That is why Premier maintains an informative, easy-to-navigate Web site.[58]

Visit the Premier Pet Insurance site <*www.ppins.com*>, review the home page, then follow the links to find out more about the various insurance plans, how much buyers can save, FAQs (frequently asked questions), and online quotes and ordering. How does the company address the social and personal factors most likely to affect the purchase of this product? What attitudes and beliefs about this purchase does Premier directly address on its Web site? What type of buying behavior would you expect consumers to follow when buying pet health insurance, and how does the company's online marketing reflect a good understanding of this buying behavior?

you're the marketer: sonic pda marketing plan

Marketing Plan Pro

Every company has to study consumer markets and behavior prior to developing a marketing plan for its products. This enables marketers to understand who constitutes the market, what and why the market buys, who participates in and influences the buying process, and how, when, and where consumers buy.

You are responsible for researching and analyzing the consumer market for Sonic's forthcoming PDA. Look again at the data you have already entered about the company's current situation and macroenvironment, especially the market being targeted. Now answer these questions about the market and buyer behavior:

- What cultural, social, personal, and psychological factors have the most influence on consumers buying PDAs? What research tools would help you better understand the effect on buyer attitudes and behavior?
- Which specific factors should Sonic's marketing plan emphasize and why?

- What consumer buying roles and buying behaviors are particularly relevant for PDA products?
- What kind of marketing activities should Sonic plan to coincide with each stage of the consumer buying process?

After you have analyzed your markets and consumer behavior, consider the implications for Sonic's marketing efforts supporting the launch of its PDA. Finally, document your findings and conclusions in a written marketing plan or type them into the Market Analysis, Situation Analysis, Target Markets, and Market Summary sections of the *Marketing Plan Pro* software.

notes

1. Tobi Elkin, "Product Pampering," *Brandweek*, June 16, 1997, pp. 38–40.
2. <*www.net-temps.com*>; Judith N. Mottl, "Customer Tracking; It's Not Just Website Hits," *InformationWeek*, February 7, 2000.
3. Adrienne Sanders, "Yankee Imperialism, " *Forbes*, December 13, 1999, p.56.
4. Leon G. Schiffman and Leslie Lazar Kanuk, *Consumer Behavior*, 6th ed. (Upper Saddle River, NJ: Prentice Hall, 1997).
5. Ibid.
6. Courteny Kane, "Advertising: TBWA/Chiat Day Brings Street Culture to a Campaign for Levi Strauss Silver Tab Clothing," *New York Times*, August 14, 1998, p. D8.
7. Abigail Goodman, "Store Most Likely to Succeed," *Los Angeles Times*, April 3, 1999.
8. Rosann L. Spiro, "Persuasion in Family Decision Making," *Journal of Consumer Research* (March 1983): 393–402; Lawrence H. Wortzel, "Marital Roles and Typologies as Predictors of Purchase Decision Making for Everyday Household Products: Suggestions for Research," in Jerry C. Olsen, (ed.), *Advances in Consumer Research*, Vol. 7 (Chicago: American Marketing Association, 1989), pp. 212–15; David J. Burns, "Husband-Wife Innovative Consumer Decision Making: Exploring the Effect of Family Power," *Psychology & Marketing* (May–June 1992): 175–89; Robert Boutilier, "Pulling the Family's Strings," *American Demographics* (August 1993): 44–48. For cross-cultural comparisons of husband-wife buying roles, see John B. Ford, Michael S. LaTour, and Tony L. Henthorne, "Perception of Marital Roles in Purchase-Decision Processes: A Cross-Cultural Study, "*Journal of the Academy of Marketing Science* (Spring 1995): 120–31.
9. George Moschis, "The Role of Family Communication in Consumer Socialization of Children and Adolescents," *Journal of Consumer Research* (March 1985): 898–913.
10. John Steere, "How Asian-Americans Make Purchase Decisions," *Marketing News*, March 13, 1995, p. 9.
11. Tom Peters, "Opportunity Knocks," *Forbes*, June 2, 1997, p. 132.
12. Marilyn Lavin, "Husband-Dominant, Wife-Dominant, Joint: A Shopping Typology for Baby Boom Couples?" *Journal of Consumer Marketing* 10, no. 3 (1993): 33–42.
13. Alan Alder, "Purchasing Power: Women's Buying Muscle Shops Up in Car Design, Marketing," *Chicago Tribune*, September 29, 1996, p. 21A; Matt Nauman, "Cadillac Attracts New Buyer Groups with Escalade Sport-Utility," *San Jose Mercury News*, January 19, 2001.
14. James U. McNeal, "Tapping the Three Kids' Markets," *American Demographics* (April 1998): 37–41.
15. Lisa Bannon, "Mattel's Print Ads Will Play Up to Moms to Boost Barbie Brand," *Wall Street Journal*, September 19, 2000.
16. David Leonhardt, "Hey Kid, Buy This," *BusinessWeek*, June 30, 1997, pp. 62–67.
17. Lawrence Lepisto, "A Life Span Perspective of Consumer Behavior," in Elizabeth Hirshman and Morris Holbrook (eds.), *Advances in Consumer Research*, Vol. 12 (Provo, UT: Association for Consumer Research, 1985), p. 47. Also see Gail Sheehy, *New Passages: Mapping Your Life Across Time* (New York: Random House, 1995).
18. Arnold Mitchell, *The Nine American Lifestyles* (New York: Warner Books), pp. viii–x, 25–31; Personal communication from the VALS Program, Business Intelligence Center, SRI Consulting, Menlo Park, CA, February 1, 1996. See also Wagner A. Kamakura and Michel Wedel, "Lifestyle Segmentation with Tailored Interviewing," *Journal of Marketing Research* 32, no. 3 (August 1995): 308–17.
19. Stuart Elliott, "Sampling Tastes of a Changing Russia," *New York Times*, April 1, 1992, pp. D1, D19.
20. Harold H. Kassarjian and Mary Jane Sheffet, "Personality and Consumer Behavior: An Update," in Harold H. Kassarjian and Thomas S. Robertson (eds.), *Perspectives in Consumer Behavior* (Glenview, IL: Scott, Foresman, 1981), pp. 160–80.
21. Jennifer Aaker, "Dimensions of Measuring Brand Personality," *Journal of Marketing Research* 34 (August 1997): 347–56.
22. M. Joseph Sirgy, "Self-Concept in Consumer Behavior: A Critical Review," *Journal of Consumer Research* (December 1982): 287–300. Jennifer L. Aaker, "The Malleable Self: The Role of Self-expression in Persuasion," *Journal of Marketing Research* (May 1999): pp. 45–57.
23. Thomas J. Reynolds and Jonathan Gutman, "Laddering Theory, Method, Analysis, and Interpretation," *Journal of Advertising Research* (February–March 1988): 11–34.
24. Jan Callebaut et al., *The Naked Consumer: The Secret of Motivational Research in Global Marketing* (Antwerp, Belgium: Censydiam Institute, 1994).
25. Jack Hitt, "Does the Smell of Coffee Brewing Remind You of Your Mother?" *New York Times Magazine,* May 7, 2000, pp. 71–74.
26. Abraham Maslow, *Motivation and Personality* (New York: Harper and Row, 1954), pp. 80–106.
27. See Frederick Herzberg, *Work and the Nature of Man* (Cleveland: William Collins, 1966); Henk Thierry and Agnes M. Koopman-Iwerna, "Motivation and Satisfaction," in P. J. Drenth (ed.), *Handbook of Work and Organizational Psychology* (New York: John Wiley, 1984), pp. 141–42.
28. Bernard Berelson and Gary A. Steiner, *Human Behavior: An Inventory of Scientific Findings* (New York: Harcourt, Brace Jovanovich, 1964), p. 88.
29. Leslie de Chernatony and Simon Knox, "How an Appreciation of Consumer Behavior Can Help in Product Testing," *Journal of Market Research Society,* (July 1990): 333. See also Chris Janiszewski and Stiju M. J. Osselar, "A Connectionist Model Of Brand-Quality Association," *Journal of Marketing Research*, August 2000, pp. 331–51.

30. David Krech, Richard S. Crutchfield, and Egerton L. Ballachey, *Individual in Society* (New York: McGraw-Hill, 1962), ch. 2.

31. Jill Venter, "Milk Mustache Campaign Is a Hit with Teens," *St. Louis Post-Dispatch*, April 1, 1998, p. E1; Dave Fusaro, "The Milk Mustache," *Dairy Foods* (April 1997): 75; Judann Pollack, "Milk: Kurt Graetzer," *Advertising Age*, June 30, 1997, p. S1; Kevin Lane Keller, "Milk: Branding a Commodity," *Strategic Brand Management* (Upper Saddle River, NJ: Prentice Hall, 1998).

32. Chad Terhune, "Wood Folks Hope for 'Got Milk?' Success," *Wall Street Journal*, February 9, 2001.

33. See Henry Assael, *Consumer Behavior and Marketing Action* (Boston: Kent, 1987), ch. 4.

34. Herbert E. Krugman, "The Impact of Television Advertising: Learning without Involvement," *Public Opinion Quarterly* (Fall 1965): 349–56.

35. Benson Shapiro, V. Kasturi Rangan, and John Sviokla, "Staple Yourself to an Order," *Harvard Business Review* (July–August 1992): 113–22. See also Carrie M. Heilman, Douglas Bowman, and Gordon P. Wright, "The Evolution of Brand Preferences and Choice Behaviors of Consumers New to a Market," *Journal of Marketing Research* (May 2000), pp.139–55.

36. Harper W. Boyd Jr. and Sidney Levy, "New Dimensions in Consumer Analysis," *Harvard Business Review* 163 (November–December): 129–40.

37. Sandra Vandermerwe, *Customer Capitalism: Increasing Returns in New Market Spaces* (London: Nicholas Brealey Publishing), ch. 11.

38. Patricia B. Seybold, "Get Inside the Lives of Your Customers," *Harvard Business Review* (May 2001): 81–89.

39. Mohanbir Sawhney, "Making New Markets," *Business 2.0* (May 1999): 116–21.

40. Marketing scholars have developed several models of the consumer buying process. See John A. Howard and Jagdish N. Sheth, *The Theory of Buyer Behavior* (New York: Wiley, 1969); James F. Engel, Roger D. Blackwell, and Paul W. Miniard, *Consumer Behavior*, 8th ed. (Fort Worth, TX: Dryden, 1994); Mary Frances Luce, James R. Bettman, and John W. Payne, *Emotional Decisions: Tradeoff Difficulty and Coping in Consumer Choice*, (Chicago, IL: University of Chicago Press, 2001).

41. William P. Putsis Jr. and Narasimhan Srinivasan, "Buying or Just Browsing? The Duration of Purchase Deliberation," *Journal of Marketing Research* (August 1994): 393–402.

42. Chem L. Narayana and Rom J. Markin, "Consumer Behavior and Product Performance: An Alternative Conceptualization," *Journal of Marketing* (October 1975): 1–6. See also Wayne S. DeSarbo and Kamel Jedidi, "The Spatial Representation of Heterogeneous Consideration Sets," *Marketing Science* 14, no.3, pt. 2 (1995): 326–42; Lee G. Cooper and Akihiro Inoue, "Building Market Structures from Consumer Preferences," *Journal of Marketing Research* 33, no. 3 (August 1996): 293–306.

43. See Paul E. Green and Yoram Wind, *Multiattribute Decisions in Marketing: A Measurement Approach* (Hinsdale, IL: Dryden, 1973), ch. 2; Leigh McAlister, "Choosing Multiple Items from a Product Class," *Journal of Consumer Research* (December 1979): 213–24.

44. This expectancy-value model was developed by Martin Fishbein, "Attitudes and Prediction of Behavior," in Martin Fishbein (ed.), *Readings in Attitude Theory and Measurement* (New York: John Wiley, 1967), pp. 477–92. For a critical review, see Paul W. Miniard and Joel B. Cohen, "An Examination of the Fishbein-Ajzen Behavioral-Intentions Model's Concepts and

Measures," *Journal of Experimental Social Psychology* (May 1981): 309–39. Other models of consumer evaluation include the ideal-brand model, which assumes that a consumer compares actual brands to her ideal brand and chooses the brand that comes closest to her ideal brand; the conjunctive model, which assumes that a consumer sets minimum acceptable levels on all the attributes and considers only the brands that meet all the minimum requirements; and the disjunctive model, which assumes that a consumer sets minimum acceptable levels on only a few attributes and eliminates those brands falling short. For a discussion of these and other models, see Green and Wind, *Multiattribute Decisions in Marketing A Measurement Approach*.

45. Harper W. Boyd Jr., Michael L. Ray, and Edward C. Strong, "An Attitudinal Framework for Advertising Strategy," *Journal of Marketing* (April 1972): 27–33.

46. Jagdish N. Sheth, "An Investigation of Relationships among Evaluative Beliefs, Affect, Behavioral Intention, and Behavior," in John U. Farley, John A. Howard, and L. Winston Ring (eds.), *Consumer Behavior: Theory and Application* (Boston: Allyn & Bacon, 1974), pp. 89–114.

47. Fishbein, "Attitudes and Prediction of Behavior."

48. Raymond A. Bauer, "Consumer Behavior as Risk Taking," in Donald F. Cox (ed.), *Risk Taking and Information Handling in Consumer Behavior* (Boston: Division of Research, Harvard Business School, 1967); James W. Taylor, "The Role of Risk in Consumer Behavior," *Journal of Marketing* (April 1974): 54–60.

49. Priscilla A. La Barbera and David Mazursky, "A Longitudinal Assessment of Consumer Satisfaction/Dissatisfaction: The Dynamic Aspect of the Cognitive Process," *Journal of Marketing Research* (November 1983): 393–404.

50. Ralph L. Day, "Modeling Choices among Alternative Responses to Dissatisfaction," *Advances in Consumer Research*, Vol. 11 (1984): 496–99. Also see Philip Kotler and Murali K. Mantrala, "Flawed Products: Consumer Responses and Marketer Strategies," *Journal of Consumer Marketing* (Summer 1985): 27–36.

51. Barry L. Bayus, "Word of Mouth: The Indirect Effects of Marketing Efforts," *Journal of Advertising Research* (June-July 1985): 31–39.

52. Albert O. Hirschman, *Exit, Voice, and Loyalty* (Cambridge, MA: Harvard University Press, 1970).

53. Mary C. Gilly and Richard W. Hansen, "Consumer Complaint Handling as a Strategic Marketing Tool," *Journal of Consumer Marketing* (Fall 1985): 5–16.

54. James H. Donnelly Jr. and John M. Ivancevich, "Post-Purchase Reinforcement and Back-Out Behavior," *Journal of Marketing Research* (August 1970): 399–400.

55. Pam Weisz, "Avon's Skin-So-Soft Bugs Out," *Brandweek*, June 6, 1994, p. 4; Beverly Beyette, "Strange but True: Cheez Whiz Works in Laundry," *Los Angles Times*, October 22, 2000.

56. C.C DiClemente and J. O.Prochaska, "Processes and Stages of Self-Change: Coping and Competence in Smoking Behavior Change," in S.Shiffman and T. A. Willis (eds.), *Coping and Substance Abuse I* (San Diego, CA: Academic Press, 1985), pp. 319–43.

57. Sandra Vandermerwe, *Customer Capitalism: Increasing Returns in New Market Spaces* (London: Nicholas Brealey, 1999), pp. 91–95.

58. Michelle Leder, "How Much Is That $100 Deductible in the Window?" *New York Times*, July 22, 2001, sec.3, p.10; Monica Khemsurov, "Smart City Navigator," *New York*, September 11, 2000, <*www.newyorkmag.com/page.cfm?page_id=3752*>.

dealing with the competition

Kotler on Marketing

Poor firms ignore their competitors; average firms copy their competitors; winning firms lead their competitors.

In this chapter, we will address the following questions:

- Who the primary competitors are
- How to ascertain their strategies, objectives, strengths and weaknesses, and reaction patterns
- How to design a competitive intelligence system
- Whether to position as market leader, challenger, follower, or nicher
- How to balance a customer versus competitor orientation

I n the two previous chapters we examined the dynamics of consumer and business markets. This chapter examines the role competition plays and how companies position themselves relative to competitors.

Today, competition is not only rife but growing more intense every year. Many U.S., European, and Japanese companies are setting up production in lower-cost countries and bringing cheaper goods to market. Because markets have become so competitive, understanding customers is no longer enough. Companies must start paying keen attention to their competitors. Successful companies design and operate systems for gathering continuous intelligence about competitors.[1]

competitive forces

Michael Porter has identified five forces that determine the intrinsic long-run profit attractiveness of a market or market segment: industry competitors, potential entrants, substitutes, buyers, and suppliers. His model is shown in Figure 9.1. The threats these forces pose are as follows:

1. *Threat of intense segment rivalry:* A segment is unattractive if it already contains numerous, strong, or aggressive competitors. It is even more unattractive if it is stable or declining, if plant capacity additions are done in large increments, if fixed costs are high, if exit barriers are high, or if competitors have high stakes in staying in the segment. These conditions will lead to frequent price wars, advertising battles, and new-product introductions, and will make it expensive to compete.

2. *Threat of new entrants:* A segment's attractiveness varies with the height of its entry and exit barriers.[2] The most attractive segment is one in which entry barriers are high and exit barriers are low (see Figure 9.2). Few new firms can enter the industry, and poor-performing firms can easily exit. When both entry and exit barriers are high, profit potential is high, but firms face more risk because poorer-performing firms stay in and fight it out. When both entry and exit barriers are low, firms easily enter and leave the industry, and the returns are stable and low. The worst case is when entry barriers are low and exit barriers are high: Here firms enter during good times but find it hard to leave during bad times. The result is chronic overcapacity and depressed earnings for all.

3. *Threat of substitute products:* A segment is unattractive when there are actual or potential substitutes for the product. Substitutes place a limit on prices and on profits. The company has to monitor price trends closely. If technology advances or competition increases in these substitute industries, prices and profits in the segment are likely to fall.

4. *Threat of buyers' growing bargaining power:* A segment is unattractive if the buyers possess strong or growing bargaining power. Buyers' bargaining power grows when they become more concentrated or organized, when the product represents a significant fraction of the buyers' costs, when the product is undifferentiated, when the buyers' switching costs are low, when buyers are price sensitive because of low profits, or when buyers can integrate upstream. To protect

---

figure **9.1**

Five Forces Determining Segment Structural Attractiveness

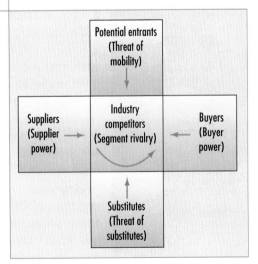

Source: Reprinted with the permission of the Free Press, an imprint of Simon & Schuster, from Michael E. Porter, *Competitive Advantage: Creating and Sustaining Superior Performance.* Copyright 1985 by Michael E. Porter.

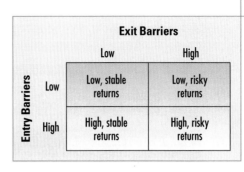

figure **9.2**

Barriers and Profitability

themselves, sellers might select buyers who have the least power to negotiate or switch suppliers. A better defense consists of developing superior offers that strong buyers cannot refuse.

5. *Threat of suppliers' growing bargaining power:* A segment is unattractive if the company's suppliers are able to raise prices or reduce quantity supplied. Suppliers tend to be powerful when they are concentrated or organized, when there are few substitutes, when the supplied product is an important input, when the costs of switching suppliers are high, and when the suppliers can integrate downstream. The best defenses are to build win–win relations with suppliers or use multiple supply sources.

identifying competitors

It would seem a simple task for a company to identify its competitors. Coca-Cola knows that PepsiCo is its major competitor; Sony knows that Matsushita is a major competitor;[3] and Petsmart.com knows that Petco.com is a major competitor. However, the range of a company's actual and potential competitors is in reality much broader. A company is more likely to be hurt by emerging competitors or new technologies than by current competitors.

In recent years, many businesses failed to look to the Internet for their most formidable competitors. A few years back, Barnes & Noble and Borders bookstore chains were competing to see who could build the most megastores, where book browsers could sink into comfortable couches and sip cappuccino. While they were deciding which products to stock, Jeffrey Bezos was building an online empire called Amazon.com. Bezos's cyber bookstore had the advantage of offering an almost unlimited selection of books without the expense of stocking inventory. Now both Barnes & Noble and Borders are playing catch-up in building their own online stores. Yet, "competitor myopia"—a focus on current competitors rather than latent ones—has rendered some businesses extinct:[4]

Encyclopaedia Britannica In 1996, 230-year-old Encyclopaedia Britannica dismissed its entire home sales force after the arrival of its $5-per-month subscription Internet site made the idea of owning a 32-volume set of books for $1,250 less appealing to parents. Britannica decided to create an online site after realizing that computer-savvy kids most often sought information online or on CD-ROMs such as Microsoft's Encarta, which sold for $50. What really smarts is that Britannica had the opportunity to partner with Microsoft in providing content for Encarta but refused. In 1999, Britannica made its entire encyclopedia available online at no cost and began earning revenues via Web advertising sales.[5]

Other publishing businesses feel similarly threatened by the Internet. Web sites that offer jobs, real estate listings, and automobiles online threaten newspapers,

marketing for the **new economy**

Displaced but Not Discouraged: What Happens When E-Commerce Edges Out the Middleman

Belair/Empress Travel in Bowie, Maryland, typifies the kind of business most threatened by the advent of online selling. In addition to having seen airline commissions drop from 62 percent of its revenue to 30 percent, Belair/Empress must now compete against giant online travel sites, such as Expedia or Travelocity, which allow consumers to surf the Web for rock-bottom ticket prices. Airlines joined the online sales fray as well. Every major airline now has a Web site offering online reservations, as well as information on routes and schedules, special deals, and other travel arrangements.

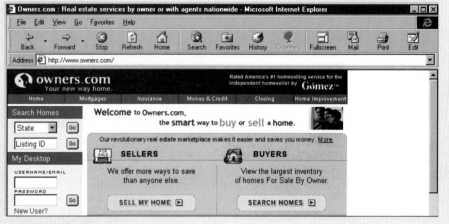

www.owners.com: "The smart way to buy or sell a home."

By facilitating direct contact between buyers and sellers, the Internet is displacing the travel agents, insurance brokers, car dealers, real estate brokers, stockbrokers, and headhunters who have traditionally been the intermediaries. There is even a fancy 17-letter word to describe the demise of the middleman: disintermediation. Here is a short list of some online pioneers that have helped bring it about.

www.expedia.com www.travelocity.com	Not only offer no-hassle ways to purchase airline tickets but also have links to and information about restaurants, hotels, car rentals, and local sights pertinent to a particular destination.
www.carpoint.com www.autobytel.com www.edmunds.com	Provide services ranging from pricing reports and test-drive reviews to leasing options and links to financing sites.
www.owners.com	Real estate sellers enter basic price and property data and even extras like pictures for a small fee, and buyers search over 200,000 listings in all 50 states. If buyer and seller link up, the price for both sides reflects savings on the commission.
www.lifequote.com	Visitors to the site can request life insurance quotes from a number of national insurance companies, compare policies and prices, and choose the best insurance plan.
www.monster.com	This online job market network connects employers with prospective employees. The site lists over 450,000 jobs and attracts more than 4 million unique visitors every quarter.

What can traditional businesses do when facing digital competition? At one end are those who wholeheartedly embrace the Internet. Palo Alto travel agent Bruce Yoxsimer teamed with Internet guru Dan Whaley to set up shop on the Web and launched Internet Travel Network (www.itn.net). In 1995, the first Web site for making travel reservations. Since then, the company (now called GetThere and owned by Sabre Holdings), has helped people book more than 10 million trips over the Internet. Others completely reject the Internet business model. Judy McLoughlin, owner of children's bookstore Reading in the

which derive a huge portion of their revenue from classified employment, real estate, and automobile ads. When you can get free news content online, why should you buy a newspaper? The businesses with the most to fear from Internet technology are the world's middlemen. (See "Marketing for the New Economy: Displaced but Not Discouraged: What Happens When E-Commerce Edges Out the Middleman.")

We can examine competition from both an industry and a marketing point of view.

Park in suburban Detroit says, "I won't want to buy or sell a book I cannot touch." McLoughlin tries to gain an edge through attentiveness to customers. Most businesses fall somewhere in between. Belair/Empress owner Phil Davidoff is now a market nicher specializing in cruises, package tours, and group vacations. The reformulated business is now replete with a Web address (www.belairtrav.com).

Many, such as brokerage firm Charles Schwab, are using the Web. The nation's largest discount stockbroker jumped onto the Internet to face a horde of price-cutting e-commerce competitors who had been there first, including E-Trade and Ameritrade. Not only did Schwab face cheaper competitors, it also had to cannibalize its own accounts. The gamble paid off because the volume of trades grew tremendously. The key to Schwab's success was providing a wealth of financial and company information to help customers research and manage their accounts. The company acquired more than 7 million customer accounts and propelled Schwab to record revenues, which surpassed $6 billion in 2000.

In truth, most consumers appreciate hand-holding from real persons, especially when purchasing such complex or costly products and services as cars, life insurance, or a three-week vacation that includes stops in the Galapagos Islands and Tierra del Fuego. Although the Internet has created a new breed of competitors for traditional middlemen, it has also opened up a great opportunity for a human intermediary to lead consumers through the maze.

GetThere.com launched as the Internet Travel Network in 1995, was the first company to book trips over the Web.

Sources: Marcia Stepanek, "Rebirth of the Salesman," BusinessWeek, June 22, 1998, p. 146; Evan J. Schwartz, "How Middlemen Can Come Out on Top," BusinessWeek, February 9, 1998, pp. ENT4–ENT7; Bernard Warner, "Prepare for Takeoff," Brandweek, January 19, 1998, pp. 38–40; Ira Lewis, Janjaap Semeijn, and Alexander Talalayevsky, "The Impact of Information Technology on Travel Agents," Transportation Journal (Summer 1998): 20–25; Mary J. Cronin, "The Travel Agents' Dilemma," Fortune, May 11, 1998, pp. 163–64; John Hughes, "Auto Dealers See Future in Internet," Marketing News, March 2, 1998, p. 13; Saroja Girishankar, "Virtual Markets Create New Roles for Distributors," Internetweek, April 6, 1998, p. S10; Laurie J. Flynn, "Eating Your Young," Context (Summer 1998): 45–51; <www.schwab.com>.

industry concept of competition

What exactly is an industry? An **industry** is a group of firms that offer a product or class of products that are close substitutes for one another. Industries are classified according to number of sellers; degree of product differentiation; presence or absence of entry, mobility, and exit barriers; cost structure; degree of vertical integration; and degree of globalization.

NUMBER OF SELLERS AND DEGREE OF DIFFERENTIATION   The starting point for describing an industry is to specify the number of sellers and whether the product is homogeneous or highly differentiated. These characteristics give rise to four industry structure types:

1. *Pure monopoly:* Only one firm provides a certain product or service in a certain country or area (local electricity or gas company). An unregulated monopolist might charge a high price, do little or no advertising, and offer minimal service. If partial substitutes are available and there is some danger of competition, the monopolist might invest in more service and technology. A regulated monopolist is required to charge a lower price and provide more service as a matter of public interest.

2. *Oligopoly:* A small number of (usually) large firms produce products that range from highly differentiated to standardized. *Pure oligopoly* consists of a few companies producing essentially the same commodity (oil, steel). Such companies would find it hard to charge anything more than the going price. If competitors match on price and services, the only way to gain a competitive advantage is through lower costs. *Differentiated oligopoly* consists of a few companies producing products (autos, cameras) partially differentiated along lines of quality, features, styling, or services. Each competitor may seek leadership in one of these major attributes, attract the customers favoring that attribute, and charge a price premium for that attribute.

3. *Monopolistic competition:* Many competitors are able to differentiate their offers in whole or in part (restaurants, beauty shops). Competitors focus on market segments where they can meet customer needs in a superior way and command a price premium.

4. *Pure competition:* Many competitors offer the same product and service (stock market, commodity market). Because there is no basis for differentiation, competitors' prices will be the same. No competitor will advertise unless advertising can create psychological differentiation (cigarettes, beer), in which case it would be more proper to describe the industry as monopolistically competitive.

An industry's competitive structure can change over time.

Palm Pilot   When Palm Computing innovated the Palm Pilot, a Personal Digital Assistant (PDA) with a touch-screen interface, it rolled out over 1 million units in 18 months and found itself an instant monopolist. There was simply no other product like it on the market. Soon, however, a few other companies entered the PDA market, turning it into an oligopoly. The market took on a monopolistically competitive structure by 2000, as PDAs proliferated from a variety of companies such as Sony, Handspring, Hewlett-Packard, and Casio. When demand growth slows, however, we can expect some competitors to exit, returning the market to an oligopoly dominated by a few key competitors.[6]

ENTRY, MOBILITY, AND EXIT BARRIERS   Industries differ greatly in ease of entry. It is easy to open a new restaurant but difficult to enter the aircraft industry. Major *entry barriers* include high capital requirements; economies of scale; patents and licensing requirements; scarce locations, raw materials, or distributors; and reputation requirements. Even after a firm enters an industry, it might face *mobility barriers* when it tries to enter more attractive market segments.

Firms often face *exit barriers,*[7] such as legal or moral obligations to customers, creditors, and employees; government restrictions; low asset salvage value due to overspecialization or obsolescence; lack of alternative opportunities; high vertical integration; and emotional barriers. Many firms stay in an industry as long as they cover their variable costs and some or all of their fixed costs. Their continued presence, however, dampens profits for everyone.

Even if some firms do not want to exit the industry, they might decrease their size. Companies can try to reduce shrinkage barriers to help ailing competitors get smaller gracefully.[8]

COST STRUCTURE   Each industry has a certain cost burden that shapes much of its strategic conduct. For example, steelmaking involves heavy manufacturing and raw-material costs; toy manufacturing involves heavy distribution and marketing costs.

Firms strive to reduce their largest costs. The integrated steel company with the most cost-efficient plant will have a great advantage over other integrated steel companies; but even they have higher costs than the new steel minimills.

DEGREE OF VERTICAL INTEGRATION Companies find it advantageous to integrate backward or forward (**vertical integration**). Major oil producers carry on oil exploration, oil drilling, oil refining, chemical manufacture, and service-station operation. Vertical integration often lowers costs, and the company gains a larger share of the value-added stream. In addition, vertically integrated firms can manipulate prices and costs in different parts of the value chain to earn profits where taxes are lowest. There can be disadvantages, such as high costs in certain parts of the value chain and a lack of flexibility. Companies are increasingly questioning how vertical they should be. Many are outsourcing more activities, especially those that can be done better and more cheaply by specialist firms.

DEGREE OF GLOBALIZATION Some industries are highly local (such as lawn care); others are global (such as oil, aircraft engines, cameras). Companies in global industries need to compete on a global basis if they are to achieve economies of scale and keep up with the latest advances in technology.[9]

market concept of competition

In addition to the industry approach, we can identify competitors using the market approach: Competitors are companies that satisfy the same customer need. For example, a customer who buys a word-processing package really wants "writing ability"—a need that can also be satisfied by pencils, pens, or typewriters.

The market concept of competition reveals a broader set of actual and potential competitors. Rayport and Jaworski suggest profiling a company's direct and indirect competitors by mapping the buyer's steps in obtaining and using the product. Figure 9.3 illustrates

figure **9.3**

Competitor Map – Eastman Kodak

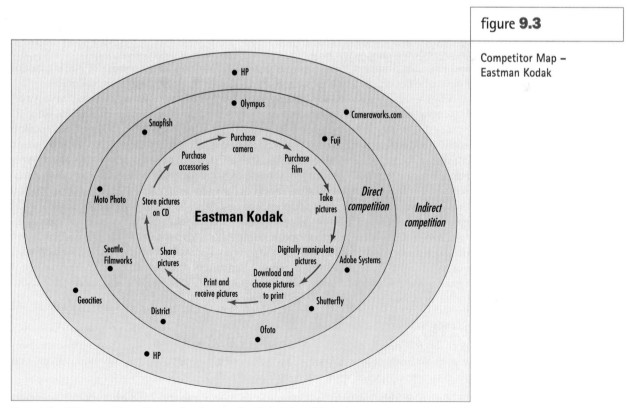

Source: Jeffrey F. Rayport and Bernard J. Jaworski, *e-Commerce* (New York: McGraw-Hill, 2001), p. 53.

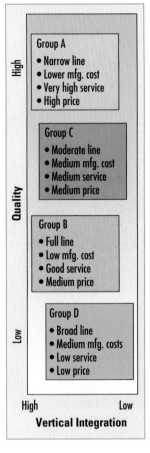

their *competitor map* of Eastman Kodak in the film business. In the center is a listing of consumer activities: buying a camera, buying film, taking pictures, and so on. The first outer ring lists Kodak's main competitors with respect to each consumer activity: Olympus for buying a camera, Fuji for purchasing film, and so on. The second outer ring lists indirect competitors—HP, Intel, cameraworks.com—who may become direct competitors. This type of analysis highlights both the opportunities and the challenges a company faces.[10]

analyzing competitors

Once a company identifies its primary competitors, it must ascertain their characteristics, specifically, their strategies, objectives, strengths and weaknesses, and reaction patterns.

strategies

A group of firms following the same strategy in a given target market is called a **strategic group**.[11] Suppose a company wants to enter the major appliance industry. What is its strategic group? It develops the chart shown in Figure 9.4 and discovers four strategic groups based on product quality and level of vertical integration. Group A has one competitor (Maytag), group B has three (General Electric, Whirlpool, and Sears), group C has four, and group D has two. Important insights emerge from this exercise. First, the height of the entry barriers differs for each group. Second, if the company successfully enters a group, the members of that group become its key competitors.

A company must continuously monitor competitors' strategies. When U.S. automakers just about caught up in mechanical quality, Japanese automakers shifted to sensory qualities. A Ford engineer explained: "It's the turn-signal lever that doesn't wobble . . . the speed of the power window up and down . . . the feel of a climate-control knob . . . this is the next nuance of customer competition."[12]

objectives

Once a company has identified its main competitors and their strategies, it must ask: What is each competitor seeking in the marketplace? What drives each competitor's behavior? Many factors shape a competitor's objectives, including size, history, current management, and financial situation. If the competitor is a division of a larger company, it is important to know whether the parent company is running it for growth, profits, or milking it.[13]

One useful initial assumption is that competitors strive to maximize profits. However, companies differ in the emphasis they put on short-term versus long-term profits. Most U.S. firms operate on a short-run model, largely because current performance is judged by stockholders who might lose confidence, sell their stock, and cause the company's cost of capital to rise. Japanese firms operate largely on a market-share-maximization model. They receive much of their funds from banks at a lower interest rate and in the past have readily accepted lower profits. An alternative assumption is that each competitor pursues some mix of objectives: current profitability, market-share growth, cash flow, technological leadership, service leadership.

Finally, a company must monitor competitors' expansion plans. Figure 9.5 shows a product-market battlefield map for the personal computer industry. Dell, which started out as a strong force in selling personal computers to individual users, is now a major force in the commercial and industrial market. Other incumbents may try to set up mobility barriers to Dell's further expansion.

strengths and weaknesses

A company needs to gather information on each competitor's strengths and weaknesses. According to the Arthur D. Little consulting firm, a company will occupy one of six competitive positions in the target market:[14]

1. *Dominant:* This firm controls the behavior of other competitors and has a wide choice of strategic options.

2. *Strong:* This firm can take independent action without endangering its long-term position and can maintain its long-term position regardless of competitors' actions.

3. *Favorable:* This firm has an exploitable strength and a more-than-average opportunity to improve its position.

4. *Tenable:* This firm is performing at a sufficiently satisfactory level to warrant continuing in business, but it exists at the sufferance of the dominant company and has a less-than-average opportunity to improve its position.

5. *Weak:* This firm has unsatisfactory performance, but an opportunity exists for improvement. The firm must change or else exit.

6. *Nonviable:* This firm has unsatisfactory performance and no opportunity for improvement.

This assessment helped one company decide whom to attack in the programmable-controls market:

> The company faced three entrenched competitors: Allen Bradley, Texas Instruments, and Gould. Its research showed that Allen Bradley had an excellent reputation for technological leadership; Texas Instruments had low costs and engaged in bloody battles for market share; and Gould did a good job but not a distinguished job. The company concluded that its best target was Gould.

Table 9.1 shows the results of a company survey that asked customers to rate its three competitors, A, B, and C, on five attributes. Competitor A turns out to be well-known and respected for producing high-quality products sold by a good sales force. Competitor A is poor at providing product availability and technical assistance. Competitor B is good across the board and excellent in product availability and sales force. Competitor C rates poor to fair on most attributes. This suggests that the company could attack Competitor A

	Customer Awareness	Product Quality	Product Availability	Technical Assistance	Selling Staff
Competitor A	E	E	P	P	G
Competitor B	G	G	E	G	E
Competitor C	F	P	G	F	F

Note: E = excellent, G = good, F = fair, P = poor.

table **9.2**

Market Share, Mind
Share, and Heart
Share

	Market Share			Mind Share			Heart Share		
	2000	2001	2002	2000	2001	2002	2000	2001	2002
Competitor A	50%	47%	44%	60%	58%	54%	45%	42%	39%
Competitor B	30	34	37	30	31	35	44	47	53
Competitor C	20	19	19	10	11	11	11	11	8

on product availability and technical assistance and Competitor C on almost anything, but should not attack B, which has no glaring weaknesses.

In general, a company should monitor three variables when analyzing competitors:

1. *Share of market:* The competitor's share of the target market.
2. *Share of mind:* The percentage of customers who named the competitor in responding to the statement "Name the first company that comes to mind in this industry."
3. *Share of heart:* The percentage of customers who named the competitor in responding to the statement "Name the company from which you would prefer to buy the product."

There is an interesting relationship among these three measures. Table 9.2 shows the numbers for these three measures for the three competitors listed in Table 9.1. Competitor A enjoys the highest market share but is slipping. Its mind share and heart share are also slipping, probably because it is not providing good product availability and technical assistance. Competitor B is steadily gaining market share, probably due to strategies that are increasing its mind share and heart share. Competitor C seems to be stuck at a low level of market share, mind share, and heart share, probably because of its poor product and marketing attributes. We could generalize as follows: *Companies that make steady gains in mind share and heart share will inevitably make gains in market share and profitability.*

To improve market share, many companies benchmark their most successful competitors, as well as world-class performers. The technique and its benefits are described in "Marketing Memo: How Benchmarking Helps Improve Competitive Performance."

reaction patterns

Companies react differently to competitive assaults. Some are slow to respond. Others respond only to certain types of attacks, such as price cuts. Still others strike back swiftly and strongly to any assault. Some industries are marked by relative accord among the competitors, and others by constant fighting. Bruce Henderson thinks that much depends on the industry's "competitive equilibrium." Here are his observations:[15]

1. *If competitors are nearly identical and make their living in the same way, then their competitive equilibrium is unstable.* Perpetual conflict characterizes industries such as steel or newsprint, where differentiation is hard to maintain. Equilibrium will be upset if any firm lowers its price to relieve overcapacity. Price wars are frequent.
2. *If a single major factor is the critical factor, then the competitive equilibrium is unstable.* This is the case in industries where cost-differentiation opportunities exist through economies of scale, advanced technology, or experience. Any company that achieves a cost breakthrough can cut its price and win market share at the expense of others, who can defend their market shares only at great cost. Price wars are frequent as a result of cost breakthroughs.
3. *If multiple factors may be critical factors, then it is possible for each competitor to have some advantage and be differentially attractive to some customers. The more factors that may provide an advantage, the more competitors who can coexist. Competitors all have their segment, defined by the preference for the factor trade-offs they offer.* Multiple factors exist in industries that can differentiate quality, service, convenience, and so on.

Marketing
MEMO

How Benchmarking Helps Improve Competitive Performance

Benchmarking is the art of learning from companies that perform certain tasks better than other companies. There can be as much as a tenfold difference in the quality, speed, and cost performance of a world-class company and an average company. The aim of benchmarking is to copy or improve on "best practices," either within an industry or across industries. Benchmarking involves seven steps: (1) Determine which functions to benchmark; (2) identify the key performance variables to measure; (3) identify the best-in-class companies; (4) measure performance of best-in-class companies; (5) measure the company's performance; (6) specify programs and actions to close the gap; and (7) implement and monitor results.

How can companies identify best-practice companies? A good starting point is asking customers, suppliers, and distributors whom they rate as doing the best job. In addition, major consulting firms have built voluminous files of best practices. The accounting and consulting firm Arthur Andersen has invested millions creating a Global Best Practices Knowledge Base to uncover breakthrough thinking at world-class companies. Some of the findings are condensed in the book *Best Practices: Building Your Business with Customer-Focused Solutions*. Data can also be accessed at the Andersen Web site www.globalbestpractices.com

Sources: Robert C. Camp, *Benchmarking: The Search for Industry-Best Practices that Lead to Superior Performance* (White Plains, NY: Quality Resources, 1989); Michael J. Spendolini, *The Benchmarking Book* (New York: Amacom, 1992); Jeremy Main, "How to Steal the Best Ideas Around," *Fortune*, October 19, 1992; A. Steven Walleck et al., "Benchmarking World Class Performance," *McKinsey Quarterly*, no. 1 (1990): 3–24; Otis Port, "Beg, Borrow—and Benchmark," *BusinessWeek*, November 30, 1992, pp. 74–75; Stanley Brown, "Don't Innovate—Imitate!" *Sales & Marketing Management* (January 1995): 24–25; Tom Stemerg, "Spies Like Us," *Inc.* (August 1998): 45–49. See also <www.benchmarking.org>; Michael Hope, "Contrast and Compare," *Marketing*, August 28, 1997, pp. 11–13; Robert Hiebeler, Thomas B. Kelly, and Charles Ketteman, *Best Practices: Building Your Business with Customer-Focused Solutions* (New York: Arthur Andersen/Simon & Schuster, 1998).

4. *The fewer the number of critical competitive variables, the fewer the number of competitors.* If only one factor is critical, then no more than two or three competitors are likely to coexist.

5. *A ratio of 2 to 1 in market share between any two competitors seems to be the equilibrium point at which it is neither practical nor advantageous for either competitor to increase or decrease share.* At this level, the costs of extra promotion or distribution would outweigh the gains in market share.

designing the competitive intelligence system
four main steps

There are four main steps in designing a competitive intelligence system: setting up the system, collecting the data, evaluating and analyzing the data, and disseminating information and responding to queries.

SETTING UP THE SYSTEM   The first step calls for identifying vital types of competitive information, identifying the best sources of this information, and assigning a person who will manage the system and its services. In smaller companies that cannot afford to set up a formal competitive intelligence office, specific executives should be assigned to watch specific competitors. A manager who used to work for a competitor would closely follow that competitor and serve as the in-house expert on that competitor. Any manager who needs to know about a specific competitor would contact the corresponding in-house expert.[16]

COLLECTING THE DATA   The data are collected on a continuous basis from the field (sales force, channels, suppliers, market research firms, trade associations), from people who do business with competitors, from observing competitors, and from published data. In addition, a vast store of data on both domestic and overseas companies is available via CD-ROM and online services.

The Internet is creating a new arsenal for those skilled at gathering intelligence. Now companies place volumes of information on their Web sites to attract customers, partners, suppliers, or franchisees, and that same information is available to competitors at the click of a mouse. Press releases that never made it into the media are published on Web sites, so you can keep abreast of new products and organizational changes. Help wanted ads posted on the Web quickly let you know competitors' expansion priorities.

Marketing
MEMO

Outsmarting the Competition with Guerrilla Marketing Research

Directories, annual reports, brochures, and press releases are good sources of historical information, but they are often not good enough if a company hopes to compete against a recently introduced new product. The following eight techniques could give a company a lead of two or more years on the competition:

1. *Watch the small companies in your industry and related industries.* True innovation often comes from small, inconspicuous companies. Who would have thought, for instance, that Arizona Iced Tea from Ferolito Vultagio & Sons of Brooklyn would make serious inroads in the soft-drink and fruit juice markets?
2. *Follow patent applications.* Not all applications lead to products. Still, patent filings indicate a company's direction. Patent application information can be found in various online and CD-ROM databases.
3. *Track the job changes and other activities of industry experts.* Who have the competitors hired? Have the new hires written papers or made presentations at conferences? What is the value of their expertise to the competitor? If the company gains this expertise, will it affect your firm's position? For instance, when a pulp and paper company hires a marketing director with significant experience in Eastern Europe, the company could be looking toward that market.
4. *Be aware of licensing agreements.* These provide useful information about where, how, and when a company can sell a new product.
5. *Monitor the formation of business contracts and alliances.* These pose new threats to the firm.
6. *Find out about new business practices that are saving your competitors money.* What does it mean if a competing insurance company has bought thousands of laptops and portable printers? Very likely, that its claims adjusters soon will be writing estimates and generating checks on the spot, saving time and overhead.
7. *Follow changes in pricing.* For instance, when luxury items become cheap enough for the mass market, they supplant some of the more expensive equipment, as when camcorders supplanted home movie cameras in the late 1980s.
8. *Be aware of social changes and changes in consumer tastes and preferences that could alter the business environment.* Consumers are fickle. During the past 15 years, jogging has given way to aerobics, and now walking is a preferred leisure activity. By anticipating changing fads, some shoe companies were able to introduce new types of athletic shoes.

Source: Adapted from Ruth Winett, "Guerrilla Marketing Research Outsmarts the Competition," *Marketing News,* January 2, 1995, p. 33.

It is not only company-sponsored Web sites that hold the richest competitor intelligence booty: Trade association sites also hold valuable nuggets of information. When he was controller of Stone Container's specialty-packaging division, Gary Owen visited a trade association Web site and noticed that a rival had won an award for a new process using ultraviolet-resistant lacquers. The site revealed the machines' configuration and run rate, which Stone's engineers used to figure out how to replicate the process.[17]

Although most information-gathering techniques are legal, some involve questionable ethics. Companies have been known to advertise and hold interviews for nonexistent jobs in order to pump competitors' employees for information. Although it is illegal for a company to photograph a competitor's plant from the air, aerial photos are often on file with the U.S. Geological Survey or Environmental Protection Agency. Some companies even buy their competitors' garbage. Once it has left the competitor's premises, refuse is legally considered abandoned property.[18] Companies need to develop ways of acquiring information about competitors without violating legal or ethical standards. (See "Marketing Memo: Outsmarting the Competition with Guerrilla Marketing Research.")

EVALUATING AND ANALYZING THE DATA   The data are checked for validity and reliability, interpreted, and organized.

DISSEMINATING INFORMATION AND RESPONDING   Key information is sent to relevant decision makers, and managers' inquiries are answered. With a well-designed system, company managers receive timely information about competitors via e-mail, phone calls, bulletins, newsletters, and reports. Managers can also contact the market intelligence department or colleagues on the company's intranet when they need help interpreting a competitor's sudden move, when they need to know a competitor's weaknesses and strengths, or when they want to discuss a likely response to a contemplated company move.

selecting competitors

With good competitive intelligence, managers will find it easier to formulate competitive strategies. They can begin with a technique called customer value analysis.

CUSTOMER VALUE ANALYSIS (CVA)   We believe customers choose between competitive brand offerings on the basis of which delivers the most customer value. Customer value is given by:

Customer Value = Customer Benefits − Customer Costs

Customer benefits include *product benefits, service benefits, personnel benefits,* and *image benefits.* We will assume the customer can judge the relative benefit level or worth of different brands. Suppose the customer is considering three brands, A, B, and C, and judges the customer benefits to be worth $150, $140, and $135, respectively. If the customer costs are the same, the customer would clearly choose brand A.

However, the costs are rarely the same. In addition to *purchase price,* costs include *acquisition costs, usage costs, maintenance costs, ownership costs,* and *disposal costs.* Often a customer will buy a more expensive brand because that particular brand will impose lower costs of the other kinds. Consider Table 9.3. A, the highest-priced brand, also involves a lower total cost than lower-priced brands B and C. Clearly, supplier A has done a good job of reducing customers' other costs.

Now we can compare the customer value of the three brands:

Customer value of A = $150 − $130 = $20
Customer value of B = $140 − $135 = $5
Customer value of C = $135 − $140 = −$5

The customer will prefer brand A both because the benefit level is higher and the customer costs are lower, but this does not have to be the case. Suppose A decided to charge $120 instead of $100 to take advantage of its higher perceived benefit level. Then A's customer cost would have been $150 instead of $130 and just offset its higher perceived benefit. Brand A, because of its greed, would lose the sale to brand B.

Very often, managers conduct a **customer value analysis** to reveal the company's strengths and weaknesses relative to various competitors. The major steps in such an analysis are:

1. *Identify the major attributes customers value.* Customers are asked what attributes and performance levels they look for in choosing a product and vendors.
2. *Assess the quantitative importance of the different attributes.* Customers are asked to rate the importance of the different attributes. If the customers diverge too much in their ratings, they should be clustered into different segments.

	A	B	C
Price	$100	$ 90	$ 80
Acquisition costs	15	25	30
Usage costs	4	7	10
Maintenance costs	2	3	7
Ownership costs	3	3	5
Disposal costs	6	5	8
Total Cost	$130	$135	$140

table **9.3**

Customer Costs of Three Brands

3. *Assess the company's and competitors' performances on the different customer values against their rated importance.* Customers describe where they see the company's and competitors' performances on each attribute.

4. *Examine how customers in a specific segment rate the company's performance against a specific major competitor on an attribute-by-attribute basis.* If the company's offer exceeds the competitor's offer on all important attributes, the company can charge a higher price (thereby earning higher profits), or it can charge the same price and gain more market share.

5. *Monitor customer values over time.* The company must periodically redo its studies of customer values and competitors' standings as the economy, technology, and features change.

CLASSES OF COMPETITORS   After the company has conducted its customer value analysis, it can focus its attack on one of the following classes of competitors: strong versus weak, close versus distant, and "good" versus "bad."

Strong versus Weak   Most companies aim their shots at weak competitors, because this requires fewer resources per share point gained. Yet, in attacking weak competitors, the firm will achieve little in the way of improved capabilities. The firm should also compete with strong competitors to keep up with the best. Even strong competitors have some weaknesses.

Close versus Distant   Most companies compete with competitors who resemble them the most. Chevrolet competes with Ford, not with Jaguar. Yet companies should also recognize distant competitors. Coca-Cola states that its number one competitor is tap water, not Pepsi. U.S. Steel worries more about plastic and aluminum than about Bethlehem Steel; and museums now worry about theme parks and malls.

At the same time, the company should avoid trying to destroy the closest competitor. Porter cites an example of a counterproductive victory:

> Bausch and Lomb in the late 1970s moved aggressively against other soft contact lens manufacturers with great success. However, this led each weak competitor to sell out to larger firms, such as Revlon, Johnson & Johnson, and Schering-Plough, with the result that Bausch and Lomb now faced much larger competitors.

"Good" versus "Bad"   Every industry contains "good" and "bad" competitors.[19] A company should support its good competitors and attack its bad competitors. Good competitors play by the industry's rules; they make realistic assumptions about the industry's growth potential; they set prices in reasonable relation to costs; they favor a healthy industry; they limit themselves to a portion or segment of the industry; they motivate others to lower costs or improve differentiation; and they accept the general level of their share and profits. Bad competitors try to buy share rather than earn it; they take large risks; they invest in overcapacity; and they upset industrial equilibrium.

designing competitive strategies

We can gain further insight by classifying firms by the roles they play in the target market: leader, challenger, follower, or nicher. Suppose a market is occupied by the firms shown in Figure 9.6. Forty percent of the market is in the hands of a *market leader*; another 30 percent is in the hands of a *market challenger*; another 20 percent is in the hands of a *market follower*, a firm that is willing to maintain its market share and not rock the boat. The remaining 10 percent is in the hands of *market nichers*, firms that serve small market segments not being served by larger firms.

market-leader strategies

Many industries contain one firm that is the acknowledged market leader. This firm has the largest market share in the relevant product market, and usually leads the other firms in price changes, new-product introductions, distribution coverage, and promotional intensity. Some of the best-known market leaders are Kodak (photography),

Microsoft (computer software), Intel (microprocessors), Procter & Gamble (consumer packaged goods), Caterpillar (earth-moving equipment), Coca-Cola (soft drinks), McDonald's (fast food), and Gillette (razor blades).

Unless a dominant firm enjoys a legal monopoly, its life is not altogether easy. It must maintain constant vigilance. A product innovation may come along and hurt the leader (Nokia's and Ericsson's digital cell phones taking over from Motorola's analog models). The leader might spend conservatively whereas a challenger spends liberally (Montgomery Ward's loss of its retail dominance to Sears after World War II). The leader might misjudge its competition and find itself left behind (as Sears did when it underestimated Kmart and Wal-Mart). The dominant firm might look old-fashioned against new and peppier rivals (Levi's ceding ground to more stylish megabrands like Tommy Hilfiger, Calvin Klein, and GAP). The dominant firm's costs might rise excessively and hurt its profits.

Remaining number one calls for action on three fronts. First, the firm must find ways to expand total market demand. Second, the firm must protect its current market share through good defensive and offensive actions. Third, the firm can try to increase its market share, even if market size remains constant.

EXPANDING THE TOTAL MARKET   The dominant firm normally gains the most when the total market expands. If Americans increase their picture taking, Kodak stands to gain the most because it sells over 80 percent of the country's film. If Kodak can convince more Americans to buy cameras and take pictures, or to take pictures on other occasions besides holidays, or to take more pictures on each occasion, Kodak will benefit considerably. In general, the market leader should look for new users, new uses, and more usage of its products.

New Users   Every product class has the potential of attracting buyers who are unaware of the product or who are resisting it because of price or lack of certain features. A company can search for new users among three groups: those who might use it but do not *(market-penetration strategy)*, those who have never used it *(new-market segment strategy)*, or those who live elsewhere *(geographical-expansion strategy)*.

Selfridges   London retailer Selfridges, founded in 1909 by an American entrepreneur, undertook a $139 million, seven-year makeover of its Oxford Street flagship store when it became evident that big-spending young fashion enthusiasts had all but abandoned the store. Selfridges restored the interior to reflect the building's classical heritage, eliminated the hardware section, added high-fashion labels like Prada and Valentino, plus displays for wireless devices and other high-tech items. The Oxford Street store reported an 11 percent increase in sales for the first six weeks of 2001, a time during which many competitors suffered.[20]

New Uses   Markets can be expanded through discovering and promoting new uses for the product. For example, the average American eats dry breakfast cereal three mornings a week. Cereal manufacturers would gain if they could promote cereal eating on other occasions—perhaps as a snack.

In many cases, customers deserve credit for discovering new uses. Vaseline petroleum jelly started out as a lubricant in machine shops. Over the years, consumers have reported many new uses for the product, including a skin ointment, a healing agent, and a hair dressing. Arm & Hammer, the baking soda brand made by Church and Dwight, had downward-drifting sales for 125 years! Then the company discovered consumers used it as a refrigerator deodorant. It launched a heavy promotion campaign focusing on this single use and succeeded in getting half of the homes in America to place an open box of baking soda in the refrigerator. A few years later, Arm & Hammer discovered consumers who used its product to quell kitchen grease fires, and it promoted this use with great results.

figure **9.6**

Hypothetical Market Structure

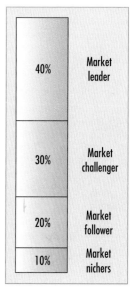

More Usage   A third market-expansion strategy is to convince people to use more product per use occasion. Shampoo manufacturers convince consumers to use more shampoo by printing the directions "lather, rinse, and repeat" on every bottle when no one really knows if there is any benefit to washing one's hair twice![21] Consider what Michelin did.

Michelin Tire Company (French)   Michelin wanted to encourage French car owners to drive their cars more miles per year—thus leading to more tire replacement. It conceived the idea of rating French restaurants on a three-star system. Michelin promoted the names of many of the best restaurants in the south of France, leading Parisians to take weekend drives to Provence and the Riviera. Michelin also published guidebooks with maps and lists of sights along the way to encourage additional driving.

Companies have long used a strategy to get people to replace products. Called "planned obsolescence," it is the idea of spurring repeat sales by making goods that break down or wear out. Ever wonder why no one has yet marketed a lightbulb that never burns out or a battery that never wears down? Now manufacturers have taken this concept further by making products that actually "tell" consumers when they are breaking down or wearing out. Gillette's new Mach3 shaving system is a prime example.

Gillette   Each Gillette Mach3 cartridge features a blue stripe that slowly fades with repeated use. After about a dozen shaves, it fades away completely, signaling the user to move on to the next cartridge or in Gillette's more subtle wording, this "alerts men that they're not getting the optimal Mach3 shaving experience," regardless of whether the blade really needs replacing. As Gillette executive Robert King said bluntly, "I wish we could get men to change the cartridge every 4 days. The more they change it, the more we sell."

DEFENDING MARKET SHARE   While trying to expand total market size, the dominant firm must continuously defend its current business. The leader is like a large elephant being attacked by a swarm of bees. Coca-Cola must constantly guard against PepsiCo; Gillette against Bic; Hertz against Avis; McDonald's against Burger King; General Motors against Ford; and Kodak against Fuji.[22] Sometimes the competitor is domestic; sometimes it is foreign.

Kodak and Fuji   For more than 100 years, Eastman Kodak has been known for its easy-to-use cameras, high-quality film, and solid profits. During the past decade, Kodak's sales have flattened and its profits have declined. Kodak has been outpaced by more innovative competitors, many of whom are Japanese, who introduced or improved on 35-mm cameras, videocameras, and digital cameras. Then Fuji Photo Film Company moved in on Kodak's bread-and-butter color film business by offering high-quality color films at prices 10 percent lower than Kodak's. Kodak fought back fiercely, matching Fuji's lower prices, improving its products, and outspending Fuji 20 to 1 on advertising and promotion. Kodak successfully defended its U.S. market position, and by the early 1990s, its share of the domestic film market had stabilized at 80 percent.

But Kodak took the battle a step further by setting up a separate subsidiary—Kodak Japan—to do battle on Fuji's home turf. Kodak bought out a Japanese distributor and set up its own Japanese marketing and sales staff. It invested in a new technology center and research facility. Finally, Kodak greatly increased its Japanese promotion and publicity. Kodak Japan now sponsors everything from Japanese television talk shows to sumo wrestling tournaments.

Kodak sought to take advantage of several benefits of its stepped-up attack on Japan. First, Japan's film and photographic paper market is second only to the

United States in size. Second, much of the new photographic technology originates in Japan. Third, having ownership and joint ventures in Japan helps Kodak to better understand Japanese manufacturing and to better develop new products. As a consequence of Kodak's ramped-up attack, Fuji devoted heavy resources to defending its home turf, and therefore had fewer resources to use against Kodak in the United States. In 1998, Kodak had a 10 percent share of the Japanese color film market, compared with Fuji's two-thirds share.[23]

What can the market leader do to defend its terrain? Twenty centuries ago, in a treatise called *The Art of War*, the famed Chinese military strategist Sun Tsu told his warriors: "One does not rely on the enemy not attacking, but on the fact that he himself is unassailable." The most constructive response is *continuous innovation*. The leader leads the industry in developing new product and customer services, distribution effectiveness, and cost cutting. It keeps increasing its competitive strength and value to customers. *The leader applies the military principle of the offensive: The commander exercises initiative, sets the pace, and exploits enemy weaknesses.* The best defense is a good offense.

IGT   International Game Technology (IGT), a company that manufactures slot machines and video poker machines for casinos around the world, has achieved the feat of maintaining a 64 percent domestic market share. Unlike the people who use its products, the company does not rely on luck. IGT has formed partnerships with casino operators and competitive gaming manufacturers to develop innovative new equipment to replace the old. IGT spends aggressively on R&D, allocating $55 million in 2001 to create new games. Dedication to service is also a company mantra. "We know months, years, in advance what our customers want," says Robert Shay, national product executive for IGT. That is because it involves casino operators throughout the sales process, from initial product development to final placement on the casino floor.[24]

Even when it does not launch offensives, the market leader must not leave any major flanks exposed. It must keep its costs down, and its prices must be consonant

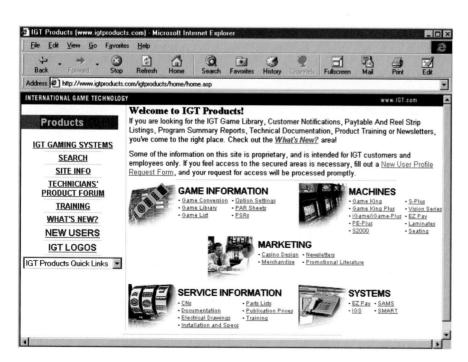

IGT's home page focuses on customer service.

with the value the customers see in the brand. Here is a dramatic example of how a company ignored this vital principle at its peril.

Johnson & Johnson   The cardiac stent is a tiny metal scaffold used to prop open obstructed heart vessels. In just 37 months after introducing this breakthrough device, Johnson & Johnson tallied more than $1 billion in sales and garnered more than 90 percent of a remarkably profitable market. In the fall of 1997, Guidant Corporation launched a competing product, and within 45 days it had gained a 70 percent market position. Other competitors moved in, and by the end of that year J&J's share had plummeted to a mere 8 percent. What went wrong? For one thing, J&J was so focused on getting the product to market that it devoted little time or resources to the next generation of the stent. The other stumbling block was its refusal to budge on price or offer discounts. At $1,595, the device was an expensive buy at a time when managed care was putting tremendous pressure on health care providers to keep costs down. With no comparable options on the market, doctors felt gouged.[25]

Clearly, the market leader must consider carefully which terrains are important to defend, even at a loss, and which can be surrendered.[26] The aim of defensive strategy is to reduce the probability of attack, divert attacks to less threatening areas, and lessen their intensity. The defender's speed of response can make an important difference in the profit consequences. Researchers are currently exploring the most appropriate forms of response to price and other attacks. A dominant firm can use the six defense strategies summarized in Figure 9.7 and described in the following paragraphs.[27]

DEFENSE STRATEGIES
Position Defense   Position defense involves building superior brand power, making the brand almost impregnable.

Heinz and Hunt's   Heinz let Hunt's carry out its massive attack in the ketchup market without striking back. Hunt's attacked Heinz with two new flavors of ketchup; it lowered its price to 70 percent of Heinz's price; it offered heavy trade allowances to retailers; it raised its advertising budget to over twice the level of Heinz's. The strategy failed because Hunt's ketchup did not deliver the same quality and the Heinz brand continued to enjoy consumer preference. Heinz showed great confidence in the superiority of its brand, which as of 2000 has over 50 percent market share in the United States, compared with Hunt's 17 percent.[28]

figure **9.7**

Six Types of Defense
Strategies

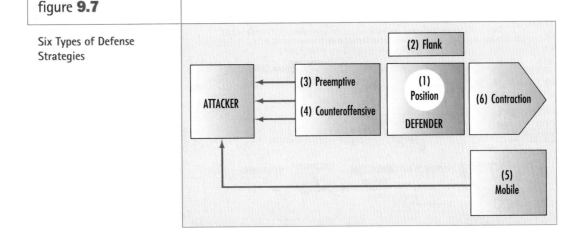

Flank Defense   Although position defense is important, leaders under attack would be foolish to rely on building fortifications around their current product; the market leader should also erect outposts to protect a weak front or possibly serve as an invasion base for counterattack. Here is a good example of a flank defense.

Heublein   Heublein's brand Smirnoff, which had 23 percent of the U.S. vodka market, was attacked by another brand, Wolfschmidt, priced at $1 less per bottle. Instead of lowering the price of Smirnoff by $1, Heublein raised the price by $1 and put the increased revenue into advertising. At the same time, Heublein introduced another brand, Relska, to compete with Wolfschmidt and still another, Popov, to sell for less than Wolfschmidt. This strategy effectively bracketed Wolfschmidt and protected Smirnoff's flanks.

Goodyear   In the 1990s, Goodyear Tire & Rubber Company was faced with fierce competition from the likes of Bridgestone/Firestone and Michelin. To stay ahead of this mounting competition, Goodyear employed a number of flank defenses. The company developed innovative new products, such as the Aquatred, a tire that uses deep grooves to dispel water from the tire's surface, and the Extended Mobility Tire, which, even when completely flat, can be driven 50 miles at 55 miles per hour. Goodyear also acquired other tire companies, such as Debica, the leading tire manufacturer in Poland, and Dunlop, a subsidiary of Sumitomo Rubber Industries, which, in combination with its value-priced Kelly-Springfield brand, provided much competitive breadth and strength. With the Dunlop acquisition, Goodyear once again became the world's largest tire manufacturer.[29]

Preemptive Defense   A more aggressive maneuver is to attack *before* the enemy starts its offense. A company can launch a preemptive defense in several ways. It can wage guerrilla action across the market—hitting one competitor here, another there—and keep everyone off balance; or it can try to achieve a grand market envelopment, as Seiko has done with 2,300 watch models distributed worldwide. It can begin sustained price attacks, as Texas Instruments often did; or it can send out market signals to dissuade competitors from attacking.[30]

Chrysler   In the 1990s, Chrysler had the largest market share of the newly popular minivans. The minivans were priced at $18,000 and highly profitable. Chairman Lee Iacocca knew that competitors would try to enter the market at a lower price, so in an interview with *USA Today,* he indicated that Chrysler was considering introducing a cut-rate minivan. This signal was sent to discourage competitors from thinking they could win by launching a lower-price minivan.

Counteroffensive Defense   When attacked, most market leaders will respond with a counterattack. In a counteroffensive, the leader can meet the attacker frontally or hit its flank or launch a pincer movement. An effective counterattack is to invade the attacker's main territory so that it will have to pull back some troops to defend the territory. One of Northwest Airlines's most profitable routes is Minneapolis to Atlanta. A smaller air carrier launched a deep fare cut and advertised it heavily to expand its share in this market. Northwest retaliated by cutting its fares on the Minneapolis/Chicago route, which the attacking airline depended on for revenue. With its major revenue source hurting, the attacking airline restored its Minneapolis/Atlanta fare to a normal level.

Another common form of counteroffensive is the exercise of economic or political clout. The leader may try to crush a competitor by subsidizing lower prices for the vulnerable product with revenue from its more profitable products; or the leader may prematurely announce that a product upgrade will be available, to prevent customers from buying the competitor's product; or the leader may lobby legislators to take political action that would inhibit or cripple the competition.

Mobile Defense   In mobile defense, the leader stretches its domain over new territories that can serve as future centers for defense and offense. It spreads through market broadening and market diversification.

Market broadening involves the company in shifting its focus from the current product to the underlying generic need. The company gets involved in R&D across the whole range of technology associated with that need. Thus "petroleum" companies sought to recast themselves into "energy" companies. Implicitly, this change demanded that they dip their research fingers into the oil, coal, nuclear, hydroelectric, and chemical industries.

Such a strategy should not be carried too far, lest it fault two fundamental military principles—the *principle of the objective* (pursue a clearly defined, decisive, and attainable objective) and the *principle of mass* (concentrate your efforts at a point of enemy weakness). Reasonable broadening, however, makes sense.

Wal-Mart   Wal-Mart's supercenters already stock groceries, so the giant chain did not consider it too much of a leap to broaden into the grocery business. In 1998, Wal-Mart Stores Inc., announced plans for three experimental grocery stores in Arkansas. The 40,000-square-foot "Neighborhood Markets" offer traditionally low Wal-Mart prices on a smaller scale with a store modeled after stand-alone grocery chains. The markets use the now-familiar low everyday price concept, while offering more convenience than Wal-Mart supercenters. After initial success in Arkansas, Wal-Mart expanded its Neighborhood Markets into other states. Wal-Mart's move into conventional grocery stores prompted supermarket giants Kroger and Safeway to cut prices and boost service.[31]

Market diversification into unrelated industries is the other alternative. When U.S. tobacco companies like Reynolds and Philip Morris acknowledged the growing curbs on cigarette smoking, they were not content with position defense or even with looking for cigarette substitutes. Instead they moved quickly into new industries, such as beer, liquor, soft drinks, and frozen foods.

Contraction Defense   Large companies sometimes recognize that they can no longer defend all of their territory. The best course of action then appears to be *planned contraction* (also called *strategic withdrawal*). Planned contraction means giving up weaker territories and reassigning resources to stronger territories. It is a move to consolidate competitive strength in the market and concentrate mass at pivotal positions. Heinz, General Mills, Del Monte, General Electric, American Can, and Georgia-Pacific are among companies that have significantly pruned their product lines in recent years.

EXPANDING MARKET SHARE   Market leaders can improve their profitability by increasing their market share. In many markets, one share point is worth tens of millions of dollars. A one-share-point gain in coffee is worth $48 million and in soft drinks, $120 million! No wonder normal competition has turned into marketing warfare.

A study by the Strategic Planning Institute (called Profit Impact of Market Strategy, or PIMS) found that a company's profitability, measured by pretax return on investment (ROI), rises with its *relative market share* of its served market,[32] as shown in Figure 9.8(a).[33] The average ROI for businesses with under 10 percent market share was about 11 percent. A difference of 10 percentage points in market share is accompanied by a difference of about 5 points in pretax ROI. The PIMS study shows that businesses with market shares over 40 percent earn an average ROI of 30 percent, or three times that of those with shares under 10 percent.[34] These findings led many companies to pursue market-share expansion and leadership as their objective. General Electric decided it must be number one or two in each market or else get out. GE divested its computer

figure **9.8**   Relationship Between Market Share and Profitability

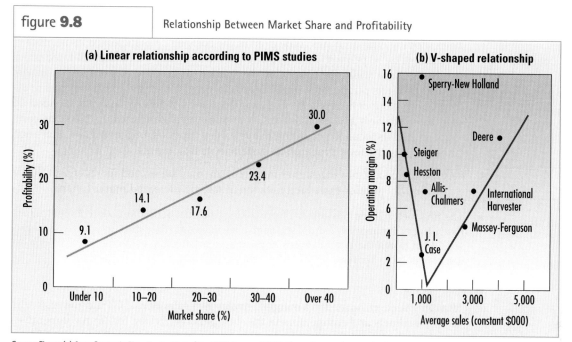

Source: Figure (a) from Strategic Planning Institute (The PIMS Program) 1030 Massachusetts Avenue, Cambridge, MA 02138.

business and its air-conditioning business because it could not achieve leadership in these industries.

Some critics have attacked the PIMS findings as being either weak or spurious. Hamermesh cited many profitable companies with low market shares.[35] Woo and Cooper identified 40 low-share businesses that enjoyed pretax ROIs of 20 percent or more; these businesses tended to have high relative product quality, medium-to-low prices, narrow product lines, and low total costs.[36] Most of these companies produced industrial components or supplies.

Some industry studies yield a V-shaped relationship between market share and profitability.[37] Figure 9.8(b) shows a V-curve for agricultural-equipment firms. The industry leader, Deere & Company, earns a high return. However, two small specialty firms, Hesston and Steiger, also earn high returns. J. I. Case and Massey-Ferguson are trapped in the valley, and at the time International Harvester commanded substantial market share but earned lower returns. Thus, such industries have one or a few highly profitable large firms, several profitable small and more-focused firms, and several medium-sized firms with poorer profit performance.

How can the two graphs in Figure 9.8 be reconciled? The PIMS findings argue that profitability increases as a business gains share relative to its competitors in its *served (target) market*. The V-shaped curve ignores market segments and looks at profitability relative to size in the *total market*. Mercedes earns high profits because it is a high-share company in its served market of luxury cars, even though it is a low-share company in the total auto market; and it has achieved this high share in its served market because it does many things right, such as producing high relative product quality.

However, gaining increased market share in the served market does not automatically produce higher profits. Much depends on the company's strategy for gaining increased market share.

figure **9.9**

The Concept of Optimal Market Share

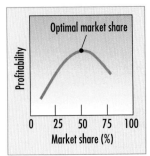

McDonald's   Since 1987, McDonald's share of fast-food sales in the United States has been slipping. The drop has come even as the company has increased its number of restaurants by 50 percent, far outpacing the industry expansion rate. Ill-fated product innovations took the blame for the market-share drop. Customers were not thrilled about its pizza and veggie burger offerings. When the company tried to expand its way out of the crisis by building thousands of new restaurants, it ended up stealing customers and profits from its own existing franchises. In 2000, the company shifted its focus to providing healthy menu options, improving the ambiance, and changing the food preparation system in its restaurants.

Because the cost of buying higher market share may far exceed its revenue value, a company should consider three factors before pursuing increased market share:

■   The first factor is the possibility of provoking antitrust action. Jealous competitors are likely to cry "monopoly" if a dominant firm makes further inroads. This rise in risk would cut down the attractiveness of pushing market-share gains too far. This is what has happened to Verizon.

Verizon   Verizon, formed in a merger between Bell Atlantic and GTE, came under fire from consumers and competitors in the state of Pennsylvania for "anti-competitive" practices. Public outcry ensued when Verizon, which controlled 90 percent of local phone lines in the state, announced plans to enter the long-distance market. A 2001 ruling by the state's Public Utilities Commission ordered Verizon to establish "functional structural separation" of its retail and wholesale units, but refrained from breaking the company into two separate parts, as many consumers and competitors had hoped it would do.[39]

■   The second factor is economic cost. Figure 9.9 shows that profitability might fall with further market-share gains after some level. In the illustration, the firm's *optimal market share* is 50 percent. The cost of gaining further market share might exceed the value. A company that has, say, 60 percent of the market must recognize that the "holdout" customers may dislike the company, be loyal to competitive suppliers, have unique needs, or prefer dealing with smaller suppliers. The cost of legal work, public relations, and lobbying rises with market share. Pushing for higher market share is less justified when there are few scale or experience economies, unattractive market segments exist, buyers want multiple sources of supply, and exit barriers are high. Some market leaders have even increased profitability by selectively decreasing market share in weaker areas.[40]
■   The third factor is that companies might pursue the wrong marketing-mix strategy in their bid for higher market share. Companies that win more market share by cutting price are buying, not earning, a larger share, and their profits may be lower.

Buzzell and Wiersema found that share-gaining companies typically outperform competitors in three areas: new-product activity, relative product quality, and marketing expenditures.[41] Specifically: Share-gaining companies typically develop and add more new products. Companies that increase product quality relative to competitors enjoy greater share gains. Companies that increase marketing expenditures faster than the rate of market growth typically achieve share gains. Increases in sales force expenditures are effective in producing share gains for both industrial and consumer markets. Increased advertising expenditures produce share gains mainly for consumer-goods companies. Increased sales-promotion expenditures are effective in producing share gains for all kinds of companies. Companies that cut prices more deeply than competitors do not achieve significant market-share gains. Presumably, enough rivals meet the price cuts, and others offer other values to buyers, so that buyers do not switch to the price cutter.

two case studies: procter & gamble and caterpillar

Market leaders who stay on top have learned the art of expanding the total market, defending their current territory, and increasing market-share profitably. Here we look at two companies, Procter & Gamble and Caterpillar, which have shown a remarkable ability to protect their market shares against able challengers.

PROCTER & GAMBLE   Procter & Gamble (P&G) is one of the most skilled marketers of consumer packaged goods. It markets the leading brand in 19 of the 39 categories in which it competes. Its average market share is close to 25 percent. Its market leadership rests on several principles:

- *Customer knowledge:* P&G studies its customers—both final consumers and the trade—through continuous marketing research and intelligence gathering. It prints its toll-free 800 number on every product.

- *Long-term outlook:* P&G takes the time to analyze each opportunity carefully and prepare the best product, then commits itself to making this product a success. It struggled with Pringles potato chips for almost a decade before achieving market success.

- *Product innovation:* P&G is an active product innovator, devoting $1.2 billion (3.4 percent of sales) to research and development, an impressively high amount for a packaged-goods company. It holds more than 2,500 active patents protecting 250 proprietary technologies. Part of its innovation process is developing brands that offer new consumer benefits. P&G spent 10 years researching and developing the first effective anticavity toothpaste, Crest.[42]

- *Quality strategy:* P&G designs products of above-average quality and continuously improves them. When P&G announces "new and improved," it means it.

- *Line-extension strategy:* P&G produces its brands in several sizes and forms. This strategy gains more shelf space and prevents competitors from moving in to satisfy unmet market needs.

- *Brand-extension strategy:* P&G often uses its strong brand names to launch new products. The Ivory brand has been extended from a soap to include a liquid soap, a dishwashing detergent, and a shampoo. Launching a new product under a strong existing brand name gives the new brand instant recognition and credibility with much less advertising outlay.

- *Multibrand strategy:* P&G markets several brands in the same product category. It produces eight brands of hand soap and six shampoo brands. Each brand meets a different consumer want and competes against specific competitors' brands. Each brand manager competes for company resources. More recently, P&G has begun to reduce its vast array of products, sizes, flavors, and varieties to bring down costs.[43]

- *Heavy advertising and media pioneer:* P&G is the nation's second largest consumer-packaged-goods advertiser, spending over $3 billion a year on advertising. A pioneer in using the power of television to create strong consumer awareness and preference, P&G is now taking a leading role in building its brand on the Web. In 1998, P&G hosted a high-powered industry "summit" meeting that brought together some 400 top executives from Internet and consumer marketing companies. The goal: figuring out how to best sell products over the Internet.[44]

- *Aggressive sales force:* In 1998, P&G's sales force was named one of the top 25 sales forces by *Sales & Marketing Management* magazine. A key to P&G's success is the close ties its sales force forms with retailers, notably Wal-Mart. The 150-person team that serves the retail giant works closely with Wal-Mart to improve both the products that go to the stores and the process by which they get there.

- *Effective sales promotion:* P&G's sales-promotion department counsels its brand managers on the most effective promotions to achieve particular objectives. The department develops an expert sense of these deals' effectiveness under varying circumstances. At the same time, P&G tries to minimize the use of sales promotion and move toward "every-day low prices."

- *Competitive toughness:* P&G carries a big stick when it comes to aggressors. It is willing to spend large sums of money to outpromote new competitive brands and prevent them from gaining a foothold.

- *Manufacturing efficiency and cost cutting:* P&G's reputation as a great marketing company is matched by its excellence as a manufacturing company. P&G spends large sums developing and improving production operations to keep its costs among the lowest in the industry; and P&G has recently begun slashing its costs even further, allowing it to reduce the premium prices at which some of its goods sell.
- *Brand-management system:* P&G originated the brand-management system, in which one executive is responsible for each brand. The system has been copied by many competitors but frequently without P&G's success. Recently, P&G modified its general management structure so that each brand category is now run by a category manager with volume and profit responsibility. Although this new organization does not replace the brand-management system, it helps to sharpen strategic focus on key consumer needs and competition in the category.

Thus P&G's market leadership is not based on doing one thing well, but on the successful orchestration of myriad factors that contribute to market leadership.

CATERPILLAR   Caterpillar is the dominant leader in the construction-equipment industry. Its tractors, crawlers, and loaders, painted in the familiar yellow, are a common sight at any construction area. Caterpillar has retained leadership in spite of charging a premium price and being challenged by a number of able competitors, including John Deere, J. I. Case, Komatsu, and Hitachi. Several policies combine to explain Caterpillar's success:

- *Premium performance:* Caterpillar produces high-quality equipment known for its reliability and durability. These are key buyer considerations in the choice of heavy industrial equipment.
- *Extensive and efficient dealership system:* Caterpillar maintains the largest number of independent construction-equipment dealers in the industry. Its 220 dealers throughout the world carry a complete line of Caterpillar equipment. Competitors' dealers normally lack a full line and carry complementary, noncompeting lines. Caterpillar can choose the best dealers and spends the most money in training, servicing, and motivating them.
- *Superior service:* Caterpillar has built a worldwide parts and service system second to none in the industry. Caterpillar can ship replacement parts and deliver service anywhere in the world within 24 hours of equipment breakdown. Competitors would have to make a substantial investment to duplicate this service level and would only neutralize Caterpillar's advantage rather than score a new advantage.
- *Full-line strategy:* Caterpillar produces a full line of construction equipment to enable customers to do one-stop buying.
- *Good financing:* Caterpillar provides a wide range of financial terms for customers who buy its equipment.

In the 1980s, Caterpillar experienced difficulties because of the depressed global construction-equipment market and cutthroat competition from Komatsu, Japan's number-one construction firm, which adopted the internal slogan "Encircle Caterpillar." Komatsu attacked market niches, sometimes pricing its equipment as much as 40 percent lower. Caterpillar fought back by cutting costs and meeting Komatsu's prices and sometimes even initiating price cutting. The price wars drove competitors like International Harvester and Clark Equipment to the brink of ruin. The long and damaging price wars appear to be coming to an end, with both sides settling for improved profits.

market-challenger strategies

Firms that occupy second, third, and lower ranks in an industry are often called runner-up, or trailing firms. Some, such as Colgate, Ford, Avis, and PepsiCo, are quite large in their own right. These firms can adopt one of two postures. They can attack the leader and other competitors in an aggressive bid for further market share (market challengers), or they can play ball and not "rock the boat" (market followers).

Many market challengers have gained ground or even overtaken the leader. Toyota today produces more cars than General Motors, and British Airways flies more international passengers than the former leader, Pan Am, did in its heyday. These challengers set high aspirations and leveraged their smaller resources while the market leaders ran their businesses as usual.

Robert Dolan found that competitive rivalry and price cutting are most intense in industries with high fixed costs, high inventory costs, and stagnant primary demand, such as steel, auto, paper, and chemicals.[45] We will now examine the competitive attack strategies available to market challengers.

DEFINING THE STRATEGIC OBJECTIVE AND OPPONENT(S)   A market challenger must first define its strategic objective. Most aim to increase market share. The challenger must decide whom to attack:

- *It can attack the market leader.* This is a high-risk but potentially high-payoff strategy and makes good sense if the leader is not serving the market well. Miller's "lite beer" campaign was successful because it pivoted on discovering consumers who wanted a less caloric, less filling beer. The alternative strategy is to out-innovate the leader across the whole segment. Xerox wrested the copy market from 3M by developing a better copying process. Later, Canon grabbed a large chunk of Xerox's market by introducing desk copiers.
- *It can attack firms of its own size that are not doing the job and are underfinanced.* These firms have aging products, are charging excessive prices, or are not satisfying customers in other ways.
- *It can attack small local and regional firms.* Several major beer companies grew to their present size by gobbling up smaller firms, or "guppies."

If the attacking company goes after the market leader, its objective might be to wrest a certain share. Bic is under no illusion that it can topple Gillette in the razor market—it is simply seeking a larger share. If the attacking company goes after a small local company, its objective might be to drive that company out of existence.

CHOOSING A GENERAL ATTACK STRATEGY   Given clear opponents and objectives, what attack options are available? We can distinguish among five attack strategies shown in Figure 9.10: frontal, flank, encirclement, bypass, and guerilla attacks.

Frontal Attack   In a pure *frontal attack*, the attacker matches its opponent's product, advertising, price, and distribution. The principle of force says that the side with the greater manpower (resources) will win. The military dogma is that for a frontal attack to succeed against a well-entrenched opponent or one controlling the high ground, the attacking forces must have at least a 3-to-1 advantage in combat firepower. The runner-up razor-blade manufacturer in Brazil attacked Gillette, the market leader. The attacker was asked if it offers the consumer a better razor blade. "No" was the reply. "A lower price?" "No." "A better package?" "No." "A clever advertising campaign?" "No." "Better allowances to the trade?" "No." "Then how do you expect to take share away from Gillette?" "Sheer determination" was the reply. Needless to say, the offensive failed.

A modified frontal attack, such as cutting price vis-à-vis the opponent's, can work if the market leader does not retaliate and if the competitor convinces the market that its product is equal to the leader's. Helene Curtis is a master at convincing the market that its brands—such as Suave and Finesse—are equal in quality but a better value than higher-priced brands.

Flank Attack   The major principle of offensive warfare is concentration of strength against weakness. The enemy's weak spots are natural targets. A *flank attack* can be directed along two strategic dimensions—geographical and segmental. In a geographical attack, the challenger spots areas where the opponent is underperforming. For example, some of IBM's former mainframe rivals, such as Honeywell, chose to set up strong sales branches in medium- and smaller-sized cities that were relatively neglected by IBM. The other flanking strategy is to serve uncovered market needs, as Japanese automakers did

figure **9.10**

Attack Strategies

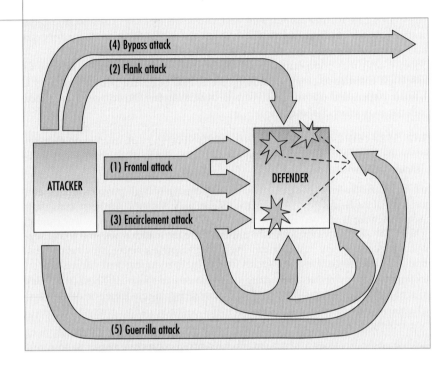

when they developed more fuel-efficient cars, and as Miller Brewing Company did when it introduced light beer.

A flanking strategy is another name for identifying shifts in market segments that are causing gaps to develop, then rushing in to fill the gaps and develop them into strong segments. Flanking is in the best tradition of modern marketing, which holds that the purpose of marketing is to discover needs and satisfy them. Flank attacks are particularly attractive to a challenger with fewer resources than its opponent and are much more likely to be successful than frontal attacks.

Encirclement Attack   The encirclement maneuver is an attempt to capture a wide slice of the enemy's territory through a "blitz." It involves launching a grand offensive on several fronts. Encirclement makes sense when the challenger commands superior resources and believes a swift encirclement will break the opponent's will.

Sun Microsystems Inc.   In making a stand against arch rival Microsoft, Sun Microsystems is licensing its Java software for all sorts of consumer devices. As consumer-electronics products began to go digital, Java started appearing in a wide range of gadgets. Motorola uses Java in everything from pagers and cell phones to fax machines and smartcards. Dallas Semiconductor makes the iButton, a key chain attachment with a Java-encoded chip that provides more secure access to hotel rooms or e-mail stations at public kiosks. As of January 2001, Java was licensed by 200 companies and used by more than 2.5 million software developers.[46]

Bypass Attack   The most indirect assault strategy is the *bypass*. It means bypassing the enemy and attacking easier markets to broaden one's resource base. This strategy offers three lines of approach: diversifying into unrelated products, diversifying into new geographical markets, and leapfrogging into new technologies to supplant existing products. Although PepsiCo and Coca-Cola often go head to head, the bypass attack is also part of their competitive battle plan. Here's how Pepsi used a bypass strategy against Coke:

PepsiCo In the summer of 1998, many people wondered why PepsiCo paid $3.3 billion for juice giant Tropicana. Unlike soda, juice is a perishable product subject to commodity markets, bad weather, and crop failures. Yet, as the world's largest juice company—with 42 percent of the $3 billion orange juice market—Tropicana armed Pepsi with a powerful new weapon for the war against Coca-Cola, which has only 24 percent of the orange juice market with its own Minute Maid. Pepsi added the dominant player in the sports beverage category to its roster in 2000, when it outbid Coca-Cola and Dannon to buy Quaker Oats, owners of the Gatorade brand, for $14 billion. Gatorade, which boasts over an 80 percent share of the sports drink market, gives Pepsi another non-soft-drink advantage over Coca-Cola, which markets the also-ran sports beverage Powerade.[47]

Technological leapfrogging is a bypass strategy practiced in high-tech industries. The challenger patiently researches and develops the next technology and launches an attack, shifting the battleground to its territory, where it has an advantage. Nintendo's successful attack in the video-game market was precisely about wresting market share by introducing a superior technology and redefining the "competitive space." Then Sega/Genesis did the same with more advanced technology, and now Sony's Playstation is grabbing the technological lead. Here is another example of a technological bypass attack strategy.

SCA SCA, the Swedish competitor to P&G, has pursued an innovative Internet strategy to outsmart P&G in the baby-diaper market with a much smaller budget. SCA saw an opportunity for real dialogue with expectant and new parents through the Internet, and created the Web site *www.libero.se* as a community for parents. The site contains a large encyclopedia on parenting plus tools like a "baby namefinder." The site also suggests how to choose the right diaper. It hosts debates, encouraging consumers to help each other out. Users can buy and sell child-related equipment free. In its "baby's own Web site," users can upload pictures, write small stories, and make child wish lists, allowing relatives all over the world to follow the child's progress.[48]

Swedish firm SCA's www.libero.se site creates a dialogue with expectant and new parents and even allows users to send pictures, brief stories, and child wish lists to family all over the world.

Guerrilla Warfare   **Guerrilla warfare** consists of waging small, intermittent attacks to harass and demoralize the opponent and eventually secure permanent footholds. The guerrilla challenger uses both conventional and unconventional means of attack. These include selective price cuts, intense promotional blitzes, and occasional legal actions. Here is an example of a very successful guerrilla strategy.

The Princeton Review   In 1938, Stanley H. Kaplan founded Kaplan Educational Centers, which became the largest test-preparation business in the United States. Then a young Princeton graduate named John Katzman created The Princeton Review, and engaged in guerrilla marketing, particularly attacking Kaplan's image. The Princeton Review ads were brash: "Stanley's a wimp," or "Friends don't let friends take Kaplan," while touting the Princeton Review's smaller, livelier classes. Katzman posted horror stories about Kaplan on the Internet, and even picked fights with the Educational Testing Service (ETS), which administers the standardized tests that the test-preparation companies coach students to take. By the 1990s, Princeton Review's guerrilla warfare had paid off. The company is now one of the leading test-preparation companies.

Normally, guerrilla warfare is practiced by a smaller firm against a larger one. The smaller firm launches a barrage of attacks in random corners of the larger opponent's market in a manner calculated to weaken the opponent's market power. Military dogma holds that a continual stream of minor attacks usually creates more cumulative impact, disorganization, and confusion in the enemy than a few major attacks.

A guerrilla campaign can be expensive, although admittedly less expensive than a frontal, encirclement, or flank attack. Guerrilla warfare is more a preparation for war than a war itself. Ultimately, it must be backed by a stronger attack if the challenger hopes to beat the opponent.

CHOOSING A SPECIFIC ATTACK STRATEGY   The challenger must go beyond the five broad strategies and develop more specific strategies:

- *Price discount:* The challenger can offer a comparable product at a lower price. This is the strategy of discount retailers. Three conditions must be fulfilled. First, the challenger must convince buyers that its product and service are comparable to the leader's. Second, buyers must be price sensitive. Third, the market leader must refuse to cut its price in spite of the competitor's attack.
- *Lower price goods:* The challenger can offer an average- or lower-quality product at a much lower price. Little Debbie Snack Cakes is priced lower than Drake's and outsells Drake's by 20 to 1. Firms that establish themselves through a lower-price strategy, however, can be attacked by firms whose prices are even lower.
- *Prestige goods:* A market challenger can launch a higher-quality product and charge a higher price than the leader. Mercedes gained on Cadillac in the U.S. market by offering a car of higher quality at a higher price.
- *Product proliferation:* The challenger can attack the leader by launching a larger product variety, thus giving buyers more choice. Baskin-Robbins achieved its growth in the ice cream business by promoting more flavors—31—than its larger competitors.
- *Product innovation:* The challenger can pursue product innovation. 3M typically enters new markets by introducing a product improvement or breakthrough.
- *Improved services:* The challenger can offer new or better services to customers. Avis's famous attack on Hertz, "We're only second. We try harder," was based on promising and delivering cleaner cars and faster service than Hertz.
- *Distribution innovation:* A challenger might develop a new channel of distribution. Avon became a major cosmetics company by perfecting door-to-door selling instead of battling other cosmetic firms in conventional stores.

- *Manufacturing-cost reduction:* The challenger might achieve lower manufacturing costs than its competitors through more efficient purchasing, lower labor costs, and more modern production equipment.
- *Intensive advertising promotion:* Some challengers attack the leader by increasing expenditures on advertising and promotion. Miller Beer outspent Budweiser in its attempt to increase its share of the U.S. beer market. Substantial promotional spending, however, is usually not a sensible strategy unless the challenger's product or advertising message is superior.

A challenger's success depends on combining several strategies to improve its position over time.

market-follower strategies

Some years ago, Theodore Levitt wrote an article entitled "Innovative Imitation," in which he argued that a strategy of *product imitation* might be as profitable as a strategy of *product innovation.*[49] The innovator bears the expense of developing the new product, getting it into distribution, and informing and educating the market. The reward for all this work and risk is normally market leadership. However, another firm can come along and copy or improve on the new product. Although it probably will not overtake the leader, the follower can achieve high profits because it did not bear any of the innovation expense.

Many companies prefer to follow rather than challenge the market leader. Patterns of "conscious parallelism" are common in capital-intensive, homogeneous-product industries, such as steel, fertilizers, and chemicals. The opportunities for product differentiation and image differentiation are low; service quality is often comparable; and price sensitivity runs high. The mood in these industries is against short-run grabs for market share because that strategy only provokes retaliation. Most firms decide against stealing one another's customers. Instead, they present similar offers to buyers, usually by copying the leader. Market shares show a high stability.

This is not to say that market followers lack strategies. A market follower must know how to hold current customers and win a fair share of new customers. Each follower tries to bring distinctive advantages to its target market—location, services, financing; and because the follower is often a major target of attack by challengers, it must keep its manufacturing costs low and its product quality and services high. It must also enter new markets as they open up. The follower has to define a growth path, but one that does not invite competitive retaliation. Four broad strategies can be distinguished:

1. *Counterfeiter:* The counterfeiter duplicates the leader's product and package and sells it on the black market or through disreputable dealers. Music record firms, Apple Computer, and Rolex have been plagued with the counterfeiter problem, especially in the Far East.
2. *Cloner:* The cloner emulates the leader's products, name, and packaging, with slight variations. For example, Ralcorp Holding Inc. sells imitations of name-brand cereals in lookalike boxes. Its Tasteeos, Fruit Rings, and Corn Flakes sell for nearly a $1 a box less than the leading name brands.[50] In the computer business, clones are a fact of life.
3. *Imitator:* The imitator copies some things from the leader but maintains differentiation in terms of packaging, advertising, pricing, or location. The leader does not mind the imitator as long as the imitator does not attack the leader aggressively.

TelePizza Fernandez Pujals grew up in Fort Lauderdale, Florida, and took Domino's home delivery idea to Spain, where he borrowed $80,000 to open his first store in Madrid. He now operates over 500 stores in Europe, with a business valued at $1.85 billion.

4. *Adapter:* The adapter takes the leader's products and adapts or improves them. The adapter may choose to sell to different markets, but often the adapter grows into the future challenger, as many Japanese firms have done after adapting and improving products developed elsewhere.

S&S Cycle S&S Cycle is the biggest supplier of complete engines and major motor parts to more than 15 companies that build several thousand Harley-like cruiser bikes each year. These cloners charge as much as $30,000 for their customized creations. S&S has built its name by improving on Harley-Davidson's handiwork. Its customers are often would-be Harley buyers frustrated by long waiting lines at the dealers. Other customers simply want the incredibly powerful S&S engines. S&S stays abreast of its evolving market by ordering a new Harley bike every year and taking apart the engine to see what it can improve upon.[51]

What does a follower earn? Normally, less than the leader. For example, a study of food processing companies showed the largest firm averaging a 16 percent return on investment; the number-two firm, 6 percent; the number-three firm, –1 percent, and the number-four firm, –6 percent. In this case, only the top two firms have profits. No wonder Jack Welch, former CEO of GE, told his business units that each must reach the number-one or -two position in its market or else! Followership is often not a rewarding path.

market-nicher strategies

An alternative to being a follower in a large market is to be a leader in a small market, or niche. Smaller firms normally avoid competing with larger firms by targeting small markets of little or no interest to the larger firms. Here is an example.

Logitech International Logitech has become a $750 million global success story by making every variation of computer mouse imaginable. The company turns out mice for left- and right-handed people, cordless mice that use radio waves, mice shaped like real mice for children, and 3-D mice that let the user appear to move behind screen objects. Its global dominance in the mouse category enabled the company to expand into other computer peripherals, such as keyboards, speakers, joysticks, and Internet video cameras.[52]

Even large firms are now setting up business units, or companies, to serve niches. Here are examples of large, profitable companies that have pursued niching strategies.

Beer Industry Microbrewers' specialty beers—such as Pyramid Ale and Pete's Wicked Ale—was the only beer market showing any growth potential in the late 1990s. That fact prompted the Big Four brewers—Anheuser-Busch, Miller, Coors, and Stroh Brewery—to launch their own specialty beers. There is Anheuser's Red Wolf and Killarney's Red, Miller's Red Dog and Icehouse beers, and Coors' George Killian's. However, because some consumers resisted the idea of buying specialty beer from a big player, some companies kept their name off the label. Miller even advertises its Red Dog and Icehouse beers as coming from Plank Road Brewery, with no mention of Miller.[53]

ITW Illinois Tool Works (ITW) manufactures thousands of products, including nails, screws, plastic six-pack holders for soda cans, bicycle helmets, backpacks, plastic buckles for pet collars, resealable food packages, and more. Since the late 1980s, the company has made between 30 and 40 acquisitions each year, which added new products to the product line. ITW has more than 500 highly autonomous and decentralized business units. When one division commercializes a new product, the product and personnel are spun off into a new entity.[54]

Thus, firms with low shares of the total market can be highly profitable through smart niching. Clifford and Cavanagh identified over two dozen highly successful mid-sized companies and studied their success factors.[55] They found that virtually all these companies were nichers. A. T. Cross niched itself in the high-price writing instruments market with its famous gold and silver items. Such companies tend to offer high value, charge a premium price, achieve lower manufacturing costs, and shape a strong corporate culture and vision. Alberto Culver Company is a classic example of a midsized company that has successfully used market-nicher strategies.

Alberto Culver Company   Alberto Culver used market-nicher strategies to grow earnings in 2000 by 13 percent over the previous year to $97.2 million on sales of $2.25 billion. CEO Howard Bernick explains the Alberto Culver philosophy: "We know who we are and, perhaps more importantly, we know who we are not. We know that if we try to out-Procter Procter, we will fall flat on our face." Instead, the company, known mainly for its Alberto VO5 hair products, focused its marketing muscle on acquiring a stable of smaller niche brands, including such nonbeauty items as flavor enhancers Molly McButter and Mrs. Dash, and static-cling fighter Static Guard.[56]

In a study of hundreds of business units, the Strategic Planning Institute found that the return on investment averaged 27 percent in smaller markets, but only 11 percent in larger markets.[57] Why is niching so profitable? The main reason is that the market nicher ends up knowing the target customers so well that it meets their needs better than other firms selling to this niche casually. As a result, the nicher can charge a substantial price over costs. The nicher achieves *high margin*, whereas the mass-marketer achieves *high volume*.

Nichers have three tasks: creating niches, expanding niches, and protecting niches. Niching carries a major risk in that the market niche might dry up or be attacked. The company is then stuck with highly specialized resources that may not have high-value alternative uses. Consider Arm & Hammer.

Arm & Hammer   Church & Dwight Co., makers of Arm & Hammer baking soda, created a new toothpaste category when it unveiled its Arm & Hammer Dental Care toothpaste with baking soda. Arm & Hammer Dental Care was a hit with consumers, and the product quickly became the leading baking soda toothpaste, helping the company capture an 11 percent share of the global toothpaste market in 1993. As major toothpaste brands like Crest, Colgate, and Mentadent all developed baking soda toothpastes, however, Arm & Hammer's market share fell to 7 percent in the global market in 2000, compared with 50 percent for market leader Colgate.[58]

The key idea in nichemanship is specialization. The following specialist roles are open to nichers:

- *End-user specialist:* The firm specializes in serving one type of end-use customer. For example, a *value-added reseller (VAR)* customizes the computer hardware and software for specific customer segments and earns a price premium in the process.[59]
- *Vertical-level specialist:* The firm specializes at some vertical level of the production-distribution value chain. A copper firm may concentrate on producing raw copper, copper components, or finished copper products.
- *Customer-size specialist:* The firm concentrates on selling to either small, medium-sized, or large customers. Many nichers specialize in serving small customers who are neglected by the majors.
- *Specific-customer specialist:* The firm limits its selling to one or a few customers. Many firms sell their entire output to a single company, such as Sears or General Motors.
- *Geographic specialist:* The firm sells only in a certain locality, region, or area of the world.
- *Product or product-line specialist:* The firm carries or produces only one product line or product. A firm may produce only lenses for microscopes. A retailer may carry only ties.
- *Product-feature specialist:* The firm specializes in producing a certain type of product or product feature. Rent-a-Wreck, for example, is a California car-rental agency that rents only "beat-up" cars.

- *Job-shop specialist:* The firm customizes its products for individual customers.
- *Quality-price specialist:* The firm operates at the low- or high-quality ends of the market. Hewlett-Packard specializes in the high-quality, high-price end of the hand-calculator market.
- *Service specialist:* The firm offers one or more services not available from other firms. An example would be a bank that takes loan requests over the phone and hand-delivers the money to the customer.
- *Channel specialist:* The firm specializes in serving only one channel of distribution. For example, a soft-drink company decides to make a very large-sized soft drink available only at gas stations.

Because niches can weaken, the firm must continually create new ones. The firm should "stick to its niching" but not necessarily to its niche. That is why *multiple niching* is preferable to *single niching*. By developing strength in two or more niches, the company increases its chances for survival.

Firms entering a market should aim at a niche initially rather than the whole market. (See "Marketing Insight: Strategies for Entering Markets Held by Incumbent Firms.")

marketing **insight**

Strategies for Entering Markets Held by Incumbent Firms

What marketing strategies can companies use to enter a market held by incumbent firms? Biggadike examined the strategies of 40 invading firms. He found that 10 entered at a lower price, 9 matched incumbents' prices, and 21 entered at a higher price. On quality, 28 claimed superior quality, 5 matched incumbents' quality, and 7 reported inferior product quality. Most entrants offered a specialist product line and served a narrower market segment. Less than 20 percent innovated a new distribution channel. Over half offered a higher level of customer service. Over half spent less than incumbents on sales force, advertising, and promotion. The winning marketing mix was (1) higher prices and higher quality; (2) narrower product line; (3) narrower market segment; (4) similar distribution channels; (5) superior service; and (6) lower expenditure on sales force, advertising, and promotion.

Schnaars examined the strategies of successful invading firms that entered occupied markets and eventually took leadership. He detailed more than 30 cases in which the imitator displaced the innovator, including:

Product	Innovator	Imitator
Word-processing software	Word Star	WordPerfect
Spreadsheet software	Unicalc	Later Word
Credit cards	Diners' Club	Visa and MasterCard
Ball-point pens	Reynolds	Parker
CAT scanners	EMI	General Electric
Hand calculators	Bowmar	Texas Instruments
Food processors	Cuisinart	Black & Decker

The imitators captured the market by offering lower prices, selling an improved product, or using superior market power and resources.

Carpenter and Nakamoto examined strategies for launching a new product into a market dominated by one brand, such as Jell-O or FedEx. (These brands, which include many market pioneers, are particularly difficult to attack because many are the standard against which others are judged.) They identified four strategies that have good profit potential in this situation:

1. *Differentiation:* Positioning away from the dominant brand with a comparable or premium price and heavy advertising spending to establish the new brand as a credible alternative. Example: Honda's motorcycle challenges Harley-Davidson.

2. *Challenger:* Positioning close to the dominant brand with heavy advertising spending and comparable or premium price to challenge the dominant brand as the category standard. Example: Pepsi competing against Coke.

3. *Niche:* Positioning away from the dominant brand with a high price and a low advertising budget to exploit a profitable niche. Example: Tom's of Maine all-natural toothpaste competing against Crest.

4. *Premium:* Positioning near the dominant brand with little advertising spending but a premium price to move "up market" relative to the dominant brand. Examples: Godiva chocolate and Haagen-Dazs ice cream competing against standard brands.

Sources: See Ralph Biggadike, *Entering New Markets: Strategies and Performance* (Cambridge, MA: Marketing Science Institute, 1977), pp. 12–20; Steven P. Schnaars, *Managing Imitation Strategies: How later Entrants Seize Markets from Pioneers* (New York: The Free Press, 1994); Gregory S. Carpenter and Kent Nakamoto, "Competitive Strategies for Late Entry into a Market with a Dominant Brand," *Management Science* (October 1990): 1268–78; Gregory S. Carpenter and Kent Nakamoto, "Competitive Late Mover Strategies," working paper, Northwestern University, 1993.

balancing customer and competitor orientations

We have stressed the importance of a company's positioning itself competitively as a market leader, challenger, follower, or nicher. Yet a company must not spend all its time focusing on competitors. We can distinguish between two types of companies: competitor-centered and customer-centered. A *competitor-centered company* sets its course as follows:

Situation

- Competitor W is going all out to crush us in Miami.
- Competitor X is improving its distribution coverage in Houston and hurting our sales.
- Competitor Y has cut its price in Denver, and we lost three share points.
- Competitor Z has introduced a new service feature in New Orleans, and we are losing sales.

Reactions

- We will withdraw from the Miami market because we cannot afford to fight this battle.
- We will increase our advertising expenditure in Houston.
- We will meet competitor Y's price cut in Denver.
- We will increase our sales-promotion budget in New Orleans.

This kind of planning has some pluses and minuses. On the positive side, the company develops a fighter orientation. It trains its marketers to be on constant alert, to watch for weaknesses in its competitors' and its own position. On the negative side, the company is too reactive. Rather than formulating and executing a consistent, customer-oriented strategy, it determines its moves based on its competitors' moves. It does not move toward its own goals. It does not know where it will end up, because so much depends on what its competitors do.

A *customer-centered company* focuses more on customer developments in formulating its strategies.

Situation

- The total market is growing at 4 percent annually.
- The quality-sensitive segment is growing at 8 percent annually.
- The deal-prone customer segment is also growing fast, but these customers do not stay with any supplier very long.
- A growing number of customers have expressed an interest in a 24-hour hot line, which no one in the industry offers.

Reactions

- We will focus more effort on reaching and satisfying the quality segment of the market. We will buy better components, improve quality control, and shift our advertising theme to quality.
- We will avoid cutting prices and making deals because we do not want the kind of customer that buys this way.
- We will install a 24-hour hot line if it looks promising.

Clearly, the customer-centered company is in a better position to identify new opportunities and set a course that promises to deliver long-run profits. By monitoring customer needs, it can decide which customer groups and emerging needs are the most important to serve, given its resources and objectives. Jeff Bezos, founder of Amazon.com, strongly favors a customer-centered orientation. "Amazon.com's mantra has been that we were going to obsess over our customer and not our competitors. We watch our competitors, learn from them, see the things that they were doing good for customers and copy those things as much as we can. But we were never going to obsess over them."[60]

summary

1. To prepare an effective marketing strategy, a company must study its competitors as well as its actual and potential customers. Companies need to identify competitors' strategies, objectives, strengths, weaknesses, and reaction patterns. They also need to know how to design an effective competitive intelligence system.

2. A company's closest competitors are those seeking to satisfy the same customers and needs and making similar offers. A company should also pay attention to latent competitors, who may offer new or other ways to satisfy the same needs. A company should identify competitors by using both industry and market-based analyses.

3. Competitive intelligence needs to be collected, interpreted, and disseminated continuously. Managers should be able to receive timely information about competitors.

4. Managers need to conduct a customer value analysis to reveal the company's strengths and weaknesses relative to competitors. The aim of this analysis is to determine the benefits customers want and how they perceive the relative value of competitors' offers.

5. A market leader has the largest market share in the relevant product market. To remain dominant, the leader looks for ways to expand total market demand, attempts to protect its current market share, and perhaps tries to increase its market share.

6. A market challenger attacks the market leader and other competitors in an aggressive bid for more market share. Challengers can choose from five types of general attack; challengers must also choose specific strategies: discount prices, produce cheaper goods, produce prestige goods, produce a wide variety of goods, innovate in products or distribution, improve services, reduce manufacturing costs, or engage in intensive advertising.

7. A market follower is a runner-up firm that is willing to maintain its market share and not rock the boat. A follower can play the role of counterfeiter, cloner, imitator, or adapter.

8. A market nicher serves small market segments not being served by larger firms. The key to nichemanship is specialization.

9. As important as a competitive orientation is in today's global markets, companies should not overdo the emphasis on competitors. They should maintain a good balance of consumer and competitor monitoring.

applications

marketing debate – how do you attack a category leader?

Attacking a leader is always difficult. Some strategists recommend attacking a leader "head-on" by targeting its strengths. Other strategists disagree and recommend flanking and attempting to avoid the leader's strengths.

Take a position: The best way to challenge a leader is to attack its strengths versus The best way to attack a leader is to avoid a head-on assault and to adopt a flanking strategy.

marketing and advertising

1. Few product categories have as many competing products and brands as the detergent category. The ad in Figure 1 shows how Surf is responding to competitive pressure from other brands—by suggesting that customers try one of the other Surf products.

   a. What kind of competitive strategy does this ad represent? Explain.

   b. What are the arguments for and against Surf using a price-discount strategy instead of the strategy represented in the ad?

   c. Does Surf appear to have a customer or competitor orientation?

2. This Listerine Essential Care Toothpaste ad (Figure 2) promotes a mouth-care product closely related to Listerine's well-known mouthwash products. The highlighted feature (germ-killing ability) is the same as the main feature of Listerine mouthwash. In this case, however, the highlighted benefit is preventing (or reversing) gingivitis.

   a. Does Listerine appear to be a market leader, challenger, follower, or nicher in the toothpaste category?

   b. How does this ad incorporate competitive strengths and weaknesses?

   c. Colgate is one of the leading toothpaste brands. From its perspective, how can Listerine be classified as a competitor?

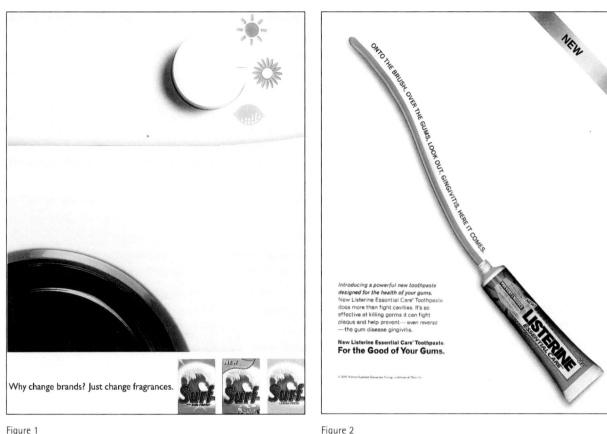

Figure 1   Figure 2

online marketing today

NetFlix is a fast-growing DVD rental site that has carved out a popular niche between retail giants like Blockbuster and online retailers like Amazon.com. The company invites movie fans to pay $19.95 per month for all the DVD movies they can see in a month. Although customers can only rent three movies at one time, they can rent up to three more as soon as they return the first three. DVDs arrive in the mail and include a postage-paid envelope for returning rentals. NetFlix does not levy late fees or set deadlines for returns, so customers can watch at their leisure without incurring penalties. This combination of convenience and value propelled NetFlix into the top five e-commerce sites and helped it attract more than 300,000 regular monthly customers in less than two years of operation.[61]

Go to the NetFlix site (*www.netflix.com*) and read about what the company offers. Next, move to the Customer Service page and browse the top customer questions. As a nicher, which of the specialist roles does NetFlix appear to be adopting? What are the risks of this strategy? What entry, mobility, and exit barriers can you identify for the industry in which NetFlix is currently operating?

you're the marketer: sonic pda marketing plan

Marketing Plan Pro

Competitive strategy comes into play in two areas of the marketing plan. First, in assessing the current marketing situation, businesses must identify their competitors and learn more about each rival's strengths and weaknesses. Second, they have to use competitive intelligence and analysis to shape their overall competitive strategy, which is supported by the marketing mix.

Sonic is a new entrant in an established industry characterized by competitors with relatively high brand identity and strong market positions. In your role of assisting Jane Melody with the development of Sonic's marketing plan, use your knowledge of competitive strategy to consider the following key issues that will affect the company's ability to successfully introduce a new personal digital assistant product:

- What is the strategic group for Sonic?
- Which firm is the market leader, and what are its objectives, strengths, and weaknesses? What additional competitive intelligence is needed to answer this question more completely?
- How would you classify Sonic's main competitors in terms of strength, closeness, and good versus bad?
- Which competitive strategy would be most effective for Sonic?

Think carefully about how Sonic's competitive strategy will affect its marketing strategy and tactics. Then summarize your ideas in a written marketing plan or enter them into the Competition, SWOT Analysis, Situation Analysis, Market Summary, and Critical Issues sections of the *Marketing Plan Pro* software.

notes

1. Leonard M. Fuld, *The New Competitor Intelligence: The Complete Resource for Finding, Analyzing, and Using Information about Your Competitors* (New York: John Wiley, 1995); John A. Czepiel, *Competitive Marketing Strategy* (Upper Saddle River, NJ: Prentice Hall, 1992).

2. Michael E. Porter, *Competitive Strategy* (New York: The Free Press, 1980), pp. 22–23.

3. Hans Katayama, "Fated to Feud: Sony versus Matsushita," *Business Tokyo* (November 1991): 28–32.

4. Michael Krantz, "Click Till You Drop," *Time*, July 20, 1998, pp. 34–39; Michael Krauss, "The Web Is Taking Your Customers for Itself," *Marketing News*, June 8, 1998, p. 8.

5. Jonathan Gaw, "Britannica Gives in and Gets Online," *Los Angeles Times*, October 19, 2000, p. A-1.

6. Jay Palmer, "Palmed Off: Handy Gadgets Are Hot Today, but the Future Belongs to Wireless Phones," *Barron's*, February 28, 2000.

7. Kathryn Rudie Harrigan, "The Effect of Exit Barriers upon Strategic Flexibility," *Strategic Management Journal* 1 (1980): 165–76.

8. Michael E. Porter, *Competitive Advantage* (New York: The Free Press, 1985), pp. 225, 485.

9. Porter, *Competitive Strategy*, ch. 13.

10. Jeffrey F. Rayport and Bernard J. Jaworski, *e-Commerce* (New York: McGraw-Hill, 2001), p. 53.

11. Porter, *Competitive Strategy*, ch. 7.

12. "The Hardest Sell," *Newsweek*, March 30, 1992, p. 41.

13. William E. Rothschild, *How to Gain (and Maintain) the Competitive Advantage* (New York: McGraw-Hill, 1989), ch. 5.

14. Robert V. L. Wright, *A System for Managing Diversity* (Cambridge, MA: Arthur D. Little, 1974).

15. The following has been drawn from Bruce Henderson's various writings, including "The Unanswered Questions, the Unsolved Problems" (paper delivered in a speech at Northwestern University in 1986); *Henderson on Corporate Strategy* (New York: Mentor, 1982); and "Understanding the Forces of Strategic and Natural Competition," *Journal of Business Strategy* (Winter 1981): 11–15.

16. For more discussion, see Leonard M. Fuld, *Monitoring the Competition* (New York: John Wiley, 1988).

17. "Spy/Counterspy," *Context* (Summer 1998): 20–21.

18. Steven Flax, "How to Snoop on Your Competitors," *Fortune*, May 14, 1984, pp. 29–33.

19. Porter, *Competitive Advantage*, Ch. 6.

20. Ogale Idudu, "London's Once-Stuffy Selfridges Now Woos Hipsters," *Wall Street Journal*, September 19, 2000, p. B1.

21. Paul Lukas, "First: Read Column, Rinse, Repeat," *Fortune*, August 3, 1998, p. 50.

22. Carla Rapoport, "You Can Make Money in Japan," *Fortune*, February 12, 1990, pp. 85–92; Keith H. Hammonds, "A Moment Kodak Wants to Capture," *BusinessWeek*, August 27, 1990, pp. 52–53; Alison Fahey, "Polaroid, Kodak, Fuji Get Clicking," *Advertising Age*, May 20, 1991, p. 18; Peter Nulty, "The New Look of Photography," *Fortune*, July 1, 1991, pp. 36–41.

23. "Kodak Develops Own Strategy," *Nikkei Weekly*, May 15, 2000.

24. Erika Rasmusson, "The Jackpot," *Sales & Marketing Management* (June 1998): 35–41.

25. Ron Winslow, "Missing a Beat: How a Breakthrough Quickly Broke Down for Johnson & Johnson: Its Stent Device Transformed Cardiac Care, Then Left a Big Opening for Rivals: 'Getting Kicked in the Shins,' " *Wall Street Journal*, September 18, 1998, p. A1.

26. The intensified competition that has taken place worldwide in recent years has sparked management interest in models of military warfare; see Sun Tsu, *The Art of War* (London: Oxford University Press, 1963); Miyamoto Mushashi, *A Book of Five Rings* (Woodstock, NY: Overlook Press, 1974); Carl von Clausewitz, *On War* (London: Routledge & Kegan Paul, 1908); B. H. Liddell-Hart, *Strategy* (New York: Praeger, 1967).

27. These six defense strategies, as well as the five attack strategies, are taken from Philip Kotler and Ravi Singh, "Marketing Warfare in the 1980s," *Journal of Business Strategy* (Winter 1981): 30–41. For additional reading, see Gerald A. Michaelson, *Winning the Marketing War: A Field Manual for Business Leaders* (Lanham, MD: Abt Books, 1987); AL Ries and Jack Trout, *Marketing Warfare* (New York: New American Library, 1986); Jay Conrad Levinson, *Guerrilla Marketing* (Boston: Houghton-Mifflin Co., 1984); and Barrie G. James, *Business Wargames* (Harmondsworth, England: Penguin Books, 1984).

28. "Leader of the Pack," *Pittsburgh Post-Gazette*, April 1, 2000.

29. "Goodyear Timeline: 1990s," <*www.goodyear.com.*>.

30. Porter, *Competitive Strategy*, ch. 4.

31. Richard Thomkins, "Wal-Mart Invades Food Chain Turf," *St. Louis Post-Dispatch*, October 7, 1998, p. C1; Maria Halkias, "Wal-Mart to Debut Local Grocery Store," *Dallas Morning News*, August 4, 2000.

32. Relative market share is the business's market share in its served market relative to the combined market share of its three leading competitors, expressed as a percentage. For example, if this business has 30 percent of the market and its three largest competitors have 20 percent, 10 percent, and 10 percent: 30/(20110110)575 percent relative market share.

33. Sidney Schoeffler, Robert D. Buzzell, and Donald F. Heany, "Impact of Strategic Planning on Profit Performance," *Harvard Business Review* (March–April 1974): 137–45; Robert D. Buzzell, Bradley T. Gale, and Ralph G. M. Sultan, "Market Share: A Key to Profitability," *Harvard Business Review* (January–February 1975): 97–106.

34. Buzzell et al., "Market Share," pp. 97, 100. The results held up in more recent PIMS studies, where the database now includes 2,600 business units in a wide range of industries. See Robert D. Buzzell and Bradley T. Gale, *The PIMS Principles: Linking Strategy to Performance* (New York: The Free Press, 1987).

35. Richard G. Hamermesh, M. J. Anderson Jr., and J. E. Harris, "Strategies for Low Market Share Businesses," *Harvard Business Review* (May–June 1978): 95–102.

6. Carolyn Y. Woo and Arnold C. Cooper, "The Surprising Case for Low Market Share," *Harvard Business Review* (November–December 1982): 106–13; also see their "Market-Share Leadership: Not Always So Good," *Harvard Business Review* (January–February 1984): 2–4.

7. This curve assumes that pretax return on sales is highly correlated with profitability and that company revenue is a surrogate for market share. Michael Porter, in his *Competitive Strategy* (p. 43), shows a similar V-shaped curve.

8. Patricia Sellers, "McDonald's Starts Over," *Fortune*, June 22, 1998, pp. 34–35; David Leonhardt, "McDonald's: Can It Regain Its Golden Touch?" *Miami Herald*, August 3, 2000.

9. Yochi J. Dreazen and Shawn Young, "Regulators Stop Short of a Verizon Split," *Wall Street Journal*, March 23, 2001, p. A3.

10. Philip Kotler and Paul N. Bloom, "Strategies for High Market-Share Companies," *Harvard Business Review* (November–December 1975): 63–72. Also see Porter, *Competitive Advantage*, pp. 221–26.

11. Robert D. Buzzell and Frederick D. Wiersema, "Successful Share-Building Strategies," *Harvard Business Review* (January–February 1981): 135–44.

12. Ronald Henkoff, "P&G: New & Improved," *Fortune*, October 14, 1996, pp. 151–60.

13. Zachary Schiller, "Ed Artzt's Elbow Grease Has P&G Shining," *BusinessWeek*, October 10, 1994, pp. 84–85.

14. Sarah Lorge, "Top of the Charts: Procter & Gamble," *Sales & Marketing Management* (July 1998): 50; Jane Hodges, "P&G Tries to Push Online Advertising," *Fortune*, September 28, 1998, p. 280.

15. Robert J. Dolan, "Models of Competition: A Review of Theory and Empirical Evidence," in Ben M. Enis and Kenneth Roering, (eds.), *Review of Marketing* (Chicago: American Marketing Association, 1981), pp. 224–34.

16. Kevin Maney, "Sun Rises on Java's Promise: CEO McNealy Sets Sights on Microsoft," *USA Today*, July 14, 1997, p. B1; Robert D. Hof, "A Java in Every Pot? Sun Aims to Make It the Language of All Smart Appliances," *BusinessWeek*, July 27, 1998, p. 71; Daniel Lyons, "Solar Power," *Forbes*, January 22, 2001, p. 82.

17. Holman W. Jenkins Jr., "Business World: On a Happier Note, Orange Juice," *Wall Street Journal*, September 23, 1998, p. 23; Robert J. O'Harrow Jr., "PepsiCo to Acquire Quaker for Billion," *Washington Post*, December 5, 2000, p. E-01.

48. Martin Linstrom and Tim Frank Andersen, *Brand Building on the Internet* (London: Kogan Page, 2000), p. 44.

49. Theodore Levitt, "Innovative Imitation," *Harvard Business Review* (September–October 1966): 63. Also see Steven P. Schnaars, *Managing Imitation Strategies: How Later Entrants Seize Markets from Pioneers* (New York: The Free Press, 1994).

50. Greg Burns, "A Fruit Look by Any Other Name," *BusinessWeek*, June 26, 1995, pp. 72, 76.

51. Stuart F. Brown, "The Company that Out-Harleys Harley," *Fortune*, September 28, 1998, pp. 56–57.

52. Allen J. McGrath, "Growth Strategies with a '90s Twist," *Across the Board* (March 1995): 43–46; Antonio Ligi, "The Bottom Line: Logitech Plots Its Escape from Mouse Trap," Dow Jones Newswire, February 20, 2001.

53. Richard A. Melcher, "From the Microbrewers Who Brought You Bud, Coors…," *BusinessWeek*, April 24, 1995, pp. 66–70.

54. Melita Marie Garza, "Illinois Tool Works Stock Continues to Suffer Since Acquisition of Firm," *Chicago Tribune*, November 16, 2000.

55. Donald K. Clifford and Richard E. Cavanaugh, *The Winning Performance· How America's High- and Midsize Growth Companies Succeed* (New York: Bantam Books, 1985).

56. Jim Kirk, "Company Finds Itself, Finds Success, Alberto-Culver Adopts Strategy of Knowing Its Strengths and Promoting Small Brands, Rather Than Tackling Giants," *Chicago Tribune*, January 22, 1998, p. 1; Ameet Sachdev, "Melrose Park, Ill.-Based Hair, Skin Firm Sees Shares Surge in 2000," *Chicago Tribune*, January 18, 2001.

57. Reported in E. R. Linneman and L. J. Stanton, *Making Niche Marketing Work* (New York: McGraw-Hill, 1991).

58. Gabriella Stern, "Arm & Hammer Is Losing Lead in Baking-Soda Toothpaste Sales," *Wall Street Journal*, December 28, 1993; p. B-8; Nikhil Deogun,and Emily Nelson, "SmithKline Is a Leading Bidder for Block, *Wall Street Journal*, October 6, 2000, p. B-6.

59. Bro Uttal, "Pitching Computers to Small Businesses," *Fortune*, April 1, 1985, pp. 95–104; also see Stuart Gannes, "The Riches in Market Niches," *Fortune*, April 27, 1987, pp. 227–30.

60. Robert Spector, *Amazon.com: Get Big Fast* (New York: HarperBusiness, 2000), p. 151.

61. "Online Purchases Rebound, Says E-Commerce Index from NextCard," *CnetNews.com*, September 11, 2001, <investor.cnet.com/investor/news/newsitem/)-9900-1028-7128874-0.html>.

positioning and differentiating the market offering through the product life cycle

Kotler on Marketing

Watch the product life cycle; but more important, watch the market life cycle.

In this chapter, we will address the following questions:

- How can a firm choose and communicate an effective positioning in the market?
- What are the major differentiating attributes available to firms?
- What marketing strategies are appropriate at each stage of the product life cycle?
- What marketing strategies are appropriate at each stage of the market's evolution?

Today's economies are afflicted with surpluses, not shortages. In a U.S. supermarket, there are not only several brands of toothpaste but one brand, Colgate, offers a dozen varieties—with baking soda or peroxide, or loaded with "sparkling white" or tartar control. Kellogg's Eggo waffles come in 16 flavors, and Kleenex tissue comes in nine varieties. Consider other markets. Investors can choose among 8,000 mutual funds. Students can choose among hundreds of business schools. For the seller, this spells hypercompetition. For the buyer, this spells overchoice.

No company can win if its product and offering resembles every other product and offering. Today, most companies are guilty of strategy convergence—namely, undifferentiated strategies. Companies must pursue meaningful and *relevant positioning and differentiation. Each company and offering must represent a distinctive big idea in the mind of the target market; and each company must dream up new features, services and guarantees, special rewards for loyal users, and new conveniences and enjoyments.*

Yet even when a company succeeds in distinguishing itself, the differences are short-lived. Competitors are quicker than ever in copying good ideas; therefore companies constantly need to think up new value-adding features and benefits to win the attention and interest of choice-rich, price-prone consumers.

Companies normally reformulate their marketing strategies and offerings several times. Economic conditions change, competitors launch new assaults, and the product passes through new stages of buyer interest and requirements. Consequently, strategies appropriate to each stage in the product's life cycle must be developed. The goal is to extend the product's life and profitability, keeping in mind that the product will not last forever. This chapter explores specific ways a company can effectively position and differentiate its offerings to achieve competitive advantage throughout the life cycle of a product or an offering.

developing and communicating a positioning strategy

All marketing strategy is built on STP—Segmentation, Targeting, and Positioning. A company discovers different needs and groups in the marketplace, targets those needs and groups that it can satisfy in a the superior way, and then positions its offering so that the target market recognizes the company's distinctive offering and image. If a company does a poor job of positioning, the market will be confused as to what to expect. If a company does an excellent job of positioning, then it can work out the rest of its marketing planning and differentiation from its positioning strategy.

We define positioning as follows: **Positioning** is the act of designing the company's offering and image to occupy a distinctive place in the mind of the target market. The end result of positioning is the successful creation of a customer-focused **value proposition**, a cogent reason why the target market should buy the product. Table 11.1 shows how three companies—Perdue, Volvo, and Domino's—defined their value proposition given their target customers, benefits, and prices.

table **11.1**	Examples of Value Propositions Demand States and Marketing Tasks

Company and Product	Target Customers	Benefits	Price	Value Proposition
Perdue (chicken)	Quality-conscious consumers of chicken	Tenderness	10% premium	More tender golden chicken at a moderate premium price
Volvo (station wagon)	Safety-conscious "upscale" families	Durability and safety	20% premium	The safest, most durable wagon in which your family can ride
Domino's (pizza)	Convenience-minded pizza lovers	Delivery speed and good quality	15% premium	A good hot pizza, delivered to your door within 30 minutes of ordering, at a moderate price

positioning according to ries and trout

The word *positioning* was popularized by two advertising executives, Al Ries and Jack Trout. They see positioning as a creative exercise done with an existing product:[1]

> Positioning starts with a product. A piece of merchandise, a service, a company, an institution, or even a person. . . . But positioning is not what you do to a product. Positioning is what you do to the mind of the prospect. That is, you position the product in the mind of the prospect.

Ries and Trout argue that well-known products generally hold a distinctive position in consumers' minds. Hertz is thought of as the world's largest auto-rental agency, Coca-Cola as the world's largest soft-drink company, and Porsche as one of the world's best sports cars. These brands own these positions, and it would be hard for a competitor to claim them.

A competitor has three strategic alternatives:

The first is to strengthen its own current position in the consumer's mind. Avis acknowledged its second position in the rental car business and claimed: "We're number two. We try harder." 7-Up capitalized on not being a cola drink by advertising itself as "the Uncola."

The second strategy is to grab an unoccupied position. Three Musketeers chocolate bar advertised itself as having 45 percent less fat than other chocolate bars. United Jersey Bank, noting that giant banks were usually slower in arranging loans, positioned itself as "the fast-moving bank."

The third strategy is to *de-position* or *re-position* the competition in the customer's mind. Most U.S. buyers of dinnerware thought that Lenox and Royal Doulton china both come from England. Royal Doulton de-positioned Lenox china by showing that it is made in New Jersey. BMW attempts to de-position Mercedes Benz with the comparison: "The ultimate sitting machine versus the ultimate driving machine." Popeye cajunstyle fried chicken aims to "save America from bland chicken" (implying an attack on KFC). Wendy's famous commercial, in which a 70-year-old woman named Clara looked at a competitor's hamburger and said "Where's the beef?" showed how an attack could destabilize consumer confidence in the leader.

Ries and Trout argue that, in an overadvertised society, the mind often knows brands in the form of *product ladders*, such as Coke-Pepsi-RC Cola or Hertz-Avis-National. The top firm is remembered best. For example, when asked "Who was the first person to fly alone across the Atlantic Ocean successfully?" we answer "Charles Lindbergh." When asked, "Who was the second person to do it?" we draw a blank. This is why companies fight for the number-one position. The "largest firm" position can be held by only one brand. The second brand should invent and lead in a new category. Thus 7-Up is the number-one Uncola, Porsche is the number-one small sports car, and Dial is the number-one deodorant soap. A fourth strategy is the exclusive-club strategy. For example, a company can promote the idea that it is one of the Big Three. The Big Three idea was invented by the third-largest U.S. auto firm, Chrysler. (The market leader never invents this concept.) The implication is that those in the club are the "best."

Ries and Trout essentially deal with communication strategies for positioning or re-positioning a brand in the consumer's mind. Yet they acknowledge that positioning requires every tangible aspect of product, price, place, and promotion to support the chosen to positioning strategy.

positioning according to treacy and wiersema

Two consultants, Michael Treacy and Fred Wiersema, proposed a positioning framework called *value disciplines*.[2] Within its industry, a firm could aspire to be the *product leader*, the *operationally excellent firm*, or the *customer intimate firm*. This is based on the notion that in every market there is a mix of three types of customers. Some customers favor the firm that is advancing on the technological frontier (product leadership); other customers want highly reliable performance (operational excellence), and still others want high responsiveness in meeting their individual needs (customer intimacy).

Treacy and Wiersema observed that a firm cannot normally be best in all three ways, or even in two ways. It lacks sufficient funds, and each value discipline requires different managerial mind-sets and investments that often conflict. Thus McDonald's excels at operational excellence, but could not afford to slow down its service to prepare hamburgers differently for each customer. Nor could McDonald's lead in new products because each addition would disrupt the smooth functioning of its normal operations. Even within a large company, such as GE, each division might follow a different value discipline: GE's major appliance division pursues operational excellence, its engineered plastics division pursues customer intimacy, and its jet engine division pursues product leadership.

Treacy and Wiersema propose that a business should follow four rules for success:

1. Become best at one of the three value disciplines.
2. Achieve an adequate performance level in the other two disciplines.
3. Keep improving one's superior position in the chosen discipline so as not to lose out to a competitor.
4. Keep becoming more adequate in the other two disciplines, because competitors keep raising customers' expectations.

positioning: how many ideas to promote?

A company must decide how many ideas (e.g., benefits, features) to convey in its positioning to its target customers. Many marketers advocate promoting only one central benefit. Rosser Reeves believes a company should develop a *unique selling proposition* (USP) for each brand and stick to it.[3] Crest toothpaste consistently promotes its anticavity protection, and Mercedes promotes its great engineering. Ries and Trout favor one consistent positioning message.[4] This makes for easier communication to the target market; it results in employees being clearer about what counts; and it makes it easier to align the whole organization with the central positioning.

The brand should tout itself as "number one" on the benefit it selects. Number-one positionings include "best quality," "best performance," "best service," "best styling," "best value," "lowest price," "safest," "fastest," "most customized," "most convenient," "most technological," "most reliable," or "most prestigious." If a company consistently hammers away at one positioning and delivers on it, it will probably be best known and recalled for this benefit. For example, Home Depot has gained a reputation for "best service" among home-improvement product retailers:

Home Depot Since Home Depot opened its first store in 1978 in Atlanta, the company has emphasized exemplary customer service. Its sales staff is trained to offer on-the-spot lessons in tile laying, electrical installations, and other projects; they are experienced tradespersons—plumbers, electricians, and carpenters. In recent years there have been customer complaints about clutter in the aisles and salespeople stocking items instead of providing service, so starting in 2001, Home Depot gave its stores a makeover called Service Performance Improvement (SPI). SPI limits restocking to off-peak hours and prohibits forklifts in store aisles during the day. The program resulted in up to a 70 percent increase in employee interactions with customers. Before SPI was introduced, employees spent as little as 40 percent of their time with customers.[5]

Not everyone agrees that single-benefit positioning is always best. What if the market tires of the benefit or believes that most competitors now deliver it? Today people believe that most cars are safe and that most cars have pretty good quality. Double-benefit positioning may be more distinctive. Steelcase, Inc., a leading office-furniture-systems company, claims two benefits: "best on-time delivery" and "best installation support." Volvo double-positions its automobiles as "safest" and "most durable."

There are even cases of successful triple-benefit positioning. Smith Kline Beecham promotes its Aquafresh toothpaste as offering three benefits: anticavity protection, better breath, and whiter teeth. The challenge is to convince consumers that the brand delivers all three. Smith Kline's solution was to create a toothpaste that squeezes out of the tube in three colors, thus visually confirming the three benefits. In doing this, Smith Kline "countersegmented"; that is, it attracted three segments instead of one.

As companies increase the number of claimed benefits for their brand, they risk disbelief and a loss of clear positioning. In general, a company must avoid four major positioning errors:

1. *Underpositioning:* Some companies discover that buyers have only a vague idea of the brand. The brand is seen as just another entry in a crowded marketplace. When Pepsi introduced its clear Crystal Pepsi in 1993, customers were distinctly unimpressed. They didn't see "clarity" as an important benefit in a soft drink.

2. *Overpositioning:* Buyers may have too narrow an image of the brand. Thus a consumer might think that diamond rings at Tiffany start at $5,000 when in fact Tiffany now offers affordable diamond rings starting at $1,000.

3. *Confused positioning:* Buyers might have a confused image of the brand resulting from the company's making too many claims or changing the brand's positioning too frequently. This was the case with Stephen Jobs's sleek and powerful NeXT desktop computer, which was positioned first for students, then for engineers, and then for businesspeople, all unsuccessfully.

4. *Doubtful positioning:* Buyers may find it hard to believe the brand claims in view of the product's features, price, or manufacturer. When GM's Cadillac division introduced the Cimarron, it positioned the car as a luxury competitor with BMW, Mercedes, and Audi. Although the car featured leather seats, a luggage rack, lots of chrome, and a Cadillac logo stamped on the chassis, customers saw it as a dolled-up version of Chevy's Cavalier and Oldsmobile's Firenza. The car was positioned as "more for more": customers saw it as "less for more."

Solving the positioning problem enables the company to solve the marketing-mix problem. Seizing the "high-quality position" requires the firm to produce high-quality products, charge a high price, distribute through high-class dealers, and advertise in high-quality magazines.

How do companies select their positioning? Consider the following example:

A theme park company wants to build a new park in the Los Angeles area to cater to the large number of tourists. Seven theme parks now operate in this area: Disneyland, Magic Mountain, Knott's Berry Farm, Busch Gardens, Japanese Deer Park, Marineland of the Pacific, and Lion Country Safari.

The company presented tourists with a series of trios (for example, Busch Gardens, Japanese Deer Park, and Disneyland) and asked them to choose the two most similar attractions and the two least similar attractions in each. A statistical analysis led to the *perceptual map* in Figure 11.1 The map contains two features. The seven dots represent the seven tourist attractions. The closer any two attractions are, the more similar they are in tourists' minds. Thus Disneyland and Magic Mountain are perceived as similar, whereas Disneyland and Lion Country Safari are perceived as very different.

The map also shows nine satisfactions that people look for in tourist attractions. These are indicated by arrows. Marineland of the Pacific is perceived as involving the "least waiting time," so it is farthest along the imaginary line of the "little waiting" arrow. Consumers think of Busch Gardens as the most economical choice.[6]

The theme park company can now choose from several different positioning possibilities:[7]

- *Attribute positioning:* A company positions itself on an attribute, such as size or number of years in existence. Disneyland can advertise itself as the largest theme park in the world.
- *Benefit positioning:* The product is positioned as the leader in a certain benefit. Knott's Berry Farm may try to position itself as a theme park that delivers a fantasy experience, such as living in the Old West.

| figure **11.1** | Perceptual Map |

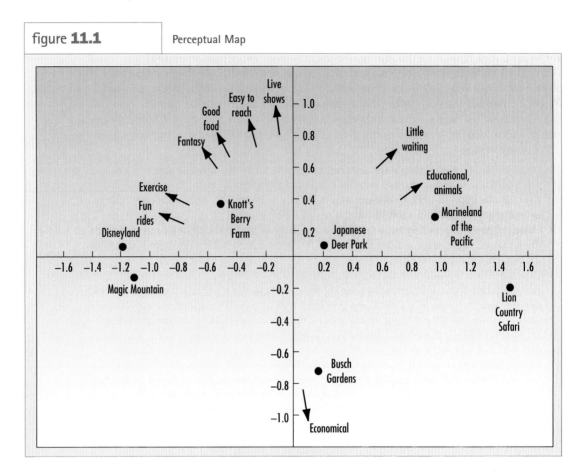

- *Use or application positioning:* Positioning the product as best for some use or application. Japanese Deer Park can position itself for the tourist who has only an hour to catch some quick entertainment.
- *User positioning:* Positioning the product as best for some user group. Magic Mountain can advertise itself as best for "thrill seekers."
- *Competitor positioning:* The product claims to be better in some way than a named competitor. For example, Lion Country Safari can advertise having a greater variety of animals than Japanese Deer Park.
- *Product category positioning:* The product is positioned as the leader in a certain product category. Marineland of the Pacific can position itself not as a "recreational theme park" but as an "educational institution."
- *Quality or price positioning:* The product is positioned as offering the best value. Busch Gardens can position itself as offering the "best value" for the money.

which positioning to promote?

Suppose a company has identified four alternative positioning platforms: technology, cost, quality, and service (Table 11.2). It has one major competitor. Both companies stand at 8 on technology (1 = low score, 10 = high score), which means they both have good technology. The competitor has a better standing on cost (8 instead of 6). The company offers higher quality than its competitor (8 compared to 6). Finally, both companies provide below-average service.

table **11.2**			Method for Competitive–Advantage Selection			
(1)	(2)	(3)	(4)	(5)	(6)	(7)
			Importance of Improving	Affordability	Competitor's Ability to	
Competitive Advantage	Company Standing	Competitor Standing	Standing (H–M–L)*	and Speed (H–M–L)	Improve Standing (H–M–L)	Recommended Action
Technology	8	8	L	L	M	Hold
Cost	6	8	H	M	M	Monitor
Quality	8	6	L	L	H	Monitor
Service	4	3	H	H	L	Invest

*H=high; M=medium; L=low

It would seem that the company should go after cost or service to improve its market appeal. However, other considerations arise. The first is how target customers feel about improvements in each of these attributes. Column 4 indicates that improvements in cost and service would be of high importance to customers, but can the company afford to make the improvements and how fast can it provide them? Column 5 shows that improving service would have high affordability and speed, but would the competitor be able to match the improved service? Column 6 shows that the competitor's ability to improve service is low. Based on this information, column 7 shows the appropriate actions to take. The one that makes the most sense is for the company to improve its service and promote this improvement. This was the conclusion Monsanto reached in one of its chemical markets. Monsanto hired additional technical service people. When they were trained and ready, Monsanto promoted itself as the "technical service leader."

communicating the company's positioning

To communicate a company or brand positioning, a marketing plan should include a *positioning statement*. The statement should follow the form: To *(target group and need)* our *(Brand)* is *(concept)* that *(point-of-difference)*.[8] For example: "To *busy professionals who need to stay organized, Palm Pilot* is *an electronic organizer* that *allows you to back up files on your PC more easily and reliably than competitive products*." Sometimes the positioning statement is more detailed:

> *Mountain Dew:* To young, active soft-drink consumers who have little time for sleep, Mountain Dew is the soft drink that gives you more energy than any other brand because it has the highest level of caffeine. With Mountain Dew, you can stay alert and keep going even when you haven't been able to get a good night's sleep.[9]

Note that the positioning first states the product's membership in a category (e.g., Mountain Dew is a soft drink) and then shows its point-of-difference from other members of the group (e.g., has more caffeine). The product's membership in the category suggests the points-of-parity that it might have with other products in the category, but the case for the product rests on its points-of-difference. Sometimes the marketer will put the product in a surprisingly different category before indicating the points of difference.

Mountain Dew's Web site
supports its positioning.

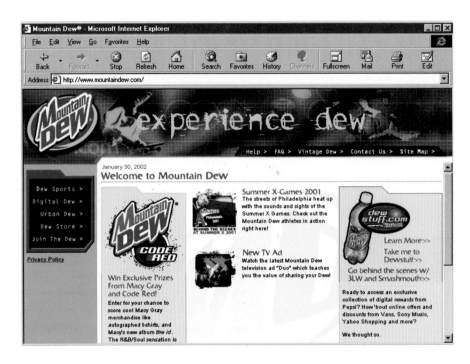

DiGiorno's pizza   DiGiorno's is a frozen pizza whose crust rises when the pizza is heated. Instead of putting it in the frozen pizza category, the marketers positioned it in the delivered pizza category. Their ad shows party guests asking which pizza delivery service the host used, but he says: "It's not delivery, its DiGiorno!" This helped highlight DiGiorno's fresh quality and superior taste over the normal frozen pizza.[10]

Once the company has developed a clear positioning statement, it must communicate that positioning effectively through all the elements of the marketing mix. Suppose a company chooses the "best quality" positioning. Quality is communicated by choosing those physical signs and cues that people normally use to judge quality. Here are some examples:

> A lawnmower manufacturer claims its lawn mower is "powerful" and has a noisy motor because buyers think noisy lawnmowers are more powerful.
> A truck manufacturer undercoats the chassis not because it needs undercoating but because undercoating suggests concern for quality.
> A car manufacturer makes cars with good-slamming doors because many buyers slam the doors in the showroom to test how well the car is built.
> Ritz Carlton hotels signal high quality by training employees to answer calls within three rings, to answer with a genuine "smile" in their voices, and to be extremely knowledgeable about all hotel services.

Quality is also communicated through other marketing elements. A high price usually signals a premium-quality product. The product's quality image is also affected by packaging, distribution, advertising, and promotion. Here are some cases where a brand's quality image was hurt:

- A well-known frozen-food brand lost its prestige image by being on sale too often.
- A premium beer's image was hurt when it switched from bottles to cans.
- A highly regarded television receiver lost its quality image when mass-merchandise outlets began to carry it.

A manufacturer's reputation also contributes to the perception of quality. Certain companies are sticklers for quality; consumers expect Nestlé and IBM products to be well made. Smart companies communicate their quality to buyers and guarantee "customer satisfaction or your money back."

As important as positioning is to a company's success, most ads fail to communicate the company or the brand's positioning. Kevin Clancy, CEO of Copernicus, a marketing strategy consulting firm, examined 340 commercials and found that only 7 percent communicated any sort of positioning; and only 50 percent mentioned product features. Not only is this a waste of advertising money, but unpositioned brands in overcrowded categories tend to devolve into price-driven brands.[11]

adding further differentiation

The task of positioning is to deliver a central idea about a company or an offering to the target market. Positioning simplifies what we think of the entity. Differentiation goes beyond positioning to spin a complex web of differences characterizing that entity. We define **differentiation** as the process of adding a set of meaningful and valued differences to distinguish the company's offering from competitors' offerings. Consider IKEA.

IKEA   IKEA, the world's largest furniture retailer, is positioned as a company offering "good quality furniture at a low price"; but IKEA has spun further differences to distinguish itself from normal furniture stores. It operates an excellent restaurant in each store (rare among furniture stores); it offers child care services while the parents shop; it offers a membership program entitling members to special discounts on their purchases beyond the normal low price; and it mails out millions of catalogs featuring the latest furniture. All this creates a highly differentiated picture of IKEA in the target market's mind.

All products can be differentiated to some extent,[12] but not all brand differences are meaningful or worthwhile. A difference will be stronger to the extent that it satisfies the following criteria:

- *Important:* The difference delivers a highly valued benefit to a sufficient number of buyers.
- *Distinctive:* The difference is delivered in a distinctive way.
- *Superior:* The difference is superior to other ways of obtaining the benefit.
- *Preemptive:* The difference cannot be easily copied by competitors.
- *Affordable:* The buyer can afford to pay for the difference.
- *Profitable:* The company will find it profitable to introduce the difference.

Many companies have introduced differentiations that failed on one or more of these tests. The Westin Stamford hotel in Singapore advertises that it is the world's tallest hotel, but a hotel's height is not important to many tourists. Polaroid's Polarvision, although distinctive and preemptive, was inferior to another way of capturing motion—namely, video cameras. When the Turner Broadcasting System installed TV monitors to beam Cable News Network (CNN) to bored shoppers in store checkout lines, it did not pass the "superior" test. Customers were not looking for a new source of entertainment in supermarkets, and Turner took a $16 million tax write-down.

Carpenter, Glazer, and Nakamoto posit that brands can sometimes be successfully differentiated on irrelevant attributes.[13] Procter & Gamble differentiates its Folger's instant coffee by its "flaked coffee crystals" created through a "unique patented process." In reality, the coffee particle's shape is irrelevant because the crystal immediately dissolves in the hot water. Saying that a brand of coffee is "mountain grown" is irrelevant because most coffee is mountain grown. Alberto Culver's Alberto Natural Silk shampoo is advertised with the slogan "We put silk in a bottle." However, a company spokesman conceded that silk does not really do anything for hair.

Sony is a good example of a company that constantly comes up with new features and benefits. As soon as Sony develops a new product, it might assemble up to three teams to view the new product as if it were a competitor's. The first team thinks of minor improvements, the second team thinks of major improvements, and the third team thinks of ways to make the product obsolete.

A major chemical company held a brainstorming session and came up with a dozen ways to create extra value for customers, among them were: helping reduce process costs by improving yield and reducing waste; helping reduce inventory by consignments, just-in-time delivery, and reduced cycle time; helping reduce administrative costs by simplified billing and electronic data interchange; improving safety for customer's employees; and reducing price to the customer by substituting components and reducing supplier costs. For more examples of differentiation, see "Marketing for the New Economy: Airlines Show They Aren't Commodities as They Jockey for Position."

Crego and Schiffrin have proposed that customer-centered organizations should study what customers value and then prepare an offering that exceeds their expectations.[14] They see this as a three-step process:

1. *Defining the customer value model:* The company first lists all the product and service factors that might influence the target customers' perception of value.

marketing for the **new economy**

Airlines Show They Aren't Commodities as They Jockey for Position

It used to be that air travel was regarded as a commodity. In 1978, deregulation kicked off an era of fierce competition. It also opened the way for some upstart "Davids" to differentiate themselves and steal passengers from airline "Goliaths." Two airlines that have been successful at differentiating themselves are Virgin Atlantic and Southwest Airlines.

Virgin Atlantic
Founded in 1983, this classy, iconoclastic airline was widely predicted to follow Laker Airway's Skytrain, a no-frills airline started by British businessman Freddy Laker, as another doomed transatlantic start-up. But in its 18-year history, Virgin has shaken up the airline industry. Richard Branson, the company's founder and current chairman and CEO, is a charismatic and talented entrepreneur. At a press conference where he launched the airline, Branson appeared wearing an old-fashioned leather flying jacket, goggles, and a helmet. When asked why he was going into the airline business, Branson quipped, "If we didn't do it, nobody else would have." Branson's personality has been a point-of-difference for Virgin Airlines. His most daring stunts, including several failed attempts to circumnavigate the globe in a hot air balloon, give the airline a certain cachet.

Southwest Airlines
The Dallas-based airline carved its niche in short-haul flights with low prices and no frills. Two Texans, Rollin King and Herb Kelleher, founded the company, originally called Air Southwest, in 1967. Southwest was a commuter service linking Dallas, Houston, and San Antonio. Eventually, it grew into a national airline operating in 55 cities across 29 states. By flying from smaller airports and avoiding major airport hubs, the airline has avoided direct competition from other airlines. Southwest also offers many short-hop flights connecting nearby cities, and its low prices on those flights lure passengers who would normally drive. The company reduced costs further by offering only basic in-flight service (no meals, no movies), and for many years the transfer of luggage between airlines was the passengers' responsibility.

Southwest knew that it could not differentiate on price alone, because competitors could easily muscle into the market with their own cheaper versions. The airline has distinguished itself as a "fun" airline, noted for humorous in-flight commentary from pilots and cabin crew members. Herb Kelleher has been known to dress up like Elvis Presley to greet passengers on occasion, and even handed out peanuts on a flight one Easter while dressed in a bunny suit. Another popular feature of Southwest flights is the first-come, first-served open seating: Passengers are given numbered cards based on when they arrive at the gate.

Kelleher, who stepped down from his CEO position in 2001, saw the company through unprecedented growth for a start-up airline. Today, Southwest is the nation's seventh-largest airline, and holds the distinction of being the only low-fare airline to achieve long-term success.

Sources: Jane Woolridge, "Baby-boom Airline Is Unknown, Cheap," *San Diego Union-Tribune,* December 30, 1984; Melanie Wells, "Red Baron: The Sun Never Sets on Richard Branson's Empire," *Forbes,* July 3, 2000; Katrina Brooker, "The Chairman of the Board Looks Back," *Fortune,* May 28, 2001.

2. *Building the customer value hierarchy:* The company now assigns each factor to one of four groups: basic, expected, desired, and unanticipated. Consider the set of factors at a fine restaurant:
   - *Basic:* The food is edible and delivered in a timely fashion. (If this is all the restaurant does right, the customer would normally not be satisfied.)
   - *Expected:* There is good china and tableware, a linen tablecloth and napkin, flowers, discreet service, and well-prepared food. (These factors make the offering acceptable, but not exceptional.)
   - *Desired:* The restaurant is pleasant and quiet, and the food is especially good and interesting.
   - *Unanticipated:* The restaurant serves a complimentary sorbet between the courses and places candy on the table after the last course is served.
3. *Deciding on the customer value package:* Now the company chooses that combination of tangible and intangible items, experiences, and outcomes designed to outperform competitors and win the customers' delight and loyalty.

differentiation tools

The number of differentiation opportunities varies with the type of industry. The Boston Consulting Group (BCG) has distinguished four types of industries based on the number of available competitive advantages and their size (see Figure 11.2):

figure **11.2**

The BCG Competitive Advantage Matrix

1. *Volume industry:* One in which companies can gain only a few, but rather large, competitive advantages. In the construction-equipment industry, a company can strive for the low-cost position or the highly differentiated position and win big on either basis. Profitability is correlated with company size and market share.
2. *Stalemated industry:* One in which there are few potential competitive advantages and each is small. In the steel industry, it is hard to differentiate the product or decrease manufacturing costs. Companies can try to hire better salespeople, entertain more lavishly, and the like, but these are small advantages. Profitability is unrelated to company market share.
3. *Fragmented industry:* One in which companies face many opportunities for differentiation, but each opportunity for competitive advantage is small. A restaurant can differentiate in many ways but end up not gaining a large market share. Both small and large restaurants can be profitable or unprofitable.
4. *Specialized industry:* One in which companies face many differentiation opportunities, and each differentiation can have a high payoff. Among companies making specialized machinery for selected market segments, some small companies can be as profitable as some large companies.

Miland Lele observed that companies differ in their potential *maneuverability* along five dimensions: *target market, product, place (channels), promotion,* and *price*.[15] The company's freedom of maneuver is affected by the industry structure and the firm's position in the industry. For each potential maneuver, the company needs to estimate the return. Those maneuvers that promise the highest return define the company's *strategic leverage*. Companies in a stalemated industry have very little maneuverability and strategic leverage, and those in specialized industries enjoy great maneuverability and strategic leverage.

Yet even in stalemated, commodity-type industries, some real or image differentiation is possible. Commodities such as bananas, salt, chicken, and milk can be differentiated. Shoppers look for the Chiquita label on bananas, the Dole label on pineapples, and the Green Giant on frozen vegetables; these brands give them an assurance of quality. Most people buy Morton salt and pay a little more; and they prefer Frank Perdue's chicken because "it takes a tough man to make a tender chicken." There are now several varieties of milk—calcium fortified, lactose free, soymilk, and so on. The marketer must start with the belief that "you can differentiate anything."

Here we will examine how a company can differentiate its market offering along five dimensions: product, services, personnel, channel, and image (see Table 11.3).

table **11.3**					
Differentiation Variables	**Product** Form	**Services** Ordering ease	**Personnel** Competence	**Channel** Coverage	**Image** Symbols
	Features	Delivery	Courtesy	Expertise	Media
	Performance	Installation	Credibility	Performance	Atmosphere
	Conformance	Customer training	Reliability		Events
	Durability	Customer consulting	Responsiveness		
	Reliability	Maintenance and repair	Communication		
	Repairability	Miscellaneous			
	Style				
	Design				

product differentiation

Physical products vary in their potential for differentiation. At one extreme we find products that allow little variation: chicken, steel, aspirin. Yet even here, some differentiation is possible. Procter & Gamble makes several brands of laundry detergent, each with a separate brand identity. At the other extreme are products capable of high differentiation, such as automobiles, commercial buildings, and furniture. Here the seller faces an abundance of design parameters, including form, features, performance quality, conformance quality, durability, reliability, repairability, style, and design.[16]

FORM   Many products can be differentiated in *form*—the size, shape, or physical structure of a product. Consider the many possible forms taken by products such as aspirin. Although aspirin is essentially a commodity, it can be differentiated by dosage size, shape, color, coating, or action time.

FEATURES   Most products can be offered with varying features that supplement the product's basic function. Being the first to introduce valued new features is one of the most effective ways to compete. Oral-B managed to differentiate its toothbrush by introducing a blue dye in the center bristles that fades and tells customers when they need a new toothbrush.

General Motors   General Motors offers the OnStar system on selected vehicles. It includes GPS (global positioning system) for locating the car's exact position. The driver can locate the nearest ATM, hospital, convenience store, gas station and hotel, and even book a room. The driver can press a button in case of an emergency to get immediate aid.

McDonald's   McDonald's has added PlayLands at a number of its U.S. and Mexican restaurants to cater to young customers. In Paraguay, McDonald's has installed a number of computer stations to cater to Internet-inclined customers.

How can a company identify and select appropriate new features? It can ask recent buyers: How do you like the product? Are there any features we could add that would improve your satisfaction? How much would you pay for each? How do you feel about the following features that other customers have suggested?

table **11.4**

Measuring Customer
Effectiveness Value

Feature	Company Cost (a)	Customer Value (b)	Customer Value/ Customer Cost (c=b/a)
Rear-window defrosting	$100	$ 200	2
Cruise control	600	600	1
Automatic transmission	800	2,400	3

The next task is to decide which features are worth adding. For each potential feature, the company should calculate *customer value* versus *company cost*. Suppose an auto manufacturer is considering the three possible improvements shown in Table 11.4. Rear-window defrosting would add $100 of cost per car at the factory level. The average customer said this feature was worth $200. The company could therefore generate $2 of incremental customer satisfaction for every $1 increase in company cost. Looking at the other two features, it appears that automatic transmission would create the most customer value per dollar of company cost. The company would also need to consider how many people want each feature, how long it would take to introduce each feature, and whether competitors could easily copy the feature.

Companies must also think in terms of feature bundles or packages. Auto companies often manufacture cars at several "trim levels." This lowers manufacturing and inventory costs. Each company must decide whether to offer feature customization at a higher cost or a few standard packages at a lower cost.

PERFORMANCE QUALITY   Most products are established at one of four performance levels: low, average, high, or superior. **Performance quality** is the level at which the product's primary characteristics operate. The important question here is: Does offering higher product performance produce higher profitability? The Strategic Planning Institute studied the impact of higher relative product quality and found a significantly positive correlation between relative product quality and return on investment (ROI). High-quality business units earned more because premium quality allowed them to charge a premium price; they benefited from more repeat purchasing, consumer loyalty, and positive word of mouth; and their costs of delivering more quality were not much higher than for business units producing low quality.

Quality's link to profitability does not mean that the firm should design the highest performance level possible. The manufacturer must design a performance level appropriate to the target market and competitors' performance levels. A company must also manage performance quality through time. Continuously improving the product often produces the highest return and market share. The second strategy is to maintain product quality at a given level. Many companies leave quality unaltered after its initial formulation unless glaring faults or opportunities occur. The third strategy is to reduce product quality through time. Some companies cut quality to offset rising costs; others reduce quality deliberately in order to increase current profits, although this course of action often hurts long-run profitability. See what happened to Schlitz.

Schlitz   Schlitz, the number-two beer brand in the United States in the 1960s and 1970s, was driven into the dust because management adopted a financially motivated strategy to increase its short-term profits and curry favor with shareholders. When it decided to cut the aging time and use less expensive hops, sales of Schlitz dropped from 17.8 million barrels in 1974 to 7.5 million in 1980. By then, its stock price had plummeted to less than 9 percent of its 1974 value. Heavy marketing expenditures and a product reformulation back to the classic recipe could not revive the brand.[17]

CONFORMANCE QUALITY   Buyers expect products to have a high **conformance quality**, which is the degree to which all the produced units are identical and meet the promised specifications. Suppose a Porsche 944 is designed to accelerate to 60 miles per hour within 10 seconds. If every Porsche 944 coming off the assembly line does this, the model is said to have high conformance quality. The problem with low conformance quality is that the product will disappoint some buyers.

DURABILITY   **Durability**, a measure of the product's expected operating life under natural or stressful conditions, is a valued attribute for certain products. Buyers will generally pay more for vehicles and kitchen appliances that have a reputation for being long lasting. However, this rule is subject to some qualifications. The extra price must not be excessive. Furthermore, the product must not be subject to rapid technological obsolescence, as is the case with personal computers and videocameras.

RELIABILITY   Buyers normally will pay a premium for more reliable products. **Reliability** is a measure of the probability that a product will not malfunction or fail within a specified time period. Maytag, which manufactures major home appliances, has an outstanding reputation for creating reliable appliances.

REPAIRABILITY   Buyers prefer products that are easy to repair. **Repairability** is a measure of the ease of fixing a product when it malfunctions or fails. An automobile made with standard parts that are easily replaced has high repairability. Ideal repairability would exist if users could fix the product themselves with little cost in money or time. Some products include a diagnostic feature that allows service people to correct a problem over the telephone or advise the user how to correct it. Many computer hardware and software companies offer technical support over the phone, or by fax or e-mail. Consider the steps taken by Cisco.

Cisco   Cisco, a major manufacturer of Internet components, now conducts over 85 percent of all sales via the Web. Its customers often need answers to questions about its equipment, and Cisco needs a large staff for its telephone support system. To handle the problem, Cisco put together a Knowledge Base of Frequently Asked Questions (FAQs) on its Web site. Cisco estimates that its Knowledge Base handles about 80 percent of the roughly 4 million monthly requests for information, which saves the company $250 million annually. Each new call and solution goes to a tech writer who adds the solution to the FAQs, thus reducing the number of future phone calls.[18]

STYLE   *Style* describes the product's look and feel to the buyer. Car buyers pay a premium for Jaguars because of their extraordinary look. Aesthetics play a key role in such brands as Absolut vodka, Apple computers, Montblanc pens, Godiva chocolate, and Harley-Davidson motorcycles.[19]

Starbucks   Integrated retail design has played a large role in Starbucks' ability to charge $2 for a cup of coffee. The elements include light wood tones at the counters; polished dark-marble countertops; lamps, walls, and tables imitating coffee tones from green to light and darker browns; comfortable chairs, well-designed cups; and coffee packages smooth and soft to the touch.

Style has the advantage of creating distinctiveness that is difficult to copy. On the negative side, strong style does not always mean high performance. A car may look sensational but spend a lot of time in the repair shop.

We must include packaging as a styling weapon, especially in food products, cosmetics, toiletries, and small consumer appliances. The package is the buyer's first encounter with the product and is capable of turning the buyer on or off. For Arizona Iced Tea, packaging is definitely a turn-on.[20]

Arizona Iced Tea   Arizona Iced Tea marketer Ferolito, Vultaggio & Sons has gained success by taking a rather straightforward drink—tea—and putting it into unusual bottles with elaborate designs. The wide-mouthed, long-necked bottles have been trendsetters in the New Age beverage category, and customers often buy the tea just for the bottle. Because consumers are known to hang on to their empties or convert them into lamps and other household objects, the company uses unique bottle shapes for its line extensions. It uses a ridged grip design on Arizona Rx Elixirs, miniature jugs for Arizona Iced Coffees, and a pint-sized deep-blue urn for Blue Luna Café Latte.[21]

DESIGN: THE INTEGRATING FORCE   As competition intensifies, design offers a potent way to differentiate and position a company's products and services.[22] In increasingly fast-paced markets, price and technology are not enough. Design is the factor that will often give a company its competitive edge. Design is the totality of features that affect how a product looks and functions in terms of customer requirements.

Design is particularly important in making and marketing retail services, apparel, packaged goods, and durable equipment. All the qualities we have discussed are design parameters. The designer has to figure out how much to invest in form, feature development, performance, conformance, durability, reliability, repairability, and style. To the company, a well-designed product is one that is easy to manufacture and distribute. To the customer, a well-designed product is one that is pleasant to look at and easy to open, install, use, repair, and dispose of. The designer has to take all these factors into account.

Here are two companies with products that embody the form-follows-function maxim.

Apple Computers   Who said that computers have to be beige and boxy? Apple's newest computer, the iMac, is anything but. The iMac features a sleek, curvy monitor and hard drive, all in one unit, in a translucent casing. There is no clunky tower or desktop hard drive to clutter up the office area. There is also no floppy drive, simply because Apple feels the floppy is on the verge of extinction. With its one-button Internet access, this machine is designed specifically for cruising the Internet (that is what the "i" in "iMac" stands for). Only one month after the iMac hit the stores in the summer of 1998, it was the number-two best-selling computer. Strong iMac sales contributed to earnings of $309 million in 1998 and $601 million in 1999.[23]

Black & Decker   What could be handier than a flashlight you do not have to hold while probing under the sink for the cause of a leaky faucet? Black & Decker's Snakelight looks just like its name and attaches itself to almost anything, leaving your hands free. It can also stand up like an illuminated cobra to light your workspace. In a market where the average flashlight cost is just $6, consumers are paying $30 for this flashlight, which was a gold medalist in the Industrial Design Excellence Awards (IDEA).[24]

Certain countries are winning on design: Italian design in apparel and furniture; Scandinavian design for functionality, aesthetics, and environmental consciousness. Braun, a German division of Gillette, has elevated design to a high art in its electric shavers, coffeemakers, hair dryers, and food processors. The company's design department enjoys equal status with engineering and manufacturing. The Danish firm Bang & Olufsen has received many kudos for the design of its stereos, TV equipment, and telephones.

services differentiation

When the physical product cannot easily be differentiated, the key to competitive success may lie in adding valued services and improving their quality. The main service differentiators are ordering ease, delivery, installation, customer training, customer consulting, and maintenance and repair.

ORDERING EASE   *Ordering ease* refers to how easy it is for the customer to place an order with the company. Baxter Healthcare has eased the ordering process by supplying hospitals with computer terminals through which they send orders directly to Baxter. Many banks now provide home banking software to help customers get information and do transactions more efficiently. Consumers are now even able to order and receive groceries without going to the supermarket.

Peapod   Peapod (*www.peapod.com*) takes computer orders and delivers groceries to the doors of over 120,000 customers in cities such as Boston, Chicago, and Washington, D.C. As the nation's largest online grocer, Peapod allows consumers to choose from between 8,000 and 10,000 food items online, and then home-delivers customers' orders as soon as the next day after they are placed. While several competitors struggled to avoid the dot-com crash (and most failed), Peapod reported achieving an operating profit in its Chicago market in the first quarter of 2001. It was subsequently purchased by Dutch food retailer Royal Ahold. The service has been integrated with Ahold's brick-and-mortar supermarket companies in the United States.[25]

DELIVERY   *Delivery* refers to how well the product or service is delivered to the customer. It includes speed, accuracy, and care attending the delivery process. Today's customers have grown to expect delivery speed: pizza delivered in one-half hour, film developed in one hour, eyeglasses made in one hour, cars lubricated in 15 minutes. A company such as Deluxe Check Printers, Inc., has built an impressive reputation for shipping out its checks one day after receiving an order—without being late once in 18 years. Levi Strauss, Benetton, and The Limited have adopted computerized *quick*

The home page for Peapod, the nation's largest online grocer.

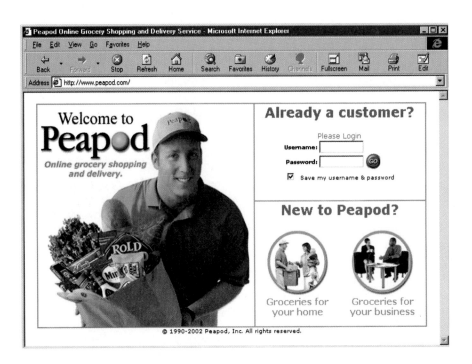

response systems (QRS) that link the information systems of their suppliers, manufacturing plants, distribution centers, and retailing outlets. Buyers will often choose a supplier with a better reputation for speedy or on-time delivery.[26]

Krones   Krones, the world leader in bottle labeling machines, deploys 250 service and installation technicians around the world. The company stores data for each machine, totaling 20,000, in its central computer. These data can be made available at every one of its locations in the world within half a minute. The data are fed directly into numerically controlled machines, and the spare parts are manufactured immediately. Parts ordered before 7:00 A.M. are sent in the afternoon, by truck, to Frankfurt Airport; from there they are air freighted the same evening to their destination. At the same time, the subsidiary receives the flight and freight numbers so that the shipment can be cleared through customs without delay.[27]

Cemex   Cemex, a giant cement company based in Mexico, has transformed the cement business by promising to deliver concrete faster than pizza. Cemex equips every truck with a *global positioning system* (GPS) so that its real-time location is known and full information is available to drivers and dispatchers. Cemex is able to promise that if your load is more than 10 minutes late, you get a 20 percent discount. It has managed to digitalize the cement business; if one can digitalize the cement business, any business can be digitalized![28]

INSTALLATION   *Installation* refers to the work done to make a product operational in its planned location. Buyers of heavy equipment expect good installation service. Differentiating at this point in the consumption chain is particularly important for companies with complex products. Ease of installation becomes a true selling point, especially when the target market is technology novices who are notoriously intolerant of on-screen messages such as "Disk Error 23."

Pacific Bell   Consumers wishing to connect to the Internet using a high-speed digital subscriber line (DSL) often require the help of a trained phone-company technician to help them with the setup. Even with trained assistance, the process can take hours, or in some cases days, to complete. To make installation easier for its new DSL customers, in 2000 Pacific Bell developed installation kits that included an interactive software setup program. The company found that most consumers who used the kits could complete their DSL setup in less than an hour.[29]

CUSTOMER TRAINING   *Customer training* refers to training the customer's employees to use the vendor's equipment properly and efficiently. General Electric not only sells and installs expensive X-ray equipment in hospitals; it also gives extensive training to users of this equipment. McDonald's requires its new franchisees to attend Hamburger University in Oakbrook, Illinois, for two weeks, to learn how to manage their franchise properly.

CUSTOMER CONSULTING   *Customer consulting* refers to data, information systems, and advice services that the seller offers to buyers. One of the best providers of value-adding consulting service is Milliken & Company.

Milliken & Company   Milliken sells shop towels to industrial launderers, who rent them to factories. Although the towels are physically similar to competitors' towels, Milliken charges a higher price and enjoys the leading market share. How can it do this? Milliken adds continuous service enhancements for customers. It trains customers' salespeople, supplies prospect leads and sales-promotional material, supplies online computer-order-entry and route-optimization systems, does marketing research, sponsors quality-improvement workshops, and sends its salespeople to work with customers. Customers are more than willing to pay a price premium because the extra services improve their profitability.[30]

In consumer marketing, Rite Aid drugstores has launched a successful consumer consulting initiative.

Rite Aid With a mandate to increase sales, Rite Aid lowered prices, and in 1997 the company launched the Vitamin Institute, designed to make consumers more comfortable asking for help at the pharmacy window. Rite Aid pharmacists now provide interested customers with available research to help them make more educated judgments. The Vitamin Institute has been hugely successful, but Rite Aid's approach is actually reminiscent of the "good old days," when people relied on their local druggists, sometimes even more than their doctors. Rite Aid extended its in-store consultation practice to the Internet when it added an "Ask Your Pharmacist" feature to its Web site.[31]

MAINTENANCE AND REPAIR *Maintenance and repair* describes the service program for helping customers keep purchased products in good working order. Consider Hewlett-Packard's e-support system.

Hewlett-Packard Hewlett-Packard is one of several PC manufacturers offering online technical support, or "e-support," for their customers. In the event of a service problem, customers can use various online tools to find a solution. Those aware of the specific problem can search an online database for fixes; those unaware can use diagnostic software that finds the problem and searches the online database for an automatic fix. Customers can also seek online help from a technician. "Research suggests PC users want help, but they don't necessarily want problems solved for them," says Bruce Greenwood, a Hewlett-Packard marketing manager. "Many users want to understand the issues and their solutions so they can become more self-sufficient."[32]

Hewlett-Packard's online support page, which allows customers to solve their own problems.

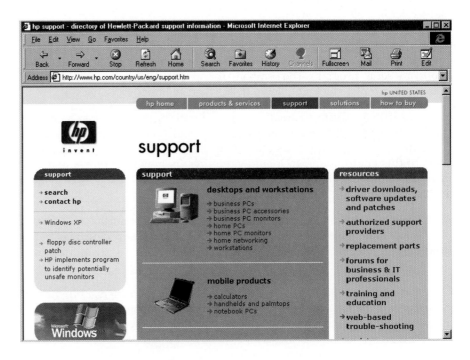

MISCELLANEOUS SERVICES   Companies can find other ways to differentiate customer services. They can offer an improved product warranty or maintenance contract. They can offer rewards.

MacMillan and McGrath say companies have opportunities to differentiate at every stage of the consumption chain. They point out that companies can even differentiate at the point when their product is no longer in use:[33]

Canon   Canon has developed a system that allows customers to return spent printer cartridges at Canon's expense. The cartridges are then rehabilitated and sold as such. Canon makes it easy for customers to return used cartridges: All they need to do is drop the prepaid package off at a United Parcel Service collection station. Canon reported collection of 12,175 tons of toner cartridges worldwide in 1999, which represented a 100 percent recycling ratio. The program has helped build Canon's reputation as an environmentally friendly company.[34]

personnel differentiation

Companies can gain a strong competitive advantage through having better-trained people. Singapore Airlines enjoys an excellent reputation in large part because of its flight attendants. The McDonald's people are courteous, the IBM people are professional, and the Disney people are upbeat. The sales forces of such companies as General Electric, Cisco, Frito-Lay, Northwestern Mutual Life, and Pfizer enjoy an excellent reputation.[35] Better-trained personnel exhibit six characteristics: *Competence*: They possess the required skill and knowledge; *courtesy*: They are friendly, respectful, and considerate; *credibility*: They are trustworthy; *reliability*: They perform the service consistently and accurately; *responsiveness*: They respond quickly to customers' requests and problems; and *communication*: They make an effort to understand the customer and communicate clearly.[36]

In an age when competitors can knock off products or services in an instant, some savvy companies are marketing their employees' unique know-how.

The Orvis Company   The Orvis Company is a mail-order and retail supplier of "country" clothing, gifts, and sporting gear that competes with the likes of L.L. Bean and Eddie Bauer. Orvis, founded in 1856, differentiates itself by selling its long history of fly-fishing expertise. Its fly-fishing schools, all situated in scenic areas from California to Florida, make a tough sport accessible to novices. The schools, not coincidentally, are usually located near Orvis retail outlets. Orvis had sales of less than $1 million in 1968, when it opened its first fly-fishing school. Now company sales are at about $500 million. Although actual fly-fishing products account for only a small portion of this, catalog manager and vice president Tom Rosenbauer says, "Without our fly-fishing heritage, we'd be just another rag vendor."[37]

channel differentiation

Companies can achieve competitive advantage through the way they design their distribution channels' coverage, expertise, and performance. Caterpillar's success in the construction-equipment industry is based partly on superior channel development. Its dealers are found in more locations than competitors' dealers, and they are typically better trained and perform more reliably. Dell in computers and Avon in cosmetics distinguish themselves by developing and managing high-quality direct-marketing channels. Iams pet food provides an instructive case on how developing a different channel can pay off.

Iams Pet Food   Back in 1946, when Paul Iams founded the company in Dayton, Ohio, pet food was cheap, not too nutritious, and sold exclusively in supermarkets and the occasional feed store. Iams went instead to regional veterinarians, breeders, and pet stores. After the company implemented this marketing strategy on a national scale in the early 1970s, annual sales soared from $16 million in 1982 to $800 million in 1999. Procter & Gamble bought Iams for $2.1 billion in 2000 and decided to expand distribution into supermarkets and other major retail outlets, but Iams' premium brand, Eukanuba, would continue to be available only in specialty outlets.[38]

image differentiation

Buyers respond differently to company and brand images. The primary way to account for Marlboro's extraordinary worldwide market share (around 30 percent) is that Marlboro's "macho cowboy" image has struck a responsive chord with much of the cigarette-smoking public. Wine and liquor companies also work hard to develop distinctive images for their brands.

Identity and image need to be distinguished. *Identity* comprises the ways that a company aims to identify or position itself or its product. *Image* is the way the public perceives the company or its products. Image is affected by many factors beyond the company's control, as the case of Vans' counterculture marketing versus Nike, Reebok, and Adidas shows.

Vans   In the 1990s, several shoe companies found success marketing "counterculture" alternatives to established athletic shoe companies like Nike, Reebok, and Adidas. Vans Inc., a Santa Fe Springs, California, shoe and apparel manufacturer, started in 1966 selling handmade shoes from a single retail location. The publicly traded company now does big business in retail centers and company-owned stores throughout the nation; sales topped $274 million in 2000. Its popularity among action sports enthusiasts is bolstered by a marketing program that includes brand name indoor and outdoor skate parks, sponsorship of the Vans Warped Tour summer concert series, signature shoe models associated with famous pro athletes, and offbeat advertising.[39]

An effective identity does three things. First, it establishes the product's character and value proposition. Second, it conveys this character in a distinctive way. Third, it delivers emotional power beyond a mental image. For the identity to work, it must be conveyed through every available communication vehicle and brand contact. It must be worked into ads and media that convey a story, a mood, a claim—something distinctive. It should be diffused in annual reports, brochures, catalogs, packaging, company stationery, and business cards. If "IBM means service," this message must be expressed in symbols, colors and slogans, atmosphere, events, and employee behavior.

SYMBOLS, COLORS, SLOGANS, SPECIAL ATTRIBUTES   Identity can be built by strong symbols. The company can choose a symbol such as the lion (Harris Bank), apple (Apple Computer), or doughboy (Pillsbury). A brand can be built around a famous person, as with Elizabeth Taylor perfumes. Companies may choose a color identifier such as blue (IBM), yellow (Kodak), or red (Campbell Soup), or a specific piece of sound or music.

Every company would benefit by adopting and repeating a short slogan or "tag line" after every mention of its name. AT&T called itself "The Right Choice"; Ford said "Quality is Our Number One Job"; and DuPont described its output as "Better Living Through Chemistry." The slogan must be chosen carefully, however. Holiday Inns once described itself as the "No Surprise" hotel. After several embarrassments, it quickly withdrew this slogan. Philips, the large Dutch electronics firm, used the slogan "From

Sand to Chips" in an effort to convey that it made lightbulbs and silicon chips, all from sand. People not only did not understand this, but the slogan was about the company, not the consumer.

A company can further differentiate its image using its special attributes, such as the company's heritage, its being the first to enter the field, its being the largest or oldest company in its industry, or its being the most preferred according to opinion polls.[40]

PHYSICAL PLANT   The seller's physical space can be another powerful image generator. Hyatt Regency hotels developed a distinctive image through its atrium lobbies. A bank that wants to convey the image of a safe bank must communicate this through the building's architecture, interior design, layout, colors, materials, and furnishings.

Companies can create a strong image by inviting prospects and customers to visit their well-laid-out headquarters and factories. Boeing, Ben & Jerry's, Hershey's, Saturn, and Crayola all sponsor excellent company tours that draw millions of visitors a year.[41] Companies such as Hallmark and Kohler have built corporate museums at their headquarters that display their history and the drama of producing and marketing their products.

EVENTS AND SPONSORSHIPS   A company can build its brand image through creating or sponsoring various events. Event marketers have favored sports events and are now using other venues such as art museums, zoos, or ice shows to entertain clients and employees. AT&T and IBM sponsor symphony performances and art exhibits; Visa is an active sponsor of the Olympics; Harley-Davidson sponsors annual motorcycle rallies; and Perrier sponsors sports events. Companies are searching for better ways to quantify the benefits of sponsorship and they are demanding greater accountability from event owners and organizers.

Companies can also create events designed to surprise the public and create a buzz. Many amount to guerrilla marketing tactics. Here are some examples:

- Driver 2, a new car-chase video game, arranged for a convoy of 20 car wrecks with smoke pouring from their engines to crawl through Manhattan and Los Angeles to attract attention to the new game.
- Ask Jeeves, the Internet search engine, sent 35 actors in British butler's outfits to guide visitors to their seats and answer tennis trivia questions at the U.S. Open tennis tournament.
- Kibu.com pays hundreds of school girls to do "peer marketing" by hanging around with their peers, handing out free lip gloss, and talking up Kibu's cosmetic site.[42]

The increased use of attention-getting events is a response to the fragmentation of media: Consumers can turn to hundreds of cable channels, thousands of magazine titles, and millions of Internet pages. Events can create attention, although whether they have a lasting effect on brand awareness, knowledge, or preference will vary considerably, depending on the quality of the product, the event itself, and its execution.

USING MULTIPLE IMAGE-BUILDING TECHNIQUES   Swatch watch provides an excellent example of how to use multiple image-building techniques to etch a lasting image in the public's mind.

Swatch   Nicholas G. Hayek, Swatch's founder, launched Swatch watches in 1983 by hanging a 500-foot-long sign from the tallest bank in Frankfurt. Within a few weeks, every German knew Swatch. Swatch is a lightweight, water-resistant, shockproof electronic analog watch with a wide variety of colorful faces and bands celebrating famous artists, sports and space events, and anniversaries. Over 200 million Swatches have been sold in over 70 markets worldwide. Here are some examples of Swatch's promotion and advertising:

Swatch issues new watches throughout the year but launches limited editions of "snazzy" watch designs only twice a year. Only Swatch Club members can bid to buy them. Swatch may produce only 40,000 units and yet receive orders from 100,000 or more collectors. The company will sponsor a drawing to choose the lucky collectors who can buy the watch.

Christie's, the auction house, holds periodic auctions of early Swatch watches. One collector paid $60,000 for one of the rarer ones.

Swatch continues to innovate and keep people buzzing about its state-of-the-art products. Alongside the standard plastic watches there are new developments such as the Irony (a metal Swatch), a light-powered Swatch Solar, and a melodious alarm clock called the Swatch Musicall. Swatch has created the world's first pager in a wristwatch, the Swatch the Beep, as well as an "e-watch" equipped with electronic mail and Internet access.

Swatch clearly has written the marketing book on how to build a cult following by applying superior styling, merchandising, and promotion.[43]

product life–cycle marketing strategies

A company's positioning and differentiation strategy must change as the product, market, and competitors change over time. Here we will describe the concept of the product life cycle (PLC) and the normal changes as the product passes through each life-cycle stage.

To say that a product has a life cycle is to assert four things:

1. Products have a limited life.
2. Product sales pass through distinct stages, each posing different challenges, opportunities, and problems to the seller.
3. Profits rise and fall at different stages of the product life cycle.
4. Products require different marketing, financial, manufacturing, purchasing, and human resource strategies in each life-cycle stage.

product life cycles

Most product life-cycle curves are portrayed as bell-shaped (see Figure 11.3). This curve is typically divided into four stages: introduction, growth, maturity, and decline.[44]

1. *Introduction:* A period of slow sales growth as the product is introduced in the market. Profits are nonexistent because of the heavy expenses incurred with product introduction.
2. *Growth:* A period of rapid market acceptance and substantial profit improvement.

figure **11.3**

Sales and Profit Life Cycles

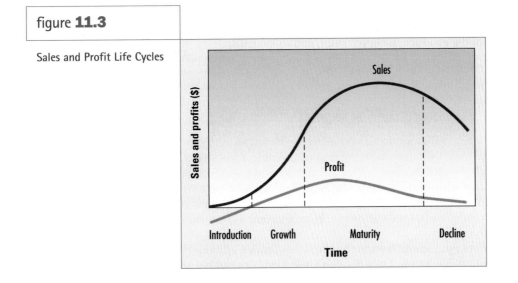

figure **11.4**	Common Product Life-Cycle Patterns

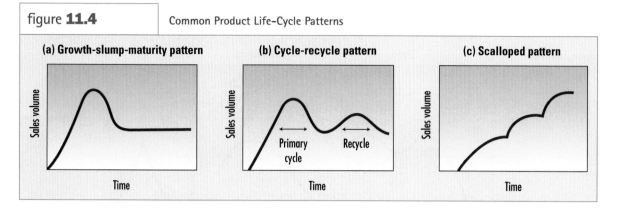

3. *Maturity:* A period of a slowdown in sales growth because the product has achieved acceptance by most potential buyers. Profits stabilize or decline because of increased competition.
4. *Decline:* The period when sales show a downward drift and profits erode.

The PLC concept can be used to analyze a product category (liquor), a product form (white liquor), a product (vodka), or a brand (Smirnoff). Not all products exhibit a bell-shaped PLC.[45] Three common alternate patterns are shown in Figure 11.4. Figure 11.4(a) shows a *growth-slump-maturity pattern*, often characteristic of small kitchen appliances. Some years ago, sales of electric knives grew rapidly when the product was first introduced and then fell to a "petrified" level. The petrified level is sustained by late adopters buying the product for the first time and early adopters replacing the product.

The *cycle-recycle pattern* in Figure 11.4(b) often describes the sales of new drugs. The pharmaceutical company aggressively promotes its new drug, and this produces the first cycle. Later, sales start declining and the company gives the drug another promotion push, which produces a second cycle (usually of smaller magnitude and duration).[46]

Another common pattern is the *scalloped PLC* in Figure 11.4(c). Here sales pass through a succession of life cycles based on the discovery of new-product characteristics, uses, or users. Nylon's sales, for example, show a scalloped pattern because of the many new uses—parachutes, hosiery, shirts, carpeting, boat sails, automobile tires—that continue to be discovered over time.[47]

STYLE, FASHION, AND FAD LIFE CYCLES   Three special categories of product life cycles should be distinguished—styles, fashions, and fads (Figure 11.5). A **style** is a basic and distinctive mode of expression appearing in a field of human endeavor. Styles appear in homes (colonial, ranch, Cape Cod); clothing (formal, casual, funky); and art (realistic, surrealistic, abstract). A style can last for generations, and go in and out of vogue. A **fashion** is a currently accepted or popular style in a given field. Fashions pass through four stages:[48] distinctiveness, emulation, mass-fashion, and decline.

The length of a fashion cycle is hard to predict. Chester Wasson believes that fashions end because they represent a purchase compromise, and consumers start looking for missing attributes.[49] For example, as automobiles become smaller, they become less comfortable, and then a growing number of buyers start wanting larger cars. Furthermore, too many consumers adopt the fashion, thus turning others away. William Reynolds suggests that the length of a particular fashion cycle depends on the extent to which the fashion meets a genuine need, is consistent with other trends in the society, satisfies societal norms and values, and does not exceed technological limits as it develops.[50]

Fads are fashions that come quickly into public view, are adopted with great zeal, peak early, and decline very fast. Their acceptance cycle is short, and they tend to attract only a limited following of those who are searching for excitement or want to distinguish

figure **11.5**

Style, Fashion, and Fad
Life Cycles

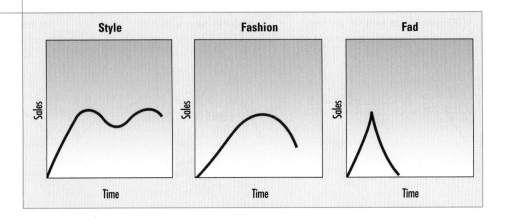

themselves from others. They often have a novel or capricious aspect, such as body piercing and tattooing. Fads do not survive because they do not normally satisfy a strong need. The marketing winners are those who recognize fads early and leverage them into products with staying power. Here is a success story of a company that managed to extend a fad's life span:

Trivial Pursuit Since its debut at the International Toy Fair in 1982, Trivial Pursuit has sold 65 million copies in 18 languages in 32 countries, and it remains the best-selling adult game. Parker Brothers has kept the product's popularity going by making a new game with updated questions every year. It also keeps creating offshoots—travel packs, a children's version, Trivial Pursuit Genus IV, and an interactive CD-ROM from Virgin Entertainment Interactive. The game has its own Web site (*www.trivialpursuit.com*), which received 100,000 visitors in its initial two-month test period. If you are having trouble making dinner conversation on a date—no problem: NTN Entertainment Network has put Trivial Pursuit in about 3,000 restaurants.[51]

marketing strategies: introduction stage

Because it takes time to roll out a new product and fill dealer pipelines, sales growth tends to be slow at this stage. Robert Buzzell identified several causes for the slow growth: delays in the expansion of production capacity; technical problems ("working out the bugs"); delays in obtaining adequate distribution through retail outlets; and customer reluctance.[52] Sales of expensive new products such as high-definition TV are retarded by additional factors such as product complexity and fewer buyers.

Profits are negative or low in the introduction stage. Promotional expenditures are at their highest ratio to sales because of the need to (1) inform potential consumers, (2) induce product trial, and (3) secure distribution in retail outlets. Firms focus on those buyers who are the readiest to buy, usually higher-income groups. Prices tend to be high because costs are high.

THE PIONEER ADVANTAGE   Companies that plan to introduce a new product must decide when to enter the market. To be first can be highly rewarding, but risky and expensive. To come in later makes sense if the firm can bring superior technology, quality, or brand strength.

Speeding up innovation time is essential in an age of shortening product life cycles. Those companies that first reach practical solutions will enjoy "first-mover" advantages in the market. Being early pays off. One study found that products that came out six months late but on budget earned an average of 33 percent less profit in their first five years; products that came out on time but 50 percent over budget cut their profits by only 4 percent.

Most studies indicate that the market pioneer gains the most advantage. Companies like Amazon.com, Campbell, Coca-Cola, Eastman Kodak, Hallmark, Peapod.com, and Xerox developed sustained market dominance. Robinson and Fornell studied a broad range of mature consumer- and industrial-goods businesses, and found that market pioneers generally enjoy a substantially higher market share than do early followers and late entrants:[53] Glen Urban's study also found a pioneer advantage: It appears that the second entrant obtained only 71 percent of the pioneer's market share, and the third entrant obtained only 58 percent.[54] Carpenter and Nakamoto found that 19 out of 25 companies who were market leaders in 1923 were still the market leaders in 1983, 60 years later.[55]

What are the sources of the pioneer's advantage?[56] Early users will recall the pioneer's brand name if the product satisfies them. The pioneer's brand also establishes the attributes the product class should possess. The pioneer's brand normally aims at the middle of the market and so captures more users. Customer inertia also plays a role; and there are producer advantages: economies of scale, technological leadership, patents, ownership of scarce assets, and other barriers to entry. An alert pioneer, according to Robertson and Gatignon, can maintain its leadership indefinitely by pursuing various strategies.[57]

However, the pioneer advantage is not inevitable. One only has to reflect on the fate of Bowmar (hand calculators), Apple's Newton (personal digital assistant), Netscape (web browser), Reynolds (ballpoint pens), and Osborne (portable computers), market pioneers who were overtaken by later entrants. Steven Schnaars studied 28 industries where the imitators surpassed the innovators.[58] He found several weaknesses among the failing pioneers, including new products that were too crude, were improperly positioned, or appeared before there was strong demand; product-development costs that exhausted the innovator's resources; a lack of resources to compete against entering larger firms; and managerial incompetence or unhealthy complacency. Successful imitators thrived by offering lower prices, improving the product more continuously, or using brute market power to overtake the pioneer.

Golder and Tellis raise further doubts about the pioneer advantage.[59] They distinguish between an *inventor* (first to develop patents in a new-product category), a *product pioneer* (first to develop a working model), and a *market pioneer* (first to sell in the new-product category). They also include nonsurviving pioneers in their sample. They conclude that although pioneers may still have an advantage, a larger number of market pioneers fail than has been reported and a larger number of early market leaders (though not pioneers) succeed. Examples of later entrants overtaking market pioneers are IBM over Sperry in mainframe computers, Matsushita over Sony in VCRs, Texas Instruments over Bowmar in hand calculators, and GE over EMI in CAT scan equipment. Tellis and Golder, in a more recent study, identify the following five factors as underpinning long-term market leadership: vision of a mass market, persistence, relentless innovation, financial commitment, and asset leverage.[60]

The pioneer should visualize the various product markets it could initially enter, knowing that it cannot enter all of them at once. Suppose market-segmentation analysis reveals the product market segments shown in Figure 11.6. The pioneer should analyze the profit potential of each product market singly and in combination and decide on a market expansion path. Thus the pioneer in Figure 11.6 plans first to enter product market P_1M_1, then move the product into a second market (P_1M_2), then surprise the competition by developing a second product for the second market (P_2M_2), then take the second product back into the first market (P_2M_1), and then launch a third product for the first market (P_3M_1). If this game plan works, the pioneer firm will own a good part of the first two segments and serve them with two or three products.

figure **11.6**

Long-Range Product Market Expansion Strategy (P_i=product i; M_j=Market j)

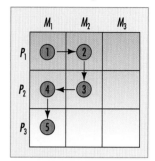

figure **11.7**

Stages of the Competitive
Cycle

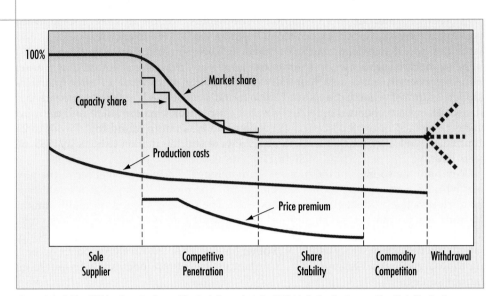

Source: John B. Frey, "Pricing Over the Competitive Cycle," speech at the 1982 Marketing Conference. New York: The Conference Board, 1982.

THE COMPETITIVE CYCLE   The pioneer knows that competition will eventually enter and cause prices and its market share to fall. When will this happen? What should the pioneer do at each stage? Frey describes five stages of the *competitive cycle* that the pioneer has to anticipate (Figure 11.7).[61]

1. Initially the pioneer is the *sole supplier,* with 100 percent of production capacity and sales.
2. *Competitive penetration* starts when a new competitor has built production capacity and begins commercial sales. The leader's share of production capacity and share of sales falls. As more competitors enter the market and charge a lower price, the perceived relative value of the leader's offer declines, forcing a reduction in the leader's price premium.
3. Capacity tends to be overbuilt during rapid growth. When a cyclical slowdown occurs, industry overcapacity drives down margins to lower levels. New competitors decide not to enter, and existing competitors try to solidify their positions. This leads to *share stability.*
4. Stability is followed by *commodity competition.* The product is viewed as a commodity, buyers no longer pay a price premium, and the suppliers earn only an average rate of return.
5. At this point, *withdrawal* begins. The pioneer might decide to build share further as other firms withdraw.

marketing strategies: growth stage

The growth stage is marked by a rapid climb in sales. Early adopters like the product, and additional consumers start buying it. New competitors enter, attracted by the opportunities. They introduce new product features and expand distribution.

Prices remain where they are or fall slightly, depending on how fast demand increases. Companies maintain their promotional expenditures at the same or at a slightly increased level to meet competition and to continue to educate the market. Sales rise much faster than promotional expenditures, causing a welcome decline in the promotion–sales ratio. Profits increase during this stage as promotion costs are spread over a larger volume and unit manufacturing costs fall faster than price declines owing to the producer learning effect. Firms have to watch for a change from an accelerating to a decelerating rate of growth in order to prepare new strategies.

During this stage, the firm uses several strategies to sustain rapid market growth:

- It improves product quality and adds new product features and improved styling.
- It adds new models and flanker products (i.e., products of different sizes, flavors, and so forth that protect the main product).
- It enters new market segments.
- It increases its distribution coverage and enters new distribution channels.
- It shifts from product-awareness advertising to product-preference advertising.
- It lowers prices to attract the next layer of price-sensitive buyers.

These market expansion strategies strengthen the firm's competitive position. Consider the following cases.

Starbucks Coffee Company   Starbucks Coffee is one of the best-known brands in the world. Starbucks is able to sell a cup of coffee for $1.40 while the store next door can only get $.50. And if you want the popular café latte, it's $2. Howard Schultz, the genius behind the brand, not only delivers a great-tasting cup of coffee, but serves it in attractive "coffee houses." You can meet friends at Starbucks, or enjoy a moment of solitude. Starbucks consists of more than 3,000 retail outlets in stores, airports, and bookstore chains all over the world. Not surprisingly, competitors have sprung up ranging from Dunkin' Donuts to smaller chains such as Tully's Coffee in Seattle and Coffee Station in New York City. Starbucks is using a number of flank defenses. For one thing, it is trying to push out innovative non-coffee-related products, such as its combo of teas and juice named Tiazzi and its ice cream products. It is also selling its premium beans in supermarkets and is getting into the restaurant business. The first Cafe Starbucks opened to capacity crowds in the fall of 1998, and the company opened another restaurant by the end of the year. Starbucks continues to expand globally, entering China, Kuwait, Korea, and Lebanon in 1999 and opening locations in Hong Kong in 2000.[62]

Yahoo!   Founded in 1994 by Web-surfing grad students, Yahoo! became the number-one place to be on the Web. The company grew into more than just a search engine; it became a portal, offering a full-blown package of information and services. In 1998, Yahoo! stock soared to $200 a share and its market capitalization was $9.1 billion. Yet as the dot-com crash took its toll on Yahoo!'s core stable of advertisers—Internet start-ups—the company began a long earnings and share price slide. It sought to broaden its content and limit its reliance on the previously bulletproof Web advertising model by focusing on e-commerce, licensing, and wireless applications. Still, Yahoo!'s problems worsened. Its stock languished under $25 for much of the first half of 2001 and its CEO (Tim Koogle) resigned in March of that year. The company hired former Warner Bros. Studio chief Terry Semel to replace Koogle, an indication that the company was eager to embrace a future as a media company. As the only portal company not to merge with a giant media company, Yahoo! remained a rugged individualist in spite of its financial difficulties.[63]

A firm in the growth stage faces a trade-off between high market share and high current profit. By spending money on product improvement, promotion, and distribution, it can capture a dominant position. It forgoes maximum current profit in the hope of making even greater profits in the next stage.

marketing strategies: maturity stage

At some point, the rate of sales growth will slow, and the product will enter a stage of relative maturity. This stage normally lasts longer than the previous stages, and poses formidable challenges to marketing management. *Most products are in the maturity stage of the life cycle, and most marketing managers cope with the problem of marketing the mature product.*

The maturity stage divides into three phases: growth, stable, and decaying maturity. In the first phase, the sales growth rate starts to decline. There are no new distribution channels to fill. In the second phase, sales flatten on a per capita basis because of market saturation. Most potential consumers have tried the product, and future sales are governed by population growth and replacement demand. In the third phase, decaying maturity, the absolute level of sales starts to decline, and customers begin switching to other products.

The sales slowdown creates overcapacity in the industry, which leads to intensified competition. Competitors scramble to find niches. They engage in frequent markdowns. They increase advertising and trade and consumer promotion. They increase R&D budgets to develop product improvements and line extensions. They make deals to supply private brands. A shakeout begins, and weaker competitors withdraw. The industry eventually consists of well-entrenched competitors whose basic drive is to gain or maintain market share.

Dominating the industry are a few giant firms—perhaps a quality leader, a service leader, and a cost leader—that serve the whole market and make their profits mainly through high volume and lower costs. Surrounding these dominant firms is a multitude of market nichers, including market specialists, product specialists, and customizing firms. The issue facing a firm in a mature market is whether to struggle to become one of the "big three" and achieve profits through high volume and low cost or to pursue a niching strategy and achieve profits through low volume and a high margin.

Some companies abandon weaker products and concentrate on more profitable products and on new products. Yet they may be ignoring the high potential many mature markets and old products still have. Industries widely thought to be mature— autos, motorcycles, television, watches, cameras—were proved otherwise by the Japanese, who found ways to offer new values to customers. Seemingly moribund brands like Jell-O, Ovaltine, and Arm & Hammer baking soda have achieved major sales revivals several times, through the exercise of marketing imagination.[64] The resurgence in Hush Puppies' popularity in the footwear category is a case study in reviving old, nearly forgotten brands.

Hush Puppies   Once the ruler of the casual footwear industry, the Hush Puppies brand slid into irrelevance in the 1980s when the parent company, Wolverine World, overextended itself by acquiring companies that had nothing to do with footwear. It took a bit of luck, plus some savvy marketing moves, to bring the brand back. In 1994, New York fashion designer John Barrett took some Hush Puppies classic styles and dyed them in colors—purple, green, and orange—to match the clothing in his runway shows. Soon afterword, a menswear trade publication ran a headline saying Hush Puppies were back. Then the company did some smart marketing: It brought out new Hush Puppies in updated colors such as powder blue, lime green, and electric orange and limited distribution to six of the most avant-garde shoe stores in the country. Wolverine also jacked the price up to $70 from $40, and showered free shoes on Hollywood celebrities. Once the shoes had garnered enough buzz, the company made them more widely available by distributing them to better department stores. Hush Puppies sales rose to more than 1.7 million pairs in 1996, from 30,000 pairs in 1994. When fashions shifted a few years later, Hush Puppies expanded into sandals and walking shoes to keep profits going.[65]

MARKET MODIFICATION   The company might try to expand the market for its mature brand by working with the two factors that make up sales volume:

$$\text{Volume} = \text{number of brand users} \times \text{usage rate per user}$$

It can try to expand the number of brand users by (1) *Converting nonusers:* The key to the growth of air freight service is the constant search for new users to whom air carriers can demonstrate the benefits of using air freight rather than ground transportation. (2) *Entering new market segments*: Johnson & Johnson successfully promoted its baby shampoo to adult users. (3) *Winning competitors' customers*: PepsiCo is constantly tempting Coca-Cola users to switch.

Volume can also be increased by convincing current users to increase their brand usage: (1) *Use the product on more occasions.* Serve Campbell's soup for breakfast. Use Heinz vinegar to clean windows. Take Kodak pictures of your pets. (2) *Use more of the product on each occasion.* Drink a larger glass of orange juice. (3) *Use the product in new ways.* Use Arm & Hammer Baking Soda as a refrigerator deodorant or to extinguish grease fires.[66]

PRODUCT MODIFICATION   Managers also try to stimulate sales by modifying the product's characteristics through quality improvement, feature improvement, or style improvement.

Quality improvement aims at increasing the product's functional performance. A manufacturer can often overtake its competition by launching a "new and improved" product. Grocery manufacturers call this a "plus launch" and promote a new additive or advertise something as "stronger," "bigger," or "better." This strategy is effective to the extent that the quality is improved, buyers accept the claim of improved quality, and a sufficient number of buyers will pay for higher quality. However, customers are not always willing to accept an "improved" product, as the classic tale of New Coke illustrates.

Coca-Cola   Battered by competition from the sweeter Pepsi-Cola, Coca-Cola decided in 1985 to replace its old formula with a sweeter variation, dubbed the New Coke. Coca-Cola spent $4 million on market research. Blind taste tests showed that Coke drinkers preferred the new, sweeter formula, but the launch of New Coke provoked a national uproar. Market researchers had measured the taste but had failed to measure the emotional attachment consumers had to Coca-Cola. There were angry letters, formal protests, and even lawsuit threats, to force the retention of "The Real Thing." Ten weeks later, the company withdrew New Coke and reintroduced its century-old formula as "Classic Coke," giving the old formula even stronger status in the marketplace.

Feature improvement aims at adding new features (for example, size, weight, materials, additives, accessories) that expand the product's versatility, safety, or convenience. You would not think one could do much to change a sliced pickle, but Vlasic R&D people worked for years to modify its core product.

Vlasic Foods International   Pickle consumption has been declining about 2 percent a year since the 1980s. Vlasic began its quest for a blockbuster pickle in the mid-1990s, after focus groups revealed that people hate it when pickle slices slither out the sides of hamburgers and sandwiches. At first the company decided to slice its average pickles horizontally into strips and marketed them as "Sandwich Stackers." The only problem was that the strips usually contained the soft seedy part of the cucumber, not the crunchy part. The company then embarked on "Project Frisbee," an effort to create a giant pickle chip. In 1998, after years of research and development, Vlasic created a cucumber 10 times larger than the traditional pickle cucumber. The chips, sold as "Hamburger Stackers," are large enough to cover the entire surface of a hamburger and are stacked a dozen high in jars.[67]

This strategy has several advantages. New features build the company's image as an innovator and win the loyalty of market segments that value these features. They provide an opportunity for free publicity and they generate sales force and distributor enthusiasm. The chief disadvantage is that feature improvements are easily imitated; unless there is a permanent gain from being first, the feature improvement might not pay off in the long run.[68]

A strategy of style improvement aims at increasing the product's aesthetic appeal. The periodic introduction of new car models is largely about style competition, as is the introduction of new packaging for consumer products. A style strategy might give the product a unique market identity. Yet style competition has problems. First, it is difficult to predict whether people—and which people—will like a new style. Second, a style change usually requires discontinuing the old style, and the company risks losing customers. Consumers may become attached to something as seemingly insignificant as a peanut shell. In the United States, eating unshelled peanuts at baseball games is a time-honored tradition. During the 1986 major league baseball season at New York's Shea Stadium, the concessionaire began selling preshelled peanuts in cellophane packages. Sales fell 15 percent and consumers complained strongly.[69]

MARKETING-MIX MODIFICATION Product managers might also try to stimulate sales by modifying other marketing-mix elements. They should ask the following questions:

- *Prices:* Would a price cut attract new buyers? If so, should the list price be lowered, or should prices be lowered through price specials, volume or early-purchase discounts, freight cost absorption, or easier credit terms? Or would it be better to raise the price to signal higher quality?
- *Distribution:* Can the company obtain more product support and display in existing outlets? Can more outlets be penetrated? Can the company introduce the product into new distribution channels? When Goodyear decided to sell its tires via Wal-Mart, Sears, and Discount Tire, it boosted market share from 14 percent to 16 percent in the first year.[70]
- *Advertising:* Should advertising expenditures be increased? Should the message or copy be changed? Should the media mix be changed? Should the timing, frequency, or size of ads be changed?
- *Sales promotion:* Should the company step up sales promotion—trade deals, cents-off coupons, rebates, warranties, gifts, and contests?
- *Personal selling:* Should the number or quality of salespeople be increased? Should the basis for sales force specialization be changed? Should sales territories be revised? Should sales force incentives be revised? Can sales-call planning be improved?
- *Services:* Can the company speed up delivery? Can it extend more technical assistance to customers? Can it extend more credit?

Marketers often debate which tools are most effective in the mature stage. For example, would the company gain more by increasing its advertising or its sales-promotion budget? Sales promotion has more impact at this stage because consumers have reached an equilibrium in their buying habits and preferences, and psychological persuasion (advertising) is not as effective as financial persuasion (sales-promotion deals). Many consumer-packaged-goods companies now spend over 60 percent of their total promotion budget on sales promotion to support mature products. Other marketers argue that brands should be managed as capital assets and supported by advertising. Advertising expenditures should be treated as a capital investment. Brand managers, however, use sales promotion because its effects are quicker and more visible to their superiors; but excessive sales-promotion activity can hurt the brand's image and long-run profit performance.

"Marketing Memo: Breaking Through the Mature-Product Syndrome" shows how *gap analysis* can be used to discover possible growth opportunities in a mature market.

marketing strategies: decline stage

Sales decline for a number of reasons, including technological advances, shifts in consumer tastes, and increased domestic and foreign competition. All lead to overcapacity, increased price cutting, and profit erosion. The decline might be slow, as in the case of oatmeal; or rapid, as in the case of the Edsel automobile. Sales may plunge to zero, or they may petrify at a low level.

Marketing
MEMO

Breaking Through the Mature-Product Syndrome

Managers of mature products need a systematic framework for identifying possible "breakthrough" ideas. Professor John A. Weber of Notre Dame developed the following framework, which he calls gap analysis, to guide the search for growth opportunities. We will apply this to a mature beverage product such as Kool-Aid:

1. *Natural changes in the size of industry market potential*: Will current birth rates and demographics favor more consumption of Kool-Aid? How will the economic outlook affect Kool-Aid consumption?
2. *New uses or new user segments*: Can Kool-Aid be made to appeal to teenagers, young adult singles, young adult parents, and so on?
3. *Innovative product differentiations*: Can Kool-Aid be made in different versions such as low calorie or super-sweet?
4. *Add new product lines*: Can the Kool-Aid name be used to launch a new soft-drink line?
5. *Stimulate nonusers*: Can elderly people be persuaded to try Kool-Aid?
6. *Stimulate light users*: Can children be reminded to drink Kool-Aid daily?
7. *Increase amount used on each use occasion*: Can more Kool-Aid be put in each package at a higher price?
8. *Close existing product and price gaps*: Should new sizes of Kool-Aid be introduced?
9. *Create new product-line elements*: Should Kool-Aid introduce new flavors?
10. *Expand distribution coverage*: Can Kool-Aid distribution coverage be expanded to Europe and the Far East?
11. *Expand distribution intensity*: Can the percentage of convenience stores in the Midwest that carry Kool-Aid be increased from 70 to 90 percent?
12. *Expand distribution exposure*: Can offers to the trade win more shelf space for Kool-Aid?
13. *Penetrate substitutes' positions*: Can consumers be convinced that Kool-Aid is better than other soft drinks?
14. *Penetrate direct competitors' position(s)*: Can consumers of other brands be convinced to switch to Kool-Aid?
15. *Defend firm's present position*: Can Kool-Aid satisfy the current users more so that they remain loyal?

Source: John A. Weber, *Identifying and Solving Marketing Problems with Gap Analysis* (Notre Dame, IN: Strategic Business Systems, 1986).

As sales and profits decline, some firms withdraw from the market. Those remaining may reduce the number of products they offer. They may withdraw from smaller market segments and weaker trade channels, and they may cut their promotion budgets and reduce prices further.

Unfortunately, most companies have not developed a policy for handling aging products. Sentiment often plays a role:

> Putting products to death—or letting them die—is a drab business, and often engenders much of the sadness of a final parting with old and tried friends. The portable, six-sided pretzel was the first product The Company ever made. Our line will no longer be our line without it.[71]

Logic may also play a role. Management believes that product sales will improve when the economy improves, or when the marketing strategy is revised, or when the product is improved; or the weak product may be retained because of its alleged contribution to the sales of the company's other products; or its revenue may cover out-of-pocket costs, even if it is not turning a profit.

Unless strong reasons for retention exist, carrying a weak product is very costly to the firm—and not just by the amount of uncovered overhead and profit: There are many hidden costs. Weak products often consume a disproportionate amount of management's time; require frequent price and inventory adjustments; generally involve short production runs in spite of expensive setup times; require both advertising and sales force attention that might be better used to make the healthy products more profitable; and can cast a shadow on the company's image. The biggest cost might well lie in the future. Failing to eliminate weak products delays the aggressive search for replacement products. The weak products create a lopsided product mix, long on yesterday's breadwinners and short on tomorrow's.

In handling aging products, a company faces a number of tasks and decisions. The first task is to establish a system for identifying weak products. Many companies appoint a product-review committee with representatives from marketing, R&D, manufacturing, and finance. The controller's office supplies data for each product showing trends in market size, market share, prices, costs, and profits. A computer program then analyzes this information. The managers responsible for dubious products fill out rating forms showing where they think sales and profits will go, with and without any changes in marketing strategy. The product-review committee makes a recommendation for each product—leave it alone, modify its marketing strategy, or drop it.[72]

Some firms will abandon declining markets earlier than others. Much depends on the presence and height of exit barriers in the industry.[73] The lower the exit barriers, the easier it is for firms to leave the industry, and the more tempting it is for the remaining firms to stay and attract the withdrawing firms' customers. For example, Procter & Gamble stayed in the declining liquid-soap business and improved its profits as others withdrew.

In a study of company strategies in declining industries, Kathryn Harrigan identified five decline strategies available to the firm:

1. Increasing the firm's investment (to dominate the market or strengthen its competitive position).
2. Maintaining the firm's investment level until the uncertainties about the industry are resolved.
3. Decreasing the firm's investment level selectively, by dropping unprofitable customer groups, while simultaneously strengthening the firm's investment in lucrative niches.
4. Harvesting ("milking") the firm's investment to recover cash quickly.
5. Divesting the business quickly by disposing of its assets as advantageously as possible.[74]

The appropriate strategy depends on the industry's relative attractiveness and the company's competitive strength in that industry. A company that is in an unattractive industry but possesses competitive strength should consider shrinking selectively. A company that is in an attractive industry and has competitive strength should consider strengthening its investment. Boston Market is an example.

Boston Market   Just five years after its 1993 initial public offering, fast-food chain Boston Market declared bankruptcy. McDonald's bought the struggling chain in 2000 for $173 million, planning to convert its locations into new McDonald's franchises. The burger giant soon realized that the Boston Market brand still had value, and decided to try to revitalize the company. Boston Market now grosses more than $700 million a year. Based on successful test-market results, McDonald's plans to give every Boston Market store a makeover that includes warmer décor and more menu options.[75]

If the company were choosing between harvesting and divesting, its strategies would be quite different. *Harvesting* calls for gradually reducing a product or business's costs while trying to maintain its sales. The first step is to cut R&D costs and plant and equipment investment. The company might also reduce product quality, sales force size, marginal services, and advertising expenditures. It would try to cut these costs without letting customers, competitors, and employees know what is happening. Harvesting is an ethically ambivalent strategy, and it is also difficult to execute. Yet many mature products warrant this strategy. Harvesting can substantially increase the company's current cash flow.[76]

Companies that successfully restage or rejuvenate a mature product often do so by adding value to the original product. Consider the experience of Pitney Bowes Inc., the dominant producer of postage meters.

Pitney Bowes   In 1996, critics, and even Pitney Bowes insiders, predicted that faxes would kill regular mail, on which Pitney's business relies. Then they predicted that e-mail would kill faxes and that all these technological advances combined would kill Pitney's profits. As it happens, the surge in direct mail and Internet-related bills has generated more mail, not less, but the Internet also enabled new companies such as e-Stamps and stamps.com to enter Pitney's territory by offering a way to download stamps over the Internet. Pitney recast itself as a messaging company, not merely a mailing company. It developed software products that let customers track incoming materials and outgoing products, convert bills and print files to fax or e-mail, and track when a document has been acted upon. Pitney also provides electronic billing services for e-commerce companies and even added an electronic-stamp business to compete with the stamp start-ups. Pitney's saving view: The Internet is not the enemy; rather, it is a vehicle for becoming a broad-based messaging company.[77]

When a company decides to drop a product, it faces further decisions. If the product has strong distribution and residual goodwill, the company can probably sell it to another firm. If the company can't find any buyers, it must decide whether to liquidate the brand quickly or slowly. It must also decide on how much inventory and service to maintain for past customers.

the product life-cycle concept: critique

The PLC concept helps interpret product and market dynamics. It can be used for planning and control, although as a forecasting tool it is less useful. PLC theory has its share of critics. They claim that life-cycle patterns are too variable in shape and duration. PLCs lack what living organisms have—namely, a fixed sequence of stages and a fixed length of each stage. Critics also charge that marketers can seldom tell what stage the product is in. A product may appear to be mature when actually it has reached a plateau prior to another upsurge. They charge that the PLC pattern is the result of marketing strategies rather than an inevitable course that sales must follow:

> Suppose a brand is acceptable to consumers but has a few bad years because of other factors—for instance, poor advertising, delisting by a major chain, or entry of a "me-too" competitive product backed by massive sampling. Instead of thinking in terms of corrective measures, management begins to feel that its brand has entered a declining stage. It therefore withdraws funds from the promotion budget to finance R&D on new items. The next year the brand does even worse, panic increases. . . . Clearly, the PLC is a dependent variable which is determined by marketing actions; it is not an independent variable to which companies should adapt their marketing programs.[78]

Table 11.5 summarizes the characteristics, marketing objectives, and marketing strategies of the four stages of the PLC.

market evolution

Because the PLC focuses on what is happening to a particular product or brand rather than on what is happening to the overall market, it yields a product-oriented picture rather than a market-oriented picture. Firms need to visualize a market's evolutionary path as it is affected by new needs, competitors, technology, channels, and other developments.

In the course of a product's or brand's existence, its positioning must change to keep pace with market developments. Consider the case of Lego.

LEGO Group   LEGO Group, the Danish toy company, enjoyed a 72 percent global market share of the construction toy market; but children were spending more of their spare time with video games, computers, and television and less time with

table **11.5**	Summary of Product Life–Cycle Characteristics, Objectives, and Strategies

	Introduction	**Growth**	**Maturity**	**Decline**
Characteristics				
Sales	Low sales	Rapidly rising sales	Peak sales	Declining sales
Costs	High cost per customer	Average cost per customer	Low cost per customer	Low cost per customer
Profits	Negative	Rising profits	High profits	Declining profits
Customers	Innovators	Early adopters	Middle majority	Laggards
Competitors	Few	Growing Number	Stable number beginning to decline	Declining number
Marketing Objectives				
	Create product awareness and trial	Maximize market share	Maximize profit while defending market share	Reduce expenditure and milk the brand
Strategies				
Product	Offer a basic product	Offer product extensions, service, warranty	Diversify brands and items models	Phase out weak
Price	Charge cost-plus	Price to penetrate market	Price to match or best competitors'	Cut price
Distribution	Build selective distribution	Build intensive distribution	Build more intensive distribution	Go selective: phase out unprofitable outlets
Advertising	Build product awareness among early adopters and dealers	Build awareness and interest in the mass-market	Stress brand differences and benefits	Reduce to level needed to retain hard-core loyals
Sales Promotion	Use heavy sales promotion to entice trial	Reduce to take advantage of heavy consumer demand	Increase to encourage brand switching	Reduce to minimal level

Sources: Chester R. Wasson, *Dynamic Competitive Strategy and Product Life Cycles* (Austin, TX: Austin Press, 1978); John A. Weber, "Planning Corporate Growth with Inverted Product Life Cycles," *Long Range Planning* (October 1976): 12–29; Peter Doyle, "The Realities of the Product Life Cycle," *Quarterly Review of Marketing* (Summer 1976).

traditional toys. So Lego recognized the need to change or expand its market space. It redefined its market space as "family edutainment," which included toys, education, interactive technology, software, computers, and consumer electronics. All involved exercising the mind and having fun. Part of LEGO Group's plan is to capture an increasing share of customer spending as children become young adults and then parents.

stages in market evolution

Like products, markets evolve through four stages: emergence, growth, maturity, and decline.

EMERGENCE   Before a market materializes, it exists as a latent market. For example, for centuries people have wanted faster means of calculation. This need was successively satisfied through abacuses, slide rules, and large adding machines. Suppose an entrepreneur recognizes this need and imagines a technological solution in the form of a small, handheld electronic calculator. He now has to determine the product attributes,

including physical size and number of mathematical functions. Because he is market-oriented, he interviews potential buyers. He finds that target customers vary greatly in their preferences. Some want a four-function calculator (adding, subtracting, multiplying, and dividing) and others want more functions (calculating percentages, square roots, and logs). Some want a small hand calculator and others want a large one. This type of market, in which buyer preferences scatter evenly, is called a *diffused-preference market*.

The entrepreneur's problem is to design an optimal product for this market. He or she has three options:

1. The new product can be designed to meet the preferences of one of the corners of the market (*a single-niche strategy*).
2. Two or more products can be simultaneously launched to capture two or more parts of the market (*a multiple-niche strategy*).
3. The new product can be designed for the middle of the market (*a mass-market strategy).*

For small firms, a single-niche market strategy makes the most sense. A small firm does not have the resources for capturing and holding the mass-market. A large firm might go after the mass-market by designing a product that is medium in size and number of functions. A product in the center minimizes the sum of the distances of existing preferences from the actual product, thereby minimizing total dissatisfaction. Assume that the pioneer firm is large and designs its product for the mass market. On launching the product, the *emergence* stage begins.

GROWTH   If the new product sells well, new firms will enter the market, ushering in a *market-growth stage*. Where will a second firm enter the market, assuming that the first firm established itself in the center? The second firm has three options:

1. It can position its brand in one of the corners (single-niche strategy).
2. It can position its brand next to the first competitor (mass-market strategy).
3. It can launch two or more products in different, unoccupied corners (multiple-niche strategy).

If the second firm is small, it is likely to avoid head-on competition with the pioneer and to launch its brand in one of the market corners. If the second firm is large, it might

figure **11.8**

Market Fragmentation and
Market Consolidation
Strategies

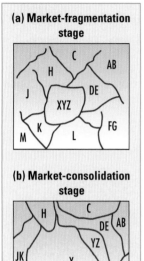

(a) Market-fragmentation stage

(b) Market-consolidation stage

launch its brand in the center against the pioneer. The two firms can easily end up shar-ing the mass market; or a large second firm can implement a multiniche strategy and surround and box in the pioneer.

MATURITY   Eventually, the competitors cover and serve all the major market segments and the market enters the *maturity stage*. In fact, they go further and invade each other's seg-ments, reducing everyone's profits in the process. As market growth slows down, the mar-ket splits into finer segments and high *market fragmentation* occurs. This situation is illus-trated in Figure 11.8(a) where the letters represent different companies supplying various segments. Note that two segments are unserved because they are too small to yield a profit.

Market fragmentation is often followed by a *market consolidation* caused by the emer-gence of a new attribute that has strong appeal. Market consolidation took place in the toothpaste market when P&G introduced Crest, which effectively retarded dental decay. Suddenly, toothpaste brands that claimed whitening power, cleaning power, sex appeal, taste, or mouthwash effectiveness were pushed into the corners because con-sumers primarily wanted dental protection. Crest won a lion's share of the market, as shown by the X territory in Figure 11.8(b).

However, even a consolidated market condition will not last. Other companies will copy a successful brand, and the market will eventually splinter again. Mature markets swing between fragmentation and consolidation. The fragmentation is brought about by competition, and the consolidation is brought about by innovation.

DECLINE   Eventually, demand for the present products will begin to decrease, and the market will enter the *decline stage*. Either society's total need level declines or a new technology replaces the old. Thus an entrepreneur might invent a mouth-rinse liquid that is superior to toothpaste. In this case, the old technology will eventually disappear and a new life cycle will emerge.

AN EXAMPLE: THE PAPER-TOWEL MARKET   Consider the evolution of the paper-towel market. Originally, homemakers used cotton and linen dishcloths and towels in their kitchens. A paper company, looking for new markets, developed paper towels. This development crystallized a latent market. Other manufacturers entered the market. The number of brands proliferated and created market fragmentation. Industry overca-pacity led manufacturers to search for new features. One manufacturer, hearing con-sumers complain that paper towels were not absorbent, introduced "absorbent" towels and increased its market share. This market consolidation did not last long because competitors came out with their own versions of absorbent paper towels. The market fragmented again. Then another manufacturer introduced a "superstrength" towel. It was soon copied. Another manufacturer introduced a "lint-free" paper towel, which was subsequently copied. Thus paper towels evolved from a single product to one with various absorbencies, strengths, and applications. Market evolution was driven by the forces of innovation and competition.

dynamics of attribute competition

Competition produces a continuous round of new product attributes. If a new attribute succeeds, several competitors soon offer it. To the extent that many airlines serve in-flight meals, meals are no longer a basis for air-carrier choice. *Customer expectations are progressive*. This fact underlines the strategic importance of a maintaining the lead in introducing new attributes. Each new attribute, if successful, creates a competitive advantage for the firm, leading to temporarily higher-than-average market share and profits. The market leader must learn to routinize the innovation process.

Can a firm look ahead and anticipate the succession of attributes that are likely to win favor and be technologically feasible? How can the firm discover new attributes? There are four approaches.

1. *A customer-survey process:* The company asks consumers what benefits they would like added to the product and their desire level for each. The firm also examines the cost of developing each new attribute and likely competitive responses.

2. *An intuitive process:* Entrepreneurs get hunches and undertake product development without much marketing research. Natural selection determines winners and losers. If a manufacturer has intuited an attribute that the market wants, that manufacturer is considered smart or lucky.

3. *A dialectical process:* Innovators should not march with the crowd. Thus blue jeans, starting out as an inexpensive clothing article, over time became fashionable and more expensive. This unidirectional movement, however, contains the seeds of its own destruction. Eventually, the price falls again or some manufacturer introduces another cheap material for pants.

4. *A needs-hierarchy process:* (See Maslow's theory in Chapter 7.) We would predict that the first automobiles would provide basic transportation and be designed for safety. Later, automobiles would start appealing to social acceptance and status needs. Still later, automobiles would be designed to help people "fulfill" themselves. The innovator's task is to assess when the market is ready to satisfy a higher-order need.

The actual unfolding of new attributes in a market is more complex than simple theories suggest.[79] We should not underestimate the role of technology and societal processes. For example, the strong consumer wish for portable computers remained unmet until miniaturization technology was sufficiently developed. Developments such as inflation, shortages, environmentalism, consumerism, and new lifestyles lead consumers to reevaluate product attributes. Inflation increases the desire for a smaller car, and a desire for car safety increases the desire for a heavier car. The innovator must use marketing research to gauge the demand potency of different attributes in order to determine the company's best move.

summary

1. Many marketers advocate promoting only one product benefit, thus creating a unique selling proposition as they position their product. People tend to remember "number one." Double-benefit position and triple-benefit positioning can also be successful, but must be used carefully.

2. The key to competitive advantage is product differentiation. A market offering can be differentiated along five dimensions: product (form, features, performance quality, conformance quality, durability, reliability, repairability, style, design); services (order ease, delivery, installation, customer training, customer consulting, maintenance and repair, miscellaneous services); personnel, channel, or image (symbols, media, atmosphere, and events). A difference is worth establishing to the extent that it is important, distinctive, superior, preemptive, affordable, and profitable.

3. Because economic conditions change and competitive activity varies, companies normally find it necessary to reformulate their marketing strategy several times during a product's life cycle. Technologies, product forms, and brands also exhibit life cycles with distinct stages. The general sequence of stages

in any life cycle is introduction, growth, maturity, and decline. The majority of products today are in the maturity stage.

4. Although many products exhibit a bell-shaped product life cycle (PLC), there are many other patterns, including the growth-slump-maturity pattern, the cycle-recycle pattern, and the scalloped pattern. The PLCs of styles, fashions, and fads can be erratic; the key to success in these areas lies in creating products with staying power.

5. Each stage of the PLC calls for different marketing strategies. The introduction stage is marked by slow growth and minimal profits. If successful, the product enters a growth stage marked by rapid sales growth and increasing profits. There follows a maturity stage in which sales growth slows and profits stabilize. Finally, the product enters a decline stage. The company's task is to identify the truly weak products; develop a strategy for each one; and finally, phase out weak products in a way that minimizes the hardship to company profits, employees, and customers.

6. Like products, markets evolve through four stages: emergence, growth, maturity, and decline.

applications

marketing debate – do brands have finite lives?

Often, after a brand begins to slip in the marketplace or disappears all together, commentators observe, "all brands have their day." Their rationale is that all brands, in some sense, have a finite life and cannot be expected to be leaders forever. Other experts contend, however, that brands can live forever, and their long-term success depends as much on the skill and insight of the marketers involved.

Take a position: Brands cannot be expected to last forever versus There is no reason for a brand to ever become obsolete.

marketing and advertising

1. When T-Fal sells its pans around the world, it takes into account each market's unique characteristics. The headline of the ad in Figure 1 reads, "Pan for the Index Finger," showing how Japanese customers can use one finger to detach the handle so the pan can be used in different ways and stored in tight spaces.

   a. What unique selling proposition is this ad promoting?

   b. Which of the nine product differentiation variables is being communicated in this ad? Why is this variable important to the target market?

   c. State the value proposition suggested by this T-Fal ad.

2. The ad in Figure 2, placed by the U.S. Postal Service for its NetPost Mailing Online service, targets businesses that use direct mail to reach their customers.

   a. Is this ad illustrating attribute, benefit, use, user, competitor, product category, or quality/price positioning?

   b. Which of the main service differentiators is being communicated by this ad? Why would customers value this difference?

   c. The market for postal services is in the maturity stage. Does the U.S. Postal Service appear to be using market modification, product modification, or marketing-mix modification to stimulate sales?

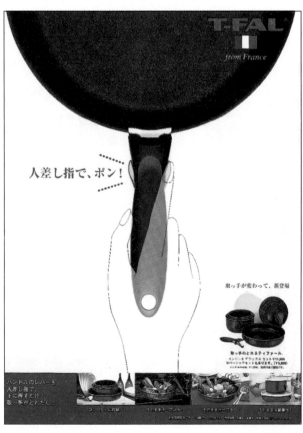

Figure 1

Figure 2

online marketing today

Although pioneering a market can be expensive and difficult, companies that do it effectively will reap first-mover advantages. The online auction site eBay is a good case in point. When the Internet was in its infancy, eBay invented the online auction concept and revolutionized the way consumers buy and sell products among themselves. Now 30 million consumers are registered as eBay buyers or sellers, and 2 million more register every month. In recent years, companies have begun using eBay's auction facilities to sell a range of new products. JCPenney, for example, has auctioned clothing on eBay, while Mitsubishi Electric has auctioned factory automation equipment.[80]

Visit the eBay site (*www.ebay.com*) and see how the company orients new users to its services. Also look at the goods and services featured on the home page; follow the link to eBay Motors or another of the specialty sites; and follow the link to read "About eBay." Based on your observations of eBay's online marketing efforts, does this market appear to be in the emergence, growth, maturity, or decline stage? How are eBay's marketing efforts intended to affect the market? How is eBay using its site to create an effective image?

you're the marketer: sonic pda marketing plan

Marketing Plan Pro

In the course of developing a marketing strategy, marketers must select and communicate an effective positioning to differentiate their offerings. They also have to plan appropriate marketing strategies for each stage of the product life cycle and the market's evolution.

As before, you are working with Jane Melody on Sonic's marketing plan for launching a new PDA. Review your work on previous sections of the marketing plan. Then answer these questions about positioning and life-cycle strategies for Sonic:

- Which of the differentiation variables related to product, services, personnel, channels, and image are best suited to Sonic's situation, strategy, and goals? Include the rationale for your selection.

- In developing your positioning, identify the benefits most valued by your target customers. Will you stress one or more than one benefit in your positioning? In a sentence, what is the value proposition for Sonic's PDA?
- Knowing the stage of Sonic's PDA in the product life cycle, what are the implications for the marketing mix, product management strategy, service strategy, and R&D strategy?
- In which stage of its evolution does the PDA market appear to be? What does this mean for Sonic's marketing plans?

Once you have answered these questions and considered the effects on Sonic's marketing, either summarize your ideas in a written marketing plan or type them in the Positioning sections of the *Marketing Plan Pro* software. Also note any additional research you may need in the Marketing Research section of the software.

notes

1. Al Ries and Jack Trout, *Positioning: The Battle for Your Mind* (New York: Warner Books, 1982).
2. Michael Treacy and Fred Wiersema, *The Disciplines of Market Leaders* (Reading, MA: Addison-Wesley, 1994).
3. Rosser Reeves, *Reality in Advertising* (New York: Alfred A. Knopf, 1960).
4. Ries and Trout, *Positioning*.
5. Chad Terhune, "Home Depot's Home Improvement," *Wall Street Journal*, March 8, 2001, p. B1.
6. Robert V. Stumpf, "The Market Structure of the Major Tourist Attractions in Southern California," *Proceedings of the 1976 Sperry Business Conference* (Chicago: American Marketing Association, 1976), pp. 101–6.
7. Yoram J. Wind, *Product Policy: Concepts, Methods and Strategy* (Reading, MA: Addison-Wesley, 1982), pp. 79–81; David Aaker and J. Gary Shansby, "Postioning Your Product," *Business Horizons* (May–June 1982): 56–62.
8. Bobby J. Calder and Steven J. Reagan, "Brand Design," in *Kellogg on Marketing*, ed. Dawn Iacobucci (New York: John Wiley & Sons, 2001), p. 61.
9. The Palm Pilot and Mountain Dew examples are taken from Alice M. Tybout and Brian Sternthal, "Brand Positioning," in *Kellogg on Marketing*, ed. Dawn Iacobucci (New York: John Wiley & Sons, 2001), p. 54.

10. Alice M. Tybout and Brian Sternthal, "Brand Positioning," in *Kellogg on Marketing*, ed. Dawn Iacobucci (New York: John Wiley & Sons, 2001), p. 35.
11. Kevin Clancy, Copernicus newsletter, May 2001.
12. Theodore Levitt, "Marketing Success through Differentiation: Of Anything," *Harvard Business Review* (January–February 1980).
13. Gregory S. Carpenter, Rashi Glazer, and Kent Nakamoto, "Meaningful Brands from Meaningless Differentiation: The Dependence on Irrelevant Attributes," *Journal of Marketing Research* (August 1994): 339–50.
14. Edwin T. Crego Jr. and Peter D. Schiffrin, *Customer Centered Reengineering* (Homewood, IL: Irwin, 1995).
15. Miland M. Lele, *Creating Strategic Leverage* (New York: John Wiley, 1992).
16. Some of these bases are discussed in David A. Garvin, "Competing on the Eight Dimensions of Quality," *Harvard Business Review* (November–December 1987): 101–9.
17. David A. Aaker, *Managing Brand Equity* (New York: The Free Press, 1991).
18. Elizabeth Corcoran, "The E Gang," *Forbes*, July 24, 2000, p. 145.
19. Bernd Schmitt and Alex Simonson, *Marketing Aesthetics: The Strategic Management of Brand, Identity, and Image* (New York: The Free Press, 1997).

20. Gerry Khermouch, "Zona Sets Collectible Max-packs," *Brandweek*, April 20, 1998, p. 16.

21. <*www.arizonabev.com*>.

22. Philip Kotler, "Design: A Powerful but Neglected Strategic Tool," *Journal of Business Strategy* (Fall 1984): 16–21. Also see Christopher Lorenz, *The Design Dimension* (New York: Basil Blackwell, 1986).

23. "Hot R.I.P: The Floppy Disk," *Rolling Stone*, August 20, 1998, p. 86; Owen Edwards, "Beauty and the Box," *Forbes*, October 5, 1998, p. 131; Brent Schlender, "Steve Jobs: The Graying Prince of a Shrinking Kingdom," *Fortune*, May 14, 2001, p. 118.

24. Joseph Weber, "A Better Grip on Hawking Tools," *BusinessWeek*, June 5, 1995, p. 99.

25. "Internet Grocer Peapod Achieves Operating Profitability in Chicago," *Business Wire*, April 23, 2001; James Turner, "Online Grocers Try to Extend Their Shelf Life," *Christian Science Monitor*, February 12, 2001, p. 16.

26. For further reading, George Stalk Jr. and Thomas M. Hout, *Competing Against Time* (New York: The Free Press, 1990); Joseph D. Blackburn, *Time-Based Competition* (Homewood, IL: Irwin, 1991); Christopher Meyer, *Fast Cycle Time* (New York: The Free Press, 1993); "The Computer Liked Us," *U.S. News & World Report*, August 14, 1995, pp. 71–72.

27. Hermann Simon, *Hidden Champions* (Boston: Harvard Business School Press, 1996).

28. For a comprehensive discussion of Cemex, see Adrian J. Slywotzky and David J. Morrison, *How Digital Is Your Business* (New York: Crown Business, 2000), ch. 5.

29. "Pac Bell to Offer DSL, You Can Install," *San Francisco Chronicle*, March 20, 2000.

30. Adapted from Tom Peters's description in *Thriving on Chaos* (New York: Alfred A. Knopf, 1987), pp. 56–57.

31. Susan Hirsh, "At Rite Aid, the Medicine 'Is Working'," *Baltimore Sun*, January 10, 2001, p. 1C.

32. Linda Knapp, "A Sick Computer?" *Seattle Times*, January 28, 2001, p. D-8.

33. Ian C. MacMillan and Rita Gunther McGrath, "Discovering New Points of Differentiation," *Harvard Business Review* (July–August 1997): 133–45.

34. *Canon Environmental Report*, 2000.

35. "The 25 Best Sales Forces," *Sales & Marketing Management* (July 1998): 32–50.

36. For a similar list, see Leonard L. Berry and A. Parasuraman, *Marketing Services: Competing Through Quality* (New York: The Free Press, 1991), p. 16.

37. Susan Greco, "Inside-Out Marketing," *Inc.*, January 1998, pp. 51–59; James P. Sterba, "Hunting with the Man Who Made Orvis a Winner," *Wall Street Journal*, November 2, 1999, p. A24.

38. Erin Davies, "Selling Sex and Cat Food," *Fortune*, June 9, 1997, p. 36; Shelly Branch, "P&G Is Out to Fetch Distribution Gains for Iams Pet Food," *Wall Street Journal*, January 6, 2000, p. A6.

39. <*www.vans.com*>.

40. Jack Trout and Steve Rivkin, *Differentiate or Die* (New York: Wiley, 2000).

41. Karen Axelrod and Bruce Brumberg, *Watch It Made in the U.S.A.* (Santa Fe: John Muir Publications, 1997).

42. "Guerrillas in Our Midst," *The Economist*, October 14, 2000, pp. 80–81.

43. "Swatch: Ambitious," *The Economist*, April 18, 1992, pp. 74–75. See also <*www.swatch.com*>.

44. Some authors distinguished additional stages. Wasson suggested a stage of competitive turbulence between growth and maturity. See Chester R. Wasson, *Dynamic Competitive Strategy and Product Life Cycles* (Austin, TX: Austin Press, 1978). Maturity describes a stage of sales growth slowdown and saturation, a stage of flat sales after sales have peaked.

45. John E. Swan and David R. Rink, "Fitting Market Strategy to Varying Product Life Cycles," *Business Horizons* (January–February 1982): 72–76; and Gerald J. Tellis and C. Merle Crawford, "An Evolutionary Approach to Product Growth Theory," *Journal of Marketing* (Fall 1981): 125–34.

46. William E. Cox Jr., "Product Life Cycles as Marketing Models," *Journal of Business* (October 1967): 375–84.

47. Jordan P. Yale, "The Strategy of Nylon's Growth," *Modern Textiles Magazine*, February 1964, p. 32. Also see Theodore Levitt, "Exploit the Product Life Cycle," *Harvard Business Review* (November–December 1965): 81–94.

48. Chester R. Wasson, "How Predictable Are Fashion and Other Product Life Cycles?" *Journal of Marketing* (July 1968): 36–43.

49. Ibid.

50. William H. Reynolds, "Cars and Clothing: Understanding Fashion Trends," *Journal of Marketing* (July 1968): 44–49.

51. Patrick Butters, "What Biggest Selling Adult Game Still Cranks Out Vexing Questions?" *Insight on the News*, January 26, 1998, p. 39.

52. Robert D. Buzzell, "Competitive Behavior and Product Life Cycles," in *New Ideas for Successful Marketing*, ed. John S. Wright and Jack Goldstucker (Chicago: American Marketing Association, 1956), p. 51.

53. William T. Robinson and Claes Fornell, "Sources of Market Pioneer Advantages in Consumer Goods Industries," *Journal of Marketing Research* (August 1985): 305–17.

54. Glen L. Urban et al., "Market Share Rewards to Pioneering Brands: An Empirical Analysis and Strategic Implications," *Management Science* (June 1986): 645–59.

55. Gregory S. Carpenter and Kent Nakamoto, "Consumer Preference Formation and Pioneering Advantage," *Journal of Marketing Research* (August 1989): 285–98.

56. Frank R. Kardes, Gurumurthy Kalyanaram, Murali Chankdrashekaran, and Ronald J. Dornoff, "Brand Retrieval, Consideration Set Composition, Consumer Choice, and the Pioneering Advantage," *Journal of Consumer Research* (June 1993): 62–75. See also Frank H. Alpert and Michael A. Kamins, "Pioneer Brand Advantage and Consumer Behavior: A Conceptual Framework and Propositional Inventory," *Journal of the Academy of Marketing Science* (Summer 1994): 244–53.

57. Thomas S. Robertson and Hubert Gatignon, "How Innovators Thwart New Entrants into Their Market," *Planning Review* (September–October 1991): 4–11, 48.

58. Steven P. Schnaars, *Managing Imitation Strategies* (New York: The Free Press, 1994). See also Jin K. Han, Namwoon Kim, and Hony-Bom Kin, "Entry Barriers: A Oull-, One-, or Two-Edged Sword for Incumbents? Unraveling the Paradox from a Contingency Perspective," *Journal of Marketing* (January 2001): 1–14.

59. Peter N. Golder and Gerald J. Tellis, "Pioneer Advantage: Marketing Logic or Marketing Legend?" *Journal of Marketing*

Research (May 1992): 34–46; Shizhang and Arthur B. Markman "Overcoming the Early Advantge: The Role of Alignable and Nanalignable Differences, *Journal of Marketing Research* (November 1998): 1–15.

Gerald Tellis and Peter Golder, *Will & Vision: How Latecomers Can Grow to Dominate Markets* (New York: McGraw-Hill, 2001). Rajesh K. Chanely and Gerald J. Tellis, "The Incumbent's Curse? Incumbency, Size, and Radical Product Innovation," *Journal of Marketing Research* (July 2000): 1–17.

John B. Frey, "Pricing Over the Competitive Cycle," speech presented at the 1982 Marketing Conference, Conference Board, New York.

Seanna Broder, "Reheating Starbucks," *BusinessWeek*, September 28, 1998, p. A1, <*www. Starbucks.com*>.

Linda Himelstein, "Yahoo! The Company, the Strategy, the Stock," *BusinessWeek*, September 7, 1998, pp. 66–76. Marc Gunther, "The Cheering Fades for Yahoo," *Fortune*, November 12, 2001; Ben Elgin, "Inside Yahoo! The untold story of how arrogance, infighting, and management missteps derailed one of the hottest companies on the Web," *BusinessWeek*, May 21, 2001, p. 114.

Joulee Andrews and Daniel C. Smith, "In Search of the Marketing Imagination: Factors Affecting the Creativity of Marketing Programs for Mature Products," *Journal of Marketing Research* (May 1996): 174–87; William Boulding, Eunkyu Lee, and Richard Staelin, "Mastering the Mix: Do Advertising, Promotion, and Sales Force Activities Lead to Differentiation?" *Journal of Marketing Research* (May 1994): 159–72.

John Bigness, "New Twists Revive Past Product Hits," *Houston Chronicle*, October 11, 1998, p. 8; Denise Gellene, "An Old Dog's New Tricks: Hush Puppies' Return in the '90s Is No Small Feet," *Los Angeles Times*, August 30, 1997, p. D1; Malcolm Gladwell, "How to Start an Epidemic," *The Guardian*, April 22, 2000.

Brian Wansink and Michael L. Ray, "Advertising Strategies to Increase Usage Frequency," *Journal of Marketing* (January 1996): 31–46. Also see Brian Wansink, "Expansion Advertising," in *How Advertising Works*, ed. John Philip Jones (Thousand Oaks, CA: Sage Publications), pp. 95–103.

Vanessa O'Connell, "Food: After Years of Trial and Error, a Pickle Slice That Stays Put," *Wall Street Journal*, October 6,

1998, p. B1; "Vlasic's Hamburger-Size Pickles," *Wall Street Journal*, October 5, 1998, p. A26, <*www.vlasic.com*>.

68. Stephen M. Nowlis and Itamar Simmonson, "The Effect of New Product Features on Brand Choice," *Journal of Marketing Research* (February 1996): 36–46.

69. Donald W. Hendon, *Classic Failures in Product Marketing* (New York: Quorum Books, 1989), p. 29.

70. Allen J. McGrath, "Growth Strategies with a '90s Twist," *Across the Board*, March 1995, pp. 43–46.

71. R. S. Alexander, "The Death and Burial of 'Sick Products,'" *Journal of Marketing* (April 1964): 1.

72. Philip Kotler, "Phasing Out Weak Products," *Harvard Business Review* (March–April 1965): 107–18; Richard T. Hise, A. Parasuraman, and R. Viswanathan, "Product Elimination: The Neglected Management Responsibility," *Journal of Business Strategy* (Spring 1984): 56–63; George J. Avlonitis, "Product Elimination Decision Making: Does Formality Matter," *Journal of Marketing* (Winter 1985): 41–52.

73. Kathryn Rudie Harrigan, "The Effect of Exit Barriers upon Strategic Flexibility," *Strategic Management Journal* 1 (1980): 165–76.

74. Kathryn Rudie Harrigan, "Strategies for Declining Industries," *Journal of Business Strategy*, (Fall 1980): 27.

75. Michael Arndt, "There's Life in the Old Bird Yet," *Business Week*, May 14, 2001, p. 77.

76. Philip Kotler, "Harvesting Strategies for Weak Products," *Business Horizons* (August 1978): 15–22; Laurence P. Feldman and Albert L. Page, "Harvesting: The Misunderstood Market Exit Strategy," *Journal of Business Strategy* (Spring 1985): 79–85.

77. Claudia H. Deutsch, "Pitney Bowes Survives Faxes, E-Mail and the Internet," *New York Times*, August 18, 1998, p. D1; Matthew Lubanko, "Pitney Bowes Faces E-Foes Despite Lion's Share of the Market," *Hartford Courant*, March 18, 2000, p. E1.

78. Nariman K. Dhalla and Sonia Yuspeh, "Forget the Product Life Cycle Concept!" *Harvard Business Review* (January–February 1976): 105.

79. Marnik G. Dekimpe and Dominique M. Hanssens, "Empirical Generalizations about Market Evolution and Stationarity," *Marketing Science* 14, no. 3, pt. 1 (1995): G109–21.

80. Leslie Walker, "Retail's Piece of the Auction: Big-Business Strategy Emerging on eBay," *Washington Post*, July 19, 2001, p. A1.

14

setting the product and branding strategy

In this chapter, we will address the following questions:

- What are the characteristics of products?
- How can a company build and manage its product mix and product lines?
- How can a company make better brand decisions?
- How can packaging and labeling be used as marketing tools?

Kotler on Marketing

The best way to get and keep customers is to constantly figure out how to give them more for less.

W hat do business executives *Ray Kroc (McDonald's), Dave Thomas (Wendy's), and Colonel Sanders (Kentucky Fried Chicken) have in common? They all have led or lead lives interesting enough to feature on A&E's award-winning television show* Biography. *A&E's* Biography *offers excellent lessons in product and brand management.*

Arts & Entertainment Network A&E is steadily building *Biography*, its nightly look at famous figures, into its trademark masterbrand, one that is crossing a spectrum of media to reach a broad audience. So far, the cable series has profiled over 500 people. Executives at A&E are practicing line extension into new formats. Home video was the obvious first extension. Videos are sold through direct response, through catalogs, online, and in dedicated space at some 500 Barnes & Noble bookstores. A Biography Web site, born in 1996, has grown to include 22,000 personalities; its traffic surpasses that of A&E's own site; and A&E now offers a separate Biography cable channel, a Biography magazine, Biography books, and Biography CDs, which feature music from musicians profiled on the show.[1]

A&E's success story underscores the importance of the first and most important element of the marketing mix: the product. All the advertising and promotion in the world will not make consumers turn on a television show if they find it boring, irritating, or irrelevant.[2]

Product is a key element in the market offering. *Marketing-mix planning begins with formulating an offering to meet target customers' needs or wants. The customer will judge the offering by three basic elements: product features and quality, services mix and quality, and price (see Figure 14.1). In this chapter, we examine product; in Chapter 15, services; and in Chapter 16, prices. All three elements must be meshed into a competitively attractive offering.*

the product and the product mix

A **product** is anything that can be offered to a market to satisfy a want or need. Products that are marketed include *physical goods, services, experiences, events, persons, places, properties, organizations, information,* and *ideas.*

product levels

In planning its market offering, the marketer needs to think through five levels of the product (see Figure 14.2).[3] Each level adds more customer value, and the five constitute a **customer value hierarchy**. The most fundamental level is the **core benefit**: the fundamental service or benefit that the customer is really buying. A hotel guest is buying "rest and sleep." The purchaser of a drill is buying "holes." Marketers must see themselves as benefit providers.

At the second level, the marketer has to turn the core benefit into a **basic product**. Thus a hotel room includes a bed, bathroom, towels, desk, dresser, and closet.

At the third level, the marketer prepares an **expected product**, a set of attributes and conditions buyers normally expect when they purchase this product. Hotel guests expect a clean bed, fresh towels, working lamps, and a relative degree of quiet. Because most hotels can meet this minimum expectation, the traveler normally will settle for whichever hotel is most convenient or least expensive.

At the fourth level, the marketer prepares an **augmented product** that exceeds customer expectations. Consider BabyCenter.com.

BabyCenter.com BabyCenter.com's mission is to help mothers raise a healthy baby. Instead of simply setting itself up to sell baby products online, it has set itself up as a *metamediary* to provide a wide variety of information and services. Mothers will find helpful hints and checklists; a search engine for retrieving high-quality medical information; an opportunity to personalize the site; and access to a community of supportive fellow parents. As Elmer Wheeler once observed, "Don't sell the steak—sell the sizzle."

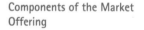

figure **14.1**

Components of the Market Offering

figure **14.2**

Five Product Levels

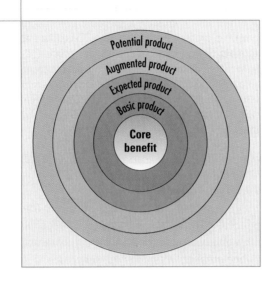

Today's competition essentially takes place at the product-augmentation level. (In less developed countries, competition takes place mostly at the expected product level.) Product augmentation leads the marketer to look at the user's total **consumption system**: the way the user performs the tasks of getting and using products and related services.[4] According to Levitt:

> The new competition is not between what companies produce in their factories, but between what they add to their factory output in the form of packaging, services, advertising, customer advice, financing, delivery arrangements, warehousing, and other things that people value.[5]

BabyCenter.com is not just an online merchant, it's a metamediary.

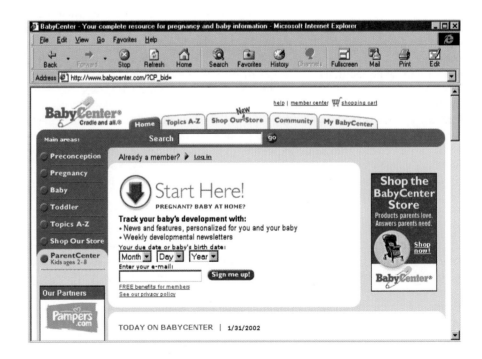

Some things should be noted about product-augmentation strategy. First, each augmentation adds cost. Second, augmented benefits soon become expected benefits. Today's hotel guests expect a remote-control television set. This means competitors will have to search for still other features and benefits. Third, as companies raise the price of their augmented product, some competitors offer a "stripped-down" version at a much lower price. Thus, alongside the growth of fine hotels like Four Seasons and Ritz Carlton, we see the emergence of lower-cost hotels and motels (Motel Six, Comfort Inn) catering to clients who simply want the basic product. Virgin Atlantic provides a good example of a company always searching to expand and differentiate its services from those offered by competitors.

Virgin Atlantic Airlines   Virgin seeks to provide an integrated travel experience. It joined with limousine companies to provide free transportation for business-class passengers to airports. Once there, they check into Virgin's Clubhouse lounge. At the Clubhouse, passengers can shower, take a hydrotherapy bath, have a free manicure, pedicure, facial, or haircut. They can sit at the bar, in the restaurant, library, or music room. On certain planes, they can take a shower or use the Jacuzzi, sleep in a ship-style sleeper cabin, or surf the Internet.

At the fifth level stands the **potential product**, which encompasses all the possible augmentations and transformations the product or offering might undergo in the future. Here is where companies search for new ways to satisfy customers and distinguish their offer. Richard Branson of Virgin Atlantic is thinking of adding a casino and a shopping mall in the 600-passenger planes that his company will acquire in the next few years; and consider the customization platforms new e-commerce sites are offering, from which companies can learn by seeing what different customers prefer.

MyCereal.com, Personalblends.com, and Reflect.com   General Mills' mycereal.com, which was available during 2000 and 2001, let users create their own cereal blends from ingredients that met their specific tastes or health needs. One woman received her cereal package with corn flakes, almond-coated raisins, sliced almonds, and dried banana bits; the package included the name she gave it: "Lisa's Yummy-to-My-Tummy" cereal. Proctor & Gamble has developed personalblends.com, where coffee lovers can customize their coffee by answering a few questions. P&G also developed Reflect.com, which offers customized beauty products created interactively on the Web site.

Successful companies add benefits to their offering that not only *satisfy* customers but also surprise and *delight* them. Delighting customers is a matter of exceeding expectations.

Ritz–Carlton Hotels   Ritz-Carlton Hotels remember guests' preferences and assign rooms with these preferences in mind. They empower employees to make decisions and spend money to solve customer-service issues. They review the service delivery process to imagine everything that could go wrong and then take preventive steps.

product hierarchy

Each product is related to certain other products. The product hierarchy stretches from basic needs to particular items that satisfy those needs. We can identify six levels of the product hierarchy (here for life insurance):

1. *Need family:* The core need that underlies the existence of a product family. Example: security.
2. *Product family:* All the product classes that can satisfy a core need with reasonable effectiveness. Example: savings and income.
3. *Product class:* A group of products within the product family recognized as having a certain functional coherence. Example: financial instruments.

General Mills' Mycereal.com Web site, available in 2000 and 2001, allowed consumers to create their own cereal blend.

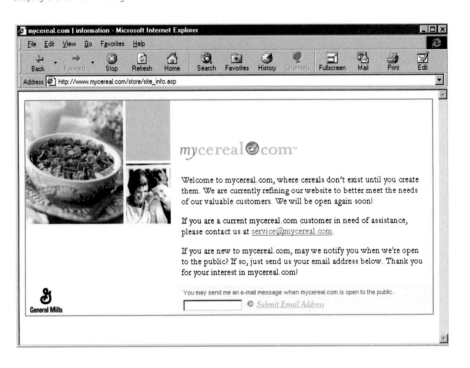

4. *Product line:* A group of products within a product class that are closely related because they perform a similar function, are sold to the same customer groups, are marketed through the same channels, or fall within given price ranges. Example: life insurance.

5. *Product type:* A group of items within a product line that share one of several possible forms of the product. Example: term life.

6. *Item (also called stockkeeping unit or product variant):* A distinct unit within a brand or product line distinguishable by size, price, appearance, or some other attribute. Example: Prudential renewable term life insurance.

Two other terms are frequently used with respect to the product hierarchy. A **product system** is a group of diverse but related items that function in a compatible manner. For example, the Handspring personal digital assistant comes with attachable Visor products including a phone, radio, pager, video games, e-books, MP3 player, digital camera, and voice recorder. A **product mix** (or product assortment) is the set of all products and items that a particular seller offers for sale to buyers.

product classifications

Marketers have traditionally classified products on the basis of characteristics: durability, tangibility, and use (consumer or industrial). Each product type has an appropriate marketing-mix strategy.[6]

DURABILITY AND TANGIBILITY   Products can be classified into three groups, according to durability and tangibility:

1. *Nondurable goods* are tangible goods normally consumed in one or a few uses, like beer and soap. Because these goods are consumed quickly and purchased frequently, the appropriate strategy is to make them available in many locations, charge only a small markup, and advertise heavily to induce trial and build preference.

2. *Durable goods* are tangible goods that normally survive many uses: refrigerators, machine tools, and clothing. Durable products normally require more personal selling and service, command a higher margin, and require more seller guarantees.

3. *Services* are intangible, inseparable, variable, and perishable products. As a result, they normally require more quality control, supplier credibility, and adaptability. Examples include haircuts and repairs.

CONSUMER-GOODS CLASSIFICATION   The vast array of goods consumers buy can be classified on the basis of shopping habits. We can distinguish among convenience, shopping, specialty, and unsought goods.

Convenience goods are those the customer usually purchases frequently, immediately, and with a minimum of effort. Examples include tobacco products, soaps, and newspapers. Convenience goods can be further divided. *Staples* are goods consumers purchase on a regular basis. A buyer might routinely purchase Heinz ketchup, Crest toothpaste, and Ritz crackers. *Impulse goods* are purchased without any planning or search effort. Candy bars and magazines are impulse goods. *Emergency goods* are purchased when a need is urgent—umbrellas during a rainstorm, boots and shovels during the first winter snowstorm. Manufacturers of emergency goods will place them in many outlets to capture the sale.

Shopping goods are goods that the customer, in the process of selection and purchase, characteristically compares on such bases as suitability, quality, price, and style. Examples include furniture, clothing, used cars, and major appliances. Shopping goods can be further divided. *Homogeneous shopping goods* are similar in quality but different enough in price to justify shopping comparisons. *Heterogeneous shopping goods* differ in product features and services that may be more important than price. The seller of heterogeneous shopping goods carries a wide assortment to satisfy individual tastes and must have well-trained salespeople to inform and advise customers.

Specialty goods have unique characteristics or brand identification for which a sufficient number of buyers is willing to make a special purchasing effort. Examples include cars, stereo components, photographic equipment, and men's suits. A Mercedes is a specialty good because interested buyers will travel far to buy one. Specialty goods do not involve making comparisons; buyers invest time only to reach dealers carrying the wanted products. Dealers do not need convenient locations; however, they must let prospective buyers know their locations.

Unsought goods are those the consumer does not know about or does not normally think of buying, like smoke detectors. The classic examples of known but unsought goods are life insurance, cemetery plots, gravestones, and encyclopedias. Unsought goods require advertising and personal-selling support.

INDUSTRIAL-GOODS CLASSIFICATION   Industrial goods can be classified in terms of how they enter the production process and their relative costliness. We can distinguish three groups of industrial goods: materials and parts, capital items, and supplies and business services. **Materials and parts** are goods that enter the manufacturer's product completely. They fall into two classes: raw materials and manufactured materials and parts.

Raw materials fall into two major classes: *farm products* (e.g., wheat, cotton, livestock, fruits, and vegetables) and *natural products* (e.g., fish, lumber, crude petroleum, iron ore). Farm products are supplied by many producers, who turn them over to marketing intermediaries, who provide assembly, grading, storage, transportation, and selling services. Their perishable and seasonal nature gives rise to special marketing practices. Their commodity character results in relatively little advertising and promotional activity, with some exceptions. At times, commodity groups will launch campaigns to promote their product—potatoes, prunes, milk. Some producers brand their product—Sunkist oranges, Chiquita bananas.

Natural products are limited in supply. They usually have great bulk and low unit value and must be moved from producer to user. Fewer and larger producers often market them directly to industrial users. Because the users depend on these materials, long-term supply contracts are common. The homogeneity of natural materials limits the amount of demand-creation activity. Price and delivery reliability are the major factors influencing the selection of suppliers.

Manufactured materials and parts fall into two categories: component materials (iron, yarn, cement, wires) and component parts (small motors, tires, castings). *Component* *material*s are usually fabricated further—pig iron is made into steel, and yarn is woven into cloth. The standardized nature of component materials usually means that price and supplier reliability are key purchase factors. *Component parts* enter the finished product with no further change in form, as when small motors are put into vacuum cleaners, and tires are put on automobiles. Most manufactured materials and parts are sold directly to industrial users. Price and service are major marketing considerations, and branding and advertising tend to be less important.

Capital items are long-lasting goods that facilitate developing or managing the finished product. They include two groups: installations and equipment. *Installations* consist of buildings (factories, offices) and equipment (generators, drill presses, mainframe computers, elevators). Installations are major purchases. They are usually bought directly from the producer, with the typical sale preceded by a long negotiation period. The producer's sales force includes technical personnel. Producers have to be willing to design to specification and to supply postsale services. Advertising is much less important than personal selling.

Equipment comprises portable factory equipment and tools (hand tools, lift trucks) and office equipment (personal computers, desks). These types of equipment do not become part of a finished product. They have a shorter life than installations but a longer life than operating supplies. Although some equipment manufacturers sell direct, more often they use intermediaries, because the market is geographically dispersed, the buyers are numerous, and the orders are small. Quality, features, price, and service are major considerations. The sales force tends to be more important than advertising, although the latter can be used effectively.

Supplies and business services are short-lasting goods and services that facilitate developing or managing the finished product. Supplies are of two kinds: *maintenance and repair items* (paint, nails, brooms), and *operating supplies* (lubricants, coal, writing paper, pencils). Together, they go under the name of MRO goods. Supplies are the equivalent of convenience goods; they are usually purchased with minimum effort on a straight rebuy basis. They are normally marketed through intermediaries because of their low unit value and the great number and geographic dispersion of customers. Price and service are important considerations, because suppliers are standardized and brand preference is not high.

Business services include *maintenance and repair services* (window cleaning, copier repair) and *business advisory services* (legal, management consulting, advertising). Maintenance and repair services are usually supplied under contract by small producers or are available from the manufacturers of the original equipment. Business advisory services are usually purchased on the basis of the supplier's reputation and staff.

product mix

A **product mix** (also called **product assortment**) is the set of all products and items that a particular seller offers for sale. Kodak's product mix consists of two strong product lines: information products and image products. NEC's (Japan) product mix consists of communication products and computer products. Michelin has three product lines: tires, maps, and restaurant-rating services.

A company's product mix has a certain width, length, depth, and consistency. These concepts are illustrated in Table 14.1 for selected Procter & Gamble consumer products.

- The *width* of a product mix refers to how many different product lines the company carries. Table 14.1 shows a product-mix width of five lines. (In fact, P&G produces many additional lines.)

- The *length* of a product mix refers to the total number of items in the mix. In Table 14.1, it is 25. We can also talk about the average length of a line. This is obtained by dividing the total length (here 25) by the number of lines (here 5), or an average product length of 5.

- The width of a product mix refers to how many variants are offered of each product in the line. If Crest comes in three sizes and two formulations (regular and mint), Crest has a depth of six. The average depth of P&G's product mix can be calculated by averaging the number of variants within the brand groups.

table **14.1**	Product–Mix Width and Product–Line Length for Procter & Gamble Products (Including Dates of Introduction)

	Product–Mix Width				
	Detergents	Toothpaste	Disposable Bar Soap	Diapers	Paper Tissue
	Ivory Snow (1930)	Gleem (1952)	Ivory (1879)	Pampers (1961)	Charmin (1928)
	Dreft (1933)	Crest (1955)	Kirk's (1885)	Luvs (1976)	Puffs (1960)
	Tide (1946)		Lava (1893)		Banner (1982)
PRODUCT-LINE LENGTH	Cheer (1950)		Camay (1926)		Summit (1992)
	Oxydol (1954)		Zest (1952)		
	Dash (1954)		Safeguard (1963)		
	Bold (1965)		Coast (1974)		
	Gain (1966)		Oil of Olay (1993)		
	Era (1972)				

- The *consistency* of the product mix refers to how closely related the various product lines are in end use, production requirements, distribution channels, or some other way. P&G's product lines are consistent insofar as they are consumer goods that go through the same distribution channels. The lines are less consistent insofar as they perform different functions for the buyers.

These four product-mix dimensions permit the company to expand its business in four ways. It can add new product lines, thus widening its product mix. It can lengthen each product line. It can add more product variants to each product and deepen its product mix. Finally, a company can pursue more product-line consistency.

product–line decisions

A product mix consists of various product lines. In General Electric's Consumer Appliance Division, there are product-line managers for refrigerators, stoves, and washing machines. At Northwestern University, there are separate academic deans for the medical school, law school, business school, engineering school, music school, speech school, journalism school, and liberal arts school.

In offering a product line, companies normally develop a basic platform and modules that can be added to meet different customer requirements. Car manufacturers build their cars around a basic platform. Homebuilders show a model home to which additional features can be added. This modular approach enables the company to offer variety while lowering production costs.

product-line analysis

Product-line managers need to know the sales and profits of each item in their line in order to determine which items to build, maintain, harvest, or divest. They also need to understand each product line's market profile.

SALES AND PROFITS   Figure 14.3 shows a sales and profit report for a five-item product line. The first item accounts for 50 percent of total sales and 30 percent of total profits. The first two items account for 80 percent of total sales and 60 percent of total profits. If these two items were suddenly hurt by a competitor, the line's sales and profitability

figure **14.3**

Product–Item
Contributions to a
Product Line's Total
Sales and Profits

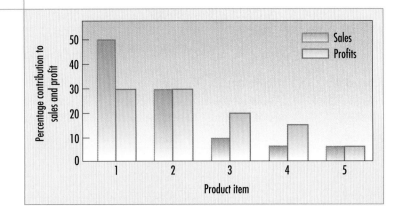

could collapse. These items must be carefully monitored and protected. At the other end, the last item delivers only 5 percent of the product line's sales and profits. The product-line manager may consider dropping this item unless it has strong growth potential.

Every company's product portfolio contains products with different margins. Supermarkets make almost no margin on bread and milk; reasonable margins on canned and frozen foods; and even better margins on flowers, ethnic food lines, and freshly baked goods. A local telephone company makes different margins on its core telephone service, call waiting, caller ID, and voice mail.

A company can classify its products into four types that yield different gross margins, depending on sales volume and promotion. To illustrate with personal computers:

■ *Core product:* Basic computers that produce high sales volume and are heavily promoted but with low margins because they are viewed as undifferentiated commodities.

■ *Staples:* Items with lower sales volume and no promotion, such as faster CPUs or bigger memories. These yield a somewhat higher margin.

■ *Specialties:* Items with lower sales volume but which might be highly promoted, such as digital movie-making equipment; or might generate income for services, such as personal delivery, installation, or on-site training.

■ *Convenience items:* Peripheral items that sell in high volume but receive less promotion, such as computer monitors, printers, upscale video or sound cards, and software. Consumers tend to buy them where they buy the original equipment because it is more convenient than making further shopping trips. These items can carry higher margins.

The main point is that companies should recognize that these items differ in their potential for being priced higher or advertised more as ways to increase their sales, margins, or both.[7]

MARKET PROFILE   The product-line manager must review how the line is positioned against competitors' lines. Consider paper company X with a paper-board product line.[8] Two paper-board attributes are weight and finish quality. Paper weight is usually offered at standard levels of 90, 120, 150, and 180 weight. Finish quality is offered at low, medium, and high levels. Figure 14.4 shows the location of the various product-line items of company X and four competitors, A, B, C, and D. Competitor A sells two product items in the extra-high weight class ranging from medium to low finish quality. Competitor B sells four items that vary in weight and finish quality. Competitor C sells three items in which the greater the weight, the greater the finish quality. Competitor D sells three items, all lightweight but varying in finish quality. Company X offers three items that vary in weight and finish quality.

figure **14.4**

Product Map for a
Paper–Product Line

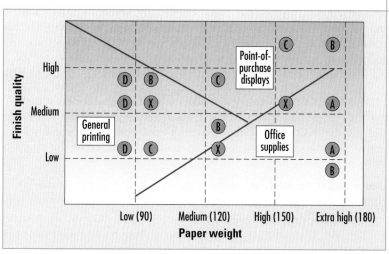

Source: Benson P. Shapiro, *Industrial Product Policy: Managing the Existing Product Line.* Cambridge, MA: Marketing Science Institute Report No. 77-110.

The product map shows which competitors' items are competing against company X's items. For example, company X's low-weight, medium-quality paper competes against competitor D's and B's papers, but its high-weight, medium-quality paper has no direct competitor. The map also reveals possible locations for new items. No manufacturer offers a high-weight, low-quality paper. If company X estimates a strong unmet demand and can produce and price this paper at low cost, it could consider adding this item to its line.

Another benefit of product mapping is that it identifies market segments. Figure 14.4 shows the types of paper, by weight and quality, preferred by the general printing industry, the point-of-purchase display industry, and the office-supply industry. The map shows that company X is well positioned to serve the needs of the general printing industry but is less effective in serving the other two industries.

After performing a product-line analysis, the product-line manager has to consider decisions on product-line length, line modernization, line featuring, and line pruning.

product-line length

A product line is too short if profits can be increased by adding items; the line is too long if profits can be increased by dropping items.

Company objectives influence product-line length. One objective is to create a product line to induce upselling: Thus BMW would like to move customers up from the BMW 3 series to the 5 to 7 series. A different objective is to create a product line that facilitates cross-selling: Hewlett-Packard sells printers as well as computers. Still another objective is to create a product line that protects against economic ups and downs; thus the GAP runs various clothing-store chains (Old Navy, GAP, Banana Republic) covering different price points in case the economy moves up or down. Companies seeking high market share and market growth will generally carry longer product lines. Companies that emphasize high profitability will carry shorter lines consisting of carefully chosen items.

Product lines tend to lengthen over time. Excess manufacturing capacity puts pressure on the product-line manager to develop new items. The sales force and distributors also pressure the company for a more complete product line to satisfy customers; but as items are added, several costs rise: design and engineering costs, inventory-carrying costs, manufacturing-changeover costs, order-processing costs, transportation costs, and new-item promotional costs. Eventually, someone calls a halt: Top management may stop development because of insufficient funds or manufacturing capacity. The controller may call for a study of money-losing items. A pattern of product-line growth followed by massive pruning may repeat itself many times.

A company lengthens its product line in two ways: by line stretching and line filling.

LINE STRETCHING   Every company's product line covers a certain part of the total possible range. For example, BMW automobiles are located in the upper price range of the automobile market. **Line stretching** occurs when a company lengthens its product line beyond its current range. The company can stretch its line downmarket, upmarket, or both ways.

Downmarket Stretch   A company positioned in the middle market may want to introduce a lower-priced line for any of three reasons:

1. The company may notice strong growth opportunities as mass-retailers such as Wal-Mart, Best Buy, and others attract a growing number of shoppers who want value-priced goods.
2. The company may wish to tie up lower-end competitors who might otherwise try to move up-market. If the company has been attacked by a low-end competitor, it often decides to counterattack by entering the low end of the market.
3. The company may find that the middle market is stagnating or declining.

A company faces a number of naming choices in deciding to move downmarket. Sony, for example, faced three choices:

1. Use the name Sony on all of its offerings. (Sony did this.)
2. Introduce the lower-priced offerings using a sub-brand name, such as Sony Value Line. Other companies have done this, such as Gillette with Gillette Good News and United Airlines with United Express. The risks are that the Sony name loses some of its quality image and that some Sony buyers might switch to the lower-priced offerings.
3. Introduce the lower-priced offerings under a different name, without mentioning Sony; but Sony would have to spend a lot of money to build up the new brand name, and the mass-merchants may not even accept a brand that lacks the Sony name.

Moving downmarket carries risks. Kodak introduced Kodak Funtime film to counter lower-priced brands, but it did not price Kodak Funtime low enough to match the lower-priced film. It also found some of its regular customers buying Funtime, thereby cannibalizing its core brand. So it withdrew the product. On the other hand, Mercedes successfully introduced its C-Class cars at $30,000 without injuring its ability to sell other Mercedes cars for $100,000 and up. John Deere introduced a lower-priced line of lawn tractors called Sabre from John Deere while still selling its more expensive tractors under the John Deere name.

Upmarket Stretch   Companies may wish to enter the high end of the market for more growth, higher margins, or simply to position themselves as full-line manufacturers. Many markets have spawned surprising upscale segments: Starbucks in coffee, Haagen-Dazs in ice cream, and Evian in bottled water. The leading Japanese auto companies have each introduced an upscale automobile: Toyota's Lexus; Nissan's Infinity; and Honda's Acura. Note that they invented entirely new names rather than using or including their own names.

Other companies have included their own name in moving upmarket. Gallo introduced Ernest and Julio Gallo Varietals and priced these wines more than twice as high as their regular wines. General Electric introduced the GE Profile brand for its large appliance offerings in the upscale market.[9]

Two-Way Stretch   Companies serving the middle market might decide to stretch their line in both directions. Texas Instruments (TI) introduced its first calculators in the medium-price-medium-quality end of the market. Gradually, it added calculators at the

Marriott's Web site lists all the hotels in its product line.

lower end, taking market share away from Bowmar, and at the higher end to compete with Hewlett-Packard. This two-way stretch won TI early market leadership in the hand-calculator market.

The Marriott Hotel group also has performed a two-way stretch of its hotel product line. Marriott International develops lodging brands in the most profitable segments in the industry. In order to determine where these opportunities lie, Marriott conducts extensive consumer research to uncover distinct consumer targets and develop products targeted to those needs in the most profitable areas. Examples of this are the development of the JW Marriott line in the upper upscale segment, Courtyard by Marriott in the upper mid-scale segment and Fairfield Inn in the lower mid-scale segment. By basing the development of these brands on distinct consumer targets with unique needs, Marriott is able to ensure against overlap between brands.

LINE FILLING   A product line can also be lengthened by adding more items within the present range. There are several motives for *line filling*: reaching for incremental profits, trying to satisfy dealers who complain about lost sales because of missing items in the line, trying to utilize excess capacity, trying to be the leading full-line company, and trying to plug holes to keep out competitors.

Line filling is overdone if it results in self-cannibalization and customer confusion. The company needs to differentiate each item in the consumer's mind. Each item should possess a *just-noticeable difference*. According to Weber's law, customers are more attuned to relative than to absolute difference.[10] They will perceive the difference between boards 2 and 3 feet long and boards 20 and 30 feet long but not between boards 29 and 30 feet long. The company should also check that the proposed item meets a market need and is not being added simply to satisfy an internal need. The Edsel automobile, on which Ford lost $350 million, met Ford's internal positioning needs for a car between its Ford and Lincoln lines but not the market's needs.

line modernization, featuring, and pruning

Product lines need to be modernized. A company's machine tools might have a 1950s look and lose out to newer-styled competitors' lines. The issue is whether to overhaul the line piecemeal or all at once. A piecemeal approach allows the company to see how customers and dealers take to the new style. It is also less draining on the company's cash flow, but it allows competitors to see changes and to start redesigning their own lines.

In rapidly changing product markets, modernization is carried on continuously. Companies plan improvements to encourage customer migration to higher-valued, higher-priced items. Microprocessor companies such as Intel and Motorola, and software companies such as Microsoft and Lotus, continually introduce more advanced versions of their products. A major issue is timing improvements so they do not appear too early (damaging sales of the current line) or too late (after the competition has established a strong reputation for more advanced equipment).

The product-line manager typically selects one or a few items in the line to feature. Sears will announce a special low-priced washing machine to attract customers. At other times, managers will feature a high-end item to lend prestige to the product line. Sometimes a company finds one end of its line selling well and the other end selling poorly. The company may try to boost demand for the slower sellers, especially if they are produced in a factory that is idled by lack of demand. This situation faced Honeywell when its medium-sized computers were not selling as well as its large computers; but it could be counterargued that the company should promote items that sell well rather than try to prop up weak items.

Product-line managers must periodically review the line for deadwood that is depressing profits. Unilever recently cut down its portfolio of brands from 1,600 to 970 and may even prune more, to 400 by 2005. The weak items can be identified through sales and cost analysis. A chemical company cut down its line from 217 to the 93 products with the largest volume, the largest contribution to profits, and the greatest long-term potential. Pruning is also done when the company is short of production capacity. Companies typically shorten their product lines in periods of tight demand and lengthen their lines in periods of slow demand.

brand decisions

Branding is a major issue in product strategy. As Russell Hanlin, the CEO of Sunkist Growers, observed: "An orange is an orange . . . is an orange. Unless . . . that orange happens to be Sunkist, a name 80% of consumers know and trust." Well-known brands command a price premium. Japanese companies such as Sony and Toyota have built a huge brand-loyal market. At the same time, developing a branded product requires a great deal of long-term investment, especially for advertising, promotion, and packaging.

what is a brand?

Perhaps the most distinctive skill of professional marketers is their ability to create, maintain, protect, and enhance brands. Branding is the art and cornerstone of marketing. The American Marketing Association defines a **brand** as: a name, term, sign, symbol, or design, or a combination of them, intended to identify the goods or services of one seller or group of sellers and to differentiate them from those of competitors. Thus a brand identifies the seller or maker. Under trademark law, the seller is granted exclusive rights to the use of the brand name in perpetuity. Brands differ from other assets such as patents and copyrights, which have expiration dates.

A brand is a complex symbol that can convey up to six levels of meaning:[11]

1. *Attributes:* A brand brings to mind certain attributes. Mercedes suggests expensive, well-built, well-engineered, durable, high-prestige automobiles.
2. *Benefits:* Attributes must be translated into functional and emotional benefits. The attribute "durable" could translate into the functional benefit "I won't have to buy another car for several

years." The attribute "expensive" translates into the emotional benefit "The car makes me feel important and admired."

3. *Values:* The brand also says something about the producer's values. Mercedes stands for high performance, safety, and prestige.

4. *Culture:* The brand may represent a certain culture. The Mercedes represents German culture: organized, efficient, high quality.

5. *Personality:* The brand can project a certain personality. Mercedes may suggest a no-nonsense boss (person), a reigning lion (animal), or an austere palace (object).

6. *User:* The brand suggests the kind of consumer who buys or uses the product. We would expect to see a 55-year-old top executive behind the wheel of a Mercedes, not a 20-year-old secretary.

Companies need to research the position their brand occupies in the customers' minds. According to Kevin Keller, "What distinguishes a brand from its unbranded commodity counterparts is the consumer's perceptions and feelings about the product's attributes and how they perform. Ultimately, a brand resides in the minds of consumers." There are three commonly used research approaches to get at brand meaning:

1. *Word associations:* People can be asked what words come to mind when they hear the brand's name. In the case of McDonald's, they probably would mention hamburgers, fast food, friendly service, fun, and children. They may mention some negative words such as high calories and fatty food. They may mention some words unique to McDonald's such as Ronald McDonald, Golden Arches, and children's hospitals. McDonald's would try to emphasize the positive and unique words and try to reduce the causes giving rise to the negative words.

2. *Personifying the brand:* People can be asked to describe what kind of person or animal they think of when the brand is mentioned. For example, they may say that the John Deere brand makes them think of a rugged Midwestern male who is hardworking and trustworthy. The brand persona delivers a picture of the more human qualities of the brand.

3. *Laddering up to find the brand essence:* **Brand essence** relates to the deeper, more abstract goals consumers are trying to satisfy with the brand. Ask why someone wants to buy a Nokia cellular phone. "They look well built" (attribute). "Why is it important that the phone be well built?" "It suggests that the Nokia is reliable" (a functional benefit). "Why is reliability important?" "Because my colleagues or family can be sure to reach me" (an emotional benefit). "Why must you be available to them at all times?" "I can help them if they are in trouble" (brand essence). The brand makes this person feel like a Good Samaritan, ready to help others.

   These "why" questions constitute a technique known as **laddering up.** They help the marketer get a deeper understanding of the person's motivation. The answers suggest some possible campaigns. The campaign can center on the brand essence, or the marketer can ladder down and feature Nokia at a more concrete level, such as its emotional benefit (easy to be reached), functional benefit (reliability), or attribute (well built).

Marketers must decide at which level(s) to anchor the brand's identity. Scott Davis suggests visualizing a *brand pyramid* in constructing the image of a brand.[12] At the lowest level are the *brand attributes*, at the next level are the *brand's benefits*, and at the top are the brand's *beliefs and values*. Thus marketers of Dove soap can talk about its attribute of one-quarter cleansing cream; or its benefit of softer skin; or its value, being more attractive. The attribute is the least desirable level. First, the buyer is more interested in benefits. Second, competitors can easily copy attributes. Third, the current attributes may become less desirable.

Compaq In 1999, the computer manufacturer Compaq increased its global advertising budget by 50 percent to $300 million. The campaign was to promote the PC maker's "bigness" and the depth of its offerings. Bigness is an attribute that does not necessarily translate into a distinctive benefit. Furthermore, there are other "big" computer brands. This campaign failed to position Compaq with a "reason to prefer."

A brand can be better positioned by associating its name with a desirable benefit. Some successful brand positioning examples are Volvo (*safety*), Hallmark (*caring*),

Harley-Davidson (*adventure*), FedEx (*guaranteed overnight delivery*), Nike (*performance*), and Lexus (*quality*). These positionings work best when they are passionately felt by everyone in the organization, and the target market believes that the company is best at delivering that benefit.

Volvo   At Volvo, engineers think safety in every design decision. When they decided to add a Global Positioning System to the dashboard of a recent model, they wanted to be sure that the screen would be easy to read and close to the driver's viewing point so it would not act as a distraction; and when some customers asked Volvo to make a convertible car, the company decided against it because "convertible cars aren't safe."

At the same time, promoting a brand on only one benefit can be risky. Suppose Mercedes touts its main benefit as "high performance." Then several competitive brands emerge with high or higher performance; or suppose car buyers start placing less importance on high performance as compared to other benefits. Mercedes needs the freedom to maneuver into a new benefit positioning.

The strongest brands present more than a rational appeal; they pack an emotional wallop. Marc Gobe, author of *Emotional Branding*, argues that successful brands must engage customers on a deeper level, touching a universal emotion.[13] His brand design agency, Desgrippes Gobe, which has worked on such accounts as Starbucks, Victoria's Secret, Godiva, Versace, and Lancome, relies more on creating surprise, passion, and excitement surrounding a brand, and less on projecting tangible product attributes.

If the brand evokes a strong set of beliefs and values, the company must be careful not to stray from this. Thus Mercedes stands for high technology, performance, and success. Mercedes must project these qualities in its brand strategy. Some believe that Mercedes is taking a risk by making smaller and less expensive cars.

building brand identity

Building the brand identity requires additional decisions on the brand's *name, logo, colors, tagline,* and *symbol.* Here is what one new dot-com decided.

Gear.com   This e-tailer sells brand-name sporting goods at closeout prices. The name "gear" was chosen to suggest "hiking gear" or "fishing gear" clothing. The company used the tagline "The best sports deals on the planet." So far, the company has not chosen a symbol, although a symbol could be helpful in the image of the brand. Gear.com recently merged with Overstock.com, so its image may change.

At the same time, a brand is much more than a name, logo, colors, a tagline, or symbol. These are marketing tools and tactics. A brand is essentially a marketer's promise to deliver a specific set of features, benefits, and services consistently to the buyers. The marketer must establish a mission for the brand and a vision of what the brand must be and do. The marketer must think that he is offering a contract to the customer regarding how the brand will perform. The brand contract must be honest. Motel 6, for example, offers clean rooms, low prices, and good service but does not imply that the furniture is expensive or the bathroom is large.

At best, the brand campaign will create name recognition, some brand knowledge, maybe even some brand preference, but an ad campaign does not create brand bonding, no matter how much the company spends on advertising and publicity. **Brand bonding** occurs when customers experience the company as delivering on its benefit promise. The fact is that *brands are not built by advertising but by the brand experience.* All of the customers' contacts with company employees and company communications must be positive. The brand idea will not take unless *everyone in the company lives the brand.* Tosti and Stotz charge that too many companies make brand promises but fail to train employees to understand and deliver on the brand promise.[14] They suggest ways that companies can carry on *internal branding* with their employees to understand, desire, and deliver on the brand promise. Here are some examples.

Eli Lilly   In 2000, Eli Lilly launched a new brand-building initiative with the brand-line "Answers that matter." The aim was to establish Eli Lilly as a pharmaceutical firm that could give doctors, patients, hospitals, HMOs, and government trustworthy answers to questions of concern to them. This brand-building initiative could not be launched before making sure that everyone at Eli Lilly received the training and knowledge to be able to deliver right answers.

Hewlett-Packard   Hewlett-Packard does not think that its job ends with carrying out advertising and personal selling. It has appointed a senior executive in charge of the *customer experience* in each of its two divisions, consumer and B2B. Their job is to monitor, measure, and improve the customer experience with H-P products. They report directly to the presidents of their respective divisions.

building brands in the new economy

Brand-building theory developed out of the practices of consumer packaged-goods companies in the last century. The theory called for creating a product difference, real or symbolic; spending a huge amount on advertising; and hoping this would lead to trial, adoption, and loyalty. Advertising played the crucial role and its effectiveness was judged by measures of awareness, recognition, recall, or intent to buy; but look at what happened to Pets.com using this theory:

Pets.com   This company did all the right things. It hired a top-flight advertising agency and created a highly recognized brand icon (Sock Puppet) that won all kinds of awards. Pets.com spent $2 million on the Super Bowl, marched in Macy's Thanksgiving Day Parade, and even developed its own line of merchandise. Although this created plenty of "industry buzz," on November 7, 2000, Pets.com shut its doors, having spent all this money without earning a dime.

Heidi and Don Schultz believe that the Consumer Packaged Goods (CPG) model for brand building is increasingly inappropriate, especially for service firms, technology firms, financial organizations, B2B brands, and even smaller CPG companies. They charge that the proliferation of media and message delivery systems has eroded mass-advertising's power. They urge companies to use a different paradigm to build their brands in the new economy.

1. Companies should clarify the corporation's basic values and build the corporate brand. Companies such as Starbucks, Sony, Cisco Systems, Marriott, Hewlett-Packard, General Electric, and American Express have built strong corporate brands; their name on a product or service creates an image of quality and value.
2. Companies should use brand managers to carry out the tactical work, but the brand's ultimate success will depend on everyone in the company accepting and living the brand's value proposition. Prominent CEOs—such as Carly Fiorina (Hewlett-Packard) and John Chambers (Cisco)—are playing a growing role in shaping brand strategies.
3. Companies need to develop a more comprehensive brand-building plan to create positive customer experiences at every touchpoint—events, seminars, news, telephone, e-mail, person-to-person contact.
4. Companies need to define the brand's basic essence to be delivered wherever it is sold. Local executions can be varied as long as they deliver the feel of the brand.

5. Companies must use the brand-value proposition as the key driver of the company's strategy, operations, services, and product development.

6. Companies must measure their brand-building effectiveness not by the old measures of awareness, recognition, and recall, but by a more comprehensive set of measures including customer-perceived value, customer satisfaction, customer share of wallet, customer retention, and customer advocacy.[15]

brand equity

Brands vary in the amount of power and value they have in the marketplace. At one extreme are brands that are not known by most buyers. Then there are brands for which buyers have a fairly high degree of *brand awareness*. Beyond this are brands with a high degree of *brand acceptability*. Then there are brands that enjoy a high degree of *brand preference*. Finally, there are brands that command a high degree of *brand loyalty*. Tony O'Reilly, former CEO of H. J. Heinz, proposed this test of brand loyalty: "My acid test . . . is whether a housewife, intending to buy Heinz tomato ketchup in a store, finding it to be out of stock, will walk out of the store to buy it elsewhere."

Few customers are this brand-loyal. David Aaker distinguished five levels of a customer attitude toward a brand, from lowest to highest:

1. Customer will change brands, especially for price reasons. No brand loyalty.
2. Customer is satisfied. No reason to change the brand.
3. Customer is satisfied and would incur costs by changing brand.
4. Customer values the brand and sees it as a friend.
5. Customer is devoted to the brand.

Brand equity is highly related to how many customers are in classes 3, 4, or 5. It is also related, according to Aaker, to the degree of brand-name recognition, perceived brand quality, strong mental and emotional associations, and other assets such as patents, trademarks, and channel relationships.[16]

Customers will pay more for a strong brand. One study found that 72 percent of customers stated they would pay a 20 percent premium for their brand of choice relative to their closest competitive brand; 50 percent said they would pay a 25 percent premium; and 40 percent would pay up to a 30 percent premium.[17] Coke lovers are willing to pay a 50 percent premium over the closest competitor; Tide and Heinz users, a 100 percent premium; and Volvo users, a 40 percent premium; and although the Lexus and the Toyota Camry share the same exact engine, the Lexus brand commands $10,000 more than the Camry brand.[18]

VALUE OF BRAND EQUITY   Clearly, brand equity is an asset. We define **brand equity** as the positive differential effect that knowing the brand name has on customer response to the product or service. Brand equity results in customers showing a preference for one product over another when they are basically identical. The extent to which customers are willing to pay more for the particular brand is a measure of brand equity. Amazon.com, for example, is able to charge 7 to 12 percent more than lesser-known online book vendors.[19]

Brand equity needs to be distinguished from **brand valuation**, which is the job of estimating the total financial value of the brand. Certain companies base their growth on acquiring and building rich brand portfolios. Nestlé acquired Rowntree (U.K.), Carnation (U.S.), Stouffer (U.S.), Buitoni-Perugina (Italy), and Perrier (France), making it the world's largest food company.

The world's 10 most valuable brands in 2001 were (in rank order): Coca-Cola, Microsoft, IBM, General Electric, Nokia, Intel, Disney, Ford, McDonald's, and AT&T. Coca-Cola's brand value was $69 billion, Microsoft's $65 billion, and IBM's $53 billion.[20] With these well-known companies, brand value is typically over one-half of the total company market capitalization. U.S. companies do not list brand equity on their balance sheets because of the arbitrariness of the estimate. However, this is done by some companies in the United Kingdom, Hong Kong, and Australia. The estimate is based in part on the price premium the brand commands times the extra volume it moves over an average brand.[21] John Stuart, co-founder of Quaker Oats, said: "If this business were split up, I would give you the land and bricks and mortar, and I would take the brands and trade marks, and I would fare better than you."

High brand equity provides a number of competitive advantages:

- The company will have more trade leverage in bargaining with distributors and retailers because customers expect them to carry the brand.
- The company can charge a higher price than its competitors because the brand has higher perceived quality.
- The company can more easily launch extensions because the brand name carries high credibility.
- The brand offers the company some defense against price competition.

The power enjoyed by a strong brand is no better illustrated than by Virgin, the brainchild of England's flamboyant Richard Branson, now age 50.

Virgin Starting with Virgin Music, Branson's Virgin Group Ltd. now spans three continents and 170 businesses, including Virgin Atlantic Airways, Virgin Mobile (cellular phones), Virgin Energy, Virgin Direct (insurance, mortgages, and investment funds), and Virgin Hotels. In 2001, Branson set up Virgin.com as the Web portal for everything from buying wine to booking airline tickets. The Web site is attracting 1.9 million visitors a month. Nearly 2 million Britishers book train tickets through Virgin and 1 million tap Virgin's help in managing $4 billion in assets.[22]

Clearly, Branson can create almost any business he wants and gain instant customers by simply attaching the name Virgin to it. Yet some marketing and financial critics point out that he is diluting the brand, that it covers too many businesses. Allen Adamson of the brand identity consultancy Landor Associates says: "(Branson) should get out of the businesses that don't fit the Virgin/Branson personality, such as beverages, cosmetics . . . the longer he keeps his name on businesses that are failing or neutral, the more damage it will do to his aura." Branson has had some fumbles, such as Virgin Clothing and the launch of Virgin Coke in the United States, but Branson replies: "We have a strategy of using the credibility of our brand to challenge the dominant players in a range of industries where we believe the consumer is not getting value for money. . . . If the consumer benefits, I see no reason why we should be frightened about launching new products."[23]

MANAGING BRAND EQUITY   A brand needs to be carefully managed so that its equity does not depreciate. This requires maintaining or improving brand awareness, perceived quality and functionality, and positive associations. These tasks require continuous R&D investment, skillful advertising, and excellent trade and consumer service. Procter & Gamble believes that well-managed brands are not subject to a brand life cycle. Many brand leaders of 70 years ago are still today's brand leaders: Kodak, Wrigley's, Gillette, Coca-Cola, Heinz, and Campbell Soup.

Some analysts see brands as outlasting a company's specific products and facilities. They see brands as the company's major enduring asset. Every powerful brand really represents a set of loyal customers. Brand equity is a major contributor to *customer equity*. The proper focus of marketing planning is to extend *customer lifetime value*, with brand management serving as a major marketing tool.

Unfortunately, many companies have mismanaged their brands. In the quest for ever-increasing profits, it is easy for a brand to lose its focus. This is what befell

Snapple Beverage Corporation almost as soon as Quaker Oats bought it for $1.7 billion in 1994.

Snapple Beverage Corporation   Snapple had been a regional brand with an offbeat image available in only small outlets and convenience stores. Quaker bought the brand and attempted to make it a national brand with mass-market appeal. Quaker changed the ad campaign—abandoning the rotund and immensely popular Snapple Lady—and promoted it as an alternative to big brands like Coke and Pepsi. This turned off Snapple fans. According to one critic, "Quaker diluted the quirkiness." Snapple began losing money and sales plunged 23 percent in the next two years. Quaker finally sold the brand to Triarc, Inc., in 1997 at a $1.4 billion loss. The company revitalized Snapple by returning to clever advertising, using original distribution channels, creating throwback packaging, and reinstating the Snapple Lady as official spokesperson. Snapple's renewed success enabled Triarc to sell Snapple and its other beverages to Cadbury Schweppes for $1.5 billion in 2000.[24] (See "Marketing Insight: Can You Build a Cult Brand, and Do You Want To?")

In a nationwide study of companies in a wide range of industries, only 43 percent indicated that they even measured brand equity. Whereas 72 percent were confident enough in their brand equity to project that it would last two years with no financial support, over two-thirds of the respondents had no formal long-term brand strategy.[25] Also, while we normally think of brand equity as something accruing to the products of manufacturers, service companies also prize it. As Wall Street competition intensifies, financial service companies are spending millions on their brand names in order to attract investors. Just as Coke wants you to reach for a soda when you are thirsty, Merrill Lynch and Chase want you to call them when you need financial know-how.[26]

marketing **insight**

Can You Build a Cult Brand, and Do You Want To?

Some brands manage to achieve a cult status—Apple Computers, Mazda Miata automobiles, Harley-Davidson motorcycles, Krispy Kreme donuts, Ben & Jerry's ice cream, Palm personal digital assistants, Air Jordan Nike shoes. As many as 85,000 Apple Computer fans attend the annual four-day MacWorld expo in San Francisco. Every announced opening of another Krispy Kreme donut store brings long lines of fans camping out overnight waiting for the store opening.

What draws people to these brands? In part, people want to be part of something larger than themselves, something that may precede them and outlive them. Some cult brands offer a community experience, like that felt by the Hell's Angels who ride Harleys in groups and the Vespa fans who meet in Manhattan on Sundays and ride their scooters.

So why wouldn't every company launching a new product want it to gain cult status? For one thing, this is not easy to do. Most of it happens spontaneously. A cult brand captures the imagination of a small group and they spread the word to others.

A company can try to create a "buzz" around the product; it can deliberately keep the supply low so that people have to wait for it; and it can organize clubs and events. Whether these tactics work depends on how special the cult brand makes the small number of users feel, and how inclined they are to talk about it to friends and acquaintances.

A company can kill a cult brand by trying to rush it into the mass-market. Yet companies with a cult brand are sorely tempted to mass-market it. Coors beer used to sell in only 11 states; visitors from the Midwest, East, and South used to buy cases to bring back home. Once Coors expanded distribution to reach all 50 states, the brand lost its cult status and became another mainstream beer. This does not mean Coors made the wrong decision from a profit point of view, but companies must be careful. When Ford redesigned the Mustang to have broader market appeal, it lost many loyal Mustang fans.

Source: Adapted from Melanie Wells, "Cult Brands," *Forbes*, April 16, 2001, p. 150.

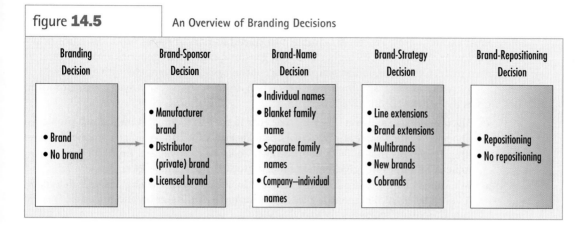

figure **14.5**   An Overview of Branding Decisions

branding challenges

Branding poses several challenges to the marketer. The key decisions are shown in Figure 14.5 and discussed in the following sections.

BRANDING DECISION: TO BRAND OR NOT TO BRAND?   The first decision is whether to develop a brand name for a product. In the past, producers and intermediaries sold their goods out of barrels, bins, and cases, without any supplier identification. Buyers depended on the seller's integrity. The earliest signs of branding were the medieval guilds' efforts to require craftspeople to put trademarks on their products to protect themselves and consumers against inferior quality. In the fine arts, too, branding began with artists signing their works.

Today, branding is such a strong force that hardly anything goes unbranded. So-called commodities do not have to remain commodities. Salt is packaged in distinctive containers, oranges are stamped with growers' names, nuts and bolts are packaged in cellophane with a distributor's label, and automobile components—spark plugs, tires, filters—bear separate brand names from the automakers. Fresh food products—such as chicken, turkey, and salmon—are increasingly being sold under strongly advertised brand names. Even bricks do not have to be seen as commodities.

Acme Brick   Acme Brick of Fort Worth, Texas, has managed to brand its bricks, with the result that it is able to charge 10 percent more and enjoy the largest market share in several of its metro markets. It makes high-quality bricks. It offers a 100-year guarantee (the norm is five years for bricks). Every time a home is built with Acme bricks, Acme contributes to the Troy Aikman Foundation for Children. Acme has also donated bricks to build 30 homes through Habitat for Humanity. A telephone survey in four major Acme markets revealed an 84 percent preference for Acme bricks, with no other supplier getting more than a 10 percent preference.[27]

In some cases, there has been a return to "no branding" of certain staple consumer goods and pharmaceuticals. Carrefours, the originator of the French hypermarket, introduced a line of "no brands" or generics in its stores in the early 1970s. Generics are unbranded, plainly packaged, less expensive versions of common products such as spaghetti, paper towels, and canned peaches. They offer standard or lower quality at a price that may be as much as 20 percent to 40 percent lower than nationally advertised brands and 10 percent to 20 percent lower than retailer private-label brands. The lower price is made possible by lower-quality ingredients, lower-cost labeling and packaging, and minimal advertising.

National brands have fought generics in a number of ways. Ralston-Purina increased its quality and targeted pet owners who identified strongly with their pets and cared most about quality. Procter & Gamble introduced its Banner paper products, a line offering lower quality than its higher lines but greater quality than generics and at a competitive price. Other companies simply have cut their prices to compete with generics.[28]

Why do sellers brand their products when doing so clearly involves costs? Branding gives the seller several advantages:

- The brand name makes it easier for the seller to process orders and track down problems.
- The seller's brand name and trademark provide legal protection of unique product features.
- Branding gives the seller the opportunity to attract a loyal and profitable set of customers. Brand loyalty gives sellers some protection from competition.
- Branding helps the seller segment markets. Instead of P&G's selling a simple detergent, it can offer eight detergent brands, each formulated differently and aimed at specific benefit-seeking segments.
- Strong brands help build the corporate image, making it easier to launch new brands and gain acceptance by distributors and consumers.

Distributors and retailers want brand names because brands make the product easier to handle, hold production to certain quality standards, strengthen buyer preferences, and make it easier to identify suppliers. Consumers want brand names to help them identify quality differences and shop more efficiently.

BRAND–SPONSOR DECISION   A manufacturer has several options with respect to brand sponsorship. The product may be launched as a *manufacturer brand* (sometimes called a national brand), a *distributor brand* (also called reseller, store, house, or private brand), or a *licensed brand name*. Another alternative is for the manufacturer to produce some output under its own name and some under reseller labels. Kellogg, John Deere & Company, and IBM sell virtually all of their output under their own brand names. Hart Schaffner & Marx sells some of its manufactured clothes under licensed names such as Christian Dior, Pierre Cardin, and Johnny Carson. Whirlpool produces both under its own name and under distributors' names (Sears Kenmore appliances).

Although manufacturers' brands dominate, large retailers and wholesalers have been developing their own brands. Sears has created several names—Diehard batteries, Craftsman tools, Kenmore appliances—that command brand preference and even brand loyalty. Retailers such as The Limited, Benetton, The Body Shop, GAP, and Marks & Spencer carry mostly own-brand merchandise. In Britain, two large supermarket chains have developed popular store-brand colas—Sainsbury Cola (from Sainsbury) and Classic Cola (from Tesco). Sainsbury, Britain's largest food chain, sells 50 percent store-label goods; U.S. supermarkets average 19.7 percent private-brand sales. Some experts believe that 50 percent is the natural limit for carrying private brands because (1) consumers prefer certain national brands, and (2) many product categories are not feasible or attractive on a private-brand basis.

Why do intermediaries bother to sponsor their own brands? They have to hunt down qualified suppliers who can deliver consistent quality, order large quantities and tie up their capital in inventories, and spend money promoting a private label. Nevertheless, private brands offer two advantages. First, they are more profitable. Intermediaries search for manufacturers with excess capacity who will produce the private label at a low cost. Other costs, such as research and development, advertising, sales promotion, and physical distribution are also much lower. This means that the private brander can charge a lower price and yet make a higher profit margin. Second, retailers develop exclusive store brands to differentiate themselves from competitors. Many consumers do not distinguish between national and store brands.

In the confrontation between manufacturers' and private brands, retailers have many advantages and increasing market power. Because shelf space is scarce, many supermarkets now charge a *slotting fee* for accepting a new brand, to cover the cost of listing and stocking it. Retailers also charge for special display space and in-store advertising space. They typically give more prominent display to their own brands and make sure they are well stocked. Retailers are now building better quality in their store brands. Consider the following case.

Loblaw   Since 1984, when its President's Choice line of foods made its debut, it has been difficult to say "private label" without Loblaw and President's Choice coming instantly to mind. Toronto-based Loblaw's supermarket chain has demonstrated that store brands can match or even exceed the quality of other brands. A finely tuned strategy involving its trademarked President's Choice and "no name" labels has helped differentiate its stores and build the retailer into a powerhouse in Canada and the United States. By bringing out private labels in new product areas—such as frozen Jambalaya, frozen bread pudding, and frozen hors d'oeuvres—Loblaw stores reduce units of expensive national and secondary brands but still increase variety. Its store brands have become so successful that Loblaw is licensing them to noncompetitive retailers in other countries, thus turning a local store brand into—believe it or not—a global brand. Today, private label sales make up 32 percent of Loblaw's total sales, compared with a Canadian average of 22 percent.[29]

Manufacturers of national brands are frustrated by the growing power of retailer brands. Kevin Price put it well: "A decade ago, the retailer was a chihuahua nipping at the manufacturer's heels—a nuisance, yes, but only a minor irritant; you fed it and it went away. Today it's a pit bull and it wants to rip your arms and legs off. You'd like to see it roll over, but you're too busy defending yourself to even try."[30] Some marketing commentators predict that private brands will eventually knock out all but the strongest manufacturers' brands.

In years past, consumers viewed the brands in a category arranged in a *brand ladder*, with their favorite brand at the top and remaining brands in descending order of preference. There are now signs that this ladder is being replaced with a consumer perception of *brand parity*—that many brands are equivalent.[31] Instead of a strongly preferred brand, consumers buy from a set of acceptable brands, choosing whichever is on sale that day. As Joel D. Weiner, a former Kraft executive, said: "People don't think the world will come to a screeching halt if they use Tide instead of Cheer." A study by DDB Needham Worldwide reported that the percentage of packaged-goods consumers saying that they bought only well-known brands fell from 77 percent to 62 percent between 1975 and 1990. A Grey Advertising Inc., study reported that 66 percent of consumers said they were trading down to lower-priced brands, particularly store brands.

The growing power of store brands is not the only factor weakening national brands. Consumers are more price-sensitive. They are noting more quality equivalence as competing manufacturers and national retailers copy and duplicate the qualities of the best brands. The continuous barrage of coupons and price specials has trained a generation of shoppers to buy on price. The fact that companies have reduced advertising to 30 percent of their total promotion budget has weakened their brand equity. The endless stream of brand extensions and line extensions has blurred brand identity and led to a confusing amount of product proliferation.

Of course, one of the newest factors that is not necessarily weakening national brands but changing the entire branding landscape is the Internet. While some "born digital" companies, like Netscape and America Online, have used the Internet to gain brand recognition seemingly overnight, other companies have poured millions of dollars into online advertising with no significant effect on brand awareness. (See "Marketing for the New Economy: The Elusive Goal of Branding on the World Wide Web.")

Manufacturers have reacted by spending substantial amounts of money on consumer-directed advertising and promotion to maintain strong brand preference. Their price has to be somewhat higher to cover the higher promotion cost. At the same time, mass-

marketing for the new economy

The Elusive Goal of Branding on the World Wide Web

Ever had a day when you could not get a TV commercial out of your head? If you are like most people, you sop up a certain amount of TV advertising. Now, try to remember the last ad you saw while surfing the Web. Drawing a blank? That is not surprising. The issue of building brands through Web advertising has so confounded marketers that Procter & Gamble held a summit on the topic in the summer of 1998. Over 400 executives converged at P&G headquarters in Cincinnati, from Internet companies such as America Online and Agency.com to packaged-goods giants like Unilever and Kraft; their goal: to harness the interactivity of the Internet to build and maintain brands. Here are some of the challenges they confronted.

The one-to-one nature of the Web does not build mass brand awareness: On the World Wide Web, it is as if millions of private conversations are going on. It is not the same as when millions of people watch the Superbowl and see the same 30-second Budweiser spot at the same time. That is why tactics that have worked on TV have failed on the Web.

- *The format of Internet advertising has been ineffective:* So far, the two most common Internet ads are banner ads and interstitials. Banner ads are those tiny rectangular ads on which you can click for more information. In a discouraging Jupiter Communications survey, 21 percent of Internet users polled said they never clicked on banner ads and another 51 percent said they clicked only rarely. Interstitial ads, which flash in the browser window before the site is loaded, have proved annoying to most consumers.
- *In the digital world consumers are in control:* Even if advertisers put larger, richer ads on the Web, they would likely face a consumer backlash. Digital developments allow Web surfers to choose products solely on real value and not just intangibles, like brand associations. Already sites like Mysimon.com, which offers a free online buyer's guide that allows users to compare features and prices on products from more than 2,000 online stores, have gained popularity with consumers.

It is therefore not surprising that some of the biggest superstars of e-commerce still conduct most of their branding efforts off-line. Cisco spends ad money for full-page ads in the *Wall Street Journal* rather than on Web banners. At the same time, the almost overnight success of Netscape Communications, Amazon.com, and Yahoo! say that a brand can grow and secure customer loyalty on the Web. How? Companies that have powerful brand awareness on the Web all have sites that help consumers do something—whether it is configuring a computer system online at Dell.com or offering a host of options for customizing services at Yahoo.com. Marketers who are set on building their brands in the online world have to offer consumers an online experience or service.

The latest theory of how to do that involves something called "rational branding." The idea is to wed the emotional pitch of traditional brand marketing with a real service offered only online. Television ads for Saturn still offer the same old-fashioned appeal, but now they point viewers to the company's Web site, which offers lots of help and very little hype. Yet there is not much potential in using the Internet as a vehicle when you are selling soap or shampoo. Still, the packaged-goods powerhouses are hardly throwing in the towel. P&G, for instance, has put most of its small online marketing budget behind brands like Pampers diapers, which have narrow target audiences with more personal subject matter. The company has turned Pampers.com into the Pampers Parenting Institute, which addresses various issues of concern to new or expectant parents. One thing consumers can be sure of is that there will be more, not less, advertising and brand building on the Web as e-commerce develops.

Sources: Jeffrey O'Brien, "Web Advertising and the Branding Mission," *Upside* (September 1998): 90–94; Don Tapscott, "Net Culture Reshapes Brand Opportunities," *Advertising Age*, November 10, 1997; Saul Hansell, "Selling Soap without the Soap Operas, Mass Marketers Seek Ways to Build Brands on the Web," *New York Times*, August 24, 1998, p. D1; Ellen Neuborne, "Branding on the Net," *BusinessWeek*, November 9, 1998, pp. 76–86.

distributors pressure manufacturers to put more promotional money into trade allowances and deals if they want adequate shelf space. Once manufacturers start giving in, they have less to spend on advertising and consumer promotion, and their brand leadership starts spiraling down. This is the national brand manufacturers' dilemma.

To maintain their power, leading brand marketers need to invest in heavy and continuous R&D to bring out new brands, line extensions, features, and quality improvements. They must sustain a strong "pull" advertising program to maintain high consumer brand recognition and preference. They must find ways to "partner" with major mass-distributors in a joint search for logistical economies and competitive strategies that produce savings.

However, what if a company is small or just starting out and cannot pump millions into expensive advertising campaigns? Technology companies in particular have been adept at achieving levels of brand recognition through less conventional marketing approaches. Here is an example.[32]

America Online Inc.   Over half of U.S. households are familiar with America Online (AOL). That is because AOL gives away its software free. For several years AOL has been blanketing the country with diskettes and now CD-ROMs, offering consumers a one-month free trial. The company cuts deals that put its product in some unlikely places: inside Rice Chex cereal boxes, United Airlines in-flight meals, and Omaha Steaks packages. Because it is hard to describe the benefits of an online service to novices, AOL believes the best approach is to let them try it. Then, once consumers start using AOL, the company reasons that the user-friendly program will lure them to subscribe. So far, this philosophy has yielded remarkable results. In 2001, AOL had 29 million U.S. subscribers, more than four times as large as the nearest Internet service provider competitor.[33]

brand-name decision

Manufacturers and service companies who brand their products must choose which brand names to use. Four strategies are available:

1. *Individual names:* This policy is followed by General Mills (Bisquick, Gold Medal, Betty Crocker, Nature Valley). A major advantage of an individual-names strategy is that the company does not tie its reputation to the product's. If the product fails or appears to have low quality, the company's name or image is not hurt. A manufacturer of good-quality watches, such as Seiko, can introduce a lower-quality line of watches (called Pulsar) without diluting the Seiko name. The strategy permits the firm to search for the best name for each new product.

2. *Blanket family names:* This policy is followed by Heinz and General Electric. A blanket family name also has advantages. Development cost is less because there is no need for "name" research or heavy advertising expenditures to create brand-name recognition. Furthermore, sales of the new product are likely to be strong if the manufacturer's name is good. Campbell soup introduces new soups under its brand name with extreme simplicity and achieves instant recognition.

3. *Separate family names for all products:* This policy is followed by Sears (Kenmore for appliances, Craftsman for tools, and Homart for major home installations). Where a company produces quite different products, it is not desirable to use one blanket family name. Swift and Company developed separate family names for its hams (Premium) and fertilizers (Vigoro). When Mead Johnson developed a diet supplement for gaining weight, it created a new family name, Nutriment, to avoid confusion with its weight-reducing products, Metrecal. Companies often invent different family names for different quality lines within the same product class.

4. *Corporate name combined with individual product names:* This policy is followed by Kellogg (Kellogg's Rice Krispies, Kellogg's Raisin Bran, and Kellogg's Corn Flakes), as well as Honda, GE, and Hewlett-Packard. The company name legitimizes, and the individual name individualizes, the new product.

Once a company decides on its brand-name strategy, it faces the task of choosing a specific brand name. The company could choose the name of a person (Honda, Estée Lauder), location (American Airlines, Kentucky Fried Chicken), quality (Safeway, Duracell), lifestyle (Weight Watchers, Healthy Choice), or an artificial name (Exxon, Kodak). Among the desirable qualities for a brand name are the following:[34]

- *It should suggest something about the product's benefits:* Examples: Beautyrest, Craftsman, Accutron.
- *It should suggest the product or service category:* Examples: Ticketron, *Newsweek.*
- *It should suggest concrete, "high imagery" qualities:* Examples: Sunkist, Spic and Span, Firebird.
- *It should be easy to spell, pronounce, recognize, and remember:* Short names help. Examples: Tide, Crest, Puffs.
- *It should be distinctive:* Examples: Mustang, Kodak, Exxon.
- *It should not carry poor meanings in other countries and languages:* Example: Nova is a poor name for a car to be sold in Spanish-speaking countries; in Spanish it means "doesn't go."

Normally, companies choose brand names by generating a list of possible names, debating their merits, eliminating all but a few, testing them with target consumers, and making a final choice. Today many companies hire a marketing research firm to develop and test names. These companies use human brainstorming sessions and vast computer databases, catalogued by association, sounds, and other qualities. Name-research procedures include *association tests* (What images come to mind?), *learning tests* (How easily is the name pronounced?), *memory tests* (How well is the name remembered?), and *preference tests* (Which names are preferred?). Of course, the firm must also conduct searches through other databases to make sure the chosen name has not already been registered. The whole process, however, is not cheap. One of the best-known specialists in the "name game" is San Francisco–based Namelab Inc., whose average fee is $90,000. Namelab is responsible for such brand names as Acura, Compaq, and CompUSA.

Many firms strive to build a unique brand name that eventually will become intimately identified with the product category. Examples are Kleenex, Kitty Litter, Levis, Jell-O, Popsicle, Scotch Tape, Xerox, and Fiberglass. In 1994, Federal Express officially shortened its marketing identity to FedEx, a term that has become a synonym for "to ship overnight." Yet identifying a brand name with a product category may threaten the company's exclusive rights to that name. Cellophane and shredded wheat are now in the public domain and available for any manufacturer to use.

Given the rapid growth of the global marketplace, companies should choose brand names that work globally. One thing Compaq liked about the name Presario for its line of home computers is that it conjures up similar meanings in various Latin-influenced languages. In French, Spanish, Latin, or Portuguese, Presario has the same, or similar, association that it does in English. It makes one immediately think of an "impresario," the magical master of the whirl and fantasy of a stage production. Companies also should not change names owned by someone in another country. For example, Anheuser-Busch cannot use the name "Budweiser" in Germany.

brand-building tools

A common misconception is that brands are basically built by advertising. It is true that TV advertising in its early days was the most effective brand-building tool. There were very few TV stations and people watched the comedies, dramas, and ads with almost equal interest. Now, viewers may be watching one of dozens of TV stations, and many are zapping or ignoring the commercials. In fact, many more are simply not watching TV. They are busy on their computers or engaged in recreational activities.

Marketers are therefore turning to other tools for attracting attention to their brands. Among the most important are:

- *Public relations and press releases:* Brands can gain a lot of attention from well-placed newspaper and magazine stories, not to mention appearing visually in Hollywood films.
- *Sponsorships:* Brands are frequently promoted in sponsored events such as world-famous bicycle and car races.
- *Clubs and consumer communities:* Brands can form the center of a customer community, such as Harley-Davidson motorcycle owners or Bradford plate collectors.
- *Factory visits:* Hershey's and Cadbury's, two candy companies, have built theme parks at their factories and they invite visitors to spend a day.
- *Trade shows:* Trade shows represent a great opportunity to build brand awareness, knowledge, and interest.
- *Event marketing:* Many automobile companies make an event out of introducing their new car models.
- *Public facilities:* Perrier, the bottled water company, etched its identity in the public mind by building running tracks in public parks to promote healthful lifestyles.
- *Social cause marketing:* Brands can achieve a following by donating money to charitable causes. Ben & Jerry's Ice Cream turns over 7 percent of its profits to charity.

- *High value for the money:* Some brands create positive word of mouth by offering exceptional value for the money. Examples include IKEA and Southwest Airlines.
- *Founder's or a celebrity personality:* A colorful founder, such as Richard Branson, or a celebrity personality, such as Michael Jordan, can create positive affect for a brand.
- *Mobile phone marketing:* Customers in the future will hear about brands on their wireless mobile phones as m-commerce grows.

Many of these tools describe efforts to build a brand through "branded experiences" or "experiential communications," terms used by the Jack Morton Company. Businesses hire Morton to create memorable experiences that engage the hearts and minds of a target audience. Morton develops trade show experiences, traveling exhibits, worldwide Webcasts of major presentations and roundtables, corporate museums, entertainments, and other first-hand experiences that go deeper than just hearing or seeing an ad for a product.[35]

brand strategy decision

Brand strategy will vary with whether the brand is a functional brand, an image brand, or an experiential brand.[36] Consumers purchase a *functional brand* to satisfy a functional need such as to shave, to clean clothes, to relieve a headache. Functional brands have the best chance to satisfy customers if they are seen as providing superior performance (Tide) or superior economy (Wal-Mart). Functional brands rely heavily on "product" and or "price" features.

Image brands arise with products or services that are difficult to differentiate, or to assess quality, or convey a statement about the user. Strategies include creating a distinctive design (Mont Blanc pens), associating them with celebrity users (Armani suit wearers include Warren Beatty, Robert De Niro, and Tom Hanks), or creating a powerful advertising image (Marlboro Man). Typically, they are designed to say something positive about the brand user. Image brands include B2B products such as Intel, McKinsey & Company, and Goldman Sachs. Image brands rely heavily on "advertising creativity" and "high advertising expenditures."

Experiential brands involve the consumer beyond simply acquiring the product. The consumer encounters "people" and "place" with these brands, as happens in a Starbucks' coffee shop or a Barnes & Noble bookstore, visiting Disneyland or Niketown, going to the Golden Door spa, or visiting a California winery.

Over time, each type of brand can be developed further. A company can introduce **line extensions** (existing brand name extended to new sizes or flavors in the existing product category), **brand extensions** (brand names extended to new-product categories), **multibrands** (new brand names introduced in the same product category), **new brands** (new brand name for a new category product), and **co-branding** (combining two or more well-known brand names).

LINE EXTENSIONS Line extensions consist of introducing additional items in the same product category under the same brand name, such as new flavors, forms, colors, added ingredients, and package sizes. Dannon introduced several Dannon yogurt line extensions, including fat-free "light" yogurt and dessert flavors such as "mint chocolate cream pie" and "caramel apple crunch." The vast majority of new-product introductions consist of line extensions.

Many companies are now introducing **branded variants**, which are specific brand lines supplied to specific retailers or distribution channels. They result from the pressure retailers put on manufacturers to enable the retailers to provide distinctive offerings. A camera company may supply its low-end cameras to mass-merchandisers while limiting its higher-priced items to specialty camera shops; or Valentino may design and supply different lines of suits and jackets to different department stores.[37]

Line extension involves risks and has provoked heated debate among marketing professionals.[38] On the downside, line extensions may lead to the brand name losing its specific meaning. Ries and Trout call this the "line-extension trap."[39] Michelob was an expensive, full-flavored premium beer; when it introduced Michelob Light and Michelob Dry, its brand suffered. In the past, when a person asked for a Coke, she received a 6.5-ounce bottle. Today the seller has to ask: New, Classic, or Cherry Coke? Regular or diet? Caffeine or caffeine-free? Bottle or can? Consider the following misfire.

Nabisco Even when a new line extension sells well, its sales may come at the expense of other items in the line. Although Fig Newton's cousins Cranberry Newtons, Blueberry Newtons, and Apple Newtons are all doing well for Nabisco, the original Fig Newton brand now seems like just another flavor. A line extension works best when it takes sales away from competing brands, not when it deflates or cannibalizes the company's other items.

However, line extensions can and often do have a positive side. They have a much higher chance of survival than brand-new products. Some marketing executives defend line extensions as the best way to build a business. Kimberly-Clark's Kleenex unit has had great success with line extensions. "We try to get facial tissue in every room of the home," says one Kimberly-Clark executive. "If it is there, it will get used." This philosophy led to 20 varieties of Kleenex facial tissues, including lotion-impregnated tissues, boxes with nursery-rhyme drawings for children's rooms, and a "man-sized" box with tissues 60 percent larger than regular Kleenex.

Line extensions are also fueled by fierce competition in the marketplace. Nabisco has had such success with its Snackwell Fat Free cookies that every competitor has had to extend its product line in defense. One study, by Reddy, Holak, and Bhat, examined what makes a line extension succeed or fail. Data on 75 line extensions of 34 cigarette brands over a 20-year period yielded these findings: Line extensions of strong brands, symbolic brands, brands given strong advertising and promotion support, and those entering earlier into a project subcategory are more successful. The size of the company and its marketing competence also play a role.[40]

BRAND EXTENSIONS A company may use its existing brand name to launch new products in other categories. Honda uses its company name to cover such different products as automobiles, motorcycles, snowblowers, lawnmowers, marine engines, and snowmobiles. This allows Honda to advertise that it can fit "six Hondas in a two-car garage." GAP stores now feature its name on soap, lotion, shampoo, conditioner, shower gel, bath salts, and perfume spray. A new trend in corporate brand building is that corporations are licensing their names to manufacturers of a wide range of products, from bedding to shoes. See "Marketing Insight: The Rise of Licensing and Corporate Branding" for a closer look at the new trend in corporate image branding.

Brand-extension strategy offers many of the same advantages as line extensions. Sony puts its name on most of its new electronic products and instantly establishes the new product's high quality. Ralph Lauren has successfully licensed his name to clothing lines, home furnishings, and even paints. Nike has successfully transitioned from sneakers to clothing, sports equipment, and watches.

Yet like line extension, brand extension also involves risks. Jack Daniels licensed its name for use as a mustard that failed; and Pierre Cardin put his name on a wine, and this failed. The brand name may be inappropriate to the new product—consider buying Shell Oil ketchup, Drano milk, or Boeing cologne. The new product might disappoint buyers and damage their respect for the company's other products. The brand name may lose its special positioning in the consumer's mind through overextension. **Brand dilution** occurs when consumers no longer associate a brand with a specific product or highly similar products and start thinking less of the brand.

Companies that are tempted to transfer their brand name must research how well the brand's associations fit the new product. The best result would occur when the brand name builds the sales of both the new product and the existing product. An

marketing **insight**

The Rise of Licensing and Corporate Branding

Corporations have seized on licensing to push the company name and image. In 1997 retail sales from licensing rights in the United States and Canada were $73.23 billion. Corporate brand licensing claimed 22 percent of that total, the same amount earned from licensing rights to entertainment properties. Licensing is a low-risk way for companies to increase revenue and raise brand awareness. Coke set up a licensing program, which started modestly but now consists of a large department overseeing more than 240 licensees and at least 10,000 products, including baby clothes, earrings, a fishing lure in the shape of a tiny coke can, and boxer shorts.

Caterpillar and John Deere are two companies with narrow markets that are now licensing a wide range of products. Caterpillar has a licensing agreement with Big Smith Brands to make Caterpillar work clothes, and Cat is also teaming up with Mattel to create a line of toys based on its construction equipment. David Aaker, author of *Building Strong Brands*, says the new branded offerings will help equipment makers reach out to younger people. Those who appreciate Deere's history "are getting older and older," he says. "They have to get people in their 20s and 30s to understand the tradition."

Sources: Adapted from Constance L. Hays, "No More Brand X: Licensing of Names Adds to Image and Profit," *New York Times*, June 12, 1998, p. D1; with additional information drawn from Carleen Hawn, "What's in a Name? Whatever You Make It," *Forbes*, July 27, 1998, pp. 84–88; Carl Quintanilla, "Advertising: Caterpillar, Deere Break Ground in Consumer-Product Territory," *Wall Street Journal*, June 20, 1996, p. B2. Also see David A. Aaker, *Building Strong Brands* (New York: The Free Press, 1995).

acceptable result would be one in which the new product sells well without affecting the sales of the existing product. The worst result would be one in which the new product fails and hurts the sales of the existing product.[41]

MULTIBRANDS, NEW BRANDS, AND CO-BRANDS   A company will often introduce additional brands in the same product category. Sometimes the company is trying to establish different features or appeal to different buying motives. Consider Black & Decker.

> Black & Decker   In the 1990s, Black & Decker, a portable power-tool company, added a line of small kitchen appliances. This resulted in an image among professionals and tradesmen that the company's power tools were mainly for homeowners. Black & Decker decided to launch a separate line of power tools under a new brand name, DeWalt, and this brand soon captured leadership with professionals and tradesmen.

A **multibrand** strategy enables a company to lock up more distributor shelf space and to protect its major brand by setting up *flanker brands*. Seiko establishes different brand names for its higher-priced (Seiko Lasalle) and lower-priced watches (Pulsar) to protect its flanks. Sometimes the company inherits different brand names in the process of acquiring competitors. Electrolux, the Swedish multinational, owns a stable of acquired brand names (Frigidaire, Kelvinator, Westinghouse, Zanussi, White, Gibson) for its appliance lines.

A major pitfall in introducing multibrand entries is that each might obtain only a small market share, and none may be particularly profitable. The company will have dissipated its resources over several brands instead of building a few highly profitable brands. Ideally, a company's brands within a category should cannibalize the competitors' brands and not each other. At the very least, the net profits with multibrands should be larger even if some cannibalism occurs.[42]

When a company launches products in a new category, it may find that none of its current brand names are appropriate. If Timex decides to make toothbrushes, it is not likely to call them Timex toothbrushes. Yet establishing a new brand name in the U.S. marketplace for a mass-consumer-packaged good can cost $100 million.

A rising phenomenon is the emergence of **co-branding** (also called **dual branding**), in which two or more well-known brands are combined in an offer. Each brand sponsor expects that the other brand name will strengthen preference or purchase intention. In the case of co-packaged products, each brand hopes it might be reaching a new audience by associating with the other brand.

Co-branding takes a variety of forms. One is *ingredient co-branding*, as when Volvo advertises that it uses Michelin tires, or Betty Crocker's brownie mix includes Hershey's chocolate syrup. DuPont has achieved success marketing its products as ingredient brands.

DuPont   Over the years, DuPont has introduced a number of innovative products for use in markets ranging from apparel to aerospace. Many products, such as Lycra® and Stainmaster® fabrics, Teflon® coating, and Kevlar® fiber, became household names as ingredient brands in consumer products manufactured by other companies. Several recent ingredient brands include Supro® isolated soy proteins used in food products, and RiboPrinter® genetic fingerprinting technology.[43]

Another form is *same-company co-branding*, as when General Mills advertises Trix and Yoplait yogurt. Still another form is *joint venture co-branding*, as in the case of General Electric and Hitachi lightbulbs in Japan and the Citibank AAdvantage credit card. Finally, there is *multiple-sponsor co-branding*, as in the case of Taligent, a technological alliance of Apple, IBM, and Motorola.[44]

Many manufacturers make components—motors, computer chips, carpet fibers—that enter into final branded products, and whose individual identity normally gets lost. Among the few component branders who have succeeded in building a separate identity are Intel, Nutrasweet, and Gortex. Intel's consumer-directed brand campaign convinced many personal computer buyers to buy only computer brands with "Intel Inside." As a result, major PC manufacturers—IBM, Dell, Compaq—purchase their chips from Intel at a premium price rather than buy equivalent chips from an unknown supplier. Searle has convinced many beverage consumers to look for Nutrasweet as an ingredient. Manufacturers of outerwear can charge a higher price if their garments include Gortex. However, most component manufacturers find it hard to convince buyers to insist on a certain component, material, or ingredient in the final product.

brand asset management

Although print and broadcast advertising have played a large role in building strong brands, other forces are now playing an increasing role. Customers come to know a brand through a range of contacts and touchpoints: personal observation and use, word of mouth, meeting company personnel, telephone experience, seeing the Web page, receiving invoices, and so on. Any of these experiences can be positive or negative. The company must put in as much quality in managing these experiences as it does in producing its ads.

Companies must balance their communication expenditures among the main communication media. These include the following seven communication vehicles: advertising, public relations, trade and sales promotion, consumer promotions, direct marketing, event marketing, and internal employee communications. Companies are increasingly moving their brand-building budgets to public relations, direct marketing, event marketing, and employee training.

One of the most potent influences on brand perception is the experience customers have with the company's personnel. If the telephone operator is curt, if the order taker is poorly informed, if the accountant will not explain the invoice—the brand image is compromised. Therefore the company needs to train its people to be customer-centered. Even better, the company should build pride in its employees regarding their products and service so that their enthusiasm will spill over to the customer. Companies such as Nordstrom and Harley-Davidson have succeeded in creating enthusiastic representatives.

Companies must go further and train and encourage their distributors and dealers to serve their customers well. Poorly trained dealers can ruin the best of efforts made by the company to build a strong brand image.

This suggests that managing a company's brand assets can no longer be entrusted to brand managers. Brand managers do not have enough power and scope to do all the things that are necessary to build and enhance their brands. Their incentive system drives them to pursue short-term results, whereas managing brands as assets calls for longer-term strategy and more inclusive teamwork.

Companies are beginning to establish brand asset management teams to manage their major brands. Canada Dry and Colgate-Palmolive have appointed *brand equity managers* to maintain and protect the brand's image, associations, and quality, and to prevent short-term tactical actions by overzealous brand managers from hurting the brand. Brand equity managers also have to handle unexpected negative publicity, as happened with the Exxon *Valdez*, Tylenol pill tainting, tainted Perrier, and Audi crashes. Coca-Cola's CEO recently resigned in part because of his slow and poor handling of Coke's contamination scare in Belgium. After all, Coca-Cola is a "giant image machine" and must handle itself as such.

Some companies are putting their branding in the hands of an entirely different company that can focus on brand management and nothing else. Henry Silverman of Cendant Corporation has made a business of managing—not owning—brands.

Cendant Corporation   Cendant's Henry Silverman has gone as far as anyone in arguing that brand is everything and in showing how a brand can even be split away from the operational aspect of the business. Cendant owns and manages brands, including motels (Days Inn, Super 8, Howard Johnson, Ramada), real estate franchises (Century 21, Coldwell Banker), and car rental agencies (Avis). The brands are all he owns. While other companies own and operate the messy, real-world parts of the business, Silverman spends his time and energy distilling, refurbishing, extending, linking, and leveraging brand names. For instance, he was able to change the brand image of Century 21. Old TV ads emphasized the company's vast real estate network, but Silverman's research showed that home buyers did not care how big Century 21 was; they cared about building good relationships with the company's real estate agents. Silverman launched a new campaign focusing on those more personal attributes, and Century 21's annual earnings have doubled.[45]

brand auditing and repositioning

Companies need to periodically audit their brands' strengths and weaknesses. Kevin Keller constructed a *brand report card* (see "Marketing Memo: The Brand Report Card") listing 10 characteristics based on his review of the world's strongest brands.[46]

A company will occasionally discover that it may have to reposition the brand because of changing customer preferences or new competitors. Consider the following repositioning stories.

Kmart   Kmart, which prospered in the 1970s as a leading discount store chain, came close to bankruptcy in the mid-1990s. It was losing out to Wal-Mart and better-looking stores such as Target. Kmart undertook a number of steps to relaunch itself as Big K. Critics saw the stores as old, dilapidated, unkept, with poor service. It built new stores that suggested it was young and hip, carried great brands and values, offered a high level of customer service, and was serving all classes. In spite of these changes, Kmart's performance remained much below its major competitors, Wal-Mart and Target. In late January 2002, Kmart filed for bankruptcy.

Marketing
MEMO

The Brand Report Card

The world's strongest brands share 10 attributes. How does your brand measure up?

1. *The brand excels at delivering the benefits consumers truly desire.* Do you focus relentlessly on maximizing your customers' product and service experiences?

2. *The brand stays relevant.* Are you in touch with your customers' tastes, current market conditions, and trends?

3. *The pricing strategy is based on consumers' perceptions of value.* Have you optimized price, cost, and quality to meet or exceed customers' expectations?

4. *The brand is properly positioned.* Have you established necessary and competitive points of parity with competitors? Have you established desirable and deliverable points of difference?

5. *The brand is consistent.* Are you sure that your marketing programs are not sending conflicting messages and that they have not done so over time?

6. *The brand portfolio and hierarchy makes sense.* Can the corporate brand create a seamless umbrella for all the brands in the portfolio? Do you have a brand hierarchy that is well thought out and well understood?

continued...

Schwinn   Schwinn, the leading U.S. bicycle manufacturer, had thrived since its beginnings in the late 1800s. It repositioned itself several times during the 1900s, first aiming its bikes at boys and their fathers, later positioning them as family bikes, then as fitness bikes. However, in the early 1980s, Schwinn paid little attention to two new markets—dirt bikes and mountain bikes. Schwinn started to become "uncool" and irrelevant in the minds of young bikers. Finally, in the 1990s, Schwinn repositioned itself by adding mountain bikes and sponsoring events featuring popular stunt riders sporting Schwinn equipment and gear. Schwinn built an image of fun and daring and its bikes were seen to be of the highest quality and durability.

packaging and labeling

Most physical products have to be packaged and labeled. Some packages—such as the Coke bottle and the L'eggs container—are world famous. Many marketers have called packaging a fifth P, along with price, product, place, and promotion. Most marketers, however, treat packaging and labeling as an element of product strategy.

packaging

We define **packaging** as all the activities of designing and producing the container for a product. The container is called the **package**, and it might include up to three levels of material. Old Spice aftershave lotion is in a bottle (*primary package*) that is in a cardboard box (*secondary package*) that is in a corrugated box (*shipping package*) containing six dozen boxes of Old Spice.

Well-designed packages can create convenience and promotional value. Various factors have contributed to the growing use of packaging as a marketing tool:

- *Self-service:* An increasing number of products are sold on a self-service basis. In an average supermarket, which stocks 15,000 items, the typical shopper passes by some 300 items per minute. Given that 53 percent of all purchases are made on impulse, the effective package operates as a "five-second commercial." The package must perform many of the sales tasks: attract attention, describe the product's features, create consumer confidence, and make a favorable overall impression.

- *Consumer affluence:* Rising consumer affluence means consumers are willing to pay a little more for the convenience, appearance, dependability, and prestige of better packages.

- *Company and brand image:* Packages contribute to instant recognition of the company or brand. The Campbell Soup Company estimates that the average shopper sees its familiar red-and-white can 76 times a year, creating the equivalent of $26 million worth of advertising.

- *Innovation opportunity:* Innovative packaging can bring large benefits to consumers and profits to producers. Companies are incorporating unique materials and features such as resealable spouts and openings. Toothpaste pump dispensers have captured 12 percent of the toothpaste market because they are more convenient and less messy. The fragrance industry is continuously developing unique bottle designs.

Developing an effective package requires several decisions. The first is to establish the packaging concept: defining what the package should basically *be* or *do* for the particular product. Decisions must be made on additional elements—size, shape, materials, color, text, and brand mark. Brian Wansink found, for example, that a larger package size will increase product usage between 7 and 43 percent.[47] Color must be carefully chosen: Blue is cool and serene, red is active and lively, yellow is medicinal and weak, pastel colors are feminine and dark colors are masculine. Decisions must also be made on the amount of text, on cellophane or other transparent films, on a plastic or a laminate tray, and so on. Decisions must be made on "tamperproof" devices. The various packaging elements must be harmonized. The packaging elements must also be harmonized with decisions on pricing, advertising, and other marketing elements. Consider this example.

Rhino Entertainment   Rhino, a music company based in Los Angeles, released a CD compilation with more than 100 songs called "Brain in a Box: The Science Fiction Collection." To get serious sci-fi fans to spend $100 for a collection of songs, Rhino designed unique packaging that would make the CD set a collector's item. Five CDs come in a box whose panels display three different views of the brain using three-dimensional holograms. The panels also show various clamps and wires attached to the brain that appear to connect with knobs and dials on the metallic lid. Since Rhino rarely records new bands, relying instead on reissues of older music, packaging has always been crucial to selling records.[48]

After the packaging is designed, it must be tested. *Engineering tests* are conducted to ensure that the package stands up under normal conditions; *visual tests*, to ensure that the script is legible and the colors harmonious; *dealer tests*, to ensure that dealers find the packages attractive and easy to handle; and *consumer tests*, to ensure favorable consumer response.

Developing effective packaging may cost several hundred thousand dollars and take several months to complete. Companies must pay attention to growing environmental and safety concerns about packaging. Shortages of paper, aluminum, and other materials suggest that marketers should try to reduce packaging. Many packages end up as broken bottles and crumpled cans littering the streets and countryside. Packaging creates a major problem in solid waste disposal, requiring huge amounts of labor and energy. Fortunately, many companies have gone "green": S. C. Johnson repackaged Agree Plus shampoo in a stand-up pouch using 80 percent less plastic. P&G eliminated outer cartons from its Secret and Sure deodorants, saving 3.4 million pounds of paper board per year.

Tetra Pak   Tetra Pak, a major Swedish multinational, provides an example of the power of innovative packaging and customer thinking. Tetra Pak invented an "aseptic" package that enables milk, fruit juice, and other perishable liquid foods to be distributed without refrigeration. So dairies can distribute milk over a wider area without investing in refrigerated trucks and facilities. Supermarkets can carry Tetra Pak packaged products on ordinary shelves, allowing them to save expensive refrigerator space. Tetra's motto is "the package should save more than it cost." Tetra Pak advertises the benefits of its packaging to consumers directly and even initiates recycling programs to save the environment. Its new American headquarters in Vernon, Illinois, used recycled materials and other environmentally sensitive building products and techniques.[49]

labeling

Sellers must label products. The label may be a simple tag attached to the product or an elaborately designed graphic that is part of the package. The label might carry only the brand name or a great deal of information. Even if the seller prefers a simple label, the law may require additional information.

Labels perform several functions. First, the label *identifies* the product or brand—for instance, the name Sunkist stamped on oranges. The label might also *grade* the product; canned peaches are grade labeled A, B, and C. The label might *describe* the product: who made it, where it was made, when it was made, what it contains, how it is to be used, and how to use it safely. Finally, the label might *promote* the product through its attractive graphics.

Labels eventually become outmoded and need freshening up. The label on Ivory soap has been redone 18 times since the 1890s, with gradual changes in the size and design of the letters. The label on Orange Crush soft drink was substantially changed when competitors' labels began to picture fresh fruits, thereby pulling in more sales. In response, Orange Crush developed a label with new symbols to suggest freshness and with much stronger and deeper colors.

7. *The brand makes use of and coordinates a full repertoire of marketing activities to build equity.* Have you capitalized on the unique capabilities of each communication option while ensuring that the meaning of the brand is consistently represented?

8. *The brand's managers understand what the brand means to consumers.* Do you know what customers like and do not like about your brand? Have you created detailed, research-driven portraits of your target customers?

9. *The brand is given proper, sustained support.* Are the successes or failures of marketing programs fully understood before they are changed? Is the brand given sufficient R&D support?

10. *The company monitors sources of brand equity.* Have you created a brand charter that defines the meaning and equity of the brand and how it should be treated? Have you assigned explicit responsibility for monitoring and preserving brand equity?

Source: Adapted from Kevin Lane Keller, "The Brand Report Card," *Harvard Business Review* (January 1, 2000), pp. 147–57.

There is a long history of legal concerns surrounding labels, as well as packaging. In 1914, the Federal Trade Commission Act held that false, misleading, or deceptive labels or packages constitute unfair competition. The Fair Packaging and Labeling Act, passed by Congress in 1967, set mandatory labeling requirements, encouraged voluntary industry packaging standards, and allowed federal agencies to set packaging regulations in specific industries. The Food and Drug Administration (FDA) has required processed-food producers to include nutritional labeling that clearly states the amounts of protein, fat, carbohydrates, and calories contained in products, as well as their vitamin and mineral content as a percentage of the recommended daily allowance. The FDA recently launched a drive to control health claims in food labeling by taking action against the potentially misleading use of such descriptions as "light," "high fiber," and "low fat." Consumerists have lobbied for additional labeling laws to require *open dating* (to describe product freshness), *unit pricing* (to state the product cost in standard measurement units), *grade labeling* (to rate the quality level), and *percentage labeling* (to show the percentage of each important ingredient).

summary

1. Product is the first and most important element of the marketing mix. Product strategy calls for making coordinated decisions on product mixes, product lines, brands, and packaging and labeling.

2. In planning its market offering, the marketer needs to think through the five levels of the product. The core benefit is the fundamental benefit or service the customer is really buying. At the second level, the marketer has to turn the core benefit into a basic product. At the third level, the marketer prepares an expected product, a set of attributes that buyers normally expect and agree to when they buy the product. At the fourth level, the marketer prepares an augmented product, one that includes additional services and benefits that distinguish the company's offer from that of competitors. At the fifth and final level, the marketer prepares a potential product, which encompasses all the augmentations and transformations the product might ultimately undergo.

3. Products can be classified in several ways. In terms of durability and reliability, products can be nondurable goods, durable goods, or services. In the consumer-goods category, products are convenience goods (staples, impulse goods, emergency goods), shopping goods (homogeneous and heterogeneous), specialty goods, or unsought goods. In the industrial-goods category, products fall into one of three categories: materials and parts (raw materials and manufactured materials and parts), capital items (installations and equipment), or supplies and business services (operating supplies, maintenance and repair items, maintenance and repair services, and business advisory services).

4. Most companies sell more than one product. A product mix can be classified according to width, length, depth, and consistency. These four dimensions are the tools for developing the company's marketing strategy and deciding which product lines to grow, maintain, harvest, and divest.

To analyze a product line and decide how many resources should be invested in that line, product-line managers need to look at sales and profits and market profile.

5. A company can change the product component of its marketing mix by lengthening its product via line stretching (downmarket, upmarket, or both) or line filling, by modernizing its products, by featuring certain products, and by pruning its products to eliminate the least profitable.

6. Branding is a major issue in product strategy. A brand is a complex symbol that can convey many levels of meaning. Branding is expensive and time-consuming, and it can make or break a product. The most valuable brands have a brand equity that is considered an important company asset and that must be carefully managed. In thinking about branding strategy, companies must decide whether or not to brand; whether to produce manufacturer brands, or distributor or private brands; which brand name to use; and whether to use line extensions, brand extensions, multibrands, new brands, or co-brands. The best brand names suggest something about the product's benefits; suggest product qualities; are easy to pronounce, recognize, and remember; are distinctive; and do not carry negative meanings or connotations in other countries or languages.

7. Many physical products have to be packaged and labeled. Well-designed packages can create convenience value for customers and promotional value for producers. In effect, they can act as "five-second commercials" for the product. Marketers develop a packaging concept and test it functionally and psychologically to make sure it achieves its desired objectives and is compatible with public policy and environmental concerns. Physical products also require labeling for identification and possible grading, description, and product promotion. Sellers may be required by law to present certain information on the label to protect and inform consumers.

applications

marketing debate – are line extensions good or bad?

Marketing consultants Al Ries and Jack Trout have vociferously denounced the practice of line extensions, referring to the "line extension trap." Others maintain that brand extensions are a critical growth strategy and source of revenue for the firm.

Take a position: Line extensions can endanger brands versus Line extensions are an important brand growth strategy.

marketing and advertising

1. Pepperidge Farm cookies are positioned as premium cookies. This magazine ad in Figure 1 features a larger-than-life Milano cookie, plus a simple headline, logo, and the tagline "Never have an ordinary day."
   a. Identify the basic, expected, and augmented products that Pepperidge Farm is offering.
   b. How would you classify this consumer product?
   c. How do the elements of this ad help convey the brand's attributes and benefits?

2. Binney & Smith is well known for marketing Crayola® crayons in a wide variety of colors, including jack-o-lantern orange, as shown in the seasonal ad in Figure 2.
   a. Can the Crayon Treat Pack be considered a line or brand extension? Why would Binney & Smith choose this strategy?
   b. Discuss Binney & Smith's packaging strategy for the Crayon Treat Pack. How does this strategy reinforce to the company's company and brand image?
   c. Are Crayola® crayons convenience goods, goods, specialty, or unsought goods? How does this classification affect Binney & Smith's marketing of its Crayon Treat Pack?

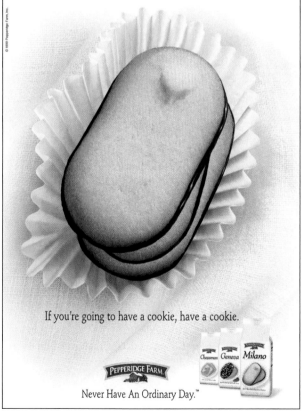

Figure 1

Figure 2

online marketing today

As noted earlier, Richard Branson is aggressively building his Virgin brand on and off the Internet. Virgin.com has evolved into a major U.K. portal with links to every Virgin company Web site and offers goods and services in numerous product categories, from travel and transport to house and home and business and finance. This site also serves as a central recruitment point for Virgin companies with job openings.

Visit the Virgin site (*www.virgin.com*), review the offers on the home page, and follow several links to featured offers and companies. Return to the home page and click to read about at least one "travel and transport" offer and one "house and home" offer. Which brand-name strategy is Virgin using? Why is this strategy appropriate for Virgin? Select two offers and determine whether they can be characterized as convenience goods, shopping goods, specialty goods, or unsought goods. Why would Virgin choose to highlight these types of products?

you're the marketer: sonic pda marketing plan

Marketing Plan Pro

Decisions about products and branding are critical elements of any marketing plan. During the planning process, marketers must consider a variety of issues related to product mix, product lines, brand equity, and brand strategies.

You are helping Sonic manage its soon-to-be-expanded line of personal digital assistant products, as well as branding for this line. After reviewing the company's current situation, target market, positioning, and other issues previously addressed in your marketing plan, consider the following questions:

■ What is the core benefit of the first PDA product Sonic will soon introduce?

■ What elements of the potential product should Sonic consider incorporating into the higher-end second product to be developed next year?

■ What are the attributes and benefits suggested by the Sonic brand?

■ How can Sonic use packaging and labeling to support its brand image and help its channel partners sell the PDA product more effectively?

Think about how your answers to these questions will influence Sonic's marketing activities. Now, as your instructor directs, summarize your ideas in a written marketing plan or type them into the Marketing Mix and Marketing Strategy sections of the *Marketing Plan Pro* software. Also indicate (in the Marketing Research section) any additional studies you will need to support decisions about managing the product line and brand.

notes

1. <*www.biography.com*>.

2. T. L. Stanley, "Brand Builders: Bio-Genetics at A&E," *Brandweek*, April 6, 1998, pp. 22–23.

3. This discussion is adapted from Theodore Levitt, "Marketing Success through Differentiation: of Anything," *Harvard Business Review* (January–February 1980): 83–91. The first level, core benefit, has been added to Levitt's discussion.

4. Harper W. Boyd Jr. and Sidney Levy, "New Dimensions in Consumer Analysis," *Harvard Business Review* (November–December 1963): 129–40.

5. Theodore Levitt, *The Marketing Mode* (New York: McGraw-Hill, 1969), p. 2.

6. For some definitions, see *Dictionary of Marketing Terms*, ed. Peter D. Bennett (Chicago: American Marketing Association, 1995). Also see Patrick E. Murphy and Ben M. Enis, "Classifying Products Strategically," *Journal of Marketing* (July 1986): 24–42.

7. Adapted from a Hamilton Consultants White Paper, December 1, 2000.

8. This illustration is found in Benson P. Shapiro, *Industrial Product Policy: Managing the Existing Product Line* (Cambridge, MA: Marketing Science Institute, September 1977), pp. 3–5, 98–101.

9. David A. Aaker, "Should You Take Your Brand to Where the Action Is?" *Harvard Business Review* (September–October 1997): 135–43; A. Kirmani, S. Sood, and S. Bridges, "The Ownership Effect in Consumer Responses to Brand Line

Stretches," *Journal of Marketing* 63 (1999): 88–101; T. Randall, K. Ulrich, and D. Reibstein, "Brand Equity and Vertical Product Line Extent," *Marketing Science* 17 (1998): 356–79.

10. Steuart Henderson Britt, "How Weber's Law Can Be Applied to Marketing," *Business Horizons* (February 1975): 21–29.

11. Jean-Noel Kapferer, *Strategic Brand Management: New Approaches to Creating and Evaluating Brand Equity* (London: Kogan Page, 1992), p. 38; Jennifer L. Aaker, "Dimensions of Brand Personality," *Journal of Marketing Research* (August 1997): 347–56. For an overview of academic research on branding, see Kevin Lane Keller, "Branding and Brand Equity," in *Handbook of Marketing*, eds., Bart Weitz and Robin Wensley (Sage Publications: in press).

12. Scott Davis, *Brand Asset Management: Driving Profitable Growth Through Your Brands* (San Francisco: Jossey-Bass, 2000); K. L. Keller, "Building Customer-Based Brand Equity: A Blueprint for Creating Strong Brands," *Marketing Management*, 10 (July/August 2001): 15–19.

13. Marc Gobe, *Emotional Branding* (New York: Allworth Press, 2001); B. H. Schmitt and A. Simonson, *Marketing Aesthetics: The Strategic Management of Brands, Identity and Image* (New York: Free Press, 1997); B. H. Schmitt, *Experiential Marketing: How to Get Customers to Sense, Feel, Think, Act and Relate to Your Company and Brands* (New York: Free Press, 1999).

14. Donald D. Tosti and Roger D. Stotz, "Building Your Brand from the Inside Out," *Marketing Management* (July–August

2001): 29–33; see also P. Berthon, J. M. Hulbert, and L. F. Pitt, "Brand Management Prognostications," *Sloan Management Review* (Winter 1999): 53–65.

15. Heidi F. Schultz and Don E. Schultz, "Why the Sock Puppet Got Sacked," *Marketing Management* (July–August 2001): 34–39.

16. David A. Akar, *Building Strong Brands* (New York: The Free Press, 1995). Also see Kavin Lane Keller, *Strategic Brand Management: Building, Measuring, and Managing Brand Equity* (Upper Saddle River, NJ: Prentice Hall, 1998); and D. A. Aaker and E. Joachimsthaler, *Brand Leadership* (New York; Free Press, 2000).

17. Scott Davis, *Brand Asset Management*; D. C. Bello and M. B. Holbrook, "Does an Absence of Brand Equity Generalize Across Product Classes?" *Journal of Business Research*, 34 (1996): 125–31.

18. Mary W. Sullivan, "How Brand Names Affect the Demand for Twin Automobiles," *Journal of Marketing Research* 35 (1998): 154–65.

19. Adrian J. Slywotzky and Benson P. Shapiro, "Leveraging to Beat the Odds: The New Marketing Mindset," *Harvard Business Review* (September–October 1993): 97–107.

20. Kurt Badenhausen with Joyce Artinian and Christopher Nikolov, "Most Valuable Brands," *Financial World* (September–October 1997): 62–63. "The Best Global Brands," *BusinessWeek*, August 6, 2001, pp. 50–64. The article ranks the 100 best global brands using a valuation method developed by Interbrand. For a discussion of methods of calculating brand value, see Kevin L. Keller, *Strategic Brand Management: Building, Measuring, and Managing Brand Equity* (Upper Saddle River, NJ: Prentice Hall, 1998), pp. 361–63.

21. Aaker, *Building Strong Brands*. Also see Patrick Barwise et al., *Accounting for Brands* (London: Institute of Chartered Accountants in England and Wales, 1990); Peter H. Farquhar, Julia Y. Han, and Yuji Ijiri, "Brands on the Balance Sheet," *Marketing Management* (Winter 1992): 16–22. Brand equity should reflect not only the capitalized value of the incremental profits from the current use of the brand name, but also the value of its potential extensions to other products.

22. Melanie Wells, "Red Baron," *Forbes*, July 3, 2000.

23. Kerry Capell, "Virgin Takes E-wing," *BusinessWeek e.biz*, January 22, 2001, pp. EB30–34; Melanie Wells, "Red Baron," *Forbes*, July 3, 2000, pp. 151–60.

24. Margaret Webb Pressler, "The Power of Branding," *Washington Post*, July 27, 1997, p. H1; "Cadbury Is Paying Triarc $1.45 Billion for Snapple Unit," *Baltimore Sun*, September 19, 2000.

25. Scott Davis and Darrell Douglass, "Holistic Approach to Brand Equity Management," *Marketing News*, January 16, 1995, pp. 4–5.

26. John F. Geer Jr., "Brand War on Wall Street," *Financial World*, May 20, 1997, pp. 54–63.

27. Bob Lamons, "Brick Brand's Mighty—Yours Can Be, Too," *Marketing News*, November 22, 1999, p. 16.

28. For further reading, see Brian F. Harris and Roger A. Strang, "Marketing Strategies in the Age of Generics," *Journal of Marketing* (Fall 1985): 70–81.

29. "President's Choice Continues Brisk Pace," *Frozen Food Age* (March 1998): 17–18; Warren Thayer, "Loblaw's Exec Predicts: Private Label to Surge," *Frozen Food Age* (May 1996): 1; Brian Dunn, "North Stars," *Supermarket News*, February 5, 2001.

30. Quoted in "Trade Promotion: Much Ado About Nothing," *Promo* (October 1991): 37.

31. Paul S. Richardson, Alan S. Dick, and Arun K. Jain, "Extrinsic and Intrinsic Cue Effects on Perceptions of Store Brand Quality," *Journal of Marketing* (October 1994): 28–36.

32. Patricia Nakache, "Secrets of the New Brand Builders," *Fortune*, June 22, 1998, pp. 167–70.

33. Marc Gunther, "Understanding AOL's Grand Unified Theory of the Media Cosmos, *Fortune*, January 8, 2001, p. 72.

34. Kim Robertson, "Strategically Desirable Brand Name Characteristics," *Journal of Consumer Marketing* (Fall 1989): 61–70; C. Kohli and D. W. LaBahn, "Creating Effective Brand Names: A Study of the Naming Process," *Journal of Advertising Research* (January/February 1997): 67–75.

35. Patricia Nakache, "Secrets of the New Brand Builders," *Fortune*, June 22, 1998, pp. 167–70.

36. Adapted from Alice M. Tybout and Gregory S. Carpenter, "Creating and Managing Brands," in *Kellogg on Marketing*, ed. Dawn Iacobucci (New York: John Wiley & Son, 2001), pp. 74–98; see also C. W. Park, S. Milberg, and R. Lawson, "Evaluation of Brand Extensions: The Role of Product Feature Similarity and Brand Concept Consistency," *Journal of Consumer Research*, 18 (1991): 185–93.

37. Steven M. Shugan, "Branded Variants," 1989 AMA Educators' Proceedings (Chicago: American Marketing Association, 1989), pp. 33–38. also M. Bergen, S. Dutta, and S. M. Shugan, "Branded Variants: A Retail Perspective," *Journal of Marketing Research*, 33 (February 1996): 9–21.

38. Robert McMath, "Product Proliferation," *Adweek* (Eastern Ed.) (Superbrands 1995 Supplement, 1995), pp. 34–40; John A. Quelch and David Kenny, "Extend Profits, Not Product Lines," *Harvard Business Review* (September–October 1994): 153–60; Bruce G. S. Hardle, Leonard M. Lodish, James V. Kilmer, and David R. Beatty et al., "The Logic of Product-Line Extensions," *Harvard Business Review* (November–December 1994): 53–62. J. Andrews and G. S. Low, "New But Not Improved: Factors That Affect the Development of Meaningful Line Extensions," Working Paper Report No. 98-124 (Cambridge, MA: Marketing Science Institute, November 1998).

39. Al Ries and Jack Trout, *Positioning: The Battle for Your Mind* (New York: McGraw-Hill, 1981).

40. From Srinivas K. Reddy, Susan L. Holak, and Subodh Bhat, "To Extend or Not to Extend: Success Determinants of Line Extensions," *Journal of Marketing Research* (May 1994): 243–62. See also Morris A. Cohen, Jehoshua Eliashberg, and Teck H. Ho, "An Anatomy of a Decision-Support System for Developing and Launching Line Extensions," *Journal of Marketing Research* (February 1997): 117–29; V. Padmanabhan, Surendra Rajiv, and Kannan Srinivasan, "New Products, Upgrades, and New Releases: A Rationale for Sequential Product Introduction," *Journal of Marketing Research* (November 1997): 456–72.

41. Barbara Loken and Deborah Roedder John, "Diluting Brand Beliefs: When Do Brand Extensions Have a Negative Impact?" *Journal of Marketing* (July 1993): 71–84; Deborah Roedder John, Barbara Loken, and Christohper Joiner, "The Negative Impact of Extensions: Can Flagship Products Be Diluted," *Journal of Marketing* (January 1998): 19–32; Susan M. Broniarcyzk and Joseph W. Alba, "The Importance of the Brand in Brand Extension," *Journal of Marketing Research* (May 1994): 214–28 (this entire issue of *JMR* is devoted to brands and brand equity). See also R. Ahluwalia and Z. Gürhan-Canli, "The Effects of Extensions on the Family Brand Name: An Accessibility-Diagnosticity Perspective,"

Journal of Consumer Research 27 (December 2000): 371–81; Z. Gürhan-Canli and M. Durairaj, "The Effects of Extensions on Brand Name Dilution and Enhancement," *Journal of Marketing Research* 35 (1998): 464–73; S. J. Milberg, C. W. Park, and M. S. McCarthy, "Managing Negative Feedback Effects Associated with Brand Extensions: The Impact of Alternative Branding Strategies," *Journal of Consumer Psychology* 6 (1997): 119–40.

42. Mark B. Taylor, "Cannibalism in Multibrand Firms," *Journal of Business Strategy* (Spring 1986): 69–75. For a general discussion of co-branding, see Shawn Clark, *The Co-Marketing Solution* (Chicago: American Marketing Association, 2000).

43. <*www.dupont.com*>.

44. Bernard L. Simonin and Julie A. Ruth, "Is a Company Known by the Company It Keeps? Assessing the Spillover Effects of Brand Alliances on Consumer Brand Attitudes," *Journal of Marketing Research* (February 1998): 30–42; see also C. W. Park, S. Y. Jun, and A. D. Shocker, "Composite Branding Alliances: An Investigation of Extension and Feedback Effects, " *Journal of Marketing Research* 33 (1996): 453–66.

45. Evan Schwartz, "The Brand Man," *Context* (Summer 1998): 54–58; Davis, *Brand Asset Management*.

46. Kevin Lane Keller, "The Brand Report Card," *Harvard Business Review* (January–February 2000): 147–57.

47. Brian Wansink, "Can Package Size Accelerate Usage Volume?" *Journal of Marketing* (July 1996): 1–14.

48. Queena Sook Kim, "This Potion's Power Is in Its Packaging," *Wall Street Journal*, December 21, 2000, p. B12.

49. "Tetra Pak Opens Innovative Environmentally Friendly Corporate Headquarters," *PR Newswire*, September 1, 1999.

16

developing price strategies and programs

In this chapter, we will address the following questions:

- How should a price be set on a product or service for the first time?
- How should the price be adapted to meet varying circumstances and opportunities?
- When should the company initiate a price change, and how should it respond to a competitor's price change?

Kotler on Marketing

Sell value, not price.

Price is the one element of the marketing mix that produces revenue; the other elements produce costs. Prices are the easiest marketing-mix element to adjust; product features, channels, and even promotion take more time. Price also communicates to the market the company's intended value positioning of its product or brand.

Today companies are wrestling with a number of difficult pricing tasks:

- *How to respond to aggressive price cutters*
- *How to price the same product when it goes through different channels*
- *How to price the same product in different countries*
- *How to price an improved product while still selling the previous version*

■ *How to price different components of an offering when the customer wants to make his own choice of components*

Price is not just a number on a tag or an item, it goes by many names:

> *Price is all around us. You pay rent for your apartment, tuition for your education, and a fee to your physician or dentist. The airline, railway, taxi, and bus companies charge you a fare; the local utilities call their price a rate; and the local bank charges you interest for the money you borrow. The price for driving your car on Florida's Sunshine Parkway is a toll, and the company that insures your car charges you a premium. The guest lecturer charges an honorarium to tell you about a government official who took a bribe to help a shady character steal dues collected by a trade association. Clubs or societies to which you belong may make a special assessment to pay unusual expenses. Your regular lawyer may ask for a retainer to cover her services. The "price" of an executive is a salary, the price of a salesperson may be a commission, and the price of a worker is a wage. Finally, although economists would disagree, many of us feel that income taxes are the price we pay for the privilege of making money.[1]*

Throughout most of history, prices were set by negotiation between buyers and sellers. "Bargaining" is still a sport in some areas. Setting one price for all buyers is a relatively modern idea that arose with the development of large-scale retailing at the end of the nineteenth century. F. W. Woolworth, Tiffany and Co., John Wanamaker, and others advertised a "strictly one-price policy," because they carried so many items and supervised so many employees.

Today the Internet is partially reversing the fixed pricing trend. On Priceline.com, the customer states the price he wants to pay for an airline ticket, hotel, or mortgage and Priceline checks whether any seller is willing to meet the customer's price. Online auction sites like eBay.com facilitate variable pricing on thousands of items—from refurbished computers to antique trains. Volume-aggregating sites combine the orders of many customers and press the supplier for a deeper discount.

Traditionally, price has operated as the major determinant of buyer choice. This is still the case in poorer nations, among poorer groups, and with commodity-type products. Although nonprice factors have become more important in recent decades, price still remains one of the most important elements determining market share and profitability. Consumers and purchasing agents have more access to price information and price discounters. Consumers put pressure on retailers to lower their prices. Retailers put pressure on manufacturers to lower their prices. The result is a marketplace characterized by heavy discounting and sales promotion.

Many companies do not handle pricing well. They make these common mistakes: Pricing is too cost-oriented; price is not revised often enough to capitalize on market changes; price is set independent of the rest of the marketing mix rather than as an intrinsic element of market-positioning strategy; and price is not varied enough for different product items, market segments, distribution channels, and purchase occasions.

Companies do their pricing in a variety of ways. In small companies, prices are often set by the boss. In large companies, pricing is handled by division and product-line managers. Even here, top management sets general pricing objectives and policies and often approves the prices proposed by lower levels of management. In industries where pricing is a key factor (aerospace, railroads, oil companies), companies will often establish a pricing department to set or assist others in determining appropriate prices. This department reports to the marketing department, finance department, or top management. Others who exert an influence on pricing include sales managers, production managers, finance managers, and accountants.

setting the price

A firm must set a price for the first time when it develops a new product, when it introduces its regular product into a new distribution channel or geographical area, and when it enters bids on new contract work. The firm must decide where to position its product on quality and price. In some markets, such as the auto market, as many as eight price points can be found:

Segment	Example
Ultimate	Rolls-Royce
Gold Standard	Mercedes-Benz
Luxury	Audi
Special Needs	Volvo
Middle	Buick
Ease/Convenience	Ford Escort
Me Too, but Cheaper	Hyundai
Price Alone	Kia

Marriott Hotels is good at developing different brands for different price points: Marriott Vacation Club—Vacation Villas (highest price), Marriott Marquis (high price), Marriott (high-medium price), Renaissance (medium-high price), Courtyard (medium price), Towne Place Suites (medium-low price), and Fairfield Inn (low price).

There can be competition between price-quality segments. Figure 16.1 shows nine price-quality strategies. The diagonal strategies 1, 5, and 9 can all coexist in the same market; that is, one firm offers a high-quality product at a high price, another offers an average-quality product at an average price, and still another offers a low-quality product at a low price. All three competitors can coexist as long as the market consists of three groups of buyers: those who insist on quality, those who insist on price, and those who balance the two.

Strategies 2, 3, and 6 are ways to attack the diagonal positions. Strategy 2 says, "Our product has the same high quality as product 1 but we charge less." Strategy 3 says the same thing and offers an even greater saving. If quality-sensitive customers believe these competitors, they will sensibly buy from them and save money (unless firm 1's product has acquired snob appeal).

Positioning strategies 4, 7, and 8 amount to overpricing the product in relation to its quality. The customers will feel "taken" and will probably complain or spread bad word of mouth about the company.

---

figure 16.1

Nine Price–Quality Strategies

		Price		
		High	Medium	Low
Product Quality	High	1. Premium strategy	2. High-value strategy	3. Super-value strategy
	Medium	4. Overcharging strategy	5. Medium-value strategy	6. Good-value strategy
	Low	7. Rip-off strategy	8. False economy strategy	9. Economy strategy

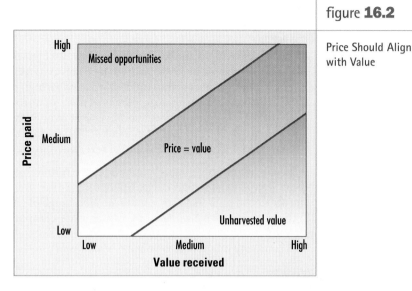

figure **16.2**

Price Should Align
with Value

The company must set its price in relation to the value delivered and perceived by the customer. If the price is higher than the value received, the company will miss potential profits; if the price is lower than the value received, the company will fail to harvest potential profits (see Figure 16.2).

The firm has to consider many factors in setting its pricing policy. We will describe a six-step procedure: (1) selecting the pricing objective; (2) determining demand; (3) estimating costs; (4) analyzing competitors' costs, prices, and offers; (5) selecting a pricing method; and (6) selecting the final price (see Figure 16.3).

step 1: selecting the pricing objective

The company first decides where it wants to position its market offering. The clearer a firm's objectives, the easier it is to set price. A company can pursue any of five major objectives through pricing: survival, maximum current profit, maximum market share, maximum market skimming, or product-quality leadership.

Companies pursue *survival* as their major objective if they are plagued with overcapacity, intense competition, or changing consumer wants. As long as prices cover variable costs and some fixed costs, the company stays in business. Survival is a short-run objective; in the long run, the firm must learn how to add value or face extinction.

Many companies try to set a price that will *maximize current profits*. They estimate the demand and costs associated with alternative prices and choose the price that produces maximum current profit, cash flow, or rate of return on investment. This strategy assumes that the firm has knowledge of its demand and cost functions; in reality, these are difficult to estimate. In emphasizing current performance, the company may sacrifice long-run performance by ignoring the effects of other marketing-mix variables, competitors' reactions, and legal restraints on price.

Some companies want to *maximize their market share*. They believe that a higher sales volume will lead to lower unit costs and higher long-run profit. They set the lowest price, assuming the market is price-sensitive. Texas Instruments (TI) practices this **market-penetration pricing**. TI will build a large plant, set its price as low as possible, win a large market share, experience falling costs, and cut its price further as costs fall. The following conditions favor setting a low price: (1) The market is highly price-sensitive, and a low price stimulates market growth; (2) production and distribution costs fall with accumulated production experience; and (3) a low price discourages actual and potential competition.

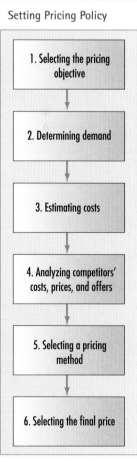

figure **16.3**

Setting Pricing Policy

1. Selecting the pricing objective

2. Determining demand

3. Estimating costs

4. Analyzing competitors' costs, prices, and offers

5. Selecting a pricing method

6. Selecting the final price

Companies unveiling a new technology favor setting high prices to "skim" the market. Sony is a frequent practitioner of *market-skimming pricing.*

Sony When Sony introduced the world's first high-definition television (HDTV) to the Japanese market in 1990, the high-tech sets cost $43,000. These televisions were purchased by customers who could afford to pay a high price for the new technology. Sony rapidly reduced the price over the next three years to attract new buyers, and by 1993 a 28-inch HDTV cost a Japanese buyer just over $6,000. In 2001, a Japanese consumer could buy a 40-inch HDTV for about $2,000, a price many could afford. In this way, Sony skimmed the maximum amount of revenue from the various segments of the market.[2]

Market skimming makes sense under the following conditions: (1) A sufficient number of buyers have a high current demand; (2) the unit costs of producing a small volume are not so high that they cancel the advantage of charging what the traffic will bear; (3) the high initial price does not attract more competitors to the market; (4) the high price communicates the image of a superior product.

A company might aim to be the *product-quality leader* in the market. Consider Maytag.

Maytag Maytag has long built high-quality washing machines and priced them higher than competitors' products (its ads featured the Maytag repairman asleep at the phone because no customers ever call for service). Now, in a change of strategy, Maytag builds on its premium-brand strengths with innovative features and benefits. The objective is to get consumers to buy Maytag appliances with attractive features at a premium price, even though their old machines are still working. To lure the price-sensitive customer, Maytag ran commercials pointing out that washers are custodians of what is often a $400 load of clothes, making them worth the higher price tag. Maytag's new Neptune washers, for example, sell for double what most other washers cost, yet company marketers argue that they use less water and electricity and prolong the life of clothing by being less abrasive.[3]

Maytag's homepage presents its "corporate family of brands."

marketing **insight**

Power Pricers: How Smart Companies Use Price to Achieve Business Strategies

Executives continually complain that pricing is a big headache—and one that is getting worse by the day. Many firms have thrown up their hands with "strategies" like this: "We determine our costs and take our industry's traditional margins." Others have a different attitude: They use price as a key strategic tool. These "power pricers" have discovered the highly leveraged effect of price on the bottom line.

- *Pricing and the value perspective:* Pharmaceutical company Glaxo introduced its ulcer medication Zantac to attack market incumbent Tagamet. The conventional wisdom was that, as the "second one in," Glaxo should price Zantac 10 percent below Tagamet. CEO Paul Girolam knew that Zantac was superior to Tagamet in terms of fewer drug interactions and side effects and more convenient dosing. Glaxo introduced Zantac at a significant price premium over Tagamet and still gained the market-leader position.
- *Customizing price and service based on segment value:* Bugs Burger's Bug Killer price was about five times that of other

firms that do battle with rodents on a commercial property. Bugs got his price premium because he focused on a particularly quality-sensitive segment of the market (hotels and restaurants) and gave them what they valued most: guaranteed pest elimination. Superior value to this chosen segment guided his pricing and enabled him to train and compensate service technicians in a way that motivated them to deliver superior service.

- *Customizing price based on segment cost and competitive situation:* Progressive Insurance collects and analyzes loss data in automobile insurance better than anyone else. Its understanding of what it costs to service various types of customers enables it to serve the lucrative high-risk customer no one else wants to insure. Free of competition and armed with a solid understanding of costs, Progressive makes good profits serving this customer base.

Source: Adapted from Robert J. Dolan and Hermann Simon, "Power Pricers," *Across the Board* (May 1997): 18–19.

Nonprofit and public organizations may adopt other pricing objectives. A university aims for *partial cost recovery*, knowing that it must rely on private gifts and public grants to cover the remaining costs. A nonprofit hospital may aim for full cost recovery in its pricing. A nonprofit theater company may price its productions to fill the maximum number of theater seats. A social service agency may set a service price geared to the income of the client.

Whatever the specific objective, businesses that use price as a strategic tool will profit more than those who simply let costs or the market determine their pricing. (See "Marketing Insight: Power Pricers: How Smart Companies Use Price to Achieve Business Strategies.")

step 2: determining demand

Each price will lead to a different level of demand and therefore have a different impact on a company's marketing objectives. The relation between alternative prices and the resulting current demand is captured in a demand curve (see Figure 16.4). In the normal case, demand and price are inversely related: the higher the price, the lower the demand. In the case of prestige goods, the demand curve sometimes slopes upward. A perfume company raised its price and sold more perfume rather than less! Some consumers take the higher price to signify a better product. However, if the price is too high, the level of demand may fall.

PRICE SENSITIVITY   The demand curve shows the market's probable purchase quantity at alternative prices. It sums the reactions of many individuals who have different price sensitivities. The first step in estimating demand is to understand what affects price sensitivity. Generally speaking, customers are most price-sensitive to products that cost a lot or are bought frequently. They are less price-sensitive to low-cost items or items they buy infrequently. They are also less price-sensitive when price is only a small

figure **16.4**

Inelastic and Elastic
Demand

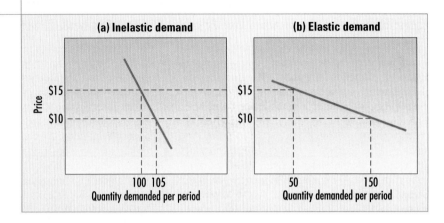

part of the total cost of obtaining, operating, and servicing the product over its lifetime. A seller can charge a higher price than competitors and still get the business if the company can convince the customer that it offers the lowest *total cost of ownership* (TCO).

Companies, of course, prefer to work with customers who are less price-sensitive. Tom Nagle offers the following list of factors associated with lower price sensitivity:

- The product is more distinctive
- Buyers are less aware of substitutes
- Buyers cannot easily compare the quality of substitutes
- The expenditure is a smaller part of the buyer's total income
- The expenditure is small compared to the total cost of the end product
- Part of the cost is borne by another party
- The product is used in conjunction with assets previously bought
- The product is assumed to have more quality, prestige, or exclusiveness
- Buyers cannot store the product[4]

On the other hand, the impact of the Internet has been to increase customers' price sensitivity. In buying a specific book online, for example, a customer can compare the prices offered by over two dozen online bookstores by just clicking mysimon.com. These prices can differ by as much as 20 percent. The Internet increases the opportunity for price-sensitive buyers to find and favor lower-price sites. At the same time, many buyers are not that price-sensitive. McKinsey conducted a study and found that 89 percent of Internet customers visited only one book site, 84 percent visited only one toy site, and 81 percent visited only one music site, which indicates that there is less price-comparison shopping taking place on the Internet than is possible.

Companies need to understand the price sensitivity of their customers and prospects and the trade-offs people are willing to make between price and product characteristics. In the words of marketing consultant Kevin Clancy, those who target only the price-sensitive are "leaving money on the table." Consider Green Mountain Power.

Green Mountain Energy Company   Green Mountain, a Vermont-based electric power company, has shown how a commodity, electric energy, can be brand-differentiated and price-differentiated. Green Mountain produces "green" energy in three grades: green (Eco-Smart), greener (EnviroBlend), and greenest (Nature's Choice). Each is blended differently from natural gas, hydro, wind, and solar energy. The greener the brand, the higher the kilowatt per hour price. Green Mountain conducted extensive marketing research and uncovered a large segment of prospects who would pay more for "greener" energy. It started an e-commerce site in 1997 called GreenMountain.com (now called Green Mountain Energy Company and head-quartered in Austin, Texas) that is currently selling electricity to more than 100,000 customers in Texas, Pennsylvania, New Jersey, and California.[5]

ESTIMATING DEMAND CURVES   Most companies make some attempt to measure their demand curves. They can use different methods.

The first involves statistically analyzing past prices, quantities sold, and other factors to estimate their relationships. The data can be longitudinal (over time) or cross-sectional (different locations at the same time). Building the appropriate model and fitting the data with the proper statistical techniques calls for considerable skill.

The second approach is to conduct price experiments. Bennett and Wilkinson systematically varied the prices of several products sold in a discount store and observed the results.[6] An alternative approach is to charge different prices in similar territories to see how sales are affected. Still another approach is to use the Internet. An e-business could test the impact of a 5 percent price increase by quoting a higher price to every fortieth visitor to compare the purchase response. However, it must do this carefully and not alienate customers, as happened when Amazon price-tested discounts of 30 percent, 35 percent, and 40 percent for DVD buyers, only to find that those receiving the 30 percent discount were upset.[7]

The third approach is to ask buyers to state how many units they would buy at different proposed prices,[8] but buyers might understate their purchase intentions at higher prices to discourage the company from setting higher prices.

In measuring the price–demand relationship, the market researcher must control for various factors that will influence demand. The competitor's response will make a difference. Also, if the company changes other marketing-mix factors besides price, the effect of the price change itself will be hard to isolate. Nagle presents an excellent summary of the various methods for estimating price sensitivity and demand.[9]

PRICE ELASTICITY OF DEMAND   Marketers need to know how responsive, or elastic, demand would be to a change in price. Consider the two demand curves in Figure 16.4. With demand curve (a), a price increase from $10 to $15 leads to a relatively small decline in demand from 105 to 100. With demand curve (b), the same price increase leads to a substantial drop in demand from 150 to 50. If demand hardly changes with a small change in price, we say the demand is *inelastic*. If demand changes considerably, demand is *elastic*. The higher the elasticity, the greater the volume growth with a 1 percent price reduction.

Demand is likely to be less elastic under the following conditions: (1) There are few or no substitutes or competitors; (2) buyers do not readily notice the higher price; (3) buyers are slow to change their buying habits; (4) buyers think the higher prices are justified. If demand is elastic, sellers will consider lowering the price. A lower price will produce more total revenue. This makes sense as long as the costs of producing and selling more units does not increase disproportionately.[10]

The effects of not considering the needs of customers for whom demand is most elastic is illustrated in the following case.

New York's Metropolitan Transit Authority   In 1997, the governor of New York announced that in the following year New York City subway riders would be able to purchase daily, weekly, or monthly passes. Riders who bought passes would also benefit from a discounted fare; for the monthly pass, the benefit kicked in if the pass was used at least 47 times. Yet a *Barron's* journalist pointed out that the special fare did not benefit those whose demand was most elastic, suburban off-peak riders who use the subway the least. Here is how he segmented New York City's subway riders in terms of price elasticity: Commuters' demand curve is perfectly inelastic; no matter what

figure **16.5**

Cost per Unit at Different
Levels of Production
per Period

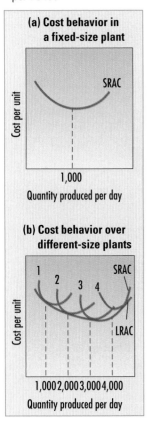

**(a) Cost behavior in
a fixed-size plant**

SRAC

Cost per unit

1,000

Quantity produced per day

**(b) Cost behavior over
different-size plants**

1 2 3 4 SRAC

Cost per unit

LRAC

1,000 2,000 3,000 4,000

Quantity produced per day

happens to the fare, these people must get to work and get back home. There are also commuters who live in the city and who might use the subway for other activities if the fare were lowered. Their demand is more elastic. Suburban off-peak riders' demand is the most elastic.[11]

Price elasticity depends on the magnitude and direction of the contemplated price change. It may be negligible with a small price change and substantial with a large price change. It may differ for a price cut versus a price increase, and there may be a *price indifference band* within which price changes have little or no effect. A McKinsey pricing study estimated that the price indifference band can range as large as 17 percent for mouthwash, 13 percent for batteries, 9 percent for small appliances, and 2 percent for certificates of deposit.

Finally, long-run price elasticity may differ from short-run elasticity. Buyers may continue to buy from a current supplier after a price increase, but they may eventually switch suppliers. Here demand is more elastic in the long run than in the short run, or the reverse may happen: Buyers may drop a supplier after being notified of a price increase but return later. The distinction between short-run and long-run elasticity means that sellers will not know the total effect of a price change until time passes.

step 3: estimating costs

Demand sets a ceiling on the price the company can charge for its product. Costs set the floor. The company wants to charge a price that covers its cost of producing, distributing, and selling the product, including a fair return for its effort and risk.

TYPES OF COSTS AND LEVELS OF PRODUCTION   A company's costs take two forms, fixed and variable. **Fixed costs** (also known as **overhead**) are costs that do not vary with production or sales revenue. A company must pay bills each month for rent, heat, interest, salaries, and so on, regardless of output.

Variable costs vary directly with the level of production. For example, each hand calculator produced by Texas Instruments involves a cost of plastic, microprocessing chips, packaging, and the like. These costs tend to be constant per unit produced. They are called variable because their total varies with the number of units produced.

Total costs consist of the sum of the fixed and variable costs for any given level of production. **Average cost** is the cost per unit at that level of production; it is equal to total costs divided by production. Management wants to charge a price that will at least cover the total production costs at a given level of production.

To price intelligently, management needs to know how its costs vary with different levels of production. Take the case in which a company such as TI has built a fixed-size plant to produce 1,000 hand calculators a day. The cost per unit is high if few units are produced per day. As production approaches 1,000 units per day, average cost falls. The reason is that the fixed costs are spread over more units. Average cost increases after 1,000 units, because the plant becomes inefficient: Workers have to queue for machines, machines break down more often, and workers get in each other's way (see Figure 16.5.[a]).

If TI believes it can sell 2,000 units per day, it should consider building a larger plant. The plant will use more efficient machinery and work arrangements, and the unit cost of producing 2,000 units per day will be less than the unit cost of producing 1,000 units per day. This is shown in the long-run average cost curve in Figure 16.5 (b). In fact, a 3,000-capacity plant would be even more efficient according to Figure 16.5 (b), but a 4,000-daily production plant would be less efficient because of increasing diseconomies of scale: There are too many workers to manage, and paperwork slows things down. Figure 16.5 (b) indicates that a 3,000-daily production plant is the optimal size if demand is strong enough to support this level of production.

ACCUMULATED PRODUCTION   Suppose TI runs a plant that produces 3,000 hand calculators per day. As TI gains experience producing hand calculators, its methods

figure **16.6**

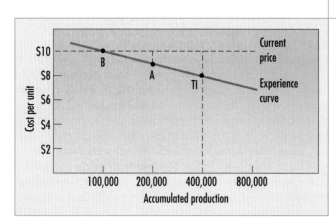

improve. Workers learn shortcuts, materials flow more smoothly, procurement costs fall. The result, as Figure 16.6 shows, is that average cost falls with accumulated production experience. Thus the average cost of producing the first 100,000 hand calculators is $10 per calculator. When the company has produced the first 200,000 calculators, the average cost has fallen to $9. After its accumulated production experience doubles again to 400,000, the average cost is $8. This decline in the average cost with accumulated production experience is called the experience curve or **learning curve.**

Now suppose three firms compete in this industry, TI, A, and B. TI is the lowest-cost producer at $8, having produced 400,000 units in the past. If all three firms sell the calculator for $10, TI makes $2 profit per unit, A makes $1 per unit, and B breaks even. The smart move for TI would be to lower its price to $9. This will drive B out of the market, and even A will consider leaving. TI will pick up the business that would have gone to B (and possibly A). Furthermore, price-sensitive customers will enter the market at the lower price. As production increases beyond 400,000 units, TI's costs will drop still further and faster and more than restore its profits, even at a price of $9. TI has used this aggressive pricing strategy repeatedly to gain market share and drive others out of the industry.

Experience-curve pricing nevertheless carries major risks. Aggressive pricing might give the product a cheap image. The strategy also assumes that the competitors are weak. Finally, the strategy leads the company into building more plants to meet demand while a competitor innovates a lower-cost technology and obtains lower costs than the market-leader company, which is now stuck with the old technology.

Most experience-curve pricing has focused on manufacturing costs, but all costs, including marketing costs, can be improved on. If three firms are each investing a large sum of money in telemarketing, the firm that has used it the longest might achieve the lowest costs. This firm can charge a little less for its product and still earn the same return, all other costs being equal.[12]

DIFFERENTIATED MARKETING OFFERS   Today's companies try to adapt their offers and terms to different buyers. Thus a manufacturer will negotiate different terms with different retail chains. One retailer may want daily delivery (to keep stock lower) while another may accept twice-a-week delivery in order to get a lower price. The manufacturer's costs will differ with each chain, and so will its profits. To estimate the real profitability of dealing with different retailers, the manufacturer needs to use **activity-based cost (ABC) accounting** instead of standard cost accounting.[13]

ABC accounting tries to identify the real costs associated with serving each customer. Both variable and overhead costs must be tagged back to each customer. Companies that

figure **16.7**

The Three Cs Model for
Price Setting

fail to measure their costs correctly are not measuring their profit correctly. They are likely to misallocate their marketing effort. Identifying the true costs arising in a customer relationship also enables a company to explain its charges to the customer.

TARGET COSTING   Costs change with production scale and experience. They can also change as a result of a concentrated effort by designers, engineers, and purchasing agents to reduce them. The Japanese use a method called **target costing**.[14] They use market research to establish a new product's desired functions. Then they determine the price at which the product will sell, given its appeal and competitors' prices. They deduct the desired profit margin from this price, and this leaves the target cost they must achieve. They then examine each cost element—design, engineering, manufacturing, sales. They consider ways to reengineer components, eliminate functions, and bring down supplier costs. The objective is to bring the final cost projections into the target cost range. If they cannot succeed, they may decide against developing the product because it could not sell for the target price and make the target profit. When they can succeed, profits are likely to follow.

step 4: analyzing competitors' costs, prices, and offers

Within the range of possible prices determined by market demand and company costs, the firm must take the competitors' costs, prices, and possible price reactions into account. The firm should first consider the nearest competitor's price. If the firm's offer contains positive differentiation features not offered by the nearest competitor, their worth to the customer should be evaluated and added to the competitor's price. If the competitor's offer contains some features not offered by the firm, their worth to the customer should be evaluated and subtracted from the firm's price. Now the firm can decide whether it can charge more, the same, or less than the competitor. The firm must be aware, however, that competitors can change their prices in reaction to the price set by the firm.

step 5: selecting a pricing method

Given the three Cs—the customers' demand schedule, the cost function, and competitors' prices—the company is now ready to select a price. Figure 16.7 summarizes the three major considerations in price setting. Costs set a floor to the price. Competitors' prices and the price of substitutes provide an orienting point. Customers' assessment of unique product features establishes the ceiling price.

Companies select a pricing method that includes one or more of these three considerations. We will examine seven price-setting methods: markup pricing, target-return pricing, perceived-value pricing, value pricing, going-rate pricing, auction-type pricing, and group pricing.

MARKUP PRICING   The most elementary pricing method is to add a standard **markup** to the product's cost. Construction companies submit job bids by estimating the total project cost and adding a standard markup for profit. Lawyers and accountants typically price by adding a standard markup on their time and costs.

Suppose a toaster manufacturer has the following costs and sales expectations:

Variable cost per unit	$ 10
Fixed cost	300,000
Expected unit sales	50,000

The manufacturer's unit cost is given by:

$$\text{Unit cost} = \text{variable cost} + \frac{\text{fixed cost}}{\text{unit sales}} = \$10 + \frac{\$300,000}{50,000} = \$16$$

Now assume the manufacturer wants to earn a 20 percent markup on sales. The manufacturer's markup price is given by:

$$\text{Markup price} = \frac{\text{unit cost}}{(1 - \text{desired return on sales})} = \frac{\$16}{1 - 0.2} = \$20$$

The manufacturer would charge dealers $20 per toaster and make a profit of $4 per unit. The dealers in turn will mark up the toaster. If dealers want to earn 50 percent on their selling price, they will mark up the toaster to $40. This is equivalent to a cost markup of 100 percent.

Markups are generally higher on seasonal items (to cover the risk of not selling), specialty items, slower-moving items, items with high storage and handling costs, and demand-inelastic items, such as prescription drugs. In the case of prescription drugs, generic (non-brand-name) drugs command an extraordinarily high markup:

Generic Drugs Drugstores and pharmacies are marking up the price of some generics by more than 1,000 percent. For example, stores charge an average of $18.08 for a prescription of the generic version of the antipsychotic drug Haldol, 2,800 percent more than the $.62 cost the generic manufacturer charges. A prescription for the generic version of Zovirax, an antiviral drug, sold at pharmacies for an average of $61.64, more than eight times the manufacturer's price of $7.22. Not only do pharmacies pocket a handsome profit, but they look like good guys when they encourage customers to use a generic to save money. Indeed, the generic is still cheaper than the brand-name counterpart. In 1999, a prescription for the generic version of the anti-anxiety drug Xanax cost an average of $17.23, versus $58.70 for the name-brand product, and the generic version of ulcer medication Zantac averaged $42.19 per prescription, versus $96.75 for the branded drug.[15]

Does the use of standard markups make logical sense? Generally, no. Any pricing method that ignores current demand, perceived value, and competition is not likely to lead to the optimal price. Markup pricing works only if the marked-up price actually brings in the expected level of sales.

Companies introducing a new product often price it high hoping to recover their costs as rapidly as possible, but this strategy could be fatal if a competitor is pricing low. This happened to Philips, the Dutch electronics manufacturer, in pricing its videodisc players. Philips wanted to make a profit on each player. Japanese competitors priced low and succeeded in building their market share rapidly, which in turn pushed down their costs substantially.

Still, markup pricing remains popular for a number of reasons. First, sellers can determine costs much more easily than they can estimate demand. By tying the price to cost, sellers simplify the pricing task. Second, where all firms in the industry use this pricing method, prices tend to be similar. Price competition is therefore minimized, which would not be the case if firms paid attention to demand variations. Third, many people feel that cost-plus pricing is fairer to both buyers and sellers. Sellers do not take advantage of buyers when the latter's demand becomes acute, and sellers earn a fair return on investment.

TARGET–RETURN PRICING   In **target-return pricing**, the firm determines the price that would yield its target rate of return on investment (ROI). Target pricing is used by General Motors, which prices its automobiles to achieve a 15 to 20 percent ROI. This method is also used by public utilities, which need to make a fair return on their investment.

Suppose the toaster manufacturer has invested $1 million in the business and wants to set a price to earn a 20 percent ROI, specifically $200,000. The target-return price is given by the following formula:

$$\text{Target-return price} = \text{unit cost} + \frac{\text{desired return} \times \text{invested capital}}{\text{unit sales}}$$

$$= \$16 + \frac{.20 \times \$1,000,000}{\$50,000} = \$20$$

The manufacturer will realize this 20 percent ROI provided its costs and estimated sales turn out to be accurate, but what if sales do not reach 50,000 units? The manufacturer can prepare a break-even chart to learn what would happen at other sales levels (see Figure 16.8). Fixed

figure **16.8**

Break–Even Chart for Determining Target–Return Price and Break–Even Volume

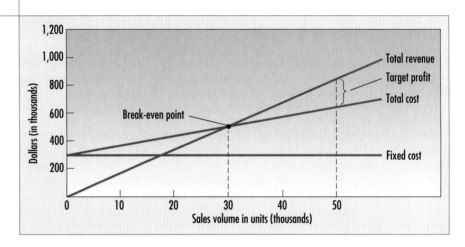

costs are $300,000 regardless of sales volume. Variable costs, not shown in the figure, rise with volume. Total costs equal the sum of fixed costs and variable costs. The total revenue curve starts at zero and rises with each unit sold.

The total revenue and total cost curves cross at 30,000 units. This is the break-even volume. It can be verified by the following formula:

$$\text{Break-even volume} = \frac{\text{fixed cost}}{(\text{price} - \text{variable cost})} = \frac{\$300,000}{\$20 - \$10} = 30,000$$

The manufacturer, of course, is hoping that the market will buy 50,000 units at $20, in which case it earns $200,000 on its $1 million investment, but much depends on price elasticity and competitors' prices. Unfortunately, target-return pricing tends to ignore these considerations. The manufacturer needs to consider different prices and estimate their probable impacts on sales volume and profits. The manufacturer should also search for ways to lower its fixed or variable costs, because lower costs will decrease its required break-even volume.

PERCEIVED-VALUE PRICING   An increasing number of companies base their price on the customer's **perceived value.** They must deliver the value promised by their value proposition, and the customer must perceive this value. They use the other marketing-mix elements, such as advertising and sales force, to communicate and enhance perceived value in buyers' minds.[16]

Perceived value is made up of several elements, such as the buyer's image of the product performance, the channel deliverables, the warranty quality, customer support, and softer attributes such as the supplier's reputation, trustworthiness, and esteem. Furthermore, each potential customer places different weights on these different elements, with the result that some will be *price buyers*, others will be *value buyers*, and still others will be *loyal buyers*. Companies need different strategies for these three groups. For price buyers, companies need to offer stripped-down products and reduced services. For value buyers, companies must keep innovating new value and aggressively reaffirming their value. For loyal buyers, companies must invest in relationship building and customer intimacy.

DuPont is a major practitioner of perceived-value pricing. When DuPont developed its new synthetic fiber for carpets, it demonstrated to carpet manufacturers that they could afford to pay DuPont as much as $1.40 per pound for the new fiber and still make their target profit. DuPont calls the $1.40 the *value-in-use price*, but pricing the new material at $1.40 per pound would leave the carpet manufacturers indifferent. So it set the price lower than $1.40 to induce manufacturers to adopt. DuPont did not use its manufacturing cost to set the price, but only to judge whether there was enough profit to go ahead in the first place. DuPont also embeds each chemical into a larger offering so that it is not seen as a commodity but rather as a solution to a customer's problem. Consider the following:

Attribute	Standard Offer	Premium Offer	Added Value
Quality	Impurities less than ten parts per million	Impurities less than one part per million	$1.40
Delivery	Within two weeks	Within one week	.15
System	Supply chemical only	Supply total system	.80
Innovation	Little R&D support	High level R&D support	2.00
Retraining	Train initially	Retrain on request	.40
Service	Through home office purchases	Locally available	.25
Price	$100/pound	$105/pound	$5.00

The chemical is part of a standard offer or a premium offer. The customer who wants the premium offer pays $105 instead of $100 a pound. The customer may end up requesting fewer added values. DuPont is willing to unbundle the premium offer and charge only for the chosen added values. Here is yet another example of DuPont's perceived value pricing approach.

DuPont DuPont educated its customers about the true value of its higher-grade polyethylene resin called Alathon. Instead of claiming only that pipes made from it were 5 percent more durable, DuPont produced a detailed analysis of the comparative costs of installing and maintaining in-ground irrigation pipe. The real savings came from the diminished need to pay the labor and crop damage costs associated with digging up and replacing the underground pipe. DuPont was able to charge 7 percent more and still see its sales double the following year.

Caterpillar also uses perceived value to set prices on its construction equipment. It might price its tractor at $100,000, although a similar competitor's tractor might be priced at $90,000. When a prospective customer asks a Caterpillar dealer why he should pay $10,000 more for the Caterpillar tractor, the dealer answers:

$ 90,000	is the tractor's price if it is only equivalent to the competitor's tractor
$ 7,000	is the price premium for Caterpillar's superior durability
$ 6,000	is the price premium for Caterpillar's superior reliability
$ 5,000	is the price premium for Caterpillar's superior service
$ 2,000	is the price premium for Caterpillar's longer warranty on parts
$ 110,000	is the normal price to cover Caterpillar's superior value
−$ 10,000	discount
$100,000	final price

The Caterpillar dealer is able to indicate why Caterpillar's tractor delivers more value than the competitor's. Although the customer is asked to pay a $10,000 premium, he is actually getting $20,000 extra value! He chooses the Caterpillar tractor because he is convinced that its lifetime operating costs will be lower.

The Scott Company is also a perceived-value marketer.

Scott Company Scott has created a new lawn care fertilizer that retards grass growth so that a homeowner can mow the lawn only once a month, instead of four times a month. If the homeowner spent $15 per week or $60 a month to cut the grass, he would be better off buying the new fertilizer if it is priced, say, at $40. He would save \$20 (\$60 − \$40 = \$20) a month. Note that Scott is basing its price on perceived value, not on the cost of producing the new fertilizer.

Yet even when a company claims that its offering delivers more total value, not all customers will respond positively. First, there is always a segment of buyers who care only about the price. Second, there are other buyers who suspect that the company is exaggerating its product quality and services. One company installed its software system in one or two plants operated by a company. The substantial and well-documented cost savings convinced the customer to buy the software for its other plants.

The key to perceived-value pricing is to deliver more value than the competitor and demonstrate this to prospective buyers. Basically, a company needs to research the customer's value drivers and understand the customer's decision-making process. The company can try to determine the value of its offering in several ways: managerial judgments within the company, value of analogous products, focus groups, surveys, experimentation, analysis of historical data, and conjoint analysis.[17]

VALUE PRICING In recent years, several companies have adopted **value pricing**, in which they win loyal customers by charging a fairly low price for a high-quality offering. Among the best practitioners of value pricing are Wal-Mart, IKEA, and Southwest Airlines. Here are two other value pricers.

Enterprise Rent-A-Car The world's largest car rental firm is not Hertz; Enterprise Rent-A-Car passed Hertz in 1996. Enterprise manages a rental fleet of nearly 500,000 vehicles from almost 4,000 rental offices that are no further than a 15-minute drive from 90 percent of the U.S. population. One of the chief draws of the company is that it charges less than its better-known competitors. It can do this for a number of reasons. First, it locates its offices in low-rent areas. Second, it works closely with insurance companies to rent cars to people whose cars have been in an accident; the typical rental period is 10 to 12 days, resulting in lower transaction costs. Third, its sales are steadier because accidents happen pretty much throughout the year.

Standard Hotel This Los Angeles hotel has beige shag carpeting lining the lobby's floor and walls, Charles Eames tables, and minimalistic décor similar to nearby Sunset Boulevard hotels that charge \$400 a night. Rooms here start at \$99! Occupancy has been running at 95 percent since the hotel opened in March 1999, and the hotel plans to expand to New York and Chicago.

A few years ago Procter & Gamble created quite a stir by reducing prices on Pampers and Luvs diapers, liquid Tide detergent, and Folger's coffee to value price them. In the past, a brand-loyal family had to pay what amounted to a \$725 premium for a year's worth of P&G products versus private-label or low-priced brands. To offer value prices, P&G underwent a major overhaul. It redesigned the way it develops, manufactures, distributes, prices, markets, and sells products to deliver better value at every point in the supply chain.[18] Value pricing is not a matter of simply setting lower prices; it is a matter of reengineering the company's operations to become a low-cost producer without sacrificing quality, and lowering prices significantly to attract a large number of value-conscious customers.

An important type of value pricing is **everyday low pricing (EDLP)**, which takes place at the retail level. A retailer who holds to an EDLP pricing policy charges a constant low price with little or no price promotions and special sales. These constant prices eliminate week-to-week price uncertainty and can be contrasted to the "high-low" pricing of promotion-oriented competitors. In **high-low pricing**, the retailer charges higher prices on an everyday basis but then runs frequent promotions in which prices are temporarily lowered below the EDLP level.[19]

In recent years, high-low pricing has given way to EDLP at such widely different venues as General Motors' Saturn car dealerships and upscale department stores such as Nordstrom; but the king of EDLP is surely Wal-Mart, which practically defined the term. Except for a few sale items every month, Wal-Mart promises everyday low prices on major brands. "It's not a short-term strategy," says one Wal-Mart executive. "You have to be willing to make a commitment to it, and you have to be able to operate with lower ratios of expense than everybody else."

The most important reason retailers adopt EDLP is that constant sales and promotions are costly and have eroded consumer confidence in the credibility of everyday shelf prices. Consumers also have less time and patience for such time-honored traditions as watching for supermarket specials and clipping coupons. Yet, there is no denying that promotions create excitement and draw shoppers. For this reason, EDLP is not a guarantee of success. As supermarkets face heightened competition from their counterparts and from alternative channels, many find that the key to drawing shoppers is using a combination of high-low and everyday low pricing strategies, with increased advertising and promotions.[20]

GOING-RATE PRICING In **going-rate pricing**, the firm bases its price largely on competitors' prices. The firm might charge the same, more, or less than major competitor(s). In oligopolistic industries that sell a commodity such as steel, paper, or fertilizer, firms normally charge the same price. The smaller firms "follow the leader," changing their prices when the market leader's prices change rather than when their own demand or costs change. Some firms may charge a slight premium or slight discount, but they preserve the amount of difference. Thus minor gasoline retailers usually charge a few cents less per gallon than the major oil companies, without letting the difference increase or decrease.

Going-rate pricing is quite popular. Where costs are difficult to measure or competitive response is uncertain, firms feel that the going price is a good solution because it is thought to reflect the industry's collective wisdom.

AUCTION-TYPE PRICING Auction-type pricing is growing more popular, especially with the growth of the Internet. There are over 2,000 electronic marketplaces selling everything from pigs to used vehicles to cargo to chemicals. One major use of auctions is to dispose of excess inventories or used goods. Companies need to be aware of the three major types of auctions and their separate pricing procedures.

- *English auctions (ascending bids).* One seller and many buyers. The seller puts up an item and bidders raise the offer price until the top price is reached. English auctions are being used today for selling antiques, cattle, real estate, and used equipment and vehicles.
- *Dutch auctions (descending bids).* One seller and many buyers, or one buyer and many sellers. In the first kind, an auctioneer announces a high price for a product and then slowly decreases the price until a bidder accepts the price. In the other, the buyer announces something that he wants to buy and then potential sellers compete to get the sale by offering the lowest price. Each seller sees what the last bid is and decides whether to go lower. General Electric uses its Trade Processing Network (TPN) to announce items that it wants to buy and sets a time limit for receiving bids. It accepts the lowest bid providing that other things are equal. As another example, the state of Pennsylvania wanted to buy rock salt and went on FreeMarkets.com. Over 600 bids came in from 9 bidders during the day, reducing the cost of rock salt by 7 percent and saving $2.5 million for the taxpayers of Pennsylvania.
- *Sealed-bid auctions.* Would-be suppliers can submit only one bid and cannot know the other bids. The U.S. government often uses this method to procure supplies. A supplier will not bid below its cost but cannot bid too high for fear of losing the job. The net effect of these two pulls can be described in terms of the bid's *expected profit* (see Table 16.1). Suppose a bid of $9,500 would yield a high chance of getting the contract (say 81 percent) but only a low profit, say $100. The expected profit is therefore $81 (= $100 x .81). If the seller bid $11,000, its expected profit would only be $16 (= $1,600 x .01). According to Table 16.1, the best bid would be $10,000, for which the expected profit is $216. Using

table **16.1**				
Effect of Different Bids on Expected Profit	**Company's Bid**	**Company's Profit**	**Probability of Getting Award with This Bid (Assumed)**	**Expected Profit**
	$ 9,500	$ 100	0.81	$ 81
	10,000	600	0.36	216
	10,500	1,100	0.09	99
	11,000	1,600	0.01	16

expected profit for setting price makes sense for the seller that makes many bids. The seller who bids only occasionally or who needs a particular contract badly will not find it advantageous to use expected profit. This criterion does not distinguish between a $1,000 profit with a 0.10 probability and a $125 profit with an 0.80 probability. Yet the firm that wants to keep production going would prefer the second contract to the first.

GROUP PRICING   The Internet is facilitating a method whereby consumers and business buyers can join groups to buy at a lower price. Consumers can go to Volumebuy.com to buy electronics, computers, subscriptions, and other items. When a consumer finds a desired product, he or she will see the current *pool price*, which is a function of the number of orders received so far. The Web page may also indicate that if (say) three more orders were to come, the price would fall by a specified amount. A major drawback is that some buyers will not wait for the volume order to be executed.

www.volumebuy.com: group or pool pricing?

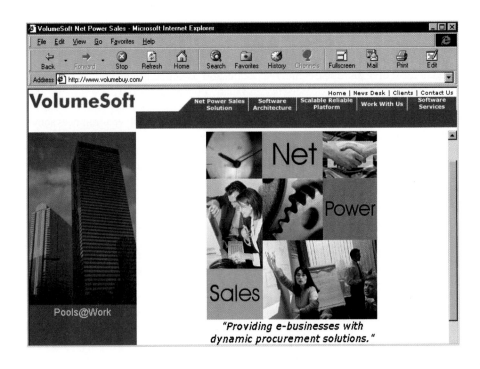

step 6: selecting the final price

Pricing methods narrow the range from which the company must select its final price. In selecting that price, the company must consider additional factors, including psychological pricing, gain-and-risk-sharing pricing, the influence of other marketing-mix elements on price, company pricing policies, and the impact of price on other parties.

PSYCHOLOGICAL PRICING   Many consumers use price as an indicator of quality. Image pricing is especially effective with ego-sensitive products such as perfumes and expensive cars. A $100 bottle of perfume might contain $10 worth of scent, but gift givers pay $100 to communicate their high regard for the receiver.

Price and quality perceptions of cars interact.[21] Higher-priced cars are perceived to possess high quality. Higher-quality cars are likewise perceived to be higher priced than they actually are. When alternative information about true quality is available, price becomes a less significant indicator of quality. When this information is not available, price acts as a signal of quality.

When looking at a particular product, buyers carry in their minds a **reference price** formed by noticing current prices, past prices, or the buying context. Sellers often manipulate these reference prices. For example, a seller can situate its product among expensive products to imply that it belongs in the same class. Department stores will display women's apparel in separate departments differentiated by price; dresses found in the more expensive department are assumed to be of better quality. Reference-price thinking is also created by stating a high manufacturer's suggested price, or by indicating that the product was priced much higher originally, or by pointing to a competitor's high price.[22]

Many sellers believe that prices should end in an odd number. Many customers see a stereo amplifier priced at $299 instead of $300 as a price in the $200 range rather than $300 range. Another explanation is that odd endings convey the notion of a discount or bargain, but if a company wants a high-price image instead of a low-price image, it should avoid the odd-ending tactic.[23]

GAIN-AND-RISK-SHARING PRICING   Buyers may resist accepting a seller's proposal because of a high perceived level of risk. The seller has the option of offering to absorb part or all of the risk if he does not deliver the full promised value. Consider the following.

Baxter Healthcare   Baxter, a leading medical products firm, approached Columbia/HCA, a leading health care provider, with an offer to develop an information management system that would save Columbia several million dollars over an eight-year period. When Columbia balked, Baxter then offered to guarantee the savings; if they were not realized, Baxter would write a check for the difference. Baxter got the order!

Baxter could have gone further and proposed that if Baxter's information system saved Columbia more than the targeted amount, Baxter would share in 30 percent of the additional savings. This would amount to offering to share in the gain as well as the risk. An increasing number of companies, especially business marketers who promise great savings with their equipment, may have to stand ready to guarantee the promised savings, and possibly participate if the gains are much greater than expected.

THE INFLUENCE OF OTHER MARKETING-MIX ELEMENTS   The final price must take into account the brand's quality and advertising relative to competition. Farris and Reibstein examined the relationships among relative price, relative quality, and relative advertising for 227 consumer businesses, and found the following:

- Brands with average relative quality but high relative advertising budgets were able to charge premium prices. Consumers apparently were willing to pay higher prices for known products than for unknown products.

- Brands with high relative quality and high relative advertising obtained the highest prices. Conversely, brands with low quality and low advertising charged the lowest prices.
- The positive relationship between high prices and high advertising held most strongly in the later stages of the product life cycle for market leaders.[24]

These findings suggest that price is not as important as quality and other benefits in the market offering. One study asked consumers to rate the importance of price and other attributes in using online retailing. Only 19 percent cared about price; far more cared about customer support (65 percent), on-time delivery (58 percent), and product shipping and handling (49 percent).[25]

COMPANY PRICING POLICIES The price must be consistent with company pricing policies. At the same time, companies are not averse to establishing pricing penalties under certain circumstances.[26]

Airlines charge $75 to those who change their reservations on discount tickets. Banks charge fees for too many withdrawals in a month or for early withdrawal of a certificate of deposit. Car rental companies charge $50-100 penalties for no shows for specialty vehicles. Although these policies are often justifiable, they must be used judiciously so as not to unnecessarily alienate customers.

Many companies set up a pricing department to develop policies and establish or approve decisions. The aim is to ensure that the salespeople quote prices that are reasonable to customers and profitable to the company. Dell Computer has developed innovative pricing techniques.

Dell Dell uses a high-tech "cost-forecasting" system that enables it to scale its selling prices based on consumer demand and the company's own costs. The company instituted this flexible pricing model in 2001 to maximize its margins during the economic slowdown. Dell managers get cost information from suppliers, which they then combine with knowledge about profit targets, delivery dates, and competition to set prices for business segments. On any given day, the same computer might sell at different prices depending on whether the purchaser is a government, small business, or home PC buyer. The cost-forecasting system may help to explain why Dell was the only U.S. PC maker among the top six to report a profit for the first quarter of 2001.[27]

IMPACT OF PRICE ON OTHER PARTIES Management must also consider the reactions of other parties to the contemplated price. How will distributors and dealers feel about it? Will the sales force be willing to sell at that price? How will competitors react? Will suppliers raise their prices when they see the company's price? Will the government intervene and prevent this price from being charged?

In the last case, marketers need to know the laws regulating pricing. U.S. legislation states that sellers must set prices without talking to competitors: Price-fixing is illegal. Many federal and state statutes protect consumers against deceptive pricing practices. For example, it is illegal for a company to set artificially high "regular" prices, then announce a "sale" at prices close to previous everyday prices.

adapting the price

Companies usually do not set a single price, but rather a pricing structure that reflects variations in geographical demand and costs, market-segment requirements, purchase timing, order levels, delivery frequency, guarantees, service contracts, and other factors. As a result of discounts, allowances, and promotional support, a company rarely realizes the same profit from each unit of a product that it sells. Here we will examine several price-adaptation strategies: geographical pricing, price discounts and allowances, promotional pricing, discriminatory pricing, and product-mix pricing.

geographical pricing (cash, countertrade, barter)

Geographical pricing involves the company in deciding how to price its products to different customers in different locations and countries. For example, should the company charge higher prices to distant customers to cover the higher shipping costs or a lower price to win additional business? Another issue is how to get paid. This issue is critical when buyers lack sufficient hard currency to pay for their purchases. Many buyers want to offer other items in payment, a practice known as **countertrade**. American companies are often forced to engage in countertrade if they want the business. Countertrade may account for 15 to 25 percent of world trade and takes several forms:[28] barter, compensation deals, buyback agreements, and offset.

- *Barter:* The direct exchange of goods, with no money and no third party involved. In 1993, Eminence S.A., one of France's major clothing makers, launched a five-year deal to barter $25 million worth of U.S.–produced underwear and sportswear to customers in eastern Europe, in exchange for a variety of goods and services, including global transportation and advertising space in eastern European magazines.

- *Compensation deal:* The seller receives some percentage of the payment in cash and the rest in products. A British aircraft manufacturer sold planes to Brazil for 70 percent cash and the rest in coffee.

- *Buyback arrangement:* The seller sells a plant, equipment, or technology to another country and agrees to accept as partial payment products manufactured with the supplied equipment. A U.S. chemical company built a plant for an Indian company and accepted partial payment in cash and the remainder in chemicals manufactured at the plant.

- *Offset:* The seller receives full payment in cash but agrees to spend a substantial amount of the money in that country within a stated time period. For example, PepsiCo sells its cola syrup to Russia for rubles and agrees to buy Russian vodka at a certain rate for sale in the United States.

More complex countertrade deals involve more than two parties. For example, Daimler-Benz agreed to sell 30 trucks to Romania and accept in exchange 150 Romanian-made jeeps, which it sold in Ecuador for bananas, which in turn were sold to a German supermarket chain for Deutsche marks. Through this circuitous transaction, Daimler-Benz finally achieved payment in German currency. Deals such as this are carried on by a separate countertrade department within the company. Other companies rely on barter houses and countertrade specialists.

price discounts and allowances

Most companies will adjust their list price and give discounts and allowances for early payment, volume purchases, and off-season buying (see Table 16.2). Companies must do this carefully or find that their profits are much less than planned.[29]

Jack Trout, author of *Positioning*, cautions that some product categories tend to self-destruct by always being on sale. Mink coats and mattresses, says Trout, never seem to be sold at anything near list price, and when automakers get rebate-happy, the market just sits back and waits for a deal. (See "Marketing Memo: Commandments of Discounting" for Trout's discounting directives.) Discount pricing has become the modus operandi of a surprising number of companies offering both products and services. Even Pepsi and Coke, two of the most popular brands in the world, engaged in a price war that ultimately tarnished their brand equity.[30]

Kevin Clancy, chairman of Copernicus, a major marketing research and consulting firm, found that only between 15 and 35 percent of buyers in most categories are price-sensitive. People with higher incomes and higher product involvement willingly pay more for features, customer service, quality, added convenience, and the brand name. So it can be a mistake for a strong, distinctive brand to plunge into price discounting to respond to low-price attacks.[31]

Marketing MEMO

Commandments of Discounting

- Thou shalt not offer discounts because everyone else does.
- Thou should be creative with your discounting.
- Thou should use discounts to clear stocks or generate extra business.
- Thou should put time limits on the deal.
- Thou should make sure the ultimate customer gets the deal.
- Thou should discount only to survive in a mature market.
- Thou should stop discounting as soon as you can.

Source: Reprinted from Jack Trout, "Prices: Simple Guidelines to Get Them Right," *Journal of Business Strategy* (November–December 1998): 13–16.

table **16.2**		
Price Discounts and Allowances	**Cash Discount:**	A price reduction to buyers who pay bills promptly. A typical example is "2/10, net 30," which means that payment is due within 30 days and that the buyer can deduct 2 percent by paying the bill within 10 days.
	Quantity Discount:	A price reduction to those who buy large volumes. A typical example is "$10 per unit for less than 100 units; $9 per unit for 100 or more units." Quantity discounts must be offered equally to all customers and must not exceed the cost savings to the seller. They can be offered on each order placed or on the number of units ordered over a given period.
	Functional Discount:	Discount (also called *trade discount*) offered by a manufacturer to trade-channel members if they will perform certain functions, such as selling, storing, and recordkeeping. Manufacturers must offer the same functional discounts within each channel.
	Seasonal Discount:	A price reduction to those who buy merchandise or services out of season. Hotels, motels, and airlines offer seasonal discounts in slow selling periods.
	Allowance:	An extra payment designed to gain reseller participation in special programs. *Trade-in allowances* are granted for turning in an old item when buying a new one. *Promotional allowances* reward dealers for participating in advertising and sales support programs.

Salespeople, in particular, are quick to give discounts in order to close a sale, but the word gets around fast that the company's list price is "soft," and discounting becomes the norm. The discounts undermine the value perceptions of the offerings.

At the same time, discounting can be a useful tool if the company can gain some concession in return:

■ the customer agrees to sign a three-year contract
■ the customer is willing to order electronically, thus saving the company money
■ the customer agrees to buy in truckload quantities

Sales management needs to monitor the proportion of customers who are receiving discounts, the average discount, and the particular salespeople who are overrelying on discounting. Higher levels of management should conduct a **net price analysis** to arrive at the "real price" of their offering. The real price is affected not only by discounts, but by many other expenses (see promotional pricing below) that reduce the realized price: Suppose the company's list price is $3,000. The average discount is $300. The company's promotional spending averages $450 (15% of the list price). Co-op advertising money of $150 is given to retailers to back the product. The company's net price is $2,100, not $3,000.

Companies in an overcapacity situation are tempted to give discounts. For example, they may agree to supply a retailer with a store brand version of their product at a deep discount. The store brand, being priced lower, may start making inroads on the manufacturer's brand. Now the manufacturer has more overcapacity and may accept a larger order from the retailer. Eventually, the manufacturer's brand may wither away and the manufacturer may become totally dependent on supplying the store brand. Manufacturers should stop to consider the implications of supplying product at a discount to retailers because they may end up losing long-run profits in an effort to meet short-run volume goals.

promotional pricing

Companies can use several pricing techniques to stimulate early purchase:

- *Loss-leader pricing:* Supermarkets and department stores often drop the price on well-known brands to stimulate additional store traffic. This pays if the revenue on the additional sales compensates for the lower margins on the loss-leader items. Manufacturers of loss-leader brands typically object because this practice can dilute the brand image and bring complaints from retailers who charge the list price. Manufacturers have tried to restrain intermediaries from loss-leader pricing through lobbying for retail-price-maintenance laws, but these laws have been revoked.

- *Special-event pricing:* Sellers will establish special prices in certain seasons to draw in more customers. Every August, there are back-to-school sales.

- *Cash rebates:* Auto companies and other consumer-goods companies offer cash rebates to encourage purchase of the manufacturers' products within a specified time period. Rebates can help clear inventories without cutting the stated list price.

- *Low-interest financing:* Instead of cutting its price, the company can offer customers low-interest financing. Automakers have even announced no-interest financing to attract customers.

- *Longer payment terms:* Sellers, especially mortgage banks and auto companies, stretch loans over longer periods and thus lower the monthly payments. Consumers often worry less about the cost (i.e., the interest rate) of a loan and more about whether they can afford the monthly payment.

- *Warranties and service contracts:* Companies can promote sales by adding a free or low-cost warranty or service contract.

- *Psychological discounting:* This strategy involves setting an artificially high price and then offering the product at substantial savings; for example, "Was $359, now $299." Illegitimate discount tactics are fought by the Federal Trade Commission and Better Business Bureaus. Discounts from normal prices are a legitimate form of promotional pricing.

Promotional-pricing strategies are often a zero-sum game. If they work, competitors copy them and they lose their effectiveness. If they do not work, they waste money that could have been put into other marketing tools, such as building up product quality and service or strengthening product image through advertising.

discriminatory pricing

Companies often adjust their basic price to accommodate differences in customers, products, locations, and so on. **Price discrimination** occurs when a company sells a product or service at two or more prices that do not reflect a proportional difference in costs. In first-degree price discrimination, the seller charges a separate price to each customer depending on the intensity of his or her demand. In second-degree price discrimination, the seller charges less to buyers who buy a larger volume. In third-degree price discrimination, the seller charges different amounts to different classes of buyers, as in the following cases:

- *Customer-segment pricing:* Different customer groups are charged different prices for the same product or service. For example, museums often charge a lower admission fee to students and senior citizens.

- *Product-form pricing:* Different versions of the product are priced differently but not proportionately to their respective costs. Evian prices a 48-ounce bottle of its mineral water at $2.00. It takes the same water and packages 1.7 ounces in a moisturizer spray for $6.00. Through product-form pricing, Evian manages to charge $3.00 an ounce in one form and about $.04 an ounce in another.

- *Image pricing:* Some companies price the same product at two different levels based on image differences. A perfume manufacturer can put the perfume in one bottle, give it a name and image, and price it at $10 an ounce. It can put the same perfume in another bottle with a different name and image and price it at $30 an ounce.

- *Channel pricing:* Coca-Cola carries a different price depending on whether it is purchased in a fine restaurant, a fast-food restaurant, or a vending machine.
- *Location pricing:* The same product is priced differently at different locations even though the cost of offering at each location is the same. A theater varies its seat prices according to audience preferences for different locations.
- *Time pricing:* Prices are varied by season, day, or hour. Public utilities vary energy rates to commercial users by time of day and weekend versus weekday. Restaurants charge less to "early bird" customers. Hotels charge less on weekends. Hotels and airlines use **yield pricing,** by which they offer lower rates on unsold inventory just before it expires.[32]

Coca-Cola considered raising its vending machine soda prices on hot days using wireless technology, and lowering the price on cold days. However, customers so disliked the idea that Coke abandoned it.

For price discrimination to work, certain conditions must exist. First, the market must be segmentable and the segments must show different intensities of demand. Second, members in the lower-price segment must not be able to resell the product to the higher-price segment. Third, competitors must not be able to undersell the firm in the higher-price segment. Fourth, the cost of segmenting and policing the market must not exceed the extra revenue derived from price discrimination. Fifth, the practice must not breed customer resentment and ill will. Sixth, the particular form of price discrimination must not be illegal.[33]

As a result of deregulation in several industries, competitors have increased their use of discriminatory pricing. Airlines charge different fares to passengers on the same flight, depending on the seating class; the time of day (morning or night coach); the day of the week (workday or weekend); the season; the person's company, past business, or status (youth, military, senior citizen); and so on. Airlines are using yield pricing to capture as much revenue as possible.

Most consumers are probably not even aware of the degree to which they are the targets of discriminatory pricing. For instance, catalog retailers like Victoria's Secret routinely send out catalogs that sell identical goods except at different prices. Consumers who live in a more free-spending zip code may see only the higher prices. Office-product superstore Staples also sends out office supply catalogs with different prices.

Computer technology is making it easier for sellers to practice discriminatory pricing. For instance, they can use software that monitors customers' movements over the Web and allows them to customize offers and prices. New software applications, however, are also allowing buyers to discriminate between sellers by comparing prices instantaneously. (See "Marketing for the New Economy: How the Internet Is Revolutionizing Pricing—for Sellers and Buyers.")

Some forms of price discrimination (in which sellers offer different price terms to different people within the same trade group) are illegal. However, price discrimination is legal if the seller can prove that its costs are different when selling different volumes or different qualities of the same product to different retailers. Predatory pricing—selling below cost with the intention of destroying competition—is unlawful.[34]

product-mix pricing

Price-setting logic must be modified when the product is part of a product mix. In this case, the firm searches for a set of prices that maximizes profits on the total mix. Pricing is difficult because the various products have demand and cost interrelationships and are subject to different degrees of competition. We can distinguish six situations involving product-mix pricing: product-line pricing, optional-feature pricing, captive-product pricing, two-part pricing, by-product pricing, and product-bundling pricing.

PRODUCT-LINE PRICING   Companies normally develop product lines rather than single products and introduce price steps.

marketing for the new economy

How the Internet Is Revolutionizing Pricing—for Sellers and Buyers

E-commerce is arguably the Web's hottest application. Yet the Internet is more than simply a new "market-space." Internet-based technologies are actually changing the rules of the market. Here is a short list of how the Internet allows sellers to discriminate between buyers and allows buyers to discriminate between sellers.

Sellers can:

- Monitor customer behavior and tailor offers to individuals. Although shopping agent software and price comparison Web sites will tell consumers published prices, they may be missing out on the special deals consumers can get with the help of new technologies. Personify, a San Francisco–based start-up, has software that lets a Web-based merchant identify individual visitors to its Web site, studies the way the person navigates through the Web site, and instantaneously targets shoppers for specific products and prices.

www.personify.com provides software that helps Web merchants find target customers.

- Give certain customers access to special prices. CDNOW, an online vendor of music albums, e-mails certain buyers a special Web site address with lower prices. Unless you know the secret address, you pay full price. Business marketers are already using extranets to get a precise handle on inventory, costs, and demand at any given moment—to adjust prices instantly.

Both buyers and sellers can:

- Negotiate prices in online auctions and exchanges. Want to sell hundreds of excess and slightly worn widgets? Post a sale on eBay. Want to purchase vintage baseball cards at a bargain price? Go to Boekhout's Collectibles Mall at *www.azww.com/mall.* Of the thousands of Internet auction sites, eBay is the largest, and unlike most Internet businesses, is actually turning a profit. About 19 million registered users bid on items in more than 20 general categories. The Internet has made the centuries-old art of haggling economical. In the brick-and-mortar world, it costs sellers too much in overhead to negotiate prices with individual buyers. Over the Internet, the cost per transaction is so low it becomes practical—even profitable—to auction an item for dollars rather than thousands of dollars. Sellers like auctions because they can get rid of excess inventory. Business marketers, whose transactions account for 68 percent of online auction sales, also use it to offer time-sensitive deals and gauge interest on possible price points for new products. Quite simply, buyers like the bargains they find.

Buyers can:

- Get instant price comparisons from thousands of vendors. New technologies make it possible to obtain price comparisons with the click of a mouse. One site, PriceScan.com, lures thousands of visitors a day, most of them corporate buyers. Intelligent shopping agents ("bots") take price comparison a step further and seek out products, prices, and reviews from as many as 2,000 merchants.

- Name their price and have it met. Using complex software that shops bids to a number of airlines, Priceline.com has brokered around 7.5 million airline tickets since it opened in April 1998. Priceline extended its services to rental and new cars, accommodations, long distance telephone service, and home mortgages. Consumers can fix their own prices, and sellers can use it too: Airlines can fill in demand for empty seats, and hotels welcome the chance to sell vacant rooms.

Sources: Amy E. Cortese, "Good-Bye to Fixed Pricing?" *BusinessWeek*, May 4, 1998, pp. 71–84; Scott Woolley, "I Got It Cheaper than You," *Forbes*, November 2, 1998, pp. 82–84; Scott Woolley, "Price War!" *Forbes*, December 14, 1998, pp. 182–84; Michael Krauss, "Web Offers Biggest Prize in Product Pricing Game," *Marketing News*, July 6, 1998, p. 8; Julie Pitta, "Competitive Shopping," *Forbes*, February 9, 1998, pp. 92–95; Matthew Nelson, "Going Once, Going Twice . . . " *InfoWorld*, November 9, 1998, pp. 1, 64; Leslie Walker, "The Net's Battle of the Bots," *Washington Post*, December 10, 1998, p. B1; Heather Green, "A Cybershopper's Best Friend," *BusinessWeek*, May 4, 1998, p. 84; Rebecca Quick, "Buying the Goods—The Attack of the Robots: Comparison-Shopping Technology is Here—Whether Retailers Like It or Not," *Wall Street Journal*, December 7, 1998, p. R14. For a discussion of some of the academic issues involved, see Florian Zettelmeyer, "Expanding to the Internet: Pricing and Communication Strategies when Firms Compete on Multiple Channels," *Journal of Marketing Research*, 37 (August 2000): 292–308.

Intel   In the fall of 1997, Intel segmented its product line into microprocessors aimed at specific markets, such as cheap PCs, mid-tier "performance" PCs, and powerful servers. This strategy let Intel balance thin profits from chips like the Celeron—new models of which sell for as little as $150 and go into low-priced PCs— with cash cows like the Itanium workstation and server chips, which cost up to $4,200 each. The company's most profitable chips are the Pentium 4 chips, priced between $300 and $600, depending on processor speed.[35]

In many lines of trade, sellers use well-established price points for the products in their line. A men's clothing store might carry men's suits at three price levels: $200, $400, and $600. Customers will associate low-, average-, and high-quality suits with the three price points. The seller's task is to establish perceived-quality differences that justify the price differences.

OPTIONAL-FEATURE PRICING   Many companies offer optional products, features, and services along with their main product. The automobile buyer can order electric window controls, defoggers, light dimmers, and an extended warranty. Pricing is a sticky problem, because companies must decide which items to include in the standard price and which to offer as options. For many years, U.S. auto companies advertised a stripped-down model for $10,000 to pull people into showrooms. The economy model was stripped of so many features that most buyers left the showroom spending $13,000.

Restaurants face a similar pricing problem. Customers can often order liquor in addition to the meal. Many restaurants price their liquor high and their food low. The food revenue covers costs, and the liquor produces the profit. This explains why servers often press hard to get customers to order drinks. Other restaurants price their liquor low and food high to draw in a drinking crowd.

CAPTIVE-PRODUCT PRICING   Some products require the use of ancillary, or **captive, products**. Manufacturers of razors and cameras often price them low and set high markups on razor blades and film, respectively. AT&T may give a cellular phone free if the person commits to buying two years of phone service.

Hewlett-Packard   In 1996, Hewlett-Packard (H-P) began drastically cutting prices on its printers, by as much as 60 percent in some cases. H-P could afford to make such dramatic cuts because the high volume of sales of aftermarket products like replacement ink cartridges and specialty paper carried profit margins as high as 70 percent. As the price of printers dropped, printer sales rose, as did the number of aftermarket sales. Ink cartridges, which cost anywhere from $20 to $200, and other aftermarket consumables contributed 12 percent of H-P's total profit in 1996. Today, these consumables account for roughly two-thirds of H-P's $647 million annual profit.[36]

There is a danger in pricing the captive product too high in the aftermarket. Caterpillar, for example, makes high profits in the aftermarket by pricing its parts and service high. This practice has given rise to "pirates," who counterfeit the parts and sell them to "shady tree" mechanics who install them, sometimes without passing on the cost savings to customers. Meanwhile, Caterpillar loses sales.[37]

TWO-PART PRICING   Service firms often engage in **two-part pricing**, consisting of a fixed fee plus a variable usage fee. Telephone users pay a minimum monthly fee plus charges for calls beyond a certain area. Amusement parks charge an admission fee plus fees for rides over a certain minimum. The service firm faces a problem similar to captive-product pricing—namely, how much to charge for the basic service and how much for the variable usage. The fixed fee should be low enough to induce purchase of the service; the profit can then be made on the usage fees.

BY-PRODUCT PRICING   The production of certain goods—meats, petroleum products, and other chemicals—often results in by-products. If the by-products have value to a customer group, they should be priced on their value. Any income earned on the by-products will make it easier for the company to charge a lower price on its main product if competition forces it to do so.

Sometimes companies do not realize how valuable their by-products are. Until Zoo-Doo Compost Company came along, many zoos did not realize that one of their by-products—their occupants' manure—could be an excellent source of additional revenue.[38]

PRODUCT-BUNDLING PRICING   Sellers often bundle products and features. **Pure bundling** occurs when a firm only offers its products as a bundle. Michael Ovitz's company, Artists Management Group, will sign up a "hot" actor if the film company will also accept other talents that Ovitz represents (directors, writers, scripts). This is a form of *tied-in sales*. In **mixed bundling**, the seller offers goods both individually and in bundles. When offering a mixed bundle, the seller normally charges less for the bundle than if the items were purchased separately. An auto manufacturer might offer an option package at less than the cost of buying all the options separately. A theater company will price a season subscription at less than the cost of buying all the performances separately. Because customers may not have planned to buy all the components, the savings on the price bundle must be substantial enough to induce them to buy the bundle.[39]

Some customers will want less than the whole bundle. Suppose a medical equipment supplier's offer includes free delivery and training. A particular customer might ask to forgo the free delivery and training in exchange for a lower price. The customer is asking the seller to "unbundle" or "rebundle" its offer. If a supplier saves $100 by not supplying delivery and reduces the customer's price by $80, the supplier has kept the customer happy while increasing its profit by $20.

initiating and responding to price changes

Companies often face situations where they may need to cut or raise prices.

initiating price cuts

Several circumstances might lead a firm to cut prices. One is excess plant capacity: The firm needs additional business and cannot generate it through increased sales effort, product improvement, or other measures. It may resort to aggressive pricing, but in initiating a price cut, the company may trigger a price war. Another circumstance is declining market share. General Motors, for example, cut its subcompact car prices by 10 percent on the West Coast when Japanese competition kept making inroads.

Companies sometimes initiate price cuts in a *drive to dominate the market through lower costs*. Either the company starts with lower costs than its competitors or it initiates price cuts in the hope of gaining market share and lower costs; but a price-cutting strategy involves possible traps:

- *Low-quality trap:* Consumers will assume that the quality is low.
- *Fragile-market-share trap:* A low price buys market share but not market loyalty. The same customers will shift to any lower-priced firm that comes along.
- *Shallow-pockets trap:* The higher-priced competitors may cut their prices and may have longer staying power because of deeper cash reserves.

Companies may have to cut their prices in a period of economic recession. During hard times, consumers reduce their spending. Some possible company responses are given in Table 16.3.

initiating price increases

A successful price increase can raise profits considerably. For example, if the company's profit margin is 3 percent of sales, a 1 percent price increase will increase profits by 33 percent if sales volume is unaffected. This situation is illustrated in Table 16.4. The

table **16.3**	Marketing–Mix Alternatives

Strategic Options	Reasoning	Consequences
1. Maintain price and perceived quality. Engage in selective customer pruning.	Firm has higher customer loyalty. It is willing to lose poorer customers to competitors.	Smaller market share. Lowered profitability.
2. Raise price and perceived quality.	Raise price to cover rising costs. Improve quality to justify higher prices.	Smaller market share. Maintained profitability.
3. Maintain price and raise perceived quality.	It is cheaper to maintain price and raise perceived quality.	Smaller market share. Short-term decline in profitability. Long-term increase in profitability.
4. Cut price partly and raise perceived quality.	Must give customers some price reduction but stress higher value of offer.	Maintained market share. Short-term decline in profitability. Long-term maintained profitability.
5. Cut price fully and maintain perceived quality.	Discipline and discourage price competition.	Maintained market share. Short-term decline in profitability.
6. Cut price fully and reduce perceived quality.	Discipline and discourage price competition and maintain profit margin.	Maintained market share. Maintained margin. Reduced long-term profitability.
7. Maintain price and reduce perceived quality.	Cut marketing expense to combat rising costs.	Smaller market share. Maintained margin. Reduced long-term profitability.
8. Introduce an economy model.	Give the market what it wants.	Some cannibalization but higher total volume.

assumption is that a company charged $10 and sold 100 units and had costs of $970, leaving a profit of $30, or 3 percent on sales. By raising its price by 10 cents (1 percent price increase), it boosted its profits by 33 percent, assuming the same sales volume.

A major circumstance provoking price increases is *cost inflation*. Rising costs unmatched by productivity gains squeeze profit margins and lead companies to regular rounds of price increases. Companies often raise their prices by more than the cost increase, in anticipation of further inflation or government price controls, in a practice called *anticipatory pricing*.

Another factor leading to price increases is *overdemand*. When a company cannot supply all of its customers, it can raise its prices, ration supplies to customers, or both. The price can be increased in the following ways. Each has a different impact on buyers.

- *Delayed quotation pricing:* The company does not set a final price until the product is finished or delivered. This pricing is prevalent in industries with long production lead times, such as industrial construction and heavy equipment.

table **16.4**			
Profits Before and After a Price Increase		**Before**	**After**
	Price	$ 10	$10.10 (a 1 percent price increase)
	Units sold	100	100
	Revenue	$1000	$1010
	Costs	−970	−970
	Profit	$ 30	$ 40 (a $33\frac{1}{3}$ percent profit increase)

- *Escalator clauses:* The company requires the customer to pay today's price and all or part of any inflation increase that takes place before delivery. An escalator clause bases price increases on some specified price index. Escalator clauses are found in contracts for major industrial projects, like aircraft construction and bridge building.

- *Unbundling:* The company maintains its price but removes or prices separately one or more elements that were part of the former offer, such as free delivery or installation. A joke in countries with high inflation is that the current price of a car no longer includes the tires and steering wheel.

- *Reduction of discounts:* The company instructs its sales force not to offer its normal cash and quantity discounts.

A company needs to decide whether to raise its price sharply on a one-time basis or to raise it by small amounts several times. Generally, consumers prefer small price increases on a regular basis to sudden, sharp increases.

In passing price increases on to customers, the company must avoid looking like a price gouger. Companies also need to think of who will bear the brunt of increased prices. Customer memories are long, and they will turn against companies they perceive as price gougers when the market softens. This happened to Kellogg, the breakfast cereal company.

Kellogg Throughout the 1980s, Kellogg pushed up the prices of its breakfast cereals and its stock price soared. Although the strategy worked for some time, in the early 1990s the company became embroiled in a bitter price war with rivals General Mills, Quaker Oats, and Post. Between 1993 and 1997, Kellogg cut prices by as much as 20 percent. The price cuts led to a 3.5 point drop in the company's U.S. market share between 1993 and 1998. To combat flagging sales, Kellogg began raising prices and used the profits to develop new products and boost advertising. Kellogg's $4 billion acquisition of Keebler in 2000 was a step toward less dependence on cereal sales, which dropped from 75 percent to 50 percent of Kellogg's $7 billion in sales.[40]

There are some techniques for avoiding this image: One is that a sense of fairness must surround any price increase, and customers must be given advance notice so they can do forward buying or shop around. Sharp price increases need to be explained in understandable terms. Making low-visibility price moves first is also a good technique: Eliminating discounts, increasing minimum order sizes, and curtailing production of low-margin products are some examples; and contracts or bids for long-term projects should contain escalator clauses based on such factors as increases in recognized national price indexes.[41]

Companies can also respond to higher costs or overdemand without raising prices. The possibilities include the following:

- Shrinking the amount of product instead of raising the price. (Hershey Foods maintained its candy bar price but trimmed its size. Nestlé maintained its size but raised the price.)

- Substituting less expensive materials or ingredients. (Many candy bar companies substituted synthetic chocolate for real chocolate to fight price increases in cocoa.)

- Reducing or removing product features. (Sears engineered down a number of its appliances so they could be priced competitively with those sold in discount stores.)

- Removing or reducing product services, such as installation or free delivery.

- Using less expensive packaging material or larger package sizes.

- Reducing the number of sizes and models offered.

- Creating new economy brands. (Jewel food stores introduced 170 generic items selling at 10 percent to 30 percent less than national brands.)

reactions to price changes

Any price change can provoke a response from customers, competitors, distributors, suppliers, and even government.

CUSTOMER REACTIONS   Customers often question the motivation behind price changes.[42] A price cut can be interpreted in different ways: The item is about to be replaced by a new model; the item is faulty and is not selling well; the firm is in financial trouble; the price will come down even further; the quality has been reduced.

A price increase, which would normally deter sales, may carry some positive meanings to customers: The item is "hot" and represents an unusually good value.

COMPETITOR REACTIONS   Competitors are most likely to react when the number of firms are few, the product is homogeneous, and buyers are highly informed.

How can a firm anticipate a competitor's reactions? One way is to assume that the competitor reacts in a set way to price changes. The other is to assume that the competitor treats each price change as a fresh challenge and reacts according to self-interest at the time. In this case, the company will have to figure out the competitor's self-interest. It will need to research the competitor's current financial situation, recent sales, customer loyalty, and corporate objectives. If the competitor has a market-share objective, it is likely to match the price change. If it has a profit-maximization objective, it may react by increasing the advertising budget or improving product quality.

The problem is complicated because the competitor can put different interpretations on a price cut: that the company is trying to steal the market, that the company is doing poorly and trying to boost its sales, or that the company wants the whole industry to reduce prices to stimulate total demand.

responding to competitors' price changes

How should a firm respond to a price cut initiated by a competitor? In markets characterized by high product homogeneity, the firm should search for ways to enhance its augmented product. If it cannot find any, it will have to meet the price reduction. If the competitor raises its price in a homogeneous product market, the other firms might not match it unless the increase will benefit the industry as a whole. Then the leader will have to rescind the increase.

In nonhomogeneous product markets, a firm has more latitude. It needs to consider the following issues: (1) Why did the competitor change the price? To steal the market, to utilize excess capacity, to meet changing cost conditions, or to lead an industrywide price change? (2) Does the competitor plan to make the price change temporary or permanent? (3) What will happen to the company's market share and profits if it does not respond? Are other companies going to respond? (4) What are the competitor's and other firms' responses likely to be to each possible reaction?

Market leaders frequently face aggressive price cutting by smaller firms trying to build market share. Using price, Fuji attacks Kodak, Bic attacks Gillette, and Compaq attacks IBM. Brand leaders also face lower-priced private-store brands. The brand leader can respond in several ways:

- *Maintain price:* The leader might maintain its price and profit margin, believing that (1) it would lose too much profit if it reduced its price, (2) it would not lose much market share, and (3) it could regain market share when necessary. However, the argument against price maintenance is that the attacker gets more confident, the leader's sales force gets demoralized, and the leader loses more share than expected. The leader panics, lowers price to regain share, and finds that regaining its market position is more difficult and costly than expected.
- *Maintain price and add value:* The leader could improve its product, services, and communications. The firm may find it cheaper to maintain price and spend money to improve perceived quality than to cut price and operate at a lower margin.
- *Reduce price:* The leader might drop its price to match the competitor's price. It might do so because (1) its costs fall with volume, (2) it would lose market share because the market is price-sensitive, and (3) it would be hard to rebuild market share once it is lost. This action will cut profits in the short run.

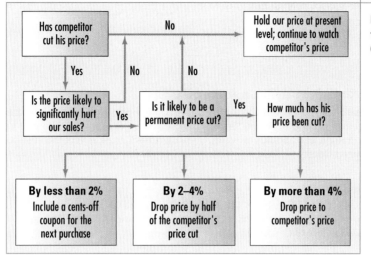

figure 16.9

Price–Reaction Program
for Meeting a
Competitor's Price Cut

- *Increase price and improve quality:* The leader might raise its price and introduce new brands to bracket the attacking brand.
- *Launch a low-price fighter line:* It might add lower-priced items to the line or create a separate, lower-priced brand.

The best response varies with the situation. The company has to consider the product's stage in the life cycle, its importance in the company's portfolio, the competitor's intentions and resources, the market's price and quality sensitivity, the behavior of costs with volume, and the company's alternative opportunities.

An extended analysis of alternatives may not be feasible when the attack occurs. The company may have to react decisively within hours or days. It would make better sense to anticipate possible competitors' price changes and to prepare contingent responses. Figure 16.9 shows a *price-reaction program* to be used if a competitor cuts prices. Reaction programs for meeting price changes find their greatest application in industries where price changes occur with some frequency and where it is important to react quickly—for example, in the meatpacking, lumber, and oil industries.

summary

1. Despite the increased role of nonprice factors in modern marketing, price remains a critical element of the marketing mix. Price is the only one of the four Ps that produces revenue; the others produce costs.

2. In setting pricing policy, a company follows a six-step procedure. First, it selects its pricing objective. Second, it estimates the demand curve, the probable quantities that it will sell at each possible price. Third, it estimates how its costs vary at different levels of output, at different levels of accumulated production experience, and for differentiated marketing offers. Fourth, it examines competitors' costs, prices, and offers. Fifth, it selects a pricing method. Finally, it selects the final price.

3. Companies do not usually set a single price, but rather a pricing structure that reflects variations in geographical demand and costs, market-segment requirements, pur-

chase timing, order levels, and other factors. Several price-adaptation strategies are available: (1) geographical pricing; (2) price discounts and allowances; (3) promotional pricing; (4) discriminatory pricing; and (5) product-mix pricing, which includes setting prices for product lines, optional features, captive products, two-part items, by-products, and product bundles.

4. After developing pricing strategies, firms often face situations in which they need to change prices. A price decrease might be brought about by excess plant capacity, declining market share, a desire to dominate the market through lower costs, or economic recession. A price increase might be brought about by cost inflation or overdemand.

5. There are several alternatives to increasing price, including shrinking the amount of product instead of raising the

price, substituting less expensive materials or ingredients, and reducing or removing product features.

6. The firm facing a competitor's price change must try to understand the competitor's intent and the likely duration of the change. The firm's strategy often depends on whether it is producing homogeneous or nonhomogeneous products. Market leaders attacked by lower-priced competitors can choose to maintain price, raise the perceived quality of their product, reduce price, increase price and improve quality, or launch a low-priced fighter line.

applications

marketing debate – is the right price a fair price?

Prices are often set to satisfy demand or to reflect the premium that consumers are willing to pay for a product or service. Some critics shudder, however, at the thought of $2 bottles of water, $150 running shoes, and $500 concert tickets.

Take a position: Prices should reflect the value that consumers are willing to pay versus Prices should primarily just reflect the cost involved in making a product or service.

marketing and advertising

1. In the ad in Figure 1, 1-800-CONTACTS reaches out to price-sensitive contact-lens users with an offer to "Get the exact same contacts delivered for less than you're paying now."

   a. What specific elements might affect price sensitivity in the consumer market for contact lenses?
   b. What pricing method does 1-800-CONTACTS appear to be using in this ad?
   c. How might 1-800-CONTACTS use product-bundling pricing to increase sales to its target market?

2. The ad in Figure 2 shows how the online auction site eBay ™ attracts price-sensitive business buyers to auctions for electronic gear such as projectors, monitors, PCs, and television monitors.

   a. Since product prices are never mentioned, what benefits does eBay emphasize to encourage business buyers to visit its Web site?
   b. Is business demand for slide projectors likely to be elastic or inelastic? What are the implications for the auction prices of projectors sold to business customers on eBay's site?
   c. Which of Nagle's nine factors affecting price sensitivity are most applicable to business demand for slide projectors?

Figure 1

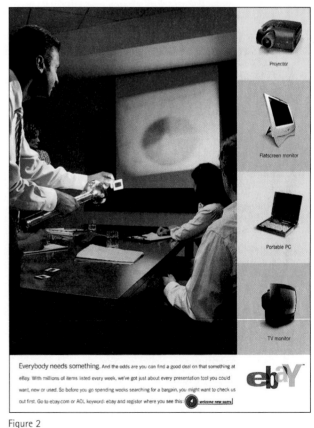

Figure 2

online marketing today

The online market for travel services will reach $63 billion within a few years, and Priceline.com is aiming to capture a significant share; already, it is high on the top-10 list of travel Web sites. After a brief period of diversification into name-your-price sales of groceries and gasoline, the company has refocused on its core travel and financial services offerings, including airline tickets, hotel rooms, rental cars, and mortgage loans. The company guarantees that a Priceline.com mortgage is the "lowest-cost loan on the market" and backs this up by paying $300 to any customer who finds a better price.[43]

See how the system works by visiting the Priceline Web site at *www.priceline.com*. Follow the link marked "How it works" to read about the name-your-price process. Then return to the home page and follow several of the links promoting discounted offerings. What can you say about the price sensitivity of Priceline's customers? What effect would Priceline's prices be likely to have on the reference prices customers bear in mind for travel and mortgage services? How does the company's lowest-cost loan guarantee affect a customer's perception of the product's value?

you're the marketer: sonic pda marketing plan

Marketing Plan Pro

Pricing is a critical element in any company's marketing plan, because it directly affects revenue and profit goals. To effectively design and manage pricing strategies, marketers must consider costs as well as the perceptions of customers and the reactions of competitors—especially in highly competitive markets.

You are in charge of pricing Sonic's first personal digital assistant for its launch early next year. Review your current situation, especially the SWOT analysis you previously prepared and your competitive environment. Also think about the markets you are targeting and the positioning you want to achieve. Now continue working on your marketing plan by responding to the following questions about pricing:

- What should Sonic's primary pricing objective be? Explain your reasoning.

- Are PDA customers likely to be price-sensitive? Is demand elastic or inelastic? What are the implications for your pricing decisions?
- How will the introductory product pricing work with the other parts of Sonic's marketing mix?
- What price adaptations (such as discounts, allowances, and promotional pricing) should Sonic include in its marketing plan?

After you have developed your pricing strategies and programs, document your recommendations in a written marketing plan or type them into the Marketing Mix section of the *Marketing Plan Pro* software, depending on your instructor's directions.

notes

1. David J. Schwartz, *Marketing Today: A Basic Approach*, 3rd ed. (New York: Harcourt Brace Jovanovich, 1981), p. 271.
2. Kara Swisher, "Electronics 2001: The Essential Guide," *Wall Street Journal*, January 5, 2001.
3. Steve Gelsi, "Spin-Cycle Doctor," *Brandweek*, March 10, 1997, pp. 38–40; Tim Stevens, "From Reliable to 'Wow,'" *Industry Week*, June 22, 1998, pp. 22–26; Juan Koncius, "A New Spin on Doing Your Laundry," *Washington Post*, April 12, 2001, p. A1.
4. Thomas T. Nagle and Reed K. Holden, *The Strategy and Tactics of Pricing*, 3rd ed. (Upper Saddle River, NJ: Prentice Hall, 2001), ch. 4. This is an excellent reference book for making pricing decisions.
5. Kevin J. Clancy, "At What Profit Price?" *Brandweek*, June 23, 1997, pp. 24–28; Monica Perin, "Vermont Energy Firm Green Mountain Moves to Texas with Increase in Capital," *Houston Business Journal*, May 12, 2000, p. 5A.
6. Sidney Bennett and J. B. Wilkinson, "Price-Quantity Relationships and Price Elasticity under In-Store Experimentation," *Journal of Business Research* (January 1974): 30–34.
7. Walter Baker, Mike Marn, and Craig Zawada, "Price Smarter on the Net," *Harvard Business Review* (February 2001): 122–27.
8. John R. Nevin, "Laboratory Experiments for Estimating Consumer Demand: A Validation Study," *Journal of Marketing Research* (August 1974): 261–68; Jonathan Weiner, "Forecasting Demand: Consumer Electronics Marketer Uses a Conjoint

Approach to Configure Its New Product and Set the Right Price," *Marketing Research: A Magazine of Management & Applications* (Summer 1994): 6–11.
9. Nagle and Holden, *The Strategy and Tactics of Pricing*, ch. 13.
10. For summary of elasticity studies, see Dominique M. Hanssens, Leonard J. Parsons, and Randall L. Schultz, *Market Response Models: Econometric and Time Series Analysis* (Boston: Kluwer Academic Publishers, 1990), pp. 187–91.
11. Gene Epstein, "Economic Beat: Stretching Things," *Barron's*, December 15, 1997, p. 65.
12. William W. Alberts, "The Experience Curve Doctrine Reconsidered," *Journal of Marketing* (July 1989): 36–49.
13. Robin Cooper and Robert S. Kaplan, "Profit Priorities from Activity-Based Costing," *Harvard Business Review* (May–June 1991): 130–35. For more on ABC, see ch. 24.
14. "Japan's Smart Secret Weapon," *Fortune*, August 12, 1991, p. 75.
15. Elyse Tanouye, "Drugs: Steep Markups on Generics Top Branded Drugs," *Wall Street Journal*, December 31, 1998, p. B1; Julie Appleby, "Drugmakers Fight Back as Patents Near Expiration," *USA Today*, November 26, 1999, p. 4B.
16. Tung-Zong Chang and Albert R. Wildt, "Price, Product Information, and Purchase Intention: An Empirical Study," *Journal of the Academy of Marketing Science* (Winter 1994): 16–27. See also G. Dean Kortge and Patrick A. Okonkwo, "Perceived

Value Approach to Pricing," *Industrial Marketing Management* (May 1993): 133–40.

17. James C. Anderson, Dipak C. Jain, and Pradeep K. Chintagunta, "Customer Value Assessment in Business Markets: A State-of-Practice Study," *Journal of Business-to-Business Marketing* 1, no. 1 (1993): 3–29.

18. Bill Saporito, "Behind the Tumult at P&G," *Fortune*, March 7, 1994, pp. 74–82. For empirical analysis of its effects, see Kusom L. Ailawadi, Donald R. Lehmann, and Scott A. Neslin, "Market Response to a Major Policy Change in the Marketing Mix: Learning from Procter & Gamble's Value Pricing Strategy," *Journal of Marketing* 65 (January 2001): 44–61.

19. Stephen J. Hoch, Xavier Dreze, and Mary J. Purk, "EDLP, Hi-Lo, and Margin Arithmetic," *Journal of Marketing* (October 1994): 16–27; Rajiv Lal and R. Rao, "Supermarket Competition: The Case of Everyday Low Pricing," *Marketing Science* 16, no. 1 (1997): 60–80.

20. Becky Bull, "No Consensus on Pricing," *Progressive Grocer* (November 1998): 87–90.

21. Gary M. Erickson and Johny K. Johansson, "The Role of Price in Multi-Attribute Product-Evaluations," *Journal of Consumer Research* (September 1985): 195–99.

22. K. N. Rajendran and Gerard J. Tellis, "Contextual and Temporal Components of Reference Price," *Journal of Marketing* (January 1994): 22–34; Goromurthy Kalyanaram and Rossell S. Winer, "Empirical Generalizations from Reference Price Research," *Marketing Science*, 14(3), G161–G169.

23. Eric Anderson and Duncan Simester, "The Role of Price Endings: Why Stores May Sell More at $49 than at $44," an unpublished conference paper, April 2001.

24. Paul W. Farris and David J. Reibstein, "How Prices, Expenditures, and Profits Are Linked," *Harvard Business Review* (November–December 1979): 173–84. See also Makoto Abe, "Price and Advertising Strategy of a National Brand against Its Private-Label Clone: A Signaling Game Approach," *Journal of Business Research* (July 1995): 241–50.

25. J. P. Morgan Report, "eTailing and the Five C's."

26. Eugene H. Fram and Michael S. McCarthy, "The True Price of Penalties," *Marketing Management* (October 1999): 49–56.

27. Gary McWilliams, "How Dell Fine-Tunes Its PC Pricing to Gain Edge in a Slow Market," *Wall Street Journal*, June 8, 2001, p. A1.

28. Michael Rowe, *Countertrade* (London: Euromoney Books, 1989); P. N. Agarwala, *Countertrade: A Global Perspective* (New Delhi: Vikas Publishing House, 1991); Christopher M. Korth, ed., *International Countertrade* (New York: Quorum Books, 1987).

29. Michael V. Marn and Robert L. Rosiello, "Managing Price, Gaining Profit," *Harvard Business Review* (September–October 1992): 84–94. See also Gerard J. Tellis, "Tackling the Retailer Decision Maze: Which Brands to Discount, How Much, When, and Why?" *Marketing Science* 14, no. 3, pt. 2 (1995): 271–99; Kusom L. Ailawadi, Scott A. Neslin, and Karen Gedeak,

"Pursuing the Value-Conscious Consumer: Store Brands Versus National Brand Promotions," *Journal of Marketing* 65 (January 2001): 71–89.

30. Jack Trout, "Prices: Simple Guidelines to Get Them Right," *Journal of Business Strategy* (November–December 1998): 13–16.

31. Kevin J. Clancy, "At What Profit Price?" *Brandweek*, June 23, 1997.

32. Robert E. Weigand, "Yield Management: Filling Buckets, Papering the House," *Business Horizons* (September–October 1999): 55–64.

33. For more information on specific types of price discrimination that are illegal, see Henry Cheesman, *Contemporary Business Law* (Upper Saddle River, NJ: Prentice Hall, 1995).

34. Mike France, "Does Predatory Pricing Make Microsoft a Predator?" *BusinessWeek*, November 23, 1998, pp. 130–32. Also see Joseph P. Guiltinan and Gregory T. Gundlack, "Aggressive and Predatory Pricing: A Framework for Analysis," *Journal of Advertising* (July 1996): 87–102.

35. Andy Reinhardt, "Who Says Intel's Chips Are Down?" *BusinessWeek*, December 7, 1998, pp. 103–4; Therese Poletti, "Computer-Chip Price War Breaks Out," *San Jose Mercury News*, April 17, 2001.

36. Lee Gomes, "Computer-Printer Price Drop Isn't Starving Makers," *Wall Street Journal*, August 16, 1996, p. B4; Simon Avery, "H-P Sees Room for Growth in Printer Market," *Wall Street Journal*, June 28, 2001, p. B6.

37. Robert E. Weigand, "Buy In-Follow On Strategies for Profit," *Sloan Management Review* (Spring 1991): 29–37.

38. Susan Krafft, "Love, Love Me Doo," *American Demographics* (June 1994): 15–16.

39. See Gerald J. Tellis, "Beyond the Many Faces of Price: An Integration of Pricing Strategies," *Journal of Marketing* (October 1986): 155. This excellent article also analyzes and illustrates other pricing strategies. Also see Dilip Soman and John T. Gourville, "Transaction Decoupling: How Price Bundling Affects the Decision to Consume," *Journal of Marketing Research*, 38 (February 2001): 30–44.

40. "Costly Cornflakes," *New York Times*, January 12, 1999, p. A1; "Bowl of Kellogg Flakes to Cost More," *New Orleans Times-Picayune*, December 15, 1998, p. C2; Steven Pearlstein, "Making Shredded Wheat of Inflation," *Washington Post*, April 14, 1994, p. A1; "Why Cookies Look Grreat," *Newsweek*, November 6, 2000, p. 56.

41. Eric Mitchell, "How Not to Raise Prices," *Small Business Reports* (November 1990): 64–67.

42. For excellent review, see Kent B. Monroe, "Buyers' Subjective Perceptions of Price," *Journal of Marketing Research* (February 1973): 70–80.

43. Robert Julavits, "Priceline.com Sticking with Web Venture," *American Banker*, October 24, 2001, p. 16; Mike Beirne, "Upping the Ante," *Brandweek*, September 10, 2001, p. 31+.

C H A P T E R

designing and managing value networks and marketing channels

Kotler on Marketing

Establish channels for different target markets and aim for efficiency, control, and adaptability.

In this chapter, we will address the following questions:

- What is a value network and marketing-channel system?
- What work is performed by marketing channels?
- What decisions do companies face in designing, managing, evaluating, and modifying their channels?
- What trends are taking place in channel dynamics?
- How can channel conflict be managed?

Companies are increasingly taking a value network *view of their businesses. Instead of limiting their focus to their immediate* suppliers, distributors, and customers, they are examining the whole supply chain *that links raw material, components, and manufactured goods and shows how they are moved toward the final consumers. Companies are looking at their suppliers' suppliers upstream and at their distributors' customers downstream.*

Even the term supply chain *can be criticized for taking a* make-and-sell *view of the business. It suggests that raw materials, productive inputs, and factory capacity should serve as the starting point for market planning. A better term would be* demand chain *because it suggests a "sense-and-respond" view of the market. The planning starting point would be a customer segment with certain needs, to which the company responds by organizing resources.*

Experts are even beginning to say that a supply chain or demand chain view of a business is still too limited because it takes a linear or vertical view of purchase-production-consumption activities. With the advent of the Internet, companies are forming more numerous and complex relationships with other firms. For example, Ford not only manages numerous supply chains, but also sponsors or transacts on many B2B Web sites and exchanges as needs arise. Ford recently formed a buying alliance with GM and DaimlerChrysler to obtain lower prices by aggregating orders for common requirements from auto parts suppliers. Companies today are engaged in building and managing a continuously evolving value network.

what is a value network and marketing-channel system?

We define a value network as follows: A **value network** is a system of partnerships and alliances that a firm creates to source, augment, and deliver its offerings. Consider Palm's value network.

Palm, Inc. Palm, the leading manufacturer of handheld devices, is a whole community of suppliers and assemblers of semiconductor components, plastic cases, LCD displays, and accessories; of off-line and online resellers; and of 45,000 complementors who have created over 5,000 applications for the Palm operating systems.

This perspective yields several insights. First, the company can estimate whether more money is made upstream or downstream, in case it might want to integrate backward or forward. Second, the company is more aware of disturbances anywhere in the supply chain that might cause costs, prices, or supplies to change suddenly. Third, more companies are eager to go online with their business partners to carry on faster and more accurate communications, transactions, and payments; this will reduce costs, speed up information, and increase accuracy.

Managing this value network has required companies to make increasing investments in information technology (IT) and software. They have invited such software firms as SAP and Oracle to design comprehensive *enterprise resource planning* (ERP) systems to manage cash flow, manufacturing, human resources, purchasing, and other major functions within a unified framework. They hope to break up department silos and carry out core business processes more seamlessly. In most cases, however, companies are still a long way from truly comprehensive ERP systems.

Marketers, for their part, have traditionally focused on the side of the value network that looks forward toward the customer. Hopefully, they will increasingly participate in and influence their companies' upstream activities and become network managers, not only product and customer managers. Most producers do not sell their goods directly to the final users; between them stands a set of intermediaries performing a variety of functions. These intermediaries constitute a **marketing channel** (also called a trade channel or distribution channel).

Some intermediaries—such as wholesalers and retailers—buy, take title to, and resell the merchandise; they are called merchants. Others—brokers, manufacturers' representatives, sales agents—search for customers and may negotiate on the producer's behalf but do not take title to the goods; they are called agents. Still others—transportation companies, independent warehouses, banks, advertising agencies—assist in the distribution process but neither take title to goods nor negotiate purchases or sales; they are called facilitators.

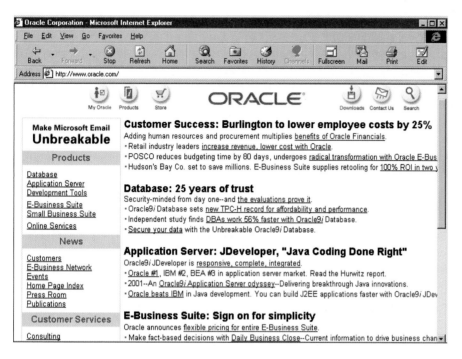

Oracle's home page.

Marketing channels are sets of interdependent organizations involved in the process of making a product or service available for use or consumption.[1] Marketing-channel decisions are among the most critical decisions facing management. The channels chosen intimately affect all the other marketing decisions. The company's pricing depends on whether it uses mass-merchandisers or high-quality boutiques. The firm's sales force and advertising decisions depend on how much training and motivation dealers need. In addition, the company's channel decisions involve relatively long-term commitments to other firms. When an automaker signs up independent dealers to sell its automobiles, the automaker cannot buy them out the next day and replace them with company-owned outlets. E. Raymond Corey observed:

> A distribution system . . . is a key external resource. Normally it takes years to build, and it is not easily changed. It ranks in importance with key internal resources such as manufacturing, research, engineering, and field sales personnel and facilities. It represents a significant corporate commitment to large numbers of independent companies whose business is distribution—and to the particular markets they serve. It represents, as well, a commitment to a set of policies and practices that constitute the basic fabric on which is woven an extensive set of long-term relationships.[2]

Today's companies are multiplying the number of "go-to-market" or **hybrid** channels:

- IBM uses its sales force to sell to large accounts, outbound telemarketing to sell to medium-sized accounts, direct mail with an inbound number for small accounts, retailers to sell to still smaller accounts, and the Internet to sell specialty items.
- Charles Schwab enables its customers to do transactions in its branches, over the phone, or on the Internet.
- Staples markets through its traditional retail channel, a direct-response Internet site, virtual malls, and 30,000 links on affiliated sites.

Companies that manage hybrid channels must make sure these channels work well together and match each target customer's preferred ways of doing business.

figure **17.1**

How a Distributor Effects
an Economy of Effort

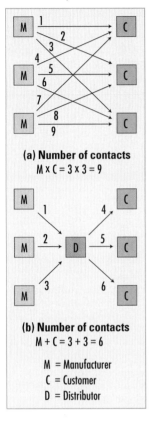

(a) Number of contacts
M x C = 3 x 3 = 9

(b) Number of contacts
M + C = 3 + 3 = 6

M = Manufacturer
C = Customer
D = Distributor

WingspanBank.com   In June 1999, Bank One launched a spin-off venture called WingspanBank to get into the online banking business, but it developed Wingspan-Bank as a separate entity; WingspanBank customers could not use Bank One branches to do their banking in person. No wonder it only garnered 144,000 accounts and had to be closed down as a separate venture.

Customers expect *channel integration,* characterized by the following features:

- The ability to order a product online and pick it up at a convenient retail location.
- The ability to return an online-ordered product to a nearby store of the retailer.
- The right to receive discounts based on total online and off-line purchases.

We will examine marketing-channel issues from the perspective of retailers, wholesalers, and physical-distribution agencies in the next chapter.

what work is performed by marketing channels?

Why would a producer delegate some of the selling job to intermediaries? Delegation means relinquishing some control over how and to whom the products are sold, but producers do gain several advantages by using intermediaries:

- Many producers lack the financial resources to carry out direct marketing. For example, General Motors sells its cars through more than 8,100 dealer outlets in North America alone. Even General Motors would be hard-pressed to raise the cash to buy out its dealers.
- In some cases direct marketing simply is not feasible. The William Wrigley Jr. Company would not find it practical to establish small retail gum shops throughout the world or to sell gum by mail order. It would have to sell gum along with many other small products and would end up in the drugstore and grocery store business. Wrigley finds it easier to work through the extensive network of privately owned distribution organizations.
- Producers who do establish their own channels can often earn a greater return by increasing their investment in their main business. If a company earns a 20 percent rate of return on manufacturing and only a 10 percent return on retailing, it does not make sense to undertake its own retailing.

Intermediaries normally achieve superior efficiency in making goods widely available and accessible to target markets. Through their contacts, experience, specialization, and scale of operation, intermediaries usually offer the firm more than it can achieve on its own. According to Stern and El-Ansary:

Intermediaries smooth the flow of goods and services. . . . This procedure is necessary in order to bridge the discrepancy between the assortment of goods and services generated by the producer and the assortment demanded by the consumer. The discrepancy results from the fact that manufacturers typically produce a large quantity of a limited variety of goods, whereas consumers usually desire only a limited quantity of a wide variety of goods.[3]

Figure 17.1 shows one major source of cost savings using intermediaries. Part (a) shows three producers, each using direct marketing to reach three customers. This system requires nine different contacts. Part (b) shows the three producers working through one distributor, who contacts the three customers. This system requires only six contacts. In this way, intermediaries reduce the number of contacts and the work.

channel functions and flows

A marketing channel performs the work of moving goods from producers to consumers. It overcomes the time, place, and possession gaps that separate goods and services from those who need or want them. Members of the marketing channel perform a number of key functions:

- They gather information about potential and current customers, competitors, and other actors and forces in the marketing environment.
- They develop and disseminate persuasive communications to stimulate purchasing.

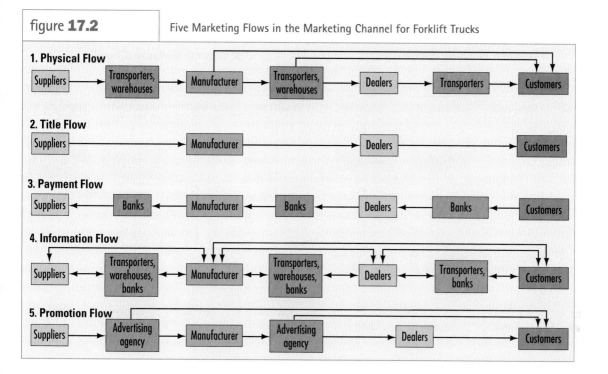

| figure **17.2** | Five Marketing Flows in the Marketing Channel for Forklift Trucks |

1. Physical Flow

2. Title Flow

3. Payment Flow

4. Information Flow

5. Promotion Flow

- They reach agreements on price and other terms so that transfer of ownership or possession can be effected.
- They place orders with manufacturers.
- They acquire the funds to finance inventories at different levels in the marketing channel.
- They assume risks connected with carrying out channel work.
- They provide for the successive storage and movement of physical products.
- They provide for buyers' payment of their bills through banks and other financial institutions.
- They oversee actual transfer of ownership from one organization or person to another.

Some functions (physical, title, promotion) constitute a *forward flow* of activity from the company to the customer; other functions (ordering and payment) constitute a *backward flow* from customers to the company. Still others (information, negotiation, finance, and risk taking) occur in both directions. Five flows are illustrated in Figure 17.2 for the marketing of forklift trucks. If these flows were superimposed in one diagram, the tremendous complexity of even simple marketing channels would be apparent. A manufacturer selling a physical product and services might require three channels: a *sales channel,* a *delivery channel,* and a *service channel.* Dell Computer uses the telephone and the Internet as sales channels, express mail services as the delivery channel, and local repair people as the service channel.

The question is not *whether* various channel functions need to be performed—they must be—but rather, *who* is to perform them. All channel functions have three things in common: They use up scarce resources; they can often be performed better through specialization; and they can be shifted among channel members. When the manufacturer shifts some functions to intermediaries, the producer's costs and prices are lower, but the intermediary must add a charge to cover its work. If the intermediaries are more efficient than the manufacturer, prices to consumers should be lower. If consumers perform some functions themselves, they should enjoy even lower prices.

Marketing functions, then, are more basic than the institutions that perform them at any given time. Changes in channel institutions largely reflect the discovery of more

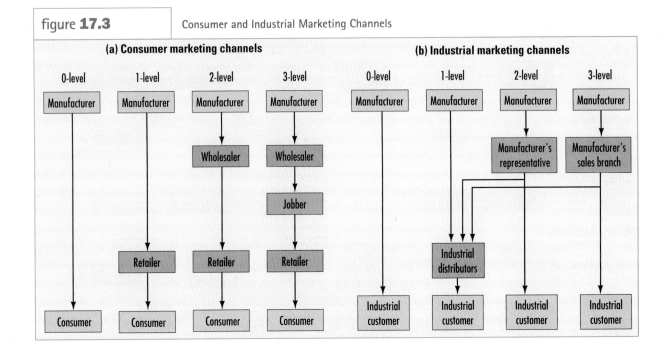

figure **17.3**   Consumer and Industrial Marketing Channels

efficient ways to combine or separate the economic functions that provide assortments of goods to target customers.

channel levels

The producer and the final customer are part of every channel. We will use the number of intermediary levels to designate the length of a channel. Figure 17.3(a) illustrates several consumer-goods marketing channels of different lengths.

A **zero-level channel** (also called a *direct-marketing channel*) consists of a manufacturer selling directly to the final customer. The major examples are door-to-door sales, home parties, mail order, telemarketing, TV selling, Internet selling, and manufacturer-owned stores. Avon sales representatives sell cosmetics door-to-door; Tupperware representatives sell kitchen goods through home parties; Franklin Mint sells collectibles through mail order; Shearson-Lehman brokers use the telephone to prospect for new customers; some exercise equipment manufacturers sell through TV commercials or hour-long "infomercials"; Amazon sells books online; and Gateway sells computers through its own stores.

A **one-level channel** contains one selling intermediary, such as a retailer. A **two-level channel** contains two intermediaries. In consumer markets, these are typically a wholesaler and a retailer. A **three-level channel** contains three intermediaries. In the meatpacking industry, wholesalers sell to jobbers, who sell to small retailers. Longer marketing channels can be found. In Japan, food distribution may involve as many as six levels. From the producer's point of view, obtaining information about end users and exercising control becomes more difficult as the number of channel levels increases.

Figure 17.3(b) shows channels commonly used in industrial marketing. An industrial-goods manufacturer can use its sales force to sell directly to industrial customers; or it can sell to industrial distributors, who sell to the industrial customers; or it can sell through manufacturer's representatives or its own sales branches directly to industrial customers, or indirectly to industrial customers through industrial distributors. Zero-, one-, and two-level marketing channels are quite common in industrial marketing channels.

Channels normally describe a forward movement of products from source to user. One can also talk about *reverse-flow channels*. They are important in the following cases: (1) to reuse products or containers (such as refillable chemical-carrying drums); (2) to refurbish products (such as circuit boards or computers) for resale; (3) to recycle products (such as paper); and (4) to dispose of products and packaging (waste products). Zikmund and Stanton have commented on reverse-flow channels for recycling or disposal:

> The recycling of solid wastes is a major ecological goal. Although recycling is technologically feasible, reversing the flow of materials in the channel of distribution—marketing trash through a "backward" channel—presents a challenge. Existing backward channels are primitive, and financial incentives are inadequate. The consumer must be motivated to undergo a role change and become a producer—the initiating force in the reverse distribution process.[4]

Several intermediaries play a role in reverse-flow channels, including manufacturers' redemption centers, community groups, traditional intermediaries such as soft-drink intermediaries, trash-collection specialists, recycling centers, trash-recycling brokers, and central-processing warehousing.[5]

service sector channels

The concept of marketing channels is not limited to the distribution of physical goods. Producers of services and ideas also face the problem of making their output available and accessible to target populations. Schools develop "educational-dissemination systems" and hospitals develop "health-delivery systems." These institutions must figure out agencies and locations for reaching a population spread out over an area.

> Hospitals must be located in geographic space to serve the people with complete medical care, and we must build schools close to the children who have to learn. Fire stations must be located to give rapid access to potential conflagrations, and voting booths must be placed so that people can cast their ballots without expending unreasonable amounts of time, effort, or money to reach the polling stations. Many of our states face the problem of locating branch campuses to serve a burgeoning and increasingly well educated population. In the cities we must create and locate playgrounds for the children. Many overpopulated countries must assign birth control clinics to reach the people with contraceptive and family planning information.[6]

As Internet technology advances, service industries such as banking, insurance, travel, and stock buying and selling will take place through new channels.

Peoples.com Connecticut-based People's Bank, a brick-and-mortar bank, added an Internet site as early as 1995 to provide additional services and convenience to its customers. The site contains a "live banker now" feature that allows its customers to "live chat" with a representative any time during 11 hours of the day, Monday through Friday, about mortgages, CD rates, and other banking questions. The customer can hit a "Call Me Now" button to request a phone call. The bank is receiving about 20,000 e-mails per month and answering them within four hours, which is considered good service. The site contains easy-to-use mortgage and savings demos. Clients can integrate their banking and brokerage accounts, pay bills online, borrow money online, and access their credit card histories. While the site's primary role is to provide access and convenience to the bank's existing clients, it is also used to attract new clients.[7]

Marketing channels also keep changing in "person" marketing. Before 1940, professional comedians could reach audiences through seven channels: vaudeville houses, special events, nightclubs, radio, movies, carnivals, and theaters. Vaudeville houses have vanished and been replaced by comedy clubs and cable television stations. Politicians also must choose a mix of channels—mass-media, rallies, coffee hours, spot TV ads, faxes, Web sites—for delivering their messages to voters.[8]

The People's Bank Internet site, with the many services it offers to make banking easier for customers.

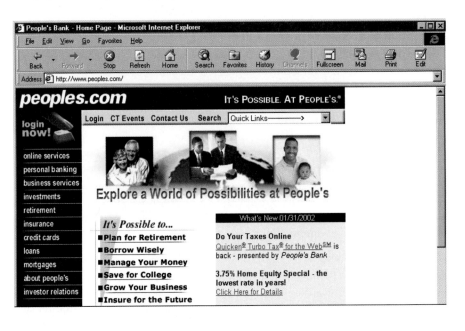

information highway channels

There was a time when information could only be passed from mouth to mouth, or by posters, or by mail. The invention of the telegraph made it possible to communicate over long distances by encrypting messages in dots and dashes. The telephone made it possible to communicate by voice using copper wires. Radio and television send voice and video signals through the wireless electromagnetic spectrum. Cable sends video content over coaxial cables. Satellite introduced the capability of beaming data, voice, text, and videos from satellites orbiting the earth.

Each information channel was originally designed to carry one type of information. Telephone carried voice, cable networks carried video programming, ATMs carried data. Today, there is a major drive to expand bandwidth so that these channels can effectively carry data, voice, video, and text. The rapid growth of the Internet, extranets, and intranets has created a huge demand for information channel capacity. Copper wires have too limited a bandwidth, so much hope lies in expanding the carrying capacity of fiber and in wireless transmission.

Marketers need to understand that these information channels require the inputs of four types of companies to function effectively: *content* companies (Disney, Time Warner, Prentice Hall), *consumer devices* companies (Nokia, Motorola, Sony, Palm), *components* companies (Lucent, Cisco), and *conduit* companies (AT&T, WorldCom, Verizon). These companies make up the information industry, and they face distinct marketing challenges in running their respective businesses.

channel-design decisions

A new firm typically starts as a local operation selling in a limited market, using existing intermediaries. The number of intermediaries in any local market is apt to be limited: a few manufacturers' sales agents, a few wholesalers, several established retailers, a few trucking companies, and a few warehouses. Deciding on the best channels might not be a problem. The problem might be to convince the available intermediaries to handle the firm's line.

If the firm is successful, it might branch into new markets. It might have to use different channels in different markets. In smaller markets, the firm might sell directly to retailers; in larger markets, it might sell through distributors. In rural areas, it might work with general-goods merchants; in urban areas, with limited-line merchants. In one part of the country, it might grant exclusive franchises; in another, it might sell through all outlets willing to handle the merchandise. In one country it might use international sales agents; in another, it might partner with a local firm.[9] In short, the channel system evolves in response to local opportunities and conditions.

In managing its intermediaries, the firm must decide how much effort to devote to push versus pull marketing. A **push strategy** involves the manufacturer using its sales force and trade promotion money to induce intermediaries to carry, promote, and sell the product to end users. Push strategy is appropriate where there is low brand loyalty in a category, brand choice is made in the store, the product is an impulse item, and product benefits are well understood. A **pull strategy** involves the manufacturer using advertising and promotion to induce consumers to ask intermediaries for the product, thus inducing the intermediaries to order it. Pull strategy is appropriate when there is high brand loyalty and high involvement in the category, when people perceive differences between brands, and when people choose the brand before they go to the store. Companies in the same industry may differ in their emphasis on push or pull.

Designing a channel system involves four steps: (1) analyzing customer needs, (2) establishing channel objectives, (3) identifying major channel alternatives, and (4) evaluating major channel alternatives.

analyze customers' desired service output levels

In designing the marketing channel, the marketer must understand the service output levels desired by target customers. Channels produce five service outputs:

1. *Lot size:* The number of units the channel permits a typical customer to purchase on one occasion. In buying cars for its fleet, Hertz prefers a channel from which it can buy a large lot size; a household wants a channel that permits buying a lot size of one.
2. *Waiting time:* The average time customers of that channel wait for receipt of the goods. Customers normally prefer fast delivery channels.
3. *Spatial convenience:* The degree to which the marketing channel makes it easy for customers to purchase the product. Chevrolet, for example, offers greater spatial convenience than Cadillac, because there are more Chevrolet dealers. Chevrolet's greater market decentralization helps customers save on transportation and search costs in buying and repairing an automobile.
4. *Product variety:* The assortment breadth provided by the marketing channel. Normally, customers prefer a greater assortment because more choices increase the chance of finding what they need.
5. *Service backup:* The add-on services (credit, delivery, installation, repairs) provided by the channel. The greater the service backup, the greater the work provided by the channel.[10]

The marketing-channel designer knows that providing greater service outputs means increased channel costs and higher prices for customers. The success of discount stores indicates that many consumers are willing to accept smaller service outputs if they can save money.

establish objectives and constraints

Channel objectives should be stated in terms of targeted service output levels. According to Louis Bucklin, under competitive conditions, channel institutions should arrange their functional tasks to minimize total channel costs with respect to desired levels of service outputs.[11] Usually, several market segments that desire differing service output levels can be identified. Effective planning requires determining which market segments to serve and the best channels to use in each case.

Channel objectives vary with product characteristics. Perishable products require more direct marketing. Bulky products, such as building materials, require channels that minimize the shipping distance and the amount of handling. Nonstandardized products, such as custom-built machinery and specialized business forms, are sold directly by company sales representatives. Products requiring installation or maintenance services, such as heating and cooling systems, are usually sold and maintained by the company or by franchised dealers. High-unit-value products such as generators and turbines are often sold through a company sales force rather than intermediaries.

Channel design must take into account the strengths and weaknesses of different types of intermediaries. For example, manufacturers' reps are able to contact customers at a low cost per customer because the total cost is shared by several clients, but the selling effort per customer is less intense than if company sales reps did the selling. Channel design is also influenced by competitors' channels.

Channel design must adapt to the larger environment. When economic conditions are depressed, producers want to move their goods to market using shorter channels and without services that add to the final price of the goods. Legal regulations and restrictions also affect channel design. U.S. law looks unfavorably on channel arrangements that may tend to substantially lessen competition or create a monopoly.

identify major channel alternatives

Companies can choose from a wide variety of channels for reaching customers—from sales forces to agents, distributors, dealers, direct mail, telemarketing, and the Internet. Each channel has unique strengths as well as weaknesses. Sales forces can handle complex products and transactions, but they are expensive. The Internet is much less expensive, but it cannot handle complex products. Distributors can create sales, but the company loses direct contact with customers.

The problem is further complicated by the fact that most companies now use a mix of channels. Each channel hopefully reaches a different segment of buyers and delivers the right products to each at the least cost. When this does not happen, there is usually channel conflict and excessive cost.

A channel alternative is described by three elements: the types of available business intermediaries, the number of intermediaries needed, and the terms and responsibilities of each channel member.

TYPES OF INTERMEDIARIES   A firm needs to identify the types of intermediaries available to carry on its channel work. Here are two examples:

A test-equipment manufacturer developed an audio device for detecting poor mechanical connections in machines with moving parts. Company executives felt this product would sell in all industries where electric, combustion, or steam engines were used, such as aviation, automobiles, railroads, food canning, construction, and oil. The sales force was small. The problem was how to reach these diverse industries effectively. The following alternatives were identified:

- Expand the company's direct sales force. Assign sales representatives to contact all prospects in an area, or develop separate sales forces for the different industries.
- Hire manufacturers' agents in different regions or end-use industries to sell the new equipment.
- Find distributors in the different regions or end-use industries who will buy and carry the device. Give them exclusive distribution, adequate margins, product training, and promotional support.

A consumer electronics company produces cellular car phones. It identified the following channel alternatives:

- The company could sell its car phones to automobile manufacturers to be installed as original equipment.
- The company could sell its car phones to auto dealers.
- The company could sell its car phones to retail automotive-equipment dealers through a direct sales force or through distributors.

- The company could sell its car phones to car phone specialist dealers through a direct sales force or dealers.
- The company could sell its car phones through mail-order catalogs.
- The company could sell its car phones through mass merchandisers such as Best Buy or Circuit City.

Companies should search for innovative marketing channels. The Conn Organ Company merchandises organs through department stores and discount stores, thus drawing more attention than it ever enjoyed in small music stores. The Book-of-the-Month Club merchandises books through the mail. Other sellers have followed with record-of-the-month clubs, candy-of-the-month clubs, flower-of-the-month clubs, fruit-of-the-month clubs, and dozens of others.

Sometimes a company chooses an unconventional channel because of the difficulty or cost of working with the dominant channel. The advantage is that the company will encounter less competition during the initial move into this channel. After trying to sell its inexpensive Timex watches through regular jewelry stores, the U.S. Time Company placed its watches in fast-growing mass-merchandise outlets. Avon chose door-to-door selling because it was not able to break into regular department stores. The company made more money than most firms selling through department stores.

Chiodo Candy Company   In the 1980s, Chiodo Candy was getting clobbered by candy mega-company E. J. Brach in the war for supermarket shelf space. The company began looking for alternative distribution channels. In 1988 it came up with a winner in the new club and warehouse stores. Club stores did not require any shelving fees and were receptive to new products. These stores wanted large packages, so Chiodo developed a plastic tub that could hold up to two pounds of penny candy. Soon club buyers were ordering more than 8,000 tubs at a time.[12]

NUMBER OF INTERMEDIARIES   Companies have to decide on the number of intermediaries to use at each channel level. Three strategies are available: exclusive distribution, selective distribution, and intensive distribution.

Exclusive distribution means severely limiting the number of intermediaries. It is used when the producer wants to maintain control over the service level and outputs offered by the resellers. Often it involves *exclusive dealing* arrangements. By granting exclusive distribution, the producer hopes to obtain more dedicated and knowledgeable selling. It requires greater partnership between seller and reseller and is used in the distribution of new automobiles, some major appliances, and some women's apparel brands. Relationships with intermediaries and the corporation can be strained when a company decides to alter an exclusive distribution relationship.

Avon   After 115 years of using only "Avon Ladies" to sell directly to consumers, in 2001, Avon Products, Inc., negotiated with Sears and JCPenney to develop in-store sales of the company's cosmetics. To avoid alienating its 500,000 U.S. representatives, the company moved cautiously at first. Avon planned to debut its in-store beauty centers, which resemble both mini-salons and typical cosmetic counters, in only 70 of JCPenney's 1,140 stores and only a few dozen of Sears' 860 stores. Avon also developed a new and separate product line called Avon Gold, which differs in price, packaging, and content from the products sold by Avon Ladies.[13]

Selective distribution involves the use of more than a few but less than all of the intermediaries who are willing to carry a particular product. It is used by established companies and by new companies seeking distributors. The company does not have to worry about too many outlets; it can gain adequate market coverage with more control and less cost than intensive distribution. Disney is a good example of selective distribution.

Disney   Disney sells its videos through five different channels: Movie rental stores like Blockbuster; the company's proprietary retail stores, called Disney Stores; retail stores like Best Buy; online retailers like Amazon.com and Disney's own online Disney Stores; the Disney catalog and other catalog sellers. These varied channels afford Disney maximum market coverage, and enable the company to offer its videos at a number of price points.[14]

Intensive distribution consists of the manufacturer placing the goods or services in as many outlets as possible. This strategy is generally used for items such as tobacco products, soap, snack foods, and gum, products for which the consumer requires a great deal of location convenience.

Manufacturers are constantly tempted to move from exclusive or selective distribution to more intensive distribution to increase coverage and sales. This strategy may help in the short term, but often hurts long-term performance, as the Calvin Klein experience illustrates.

Calvin Klein   In May 2000, designer Calvin Klein sued Linda Wachner, CEO of Warnaco Group Inc., for selling his jeans to cut-rate mass-market outlets without his permission. Warnaco, which has the license to make and distribute the jeans, was accused by Calvin Klein of making lower-quality jeans for these outlets, and therefore hurting his image. The suit was settled out of court in January 2001, and both sides said they "look forward to expanding jeanswear sales consistent with the image and prestige of Calvin Klein products." Warnaco would limit distributing jeanswear products to department and specialty stores.

TERMS AND RESPONSIBILITIES OF CHANNEL MEMBERS   The producer must determine the rights and responsibilities of participating channel members. Each channel member must be treated respectfully and given the opportunity to be profitable.[15] The main elements in the "trade-relations mix" are price policies, conditions of sale, territorial rights, and specific services to be performed by each party.

Price policy calls for the producer to establish a price list and schedule of discounts and allowances that intermediaries see as equitable and sufficient.

Conditions of sale refers to payment terms and producer guarantees. Most producers grant cash discounts to distributors for early payment. Producers might also guarantee distributors against defective merchandise or price declines. A guarantee against price declines gives distributors an incentive to buy larger quantities.

Distributors' territorial rights define the distributors' territories and the terms under which the producer will enfranchise other distributors. Distributors normally expect to receive full credit for all sales in their territory, whether or not they did the selling.

Mutual services and responsibilities must be carefully spelled out, especially in franchised and exclusive-agency channels. McDonald's provides franchisees with a building, promotional support, a record-keeping system, training, and general administrative and technical assistance. In turn, franchisees are expected to satisfy company standards regarding physical facilities, cooperate with new promotional programs, furnish requested information, and buy supplies from specified vendors.

evaluate the major alternatives

Each channel alternative needs to be evaluated against economic, control, and adaptive criteria.

figure **17.4**

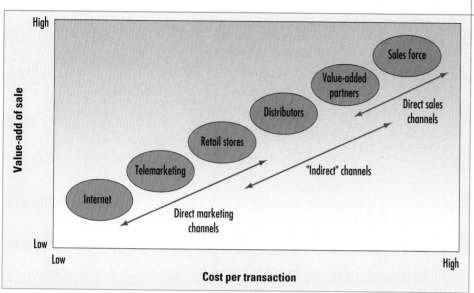

Source: Oxford Associates, adapted from Dr. Rowland T. Moriarty, Cubex Corp.

ECONOMIC CRITERIA   Each channel alternative will produce a different level of sales and costs. Figure 17.4 shows how six different sales channels stack up in terms of the value added per sale and the cost per transaction. For example, in selling industrial products costing between $2,000 and $5,000, the cost per transaction is $500 (field sales), $200 (distributors), $50 (telesales), and $10 (Internet). Banks claim that in selling retail banking services, the cost per transaction is $2 (teller), $.50 (ATM), and $.10 (Internet). Clearly, sellers would try to replace high-cost channels with low-cost channels when the value added per sale was sufficient. When sellers discover a convenient lower-cost channel, they try to get their customers to use it. The company may reward customers for switching. SAS, the Scandinavian airline, gives bonus points to customers who order electronic tickets via the Internet. Other companies may raise the fees on customers using their higher-cost channels to get them to switch. Companies that are successful in switching their customers to lower-cost channels, assuming no loss of sales or deterioration in service quality, will gain a **channel advantage**.[16]

The lower-cost channels tend to be low-touch channels. This is not important in ordering commodity items, but buyers who are shopping for more complex products prefer high-touch channels such as salespeople.

As an example of an economic analysis of channel choices, consider the following situation:

A Memphis furniture manufacturer wants to sell its line to retailers on the West Coast. The manufacturer is trying to decide between two alternatives: One calls for hiring 10 new sales representatives who would operate out of a sales office in San Francisco. They would receive a base salary plus commissions. The other alternative would be to use a San Francisco manufacturers' sales agency that has extensive contacts with retailers. The agency has 30 sales representatives, who would receive a commission based on their sales.

The first step is to determine whether a company sales force or a sales agency will produce more sales. Most marketing managers believe that a company sales force will sell more. They concentrate on the company's products; they are better trained to

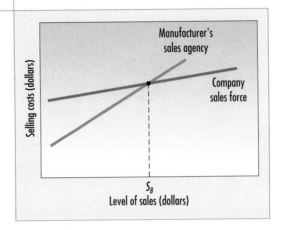

figure **17.5**

Break-even Cost Chart for the Choice Between a Company Sales Force and a Manufacturer's Sales Agency

sell those products; they are more aggressive because their future depends on the company's success; and they are more successful because many customers prefer to deal directly with the company. However, the sales agency could conceivably sell more. First, the agency has 30 representatives, not just 10. This sales force might be just as aggressive as a direct sales force, depending on the commission level. Some customers prefer dealing with agents who represent several manufacturers rather than with salespersons from one company; and the agency has extensive contacts and marketplace knowledge, whereas a company sales force would need to build these from scratch.

The next step is to estimate the costs of selling different volumes through each channel. The cost schedules are shown in Figure 17.5. The fixed costs of engaging a sales agency are lower than those of establishing a company sales office, but costs rise faster through an agency because sales agents get a larger commission than company salespeople. The final step is comparing sales and costs. As Figure 17.5 shows, there is one sales level (S_B) at which selling costs are the same for the two channels. The sales agency is thus the better channel for any sales volume below S_B, and the company sales branch is better at any volume above S_B. Given this information, it is not surprising that sales agents tend to be used by smaller firms, or by large firms in smaller territories where the volume is low.

CONTROL AND ADAPTIVE CRITERIA   Using a sales agency poses a control problem. A sales agency is an independent firm seeking to maximize its profits. Agents may concentrate on the customers who buy the most, not necessarily those who buy the manufacturer's goods. Furthermore, agents might not master the technical details of the company's product or handle its promotion materials effectively.

To develop a channel, members must make some degree of commitment to each other for a specified period of time. Yet these commitments invariably lead to a decrease in the producer's ability to respond to a changing marketplace. In rapidly changing, volatile, or uncertain product markets, the producer needs channel structures and policies that provide high adaptability.

channel-management decisions

After a company has chosen a channel alternative, individual intermediaries must be selected, trained, motivated, and evaluated. Channel arrangements must be modified over time.

selecting channel members

Companies need to select their channel members carefully. To customers, the channels are the company. Consider the negative impression customers would get of McDonald's, Shell Oil, or Ford if one or more of their outlets or dealers consistently appeared dirty, inefficient, or unpleasant.

Producers vary in their ability to attract qualified intermediaries. Toyota was able to attract many new dealers for its new Lexus. However, when Polaroid started up as a company, it could not get camera stores to carry its new cameras and was forced to use mass-merchandising outlets. Consider what happened at Epson.

Epson   Japan's Epson Corporation, a leading manufacturer of computer printers, decided to add computers to its product line. Not happy with its current distributors nor trusting their ability to sell to new types of retail outlets, Epson quietly recruited new distributors. It gave Hergenrather, a recruiting company, the following instructions: (1) Search for applicants who have two-step distribution experience (factory to distributor to dealer). (2) Applicants have to be willing and able to set up their own distributorships. (3) They will be offered $80,000 yearly salary plus bonus and $375,000 to help them set up in business; each will add $25,000 of his or her own money, and each will get equity in the business. (4) They will handle only Epson products but may stock other companies' software. Each distributor will hire a training manager and run a fully equipped service center. The recruiting firm used the Yellow Pages to get the names of existing distributors and phoned the second-in-command managers. It arranged interviews and, after much work, produced a list of highly qualified individuals, from which it chose the 12 most qualified candidates. Epson's existing distributors were given a 90-day termination notice. Yet in spite of all these steps, Epson never succeeded as a computer manufacturer.[17]

Whether producers find it easy or difficult to recruit intermediaries, they should at least determine what characteristics distinguish the better intermediaries. They should evaluate the number of years in business, other lines carried, growth and profit record, financial strength, cooperativeness, and service reputation. If the intermediaries are sales agents, producers should evaluate the number and character of other lines carried and the size and quality of the sales force. If the intermediaries are department stores that want exclusive distribution, the producer should evaluate locations, future growth potential, and type of clientele.

training channel members

Companies need to plan and implement careful training programs for their intermediaries, because they will be viewed as the company by end users. Here are some examples of reseller training programs.

Microsoft   Microsoft requires third-party service engineers to complete a set of courses and take certification exams. Those who pass are formally recognized as Microsoft Certified Professionals, and they can use this designation to promote business.

Mita Corporation   Mita, producer of photocopying equipment, uses a specially created CD-ROM to train its dealers. A dealer's sales rep walks through all the steps in selling copier equipment, and because the CD-ROM program is interactive, the sales rep can "speak" to a hypothetical customer, make a sales presentation, handle objections, and ask for the sale. The rep's performance is scored and the CD-ROM program then offers suggestions for improvement.

Marketing
MEMO

Retail Cooperation Strategies

Alert manufacturers who want to develop stronger links with their retail customers are implementing a system called *efficient consumer response (ECR)*. Four tools are involved:

1. *Activity-based cost accounting.* This accounting method enables the manufacturer to measure and demonstrate the true costs of the resources consumed in meeting a retail chain's requirements.
2. *Electronic data interchange (EDI).* This data network technique improves the manufacturer's ability to manage inventory, shipments, and promotion.
3. *Continuous replenishment program (CRP).* Continuous replenishment enables manufacturers to replenish products on the basis of actual and forecasted store demand.
4. *Flow-through cross-dock replenishment.* This distribution method allows larger shipments headed for retailer distribution centers to be reloaded for shipment to individual stores, with little or no storage time lost at the distribution center.

Manufacturers that master ECR can gain an edge over their competitors.

Source: Gary Davies, *Trade Marketing Strategies* (London: Paul Chapman, 1993).

Ford Motor Company   Ford beams training programs and technical information via its satellite-based Fordstar Network to more than 6,000 dealer sites. Service engineers at each dealership sit around a conference table and view a monitor on which an instructor explains procedures such as repairing onboard electronics, and asks and answers questions. Increasingly, Ford is developing training programs that can be delivered to dealers over the Internet.

motivating channel members

A company needs to view its intermediaries in the same way it views its end users. It needs to determine intermediaries' needs and construct a channel positioning such that its channel offering is tailored to provide superior value to these intermediaries. (See "Marketing Memo: Retail Cooperation Strategies.")

The company should provide training programs, market research programs, and other capability-building programs to improve intermediaries' performance. The company must constantly communicate its view that the intermediaries are partners in a joint effort to satisfy end users of the product.

Brewski Brewing Company   When microbrewer Brewski Brewing Company launched its business, it offered attractive incentives to the large and small distributors who had signed on to sell its products. Once distributors began selling the product, they were rewarded with leather jackets valued at $300 for reaching distribution goals in a series of short-term incentive programs. In addition, distributors are empowered to offer top customers a solid wood, hand-carved, hand-painted tap handle that features the Brewski logo.[18]

Stimulating channel members to top performance starts with understanding their needs and wants. Philip McVey listed the following propositions to help understand intermediaries:

[The intermediary often acts] as a purchasing agent for his customers and only secondarily as a selling agent for his suppliers. . . . He is interested in selling any product which these customers desire to buy from him. . . .

The [intermediary] attempts to weld all of his offerings into a family of items which he can sell in combination, as a packaged assortment, to individual customers. His selling efforts are directed primarily at obtaining orders for the assortment, rather than for individual items. . . .

Unless given incentive to do so, [intermediaries] will not maintain separate sales records by brands sold. . . . Information that could be used in product development, pricing, packaging, or promotion planning is buried in nonstandard records of [intermediaries], and sometimes purposely secreted from suppliers.[19]

Producers vary greatly in skill in managing distributors. They can draw on the following types of power to elicit cooperation:

■ *Coercive power:* A manufacturer threatens to withdraw a resource or terminate a relationship if intermediaries fail to cooperate. This power can be effective, but its exercise produces resentment and can lead the intermediaries to organize countervailing power.

■ *Reward power:* The manufacturer offers intermediaries an extra benefit for performing specific acts or functions. Reward power typically produces better results than coercive power, but can be overrated. The intermediaries may come to expect a reward every time the manufacturer wants a certain behavior to occur.

■ *Legitimate power:* The manufacturer requests a behavior that is warranted under the contract. As long as the intermediaries view the manufacturer as a legitimate leader, legitimate power works.

- *Expert power:* The manufacturer has special knowledge that the intermediaries value. Once the expertise is passed on to the intermediaries, however, this power weakens. The manufacturer must continue to develop new expertise so that the intermediaries will want to continue cooperating.
- *Referent power:* The manufacturer is so highly respected that intermediaries are proud to be associated with it. Companies such as IBM, Caterpillar, and Hewlett-Packard have high referent power.[20]

Intermediaries can aim for a relationship based on cooperation, partnership, or distribution programming.[21] Most producers see the main challenge as gaining intermediaries' cooperation. They often use positive motivators, such as higher margins, special deals, premiums, cooperative advertising allowances, display allowances, and sales contests. At times they will apply negative sanctions, such as threatening to reduce margins, slow down delivery, or terminate the relationship. The weakness of this approach is that the producer is using crude, stimulus-response thinking.

More sophisticated companies try to forge a long-term partnership with distributors. The manufacturer clearly communicates what it wants from its distributors in the way of market coverage, inventory levels, marketing development, account solicitation, technical advice and services, and marketing information. The manufacturer seeks distributor agreement with these policies and may introduce a compensation plan for adhering to the policies. Here are some examples of successful partner-building practices:

- Timken Corporation (roller bearings) has its sales reps make multilevel calls on its distributors.
- DuPont has a distributor marketing steering committee that meets regularly.
- Dayco Corporation (engineered plastics and rubber products) runs an annual week-long retreat with 20 distributors' executives and 20 Dayco executives.
- Vanity Fair, Levi Strauss, and Hanes have formed "quick response" partnerships with discounters and department stores.
- Rust-Oleum introduces a menu of marketing programs each quarter; distributors choose the programs that fit their needs.

Consider the program Ford implemented to motivate its dealers.

Ford   For dealerships that meet new standards for cleanliness, appearance, service, and training, Ford bestows the distinction Blue Oval Certified. To signal to customers which dealerships have been certified, Ford uses a blue thumbprint logo. As an incentive, certified dealers receive a 1.25 percent discount on cars from Ford. As of May 2001, 80 percent of Ford's 4,100 dealers in the United States had met the Blue Oval standards.[22]

The most advanced supply-distributor arrangement is **distribution programming**, which can be defined as building a planned, professionally managed, vertical marketing system that meets the needs of both manufacturer and distributors. The manufacturer establishes a department within the company called *distributor-relations planning*. Its job is to identify distributor needs and build up merchandising programs to help each distributor operate as efficiently as possible. This department and the distributors jointly plan merchandising goals, inventory levels, space and visual merchandising plans, sales-training requirements, and advertising and promotion plans. The aim is to convert the distributors from thinking that they make their money primarily on the buying side (through tough negotiation with the manufacturer) to seeing that they make their money on the selling side (by being part of a sophisticated, vertical marketing system). Kraft and Procter & Gamble are two companies with excellent distributor-relations planning.

Too many manufacturers think of their distributors and dealers as customers rather than working partners. Up to now, we have treated manufacturers and distributors as separate organizations, but many manufacturers are distributors of related products made by other manufacturers, and some distributors also own or contract for the manufacture of

marketing **insight**

Jeans by Any Other Name . . . Brand, or Label

Retailers and manufacturers struggle to differentiate brands by image and by distribution channel. Jeans—that staple of the American wardrobe—fall into four classes: national brands, designer labels, private labels, and retail store brands. Different types of brands have different impacts on profits.

National brands are owned by a manufacturer who advertises and sells them nationally. One of the first apparel brands to gain national recognition was Levi Strauss denim jeans in the 1870s. Examples of national brand jeans include Levi (still the number-one best-seller), Wrangler and Lee (both products of the VF Corporation), and Guess?. Levi saw great success in the 1980s and 1990s with its nondenim line of casual pants (Dockers) and its line of dress pants (Slates).

Designer labels carry the name of a designer and are usually sold at high prices ($100 and up) both nationally and internationally. The apparel industry's current mega-designers—Ralph Lauren, Calvin Klein, Tommy Hilfiger, and Donna Karan—all have their own jeans lines. Some foreign designer labels, such as Hugo Boss, are imported into the United States. Even some retired designers, such as Liz Claiborne and Gloria Vanderbilt, have active jeans lines.

A private label is owned by a retailer and found only in its stores. Examples are the Kathie Lee Gifford line sold by Wal-Mart, the Jaclyn Smith line sold by Kmart, and the Badge kids line sold by Federated Stores.

A retail store brand is the name of a chain that is used as the exclusive label on most of the items in the store or catalog. Examples include GAP, The Limited, J. Crew, L.L. Bean, and Lands' End. GAP successfully introduced the first complete store-brand jeans line in 1991. Private labels are usually priced well under national brands and far below designer brands. Store-brand prices, on the other hand, are usually close to those of national brands, and above those of private labels. Profit margins, however, are not always in proportion to selling price. The profit margin on store-brand merchandise is typically 5 to 15 percent greater than the profit on national brands.

Sources: "True Blue," *Esquire*, July 1, 1994, p. 102; George White, "Wall Street, California; Fashion Pushes Sales Forward," *Los Angeles Times*, September 8, 1998, p. B1; Sharon Haver, "Shedding Light on Denim's Dark Past," *Rocky Mountain News*, May 28, 1998, p. 6D; Stacy Perman, "Business: Levi's Gets the Blues," *Time*, November 11, 1997, p. 66.

in-house brands. "Marketing Insight: Jeans by Any Other Name . . . Brand, or Label" illustrates this situation in the jeans industry, but it is common in many others.

evaluating channel members

Producers must periodically evaluate intermediaries' performance against such standards as sales-quota attainment, average inventory levels, customer delivery time, treatment of damaged and lost goods, and cooperation in promotional and training programs. A producer will occasionally discover that it is paying too much to particular intermediaries for what they are actually doing. One manufacturer that was compensating a distributor for holding inventories found that the inventories were actually held in a public warehouse at its expense. Producers should set up functional discounts in which they pay specified amounts for the trade channel's performance of each agreed-upon service. Underperformers need to be counseled, retrained, remotivated, or terminated.

modifying channel arrangements

A producer must periodically review and modify its channel arrangements. Modification becomes necessary when the distribution channel is not working as planned, consumer buying patterns change, the market expands, new competition arises, innovative distribution channels emerge, and the product moves into later stages in the product life cycle. Consider Apple.

Apple   To combat its lowly 3.4 percent share of the U.S. personal computer market, Apple opened 25 retail locations in 2001. The stores sold Apple products exclusively and targeted tech-savvy customers with in-store product demonstrations, the full

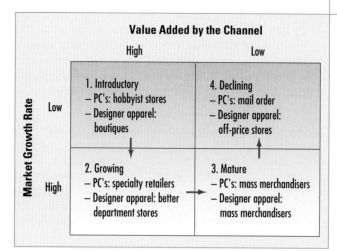

figure **17.6**

Channel Value Added
and Market Growth Rate

line of Macintosh computers, over 300 software titles, a "Genius Bar" staffed by an Apple specialist, and a host of compatible peripherals. Although the move upset existing retailers, Apple explained that since *www.apple.com* generates roughly 25 percent of sales, its own retail chain is a natural extension.[23]

No marketing channel will remain effective over the whole product life cycle. Early buyers might be willing to pay for high value-added channels, but later buyers will switch to lower-cost channels. Small office copiers were first sold by manufacturers' direct sales forces, later through office equipment dealers, still later through mass-merchandisers, and now by mail-order firms and Internet marketers.

Miland Lele developed the grid in Figure 17.6 to show how marketing channels have changed for PCs and designer apparel at different stages in the product life cycle:

- *Introductory stage:* Radically new products or fashions tend to enter the market through specialist channels (such as boutiques) that spot trends and attract early adopters.
- *Rapid growth stage:* As interest grows, higher-volume channels appear (dedicated chains, department stores) that offer services but not as many as the previous channels.
- *Maturity stage:* As growth slows, some competitors move their product into lower-cost channels (mass-merchandisers).
- *Decline stage:* As decline begins, even lower-cost channels emerge (mail-order houses, off-price discounters).[24]

In competitive markets with low entry barriers, the optimal channel structure will inevitably change over time. The change could involve adding or dropping individual channel members, adding or dropping particular market channels, or developing a totally new way to sell goods.

Adding or dropping individual channel members requires an incremental analysis. What would the firm's profits look like with and without this intermediary? An automobile manufacturer's decision to drop a dealer requires subtracting the dealer's sales and estimating the possible sales loss or gain to the manufacturer's other dealers.

Sometimes a producer considers dropping all intermediaries whose sales are below a certain amount. Consider the following.

Marketing
MEMO

**Designing a Customer–
Driven Distribution System**

Stern and Sturdivant have outlined
an excellent framework, called
*Customer-Driven Distribution
System Design*, for moving a poorly
functioning distribution system
closer to a customers' ideal system.
Companies have to reduce the
gaps between the service outputs
target customers desire, those the
existing channel system delivers,
and those management thinks are
feasible within the existing
constraints. Six steps are involved:

1. Research target customers'
   value perceptions, needs, and
   desires regarding channel
   service outputs.
2. Examine the performance of
   the company's and competitors'
   existing distribution systems in
   relation to customer desires.
3. Find service output gaps that
   need corrective action.
4. Identify major constraints that
   will limit possible corrective
   actions.
5. Design a "management-
   bounded" channel solution.
6. Implement the reconfigured
   distribution system.

Source: Louis W. Stern and Adel I. El-
Ansary, *Marketing Channels*, 5th ed.
(Upper Saddle River, NJ: Prentice Hall,
1996), p. 189.

Navistar Navistar noted at one time that 5 percent of its dealers were selling fewer than three or four trucks a year. It cost the company more to service these dealers than their sales were worth, but dropping these dealers could have repercussions on the system as a whole. The unit costs of producing trucks would be higher, because the overhead would be spread over fewer trucks; some employees and equipment would be idled; some business in these markets would go to competitors; and other dealers might become insecure. All these factors must be taken into account.

The most difficult decision involves revising the overall channel strategy.[25] Distribution channels clearly become outmoded, and a gap arises between the existing distribution system and the ideal system that would satisfy target customers' needs and desires. Examples abound: Avon's door-to-door system for selling cosmetics had to be modified as more women entered the workforce, and IBM's exclusive reliance on a field sales force had to be modified with the introduction of low-priced personal computers. (See "Marketing Memo: Designing a Customer-Driven Distribution System.")

channel dynamics

Distribution channels do not stand still. New wholesaling and retailing institutions emerge, and new channel systems evolve. We will look at the recent growth of vertical, horizontal, and multichannel marketing systems and see how these systems cooperate, conflict, and compete.

vertical marketing systems

One of the most significant recent channel developments is the rise of vertical marketing systems. A **conventional marketing channel** comprises an independent producer, wholesaler(s), and retailer(s). Each is a separate business seeking to maximize its own profits, even if this goal reduces profit for the system as a whole. No channel member has complete or substantial control over other members.

A **vertical marketing system (VMS)**, by contrast, comprises the producer, wholesaler(s), and retailer(s) acting as a unified system. One channel member, the *channel captain*, owns the others or franchises them or has so much power that they all cooperate. The channel captain can be the producer, the wholesaler, or the retailer. VMSs arose as a result of strong channel members' attempts to control channel behavior and eliminate the conflict that results when independent members pursue their own objectives. VMSs achieve economies through size, bargaining power, and elimination of duplicated services. They have become the dominant mode of distribution in the United States consumer marketplace, serving between 70 and 80 percent of the total market. There are three types of VMS: corporate, administered, and contractual.

CORPORATE AND ADMINISTERED VMS A *corporate VMS* combines successive stages of production and distribution under single ownership. For example, Sears obtains over 50 percent of the goods it sells from companies that it partly or wholly owns. Sherwin-Williams makes paint but also owns and operates 2,000 retail outlets. Giant Food Stores operates an ice-making facility, a soft-drink bottling operation, an ice cream plant, and a bakery that supplies Giant stores with everything from bagels to birthday cakes.

An *administered VMS* coordinates successive stages of production and distribution through the size and power of one of the members. Manufacturers of a dominant brand are able to secure strong trade cooperation and support from resellers. Thus Kodak, Gillette, Procter & Gamble, and Campbell Soup are able to command high levels of cooperation from their resellers in connection with displays, shelf space, promotions, and price policies.

CONTRACTUAL VMS   A *contractual VMS* consists of independent firms at different levels of production and distribution integrating their programs on a contractual basis to obtain more economies or sales impact than they could achieve alone. Johnston and Lawrence call them "value-adding partnerships" (VAPs).[26] Contractual VMSs now constitute one of the most significant developments in the economy. They are of three types:

1. *Wholesaler-sponsored voluntary chains:* Wholesalers organize voluntary chains of independent retailers to help them compete with large chain organizations. The wholesaler develops a program in which independent retailers standardize their selling practices and achieve buying economies that enable the group to compete effectively with chain organizations.
2. *Retailer cooperatives:* Retailers take the initiative and organize a new business entity to carry on wholesaling and possibly some production. Members concentrate their purchases through the retailer co-op and plan their advertising jointly. Profits are passed back to members in proportion to their purchases. Nonmember retailers can also buy through the co-op but do not share in the profits.
3. *Franchise organizations:* A channel member called a *franchisor* might link several successive stages in the production-distribution process. Franchising has been the fastest-growing retailing development in recent years. Although the basic idea is an old one, some forms of franchising are quite new.

The traditional system is the *manufacturer-sponsored retailer franchise*. Ford, for example, licenses dealers to sell its cars. The dealers are independent businesspeople who agree to meet specified conditions of sales and services. Another is the *manufacturer-sponsored wholesaler franchise*. Coca-Cola, for example, licenses bottlers (wholesalers) in various markets who buy its syrup concentrate and then carbonate, bottle, and sell it to retailers in local markets. A newer system is the *service-firm-sponsored retailer franchise*. A service firm organizes a whole system for bringing its service efficiently to consumers. Examples are found in the auto rental business (Hertz, Avis), fast-food-service business (McDonald's, Burger King), and motel business (Howard Johnson, Ramada Inn).

THE NEW COMPETITION IN RETAILING   Many independent retailers that have not joined VMSs have developed specialty stores that serve special market segments. The result is a polarization in retailing between large vertical marketing organizations and independent specialty stores, which creates a problem for manufacturers. They are strongly tied to independent intermediaries, but must eventually realign themselves with the high-growth vertical marketing systems on less attractive terms. Furthermore, vertical marketing systems constantly threaten to bypass large manufacturers and set up their own manufacturing. *The new competition in retailing is no longer between independent business units but between whole systems of centrally programmed networks (corporate, administered, and contractual) competing against one another to achieve the best cost economies and customer response.* Consider the GAP:

The GAP   The GAP is a highly successful clothing chain store that has spun off additional branded store concepts. It created a lower priceline chain store called Old Navy and acquired Banana Republic to represent a higher priceline chain store. It also started GapKids, BabyGap, and GapMaternity. Each chain has captured significant market shares. The various properties must be managed so as not to cannibalize each other. However, many GAP customers have recently switched to Old Navy, where they find lower prices and see the quality as adequate.

horizontal marketing systems

Another channel development is the **horizontal marketing system**, in which two or more unrelated companies put together resources or programs to exploit an emerging marketing opportunity. Many supermarket chains have arrangements with local banks to offer in-store banking. Each company lacks the capital, know-how, production, or marketing resources to venture alone, or it is afraid of the risk. The companies might work with each other on a temporary or permanent basis or create a joint venture company. H&R Block, Inc., for example, entered into an agreement with GEICO insurance to provide car insurance information to Block customers. Customers now can contact GEICO through a special toll-free number. Here is another example.

Kmart and Fleming　In 2001, when Kmart needed to develop an efficient procurement and inventory system but could not afford to build one from the ground up, it turned to grocery wholesaler Fleming. The two companies formed a $4.5 billion supply-chain alliance governed by a joint team based in Kmart headquarters. Fleming uses its advanced procurement and distribution system to manage Kmart's buying, inventory, and logistics. Kmart expects the alliance will save $400 million during the first three years.[27]

multichannel marketing systems

Once, many companies sold to a single market through a single channel. Today, with the proliferation of customer segments and channel possibilities, more companies have adopted multichannel marketing. **Multichannel marketing** occurs when a single firm uses two or more marketing channels to reach one or more customer segments. Here are some examples.

Parker-Hannifin　The Parker-Hannifin Corporation (PHC) sells pneumatic drills to customers in the lumber, fishing, and aircraft industries. Instead of selling them through one industrial distributor, PHC established three separate channels—*forestry equipment distributors, marine distributors,* and *industrial distributors.* There appears to be little conflict because each type of distributor sells to a separate target segment.

Stihl's product lines. The Web site includes a link to dealerships in the USA and to company locations worldwide.

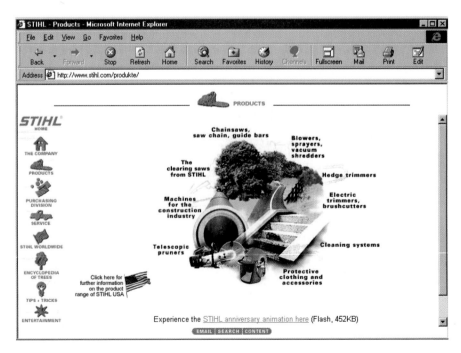

Stihl   Stihl manufactures hand-held outdoor power equipment. All Stihl products are branded under one name and Stihl does not do private label for other companies. Stihl is best known for chain saws, but has expanded into string trimmers, blowers, hedge trimmers, and cut-off machines. It distributes products through a network of geographically exclusive distribution points, then through a network of independent servicing dealers. Stihl is one of the few outdoor power equipment companies that does not sell its products through mass merchants, catalogs, or the Internet.[28]

By adding more channels, companies can gain three important benefits. The first is increased market coverage. The second is lower channel cost—selling by phone rather than personal visits to small customers. The third is more customized selling—adding a technical sales force to sell more complex equipment. The gains from adding new channels come at a price, however. New channels typically introduce conflict and control problems. Two or more channels may end up competing for the same customers. The new channels may be more independent and make cooperation more difficult.

PLANNING CHANNEL ARCHITECTURE   Clearly, companies need to think through their channel architecture. Moriarty and Moran propose using the hybrid grid shown in Figure 17.7 to plan the channel architecture.[29] The grid shows several marketing channels (rows) and several demand-generation tasks (columns). The grid illustrates why using only one channel is not efficient. Consider using only a direct sales force. A salesperson would have to find leads, qualify them, presell, close the sale, provide service, and manage account growth. It would be more efficient for the company to perform the earlier tasks, leaving the salesperson to invest his or her costly time primarily to close the sale. The company's marketing department would generate leads through telemarketing,

figure **17.7**

The Hybrid Grid

Marketing Channels and Methods	VENDOR		Lead Generation	Qualifying Sales	Presales	Close of Sale	Postsales Service	Account Management	CUSTOMER
		Internet							
		National Account Management							
		Direct Sales							
		Telemarketing							
		Direct Mail							
		Retail Stores							
		Distributors							
		Dealers and Value-Added Resellers							
		Advertising							

Demand-Generation Tasks

Source: Rowland T. Moriarty and Ursula Moran, "Marketing Hybrid Marketing Systems," *Harvard Besiness Review* (November–December 1990): 150.

direct mail, advertising, and trade shows. The leads would be sorted into hot, warm, and cool by using qualifying techniques such as checking whether a lead wants a sales call and has adequate purchasing power. The department would also run a preselling campaign informing prospects about the company's products through advertising, direct mail, and telemarketing. The salesperson comes to the prospect when the prospect is ready to talk business. This multichannel architecture optimizes coverage, customization, and control while minimizing cost and conflict.

Companies should use different channels for selling to different-size customers. A company can use its direct sales force to sell to large customers, telemarketing to sell to midsized customers, and distributors to sell to small customers; but these gains can be compromised by an increased level of conflict over who has account ownership. For example, territory-based sales representatives may want credit for all sales in their territories, regardless of the marketing channel used.

ROLES OF INDIVIDUAL FIRMS   Each firm in an industry has to define its role in the channel system. Bert McCammon has distinguished five roles:[30]

1. *Insiders* are members of the dominant channel. They enjoy access to preferred sources of supply and high respect in the industry. They want to perpetuate the existing channel arrangements and are the main enforcers of industry codes of conduct.
2. *Strivers* are firms seeking to become insiders. They have less access to preferred sources of supply, which can handicap them in periods of short supply. They adhere to the industry code because of their desire to become insiders.
3. *Complementers* are not part of the dominant channel. They perform functions not normally performed by others in the channel, serve smaller segments of the market, or handle smaller quantities of merchandise. They usually benefit from the present system and respect the industry code of conduct.
4. *Transients* are outside the dominant channel and do not seek membership. They go in and out of the market and move around as opportunities arise. They have short-run expectations and little incentive to adhere to the industry code of conduct.
5. *Outside innovators* are the real challengers and disrupters of the dominant channels. They develop a new system for carrying out the marketing work of the channel. If successful, they force major channel realignments (see "Marketing for the New Economy: How CarMax Is Transforming the Auto Business").

conflict, cooperation, and competition

No matter how well channels are designed and managed, there will be some conflict, if for no other reason than the interests of independent business entities do not always coincide. Here we examine three questions: What types of conflict arise in channels? What causes channel conflict? What can be done to resolve conflict situations?

TYPES OF CONFLICT AND COMPETITION   Suppose a manufacturer sets up a vertical channel consisting of wholesalers and retailers. The manufacturer hopes for channel cooperation that will produce greater profits for each channel member. Yet vertical, horizontal, and multichannel conflict can occur.

Vertical channel conflict means conflict between different levels within the same channel. General Motors came into conflict with its dealers in trying to enforce policies on service, pricing, and advertising. Coca-Cola came into conflict with bottlers who also agreed to bottle Dr. Pepper. (See "Marketing Memo: Managing Vertical Channel Conflict.")

Horizontal channel conflict involves conflict between members at the same level within the channel. Some Ford car dealers in Chicago complained about other Chicago Ford dealers advertising and pricing too aggressively. Some Pizza Inn franchisees complained about other Pizza Inn franchisees cheating on ingredients, providing poor service, and hurting the overall Pizza Inn image.

Multichannel conflict exists when the manufacturer has established two or more channels that sell to the same market. When Levi Strauss agreed to distribute its jeans

marketing for the **new economy**

How CarMax Is Transforming the Auto Business

For years, buying a used car was considered a dangerous and risky business; used-car salesmen were stock figures in comedy routines. Then CarMax emerged to change the face of the industry and its standards. Circuit City, a major retailer of electronic products, started CarMax, the Auto Superstore, in 1993. The first superstore opened in Richmond, Virginia: CarMax now operates 33 used-car stores and 22 new-car franchises.

What is so special about CarMax? The company locates its used-car superstores, each carrying around 500 cars, on large lots on the outskirts of a city near a major highway. Customers enter an attractive display room, where a sales associate finds out what kind of car they want and then escorts them to a computer kiosk. Using a touch screen, the associate retrieves a full listing of the cars in stock that meet the customer's criteria. A color display of each car can be shown along with the vehicle's features and its fixed selling price. There is no price negotiation. The salesperson, paid a commission on the number of cars sold rather than their value, has no incentive to push higher-priced cars. The customer is informed that CarMax mechanics carried out a 110-point inspection and made any necessary repairs beforehand. Furthermore, a car buyer receives a 5-day money-back guarantee and a 30-day comprehensive warranty. If the buyer wants financing, the CarMax associate can arrange it in 20 minutes. The entire process typically takes less than one hour.

A booming new-car market hurt CarMax at first. In fact, the company reported annual losses in each of its first six years. Recently, the company has found increased value by focusing on the used-car market. Given that today's cars are better and have longer life expectancies, many buyers now prefer to save money by buying a used car, and the substantial growth of car leasing has greatly inflated the supply of used cars. Banks are more willing to offer low-cost financing for used cars, especially when research revealed that default rates were lower for used-car buyers. Finally, dealers have reported earning a higher profit on used cars, up to $100 more than for a new car.

CarMax has been very successful in achieving even greater margins: The company's average selling price for a used vehicle is $15,000 and its average profit margin is 13 percent, compared with industry averages of $13,650 and 11 percent, respectively. As a result of these high margins, CarMax turned its first profit in fiscal 2000.

Sources: Gabriella Stern, "'Nearly New' Autos for Sale: Dealers Buff Up Their Marketing of Used Cars," *Wall Street Journal*, February 17, 1995, p. B1; Gregory J. Gilligan, "Circuit City's CarMax Superstores Pass $300 Million in Yearly Sales," *Knight-Ridder/Tribune Business News*, April 5, 1997, p. 19; Arlena Sawyers, "CarMax Is Out of the Red, In the Pink," *Automotive News*, April 16, 2001, p. 28; Mike Brennan, "Mavericks Are Changing Way Cars Are Sold," *Detroit Free Press*, January 6, 1998, p. 28.

through Sears and JCPenney in addition to its normal specialty store channel, the specialty stores complained. When clothing manufacturers like Ralph Lauren and Anne Klein opened their own stores, the department stores that carried their brands were upset. When Goodyear began selling its popular tire brands through Sears, Wal-Mart, and Discount Tire, it angered its independent dealers. (It eventually placated them by offering exclusive tire models that would not be sold in other retail outlets.) Multichannel conflict is likely to be especially intense when the members of one channel get a lower price (based on larger volume purchases) or work with a lower margin.

One of the major current examples of multichannel conflict is brick-and-mortar companies sweating over whether to add an online e-commerce channel. Barnes & Noble, Merrill Lynch, Compaq, and All State Insurance all resisted, but eventually succumbed after seeing how much online business was rushing to its competitors, Amazon, E*TRADE, Dell, and Direct Line, respectively. Yet adding an e-commerce channel creates the threat of a backlash from retailers, brokers, agents, and other intermediaries. For example, retailers were angered when Mattel decided to sell Barbie dolls via the Internet.

Mattel Just before the 2000 holiday season, Mattel began selling a wide range of toys and children's apparel on its Barbie.com Web site. The company also mailed its first ever Barbie catalog to 4 million U.S households. Retailers perceived these moves as a clear case of channel conflict: "We're supposed to be partners and this is obviously competitive," said one toy retail executive. Mattel sought to placate retailers by noting that online and catalog sales would contribute less than 1 percent of Barbie's sales during the first year, and by not advertising the e-commerce features of the site. The company views its Web site as a "self-funding" marketing and advertising tool designed to foster relationships with customers.[31]

The question is how to sell both through intermediaries and online. There are at least three strategies for trying to gain acceptance from intermediaries. One, offer different brands or products on the Internet. Two, offer the off-line partners higher commissions to cushion the negative impact on sales. Three, take orders on the Web site but have retailers deliver and collect payment.

Here are some companies that have reconciled their off-line and online marketing channels:[32]

- **Talbots.** When Talbots, a specialty women's clothing chain, runs out of an item, the sales clerk will order it at a Talbots' catalog call center. Customers pay a flat $4 shipping charge, which is less than the normal charge on regular catalog orders. The store earns credit for the catalog sale.
- **Liberty Mutual.** Liberty Mutual asks its online customers if they might prefer to work though a financial advisor; if yes, their information will be routed to an advisor.
- **Avon.** Avon showed its reps that its online sales will not overlap with their sales from existing customers and even offered to help reps set up their own Web sites.
- **JCPenny.** JCPenny offers online coupons that can be printed and redeemed in its stores, and may even sell some items online that are not profitable to sell through its stores.
- **Gibson Guitars.** Gibson started by selling accessories such as guitar strings and parts online and is eager to overcome dealers' objections to selling guitars over the Internet. It may have to give some credit to the guitar store nearest the customer who bought online.

Ultimately, companies may need to decide whether to drop some or all of their retailers and go direct.

Dell and Compaq In selling direct, Dell is outperforming all other retailer-dependent competitors. Dell manufactures a PC only after receiving a Web site order from a customer who designs the desired computer on Dell's configurator choiceboard and who pays in advance by clicking in his or her credit card number. Dell gets paid before it makes the computer and uses the customer's cash, instead of its own, to pay suppliers, so it needs less working capital. Compaq, by contrast, has to guess the level of demand for its PCs, fill its warehouses and retailer pipelines with a sufficient number, and hope that they all sell in a reasonable time before Compaq introduces its next generation of PCs.

Given the superiority of Internet-based ordering, what is to stop an auto company from offering customers the ability to design a car on the Web site, and have it assembled and delivered to the customer's premises within a week? The cost of operating a *virtual dealership* would be considerably less than the present dealership systems, where cars sit in inventory for 70 days and companies have to spend about 10 percent of the car's price on ads and promotions to get customers to buy. Our prediction is that more companies in the economy will shift from build-for-stock to build-to-order.

CAUSES OF CHANNEL CONFLICT It is important to identify the causes of channel conflict. Some are easy to resolve, others are not.

One major cause is *goal incompatibility*. For example, the manufacturer may want to achieve rapid market penetration through a low-price policy. Dealers, in contrast, may prefer to work with high margins and pursue short-run profitability. Sometimes conflict arises from *unclear roles and rights*. IBM sells personal computers to large accounts through its own sales force, and its licensed dealers are also trying to sell to large accounts. Territory boundaries and credit for sales often produce conflict.

By adding new channels, a company faces the possibility of channel conflict. The following three channel conflicts arose at IBM:

1. *Conflict between the national account managers and field sales force:* National account managers rely on field salespeople to make calls at certain national account customers located in the salesperson's territory, sometimes on a moment's notice. Requests from several national

account managers to make such calls can seriously disrupt the salesperson's normal schedule and hurt commissions. Salespeople may not cooperate with national account managers when doing so conflicts with their own interests.

2. *Conflict between the field sales force and the telemarketers:* Salespeople often resent the company's setting up a telemarketing operation to sell to smaller customers. The company tells the salespeople that telemarketers free up their time to sell to larger accounts on which they can earn more commission, but the salespeople still object.

3. *Conflict between the field sales force and the dealers:* Dealers include value-added resellers, who buy computers from IBM and add specialized software needed by the target buyer, and computer retail stores, which are an excellent channel for selling small equipment to walk-in traffic and small businesses. These dealers frequently offer specialized software installation and training, better service, and even lower prices than IBM's direct sales force. The direct sales force becomes angry when these dealers go after large accounts: They want IBM to refuse to sell through dealers who try to sell to large accounts, but IBM would lose a lot of business if it dropped these successful resellers. As an alternative, IBM decided to give partial credit to salespeople for business sold to their accounts by aggressive resellers.

Conflict can also stem from *differences in perception.* The manufacturer may be optimistic about the short-term economic outlook and want dealers to carry higher inventory. Dealers may be pessimistic. Conflict might also arise because of the intermediaries' *dependence* on the manufacturer. The fortunes of exclusive dealers, such as auto dealers, are profoundly affected by the manufacturer's product and pricing decisions. This situation creates a high potential for conflict.

MANAGING CHANNEL CONFLICT Some channel conflict can be constructive and lead to more dynamic adaptation to a changing environment, but too much is dysfunctional. The challenge is not to eliminate conflict but to manage it better. There are several mechanisms for effective conflict management.[33]

One is the adoption of superordinate goals. Channel members come to an agreement on the fundamental goal they are jointly seeking, whether it is survival, market share, high quality, or customer satisfaction. They usually do this when the channel faces an outside threat, such as a more efficient competing channel, an adverse piece of legislation, or a shift in consumer desires.

A useful step is to exchange persons between two or more channel levels. General Motors executives might agree to work for a short time in some dealerships, and some dealership owners might work in GM's dealer policy department. Hopefully, the participants will grow to appreciate the other's point of view.

Co-optation is an effort by one organization to win the support of the leaders of another organization by including them in advisory councils, boards of directors, and the like. As long as the initiating organization treats the leaders seriously and listens to their opinions, co-optation can reduce conflict, but the initiating organization may have to compromise its policies and plans to win their support.

Much can be accomplished by encouraging joint membership in and between trade associations. For example, there is good cooperation between the Grocery Manufacturers of America and the Food Marketing Institute, which represents most of the food chains; this cooperation led to the development of the universal product code (UPC). Presumably, the associations can consider issues between food manufacturers and retailers and resolve them in an orderly way.

When conflict is chronic or acute, the parties may have to resort to diplomacy, mediation, or arbitration. *Diplomacy* takes place when each side sends a person or group to meet with its counterpart to resolve the conflict. *Mediation* means resorting to a neutral third party who is skilled in conciliating the two parties' interests. *Arbitration* occurs when the two parties agree to present their arguments to one or more arbitrators and accept the arbitration decision. Sometimes, when none of these methods proves effective, a company or a channel partner may choose to file a lawsuit. Levi Strauss and U.K. retailer Tesco became locked in a legal battle beginning in 1999.

Levi's Levi's filed a suit with the European Court of Justice against Tesco claiming the retailer's selling of low-priced Levi's jeans imported from outside Britain "undermines the product experience." Tesco offers genuine Levis at roughly half the price of other U.K. retailers, and Levi's also objects to the fact that its jeans appear in the same stores that sell produce and other food items. In order to win a decision, Levi's must prove that its brand suffered material damage by being sold at a discount in Tesco.[34]

legal and ethical issues in channel relations

For the most part, companies are legally free to develop whatever channel arrangements suit them. In fact, the law seeks to prevent companies from using exclusionary tactics that might keep competitors from using a channel. Here we briefly consider the legality of certain practices, including exclusive dealing, exclusive territories, tying agreements, and dealers' rights.

Many producers like to develop exclusive channels for their products. A strategy in which the seller allows only certain outlets to carry its products is called **exclusive distribution**, and when the seller requires that these dealers not handle competitors' products, this is called **exclusive dealing**. Both parties benefit from exclusive arrangements: The seller obtains more loyal and dependable outlets, and the dealers obtain a steady source of supply of special products and stronger seller support. Exclusive arrangements are legal as long as they do not substantially lessen competition or tend to create a monopoly, and as long as both parties enter into the agreement voluntarily.

Exclusive dealing often includes exclusive territorial agreements. The producer may agree not to sell to other dealers in a given area, or the buyer may agree to sell only in its own territory. The first practice increases dealer enthusiasm and commitment. It is also perfectly legal—a seller has no legal obligation to sell through more outlets than it wishes. The second practice, whereby the producer tries to keep a dealer from selling outside its territory, has become a major legal issue. An example of bitter lawsuits is one brought by GT Bicycles of Santa Ana, California, against the giant Price-Costco chain, which sold 2,600 of its high-priced mountain bikes at a huge discount, thus upsetting GT's other U.S. dealers. GT alleges that it first sold the bikes to a dealer in Russia and that they were meant for sale only in Russia. GT maintains that it constitutes fraud when discounters work with middlemen to get exclusive goods.[35]

Producers of a strong brand sometimes sell it to dealers only if they will take some or all of the rest of the line. This practice is called full-line forcing. Such **tying agreements** are not necessarily illegal, but they do violate U.S. law if they tend to lessen competition substantially.

Producers are free to select their dealers, but their right to terminate dealers is somewhat restricted. In general, sellers can drop dealers "for cause," but they cannot drop dealers if, for example, the dealers refuse to cooperate in a doubtful legal arrangement, such as exclusive dealing or tying agreements.

summary

1. Most producers do not sell their goods directly to final users. Between producers and final users stands one or more marketing channels, a host of marketing intermediaries performing a variety of functions. Marketing-channel decisions are among the most critical decisions facing management. The company's chosen channel(s) profoundly affect all other marketing decisions.

2. Companies use intermediaries when they lack the financial resources to carry out direct marketing, when direct marketing is not feasible, and when they can earn more by doing so. The use of intermediaries largely boils down to their superior efficiency in making goods widely available and accessible to target markets. The most important functions performed by intermediaries are information, promotion, negotiation, ordering, financing, risk taking, physical possession, payment, and title.

3. Manufacturers have many alternatives for reaching a market. They can sell direct or use one-, two-, or three-level channels.

Deciding which type(s) of channel to use calls for analyzing customer needs, establishing channel objectives, and identifying and evaluating the major alternatives, including the types and numbers of intermediaries involved in the channel. The company must determine whether to distribute its product exclusively, selectively, or intensively, and it must clearly spell out the terms and responsibilities of each channel member.

4. Effective channel management calls for selecting intermediaries and training and motivating them. The goal is to build a long-term partnership that will be profitable for all channel members. Individual members must be periodically evaluated. Channel arrangements may need to be modified when market conditions change.

5. Marketing channels are characterized by continuous and sometimes dramatic change. Three of the most important trends are the growth of vertical marketing systems, horizontal marketing systems, and multichannel marketing systems.

6. All marketing channels have the potential for conflict and competition resulting from such sources as goal incompatibility, poorly defined roles and rights, perceptual differences, and interdependent relationships. Companies can manage conflict by striving for superordinate goals, exchanging people among two or more channel levels, co-opting the support of leaders in different parts of the channel, and encouraging joint membership in and between trade associations.

7. Channel arrangements are up to the company, but there are certain legal and ethical issues to be considered with regard to practices such as exclusive dealing or territories, tying agreements, and dealers' rights.

applications

marketing debate – should national brand manufacturers also supply private label brands?

One controversial move by some marketers of major brands is to actually supply private label makers. For example, Ralston-Purina, Borden, ConAgra, and Heinz have all admitted to supplying products—sometimes lower in quality—to be used for private labels. Other marketers, however, criticize this "if you can't beat them, join them" strategy, maintaining that these actions, if revealed, may create confusion or even reinforce a perception by consumers that all brands in a category are essentially the same.

Take a position: Manufacturers should feel free to sell private labels as a source of revenue versus National manufacturers should never get involved with private labels.

marketing and advertising

1. Ford has introduced a certification program to identify dealerships that are among the best in customer satisfaction. This ad alerts car and truck buyers to look for the blue thumbprint symbol at their local Ford dealerships.

   a. What type of vertical marketing system does the Blue Oval Certified Ford Dealership program represent?

   b. How might the Blue Oval certification program affect Ford's channel dynamics?

   c. Over time, how might Ford establish and apply criteria to evaluate its channel members?

Presenting the blueprint for the future of Ford Dealerships.

When you come into a Blue Oval Certified Ford Dealership, you'll see the blue thumbprint. It's something new. It means the dealership you're in has been certified as among the best in customer satisfaction. At Blue Oval Certified Ford Dealerships, we believe every experience you have should be a great one. The blue thumbprint signifies the unique and personal dedication of every one of our employees to get the job done right – whether you're buying, leasing or just in for service. So come on in and see for yourself. We're certified to satisfy.

BlueOvalCertified Ford

Come on in

For your nearest Blue Oval Certified Dealer, call 866-BLUEOVAL or visit blueoval.fordvehicles.com.

online marketing today

As mentioned earlier, People's Bank, based in Connecticut, uses its Web site as a key channel for reaching individuals, business customers, and prospects. Not only can customers e-mail the bank with questions; they can click on a link to have a bank representative call them with further information or choose another link if they want to chat online. In addition, prospects can open new accounts online, print out and fax account applications, and even order printed checks with a few keystrokes. Now the company has expanded its financial services offerings by adding insurance products for consumers and businesses.

Visit the People's Web site (www.peoples.com). After looking at the home page, follow the link to read about Online Services and click for a demonstration of People's Online. Next, follow the Insurance link and dig deeper by clicking on Auto, Home, and Other Personal Insurance. What role is Peoples.com playing in the distribution of these insurance products? What is the length of the channel the bank uses to distribute its own checking account products? How would you describe the channel positioning of People's Bank?

you're the marketer: sonic pda marketing plan

Marketing Plan Pro

Manufacturers need to pay close attention to their value networks and marketing channels. By planning the design, management, evaluation, and modification of their marketing channels, manufacturers can ensure that their products are available when and where customers want to buy.

At Sonic, you have been asked to develop a channel strategy for the company's new personal digital assistant (PDA). Based on the information you previously gathered and the decisions you have already made about the target market, the product, and the pricing, answer the following questions about your marketing channels:

- What forward and backward channel flows should Sonic plan for?

- How many levels would be appropriate for the consumer and business markets you are targeting?
- In determining the number of channel members, should you use exclusive, selective, or intensive distribution? Why?
- What levels of service output do Sonic customers desire? How do these levels affect Sonic's channel strategy?
- How should Sonic support its channel members?

After you have answered the questions, document your recommendations about marketing channels and strategy in a written marketing plan. Alternatively, type them into the Marketing Mix and the Channels sections of the *Marketing Plan Pro* software.

notes

1. Louis W. Stern and Adel I. El-Ansary, *Marketing Channels,* 5th ed. (Upper Saddle River, NJ: Prentice Hall, 1996).
2. E. Raymond Corey, *Industrial Marketing: Cases and Concepts,* 4th ed. (Upper Saddle River, NJ: Prentice Hall, 1991), ch. 5.
3. Stern and El-Ansary, *Marketing Channels,* pp. 5–6.
4. William G. Zikmund and William J. Stanton, "Recycling Solid Wastes: A Channels-of-Distribution Problem," *Journal of Marketing* (July 1971): 34.
5. For additional information on backward channels, see Marianne Jahre, "Household Waste Collection as a Reverse Channel: A Theoretical Perspective," *International Journal of Physical Distribution and Logistics* 25, no. 2 (1995): 39–55; Terrance L. Pohlen and M. Theodore Farris II, "Reverse Logistics in Plastics Recycling," *International Journal of Physical Distribution and Logistics* 22, no. 7 (1992): 35–37.
6. Ronald Abler, John S. Adams, and Peter Gould, *Spatial Organizations: The Geographer's View of the World* (Upper Saddle River, NJ: Prentice Hall, 1971), pp. 531–32.
7. Described in *Inside 1-to-1,* Peppers and Rogers Group newsletter, May 14, 2001.
8. Irving Rein, Philip Kotler, and Martin Stoller, *High Visibility* (New York: Dodd, Mead, 1987).
9. For a technical discussion of how service-oriented firms choose to enter international markets, see M. Krishna Erramilli, "Service Firms' International Entry-Mode Approach: A Modified Transaction-Cost Analysis Approach," *Journal of Marketing* (July 1993): 19–38.

10. Louis P. Bucklin, *Competition and Evolution in the Distributive Trades* (Upper Saddle River, NJ: Prentice Hall, 1972). Also see Stern and El-Ansary, *Marketing Channels.*
11. Louis P. Bucklin, *A Theory of Distribution Channel Structure* (Berkeley: Institute of Business and Economic Research, University of California, 1966).
12. Teri Lammers Prior, "Channel Surfers," *Inc.* (February 1995): 65–68.
13. Emily Nelson, "Avon Goes Store to Store," *Wall Street Journal,* September 18, 2000, p. B1
14. <*www.disney.com*>; Edward Helmore, "Media: Why House of Mouse Is Haunted by Failures," *The Observer,* February 11, 2001, p. 10.
15. For more on relationship marketing and the governance of marketing channels, see Jan B. Heide, "Interorganizational Governance in Marketing Channels," *Journal of Marketing* (January 1994): 71–85.
16. Lawrence G. Friedman and Timothy R. Furey, *The Channel Advantage: Going to Marketing with Multiple Sales Channels* (Woburn, MA: Butterworth-Heinemann, 1999). They suggest measuring a channel's profitability by the expense-to-revenue ratio, or E/R. E/R is the average transaction cost divided by the average order size. The average transaction cost is found by dividing the total expense in operating the channel by the total number of transactions. The lower the E/R, the more profitable the channel because less money is spent on selling cost for each dollar of revenue.

17. Arthur Bragg, "Undercover Recruiting: Epson America's Sly Distributor Switch," *Sales and Marketing Management*, March 11, 1985, pp. 45–49.

18. Vincent Alonzo, "Brewski," *Incentive* (December 1994): 32–33.

19. Philip McVey, "Are Channels of Distribution What the Textbooks Say?" *Journal of Marketing* (January 1960): 61–64.

20. These bases of power were identified in John R. P. French and Bertram Raven, "The Bases of Social Power," in *Studies in Social Power*, ed. Dorwin Cartwright (Ann Arbor: University of Michigan Press, 1959), pp. 150–67.

21. Bert Rosenbloom, *Marketing Channels: A Management View*, 5th ed. (Hinsdale, IL: Dryden, 1995).

22. Earl Eldridge, "Ford Forces Dealers to Tidy Up—Or Pay Up," *USA Today*, April 6, 2001, p. B8.

23. Tobi Elkin, "Apple Gambles with Retail Plan," *Advertising Age*, June 24, 2001.

24. Miland M. Lele, *Creating Strategic Leverage* (New York: John Wiley, 1992), pp. 249–51.

25. For an excellent report on this issue, see Howard Sutton, *Rethinking the Company's Selling and Distribution Channels*, research report no. 885, Conference Board, 1986, p. 26.

26. Russell Johnston and Paul R. Lawrence, "Beyond Vertical Integration: The Rise of the Value-Adding Partnership," *Harvard Business Review* (July–August 1988): 94-101. See also Judy A. Siguaw, Penny M. Simpson, and Thomas L. Baker, "Effects of Supplier Market Orientation on Distributor Market Orientation and the Channel Relationship: The Distribution Perspective," *Journal of Marketing* (July 1998): 99–111; Narakesari Narayandas and Manohar U. Kalwani, "Long-Term Manufacturer–Supplier Relationships: Do They Pay Off for Supplier Firms?" *Journal of Marketing* (January 1995): 1–16; Arnt Bovik and George John, "When Does Vertical Coordination Improve Industrial Purchasing Relationships," *Journal of Marketing* 64 (October 2000): pp. 52–64.

27. Matthew Schifrin, "Partner or Perish," *Forbes*, May 21, 2001, p. 26.

28. "2001 Industry Forecasts," *Outdoor Power Equipment*, January 1, 2001.

29. Rowland T. Moriarty and Ursula Moran, "Marketing Hybrid Marketing Systems," *Harvard Business Review* (November–December 1990): 146–55. Also see Gordon S. Swartz and Rowland T. Moriarty, "Marketing Automation Meets the Capital Budgeting Wall," *Marketing Management* 1, no. 3 (1992); Sridhar Balasubramanian, "Mail versus Mall: A Strategic Analysis of Competition Between Direct Marketers and Conventional Retailers," *Marketing Science* 17, no. 3, 1998, pp. 181–95.

30. Bert C. McCammon Jr., "Alternative Explanations of Institutional Change and Channel Evolution," in *Toward Scientific Marketing*, ed. Stephen A. Greyser (Chicago: American Marketing Association, 1963), pp. 477–90.

31. Lisa Bannon, "Selling Barbie Online May Pit Mattel vs. Stores," *Wall Street Journal*, November 17, 2000, p. B1.

32. Some of these examples are found in Stanley A. Brown, *Customer Relationship Management* (New York: John Wiley and Sons, 2000), and Chuck Martin, *Net Future* (New York: McGraw-Hill, 1999).

33. This section draws on Stern and El-Ansary, *Marketing Channels*, ch. 6. See also Jonathan D. Hibbard, Nirmalya Kumar, and Louis W. Stern, "Examining the Impact of Destructive Acts in Marketing Channel Relationships," *Journal of Marketing Research* 38 (February 2001), pp. 45–61; Kersi D. Antia and Gary L. Frazier, "The Severity of Contract Enforcement in Interfirm Channel Relationships, "*Journal of Marketing* 65 (October 2001), pp. 67–81; James R. Brown, Chekitan S. Dev, and Dong-Jin Lee, "Managing Marketing Channel Opportunism: The Efficency of Alternative Governance Mechanisms," *Journal of Marketing* 64 (April 2001), pp. 51–65.

34. Allessandra Galloni, "Levi's Doesn't Fancy Selling With Cukes," *Wall Street Journal*, April 10, 2001, p. B10.

35. Greg Johnson, "Gray Wail: Southern California Companies Are among the Many Upscale Manufacturers Voicing Their Displeasure about Middlemen Delivering Their Goods into the Hands of Unauthorized Discount Retailers," *Los Angeles Times*, March 30, 1997, p. B1. Also see Paul R. Messinger and Chakravarthi Narasimhan, "Has Power Shifted in the Grocery Channel?" *Marketing Science* 14, no. 2 (1995): 189–223.

18

managing retailing, wholesaling, and market logistics

In this chapter, we will address the following questions:

■ What major types of organizations occupy this sector?

■ What marketing decisions do organizations in this sector make?

■ What are the major trends in this sector?

Kotler on Marketing

Successful "go-to-market" strategies require integrating retailers, wholesalers, and logistical organizations.

I n the previous chapter, we examined marketing intermediaries from the viewpoint of manufacturers who wanted to build and manage marketing channels. In this chapter, we view these intermediaries—retailers, wholesalers, and logistical organizations—as requiring and forging their own marketing strategies. Some intermediaries dominate the manufacturers who deal with them. Many use strategic planning, advanced information systems, and sophisticated marketing tools. They measure performance more on a return-on-investment basis than on a profit-margin basis. They segment their markets, improve their market targeting and positioning, and aggressively pursue market expansion and diversification strategies.

retailing

Retailing includes all the activities involved in selling goods or services directly to final consumers for personal, nonbusiness use. A **retailer** or **retail store** is any business enterprise whose sales volume comes primarily from retailing.

Any organization selling to final consumers—whether it is a manufacturer, wholesaler, or retailer—is doing retailing. It does not matter *how* the goods or services are sold (by person, mail, telephone, vending machine, or Internet) or *where* they are sold (in a store, on the street, or in the consumer's home).

types of retailers

Consumers today can shop for goods and services in a wide variety of retail organizations. There are store retailers, nonstore retailers, and retail organizations. Perhaps the best-known type of retailer is the department store. Japanese department stores such as Takashimaya and Mitsukoshi attract millions of shoppers each year. These stores feature art galleries, cooking classes, and children's playgrounds

Retail-store types pass through stages of growth and decline that can be described as the *retail life cycle*.[1] A type emerges, enjoys a period of accelerated growth, reaches maturity, and then declines. Older retail forms took many years to reach maturity; newer retail forms reach maturity much more quickly. Department stores took 80 years to reach maturity, whereas warehouse retail outlets reached maturity in 10 years. The most important retail-store types are described in Table 18.1.

LEVELS OF SERVICE   The *wheel-of-retailing* hypothesis[2] explains one reason that new store types emerge. Conventional retail stores typically increase their services and raise their prices to cover the costs. These higher costs provide an opportunity for new store forms to offer lower prices and less service. New store types meet widely different consumer preferences for service levels and specific services.

Retailers can position themselves as offering one of four levels of service:

1. *Self-service:* Self-service is the cornerstone of all discount operations. Many customers are willing to carry out their own locate-compare-select process to save money.
2. *Self-selection:* Customers find their own goods, although they can ask for assistance.
3. *Limited service:* These retailers carry more shopping goods, and customers need more information and assistance. The stores also offer services (such as credit and merchandise-return privileges).
4. *Full service:* Salespeople are ready to assist in every phase of the locate-compare-select process. Customers who like to be waited on prefer this type of store. The high staffing cost, along with the higher proportion of specialty goods and slower-moving items and the many services, results in high-cost retailing.

By combining these different service levels with different assortment breadths, we can distinguish the four broad positioning strategies available to retailers, as shown in Figure 18.1 on page 537:

1. *Bloomingdale's:* Stores that feature a broad product assortment and high value added. Stores in this quadrant pay close attention to store design, product quality, service, and image. Their profit margin is high, and if they are fortunate enough to have high volume, they will be very profitable.
2. *Tiffany:* Stores that feature a narrow product assortment and high value added. Such stores cultivate an exclusive image and tend to operate on a high margin and low volume.
3. *Sunglass Hut:* Stores that feature a narrow line and low value added. Such stores keep their costs and prices low by centralizing buying, merchandising, advertising, and distribution.
4. *Wal-Mart:* Stores that feature a broad line and low value added. They focus on keeping prices low so that they have an image of being a place for good buys. They make up for low margin by high volume.

table **18.1**	Major Retailer Types

Specialty Store: Narrow product line with a deep assortment. A clothing store would be a *single-line store*; a men's clothing store would be a *limited-line store*; and a men's custom-shirt store would be a *superspecialty store. Examples:* Athlete's Foot, Tall Men, The Limited, The Body Shop.

Department Store: Several product lines—typically clothing, home furnishings, and household goods—with each line operated as a separate department managed by specialist buyers or merchandisers. *Examples:* Sears, JCPenney, Nordstrom, Bloomingdale's.

Supermarket: Relatively large, low-cost, low-margin, high-volume, self-service operation designed to serve total needs for food, laundry, and household products. *Examples:* Kroger, Food Emporium, Jewel.

Convenience Store: Relatively small store located near residential area, open long hours, seven days a week, and carrying a limited line of high-turnover convenience products at slightly higher prices, plus takeout sandwiches, coffee, soft drinks. *Examples:* 7-Eleven, Circle K.

Discount Store: Standard merchandise sold at lower prices with lower margins and higher volumes. Discount retailing has moved into specialty merchandise stores, such as discount sporting-goods stores, electronics stores, and bookstores. *Examples:* Wal-Mart, Kmart, Circuit City, Crown Bookstores.

Off-Price Retailer: Merchandise bought at less than regular wholesale prices and sold at less than retail: often leftover goods, overruns, and irregulars.

Factory outlets are owned and operated by manufacturers and normally carry the manufacturer's surplus, discontinued, or irregular goods. *Examples:* Mikasa (dinnerware), Dexter (shoes), Ralph Lauren (upscale apparel).

Independent off-price retailers are owned and run by entrepreneurs or by divisions of larger retail corporations. *Examples:* Filene's Basement, T. J. Maxx.

Warehouse clubs (or *wholesale clubs*) sell a limited selection of brand-name grocery items, appliances, clothing, and a hodgepodge of other goods at deep discounts to members who pay annual membership fees. Wholesale clubs operate in huge, low-overhead, warehouselike facilities and offer rock-bottom prices—typically 20 to 40 percent below supermarket and discount-store prices. *Examples:* Sam's Clubs, Max Clubs, Price-Costco, BJ's Wholesale Club.

Superstore: About 35,000 square feet of selling space traditionally aimed at meeting consumers' total needs for routinely purchased food and nonfood items, plus services such as laundry, dry cleaning, shoe repair, check cashing, and bill paying. A new group called *category killers* carry a deep assortment in a particular category and a knowledgeable staff. *Examples:* Borders Books and Music, Petsmart, Staples, Home Depot, IKEA.

Combination stores are combination food and drug stores that average 55,000 square feet of selling space. *Examples:* Jewel and Osco stores.

Hypermarkets range between 80,000 and 220,000 square feet and combine supermarket, discount, and warehouse retailing. Product assortment includes furniture, large and small appliances, clothing, and many other items. They feature bulk display and minimum handling by store personnel, with discounts for customers who are willing to carry heavy appliances and furniture out of the store. Hypermarkets originated in France. *Examples:* Carrefour and Casino (France); Pyrca, Continente, and Alcampo (Spain); Meijer's (Netherlands).

Catalog Showroom: Broad selection of high-markup, fast-moving, brand-name goods at discount prices. Customers order goods from a catalog, then pick these goods up at a merchandise pickup area in the store. *Example:* Service Merchandise.

Sources: For further reading, see Leah Rickard, "Supercenters Entice Shoppers," *Advertising Age,* March 29, 1995, pp. 1–10; Debra Chanil, "Wholesale Clubs: A New Era?" *Discount Merchandiser,* November 1994, pp. 38–51; Julie Nelson Forsyth, "Department Store Industry Restructures for the 90s," *Chain Store Age Executive* (August 1993): pp. 29A–30A; John Milton Fogg, "The Giant Awakens," *Success,* March 1995, p. 51; J. Douglas Eldridge, "Nonstore Retailing: Planning for a Big Future," *Chain Store Age Executive* (August 1993): 34A–35A.

Although the overwhelming bulk (97 percent) of goods and services is sold through stores, *nonstore retailing* has been growing much faster than store retailing. Nonstore retailing falls into four major categories: direct selling, direct marketing (which includes telemarketing and Internet selling), automatic vending, and buying services:

1. *Direct selling* (also called *multi-level selling, network marketing*) is a $9 billion industry, with over 600 companies selling door-to-door or at home sales parties. Well-known in one-to-one selling

figure **18.1**

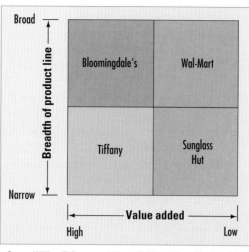

Source: William T. Gregor and Eileen M. Friars, *Money Merchandising: Retail Revolution in Consumer Financial Service* (Cambridge, MA: The MAC Group, 1982).

are Avon, Electrolux, and-Southwestern Company of Nashville (Bibles). Tupperware and Mary Kay Cosmetics are sold one-to-many: A salesperson goes to the home of a host who has invited friends; the salesperson demonstrates the products and takes orders. Pioneered by Amway, the multilevel (network) marketing sales system consists of recruiting independent businesspeople who act as distributors. The distributor's compensation includes a percentage of sales of those the distributor recruits as well as earnings on direct sales to customers. These direct selling firms, now finding fewer consumers at home, are developing multidistribution strategies.

2. *Direct marketing* has roots in direct-mail and catalog marketing (Lands' End, L.L. Bean); it includes *telemarketing* (1-800-FLOWERS), *television direct-response marketing* (Home Shopping Network, QVC), and *electronic shopping* (Amazon.com, Autobytel.com). Of these, electronic shopping experienced a major take-off in the late 1990s as consumers flocked to dot-com sites to buy books, music, toys, electronics, and other products.

3. *Automatic vending* is used for a variety of merchandise, including impulse goods like cigarettes, soft drinks, coffee, candy, newspapers, magazines, and other products like hosiery, cosmetics, hot food, condoms, and paperbacks. Coinstar, a company started by a Stanford student, has placed over 8,500 machines in supermarkets. They take loose change and return bills, keeping 8.9 percent as a fee. Vending machines are found in factories, offices, large retail stores, gasoline stations, hotels, restaurants, and many other places. They offer 24-hour selling, self-service, and merchandise that is always fresh. Japan has the most vending machines per person and is experimenting with having vending machines take orders directly from the popular DoCoMo cell phones, cost to be charged against the customer's prepaid account.

4. *Buying service* is a storeless retailer serving a specific clientele—usually employees of large organizations—who are entitled to buy from a list of retailers that have agreed to give discounts in return for membership.

CORPORATE RETAILING   Although many retail stores are independently owned, an increasing number are part of some form of **corporate retailing**. Corporate retail organizations achieve economies of scale, greater purchasing power, wider brand recognition, and better-trained employees. The major types of corporate retailing—corporate chain stores, voluntary chains, retailer cooperatives, franchises, and merchandising

table **18.2**	
Major Types of Retail Organizations	**Corporate Chain Store:** Two or more outlets commonly owned and controlled, employing central buying and merchandising, and selling similar lines of merchandise. Their size allows them to buy in large quantities at lower prices, and they can afford to hire corporate specialists to deal with pricing, promotion, merchandising, inventory control, and sales forecasting. *Examples:* Tower Records, GAP, Pottery Barn.
	Voluntary Chain: A wholesaler-sponsored group of independent retailers engaged in bulk buying and common merchandising. *Examples:* Independent Grocers Alliance (IGA), True Value Hardware.
	Retailer Cooperative: Independent retailers who set up a central buying organization and conduct joint promotion efforts. *Examples:* Associated Grocers, ACE Hardware.
	Consumer Cooperative: A retail firm owned by its customers. In consumer co-ops residents contribute money to open their own store, vote on its policies, elect a group to manage it, and receive patronage dividends.
	Franchise Organization: Contractual association between a *franchiser* (manufacturer, wholesaler, service organization) and *franchisees* (independent businesspeople who buy the right to own and operate one or more units in the franchise system). Franchising has been prominent in dozens of product and service areas. *Examples:* McDonald's, Subway, Pizza Hut, Jiffy Lube, Meineke Mufflers, 7-Eleven.
	Merchandising Conglomerate: A free-form corporation that combines several diversified retailing lines and forms under central ownership, along with some integration of distribution and management. *Examples:* Allied Domeq PLC operates Dunkin' Donuts and Baskin-Robbins, plus a number of British retailers and a wine and spirits group.

conglomerates—are described in Table 18.2. Franchising is described in detail in "Marketing Insight: Franchise Fever."

marketing decisions

In the past retailers held customers by offering convenient location, special or unique assortments of goods, greater or better services than competitors, and store credit cards. All of this has changed. Today, national brands such as Calvin Klein, Izod, and Levi's are found in department stores, in their own shops, in merchandise outlets, and in off-price discount stores. In their drive for volume, national-brand manufacturers have placed their branded goods everywhere. The result is that retail-store assortments have grown more alike.

Service differentiation also has eroded. Many department stores have trimmed services, and many discounters have increased services. Customers have become smarter shoppers. They do not want to pay more for identical brands, especially when service differences have diminished; nor do they need credit from a particular store, because bank credit cards are almost universally accepted.

In the face of increased competition from discount houses and specialty stores, department stores are waging a comeback war. In addition to locations in the centers of cities, many have branches in suburban shopping centers, where parking is plentiful and family incomes are higher. Others run more frequent sales, remodel their stores, and experiment with mail-order and online marketing, and telemarketing. Supermarkets have opened larger stores, carry a larger number and variety of items, and upgrade facilities. Supermarkets have also increased their promotional budgets and moved heavily into private brands.

We will examine retailers' marketing decisions in the areas of target market, product assortment and procurement, services and store atmosphere, price, promotion, and place. (See also "Marketing Memo: Key Lessons on Shops, Shoppers, and Shopping.")

marketing **insight**

Franchise Fever

Franchises commanded over 40 percent of retail sales in the United States in 2000, up from 35 percent in 1998. This figure should not come as a surprise in a society where it is nearly impossible to stroll down a city block or drive on a suburban thoroughfare without seeing a Wendy's, a McDonald's, a Jiffy-Lube, or a 7-Eleven.

In a franchising system, individual *franchisees* are a tightly knit group of enterprises whose systematic operations are planned, directed, and controlled by the operation's innovator, called a *franchiser*. Franchises are distinguished by three characteristics:

1. *The franchiser owns a trade or service mark and licenses it to franchisees in return for royalty payments.*
2. *The franchisee pays for the right to be part of the system.* Start-up costs include rental and lease equipment and fixtures, and usually a regular license fee. McDonald's franchisees may invest as much as $750,000 in start-up costs. The franchisee then pays McDonald's a certain percentage of sales plus a monthly base rent.
3. *The franchiser provides its franchisees with a system for doing business.* McDonald's requires franchisees to attend "Hamburger University" in Oak Brook, Illinois, for three weeks to learn how to manage the business. Additionally, the franchisees must adhere to certain procedures in buying materials.

Franchising is mutually beneficial to both franchiser and franchisee. Among the benefits reaped by franchisers are the motivation and hard work of employees who are entrepreneurs rather than "hired hands," the franchisees' familiarity with local communities and conditions, and the enormous purchasing power of the franchiser. Franchisees benefit from buying into a business with a well-known and accepted brand name. They find it easier to borrow money from financial institutions, and they receive support in areas ranging from marketing and advertising to site selection and staffing.

The franchise explosion in recent years has increasingly saturated the domestic market. Some new directions that may deliver both franchiser growth and franchisee earnings are:

- *Strategic alliances with major outside corporations:* Fuji USA arranged with Moto Photo, a one-hour photo developer, to carry its film. Fuji won instant market penetration through Moto Photo's 400 locations, and Moto Photo franchisees enjoyed Fuji's name recognition and advertising reach.
- *Expansion abroad:* Fast-food franchises have become very popular throughout the world. Today McDonald's has over 15,000 restaurants in 119 countries outside the United States, which account for nearly 60 percent of the company's sales and profits.
- *Nontraditional site locations in the United States:* Franchises are opening in airports, sports stadiums, college campuses, hospitals, gambling casinos, theme parks, convention halls, and even riverboats.

Sources: Norman D. Axelrad and Robert E. Weigand, "Franchising—A Marriage of System Members," in *Marketing Managers Handbook* (3rd ed.), ed. Sidney Levy, George Frerichs, and Howard Gordon (Chicago: Dartnell, 1994), pp. 919–34; Meg Whittemore, "New Directions in Franchising," *Nation's Business* (January 1995): 45–52; "Trouble in Franchise Nation," *Fortune*, March 6, 1995, pp. 115–29; Carol Steinberg, "Millionaire Franchisees," *Success* (March 1995): 65–69; Deepak Agrawal and Rajiv Lal, "Contractual Agreements in Franchising: An Empirical Investigation," *Journal of Marketing Research* (May 1995): 213–21.

TARGET MARKET   A retailer's most important decision concerns the target market. Until the target market is defined and profiled, the retailer cannot make consistent decisions on product assortment, store decor, advertising messages and media, price, and service levels.

Some retailers have defined their target markets quite well:

Wal-Mart   The late Sam Walton and his brother opened the first Wal-Mart discount store in Rogers, Arkansas, in 1962. It was a big, flat, warehouse-type store selling everything from apparel to automotive supplies to small appliances at the lowest possible prices. More recently, Wal-Mart has been building stores in larger cities. Today, Wal-Mart operates 2,363 discount stores in the United States, including 454 Supercenters, 444 Sam's Clubs, and 41 distribution centers. It is expanding into the Wal-Mart Neighborhood Market supermarket-pharmacy business. Its annual sales exceed $165 billion, making it the largest U.S. private employer and the world's largest retailer. Its daily movement of goods is prodigious—474,000 pairs of shoes a day, 208,000 bras a day, 279,000 large boxes of diapers a day. Wal-Mart's secrets: Listen to customers, treat the employees as partners, push for lower prices from suppliers, keep a tight rein on

Marketing
MEMO
Key Lessons on Shops, Shoppers, and Shopping

In the pursuit of higher sales volume, retailers are studying their store environments for ways to improve the shopper experience. Paco Underhill, managing director of the retail consultant Envirosell Inc., writes about the art of selling in his book *Why We Buy: The Science of Shopping*. The book offers the following advice for fine-tuning the retail space in order to keep shoppers spending:

- *Attract shoppers and keep them in the store:* The amount of time shoppers spend in a store is perhaps the single most important factor in determining how much they will buy.
- *Honor the "transition zone":* On entering a store, people need to slow down and sort out the stimuli, which means that shoppers will likely be moving too fast to respond positively to signs, merchandise, or sales clerks in the zone they cross before making that transition.
- *Make merchandise available to the touch:* It is hard to overemphasize the importance of customers' hands to the world of shopping. A store can offer the finest, cheapest, sexiest goods, but if the shopper cannot pick them up, much of their appeal can be lost.
- *Men do not ask questions:* Men always move faster than women do through store's aisles. In many settings, it is hard to get them to look at anything they had not intended to buy. Men also do not like asking where things are. If a man cannot find the section he is looking for, he will wheel about once or twice, then leave the store without ever asking for help.
- *Behold the geriatrics:* By 2025, nearly one-fifth of the American people will be 65 or older. All of retailing is going to have to cater to seniors because there will be so many of them with money to spend.

Source: Keith Hammonds, "How We Sell," *Fast Company* (November 1999): 294.

expenses, and manage with the most advanced information systems. Wal-Mart's use of everyday low pricing and EDI for speedy stock replenishment has been benchmarked by other retailers, and it was the first U.S. mega merchant to take the plunge into global retailing. It already has stores in Argentina, Brazil, China, South Korea, and Mexico, and is adding more.[3]

The Limited Leslie H. Wexner borrowed $5,000 in 1963 to create The Limited Inc., which started as a single store targeted to young, fashion-conscious women. All aspects of the store—clothing assortment, fixtures, music, colors, personnel—were orchestrated to match the target consumer. A decade later, his original customers were no longer in the "young" group. To catch the new "youngs," he started the Express. Over the years, he started or acquired other targeted store chains, including Lane Bryant, Victoria's Secret, Lerner's, and Bath and Body Works. Today, The Limited operates more than 5,300 stores in the United States plus global catalog operations. Sales totaled over $10 billion in 2000.[4]

PRODUCT ASSORTMENT AND PROCUREMENT The retailer's product assortment must match the target market's shopping expectations. The retailer has to decide on product-assortment *breadth* and *depth*. Thus a restaurant can offer a narrow and shallow assortment (small lunch counters), a narrow and deep assortment (delicatessen), a broad and shallow assortment (cafeteria), or a broad and deep assortment (large restaurant). The real challenge begins after defining the store's product assortment, and that is to develop a product-differentiation strategy. Here are some possibilities:

- *Feature exclusive national brands that are not available at competing retailers:* Thus Saks might get exclusive rights to carry the dresses of a well-known international designer.
- *Feature mostly private branded merchandise:* Benetton and GAP design most of the clothes carried in their stores. Many supermarket and drug chains carry private branded merchandise.
- *Feature blockbuster distinctive merchandise events:* Bloomingdale's will run month-long shows featuring the goods of another country, such as India or China, throughout the store.
- *Feature surprise or ever-changing merchandise:* Benetton changes some portion of its merchandise every month so that customers will want to drop in frequently. T. J. Maxx offers surprise assortments of distress merchandise (goods the owner must sell immediately because it needs cash), overstocks, and closeouts.
- *Feature the latest or newest merchandise first:* The Sharper Image leads other retailers in introducing electronic appliances from around the world.
- *Offer merchandise customizing services:* Harrod's of London will make custom-tailored suits, shirts, and ties for customers, in addition to ready-made menswear.
- *Offer a highly targeted assortment:* Lane Bryant carries goods for the larger woman. Brookstone offers unusual tools and gadgets for the person who wants to shop in an "adult toy store."[5] Circuit City's decision to drop major appliances gave it more than 200 square feet to stock more units of higher-margin electronics. Remodeling also expanded total floor space by an additional 10,000 square feet, providing even more space for higher-margin home electronics.[6]

After deciding on the product-assortment strategy, the retailer must establish procurement sources, policies, and practices. In the corporate headquarters of a supermarket chain, specialist buyers (sometimes called *merchandise managers*) are responsible for developing brand assortments and listening to presentations by salespersons. In some chains, buyers have the authority to accept or reject new items. In other chains, they are limited to screening "obvious rejects" and "obvious accepts"; they bring other items to the buying committee for approval. Even when an item is accepted by a chain-store buying committee, individual stores in the chain may not carry it. About one-third of the items must be stocked and about two-thirds are stocked at the discretion of each store manager.

The Limited's home page presents "a family of the world's best fashion brands."

Manufacturers face a major challenge trying to get new items onto store shelves. They offer the nation's supermarkets between 150 and 250 new items each week, of which store buyers reject over 70 percent. Manufacturers need to know the acceptance criteria used by buyers, buying committees, and store managers. A. C. Nielsen Company interviewed store managers and found that they are most influenced (in order of importance) by strong evidence of consumer acceptance, a well-designed advertising and sales-promotion plan, and generous financial incentives to the trade.

Retailers are rapidly improving their skills in demand forecasting, merchandise selection, stock control, space allocation, and display. They are using computers to track inventory, compute economic order quantities, order goods, and analyze dollars spent on vendors and products. Supermarket chains are using scanner data to manage their merchandise mix on a store-by-store basis.

Stores are using **direct product profitability (DPP)** to measure a product's handling costs (receiving, moving to storage, paperwork, selecting, checking, loading, and space cost) from the time it reaches their warehouse until a customer buys it in their retail store. Resellers who have adopted DPP learn to their surprise that the gross margin on a product often has little relation to the direct product profit. Some high-volume products may have such high handling costs that they are less profitable and deserve less shelf space than low-volume products. Clearly, vendors are facing increasingly sophisticated retailers.

General Electric   Before the late 1980s, GE operated a traditional system of trying to load its dealers with GE appliances. This approach created problems for smaller independent dealers who could not afford to carry a large stock and who could not meet the price competition of multibrand dealers. So GE invented an alternative model called the Direct Connect system: GE dealers carry only display models and rely on a "virtual inventory" to fill orders. Dealers can access GE's order-processing system 24 hours a day, check on model availability, and place orders for next-day delivery. They get GE's best price, GE financing, and no interest charge for the first 90 days. In exchange, dealers must commit to selling 9 major GE product categories, generating 50 percent of their sales in GE products, opening their books to GE for review, and paying

marketing for the **new economy**

Extreme Retailing

Despite the failure of many dot-coms, customers continue to validate the concept of e-commerce with their wallets. Online business-to-consumer sales in the United States totaled $29 billion during 2000, nearly a 100 percent increase over 1999. E-commerce sites harbor advantages over brick-and-mortar retailers such as ease of use, product research and comparison tools, large inventories and better selection, and in-home purchasing. Brick-and-mortar retailers do have, however, several natural advantages, such as products shoppers can actually see, touch, and test, real-life customer service, no delivery lag time for small or medium-sized purchases, and they also provide the traditional shopping experience. Jeff Bezos, chief executive of Amazon.com, readily admits that "the physical world is still the best medium ever invented."

To further entice Internet-savvy consumers to visit their stores, real-life retailers are developing a host of new services and promotions designed to increase customer traffic. The change in strategy can be noticed in practices as simple as calling each shopper a "guest" (as many stores are beginning to do) or as grandiose as building an indoor amusement park. Still others are finding ways to update the customer service model. Several stores, such as the Banana Republic, offer free home delivery during the holidays for customers who spend above a certain amount. The flagship Banana Republic in San Francisco gives free rides home to shoppers who spend at least $100.

Retailers are also creating in-store entertainment in the hopes of attracting customers who want fun and excitement. The super-regional mall developer Mills Corp. has trademarked a word for this phenomenon: "shoppertainment." Mills Corp. built a mall in Las Vegas called The Forum Shops that treats shoppers to Vegas-style spectacles. Entertainment for shoppers helps The

Forum Shops average $1,200 per square foot in annual sales, compared with a national average of about $300.

Super-regional malls often seek to anchor themselves with unique and interesting shops, rather than the brand-name department stores and national retailers that fill most traditional malls. Says Laurence C. Siegel, chairman and CEO at Mills Corp., "There are no Macy's at our centers. We want to create destination retail." One such destination is sporting-goods retailer Bass Pro Shops, which has aquariums, waterfalls, trout ponds, archery and rifle ranges, and putting greens in its stores. The Sony Style store, where Sony entertainment and electronics products are displayed in environments that encourage customers to test them, is another example of a mega-mall store.

Brick-and-mortar retailers are adding Internet content to their physical stores. Borders bookstores installed in-store kiosks called Title Sleuths that allow customers to view the full inventory from the company's Internet site and make online purchases. As the convenience of online shopping becomes more popular, more companies may adopt these Internet/brick-and-mortar in-store hybrids.

Despite the recent explosion of e-commerce, the vast majority of shoppers will do their purchasing in physical retail locations in the near future. By the highest estimate, online retail sales in the United States will be less than 5 percent of total estimated U.S. retail sales. If brick-and-mortar stores continue to find innovative ways to attract customers, this percentage could very well be lower.

Sources: Kenneth T. Rosen and Amanda L. Howard, "E-tail: Gold Rush or Fool's Gold?" *California Management Review* (April 1, 2000) 72–100; Moira Cotlier, "Census Releases First E-commerce Report," *Catalog Age*, May 1, 2001; Associated Press, "Online Sales Boomed at End of 2000," *Star-Tribune of Twin Cities*, February 17, 2001.

GE every month through electronic funds transfer. GE integrated Direct Connect with the Internet to create CustomerNet, which makes all the original Direct Connect services available on the Web. CustomerNet is also a B2B e-commerce site where GE provides Internet content for each of its 1,500 online dealers.[7]

SERVICES AND STORE ATMOSPHERE   Retailers must also decide on the *services mix* to offer customers:

- Prepurchase services include accepting telephone and mail orders, advertising, window and interior display, fitting rooms, shopping hours, fashion shows, trade-ins.
- Postpurchase services include shipping and delivery, gift wrapping, adjustments and returns, alterations and tailoring, installations, engraving.
- Ancillary services include general information, check cashing, parking, restaurants, repairs, interior decorating, credit, rest rooms, baby-attendant service.

The services mix is a key tool for differentiating one store from another; so is atmosphere. (See "Marketing for the New Economy: Extreme Retailing.") *Atmosphere* is another element in the store arsenal. Every store has a physical layout that makes it hard or easy to move around. Every store has a "look." The store must embody a planned atmosphere that suits the target market and draws consumers toward purchase. Consider Kohl's floor plan.

Kohl's   Retail giant Kohl's employs a floor plan modeled after a racetrack. Designed to smoothly convey customers past all the merchandise in the store, an eight-foot-wide main aisle moves them in a circle around the store. The design also includes a middle aisle that hurried shoppers can use as a shortcut. The racetrack loop yields higher spending levels than many competitors: Kohl's stores take in an average $279 per square foot, compared with $220 a square foot for Target and $147 for Dillard's.[8]

Victoria's Secret stores work on the concept of "retail theater": Customers feel they are in a romance novel, with lush music and faint floral scents in the background. Supermarkets have found that varying the tempo of music affects the average time spent in the store and the average expenditures. Retailers are now adding fragrances in their stores to stimulate certain moods in shoppers. London's Heathrow Airport sprays the scent of pine needles because it stimulates the sense of holidays and weekend walks. Automobile dealers will spray a "leather" scent in second-hand cars to make them smell "new."[9] Here are other examples of "packaged environments."[10]

Recreational Equipment Inc. (REI)   Seattle-based REI has been retailing outdoor equipment products since 1938 and today operates 57 stores in 23 states and Japan. Its stores work on the principle of "experiential retailing." Consumers are able to test climbing equipment on a huge wall in the store. They can test Gore-tex raincoats by going under a simulated rain shower.

Mall of America   The largest mall in the United States, the Mall of America (near Minneapolis) is a super-regional mall plus a seven-acre amusement park. Opened in 1992, it now has a total of over 500 stores that employ more than 12,000 people. Anchored by four major department stores—Nordstrom, Macy's, Bloomingdale's, and Sears—it has become a tourist destination for avid shoppers from around the world. It now attracts more than 40 million visitors yearly. Other attractions at the Mall of America include the four-story Lego Imagination Center, a miniature golf course, the UnderWater World aquarium, and a Chapel of Love, where thousands of couples have been married.[11]

PRICE DECISION   Prices are a key positioning factor and must be decided in relation to the target market, the product-and-service assortment mix, and competition. All retailers would like to achieve high volumes and high gross margins. They would like high *Turns x Earns*, but the two usually do not go together. Most retailers fall into the *high-markup, lower-volume* group (fine specialty stores) or the *low-markup, higher-volume* group (mass-merchandisers and discount stores). Within each of these groups are further gradations. Thus Bijan's on Rodeo Drive in Beverly Hills prices suits starting at $1,000 and shoes at $400. At the other extreme, Odd Lot Trading in New York City is a superdiscounter that sells odd lots and closeouts at prices below those of normal discounters.

Retailers must also pay attention to pricing tactics. Most retailers will put low prices on some items to serve as traffic builders or loss leaders. They will run storewide sales. They will plan markdowns on slower-moving merchandise. For example, shoe retailers expect to sell 50 percent of their shoes at the normal markup, 25 percent at a 40 percent markup, and the remaining 25 percent at cost. Recently, a classic pricing tactic experienced a revival.

Kmart   In 2001, as part of an initiative to revitalize ailing sales, Kmart reintroduced the classic Blue Light Specials, which it had discontinued in 1991. The Blue Light Specials, flashing blue police lights that announce unadvertised specials, were relaunched via a $25 million advertising campaign. The company anticipates the new Blue Lights will attract nostalgic shoppers who remember the specials from a decade ago.[12]

Some retailers have abandoned "sales pricing" in favor of everyday low pricing (EDLP). EDLP could lead to lower advertising costs, greater pricing stability, a stronger image of fairness and reliability, and higher retail profits. General Motors' Saturn division states a low list price for its cars and its dealers do not bargain. Wal-Mart also practices everyday low prices. Frank Feather cites a study showing that supermarket chains practicing everyday low pricing are often more profitable than those practicing sales pricing.[13]

PROMOTION DECISION   Retailers use a wide range of promotion tools to generate traffic and purchases. They place ads, run special sales, issue money-saving coupons, and run frequent shopper-reward programs, in-store food sampling, and coupons on shelves or at checkout points. Each retailer must use promotion tools that support and reinforce its image positioning. Fine stores will place tasteful full-page ads in magazines such as Vogue and Harper's. They will carefully train salespeople to greet customers, interpret their needs, and handle complaints. Off-price retailers will arrange their merchandise to promote the idea of bargains and large savings, while conserving on service and sales assistance.

PLACE DECISION   Retailers are accustomed to saying that the three keys to success are "location, location, and location." Customers generally choose the nearest bank and gas station. Department-store chains, oil companies, and fast-food franchisers exercise great care in selecting locations. The problem breaks down into selecting regions of the country in which to open outlets, then particular cities, and then particular sites. A supermarket chain might decide to operate in the Midwest; in the cities of Chicago, Milwaukee, and Indianapolis; and in 14 locations, mostly suburban, within the Chicago region. Two of the savviest location experts in recent years have been the off-price retailer T. J. Maxx and toy store giant Toys "R" Us. Both retailers put the majority of their new locations in areas with rapidly growing numbers of young families.

One retailer is adding stores in spite of a sales decline.

Staples   Despite a recent downturn in the growth rate of small businesses and home offices and a decline in PC sales in the United States, Staples office-supply stores is seeking aggressive expansion. While its two major competitors (Office Depot and Office Max) are closing stores and cutting jobs, in 2001 Staples expanded its retail space 12 percent by opening 160 new stores. Explaining the aggressive expansion, Staples' head of real estate operations said, "We like to saturate markets. We want to be a convenience operator—our customers don't want to spend a lot of time trying to find a store or driving to a store."[14]

Retailers can locate their stores in the central business district, a regional shopping center, a community shopping center, a shopping strip, or within a larger store:

- *General business districts:* This is the oldest and most heavily trafficked city area, often known as "downtown." Store and office rents are normally high. Most downtown areas were hit by a flight to the suburbs in the 1960s, resulting in deteriorated retailing facilities; but in the 1990s, a minor renaissance of interest in downtown apartments, stores, and restaurants began in many cities.
- *Regional shopping centers:* These are large suburban malls containing 40 to 200 stores. They usually draw customers from a 5- to 20-mile radius. Typically, malls feature one or two nationally known anchor stores, such as JCPenney or Lord & Taylor, and a great number of smaller stores, many under franchise operation. Malls are attractive because of generous parking, one-stop shopping, restaurants, and recreational facilities. Successful malls charge high rents and may get a share of stores' sales.
- *Community shopping centers:* These are smaller malls with one anchor store and between 20 and 40 smaller stores.
- *Strip malls* (also called *shopping strips*): These contain a cluster of stores, usually housed in one long building, serving a neighborhood's needs for groceries, hardware, laundry, shoe repair, and dry cleaning. They usually serve people within a five- to ten-minute driving range.

- *A location within a larger store:* Certain well-known retailers—McDonald's, Starbucks, Nathan's, Dunkin' Donuts—locate new, smaller units as concession space within larger stores or operations, such as airports, schools, or department stores.

In view of the relationship between high traffic and high rents, retailers must decide on the most advantageous locations for their outlets. They can use a variety of methods to assess locations, including traffic counts, surveys of consumer shopping habits, and analysis of competitive locations.[15] Several models for site location have also been formulated.[16]

Retailers can assess a particular store's sales effectiveness by looking at four indicators: (1) number of people passing by on an average day; (2) percentage who enter the store; (3) percentage of those entering who buy; and (4) average amount spent per sale.

trends in retailing

At this point, we can summarize the main developments retailers and manufacturers need to take into account in planning competitive strategies.

1. *New retail forms and combinations.* Some supermarkets include bank branches. Bookstores feature coffee shops. Gas stations include food stores. Loblaw's Supermarkets have added fitness clubs to their stores. Shopping malls and bus and train stations have peddler's carts in their aisles.

2. *Growth of intertype competition.* Different types of stores—discount stores, catalog showrooms, department stores—all compete for the same consumers by carrying the same type of merchandise.

3. *Growth of giant retailers.* Through their superior information systems, logistical systems, and buying power, giant retailers are able to deliver good service and immense volumes of product at appealing prices to masses of consumers. They are crowding out smaller manufacturers who cannot deliver enough quantity and even dictating to the most powerful manufacturers what to make, how to price and promote, when and how to ship, and even how to improve production and management. Manufacturers need these accounts; otherwise they would lose 10 to 30 percent of the market. Some giant retailers are *category killers* that concentrate on one product category, such as toys (Toys "R" Us), home improvement (Home Depot), or office supplies (Staples). Others are *supercenters* that combine grocery items with a huge selection of nonfood merchandise (Kmart, Wal-Mart). (See "Marketing Insight: Category Killers vs. the Internet.")

4. *Growing investment in technology.* Retailers are using computers to produce better forecasts, control inventory costs, order electronically from suppliers, send e-mail between stores, and even sell to customers within stores. They are adopting checkout scanning systems,[17] electronic funds transfer, electronic data interchange,[18] in-store television, store traffic radar systems,[19] and improved merchandise-handling systems.

5. *Global presence of major retailers.* Retailers with unique formats and strong brand positioning are increasingly appearing in other countries.[20] U.S. retailers such as McDonald's, The Limited, GAP, and Toys "R" Us have become globally prominent. Wal-Mart operates over 700 stores abroad. Among foreign-based global retailers are Britain's Marks and Spencer, Italy's Benetton, France's Carrefour hypermarkets, Sweden's IKEA home furnishings stores, and Japan's Yaohan supermarkets.[21]

6. *Selling an experience, not just goods.* Retailers are now adding fun and community in order to compete with other stores and online retailers.[22] There has been a marked rise in establishments that provide a place for people to congregate, such as coffeehouses, tea shops, juice bars, bookshops, and brew pubs. Brew pubs such as New York's Zip City Brewing and Seattle's Trolleyman Pub offer tastings and a place to pass the time. Bass Pro Shops, a retailer of outdoor sports equipment, feature giant aquariums, waterfalls, trout ponds, archery and rifle ranges, putting greens, and classes in everything from ice fishing to conservation—all free. The Discovery Zone, a chain of children's play spaces, offers indoor spaces where kids can go wild without breaking anything and stressed-out parents can exchange stories. Denver's two Tattered Covered bookstores host more than 250 events annually, from folk dancing to women's meetings, and Barnes & Noble turned a once-staid bookstore industry into a fun-filled village green.

Barnes & Noble   Now the nation's largest bookseller, Barnes & Noble has over 500 locations across the United States. It reached this impressive size by making its stores attractive, sponsoring community and literary events, installing public rest

marketing **insight**

Category Killers vs. the Internet

One problem with the category killer model was that it was easy to copy, which meant that any specialty niche was subject to cut-throat competitors. For example, the office supply store market is currently occupied by three chains: Office Depot, Office Max, and Staples. Another problem was the success of superstore retailers like Wal-Mart. Wal-Mart's dominance of retail in the 1990s also led many experts to question the category killer concept: Why would consumers want to travel to a different store for each category purchase when they could buy all that they need at a single location? Wal-Mart demonstrated the power of its superstore concept when it surpassed Toys "R" Us in 1998 to become the largest toy seller in the United States.

Perhaps the biggest problem for category killers in recent years has been e-commerce. Internet sites with category killer business models, like online grocer Peapod.com, toy e-tailer eToys.com, and Internet pet supply site Pets.com, attracted much investor attention. By contrast, off-line retailers that moved to e-commerce were held to normal earnings criteria that did not reward a money-losing online venture, and as a result many brick-and-mortar retailers' stock prices were punished on Wall Street. With their high valuations, pure-click e-tailers were able to attract talented employees by offering lucrative stock options, and succeeded in building efficient delivery systems that fit the online business model. Traditional retailers had neither the cachet nor the soaring stock prices to attract the most creative talent, and often had to wrestle with delivery systems designed to bring products from warehouses to store shelves, not individual homes. Although many Internet pure-clicks did not survive the dot-com crash, they made the market much tougher for category killers.

The company that pioneered the category killer retail model, Toys "R" Us, struggled in the late 1990s against online competitors like eToys. In response, Toys "R" Us developed its own e-commerce site, called Toysrus.com, in 1998. The company invested more than $75 million in infrastructure to manage delivery of products ordered on the site. The number of visitors to Toysrus.com increased more than 300 percent from 1998 to 1999. Unfortunately, the site was overwhelmed by holiday season orders in 1999, and Toys "R" Us could not deliver many Christmas orders in time. In 2000, Toys "R" Us joined its e-commerce site with Amazon.com. The partnership illustrates one method for category killers to compete with Internet pure-plays. Another method is integrating the physical retail locations with the e-commerce site, known as a "clicks-and-mortar" strategy. For example, Barnes & Noble bookstores installed Internet terminals where customers can browse and purchase titles from the company's Web site, bn.com. The clicks-and-mortar approach has several advantages. For example, store-based retailers spent an average of less than $5 per person getting existing customers to shop online, while Internet start-ups spent an average of $45 per person building a customer base from square one. Moreover, customers who purchased online and off-line (the so-called "double channel") from the same retailer increased their total purchases by 10 percent.

Sources: John D. Calkins et al., "From Retailing to E-tailing," *The McKinsey Quarterly*, Janurary 1, 2000; John Peet, "Survey of E-commerce: Something Old, Something New," *The Economist*, February 26, 2000; William M. Bulkeley, " 'Category Killers' Go from Lethal to Lame," *Wall Street Journal Europe*, March 13, 2000; Steve Weiner, "With Big Selection and Low Prices, 'Category Killer' Stores Are a Hit," *Wall Street Journal*, June 17, 1996; "Toys 'R' Us Announces Aggressive Online Retailing Strategy," *PR Newswire*, April 27, 1999; Fran Silverman, "E-sales Overwhelm Toys 'R' Us," *Hartford Courant*, December 24, 1999.

rooms and Starbucks coffee bars, having storytelling for kids, comfortable reading areas, soft music, and a huge selection of books, magazines, and music. Barnes & Noble is also a major player on the Internet, with the largest free-standing inventory of any online bookseller. To better leverage the successful brick-and-mortar retail locations in building traffic to its Web sites, Barnes and Noble spent $20 million in 2000 to install counters with Internet access in its retail locations, which enable customers to order from the e-commerce site. This move helped Barnes & Noble.com's market share rise from 19 percent in the first quarter of 2000 to 27 percent in the first quarter of 2001.[23]

7. *Competition between store-based and non-store-based retailing.* Consumers now receive sales offers through direct mail letters and catalogs, and over television, computers, and telephones. These non-store-based retailers are taking business away from store-based retailers. Some store-based retailers initially saw online retailing as a definite threat. Home Depot shocked its top vendors (Black & Decker, Stanley Tools, etc.) by issuing a memo implying that if they started to sell online, Home Depot might drop them as suppliers; but now Home Depot is finding it advantageous to work with online retailers. Wal-Mart recently joined with America Online (AOL) so that AOL will provide a low-cost Internet access service that carries the Wal-Mart

brand, and Wal-Mart will promote the service and AOL in its stores and through TV advertising. Stores such as Wal-Mart and Kmart have developed their own online Web sites, and some online retailers are finding it advantageous to own or manage physical outlets, either retail stores or warehouses.

HomePoint.com HomePoint.com, a Web-based home furnishings e-tailer, created HomePoint Advantage to link thousands of bricks-and-mortar furniture stores to its extranet. Customers visiting a furniture store can inspect items in the store or order items from the site's electronic catalog and arrange delivery. The local store thus becomes a giant furniture retailer. With HomePoint's huge inventory and regional warehouses, furniture items can be delivered in a week compared to the normal eight-week wait.

wholesaling

Wholesaling includes all the activities involved in selling goods or services to those who buy for resale or business use. Wholesaling excludes manufacturers and farmers because they are engaged primarily in production, and it excludes retailers. Wholesalers (also called *distributors*) differ from retailers in a number of ways. First, wholesalers pay less attention to promotion, atmosphere, and location because they are dealing with business customers rather than final consumers. Second, wholesale transactions are usually larger than retail transactions, and wholesalers usually cover a larger trade area than retailers. Third, the government deals with wholesalers and retailers differently in terms of legal regulations and taxes.

Why are wholesalers used at all? Why do manufacturers not sell directly to retailers or final consumers? In general, wholesalers are used when they are more efficient in performing one or more of the following functions:

- *Selling and promoting:* Wholesalers' sales forces help manufacturers reach many small business customers at a relatively low cost. Wholesalers have more contacts, and often buyers trust wholesalers more than they trust a distant manufacturer.
- *Buying and assortment building:* Wholesalers are able to select items and build the assortments their customers need, saving the customers considerable work.
- *Bulk breaking:* Wholesalers achieve savings for their customers through buying in large carload lots and breaking the bulk into smaller units.
- *Warehousing:* Wholesalers hold inventories, thereby reducing inventory costs and risks to suppliers and customers.
- *Transportation:* Wholesalers can often provide quicker delivery to buyers because they are closer to the buyers.
- *Financing:* Wholesalers finance customers by granting credit, and finance suppliers by ordering early and paying bills on time.
- *Risk bearing:* Wholesalers absorb some risk by taking title and bearing the cost of theft, damage, spoilage, and obsolescence.
- *Market information:* Wholesalers supply information to suppliers and customers regarding competitors' activities, new products, price developments, and so on.
- *Management services and counseling:* Wholesalers often help retailers improve their operations by training sales clerks, helping with store layouts and displays, and setting up accounting and inventory-control systems. They may help industrial customers by offering training and technical services.

the growth and types of wholesaling

Wholesaling has grown in the United States in recent years.[24] A number of factors explain this: the growth of larger factories located some distance from the principal buyers; production in advance of orders rather than in response to specific orders; an increase in the number of levels of intermediate producers and users; and the increasing

table **18.3**	Major Wholesaler Types

Merchant Wholesalers: Independently owned businesses that take title to the merchandise they handle. They are called *jobbers*, *distributors*, or *mill supply houses* and fall into two categories: full service and limited service.

Full-Service Wholesalers: Carry stock, maintain a sales force, offer credit, make deliveries, and provide management assistance. There are two types of full-service wholesalers: (1) *Wholesale merchants* sell primarily to retailers and provide a full range of services. *General-merchandise wholesalers* carry several merchandise lines. *General-line wholesalers* carry one or two lines. *Specialty wholesalers* carry only part of a line. (2) *Industrial distributors* sell to manufacturers rather than to retailers and provide several services—carrying stock, offering credit, and providing delivery.

Limited-Service Wholesalers: Offer fewer services to suppliers and customers. *Cash-and-carry wholesalers* have a limited line of fast-moving goods and sell to small retailers for cash. *Truck wholesalers* primarily sell and deliver a limited line of semi-perishable merchandise to supermarkets, small grocery stores, hospitals, restaurants, factory cafeterias, and hotels. *Drop shippers* operate in bulk industries, such as coal, lumber, and heavy equipment. Upon receiving an order, they select a manufacturer, who ships the merchandise directly to the customer on the agreed-upon terms and time of delivery. The drop shipper assumes title and risk from the time the order is accepted to its delivery to the customer. *Rack jobbers* serve grocery and drug retailers, mostly in nonfood items. They send delivery trucks to stores, and the delivery people set up displays, price the goods, keep them fresh, set up point-of-purchase displays, and keep inventory records. Rack jobbers retain title to the goods and bill retailers only for goods sold to consumers. *Producers' cooperatives* assemble farm produce to sell in local markets. Co-op profits are distributed to members at the end of the year. *Mail-order wholesalers* send catalogs to retail, industrial, and institutional customers featuring jewelry, cosmetics, specialty foods, and other small items. Main customers are businesses in small outlying areas. No sales force is maintained. Orders are filled and sent by mail, truck, or other means of transportation.

Brokers and Agents: Do not take title to goods, and perform only a few functions. Main function is to facilitate buying and selling, for which they earn a commission of 2 to 6 percent of the selling price. Generally specialize by product line or customer type.

Brokers: Chief function is bringing buyers and sellers together and assisting in negotiation. They are paid by the party who hired them and do not carry inventory, get involved in financing, or assume risk. The most familiar examples are food brokers, real estate brokers, insurance brokers, and security brokers.

Agents: Represent either buyers or sellers on a more permanent basis. *Manufacturers' agents* represent two or more manufacturers of complementary lines. They enter into a formal written agreement with each manufacturer covering pricing policy, territories, order-handling procedure, delivery service and warranties, and commission rates. Most manufacturers' agents are small businesses, with only a few skilled salespeople. *Selling agents* have contractual authority to sell a manufacturer's entire output in such product areas as textiles, industrial machinery and equipment, coal and coke, chemicals, and metals. *Purchasing agents* generally have a long-term relationship with buyers and make purchases for them, often receiving, inspecting, warehousing, and shipping merchandise to buyers. *Commission merchants* take physical possession of products and negotiate sales.

Manufacturers' and Retailers' Branches and Offices: Wholesaling operations conducted by sellers or buyers themselves rather than through independent wholesalers. Separate branches and offices can be dedicated to sales or purchasing. Sales branches and offices are set up by manufacturers to improve inventory control, selling, and promotion. Sales branches carry inventory and are found in such industries as lumber and automotive equipment and parts. *Sales offices* do not carry inventory and are most prominent in dry-goods and notions industries. *Purchasing offices* perform a role similar to that of brokers or agents but are part of the buyer's organization. Many retailers set up purchasing offices in major market centers.

Miscellaneous Wholesalers: A few specialized types of wholesalers are found in certain sectors of the economy. These include agricultural assemblers (which buy the agricultural output of many farms), petroleum bulk plants and terminals (which consolidate the petroleum output of many wells), and auction companies (which auction cars, equipment, and so forth, to dealers and other businesses).

need for adapting products to the needs of intermediate and final users in terms of quantities, packages, and forms. The major types of wholesalers are described in Table 18.3.

wholesaler marketing decisions

Wholesaler-distributors have faced mounting pressures in recent years from new sources of competition, demanding customers, new technologies, and more direct-buying programs by large industrial, institutional, and retail buyers. They have had to develop appropriate strategic responses. One major drive has been to increase asset productivity by managing their inventories and receivables better. They also have had to improve their strategic decisions on target markets, product assortment and services, price, promotion, and place.

TARGET MARKET   Wholesalers need to define their target markets. They can choose a target group of customers by size (only large retailers), type of customer (convenience food stores only), need for service (customers who need credit), or other criteria. Within the target group, they can identify the most profitable customers and design stronger offers to build better relationships with them. They can propose automatic reordering systems, set up management-training and advisory systems, and even sponsor a voluntary chain. They can discourage less profitable customers by requiring larger orders or adding surcharges to smaller ones.

PRODUCT ASSORTMENT AND SERVICES   The wholesalers' "product" is their assortment. Wholesalers are under great pressure to carry a full line and maintain sufficient stock for immediate delivery, but the costs of carrying huge inventories can kill profits. Wholesalers today are reexamining how many lines to carry and are choosing to carry only the more profitable ones. They are also examining which services count most in building strong customer relationships and which ones should be dropped or charged for. The key is to find a distinct mix of services valued by their customers.

PRICE DECISION   Wholesalers usually mark up the cost of goods by a conventional percentage, say 20 percent, to cover their expenses. Expenses may run 17 percent of the gross margin, leaving a profit margin of approximately 3 percent. In grocery wholesaling, the average profit margin is often less than 2 percent. Wholesalers are beginning to experiment with new approaches to pricing. They might cut their margin on some lines in order to win important new customers. They will ask suppliers for a special price break when they can turn it into an opportunity to increase the supplier's sales.

PROMOTION DECISION   Wholesalers rely primarily on their sales force to achieve promotional objectives. Even here, most wholesalers see selling as a single salesperson talking to a single customer, instead of a team effort to sell, build, and service major accounts. Wholesalers would benefit from adopting some of the image-making techniques used by retailers. They need to develop an overall promotion strategy involving trade advertising, sales promotion, and publicity. They also need to make greater use of supplier promotion materials and programs.

PLACE DECISION   In the past, wholesalers were typically located in low-rent, low-tax areas and put little money into their physical setting and offices. Often the materials-handling systems and order-processing systems lagged behind the available technologies. Today, progressive wholesalers have been improving materials-handling procedures and costs by developing *automated warehouses* and improving their supply capabilities through advanced information systems. Here is an example.[25]

McKesson   McKesson Corporation is a leading healthcare services company providing pharmaceutical and medical-surgical supply management, information solutions, pharmacy automation, and sales and marketing services to the healthcare industry. The company has unmatched depth, breadth, and reach delivering unique cost-saving and quality improvement solutions to pharmacies, hospitals, physicians, extended care sites, payor sites, and pharmaceutical and medical-surgical manufacturers. McKesson maintains a strong presence on the Internet through its Web site *www.mckesson.com*. The site offers access to information about the company, its people, products, and services. McKesson customers can use the Web site to access the company's healthcare software applications as well as order and track pharmaceutical and medical-surgical products.[26]

McKesson offers online supply
management.

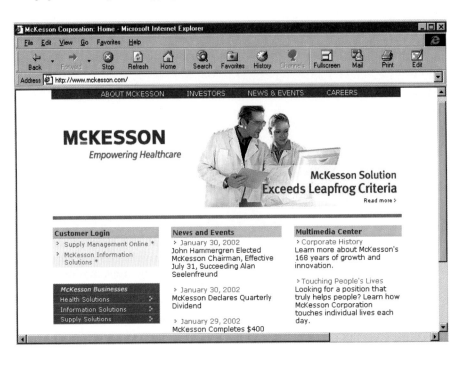

trends in wholesaling

Manufacturers always have the option of bypassing wholesalers or replacing inefficient wholesalers with better ones. Manufacturers' major complaints against wholesalers are as follows: They do not aggressively promote the manufacturer's product line, and act more like order takers; they do not carry enough inventory and therefore fail to fill customers' orders fast enough; they do not supply the manufacturer with up-to-date market, customer, and competitive information; they do not attract high-caliber managers and bring down their own costs; and they charge too much for their services.

It even appeared that wholesalers were headed for a significant decline as large manufacturers and retailers moved aggressively into direct buying programs. Savvy wholesalers rallied to the challenge and began to reengineer their businesses. The most successful wholesaler-distributors adapted their services to meet their suppliers' and target customers' changing needs. They recognized that they had to add value to the channel. They also had to reduce their operating costs by investing in more advanced materials-handling technology, information systems, and the Internet.

Grainger   W. W. Grainger, Inc., is one of the largest B2B distributors of equipment, components, and supplies in the United States and Canada. It offers over 220,000 products to clients. It has developed and stocked one national, two regional, and seven zone distribution centers to guarantee product availability and quick service. The distribution centers are linked by satellite network, which has reduced customer-response time and boosted sales. Grainger also offers a Web site to provide 24-hour-a-day online ordering.[27]

Narus and Anderson interviewed leading industrial distributors and identified four ways they strengthened their relationships with manufacturers:

1. They sought a clear agreement with their manufacturers about their expected functions in the marketing channel.
2. They gained insight into the manufacturers' requirements by visiting their plants and attending manufacturer association conventions and trade shows.

3. They fulfilled their commitments to the manufacturer by meeting the volume targets, paying bills promptly, and feeding back customer information to their manufacturers.
4. They identified and offered value-added services to help their suppliers.[28]

The wholesaling industry remains vulnerable to one of the most enduring trends— fierce resistance to price increases and the winnowing out of suppliers based on cost and quality. The trend toward vertical integration, in which manufacturers try to control or own their intermediaries, is still strong. "Marketing Memo: Strategies of High-Performance Wholesaler-Distributors" outlines some of the strategies used by successful wholesale organizations.

market logistics

Physical distribution starts at the factory. Managers choose a set of warehouses (stocking points) and transportation carriers that will deliver the goods to final destinations in the desired time or at the lowest total cost. Physical distribution has now been expanded into the broader concept of **supply chain management (SCM).** Supply chain management starts before physical distribution: It involves procuring the right inputs (raw materials, components, and capital equipment); converting them efficiently into finished products; and dispatching them to the final destinations. An even broader perspective calls for studying how the company's suppliers themselves obtain their inputs. The supply chain perspective can help a company identify superior suppliers and distributors and help them improve productivity, which ultimately brings down the company's costs.

The supply chain view sees markets as destination points and amounts to a linear view of the flow. A broader view sees a company at the center of a *value network* that includes its suppliers and its suppliers' suppliers and its immediate customers and their end customers. The value network includes valued relations with others such as university researchers, government approval agencies, and so on. A company needs to orchestrate these parties to enable it to deliver superior value to the target market. The company should first think of the target market and then design the supply chain backward from that point. This view has been called **demand chain planning. Market logistics** involves planning the infrastructure to meet demand, then implementing and controlling the physical flows of materials and final goods from points of origin to points of use, to meet customer requirements at a profit.

Market logistics planning has four steps:[29]

1. Deciding on the company's value proposition to its customers. (What on-time delivery standard should be offered? What levels should be attained in ordering and billing accuracy?)
2. Deciding on the best channel design and network strategy for reaching the customers. (Should the company serve customers directly or through intermediaries? What products to source from which manufacturing facilities? How many warehouses to maintain and where should they be located?)
3. Developing operational excellence in sales forecasting, warehouse management, transportation management, and materials management.
4. Implementing the solution with the best information systems, equipment, policies, and procedures.

Market logistics leads to an examination of the most efficient way to deliver value:

- A software company normally sees its challenge as producing and packaging software disks and manuals, then shipping them to wholesalers—who ship them to retailers, who sell them to customers. Customers bring the software package to home or office and download the software onto a hard drive. Market logistics would look at two superior delivery systems. The first involves ordering the software to be downloaded onto the customer's hard drive. Alternatively, software could be loaded onto a computer by the computer manufacturer. Both solutions eliminate the need for printing, packaging, shipping, and stocking millions of disks and manuals. The same solutions are available for distributing music, newspapers, video games, films, and other products that deliver voice, text, data, or images.

Marketing
MEMO

**Strategies for
High-Performance
Wholesaler-Distributors**

Lusch, Zizzo, and Kenderine studied 136 wholesalers in North America and concluded that the progressive ones are renewing themselves in five ways:

1. *Strengthening core operations:* Several wholesalers have put renewed focus on their core operations. They develop such expertise in distributing their particular product line that manufacturers and retailers cannot duplicate the efficiency.

2. *Expanding into global markets:* Wholesalers, especially in the chemical, electronics, and computer fields, have been expanding not only in Canada and Mexico but also in Europe and Asia. Many manufacturers prefer using these wholesaler networks to expand overseas.

3. *Doing more with less:* Wholesalers have been investing heavily in technology, including bar coding and scanning, fully automated warehouses, electronic data interchange (EDI), and advanced information technology. This has enabled them to serve manufacturers and retailers who have been unable or unwilling to make investments of their own.

continued...

■ At one time, German consumers purchased individual bottles of soft drinks. Then they said they would be willing to buy six bottles at a time in a six-pack. Retailers also favored this because the bottles could be loaded faster on the shelves, and more bottles would be purchased per occasion. A soft-drink manufacturer designed the six-packs to fit on store shelves. Then cases and pallets were designed to bring these six-packs to the store's receiving rooms. Factory operations were redesigned to produce the new six-packs. The purchasing department let out bids for the new materials. Once the six-packs hit the market, the manufacturer's market share rose substantially.

■ The IKEA Retailers, franchisees of the world-famous IKEA concept for retail sale of furniture and home furnishings, are able to sell good-quality furniture and home furnishings at a much lower cost than competitors. The IKEA concepts cost savings stem from several sources: (1) The IKEA Retailers buy such large volumes of furniture and home furnishings that they get lower prices; (2) the furniture and home furnishings are designed in "knockdown" form and therefore shipped flat at a much lower transportation cost; (3) the customer drives the furniture home, which saves delivery cost; (4) the customer assembles the furniture; and (5) the IKEA concept works on a low markup and high volume. Altogether, the IKEA Retailers can charge 20 percent less than competitors for comparable furniture and home furnishings.

The market logistics task calls for **integrated logistics systems (ILS)**, involving materials management, material flow systems, and physical distribution, abetted by information technology (IT). Third-party suppliers, such as FedEx Logistics Services or Ryder Integrated Logistics, often participate in designing or managing these systems. Volvo, working with FedEx, set up a warehouse in Memphis with a complete stock of truck parts. A dealer, needing a part in an emergency, phones a toll-free number, and the part is flown out the same day and delivered that night either at the airport or at the dealer's office or even at the roadside repair site.

Information systems play a critical role in managing market logistics, especially computers, point-of-sale terminals, uniform product bar codes, satellite tracking, electronic data interchange (EDI), and electronic funds transfer (EFT). These developments have shortened the order-cycle time, reduced clerical labor, reduced the error rate in documents, and provided improved control of operations. They have enabled companies to make promises such as "the product will be at dock 25 at 10:00 A.M. tomorrow," and control this promise through information. Consider the following two examples.

Supervalu   Supervalu, based in Eden Prairie, Minnesota, is a major wholesaler-retailer of dry groceries and the largest distributor to grocery retailers in the United States. It has been experimenting with "cross-docking," a system of moving products from the supplier's truck through the distribution center and onto a store-bound truck without putting them into pick or reserve bins. Attracted by the promise of savings on labor and time, Supervalu began cross-docking some high-volume products, such as paper products, and some milk and bread; about 12 percent of dry groceries were cross-docked in 1998. In 2000, the company expanded its cross-docking capabilities, which helped it to reduce the total number of inventory days on hand for the 1.5 billion cases of goods it shipped.[30]

Cutter & Buck   Cutter & Buck, Inc., is a high-end fashion sportswear company founded in 1990. By 1996, after successful growth, the company realized it had a problem with the contract warehouse, further compounded by the lack of an in-house embroidery capability. About half of its knit shirts needed custom embroidery, and the logistics of dealing with 14 different embroidery suppliers were difficult. So Cutter & Buck built its own warehouse and put embroidery machines in it. Fast turnaround, especially for embroidered items, greatly improved the company's profit margins. In 2000, a new warehouse management system implemented by the company helped reduce total labor costs by 20 percent.[31]

Market logistics involves several activities. The first is sales forecasting, on the basis of which the company schedules distribution, production, and inventory levels. Production plans indicate the materials the purchasing department must order. These materials arrive through inbound transportation, enter the receiving area, and are stored in raw-material inventory. Raw materials are converted into finished goods. Finished-goods inventory is the link between customer orders and manufacturing activity. Customers' orders draw down the finished-goods inventory level, and manufacturing activity builds it up. Finished goods flow off the assembly line and pass through packaging, in-plant warehousing, shipping-room processing, outbound transportation, field warehousing, and customer delivery and servicing.

Management has become concerned about the total cost of market logistics, which can amount to 30 to 40 percent of the product's cost. The grocery industry alone thinks it can decrease its annual operating costs by 10 percent, or $30 billion, by revamping its market logistics. A typical box of breakfast cereal takes 104 days to get from factory to supermarket, chugging through a labyrinth of wholesalers, distributors, brokers, and consolidators.[32] With inefficiencies like these, it is no wonder that experts call market logistics "the last frontier for cost economies." Lower market-logistics costs will permit lower prices, yield higher profit margins, or both. Even though the cost of market logistics can be high, a well-planned program can be a potent tool in competitive marketing. Companies can attract additional customers by offering better service, faster cycle time, or lower prices through market-logistics improvements.

What happens if a firm's market logistics are not set up properly? Companies lose customers when they fail to supply goods on time. Kodak launched a national advertising campaign for a new instant camera before it had delivered enough cameras to the stores. Customers found that it was not available and bought Polaroid cameras instead.

Today's large customers are making stronger demands for logistical support that will increase the supplier's costs. Customers want more frequent deliveries so that they do not have to carry as much inventory. They want shorter order-cycle times, which means that suppliers will have to carry high in-stock availability. Customers often want direct store delivery rather than shipments to distribution centers. They want mixed

4. *Committing to TQM:* Instead of just measuring sales and product movement, progressive wholesalers are moving toward managing processes to improve outcomes as perceived by customers. This includes performing quality assessment of their suppliers' products and thereby adding value. As the wholesalers move toward zero-defect customer service, manufacturers and retailers will welcome this trend as contributing to their own capacity to satisfy customers.

5. *Marketing support philosophy:* Wholesalers are recognizing that their role is not simply to represent the suppliers' interests, or their customers' interests, but to provide marketing support to both, by acting as a valued member of the marketing value chain.

Sources: Robert F. Lusch, Deborah Zizzo, and James M. Kenderdine, "Strategic Renewal in Distribution," *Marketing Management* 2, no. 2 (1993): 20–29. Also see their *Foundations of Wholesaling—A Strategic and Financial Chart Book, Distribution Research Program* (Norman, OK: College of Business Administration, University of Oklahoma, 1996).

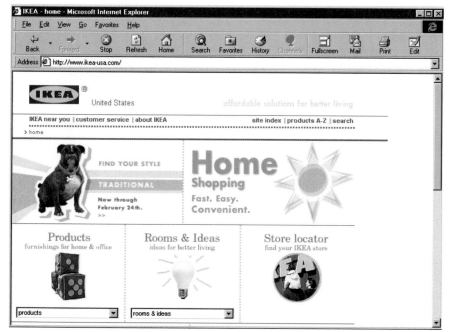

The IKEA-USA home page.

pallets of the goods they ordered rather than separate pallets. They want tighter promised delivery times. They may want custom packaging, price tagging, and display
building. Suppliers cannot say no to many of these requests, but at least they can set up
different logistical programs with different service levels and customer charges.

Smart companies will abandon "one-size-fits-all" logistics service and adjust their
offerings to each major customer's requirements. Some large retailers will want daily
shipments of smaller volumes; others will accept less frequent shipments of larger volumes. The company's trade group will set up *differentiated distribution* by offering different bundled service programs for different customers.

market-logistics objectives

Many companies state their market-logistics objective as "getting the right goods to
the right places at the right time for the least cost." Unfortunately, this objective provides little practical guidance. No system can simultaneously maximize customer
service and minimize distribution cost. Maximum customer service implies large
inventories, premium transportation, and multiple warehouses, all of which raise
market-logistics costs.

A company cannot achieve market-logistics efficiency by asking each market-logistics
manager to minimize his or her own logistics costs. Market-logistics costs interact and
are often negatively related. For example:

- The traffic manager favors rail shipment over air shipment because rail costs less. However, because the railroads are slower, rail shipment ties up working capital longer,
  delays customer payment, and might cause customers to buy from competitors who offer
  faster service.
- The shipping department uses cheap containers to minimize shipping costs. Cheaper
  containers lead to a higher rate of damaged goods and customer ill will.
- The inventory manager favors low inventories. This increases stockouts, back orders,
  paperwork, special production runs, and high-cost fast-freight shipments.

Given that market-logistics activities involve strong trade-offs, decisions must be
made on a total system basis. The starting point is to study what customers require and
what competitors are offering. Customers are interested in on-time delivery, supplier
willingness to meet emergency needs, careful handling of merchandise, supplier willingness to take back defective goods and re-supply them quickly.

The company must then research the relative importance of these service outputs.
For example, service-repair time is very important to buyers of copying equipment.
Xerox developed a service-delivery standard that "can put a disabled machine anywhere in the continental United States back into operation within three hours after
receiving the service request." It then designed a service division of personnel, parts,
and locations to deliver on this promise.

The company must also consider competitors' service standards. It will normally
want to match or exceed the competitors' service level, but the objective is to maximize
profits, not sales. The company has to look at the costs of providing higher levels of
service. Some companies offer less service and charge a lower price; other companies
offer more service and charge a premium price.

The company ultimately has to establish some promise to the market. Coca-Cola
wants to "put Coke within an arm's length of desire." Lands' End, the giant clothing
retailer, aims to respond to every phone call within 20 seconds, and to ship out every
order within 24 hours of its receipt. Some companies define standards for each service
factor. One appliance manufacturer has established the following service standards: to
deliver at least 95 percent of the dealer's orders within seven days of order receipt, to fill
the dealer's orders with 99 percent accuracy, to answer dealer inquiries on order status
within three hours, and to ensure that damage to merchandise in transit does not exceed
1 percent.

Given the market-logistics objectives, the company must design a system that will minimize the cost of achieving these objectives. Each possible market-logistics system will lead to the following cost:

$$M = T + FW + VW + S$$

where M = total market-logistics cost of proposed system
T = total freight cost of proposed system
FW = total fixed warehouse cost of proposed system
VW = total variable warehouse costs (including inventory) of proposed system
S = total cost of lost sales due to average delivery delay under proposed system

Choosing a market-logistics system calls for examining the total cost (M) associated with different proposed systems and selecting the system that minimizes it. If it is hard to measure S, the company should aim to minimize $T + FW + VW$ for a target level of customer service.

market-logistics decisions

Four major decisions must be made with regard to market logistics: (1) How should orders be handled? (order processing); (2) Where should stocks be located? (warehousing); (3) How much stock should be held? (inventory); and (4) How should goods be shipped? (transportation).

ORDER PROCESSING Most companies today are trying to shorten the *order-to-payment cycle*—that is, the elapsed time between an order's receipt, delivery, and payment. This cycle involves many steps, including order transmission by the salesperson, order entry and customer credit check, inventory and production scheduling, order and invoice shipment, and receipt of payment. The longer this cycle takes, the lower the customer's satisfaction and the lower the company's profits. Salespeople may be slow in sending in orders and use inefficient communications; these orders may pile up on the desk of order processors while they wait for credit department approval and inventory availability information from the warehouse.

Companies need to prepare criteria for the Perfect Order. Suppose the customer expects on-time delivery, order completeness, picking accuracy, and billing accuracy. Suppose the supplier has a 70 percent chance of delivering all four of these perfectly on any order. Then the probability that the supplier will fulfill perfect orders five times in a row to that customer would be $.70^5 = .168$. The customer's series of disappointments is likely to lead him to drop this supplier. A .70 standard is not good enough.

Companies are making progress, however. For example, General Electric operates an information system that checks the customer's credit standing upon receipt of an order, and determines whether and where the items are in stock. The computer issues an order to ship, bills the customer, updates the inventory records, sends a production order for new stock, and relays the message back to the sales representative that the customer's order is on its way—all in less than 15 seconds.

WAREHOUSING Every company has to store finished goods until they are sold, because production and consumption cycles rarely match. The storage function helps to smooth discrepancies between production and quantities desired by the market. The company must decide on the number of inventory stocking locations. Consumer packaged-goods companies have been reducing their number of stocking locations from 10–15 to about 5–7; and pharmaceutical and medical distributors have cut their stocking locations from 90 to about 45. On the one hand, more stocking locations means that goods can be delivered to customers more quickly, but it also means higher warehousing and inventory costs. To reduce warehousing and inventory duplication costs, the company might centralize its inventory in one place and use fast transportation to fulfill orders. After National Semiconductor shut down its six storage warehouses and set up a central distribution warehouse in Singapore, its standard delivery time decreased by 47 percent, its distribution costs fell 2.5 percent, and its sales increased 34 percent.[33]

Some inventory is kept at or near the plant, and the rest is located in warehouses in other locations. The company might own private warehouses and also rent space in public warehouses. *Storage warehouses* store goods for moderate-to-long periods of time. *Distribution warehouses* receive goods from various company plants and suppliers and move them out as soon as possible.

The older, multistoried warehouses with slow elevators and inefficient materials-handling procedures are receiving competition from newer, single-story *automated warehouses* with advanced materials-handling systems under the control of a central computer. The computer reads store orders and directs lift trucks and electric hoists to gather goods according to bar codes, move them to loading docks, and issue invoices. These warehouses have reduced worker injuries, labor costs, pilferage, and breakage and improved inventory control. When the Helene Curtis Company replaced its six antiquated warehouses with a new $32 million facility, it cut its distribution costs by 40 percent.[34]

Some warehouses are now taking on some activities formerly done in the plant. These include assembly, packaging, and constructing promotional displays. By "postponing" finalization of the offering, savings can be achieved in costs and finer matching of offerings to demand.

INVENTORY Inventory levels represent a major cost. Salespeople would like their companies to carry enough stock to fill all customer orders immediately. However, this is not cost-effective. *Inventory cost increases at an accelerating rate as the customer service level approaches 100 percent.* Management needs to know how much sales and profits would increase as a result of carrying larger inventories and promising faster order fulfillment times, and then make a decision.

Inventory decision making involves knowing when to order and how much to order. As inventory draws down, management must know at what stock level to place a new order. This stock level is called the *order (reorder) point.* An order point of 20 means reordering when the stock falls to 20 units. The order point should balance the risks of stockout against the costs of overstock.

The other decision is how much to order. The larger the quantity ordered, the less frequently an order has to be placed. The company needs to balance order-processing costs and inventory-carrying costs. *Order-processing costs* for a manufacturer consist of *setup costs* and *running costs* (operating costs when production is running) for the item. If setup costs are low, the manufacturer can produce the item often, and the average cost per item is stable and equal to the running costs. If setup costs are high, however, the manufacturer can reduce the average cost per unit by producing a long run and carrying more inventory.

Order-processing costs must be compared with *inventory-carrying costs.* The larger the average stock carried, the higher the inventory-carrying costs. These carrying costs include storage charges, cost of capital, taxes and insurance, and depreciation and obsolescence. Carrying costs might run as high as 30 percent of inventory value. This means that marketing managers who want their companies to carry larger inventories need to show that the larger inventories would produce incremental gross profit to exceed incremental carrying costs.

The optimal order quantity can be determined by observing how order-processing costs and inventory-carrying costs sum up at different order levels. Figure 18.2 shows that the order-processing cost per unit decreases with the number of units ordered because the order costs are spread over more units. Inventory-carrying charges per unit increase with the number of units ordered because each unit remains longer in inventory. The two cost curves are summed vertically into a total-cost curve. The lowest point on the total-cost curve is projected down on the horizontal axis to find the optimal order quantity Q^*.[35]

Companies are reducing their inventory costs by treating inventory items differently. They are positioning inventory items according to risk and opportunity. They distinguish between bottleneck items (high risk, low opportunity), critical items (high risk,

figure **18.2**

Determining Optimal Order Quantity

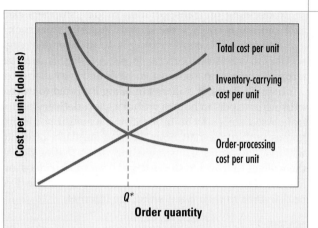

high opportunity), commodities (low risk, high opportunity), and nuisance items (low risk, low opportunity).[36] They are also keeping slow-moving items in a central location while carrying fast-moving items in warehouses closer to customers.

Just-in-time production methods have changed inventory-planning practices. **Just-in-time production (JIT)** consists of arranging for supplies to come into the factory at the rate that they are needed. If the suppliers are dependable, then the manufacturer can carry much lower levels of inventory and still meet customer-order-fulfillment standards. The basic idea is to arrange for well-timed *flows*, not *stocks*. Consider the following example.

Tesco   Tesco, the large British supermarket chain, has set up an innovative JIT market-logistics system. Tesco's management wanted to greatly reduce costly backroom storage space. It accomplished this by arranging twice-a-day delivery of replenishment stock. Ordinarily, it would have needed three separate trucks to deliver frozen goods, refrigerated goods, and regular goods on each trip. Instead, it designed new trucks with three compartments to carry the three types of goods.

The ultimate answer to carrying *near-zero inventory* is to build for order, not for stock. Sony calls it SOMA, "sell-one, make-one." Dell, for example, gets the customer to order a computer and pay for it in advance. Then Dell uses the customer's money to pay suppliers to ship the necessary components. As long as customers do not need the item immediately, money can be saved by all.

TRANSPORTATION   Marketers need to be concerned with transportation decisions. Transportation choices will affect product pricing, on-time delivery performance, and the condition of the goods when they arrive, all of which affects customer satisfaction.

In shipping goods to its warehouses, dealers, and customers, the company can choose among five transportation modes: rail, air, truck, waterway, and pipeline. Shippers consider such criteria as speed, frequency, dependability, capability, availability, traceability, and cost. For speed, air and truck are the prime contenders. If the goal is low cost, then it is water and pipeline.

Shippers are increasingly combining two or more transportation modes, thanks to containerization. **Containerization** consists of putting the goods in boxes or trailers that are easy to transfer between two transportation modes. *Piggyback* describes the use of rail and trucks; *fishyback*, water and trucks; *trainship*, water and rail; and *airtruck*, air and trucks. Each coordinated mode offers specific advantages. For example, piggyback is cheaper than trucking alone, yet provides flexibility and convenience.

In deciding on transportation modes, shippers can choose from private, contract, and common carriers. If the shipper owns its own truck or air fleet, the shipper becomes a *private carrier*. A *contract carrier* is an independent organization selling transportation services to others on a contract basis. A *common carrier* provides services between predetermined points on a scheduled basis and is available to all shippers at standard rates.

Today billions of dollars are being invested to develop "last-mile delivery systems" to bring products to homes within a short delivery period. Domino's Pizza organized its franchised stores to be in locations where it could promise to deliver hot pizzas to homes within one-half hour. Peapod similarly offers to deliver online grocery orders within a few hours. Consumers may soon think twice about whether they should exert themselves to travel to stores to get their food, videos, or clothes or simply ask the stores to bring it to them in about the same amount of time. Everything, including flowers, can be delivered to their door, using the Internet.

1-800-flowers.com. A customer can order flowers from this site to send to an address book of recipients. 1-800-Flowers uses a sophisticated regional fulfillment system. If the flower is not available in the region, the customer is notified of the shipment delay and can approve or change the order. After ordering, the customer can use the site to track the order's location. The fulfillment capabilities have been designed to give customers confidence that their gifts will be delivered in the promised time.

organizational lessons

Experience with market logistics has taught executives three major lessons:

1. Companies should appoint a senior vice president of logistics to be the single point of contact for all logistical elements. This executive should be accountable for logistical performance on both cost and customer-satisfaction criteria.

The 1-800-Flowers.com site makes online ordering easy.

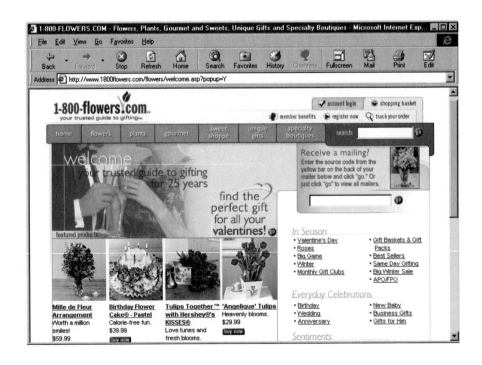

2. The senior vice president of logistics should hold periodic meetings (weekly, biweekly) with sales and operations people to review inventory, operating costs, and customer service and satisfaction, as well as to consider market conditions and whether changes should be made in production schedules.

3. New software and systems are the key to achieving competitively superior logistics performance in the future.

Here is how Sears is gaining through the use of better software:[37]

Sears   Sears, Roebuck & Company owns a huge credit-card company called Sears Credit, which serves over 60 million credit-card holders who use their cards to purchase more than 50 percent of all merchandise sold in Sears stores. To improve customer service, Sears formed a strategic alliance with Total Systems Services (TSYS), a third-party credit-card processing service. Alan J. Lacy, president of Sears Credit, stressed the ability of TSYS to track delinquent accounts more quickly and effectively, thus improving collections. The partnership with TSYS also yielded one of Sears' more successful credit-card launches—the Sears Gold MasterCard, which generated more than $1 billion in receivables within a year of its 2000 debut.[38]

Market-logistics strategies must be derived from business strategies, rather than solely from cost considerations. The logistics system must be information-intensive and establish electronic links among all the significant parties. Finally, the company should set its logistics goals to match or exceed competitors' service standards and should involve members of all relevant teams in the planning process.

summary

1. Retailing includes all the activities involved in selling goods or services directly to final consumers for personal, non-business use. Retailers can be understood in terms of store retailing, nonstore retailing, and retail organizations.

2. Like products, retail-store types pass through stages of growth and decline. As existing stores offer more services to remain competitive, their costs and prices go up, which opens the door to new retail forms that offer a mix of merchandise and services at lower prices. The major types of retail stores are specialty stores; department stores; supermarkets; convenience stores; discount stores; off-price retailers (factory outlets, independent off-price retailers, and warehouse clubs); superstores (combination stores and supermarkets); and catalog showrooms.

3. Although most goods and services are sold through stores, nonstore retailing has been growing much faster than store retailing. The major types of nonstore retailing are direct selling (one-to-one selling, one-to-many-party selling, and multilevel network marketing); direct marketing (which includes e-commerce and Internet retailing); automatic vending; and buying services.

4. Although many retail stores are independently owned, an increasing number are falling under some form of corporate retailing. Retail organizations achieve many economies of scale, such as greater purchasing power, wider brand recognition, and better-trained employees. The major types of corporate retailing are corporate chain stores, voluntary chains, retailer cooperatives, consumer cooperatives, franchise organizations, and merchandising conglomerates.

5. Like all marketers, retailers must prepare marketing plans that include decisions on target markets, product assortment and procurement, services and store atmosphere, price, promotion, and place. These decisions must take into account the major trends in retailing.

6. Wholesaling includes all the activities involved in selling goods or services to those who buy for resale or business use. Manufacturers use wholesalers because wholesalers can perform functions better and more cost-effectively than the manufacturer can. These functions include, but are not limited to, selling and promoting, buying and assortment building, bulk breaking, warehousing, transportation, financing, risk bearing, dissemination of market information, and provision of management services and consulting.

7. There are four types of wholesalers: merchant wholesalers (full-service wholesalers like wholesale merchants and industrial distributors, and limited-service wholesalers like cash-and-carry wholesalers, truck wholesalers, drop shippers, rack jobbers, producers' cooperatives, and mail-order wholesalers); brokers and agents (including manufacturers' agents, selling agents, purchasing agents, and commission merchants); manufacturers' and retailers' sales branches, sales offices, and purchasing offices; and miscellaneous wholesalers such as agricultural assemblers and auction companies.

8. Like retailers, wholesalers must decide on target markets, product assortment and services, price, promotion, and place. The most successful wholesalers are those who adapt their services to meet their suppliers' and target customers' needs.

9. Producers of physical products and services must decide on market logistics—the best way to store and move their goods and services to market destinations. The logistical task is to coordinate the activities of suppliers, purchasing agents, manufacturers, marketers, channel members, and customers. Major gains in logistical efficiency have come from advances in information technology. Although the cost of market logistics can be high, a well-planned market-logistics program can be a potent tool in competitive marketing. The ultimate goal of market logistics is to meet customers' requirements in an efficient and profitable way.

applications

marketing debate – does it matter where you are sold?

Some marketers feel that the image of the retail store in which they sell their products does not matter—all that matters is that the right customers shop there and the product is displayed in the right way. Others maintain that store images can be critical and must be consistent with the image of the product.

Take a position: Store image does not really affect the brand images of the products they sell that much versus Store image must be consistent with the product image.

marketing and advertising

1. The Mayors jewelry store ad in Figure 1 focuses on a particular type of merchandise—the diamond engagement ring—and suggests how it helps to bring luxury to the recipient.

   a. What is the target market for this ad? How is the ad using the ad graphics and copy to appeal to this target market?

   b. Based on this ad, what services and atmosphere would a consumer expect to find at a Mayors store? At the Mayors Web site?

   c. Discuss the retailer's product-assortment strategy, as suggested by the item featured here.

2. Retailers need to plan market logistics for backward channels as well as forward channels. The ad shown in Figure 2 explains how online retailers can save time and money—and satisfy customers—by incorporating a UPS system to manage merchandise returns.

   a. What flows must an online retailer consider when preparing for customer returns?

   b. How would a system for managing returns be likely to affect an online retailer's decisions about warehousing and inventory?

   c. What market-logistics objectives might a retailer using this UPS system set for its merchandise returns?

Figure 1

Figure 2

online marketing today

As discussed earlier, W. W. Grainger is a giant industrial wholesaler with branches throughout North America and a comprehensive Web site for online ordering at any hour. Despite competition from specialized Web marketplaces, Grainger.com draws more than one million users every month and rings up over $260 million in annual sales. After a months-long promotional campaign to attract online users, the site became so well established that Grainger was able to shift spending into advanced technology such as new search tools to help customers locate what they want even more quickly.[39]

Browse the home page of the Grainger Web site (www.grainger.com), noting the kinds of products that are highlighted here. Then follow the "About Us" link to read about the company's history, mission and values, and special promotions. Finally, follow the "Services" link and read about the various services being offered. Who is Grainger's target market, and what is its mission? How would you describe its product assortment and services? What is this wholesaler doing to build and strengthen customer relationships by adding extra value?

you're the marketer: sonic pda marketing plan

Marketing Plan Pro

Retailers and wholesalers play a critical role in marketing strategy because of their relationships with the final consumer. For this reason, manufacturers need to effectively manage their connections with these channel intermediaries.

You are responsible for channel management for Sonic's new personal digital assistant (PDA) product. Based on your previous strategic choices and your knowledge of the market, respond to the following questions in shaping your wholesaling and retailing decisions:

■ What types of retailers would be most appropriate for distributing Sonic's PDA? What are the advantages and disadvantages of selling through these types of retailers?

■ What role should wholesalers play in Sonic's distribution strategy? Why?
■ What market-logistics issues must Sonic consider for the launch of its first PDA?
■ What effect do your wholesale/retail decisions have on the other decisions you face about Sonic's marketing mix?

Now that you have examined Sonic's retail and wholesale opportunities and market logistics, summarize your ideas in a written marketing plan or type them into the Marketing Mix and Channels sections of the *Marketing Plan Pro* software.

notes

1. William R. Davidson, Albert D. Bates, and Stephen J. Bass, "Retail Life Cycle," *Harvard Business Review* (November–December 1976): 89–96.
2. Stanley C. Hollander, "The Wheel of Retailing," *Journal of Marketing* (July 1960): 37–42.
3. Bill Saporito, "And the Winner Is Still . . . Wal-Mart," *Fortune*, May 2, 1994, pp. 62–70; Lorrie Grant, "An Unstoppable Marketing Force: Wal-Mart Aims for Domination of the Retail Industry—Worldwide," *USA Today*, November 6, 1998, p. B1.
4. Hoover's Company Capsules, 1999; Limited Annual Report, 2001.
5. Laurence H. Wortzel, "Retailing Strategies for Today's Marketplace," *Journal of Business Strategy* (Spring 1987): 45–56.
6. Evan Ramstad, "Circuit City's CEO Gambles to Galvanize the Chain," *Wall Street Journal*, September 18, 2000, p. B4.
7. Michael Treacy and Fred Wiersema, "Customer Intimacy and Other Discipline Values," *Harvard Business Review* (January–February 1993): 84–93; "GE to Sell Appliances Online," *PR Newswire*, September 30, 1999.
8. Cametta Coleman, "Kohl's Retail Racetrack," *Wall Street Journal*, March 1, 2000.
9. Piet Vroon et al., *Smell : The Secret Seducer* (New York: Farrar, Straus & Giroux, 1997).
10. For more discussion, see Philip Kotler, "Atmospherics as a Marketing Tool," *Journal of Retailing* (Winter 1973–1974): 48–64; and Mary Jo Bitner, "Servicescapes: The Impact of Physical Surroundings on Customers and Employees," *Journal of Marketing* (April 1992): 57–71. Also see B. Joseph Pine II and

James H. Gilmore, *The Experience Economy* (Boston: Harvard Business School Press, 1999).
11. Mall of America Web site; Kristen Ostendorf, "Not Wed to Tradition," *Gannett News Service*, January 5, 1998; Carol Sottili, "Mall of America Has Stores Galore," *Plain Dealer*, April 23, 2000, p. 2K.
12. Joann Muller, "Kmart's Bright Idea," *Business Week*, April 9, 2001, p. 50.
13. Frank Feather, *The Future Consumer* (Toronto: Warwick Publishing, 1994), p. 171. Also see Stephen J. Hoch, Xavier Dreeze, and Mary E. Purk, "EDLP, Hi-Lo, and Margin Arithmetic," *Journal of Marketing* (October 1994): 1–15.
14. Paul Klebnikov, "Hair of the Dog," *Forbes*, April 16, 2001, p. 74.
15. R. L. Davies and D. S. Rogers, eds., *Store Location and Store Assessment Research* (New York: John Wiley, 1984).
16. Sara L. McLafferty, *Location Strategies for Retail and Service Firms* (Lexington, MA: Lexington Books, 1987).
17. Catherine Yang, "Maybe They Should Call Them Scammers," *BusinessWeek*, January 16, 1995, pp. 32–33; Ronald C. Goodstein, "UPC Scanner Pricing Systems: Are They Accurate?" *Journal of Marketing* (April 1994): 20–30.
18. For a listing of the key factors involved in success with an EDI system, see R. P. Vlosky, D. T. Wilson, and P. M. Smith, "Electronic Data Interchange Implementation Strategies: A Case Study," *Journal of Business & Industrial Marketing* 9, no. 4 (1994): 5–18.
19. "Business Bulletin: Shopper Scanner," *Wall Street Journal*, February 18, 1995, p. A1.

20. For further discussion of retail trends, see Louis W. Stern and Adel I. El-Ansary, *Marketing Channels*, 5th ed. (Upper Saddle River, NJ: Prentice Hall, 1996).

21. Shelley Donald Coolidge, "Facing Saturated Home Markets, Retailers Look to Rest of World," *Christian Science Monitor*, February 14, 1994, p. 7; Carla Rapoport with Justin Martin, "Retailers Go Global," *Fortune*, February 20, 1995, pp. 102–8.

22. Gherry Khermouch, "Third Places," *Brandweek*, March 13, 1995, pp. 36–40.

23. I. Jeanne Dugan, "The Baron of Books," *BusinessWeek*, June 29, 1998; Hoover's Company Profiles, 1999; Rebecca Quick, "CEO Steps Down at Barnes & Noble Online Concern," *Wall Street Journal*, January 13, 2000; Rebecca Quick, "Barnes & Noble and Its Online Sibling Enter Alliance Linking 'Bricks and Clicks,'" *Wall Street Journal*, October 27, 2000, p. B10; Erin White, "Barnes & Noble.com Expects to Report 23% Revenue Rise," *Wall Street Journal*, April 27, 2001, p. 25.

24. Bert McCammon, Robert F. Lusch, Deborah S. Coykendall, and James M. Kenderdine, *Wholesaling in Transition* (Norman: University of Oklahoma, College of Business Administration, 1989).

25. Hoover's Company Profiles, 1999; and company Web sites.

26. Michael Liedtke, "Online Goes Offline at McKesson HBOC," *Pittsburgh Post-Gazette*, February 27, 2001, p. B4.

27. <www.grainger.com>.

28. James A. Narus and James C. Anderson, "Contributing as a Distributor to Partnerships with Manufacturers, " *Business Horizons* (September–October 1987). Also see James D. Hlavecek and Tommy J. McCuistion, "Industrial Distributors—When, Who, and How," *Harvard Business Review* (March–April 1983): 96–101.

29. William C. Copacino, *Supply Chain Management* (Boca Raton, FL: St. Lucie Press, 1997).

30. Susan Reda, "Crossdocking: Can Supermarkets Catch Up?" *Stores* (February 1998); Supervalu 2001 *Annual Report*.

31. Diane Mayoros, "Cutter & Buck Chairman & CEO Interview," *Wall Street Corporate Reporter*, August 6, 1998; "Cutter & Buck Announces Two New Retail Locations;" *Business Wire*, August 21, 2000.

32. Ronald Henkoff, "Delivering the Goods," *Fortune*, November 28, 1994, pp. 64–78.

33. Ibid., pp. 64–78.

34. Rita Koselka, "Distribution Revolution," *Forbes*, May 25, 1992, pp. 54–62.

35. The optimal order quantity is given by the formula $Q^*=2DS/IC$, where D=annual demand, S=cost to place one order, and I=annual carrying cost per unit. Known as the economic-order quantity formula, it assumes a constant ordering cost, a constant cost of carrying an additional unit in inventory, a known demand, and no quantity discounts. For further reading on this subject, see Richard J. Tersine, *Principles of Inventory and Materials Management*, 4th ed. (Upper Saddle River, NJ: Prentice Hall, 1994).

36. William C. Copacino, *Supply Chain Management* (Boca Raton, FL: St. Lucie Press, 1997), pp. 122–23.

37. "Darigold Selects IMI to Enhance Order Fulfillment and Customer Service," *Business Wire*, February 2, 1998.

38. Sears Press Release, "Sears Announces Strategic Alliance with Total Systems, Inc.," May 14, 1998; <www.tsys.com>; "TSYS Extends Retail Agreement with Sears." *PR Newswire*, January 18, 2000.

39. Don Steinberg, "W. W. Grainger—Grainger.com," *Ziff Davis Smart Business for the New Economy,* September 1, 2001, p. 64.

managing integrated marketing communications

Kotler On Marketing

Integrated marketing communications is a way of looking at the whole marketing process from the viewpoint of the customer.

In this chapter, we will address the following questions:

- How does communication work?
- What are the major steps in developing an integrated marketing communications program?
- Who should be responsible for marketing communication planning?

Modern marketing calls for more than developing a good product, pricing it attractively, and making it accessible. Companies must also communicate with present and potential stakeholders, and the general public. Every company is inevitably cast into the role of communicator and promoter. For most companies, the question is not whether to communicate but rather what to say, to whom, and how often.

The **marketing communications mix** consists of five major modes of communication:

1. *Advertising:* Any paid form of nonpersonal presentation and promotion of ideas, goods, or services by an identified sponsor.

2. *Sales promotion: A variety of short-term incentives to encourage trial or purchase of a product or service.*

3. *Public relations and publicity: A variety of programs designed to promote or protect a company's image or its individual products.*

4. *Personal selling: Face-to-face interaction with one or more prospective purchasers for the purpose of making presentations, answering questions, and procuring orders.*

5. *Direct and interactive marketing: Use of mail, telephone, fax, e-mail, or Internet to communicate directly with or solicit response or dialogue from specific customers and prospects.[1]*

This chapter will describe the communication process; in the following chapters we will examine each of the communication tools.

the communications process

Today there is a new view of communications as an interactive dialogue between the company and its customers that takes place during the preselling, selling, consuming, and postconsuming stages. Companies must ask not only "How can we reach our customers?" but also, "How can our customers reach us?"

Table 19.1 lists numerous communication platforms. Thanks to technological breakthroughs, people can now communicate through traditional media (newspapers, magazines, radio, telephone, television, billboards), as well as through newer media (computers, fax machines, cellular phones, pagers, and wireless appliances). By decreasing communications costs, the new technologies have encouraged more companies to move from mass-communication to more targeted communication and one-to-one dialogue.

table **19.1**	Common Communication Platforms			
Advertising	**Sales Promotion**	**Public Relations**	**Personal Selling**	**Direct Marketing**
Print and broadcast ads	Contests, games, sweepstakes, lotteries	Press kits	Sales presentations	Catalogs
Packaging–outer		Speeches	Sales meetings	Mailings
Packaging inserts	Premiums and gifts	Seminars	Incentive programs	Telemarketing
Motion pictures	Sampling	Annual reports	Samples	Electronic shopping
Brochures and booklets	Fairs and trade shows	Charitable donations	Fairs and trade shows	TV shopping
Posters and leaflets	Exhibits	Sponsorships		Fax mail
Directories	Demonstrations	Publications		E-mail
Reprints of ads	Coupons	Community relations		Voice mail
Billboards	Rebates	Lobbying		
Display signs	Low-interest financing	Identity media		
Point-of-purchase displays	Entertainment	Company magazine		
Audiovisual material	Trade-in allowances	Events		
Symbols and logos	Continuity programs			
Videotapes	Tie-ins			

figure **19.1**

Elements in the
Communication Process

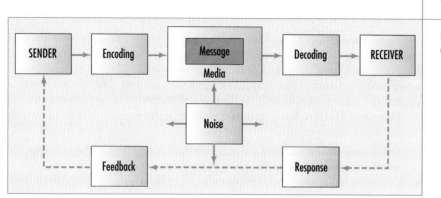

However, company communication goes beyond the specific platforms listed in Table 19.1. The product's styling and price, the shape and color of the package, the salesperson's manner and dress, the store decor, the company's stationery—all communicate something to buyers. Every *brand contact* delivers an impression that can strengthen or weaken a customer's view of the company. The whole marketing mix must be integrated to deliver a consistent message and strategic positioning.

The starting point is an audit of all the potential interactions target customers may have with the product and the company. For example, someone interested in purchasing a new computer would talk to others, see television ads, read articles, look for information on the Internet, and observe computers in a store. Marketers need to assess which experiences and impressions will have the most influence at each stage of the buying process. This understanding will help them allocate communications dollars more efficiently.

Marketers also need to understand the fundamental elements of effective communications. Figure 19.1 shows a communication model with nine elements. Two represent the major parties in a communication—sender and receiver. Two represent the major communication tools—message and media. Four represent major communication functions—*encoding, decoding, response,* and *feedback*. The last element in the system is *noise* (random and competing messages that may interfere with the intended communication).[2]

The model emphasizes the key factors in effective communication. Senders must know what audiences they want to reach and what responses they want to get. They must encode their messages so that the target audience can decode them. They must transmit the message through media that reach the target audience and develop feedback channels to monitor the responses. The more the sender's field of experience overlaps with that of the receiver, the more effective the message is likely to be.

The target audience may not receive the intended message for any of three reasons:

1. *Selective attention:* People are bombarded by about 1,600 commercial messages a day, of which 80 are consciously noticed and about 12 provoke some reaction. Selective attention explains why ads with bold headlines promising something, such as "How to Make a Million," have a high likelihood of getting attention.
2. *Selective distortion:* Receivers will hear what fits into their belief systems. As a result, receivers often add things to the message that are not there (amplification) and do not notice other things that are there (leveling). The communicator's task is to strive for simplicity, clarity, interest, and repetition to get the main points across.
3. *Selective retention:* People will retain in long-term memory only a small fraction of the messages that reach them. If the receiver's initial attitude toward the object is positive and he or she rehearses support arguments, the message is likely to be accepted and have high recall. If the initial attitude

figure **19.2**

Steps in Developing
Effective Communication

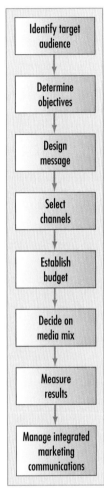

is negative and the person rehearses counterarguments, the message is likely to be rejected but to stay in long-term memory. Because persuasion requires the receiver's rehearsal of his or her own thoughts, much of what is called persuasion is actually self-persuasion.[3]

The communicator considers audience traits that correlate with persuasibility and uses them to guide message and media development. People of high education or intelligence are thought to be less persuasible, but the evidence is inconclusive. Those who accept external standards to guide their behavior and who have a weak self-concept appear to be more persuasible, as do those who have low self-confidence.[4]

Fiske and Hartley have outlined some general factors that influence the effectiveness of a communication:

■ The greater the influence of the communication source over the recipient, the greater the recipient's change or effect in favor of the source.

■ Communication effects are greatest where the message is in line with the receiver's existing opinions, beliefs, and dispositions.

■ Communication can produce the most effective shifts on unfamiliar, lightly felt, peripheral issues that do not lie at the core of the recipient's value system.

■ Communication is more likely to be effective if the source is believed to have expertise, high status, objectivity, or likability, but particularly if the source has power and can be identified with.

■ The social context, group, or reference group will mediate the communication and influence whether or not the communication is accepted.[5]

developing effective communications

Figure 19.2 shows the eight steps in developing effective communications that we discuss here.

identify the target audience

The process must start with a clear target audience in mind: potential buyers of the company's products, current users, deciders, or influencers; individuals, groups, particular publics, or the general public. The target audience is a critical influence on the communicator's decisions on what to say, how to say it, when to say it, where to say it, and to whom to say it.

IMAGE ANALYSIS   A major part of audience analysis is assessing the current image of the company, its products, and its competitors. **Image** is the set of beliefs, ideas, and impressions a person holds regarding an object. People's attitudes and actions toward an object are highly conditioned by that object's image.

The first step is to measure the target audience's knowledge of the object, using the *familiarity scale:*

Never Heard of	Heard of Only	Know a Little Bit	Know a Fair Amount	Know Very Well

If most respondents circle only the first two categories, the challenge is to build greater awareness.

Respondents who are familiar with the product can be asked how they feel toward it, using the *favorability scale:*

Very Unfavorable	Somewhat Unfavorable	Indifferent	Somewhat Favorable	Very Favorable

If most respondents check the first two categories, then the organization must overcome a negative image problem. The two scales can be combined to develop insight into the nature of the communication challenge. Suppose area residents are asked about their familiarity with and attitudes toward four local hospitals, A, B, C, and D. Their responses are averaged and shown in Figure 19.3. Hospital A has the most positive image: Most people know it and like it. Hospital B is less familiar to most people, but those who know it like it. Hospital C is viewed negatively by those who know it, but (fortunately for the hospital) not too many people know it. Hospital D is seen as a poor hospital, and everyone knows it!

Each hospital faces a different communication task. Hospital A must work at maintaining its good reputation and high awareness. Hospital B must gain the attention of more people. Hospital C must find out why people dislike it and must take steps to improve its quality while keeping a low profile. Hospital D should lower its profile, improve its quality, and then seek public attention.

Each hospital needs to research the specific content of its image. The most popular tool for this research is the **semantic differential**.[6] It involves the following steps:

1. *Developing a set of relevant dimensions:* The researcher asks people to identify the dimensions they would use in thinking about the object: "What things do you think of when you consider a hospital?" If someone suggests "quality of medical care," this dimension would be turned into a five- or seven-point bipolar adjective scale, with "inferior medical care" at one end and "superior medical care" at the other. A set of additional dimensions for a hospital is shown in Figure 19.4.
2. *Reducing the set of relevant dimensions:* The number of dimensions should be reduced to avoid respondent fatigue.
3. *Administering the instrument to a sample of respondents:* The respondents are asked to rate one object at a time. The bipolar adjectives should be randomly arranged so that the unfavorable adjectives are not all listed on one side.
4. *Averaging the results:* Figure 19.4 shows the results of averaging the respondents' pictures of hospitals A, B, and C (hospital D is left out). Each hospital's image is represented by a vertical "line of means" that summarizes average perception of that hospital. Hospital A is seen as a large, modern, friendly, and superior hospital. Hospital C, in contrast, is seen as small, dated, impersonal, and inferior.
5. *Checking on the image variance:* Because each image profile is a line of means, it does not reveal how variable the image is. Did everyone see hospital B this way, or was there considerable variation? In the first case, we would say that the image is highly specific; and in the second case, highly diffused. Some organizations prefer a diffused image so that different groups will see the organization in different ways.

figure **19.3**

Familiarity–Favorability Analysis

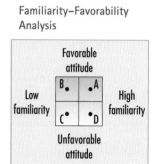

figure **19.4**

Images of Three Hospitals (Semantic Differential)

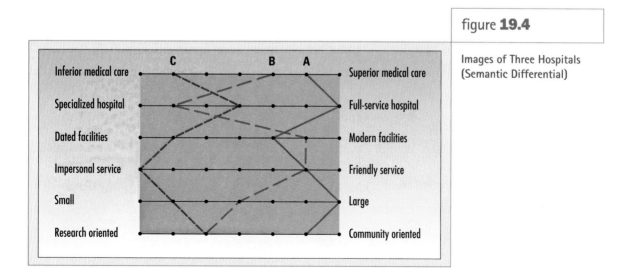

Management should now define a desired image if it differs from the current one. Suppose hospital C would like the public to view its medical care, facilities, and friendliness more favorably. Management must decide which image gaps it wants to close first. Is it more desirable to improve friendliness (through staff training programs) or the quality of its facilities (through renovation)? What would it cost to close a particular gap? How long would it take?

Images are "sticky"; they persist long after the organization has changed. Image persistence is explained by the fact that once people have a certain image, they perceive what is consistent with that image. It will take highly disconfirming information to raise doubts and open their minds, especially when people do not have continuous or new firsthand experiences with the changed object.

Wolverine   Wolverine World Wide of Rockford, Michigan, discovered this when its Hush Puppies brand of casual shoes lost its fashionable image. Then a fashion designer used Hush Puppies dyed in bright colors. The Hush Puppies image went from stodgy to avant-garde, and once the "new" Hush Puppies were in demand, sales went from under 30,000 pairs in 1994 to 1.7 million pairs in 1996.[7]

determine the communication objectives

The marketer can be seeking a *cognitive*, *affective*, or *behavioral* response. That is, the marketer might want to put something into the consumer's mind, change an attitude, or get the consumer to act. Even here, there are different models of consumer-response stages. Figure 19.5 summarizes the four best-known *response hierarchy models*.

figure **19.5**

Response Hierarchy Models

Stages	Models			
	AIDA Model[a]	Hierarchy-of-Effects Model[b]	Innovation-Adoption Model[c]	Communications Model[d]
Cognitive stage	Attention	Awareness ↓ Knowledge	Awareness	Exposure ↓ Reception ↓ Cognitive response
Affective stage	Interest ↓ Desire	Liking ↓ Preference ↓ Conviction	Interest ↓ Evaluation	Attitude ↓ Intention
Behavior stage	Action	Purchase	Trial ↓ Adoption	Behavior

Sources: [a]E. K. Strong, *The Psychology of Selling* (New York: McGraw-Hill, 1925), p. 9; [b]Robert J. Lavidge and Gary A. Steiner, "A Model for Predictive Measurements of Advertising Effectiveness," *Journal of Marketing* (October 1961): 61; [c]Everett M. Rogers, *Diffusion of Innovation* (New York: The Free Press, 1962), pp. 79–86; [d]various sources.

All these models assume that the buyer passes through a cognitive, affective, and behavioral stage, in that order. This "learn-feel-do" sequence is appropriate when the audience has high involvement with a product category perceived to have high differentiation, as in purchasing an automobile. An alternative sequence, "do-feel-learn," is relevant when the audience has high involvement but perceives little or no differentiation within the product category, as in purchasing aluminum siding. A third sequence, "learn-do-feel," is relevant when the audience has low involvement and perceives little differentiation within the product category, as in purchasing salt. By choosing the right sequence, the marketer can do a better job of planning communications.[8]

Here we will assume that the buyer has high involvement with the product category and perceives high differentiation within the category. We will illustrate the *hierarchy-of-effects model* (in the second column of Figure 19.5):

- *Awareness:* If most of the target audience is unaware of the object, the communicator's task is to build awareness, perhaps just name recognition, with simple messages repeating the product name. Suppose a small Iowa college named Pottsville seeks applicants from Nebraska but has no name recognition in Nebraska. Suppose there are 30,000 high school juniors and seniors in Nebraska who may potentially be interested in Pottsville College. The college might set the objective of making 70 percent of these students aware of Pottsville's name within one year.

- *Knowledge:* The target audience might have product awareness but not know much more. Pottsville may want its target audience to know that it is a private four-year college with excellent programs in English, foreign languages, and history. It needs to learn how many people in the target audience have little, some, or much knowledge about Pottsville. If knowledge is weak, Pottsville may decide to select product knowledge as its communication objective.

- *Liking:* If target members know the product, how do they feel about it? If the audience looks unfavorably on Pottsville College, the communicator has to find out why. If the unfavorable view is based on real problems, Pottsville will have to fix its problems and then communicate its renewed quality. Good public relations calls for "good deeds followed by good words."

- *Preference:* The target audience might like the product but not prefer it to others. In this case, the communicator must try to build consumer preference by promoting quality, value, performance, and other features. The communicator can check the campaign's success by measuring audience preference after the campaign.

- *Conviction:* A target audience might prefer a particular product but not develop a conviction about buying it. The communicator's job is to build conviction among interested students that Pottsville College is their best choice.

- *Purchase:* Finally, some members of the target audience might have conviction but may not quite get around to making the purchase. They may wait for more information or plan to act later. The communicator must lead these consumers to take the final step, perhaps by offering the product at a low price, offering a premium, or letting consumers try it out. Pottsville might invite selected high school students to visit the campus and attend some classes, or it might offer partial scholarships to deserving students.

design the message

Having defined the desired response, the communicator moves to developing an effective message. Ideally, the message should gain *attention*, hold *interest*, arouse *desire*, and elicit *action* (AIDA model—see the first column of Figure 19.5). In practice, few messages take the consumer all the way from awareness through purchase, but the AIDA framework suggests the desirable qualities of any communication.

Formulating the message will require solving four problems: what to say (message content), how to say it logically (message structure), how to say it symbolically (message format), and who should say it (message source).

MESSAGE CONTENT   In determining message content, management searches for an appeal, theme, idea, or unique selling proposition (USP). There are three types of appeals: rational, emotional, and moral.

Rational appeals engage self-interest: They claim the product will produce certain benefits. Examples are messages demonstrating quality, economy, value, or performance. It is widely believed that industrial buyers are most responsive to rational appeals. They are knowledgeable about the product, trained to recognize value, and accountable to others for their choices. Consumers, when they buy certain big-ticket items, also tend to gather information and estimate benefits.

*Emotional appe*als attempt to stir up negative or positive emotions that will motivate purchase. Marketers search for the right *emotional selling proposition* (ESP).

American Cancer Society (ACS)   The American Cancer Society launched a campaign in the 1990s to promote the use of SPF 15 sun block in order to help prevent skin cancer. It aimed the campaign at young men and women and used the selling line "Save your life!" This turned out to be too rational because young persons want to look attractive. ACS then changed the appeal to say that SPF 15 sun block would allow users to safely enjoy more time in the sun, get tan, and be more attractive.

Communicators work with both negative and positive emotional appeals. They use negative appeals such as fear, guilt, and shame to get people to do things (brush their teeth, have an annual health checkup) or stop doing things (smoking, alcohol or abuse, overeating). Fear appeals work best when they are not too strong. Research indicates that neither extremely strong nor extremely weak fear appeals are as effective as moderate ones. Furthermore, fear appeals work better when source credibility is high and when the communication promises to relieve, in a believable and efficient way, the fear it arouses.[9] Messages are most persuasive when they are moderately discrepant with what the audience believes. Messages that state only what the audience already believes at best only reinforce beliefs, and if the messages are too discrepant, they will be counterargued and disbelieved.

Communicators also use positive emotional appeals such as humor, love, pride, and joy. Advocates for humorous messages claim that they attract more attention and create more liking and belief in the sponsor. Others maintain that humor can detract from comprehension, wear out its welcome fast, and overshadow the product.[10] Here is an example of a successful use of humor.

E*TRADE   Online financial services company E*TRADE set itself apart from competitors and attracted traders to its site using humorous, high-profile advertising. During the 2000 Super Bowl, the company sponsored the halftime show and debuted a television spot that featured little more than a dancing chimpanzee and the tagline "We just wasted two million bucks. What are you doing with your money?" That year, E*TRADE spent $522 million—or nearly 40 percent of revenues—on marketing and generated 1.7 million new accounts. The company followed its Super Bowl success with an ad during the 2001 Super Bowl that poked fun at dot-com excesses and companies, such as Pets.com, that had not survived the bursting bubble. The ad earned high marks from critics and scored well in consumer polls.[11]

Moral appeals are directed to the audience's sense of what is right and proper. They are often used to exhort people to support social causes. An example is the appeal "Silence = Death," which is the slogan of Act-Up, the AIDS Coalition to Unleash Power.

Companies that sell their products in different countries must be prepared to vary their messages. In advertising its hair care products in different countries, Helene Curtis adjusts its messages. Middle-class British women wash their hair frequently, whereas

marketing for the **new economy**

Challenges in Global Advertising and Promotion

Multinational companies wrestle with a number of challenges in developing global communications programs: They must decide whether the product is appropriate for a country. They must make sure the market segment they address is both legal and customary. They must decide if the style of the ad is acceptable, and they must decide whether ads should be created at headquarters or locally.

1. **Product:** Many products are restricted or forbidden in certain parts of the world. Beer, wine, and spirits cannot be advertised or sold in Muslim countries. Tobacco products are subject to strict regulation in many countries. Sometimes a company is required to change the manner in which it sells its products. Avon China Inc., was forced to open retail stores after a resolution passed by the Chinese government banned selling directly to Chinese consumers. New advertising and promotion campaigns repositioned Avon as a retailer, rather than a direct marketer. (China and the United States reached an agreement in 1999 that would lift the ban on direct selling by 2003.)

2. **Market Segment:** Coca-Cola conducts business with more than 230 brands in 200 countries. The company has a pool of different commercials for different national market segments, and local segment managers decide which to use for which segments. When Douglas Daft took over as chairman and CEO in 2000, he gave Coca-Cola managers a new mantra: "Think locally and act locally." This local focus sometimes leaves Coke caught in the middle of a sensitive political issue. In 2000, Coca-Cola was running a campaign in mainland China featuring a popular female Taiwanese pop star. Authorities in China blacklisted the star after she sang Taiwan's national anthem at the inauguration of the island's new president. Coca-Cola had to replace all television, print, and radio advertising that used her voice.

   U.S. toy makers were surprised to learn that in many countries (Norway and Sweden, for example) no TV ads may be directed at children under 12. Sweden is lobbying to extend that ban to all EU member countries. To play it safe, McDonald's advertises itself as a family restaurant in Sweden.

3. **Style:** The style of the ad is also important. For instance, comparative ads, while acceptable and even common in the United States and Canada, are less commonly used in the United Kingdom, unacceptable in Japan, and illegal in India and Brazil. PepsiCo had a comparative taste test ad in Japan that was refused by many TV stations and eventually led to a lawsuit. China has restrictive censorship rules for TV and radio advertising; the words "the best" are banned, as are ads that "violate social customs" or present women in "improper ways."

4. **Local or Global:** Today, more and more multinational companies are attempting to build a global brand image by using the same advertising in all markets. When Daimler AG and Chrysler merged to become the world's fifth-largest automaker, they ran a three-week ad campaign in more than 100 countries consisting of a 12-page magazine insert, 9 newspaper spreads, and a 24-page brochure that was sent to business, government, and union leaders and to the news media. The campaign's tag line was "Expect the extraordinary," and it featured people from both companies working together.

Sources: Richard C. Morais, "Mobile Mayhem," *Forbes*, July, 6 1998, p. 138; Patti Bond, "Today's Topic: From Russia with Fizz, Coke Imports Ads," *Atlanta Journal and Constitution*, April 4, 1998, pp. E2; "Working in Harmony," *Soap Perfumery & Cosmetics*, July 1, 1998, p. 27; Rodger Harrabin, "A Commercial Break for Parents," *Independent*, September 8, 1998, p. 19; T. B. Song and Leo Wong, "Getting the Word Out," *The China Business Review*, September 1, 1998; "Avon Campaign Repositions Company in China," AdAgeInternational.com, July 1998; Naveen Donthu, "A Cross Country Investigation of Recall of and Attitude toward Comparative Advertising," *Journal of Advertising* 27 (June 22, 1998): 111; "EU to Try Again on Tobacco Advertising Ban," *Associated Press*, May 9, 2001; Betsy McKay, "Coca-Cola Restructuring Effort Has Yet to Prove Effective," *Asian Wall Street Journal*, March 2, 2001 p. N4; James Kynge and Mure Dickie, "Coke Forced to Dump Taiwanese Diva," *Financial Times*, May 25, 2000, p. C12.

the opposite is true among Spanish women. Japanese women avoid overwashing their hair for fear of removing protective oils. (See "Marketing for the New Economy: Challenges in Global Advertising and Promotion.")

MESSAGE STRUCTURE Effectiveness depends on structure as well as content. For example, a credit-card company contacted customers who had not used the card for three months. To one group of nonusers it sent a message explaining the benefits of using the card. To another group it sent a message explaining the losses they could suffer by not using the card. The percentage of customers who started to use the card in the loss condition was more than double and, the charges of the former customers were more than twice that of the positive message receivers.[12]

Hovland's research at Yale has shed much light on message content and its relation to conclusion drawing, one- versus two-sided arguments, and order of presentation. Some early experiments supported stating conclusions for the audience rather than allowing the audience to reach its own. Subsequent research, however, indicates that the best ads ask questions and allow readers and viewers to form their own conclusions.[13]

Conclusion drawing might cause negative reactions if the communicator is seen as untrustworthy, or the issue is seen as too simple or highly personal. Drawing too explicit a conclusion can also limit appeal or acceptance. If Ford had hammered away that the Mustang was for young people, this strong definition might have blocked older age groups from buying it. Some stimulus ambiguity can lead to a broader market definition and more spontaneous purchases.

You would think that one-sided presentations that praise a product would be more effective than two-sided arguments that also mention shortcomings. Yet two-sided messages may be more appropriate, especially when some negative association must be overcome. In this spirit, Heinz ran the message "Heinz Ketchup is slow good" and Listerine ran the message "Listerine tastes bad twice a day."[14] Two-sided messages are more effective with more educated audiences and those who are initially opposed.[15]

Finally, the order in which arguments are presented is important.[16] In the case of a one-sided message, presenting the strongest argument first has the advantage of arousing attention and interest. This is important in newspapers and other media where the audience often does not attend to the whole message. With a captive audience, however, a climactic presentation might be more effective. In the case of a two-sided message, if the audience is initially opposed, the communicator might start with the other side's argument and conclude with his or her strongest argument.[17]

MESSAGE FORMAT The message format needs to be strong. In a print ad, the communicator has to decide on headline, copy, illustration, and color. For a radio message, the communicator has to choose words, voice qualities, and vocalizations. The "sound" of an announcer promoting a used automobile has to be different from one promoting a new Cadillac. If the message is to be carried on television or in person, all these elements plus body language (nonverbal clues) have to be planned. Presenters have to pay attention to facial expressions, gestures, dress, posture, and hairstyle. If the message is carried by the product or its packaging, the communicator has to pay attention to color, texture, scent, size, and shape. BMW used a cinematic format to advertise its cars.

BMW BMW blurred the line between advertising and entertainment when it developed a series of online minifilms that featured the company's cars. The company enlisted Hollywood heavyweights like John Frankenheimer and Ang Lee to direct the films, which starred actors such as Mickey Rourke and Madonna. To build traffic to the bmwfilms.com Web site, BMW used television spots that mirrored movie trailers. In the first six weeks after their April 2001 debut, the films attracted 3 million viewers. Although the Internet films intentionally did not use hard-sell tactics, a spokesperson for BMW said that many viewers requested information about cars after seeing the movies.[18]

MESSAGE SOURCE Messages delivered by attractive or popular sources achieve higher attention and recall. This is why advertisers often use celebrities as spokespeople. Celebrities are likely to be effective when they personify a key product attribute. Catherine Deneuve's beauty did this for Chanel, and Paul Hogan's manliness did this for Subaru Outback. On the other hand, using James Garner and Cybill Shepherd to sell beef backfired: James had heart trouble and Cybill became a vegetarian.

What is important is the spokesperson's credibility. Pharmaceutical companies want doctors to testify about product benefits because doctors have high credibility. Antidrug crusaders will use ex-drug addicts because they have higher credibility for students than teachers do.

What factors underlie source credibility? The three most often identified are expertise, trustworthiness, and likability.[19] *Expertise* is the specialized knowledge the communicator possesses to back the claim. *Trustworthiness* is related to how objective and honest the source is perceived to be. Friends are trusted more than strangers or salespeople, and

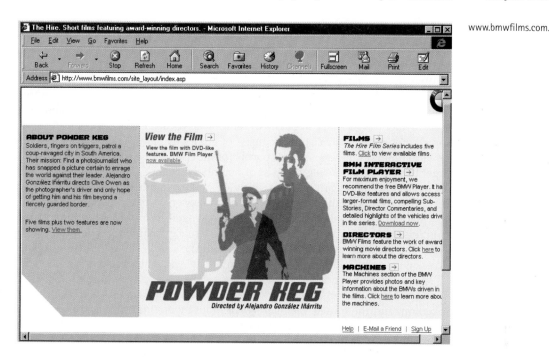

www.bmwfilms.com.

people who are not paid to endorse a product are viewed as more trustworthy than people who are paid.[20] *Likability* describes the source's attractiveness. Qualities like candor, humor, and naturalness make a source more likable. The most highly credible source would be a person who scores high on all three dimensions.

If a person has a positive attitude toward a source and a message, or a negative attitude toward both, a state of *congruity* is said to exist. What happens if the person holds one attitude toward the source and the opposite toward the message? Suppose a homemaker hears a likable celebrity praise a brand that she dislikes? Osgood and Tannenbaum posit that *attitude change will take place in the direction of increasing the amount of congruity between the two evaluations.*[21] The homemaker will end up respecting the celebrity somewhat less or respecting the brand somewhat more. If she encounters the same celebrity praising other disliked brands, she will eventually develop a negative view of the celebrity and maintain her negative attitudes toward the brands. The **principle of congruity** implies that communicators can use their good image to reduce some negative feelings toward a brand but in the process might lose some esteem with the audience.

select the communication channels

The communicator must select efficient channels to carry the message. For example, pharmaceutical company salespeople can rarely wrest more than five minutes' time from a busy physician. Their presentation must be crisp, quick, and convincing. This makes pharmaceutical sales calling extremely expensive. The industry has had to expand its battery of communication channels. These include placing ads in medical journals, sending direct mail (including audio and videotapes), passing out free samples, and even telemarketing. Pharmaceutical companies sponsor clinical conferences to which they invite and pay for a large number of physicians to spend a weekend listening to leading physicians extol certain drugs in the morning, followed by an afternoon of golf or tennis. Salespeople will arrange evening teleconferences where physicians are invited to discuss a common problem with an expert. Salespeople also will sponsor small group lunches and dinners. All of these channels are used in the hope of building physician preference for their branded therapeutic agent.

Source: Renée Dye, "The Buzz on Buzz," *Harvard Business Review* (November–December 2000): 139.

Marketing MEMO

Buzz Marketing

Research conducted by Renée Dye, a strategy expert with McKinsey, suggests that buzz evolves according to basic principles. Dye contends that companies seeking to take advantage of buzz must first overcome five misconceptions about marketing contagion. Here are "The 5 Myths of Buzz":

1. *Only outrageous or edgy products are buzz-worthy.* The most unlikely products, like prescription drugs, can generate tremendous buzz.

2. *Buzz just happens.* Buzz is increasingly the result of shrewd marketing tactics in which companies seed a vanguard group, ration supplies, use celebrities to generate buzz, leverage the power of lists, and initiate grassroots marketing.

3. *The best buzz-starters are your best customers.* Often, a counterculture has a greater ability to start buzz.

4. *To profit from buzz, you must act first and fast.* Copycat companies can reap substantial profits if they know when to jump in—and when not to.

5. *The media and advertising are needed to create buzz.* When used either too early or too much, the media and advertising can squelch buzz before it ignites.

Communication channels may be personal and nonpersonal. Within each are many subchannels.

PERSONAL COMMUNICATION CHANNELS Personal communication channels involve two or more persons communicating directly with each other face-to-face, person-to-audience, over the telephone, or through e-mail. Personal communication channels derive their effectiveness through individualized presentation and feedback.

A further distinction can be drawn among advocate, expert, and social communication channels. *Advocate channels* consist of company salespeople contacting buyers in the target market. *Expert channels* consist of independent experts making statements to target buyers. *Social channels* consist of neighbors, friends, family members, and associates talking to target buyers. In a study of 7,000 consumers in seven European countries, 60 percent said they were influenced to use a new brand by family and friends.[22]

Personal influence carries especially great weight in two situations. One is with products that are expensive, risky, or purchased infrequently. The other situation is where the product suggests something about the user's status or taste. In both cases, buyers will consult others for information or to avoid embarrassment.

Many companies are becoming acutely aware of the power of *word of mouth* or *buzz.* (See "Marketing Memo: Buzz Marketing.") Products and brands such as Beanie Babies, Pokemon, and the movie *The Blair Witch Project* were built through buzz. Companies such as Body Shop, USAA, Starbucks, Palm Pilot, BMW23 Roadster, and Amazon were essentially built by word of mouth, with very little advertising.

Amazon Jeff Bezos, founder of Amazon.com, had noticed that the celebrated department store Nordstrom never advertised its customer service and yet had the most loyal customer following. Having no money to spend on advertising when he launched Amazon, Bezos trusted that good service would do the trick. "It was seeing how successful word-of-mouth was in that first year, that really led us on this path of being obsessively, compulsively, anal-retentively focused on customer service." According to Bezos, if you make a customer unhappy he will tell five friends; if you disappoint a customer on the Internet, he is capable of telling 5,000 or 50,000 people.[23]

In some cases, positive word of mouth happens in a natural way.

Kiehl Kiehl's is a small, 148-year-old company that makes and sells hair and skin products, such as Kiehl's rosewater facial freshener-toner and pineapple papaya facial scrub. Its marketing practices defy normal wisdom. It does not advertise. Its packaging is bland and the text is difficult to read. It refuses to be carried by most stores, making exceptions only for the highest-priced stores such as Bergdorf Goodman and Barney's. It gives away vast amounts of free samples to anyone coming into its single store. It gets great coverage from the business press without ever soliciting attention. Kiehl's has the gift of being carried by word of mouth.[24]

In most cases, "buzz" is managed.[25] Regis McKenna advises a software company launching a new product to promote it initially to the trade press, opinion luminaries, and financial analysts, who can supply favorable word of mouth; then to dealers; and finally to customers.[26] MCI attracted customers with its Friends and Family program, which encourages MCI users to ask friends and family members to use MCI so that both parties will benefit from lower telephone rates.

Companies can take several steps to stimulate personal influence channels to work on their behalf:

- *Identify influential individuals and companies and devote extra effort to them:*[27] In industrial selling, the entire industry might follow the market leader in adopting innovations.

- *Create opinion leaders by supplying certain people with the product on attractive terms:* A new tennis racket might be offered initially to members of high school tennis teams at a special low price; or Toyota could offer its more satisfied customers a small gift if they are willing to advise prospective buyers.

- *Work through community influentials such as local disk jockeys, class presidents, and presidents of women's organizations:* When Ford introduced the Thunderbird, it sent invitations to executives offering them a free car to drive for the day. Of the 15,000 who took advantage of the offer, 10 percent indicated that they would become buyers, whereas 84 percent said they would recommend it to a friend.

- *Use influential or believable people in testimonial advertising:* Companies such as American Express, Nike, and Buick are using golf mega-star Tiger Woods to talk up the virtues of their respective products.

- *Develop advertising that has high "conversation value":* Ads with high conversation value often have a slogan that becomes part of the national vernacular. In the mid-1980s, Wendy's "Where's the Beef?" campaign (showing an elderly lady named Clara questioning where the hamburger was hidden in all that bread) created high conversation value. Nike's "Just do it" ads have created a popular command for those unable to make up their minds or take some action.

- *Develop word-of-mouth referral channels to build business:* Professionals will often encourage clients to recommend their services. Dentists can ask satisfied patients to recommend friends and acquaintances and subsequently thank them for their recommendations. (See "Marketing Memo: How to Develop Word-of-Mouth Referral Sources to Build Business.")

- *Establish an electronic forum:* Toyota owners who use an online service line such as America Online can hold online discussions to share experiences.

- *Use viral marketing:* Internet marketers are using **viral marketing** a form of word of mouth, to draw attention to their sites.[28] Viral marketing involves passing on company-developed products, services, or information from user to user. As a classic example, Hotmail, an Internet Service Provider (ISP), offered a free e-mail account to anyone who signed up. Each e-mail sent by a Hotmail subscriber included the simple tag at the bottom of each message: "Get your free private e-mail at *http://www.hotmail.com*." Users were in effect advertising Hotmail to others. Hotmail spent less than $500,000 on marketing and within 18 months attracted 12 million subscribers. (See "Marketing Memo: Creating a Tipping Point" for further insight into factors that help spread word of mouth.)

Marketing
MEMO

How to Develop Word-of-Mouth Referral Sources

People always ask others—friends, relatives, professionals—for a recommendation for a doctor, plumber, hotel, lawyer, accountant, architect, insurance agent, interior decorator, or financial consultant. If we have confidence in the recommendation, we normally act on the referral. In such cases, the recommender has potentially benefited the service provider as well as the service seeker. Service providers clearly have a strong interest in building referral sources. The two chief benefits of developing referrals, or word-of-mouth sources, are:

1. *Word-of-mouth sources are convincing:* Word of mouth is the only promotion method that is of consumers, by consumers, and for consumers. Not only are satisfied customers repeat buyers, but they are also walking, talking billboards for your business.
2. *Word-of-mouth sources are low cost:* Keeping in touch with satisfied customers and making them providers costs the business relatively little. The business might reciprocate by referring business to the referrer, or by giving the referrer enhanced service or a discount, or by offering a small gift.

Marketing author Michael Cafferky's Word-of-Mouth Marketing Tips Web site offers many suggestions on how to build a network of referral sources; here are five:

1. *Involve your customers in the process of making or delivering your product or service.*
2. *Solicit testimonials from your customers:* Use a response form that asks for feedback—and permission to quote it.
3. *Tell true stories to your customers:* Stories are the central vehicle for spreading reputations because they communicate on an emotional level.
4. *Educate your best customers:* You can pick any topic that is relevant to your best customers and have them become the source of credible, up-to-date information on that topic.
5. *Offer fast complaint handling:* A speedy response is vital to preventing negative word of mouth from starting, because negative feelings about a product or service may linger for years.

Sources: Scott R. Herriott, "Identifying and Developing Referral Channels," Management Decision 30, no. 1 (1992): 4–9; Peter H. Riengen and Jerome B. Kernan, "Analysis of Referral Networks in Marketing: Methods and Illustration," Journal of Marketing Research (November 1986): 37–78; Jerry R. Wilson, *Word of Mouth Marketing* (New York: John Wiley, 1991); Cafferky's Free Word-of-Mouth Marketing Tips, 1999, available at www.geocities.com/wallstreet/cafferkys. Also see Emanuel Rosen, The Anatomy of Buzz (New York: Doubleday, 2000).

Marketing
MEMO

Creating a Tipping Point

Why do certain ideas suddenly take off and everyone hears about them? What causes "the tipping point?" Malcolm Gladwell claims that three factors work to ignite public interest in an idea. He calls the first "The Law of the Few." Three types of people help spread an idea like an epidemic. First are *Mavens*, people who are very knowledgeable about big and small things. Mavens can tell you what hotel to choose in New York City, which restaurant to patronize in San Francisco, which brand of minivan to buy, all in the interest of helping you. Second are *Connectors*, people who know a great number of other people. They may even send an e-mail to a long list of friends about something they heard about. Third are *Salesmen*, those who possess great natural persuasive power. Any idea that catches the interests of Mavens, Connectors, and Salesmen is likely to be broadcast far and wide. If you are interested in starting a word-of-mouth epidemic, "The Law of the Few" says that you only need to focus on these three groups of people.

However, a second factor comes into play, that of "*stickiness*." The idea needs to be memorably expressed and must motivate people to act. Otherwise "The Law of the Few" would not lead to a self-sustaining epidemic. A third factor, the *Power of Context*, will make a difference, namely, whether those spreading an idea are able to organize groups and communities around it.

Marketers who want to create a "buzz" over their latest idea should apply Gladwell's findings.

Source: Malcolm Gladwell, *The Tipping Point: How Little Things Can Make a Big Difference* (Boston: Little, Brown & Company, 2000).

NONPERSONAL COMMUNICATION CHANNELS Nonpersonal channels include media, atmospheres, and events.

Media consist of print media (newspapers, magazines, direct mail), broadcast media (radio, television), network media (telephone, cable, satellite, wireless), electronic media (audiotape, videotape, videodisk, CD-ROM, Web page), and display media (billboards, signs, posters). Most nonpersonal messages come through paid media. Volvo attempted to market a car using only one channel, the Internet.

Volvo In 2000, Volvo developed an Internet-only launch for its new S60 sedan. The company signed an exclusive deal with America Online that placed banner ads for the car in prime locations on the AOL portal. The ads led viewers to a special Web site—called revolvolution.com—where they could learn more about the vehicle, configure a car to their tastes, and request a quote from a nearby dealer. Although over one million consumers visited the site, dealers across the nation were disappointed with the customer response: Only 2,994 vehicles were sold between the October introduction and the new year. Volvo replaced the Internet-only launch with an integrated campaign that included Web, wireless, television, and print advertising.[29]

Atmospheres are "packaged environments" that create or reinforce the buyer's leanings toward product purchase. Law offices are decorated with Oriental rugs and oak furniture to communicate "stability" and "success."[30] A five-star hotel will use elegant chandeliers, marble columns, and other tangible signs of luxury.

Events are occurrences designed to communicate particular messages to target audiences. Public-relations departments arrange news conferences, grand openings, and sports sponsorships to achieve specific communication effects with a target audience.

Sea-Doo Personal watercraft manufacturer Sea-Doo conducts a promotional tour each summer that offers consumers free test rides on a variety of Sea-Doo craft. The tour, called "Get Caught Doin' It" in a play on Sea-Doo's "Everybody's Doin' It" tagline, visits more than 40 domestic markets during the summer months. Sea-Doo works together with local dealers in each market to hold day-long events that include free food and drinks, prize giveaways, and remote radio broadcasts. About 15 percent of participants in the events become buyers of the $5,000 to $9,000 crafts.[31]

Although personal communication is often more effective than mass-communication, mass–media might be the major means of stimulating personal communication. Mass–communications affect personal attitudes and behavior through a two-step, flow-of-communication process. Ideas often flow from radio, television, and print to opinion leaders and from these to the less media-involved population groups. This two-step flow has several implications. First, the influence of mass-media on public opinion is not as direct, powerful, and automatic as supposed. It is mediated by opinion leaders, people whose opinions are sought or who carry their opinions to others. Second, the two-step flow challenges the notion that consumption styles are primarily influenced by a "trickle-down" or "trickle-up" effect from mass-media. People interact primarily within their own social groups and acquire ideas from opinion leaders in their groups. Third, two-step communication suggests that mass-communicators should direct messages specifically to opinion leaders and let them carry the message to others. Pharmaceutical firms should promote new drugs to the most influential physicians first.

Communication researchers are moving toward a social-structure view of interpersonal communication.[32] They see society as consisting of **cliques**, small groups whose members interact frequently. Clique members are similar, and their closeness facilitates effective communication but also insulates the clique from new ideas. The challenge is to create more system openness so that cliques exchange information with others in the society. This openness is helped by people who function as liaisons and bridges. A **liaison** is a person who connects two or more cliques without belonging to either. A **bridge** is a person who belongs to one clique and is linked to a person in another clique.

establish the total marketing communications budget

One of the most difficult marketing decisions is determining how much to spend on promotion. John Wanamaker, the department-store magnate, once said, "I know that half of my advertising is wasted, but I don't know which half."

Industries and companies vary considerably in how much they spend on promotion. Expenditures might amount to 30 to 50 percent of sales in the cosmetics industry and 5 to 10 percent in the industrial-equipment industry. Within a given industry, there are low- and high-spending companies. Philip Morris is a high spender. When it acquired the Miller Brewing Company, and later the 7-Up Company, it substantially increased total promotion spending. The additional spending at Miller raised its market share from 4 to 19 percent within a few years.

How do companies decide on the promotion budget? We will describe four common methods: the affordable method, percentage-of-sales method, competitive-parity method, and objective-and-task method.

AFFORDABLE METHOD   Many companies set the promotion budget at what they think the company can afford. One executive said: "Why, it's simple. First, I go upstairs to the controller and ask how much they can afford to give us this year. He says a million and a half. Later, the boss comes to me and asks how much we should spend and I say, 'Oh, about a million and a half.' "[33]

The affordable method completely ignores the role of promotion as an investment and the immediate impact of promotion on sales volume. It leads to an uncertain annual budget, which makes long-range planning difficult.

PERCENTAGE-OF-SALES METHOD   Many companies set promotion expenditures at a specified percentage of sales (either current or anticipated) or of the sales price. A railroad company executive said: "We set our appropriation for each year on December 1 of the preceding year. On that date we add our passenger revenue for the next month, and then take 2 percent of the total for our advertising appropriation for the new year."[34] Automobile companies typically budget a fixed percentage for promotion based on the planned car price. Oil companies set the appropriation at a fraction of a cent for each gallon of gasoline sold under their own label.

Supporters of the percentage-of-sales method see a number of advantages. First, promotion expenditures will vary with what the company can "afford." This satisfies financial managers, who believe that expenses should be closely related to the movement of corporate sales over the business cycle. Second, it encourages management to think of the relationship among promotion cost, selling price, and profit per unit. Third, it encourages stability when competing firms spend approximately the same percentage of their sales on promotion.

In spite of these advantages, the percentage-of-sales method has little to justify it. It views sales as the determiner of promotion rather than as the result. It leads to a budget set by the availability of funds rather than by market opportunities. It discourages experimentation with countercyclical promotion or aggressive spending. Dependence on year-to-year sales fluctuations interferes with long-range planning. There is no logical basis for choosing the specific percentage, except what has been done in the past or what competitors are doing. Finally, it does not encourage building the promotion budget by determining what each product and territory deserves.

COMPETITIVE-PARITY METHOD   Some companies set their promotion budget to achieve share-of-voice parity with competitors. This thinking is illustrated by the executive who asked a trade source, "Do you have any figures which other companies in the builders' specialties field have used which would indicate what proportion of gross sales should be given over to advertising?"[35] This executive believes that by matching competitors, he will maintain his market share.

Two arguments are made in support of the competitive-parity method. One is that competitors' expenditures represent the collective wisdom of the industry. The other is that maintaining competitive parity prevents promotion wars. Neither argument is valid. There are no grounds for believing that competitors know better. Company reputations, resources, opportunities, and objectives differ so much that promotion budgets are hardly a guide. Furthermore, there is no evidence that budgets based on competitive parity discourage promotional wars.

OBJECTIVE-AND-TASK METHOD The objective-and-task method calls upon marketers to develop promotion budgets by defining specific objectives, determining the tasks that must be performed to achieve these objectives, and estimating the costs of performing these tasks. The sum of these costs is the proposed promotion budget.

G. Maxwell Ule showed how the objective-and-task method could be used to establish an advertising budget. Suppose Helene Curtis wants to launch a new woman's anti-dandruff shampoo.[36]

1. *Establish the market-share goal:* The company estimates 50 million potential users and sets a target of attracting 8 percent of the market—that is, 4 million users.
2. *Determine the percentage of the market that should be reached by advertising:* The advertiser hopes to reach 80 percent (40 million prospects) with the advertising message.
3. *Determine the percentage of aware prospects that should be persuaded to try the brand:* The advertiser would be pleased if 25 percent of aware prospects (10 million) tried Clear. This is because it estimates that 40 percent of all triers, or 4 million people, would become loyal users. This is the market goal.
4. *Determine the number of advertising impressions per 1 percent trial rate:* The advertiser estimates that 40 advertising impressions (exposures) for every 1 percent of the population would bring about a 25 percent trial rate.
5. *Determine the number of gross rating points that would have to be purchased:* A gross rating point is one exposure to 1 percent of the target population. Because the company wants to achieve 40 exposures to 80 percent of the population, it will want to buy 3,200 gross rating points.
6. *Determine the necessary advertising budget on the basis of the average cost of buying a gross rating point:* To expose 1 percent of the target population to one impression costs an average of $3,277. Therefore, 3,200 gross rating points would cost $10,486,400 (= $3,277 × 3,200) in the introductory year.

The objective-and-task method has the advantage of requiring management to spell out its assumptions about the relationship among dollars spent, exposure levels, trial rates, and regular usage.

A major question is how much weight promotion should receive in relation to alternatives such as product improvement, lower prices, or better service. The answer depends on where the company's products are in their life cycles, whether they are commodities or highly differentiable products, whether they are routinely needed or have to be "sold," and other considerations. In theory, the total promotional budget should be established so that the marginal profit from the last promotional dollar just equals the marginal profit from the last dollar in the best nonpromotional use. Implementing this principle, however, is not easy.

deciding on the marketing communications mix

Companies must allocate the promotion budget over the five promotional tools—advertising, sales promotion, public relations and publicity, sales force, and direct marketing. Here is how one company touches several bases.

Select Comfort Corporation   A mattress is a mattress, or is it? We have heard of waterbeds. Now Select Comfort offers an "air bed." The mattress is air-inflated, and sleepers can adjust firmness by changing the air level. Two sleepers can even call for different degrees of firmness on their respective sides of the mattress. To market the mattresses, Select Comfort, headquartered in Minneapolis, has put together a strong combination of channels and promotion initiatives: 300 retail stores where prospects can take a "Test Rest on Air"; demonstration videos and collateral material discussing "Sleep Science"; a company Web site (select comfort. com) describing the products and offering advice on how to sleep better; celebrity endorsements; and giving customers who recommend others who buy the mattress a merchandise certificate.

Within the same industry, companies can differ considerably in their media and channel choices. Avon concentrates its promotional funds on personal selling, whereas Revlon spends heavily on advertising. Electrolux spends heavily on a door-to-door sales force, whereas Hoover relies more on advertising.

Companies are always searching for ways to gain efficiency by replacing one promotional tool with others. Consider: "Procter & Gamble is urging its ad agencies to focus less on TV and embrace direct mail, staged events and the Internet . . . P&G no longer believes TV advertising provides the best value."[37] Many companies are replacing some field sales activity with ads, direct mail, and telemarketing. One auto dealer dismissed his five salespeople and cut his prices, and sales exploded. Companies are shifting advertising funds into sales promotion. The substitutability among promotional tools explains why marketing functions need to be coordinated. For an account of how companies set their budgets, in practice, see "Marketing Insight: How Do Companies Set and Allocate Their Marketing Communications Budgets?"

marketing **insight**

How Companies Set and Allocate Marketing Communications Budgets

Low and Mohr interviewed managers in consumer packaged-goods companies on how the marketing communications budget is set and allocated to advertising, sales promotion, and trade promotion. They found that a brand team is formed and, after performing an extensive situation analysis, establishes marketing objectives and a broad strategy. After forecasting brand sales and profits based on the broad strategy, the team develops an initial allocation to advertising, consumer promotion, and trade promotion. The team relies heavily on the previous year's budget allocation, which may make sense if the environment is stable but not if there is rapid environmental change. The brand plan is presented to senior management, required changes are made, and the revised plan is implemented.

During the year, the brand team will adjust allocations in response to the changing environment.

In their 1998 study, Low and Mohr also found that:

- As brands move to the more mature phase of the product life cycle, managers allocate less to advertising.

- When a brand is well-differentiated from the competition, managers allocate more to advertising.
- When managers are rewarded on short-term results, they allocate less of their budgets to advertising.
- As retailers gain more power, managers allocate less of their budgets to advertising.
- As managers gain greater experience with the company, they tend to allocate proportionately more of their budgets to advertising.

Sources: See George S. Low and Jakki J. Mohr, "The Advertising Sales Promotion Trade-Off: Theory and Practice" (Cambridge, MA: Marketing Science Institute, Report No. 92-127, October 1992); and their "Brand Managers' Perceptions of the Marketing Communications Budget Allocation Process" (Cambridge, MA: Marketing Science Institute, Report No. 98-105, March 1998). Also see Gabriel J. Beihal and Daniel A. Sheinen, "Managing the Brand in a Corporate Advertising Environment: A Decision-Making Framework for Brand Managers," *Journal of Advertising* 17 (June 22, 1998): 99.

the promotional tools

Each promotional tool has its own unique characteristics and costs.[38]

Advertising   Because of the many forms and uses of advertising, it is difficult to make generalizations.[39] Yet the following qualities can be noted:

- *Public presentation:* Advertising's public nature confers a kind of legitimacy on the product and also suggests a standardized offering.
- *Pervasiveness:* Advertising permits the seller to repeat a message many times. It also allows the buyer to receive and compare the messages of various competitors. Large-scale advertising says something positive about the seller's size, power, and success.
- *Amplified expressiveness:* Advertising provides opportunities for dramatizing the company and its products through the artful use of print, sound, and color.
- *Impersonality:* The audience does not feel obligated to pay attention or respond to advertising. Advertising is a monologue in front of, not a dialogue with, the audience.

Advertising can be used to build up a long-term image for a product (Coca-Cola ads) or trigger quick sales (a Sears ad for a weekend sale). Advertising can efficiently reach geographically dispersed buyers. Certain forms of advertising (TV advertising) can require a large budget, whereas other forms (newspaper advertising) do not. Just the presence of advertising might have an effect on sales: Consumers might believe that a heavily advertised brand must offer "good value."

Sales Promotion   Sales-promotion tools—coupons, contests, premiums, and the like—offer three distinctive benefits:

1. *Communication:* They gain attention and may lead the consumer to the product.
2. *Incentive:* They incorporate some concession, inducement, or contribution that gives value to the consumer.
3. *Invitation:* They include a distinct invitation to engage in the transaction now.

Companies use sales-promotion tools to draw a stronger and quicker buyer response. Sales promotion can be used for short-run effects such as to dramatize product offers and boost sagging sales.

Public Relations and Publicity   The appeal of public relations and publicity is based on three distinctive qualities:

1. *High credibility:* News stories and features are more authentic and credible to readers than ads.
2. *Ability to catch buyers off guard:* Public relations can reach prospects who prefer to avoid salespeople and advertisements.
3. *Dramatization:* Public relations has the potential for dramatizing a company or product.

Marketers tend to underuse public relations, yet a well-thought-out program coordinated with the other promotion-mix elements can be extremely effective.

Personal Selling   Personal selling is the most effective tool at later stages of the buying process, particularly in building up buyer preference, conviction, and action. Personal selling has three distinctive qualities:

1. *Personal confrontation:* Personal selling involves an immediate and interactive relationship between two or more persons. Each party is able to observe the other's reactions.
2. *Cultivation:* Personal selling permits all kinds of relationships to spring up, ranging from a matter-of-fact selling relationship to a deep personal friendship.
3. *Response:* Personal selling makes the buyer feel under some obligation for having listened to the sales talk.

Direct Marketing   The many forms of direct marketing—direct mail, telemarketing, Internet marketing—share four distinctive characteristics. Direct marketing is:

1. *Nonpublic:* The message is normally addressed to a specific person.
2. *Customized:* The message can be prepared to appeal to the addressed individual.

3. *Up-to-date:* A message can be prepared very quickly.
4. *Interactive:* The message can be changed depending on the person's response.

factors in setting the marketing communications mix

Companies must consider several factors in developing their promotion mix: type of product market, consumer readiness to make a purchase, and stage in the product life cycle. Also important is the company's market rank. Market leaders derive more benefit from advertising than from sales promotion. Conversely, smaller competitors gain more by using sales promotion in their marketing communications mix.

TYPE OF PRODUCT MARKET   Promotional allocations vary between consumer and business markets. Consumer marketers spend on sales promotion, advertising, personal selling, and public relations, in that order. Business marketers spend on personal selling, sales promotion, advertising, and public relations, in that order. In general, personal selling is used more with complex, expensive, and risky goods and in markets with fewer and larger sellers (hence, business markets).

Although advertising is used less than sales calls in business markets, it still plays a significant role:

- Advertising can provide an introduction to the company and its products.
- If the product embodies new features, advertising can explain them.
- Reminder advertising is more economical than sales calls.
- Advertisements offering brochures and carrying the company's phone number are an effective way to generate leads for sales representatives.
- Sales representatives can use tear sheets of the company's ads to legitimize their company and products.
- Advertising can remind customers of how to use the product and reassure them about their purchase.

A number of studies have underscored advertising's role in business markets. The Morrill study showed that advertising combined with personal selling increased sales 23 percent over what they had been with no advertising. The total promotional cost as a percentage of sales was reduced by 20 percent.[40] Cyril Freeman developed a formal model for dividing promotional funds between advertising and personal selling on the basis of the selling tasks that each performs more economically.[41] Levitt's research also showed the important role advertising can play in business markets. He found:

1. A company's reputation improves its sales force's chances of getting a favorable first hearing and an early adoption of the product. Corporate advertising that can build up the company's reputation will help the sales representatives.
2. Sales representatives from well-known companies have an edge if their sales presentations are adequate; but a rep from a lesser-known company who makes a highly effective presentation can overcome the disadvantage.
3. Company reputation helps most where the product is complex, the risk is high, and the purchasing agent is less professionally trained.[42]

Gary Lilien researched business marketing practices in a major project called ADVISOR and reported the following:[43]

- The average industrial company set its marketing budget at 7 percent of its sales. It spent only 10 percent of its marketing budget on advertising. Companies spent the remainder on sales force, trade shows, sales promotion, and direct mail.
- Industrial companies spent a higher-than-average amount on advertising if their products had higher quality, uniqueness, or purchase frequency, or if there was customer growth.
- Industrial companies set a higher-than-average marketing budget when their customers were more dispersed or the customer growth rate was higher.

Personal selling can also make a strong contribution in consumer-goods marketing. Some consumer marketers use the sales force mainly to collect weekly orders from dealers

figure **19.6**

Cost-Effectiveness of Different Promotional Tools at Different Buyer-Readiness Stages

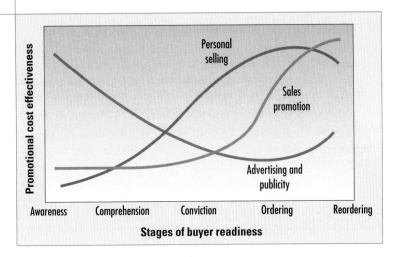

and to see that sufficient stock is on the shelf. Yet an effectively trained consumer company sales force can make four important contributions:

1. *Increased stock position:* Sales reps can persuade dealers to take more stock and devote more shelf space to the company's brand.
2. *Enthusiasm building:* Sales reps can build dealer enthusiasm by dramatizing planned advertising and sales-promotion backup.
3. *Missionary selling:* Sales reps can sign up more dealers.
4. *Key account management:* Sales reps can take responsibility for growing business with the most important accounts.

BUYER-READINESS STAGE   Promotional tools vary in cost-effectiveness at different stages of buyer readiness. Figure 19.6 shows the relative cost effectiveness of four promotional tools. Advertising and publicity play the most important roles in the awareness-building stage. Customer comprehension is primarily affected by advertising and personal selling. Customer conviction is influenced mostly by personal selling. Closing the sale is influenced mostly by personal selling and sales promotion. Reordering is also affected mostly by personal selling and sales promotion, and somewhat by reminder advertising.

PRODUCT LIFE-CYCLE STAGE   Promotional tools also vary in cost-effectiveness at different stages of the product life cycle. In the introduction stage, advertising and publicity have the highest cost-effectiveness, followed by personal selling to gain distribution coverage and sales promotion to induce trial. In the growth stage, demand has its own momentum through word of mouth. In the maturity stage, sales promotion, advertising, and personal selling all grow more important, in that order. In the decline stage, sales promotion continues strong, advertising and publicity are reduced, and salespeople give the product only minimal attention. An intriguing example of a promotion mix used in the introduction stage of the product or service life cycle is the privately held Best Friends Pet Care Company.

Best Friends Pet Care   Best Friends operates 28 pet care centers in 16 states, offering hotel services for dogs and cats, including grooming, day care, exercise, and overnight lodging. When opening a new site, the company takes out cable TV ads and sends direct mail invitations to come in and tour its state-of-the-art facility. At its grand opening in Milford, Connecticut, it brought in Beethoven, the canine movie star, and offered free pictures of him with visitors. The promotion attracted 7,000 visitors! Once on-site, a professionally trained staff used a highly personal selling approach.[44]

measure the communications' results

Senior managers want to know the *outcomes* and *revenues* resulting from their communications investments. Too often, however, their communications directors supply only *outputs* and *expenses:* press clipping counts, numbers of ads placed, media costs. In fairness, the communications directors try to translate outputs into intermediate outputs such as reach and frequency, recall and recognition scores, persuasion changes, and cost-per-thousand calculations. Ultimately, behavior change measures capture the real payoff from communications.

After implementing the promotional plan, the communicator must measure its impact on the target audience. Members of the target audience are asked whether they recognize or recall the message, how many times they saw it, what points they recall, how they felt about the message, and their previous and current attitudes toward the product and company. The communicator should also collect behavioral measures of audience response, such as how many people bought the product, liked it, and talked to others about it.

Figure 19.7 provides an example of good feedback measurement. We find that 80 percent of the consumers in the total market are aware of brand A, 60 percent have tried it, and only 20 percent who have tried it are satisfied. This indicates that the communications program is effective in creating awareness, but the product fails to meet consumer expectations. In contrast, only 40 percent of the consumers in the total market are aware of brand B, and only 30 percent have tried it, but 80 percent of those who have tried it are satisfied. In this case, the communications program needs to be strengthened to take advantage of the brand's power.

managing the integrated marketing communications process

Many companies still rely on one or two communication tools to achieve their communications aims. This practice persists in spite of the fragmenting of mass-markets into a multitude of minimarkets, each requiring its own approach; the proliferation of new types of media; and the growing sophistication of consumers. The wide range of communication tools, messages, and audiences makes it imperative that companies move toward **integrated marketing communications (IMC)**. As defined by the American Association of Advertising Agencies, IMC is a concept of marketing communications planning that recognizes the added value of a comprehensive plan. Such a plan evaluates the strategic roles of a variety of communications disciplines—for example, general advertising, direct response, sales promotion and public relations—and combines these disciplines to provide clarity, consistency, and maximum impact through the seamless integration of discrete messages.

Here are creative examples of integrated marketing communications.

Warner–Lambert   Warner-Lambert wanted to promote its antihistamine Benadryl to allergy sufferers. The company used advertising and public relations to increase brand awareness and promote a toll-free number that provided people with the pollen count in their area. People who called the number more than once received free product samples, coupons, and in-depth materials describing the product's benefits. These people also received a newsletter that includes advice on how to cope with allergy problems.[45]

Beck's Beer   Seeking a cost-effective campaign with which to compete against bigger spenders in the category, Beck's North America launched a $10 million integrated marketing campaign in late 1999. The company used 60 percent of the money to buy TV advertising on ESPN/ABC Sports networks. The remaining 40 percent went to Internet advertising on ESPN.com, radio advertising on ESPN radio, print

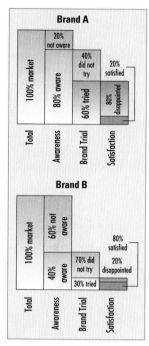

figure **19.7**

Current Consumer States for Two Brands

advertising in *ESPN Magazine*, and sponsorships and promotions at sporting events. The integrated, targeted approach enabled the company to "make an impact before its key audience," 21- to 34-year-old males.[46]

A study of top management and marketing executives in large consumer companies indicated that over 70 percent favored the concept of integrated marketing communications. Several large advertising agencies—Ogilvy & Mather, Young & Rubicam, Saatchi & Saatchi—acquired major agencies specializing in sales promotion, public relations, and direct marketing in order to provide one-stop shopping, but to their disappointment, most clients did not buy their integrated marketing communications package, preferring to put together the specialized agencies themselves.

Why the resistance? Large companies employ several communications specialists to work with their brand managers. Each specialist knows little about the other communication tools. Furthermore, the specialists usually have favorite outside agencies and oppose turning their responsibilities over to one superagency. They argue that the company should choose the best specialist agency for each purpose, not second- and third-rate agencies just because they belong to a superagency. They believe that the ad agency will still put most of the advertiser's money into the advertising budget.

Today, however, a few large agencies have substantially improved their integrated offerings. Many international clients have opted to put a substantial portion of their communications work through one agency. An example is IBM turning all of its advertising over to Ogilvy to attain uniform branding.

Integrated marketing communications does produce stronger message consistency and greater sales impact. It forces management to think about every way the customer comes in contact with the company, how the company communicates its positioning, the relative importance of each vehicle, and timing issues. It gives someone the responsibility—where none existed before—to unify the company's brand images and messages as they come through thousands of company activities. IMC will improve the company's ability to reach the right customers with the right messages at the right time and in the right place.[47] Duke Power, the North Carolina utility, found out how useful IMC can be.

Duke Power   To develop IMC, Duke Power conducted lengthy interviews with company officers, customer surveys, literature reviews, and "best practice" interviews with other companies. Out of this process came four recommendations: (1) that Duke manage its reputation as a corporate asset; (2) that the company develop and implement an integrated communications process to manage all aspects of its communications; (3) that the company train all its employees in how to communicate, because Duke's customers responded more to employees' actions than to specific planned programs; and (4) that the company develop and enhance a strategic database to help it anticipate customer interests and improve customer satisfaction and retention. Based on these recommendations, Duke Power developed integrated communications processes that are directly tied to the company's business processes.[48]

IMC advocates describe it as a way of looking at the whole marketing process instead of focusing on individual parts of it. Companies such as Motorola, Xerox, and Hewlett-Packard are bringing together their advertising, direct marketing, public relations, and employee communications experts into "supercouncils" that meet a few times each year for training and improved communication among them. Procter & Gamble recently revised its communications planning by requiring that each new program be formulated jointly, with its ad agency sitting together with P&G's public relations agencies, direct marketing units, promotion-merchandising firms, and Internet operations.

summary

1. Modern marketing calls for more than developing a good product, pricing it attractively, and making it accessible to target customers. Companies must also communicate with present and potential stakeholders, and with the general public. The marketing communications mix consists of five major modes of communication: advertising, sales promotion, public relations and publicity, personal selling, and direct marketing.

2. The communication process consists of nine elements: sender, receiver, message, media, encoding, decoding, response, feedback, and noise. To get their messages through, marketers must encode their messages in a way that takes into account how the target audience usually decodes messages. They must also transmit the message through efficient media that reach the target audience and develop feedback channels to monitor response to the message.

3. Developing effective communications involves eight steps: (1) Identify the target audience, (2) determine the communications objectives, (3) design the message, (4) select the communication channels, (5) establish the total communications budget, (6) decide on the communications mix, (7) measure the communications' results, and (8) manage the integrated marketing communications process.

4. In identifying the target audience, the marketer needs to close any gap that exists between current public perception and the image sought. Communications objectives may be cognitive, affective, or behavioral—that is, the com-

pany might want to put something into the consumer's mind, change the consumer's attitude, or get the consumer to act. In designing the message, marketers must carefully consider content, structure, format, and source. Communication channels may be personal (advocate, expert, and social channels) or nonpersonal (media, atmospheres, and events). The objective-and-task method of setting the promotion budget, which calls upon marketers to develop their budgets by defining specific objectives, is the most desirable.

5. In deciding on the marketing communications mix, marketers must examine the distinct advantages and costs of each promotional tool and the company's market rank. They must also consider the type of product market in which they are selling, how ready consumers are to make a purchase, and the product's stage in the product life cycle. Measuring the marketing communications mix's effectiveness involves asking members of the target audience whether they recognize or recall the message, how many times they saw it, what points they recall, how they felt about the message, and their previous and current attitudes toward the product and the company.

6. Managing and coordinating the entire communications process calls for integrated marketing communications (IMC): marketing communications planning which recognizes the added value of a comprehensive plan that evaluates the strategic roles of a variety of communications disciplines and combines these disciplines to provide clarity, consistency, and maximum impact through the seamless integration of discrete messages.

applications

marketing debate – what is the biggest obstacle to integrating marketing communications?

Although integrated marketing communications is a frequently espoused goal, truly integrated programs have been hard to come by. Some critics maintain the problem is an organizational one—the agencies have not done a good job of putting together all the different teams and organizations involved with a communications campaign. Others maintain that the biggest problem is the lack of managerial guidelines for evaluating IMC programs. How does a manager know when his or her IMC program is satisfactorily integrated?

Take a position: The biggest obstacle to effective IMC programs is a lack of agency coordination across communication units versus The biggest obstacle to effective IMC programs is a lack of understanding as to how to optimally design and evaluate such programs.

marketing and advertising

1. The magazine ad in Figure 1 promotes UpWords, a game marketed by the manufacturer of the Scrabble word game. Although the game is portrayed in the ad, other elements are more prominent.

   a. Who is the target audience for this advertising message? What image of the game would the advertiser like to create with this ad?

   b. How do selective attention, selective distortion, and selective retention apply to this advertising message?

   c. What communication objectives might the game manufacturer set for this advertising message?

2. Sharp incorporates a clever depiction of its imaging product's key benefit—using color to reach people—to attract attention and communicate with business decision makers in the ad shown in Figure 2.

   a. Analyze this ad in terms of the hierarchy-of-effects model.

   b. How is Sharp using message format to communicate with its target audience?

   c. How does Sharp establish source credibility in this advertisement?

Figure 1

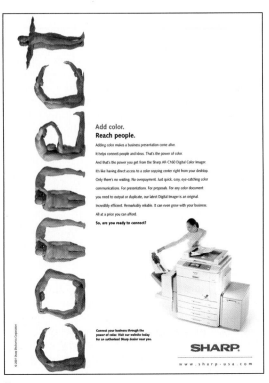

Figure 2

online marketing today

VF, which makes Lee jeans, has used the Internet to create a word-of-mouth tidal wave around its jeans. It started by creating Web sites for Buddy Lee, a kewpie-doll character, and Curry, a fictional race-car driver, and encouraging consumers to discover the sites on their own or e-mail their friends about the sites. Weeks later, VF ran media ads revealing that the characters were part of an elaborate online computer game. To advance to higher levels in the game, players needed to input code numbers found only on Lee jeans—which meant visiting a store and looking at Lee's products. This integrated marketing communications campaign helped push Lee's sales 20 percent higher than in the previous year.[49]

VF continues to operate some of the sites. The Curry site is located at *www.rubberburner.com* and one of the Buddy Lee sites is at *www.buddylee.com.* Explore both sites. Also follow the "Lee Sites" link at the Buddy Lee home page and review one or two of the featured sites. How does Lee encourage consumer participation on these sites? What is the appeal of these sites? What objectives might Lee set for campaigns that rely on word of mouth?

you're the marketer: sonic pda marketing plan

Marketing Plan Pro

Every marketing plan must include a section showing how the company will use marketing communications to connect with customers, prospects, and other stakeholders. Web-based communications must be integrated into the overall communications strategy to ensure consistency of messages.

You are responsible for planning integrated marketing communications for Sonic's introduction of its personal digital assistant (PDA). Review the data, decisions, and strategies you have previously documented in your marketing plan. Now use your knowledge of communications to answer these questions:

■ What audience(s) should Sonic be targeting? What image should it seek to create for its initial PDA product?

■ What objectives are appropriate for Sonic's initial communications campaign?
■ What message design and communication channel(s) are likely to be most effective for the target audience?
■ How should Sonic establish its marketing communications budget?
■ Which promotional tools would be most effective in Sonic's promotional mix? Why?

Be sure that your marketing communications plans will support Sonic's overall marketing efforts. Now, as your instructor directs, summarize your thoughts in a written marketing plan or type them into the Marketing Mix section of the *Marketing Plan Pro* software.

notes

1. The definitions are adapted from Peter D. Bennett, ed., *Dictionary of Marketing Terms* (Chicago: American Marketing Association, 1995).

2. For an alternate communication model developed specifically for advertising communications, see Barbara B. Stern, "A Revised Communication Model for Advertising: Multiple Dimensions of the Source, the Message, and the Recipient," *Journal of Advertising* (June 1994): 5–15. For some additional perspectives, see Tom Duncan and Sandra E. Moriarity, "A Communication-Based Marketing Model for Managing Relationships," *Journal of Marketing* (April 1998): 1–13.

3. Brian Sternthal and C. Samuel Craig, *Consumer Behavior: An Information Processing Perspective* (Upper Saddle River, NJ: Prentice Hall, 1982), pp. 97–102.

4. However, research by Cox and Bauer showed a curvilinear relation between self-confidence and persuasibility, with those moderate in self-confidence being the most persuasible. Donald F. Cox and Raymond A. Bauer, "Self-Confidence and Persuasibility in Women," *Public Opinion Quarterly* (Fall 1964): 453–66; Raymond L. Horton, "Some Relationships between Personality and Consumer Decision-Making," *Journal of Marketing Research* (May 1979): 233–46.

5. John Fiske and John Hartley, *Reading Television* (London: Methuen, 1980), p. 79. For the effects of expertise on persuasion, see also Elizabeth J. Wilson and Daniel L. Sherrell, "Source Effects in Communication and Persuasion Research: A Meta-Analysis of Effect Size," *Journal of the Academy of Marketing Science* (Spring 1993): 101–12.

6. The semantic differential was developed by C. E. Osgood, C. J. Suci, and P. H. Tannenbaum, *The Measurement of Meaning* (Urbana: University of Illinois Press, 1957).

7. John Bigness, "Back to Brand New Life," *Chicago Tribune*, October 4, 1998; Chris Reidy, "Putting on the Dog to be Arnold's Job," *Boston Globe*, August 28, 1998.

8. Michael L. Ray, *Advertising and Communications Management* (Upper Saddle River, NJ: Prentice Hall, 1982).

9. Michael R. Solomon, *Consumer Behavior*, 3rd ed. (Upper Saddle River, NJ: Prentice Hall, 1996), pp. 208–10 for references to research articles on fear appeals.

10. Kevin Goldman, "Advertising: Knock, Knock. Who's There? The Same Old Funny Ad Again," *Wall Street Journal*, November 2, 1993, p. B10. See also Marc G. Weinberger, Harlan Spotts, Leland Campbell, and Amy L. Parsons, "The Use and Effect of Humor in Different Advertising Media," *Journal of Advertising Research* (May–June 1995): 44–55.

11. Susanne Craig, "E*Trade to Cut Marketing Even as Its Losses Narrow," *Wall Street Journal*, April 12, 2001, p. B13; "Bank on It," *Brandweek*, December 11, 2000.

12. Yoav Ganzach and Nili Karashi, "Message Framing and Buying Behavior: A Field Experiment," *Journal of Business Research* (January 1995): 11–17.

13. James F. Engel, Roger D. Blackwell, and Paul W. Minard, *Consumer Behavior*, 8th ed. (Fort Worth, TX: Dryden, 1994).

14. Ayn E. Crowley and Wayne D. Hoyer, "An Integrative Framework for Understanding Two-Sided Persuasion," *Journal of Consumer Research* (March 1994): 561–74.

15. C. I. Hovland, A. A. Lumsdaine, and F. D. Sheffield, *Experiments on Mass Communication*, vol. 3 (Princeton, NJ: Princeton University Press, 1948), ch. 8; Crowley and Hoyer, "An Integrative Framework for Understanding Two-Sided Persuasion." For an alternative viewpoint, see George E. Belch, "The Effects of Message Modality on One- and Two-Sided Advertising Messages," in *Advances in Consumer Research*, ed. Richard P. Bagozzi and Alice M. Tybout (Ann Arbor, MI: Association for Consumer Research, 1983), pp. 21–26.

16. Curtis P. Haugtvedt and Duane T. Wegener, "Message Order Effects in Persuasion: An Attitude Strength Perspective," *Journal of Consumer Research* (June 1994): 205–18; H. Rao Unnava, Robert E. Burnkrant, and Sunil Erevelles, "Effects of Presentation Order and Communication Modality on Recall and Attitude," *Journal of Consumer Research* (December 1994): 481–90.

17. Sternthal and Craig, *Consumer Behavior*, pp. 282–84.

18. Michael McCarthy, "BMW Drives into New Ad World." *USA Today*, June 6, 2001, p. B3.

19. Herbert C. Kelman and Carl I. Hovland, "Reinstatement of the Communication in Delayed Measurement of Opinion Change," *Journal of Abnormal and Social Psychology* 48 (1953): 327–35.

20. David J. Moore, John C. Mowen, and Richard Reardon, "Multiple Sources in Advertising Appeals: When Product Endorsers Are Paid by the Advertising Sponsor," *Journal of the Academy of Marketing Science* (Summer 1994): 234–43.

21. C. E. Osgood and P. H. Tannenbaum, "The Principles of Congruity in the Prediction of Attitude Change," *Psychological Review* 62 (1955): 42–55.

22. Michael Kiely, "Word-of-Mouth Marketing," *Marketing* (September 1993): 6. See also Aric Rindfleisch and Christine Moorman, "The Acquistion and Utilization of Information in New Product Alliances: A Strength-of-Ties Perspective," *Journal of Marketing* (April 2001): 1–18.

23. Robert Spector, *Amazon.com: Get Big Fast* (New York: HarperBusiness, 2000), p. 149.

24. Hilary Stout, "Ad Budget: Zero. Buzz: Deafening." *Wall Street Journal*, December 29, 1999, B.1.

25. Renee Dye, "The Buzz on Buzz," *Harvard Business Review* (November–December 2000): 139–46.

26. Regis McKenna, *The Regis Touch* (Reading, MA: Addison-Wesley, 1985); Regis McKenna, *Relationship Marketing* (Reading, MA: Addison-Wesley, 1991).

27. Michael Cafferky has identified four kinds of people companies try to reach to stimulate word-of-mouth referrals: opinion leaders, marketing mavens, influentials, and product enthusiasts. Opinion leaders are people who are widely respected within defined social groups, such as fashion leaders. They have a large relevant social network, high source credibility, and a high propensity to talk. Marketing mavens are people who spend a lot of time learning the best buys (values) in the marketplace. Influentials are people who are socially and politically active; they try to know what is going on and influence the course of events. Product enthusiasts are people who are known experts in a product category, such as art connoisseurs, audiophiles, and computer wizards. See Cafferky, *Let Your Customers Do the Talking* (Chicago: Dearborn Financial Publishing, 1995), pp. 30–33.

28. Emanuel Rosen, *The Anatomy of Buzz* (New York: Currency, 2000), ch. 12; "Viral Marketing," *Sales & Marketing Automation* (November 1999): 12–14; George Silverman, *The Secrets of Word-of-Mouth Marketing* (New York: Amacom, 2001).

29. Suzanne Vranica, "Volvo Campaign Tests New Media Waters," *Wall Street Journal*, March 16, 2001 p. B5.; Karen Lundegaard. "Volvo's Web-Only Vehicle Launch Ends amid Ford Unit's Questioning of Tactic." *Wall Street Journal*, January 11, 2001, p. B13.

30. Philip Kotler, "Atmospherics as a Marketing Tool," *Journal of Retailing* (Winter 1973–1974): 48–64.

31. Theresa Howard, "Freebies Take on Brash New Form," *USA Today*, May 15, 2001, p. B1; "Sea-Doo's Plan: See It, Do It, Buy It," *Brandweek*, May 3, 1999, p. 12.

32. Everett M. Rogers, *Diffusion of Innovations*, 4th ed. (New York: The Free Press, 1995).

33. Quoted in Daniel Seligman, "How Much for Advertising?" *Fortune*, December 1956, p. 123. For a good discussion of setting promotion budgets, see Michael L. Rothschild, *Advertising* (Lexington, MA: D. C. Heath, 1987), ch. 20.

34. Albert Wesley Frey, *How Many Dollars for Advertising*? (New York: Ronald Press, 1955), p. 65.

35. Ibid., p. 49.

36. Adapted from G. Maxwell Ule, "A Media Plan for 'Sputnik' Cigarettes," *How to Plan Media Strategy* (American Association of Advertising Agencies, 1957 Regional Convention), pp. 41–52.

37. *New York Times*, July 6, 2000.

38. Sidney J. Levy, *Promotional Behavior* (Glenview, IL: Scott, Foresman, 1971), ch. 4.

39. Relatively little research has been done on the effectiveness of B2B advertising. For a survey, see Wesley J. Johnson, "The Importance of Advertising and the Relative Lack of Research," *Journal of Business & Industrial Marketing* 9, no. 2 (1994): 3–4.

40. *How Advertising Works in Today's Marketplace: The Morrill Study* (New York: McGraw-Hill, 1971), p. 4.

41. Cyril Freeman, "How to Evaluate Advertising's Contribution," *Harvard Business Review* (July–August 1962): 137–48.

42. Theodore Levitt, *Industrial Purchasing Behavior: A Study in Communication Effects* (Boston: Division of Research, Harvard Business School, 1965).

43. Gary L. Lilien and John D. C. Little, "The ADVISOR Project: A Study of Industrial Marketing Budgets," *Sloan Management Review* (Spring 1976): 17–31; Gary L. Lilien, "ADVISOR 2: Modeling the Marketing Mix Decision for Industrial Products," *Management Science* (February 1979): 191–204.

44. Danielle McDavitt, "Best Friends Pet Care CEO: Interview," CNBC-Dow Jones Business Video, October 19, 1998.

45. Paul Wang and Lisa Petrison, "Integrated Marketing Communications and Its Potential Effects on Media Planning," *Journal of Media Planning* 6, no. 2 (1991): 11–18.

46. Laurie Freeman, "Smaller Budget, Big Reach: Networks Sold on Integrated Marketing," *Electronic Media*, November 22, 1999, p. 12.

47. Don E. Shultz, Stanley I. Tannenbaum, and Robert F. Lauterborn, *Integrated Marketing Communications: Putting It Together and Making It Work* (Lincolnwood, IL: NTC Business Books, 1992); Ernan Roman, *Integrated Direct Marketing: The Cutting-Edge Strategy for Synchronizing Advertising, Direct Mail, Telemarketing, and Field Sales* (Lincolnwood, IL: NTC Business Books, 1995).

48. Don E. Schultz, "The Next Step in IMC?" *Marketing News*, August 15, 1994, pp. 8–9. Also see Birger Wernerfelt, "Efficient Marketing Communication: Helping the Customer Learn," *Journal of Marketing Research* (May 1996): 239–46.

49. Gerry Khermouch, "Buzz Marketing," *BusinessWeek*, July 30, 2001, pp. 50–56.

managing the sales force

Kotler on Marketing

The successful salesperson cares first for the customer, second for the products.

In this chapter, we will address the following questions:

- What decisions do companies face in designing a sales force?
- How do companies recruit, select, train, supervise, motivate, and evaluate a sales force?
- How can salespeople improve their skills in selling, negotiating, and carrying on relationship marketing?

U.S. firms spend over a trillion dollars annually on sales forces and sales-force materials—more than they spend on any other promotional method. Nearly 12 percent of the total workforce work full time in sales occupations. Sales forces are found in nonprofit as well as for-profit organizations. College recruiters are the university's sales-force arm. Churches use membership committees to attract new members. The U.S. Agricultural Extension Service sends agricultural specialists to sell farmers on new farming methods. Hospitals and museums use fund-raisers to contact donors and solicit donations.

The term **sales representative** *covers a broad range of positions. Robert McMurry distinguished six sales positions, ranging from the least to the most creative types of selling:*[1]

1. Deliverer: *A salesperson whose major task is the delivery of a product (milk, bread, fuel, oil).*

2. Order taker: *A salesperson who acts predominantly as an inside order taker (the salesperson standing behind the counter) or outside order taker (the soap salesperson calling on the supermarket manager).*

3. Missionary: *A salesperson who is not expected or permitted to take an order but whose major task is to build goodwill or to educate the actual or potential user (the medical "detailer" representing an ethical pharmaceutical house).*

4. Technician: *A salesperson with a high level of technical knowledge (the engineering salesperson who is primarily a consultant to the client companies).*

5. Demand creator: *A salesperson who relies on creative methods for selling tangible products (vacuum cleaners, refrigerators, siding, encyclopedias) or intangibles (insurance, advertising services, or education).*

6. Solution vendor: *A salesperson whose expertise is in the solving of a customer's problem, often with a system of the company's products and services (for example, computer and communications systems).*

No one debates the importance of the sales force in the marketing mix. However, companies are sensitive to the high and rising costs (salaries, commissions, bonuses, travel expenses, and benefits) of maintaining a sales force. Because the average cost of a personal sales call ranges from $250 to $500, and closing a sale typically requires four calls, the total cost can range from $1,000 to $2,000. Not surprisingly, companies are seeking to substitute mail- and phone-based selling units to reduce field sales expenses. They also are trying to increase the productivity of the sales force through better selection, training, supervision, motivation, and compensation.

designing the sales force

Sales personnel serve as the company's personal link to the customers. The sales representative is the company to many of its customers. It is the sales rep who brings back much-needed information about the customer. Therefore, the company needs to carefully consider issues in sales force design—namely, the development of sales force objectives, strategy, structure, size, and compensation. (See Figure 21.1.)

sales-force objectives and strategy

The old idea was that the sales force should "sell, sell, and sell." At IBM, salespeople would "push metal" and at Xerox they would "sell boxes." Salespeople had quotas, and the better salespeople met or exceeded their quotas. Later, the idea arose that sales reps should know how to diagnose a customer's problem and propose a solution. Salespeople show a customer-prospect how their company can help the customer improve its profitability. They seek to join their company with the customer's company as "partners for profit."

Companies need to define the specific objectives they want their sales force to achieve. For example, a company might want its sales representatives to spend 80 percent of their time with current customers and 20 percent with prospects, and 85 percent of their time on established products and 15 percent on new products. The specific allocation scheme depends on the kind of products and customers, but regardless of the selling context, salespeople will have one or more of the following specific tasks to perform:

- *Prospecting:* Searching for prospects, or leads.
- *Targeting:* Deciding how to allocate their time among prospects and customers.
- *Communicating:* Communicating information about the company's products and services.
- *Selling:* Approaching, presenting, answering objections, and closing sales.
- *Servicing:* Providing various services to the customers—consulting on problems, rendering technical assistance, arranging financing, expediting delivery.
- *Information gathering:* Conducting market research and doing intelligence work.
- *Allocating:* Deciding which customers will get scarce products during product shortages.

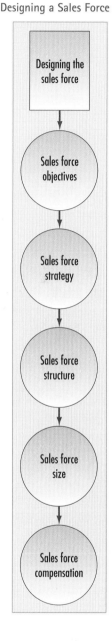

figure **21.1**

Designing a Sales Force

Because of the expense, most companies are moving to the concept of a *leveraged sales force*. A sales force should focus on selling the company's more complex and customized products to large accounts and the company should turn over low-end selling to inside sales people and to Web ordering. Tasks such as lead generation, proposal writing, order fulfillment, and postsale support should be turned over to others. Salespeople should handle fewer accounts, and be rewarded for key account growth. This is far different from expecting salespeople to sell to every possible account, which is usually the weakness of geographically based sales forces.[2]

The sales representative's focus varies with the state of the economy. During product shortages, reps have no problem selling. During periods of product abundance, reps compete vigorously to win customer preference. Companies are increasingly judging their sales reps not only on their sales volume, but also on their ability to create customer satisfaction and profit. Here is an example.

Tiffany & Co. The name *Tiffany* brings to mind expensive jewelry, and this image is cultivated in every aspect of the retailer's marketing. A purchase on the selling floor can be like an investment, so management trains its retail sales staff to be consultants. Because the consumer is not typically an expert, salespeople are trained to offer advice and information about the quality and cut of stones, the suitability of various settings, and the choices available in various price ranges. Even when selling less expensive items, such as a box of stationery or a scarf, the salespeople know that part of the purchase is the experience and prestige of shopping at Tiffany. They also know that a satisfied customer is a potential return customer.

In addition to its retail sales staff, Tiffany has 155 field reps to serve corporate customers. An initial training program for the corporate sales staff lasts for six to eight weeks, and only when new hires have demonstrated mastery of skills, knowledge, and products are they allowed to deal with customers.[3]

Companies must deploy sales forces strategically so that they call on the right customers at the right time and in the right way. Today's sales representatives act as "account managers" who arrange fruitful contact between various people in the buying and selling organizations. Selling increasingly calls for teamwork requiring the support of other personnel, such as top management, especially when national accounts or major sales are at stake; technical people, who supply technical information and service to the customer before, during, or after product purchase; customer service representatives, who provide installation, maintenance, and other services; and an office staff, consisting of sales analysts, order expediters, and secretaries.

DuPont When DuPont heard that corn growers needed a herbicide that could be applied less often, it appointed a team of chemists, sales and marketing executives, and regulatory specialists to solve the problem. They created a product that topped $57 million in sales its first year.[4]

To maintain a market focus, salespeople should know how to analyze sales data, measure market potential, gather market intelligence, and develop marketing strategies and plans. Sales representatives need analytical marketing skills, and these skills become especially important at the higher levels of sales management. Marketers believe that sales forces will be more effective in the long run if they understand marketing as well as selling.

Once the company decides on an approach, it can use either a direct or a contractual sales force. A **direct (company) sales force** consists of full- or part-time paid employees who work exclusively for the company. This sales force includes inside sales personnel who conduct business from the office using the telephone and receive visits from prospective buyers, and field sales personnel who travel and visit customers. A **contractual sales force** consists of manufacturers' reps, sales agents, and brokers, who are paid a commission based on sales.

sales-force structure

The sales-force strategy has implications for the sales-force structure. If the company sells one product line to one end-using industry with customers in many locations, it would use a territorial sales-force structure. If the company sells many products to many types of customers, it might need a product or market sales-force structure. Table 21.1 summarizes

table **21.1**	
Sales-Force Structures	**Territorial**: Each sales representative is assigned an exclusive territory. This sales structure results in a clear definition of responsibilities. It increases the rep's incentive to cultivate local business and personal ties. Travel expenses are relatively low because each rep travels within a small area.
	Territory size: Territories can be designed to provide equal sales potential or equal workload. Territories of *equal potential* provide each rep with the same income opportunities and provide the company with a means to evaluate performance. Territories can also be designed *to equalize the sales workload* so that each rep can cover the territory adequately.
	Territory shape: Territories are formed by combining smaller units, such as counties or states, until they add up to a territory of a given potential or workload. Companies can use computer programs to design territories that optimize such criteria as compactness, equalization of workload or sales potential, and minimal travel time.
	Product: The importance of sales reps' knowing their products, together with the development of product divisions and product management, has led many companies to structure their sales forces along product lines. Product specialization is particularly warranted where the products are technically complex, highly unrelated, or very numerous.
	Market: Companies often specialize their sales forces along industry or customer lines. Separate sales forces can be set up for different industries and even different customers. The advantage of market specialization is that each sales force can become knowledgeable about specific customer needs. The major disadvantage is that customers are scattered throughout the country, requiring extensive travel.
	Complex: When a company sells a wide variety of products to many types of customers over a broad geographical area, it often combines several structures. Reps can be specialized by territory-product, territory-market, product-market, and so on. A sales rep might then report to one or more line and staff managers. Motorola, for example, manages four types of sales forces: (1) a strategic market sales force composed of technical, applications, and quality engineers and service personnel assigned to major accounts; (2) a geographic sales force calling on thousands of customers in different territories; (3) a distributor sales force calling on and coaching Motorola distributors; and (4) an inside sales force doing telemarketing and taking orders via phone and fax.

marketing **insight**

Major Account Management—What It Is and How It Works

Major accounts (also called key accounts, national accounts, global accounts, or house accounts) are typically singled out for special attention. Important customers who have multiple divisions in many locations are offered *major account contracts*, which provide uniform pricing and coordinated service for all customer divisions. A **major account manager (MAM)** supervises field reps calling on customer plants within their territories. Large accounts involving collaborative work are handled by *major account programs* consisting of cross-functional personnel who handle all aspects of the relationship. The company's largest accounts may get a strategic account management team, consisting of cross-functional personnel permanently assigned to one customer, that often maintains offices at the customer's facility. For example, in 1992 Procter & Gamble stationed a strategic account management team to work with Wal-Mart in its Bentonville, Arkansas, headquarters. By 1998, P&G and Wal-Mart had already jointly saved $30 billion through supply chain improvements. Today, the P&G team in Bentonville consists of approximately 100 staffers dedicated to serving Wal-Mart.

If a company has several such accounts, it is likely to organize a major account management division. The average company manages about 75 key accounts. In a typical major account management division, the average MAM handles nine accounts. MAMs typically report to the national sales manager who reports to the vice president of marketing and sales, who in turn reports to the CEO.

Major account management is growing. As buyer concentration increases through mergers and acquisitions, fewer buyers account for a larger share of a company's sales. Many buyers are centralizing their purchases for certain items, which gives them more bargaining power. Sellers in turn need to devote more attention to these major buyers. Still another factor is that as products become more complex, more groups in the buyer's organization become involved in the purchase process. The typical salesperson might not have the skill, authority, or coverage to be effective in selling to the large buyer.

In organizing a major account program, a company faces a number of issues, including how to select major accounts; how to manage them; how to select, manage, and evaluate major account managers; how to organize a structure for major account managers; and where to locate major account management in the organization. In selecting major accounts, companies look for accounts that purchase a high volume (especially of more profitable products), purchase centrally, require a high level of service in several geographic locations, may be price-sensitive, and may want a long-term partnering relationship.

Major account managers have a number of duties: acting as the single point of contact; developing and growing customer business; understanding customer decision processes; identifying added-value opportunities; providing competitive intelligence; negotiating sales; and orchestrating customer service. MAMs are typically evaluated on their effectiveness in growing their share of the account's business and on their achievement of annual profit-and-sales volume goals. Companies often make the mistake of selecting their most productive salespeople as MAMs, but different sets of skills are required for the two jobs. One MAM said, "My position must not be as a salesman, but as a 'marketing consultant' to our customers and a salesman of my company's capabilities as opposed to my company's products."

Major accounts normally receive more favorable pricing based on their purchase volume, but marketers cannot rely exclusively on this incentive to retain customer loyalty. There is always a risk that competitors can match or beat a price or that increased costs may necessitate raising prices. Many major accounts look for added value more than for a price advantage. They appreciate having a single point of dedicated contact; single billing; special warranties; EDI links; priority shipping; early information releases; customized products; and efficient maintenance, repair, and upgraded service. In addition to these practical considerations, there is the value of goodwill. Personal relationships with personnel who value the major account's business and who have a vested interest in the success of that business are compelling reasons for being a loyal customer.

Sources: S. Tubridy, "Major Account Management," in *AMA Management Handbook* (3rd ed.), ed. John J. Hampton (New York: Amacom, 1994), pp. 3-25, 3-27; Sanjit Sengupta, Robert E. Krapfel, and Michael A. Pusateri, "The Strategic Sales Force," *Marketing Management* (Summer 1997): 29–34; Robert S. Duboff and Lori Underhill Sherer, "Customized Customer Loyalty," *Marketing Management* (Summer 1997): 21–27; Tricia Campbell, "Getting Top Executives to Sell," *Sales & Marketing Management* (October 1998): 39. More information can be obtained from NAMA (National Account Management Association), <*www.nasm.com*>; "Promotion Marketer of the Decade: Wal-Mart," *Promo*, December 1, 1999.

the most common sales-force structures, and "Marketing Insight: Major Account Management—What It Is and How It Works" discusses major account management, a specialized form of sales-force structure.

Established companies need to revise their sales-force structure as market and economic conditions change. British Airways is an excellent example.

British Airways   British Airways hired a team of consultants in 2000 to evaluate its sales force. The results of the evaluation revealed that British Airways excelled in business-to-consumer sales, but needed to focus more on B2B sales. The company kept its basic sales structure intact, under which separate sales teams cover leisure sales, field sales, and the top 200 corporate accounts. To improve its business-to-business sales, the company added "key account" managers to "focus on accounts that delivered the most value."[5]

sales-force size

Once the company clarifies its strategy and structure, it is ready to consider sales-force size. Sales representatives are one of the company's most productive and expensive assets. Increasing their number will increase both sales and costs.

Once the company establishes the number of customers it wants to reach, it can use a *workload approach* to establish sales-force size. This method consists of the following five steps:

1. Customers are grouped into size classes according to annual sales volume.
2. Desirable call frequencies (number of calls on an account per year) are established for each class.
3. The number of accounts in each size class is multiplied by the corresponding call frequency to arrive at the total workload for the country, in sales calls per year.
4. The average number of calls a sales representative can make per year is determined.
5. The number of sales representatives needed is determined by dividing the total annual calls required by the average annual calls made by a sales representative.

Suppose the company estimates that there are 1,000 A accounts and 2,000 B accounts in the nation. A accounts require 36 calls a year, and B accounts require 12 calls a year. The company needs a sales force that can make 60,000 sales calls a year. Suppose the average rep can make 1,000 calls a year. The company would need 60 full-time sales representatives.

The Internet has enabled companies to reduce their sales forces without sacrificing relationships with customers.

Bethlehem Steel   Bethlehem Steel had 220 salespeople in 1990, a number it cut in half by 2000. The company was able to reduce the number of salespeople so drastically because it embraced e-commerce early. It set up a proprietary e-commerce site, *www.bethsteel.com*, where customers can view product inventories, view order status, and track orders. Bethlehem Steel also sells its products via MetalSite, a steel trading portal. Customers are pleased with Bethlehem's e-commerce offerings, and the company plans on reducing its sales force even further.[6]

sales-force compensation

To attract top-quality sales reps, the company has to develop an attractive compensation package. Sales reps would like income regularity, extra reward for above-average performance, and fair payment for experience and longevity. Management would like to achieve control, economy, and simplicity. Some management objectives will conflict with sales rep objectives. No wonder compensation plans exhibit a tremendous variety from industry to industry and even within the same industry.

The level and components of an effective compensation plan must bear some relation to the "going market price" for the type of sales job and required abilities. For example, the average earnings of a typical U.S. sales and marketing manager in 1998 was $110,000.[7] If the market price for salespeople is well-defined, the individual firm has little choice but to pay the going rate. However, published data on industry sales-force compensation levels are infrequent and generally lack sufficient detail.

The company must next determine the four components of sales-force compensation—a fixed amount, a variable amount, expense allowances, and benefits. The *fixed amount*, a salary, is intended to satisfy the reps' need for income stability. The *variable amount*, which might be commissions, bonus, or profit sharing, is intended to stimulate and reward greater effort. *Expense allowances* enable sales reps to meet the expenses involved in travel, lodging, dining, and entertaining. Benefits, such as paid vacations, sickness or accident benefits, pensions, and life insurance, are intended to provide security and job satisfaction.

A popular rule favors making about 70 percent of the salesperson's total income fixed and allocating the remaining 30 percent among the other elements. Fixed compensation receives more emphasis in jobs with a high ratio of nonselling to selling duties and in jobs where the selling task is technically complex and involves teamwork. Variable compensation receives more emphasis in jobs where sales are cyclical or depend on individual initiative. Fixed and variable compensation give rise to three basic types of compensation plans—straight salary, straight commission, and combination salary and commission. Only one-fourth of all firms use either a straight-salary or straight-commission method. Three-quarters use a combination of the two, though the relative proportion of salary versus incentives varies widely.[8]

Straight-salary plans provide sales reps with a secure income, make them more willing to perform nonselling activities, and give them less incentive to overstock customers. From the company's perspective, they provide administrative simplicity and lower turnover. Straight-commission plans attract higher performers, provide more motivation, require less supervision, and control selling costs. On the negative side, commission plans overemphasize getting the sale rather than building the relationship. Combination plans feature the benefits of both plans while reducing their disadvantages.

With compensation plans that combine fixed and variable pay, companies may link the variable portion of a salesperson's pay to a wide variety of strategic goals. Some see a new trend toward deemphasizing volume measures in favor of factors such as gross profitability, customer satisfaction, and customer retention. For example, IBM now partly rewards salespeople on the basis of customer satisfaction as measured by customer surveys.[9]

Some companies are basing the rep's reward partly on a sales team's performance or even companywide performance. This should get reps to work more closely together for the common good. Yet some talented reps may resent carrying weaker team members.

managing the sales force

Once the company has established objectives, strategy, structure, size, and compensation, it has to recruit, select, train, supervise, motivate, and evaluate sales representatives. Various policies and procedures guide these decisions (see Figure 21.2).

recruiting and selecting representatives

At the heart of a successful sales force is the selection of effective representatives. One survey revealed that the top 27 percent of the sales force brought in over 52 percent of the sales. Beyond differences in productivity is the great waste in hiring the wrong people. The average annual turnover rate for all industries is almost 20 percent. When a salesperson quits, the costs of finding and training a new person—plus the cost of lost sales—can run as high as $50,000 to $100,000. A sales force with many new people is less productive.[10]

The financial loss due to turnover is only part of the total cost. If a new representative receives $50,000 a year, another $50,000 goes into fringe benefits, expenses, supervision, office space, supplies, and secretarial assistance. Consequently, the new representative needs to produce sales on which the gross margin at least covers the selling expenses of $100,000. If the gross margin is 10 percent, the new salesperson will have to sell at least $1,000,000 for the company to break even.

Selecting sales reps would be simple if one knew what traits to look for. One good starting point is to ask customers what traits they prefer. Most customers say they want

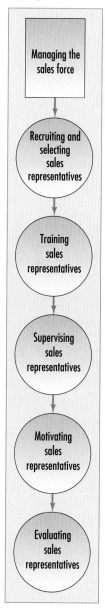

figure 21.2

Managing the Sales Force

Managing the sales force

↓

Recruiting and selecting sales representatives

↓

Training sales representatives

↓

Supervising sales representatives

↓

Motivating sales representatives

↓

Evaluating sales representatives

the rep to be honest, reliable, knowledgeable, and helpful. Another approach is to look for traits common to the most successful salespeople in the company. Here are some findings:

- Charles Garfield, in his study of superachievers, concluded that supersales performers exhibit the following traits: risk taking, powerful sense of mission, problem-solving bent, care for the customer, and careful call planning.[11]
- Robert McMurry wrote: "It is my conviction that the possessor of an effective sales personality is a habitual 'wooer,' an individual who has a compulsive need to win and hold the affection of others."[12] He listed five additional traits: "A high level of energy, abounding self-confidence, a chronic hunger for money, a well-established habit of industry, and a state of mind that regards each objection, resistance, or obstacle as a challenge."[13]
- Mayer and Greenberg offered one of the shortest lists of traits. They concluded that the effective salesperson has two basic qualities: *empathy*, the ability to feel as the customer does; and *ego drive*, a strong personal need to make the sale.[14]

After management develops its selection criteria, it must recruit. The human resources department seeks applicants by various means, including soliciting names from current sales representatives, using employment agencies, placing job ads, and contacting college students. Unfortunately, few students decide to go into selling as a career. Reasons include "Selling is a job and not a profession," and "There is insecurity and too much travel." To counter these objections, company recruiters emphasize starting salaries, income opportunities, and the fact that one-fourth of the presidents of large U.S. corporations started out in marketing and sales.

Selection procedures can vary from a single informal interview to prolonged testing and interviewing, not only of the applicant but of the applicant's spouse.[15] If the spouse is not ready to support the "away-from-home" lifestyle of the salesperson, the hire will not be a good one. Many companies give sales applicants formal tests. Although test scores are only one information element in a set that includes personal characteristics, references, past employment history, and interviewer reactions, they are weighted quite heavily by such companies as IBM, Prudential, Procter & Gamble, and Gillette. Gillette claims that tests have reduced turnover by 42 percent and have correlated well with the subsequent progress of new reps in the sales organization.

training sales representatives

Many companies send their new reps into the field almost immediately, supplied with samples, order books, and a description of the territory. Much of their selling is ineffective. A vice president of a major food company once spent a week watching 50 sales presentations to a busy buyer for a major supermarket chain. Here is what he observed:

> The majority of salesmen were ill prepared, unable to answer basic questions, uncertain as to what they wanted to accomplish during the call. They did not think of the call as a studied professional presentation. They didn't have a real idea of the busy retailer's needs and wants.[16]

Today's customers expect salespeople to have deep product knowledge, to add ideas to improve the customer's operations, and to be efficient and reliable. These demands have required companies to make a much higher investment in sales training.

One of the main problems is that salespeople give in too often when customers demand a discount. One company pinpointed this as a problem when it recognized that its sales revenue had gone up by 25 percent but its profit had remained flat. The company decided to retrain its salespeople to "sell the price," rather than "sell through price." Salespeople were given richer information about each customer's sales history and behavior. They received training to recognize value-adding opportunities rather than price-cutting opportunities. As a result, the company's sales revenue climbed further and so did its margins.[17]

Today, new reps may spend a few weeks to several months in training. The median training period is 28 weeks in industrial-products companies, 12 in service companies, and 4 in consumer-products companies. Training time varies with the complexity of the selling task and the type of person recruited into the sales organization. At IBM, new reps receive extensive initial training and may spend 15 percent of their time each year in additional training. (IBM has now switched 25 percent of the training from classroom to e-learning, saving a great deal of money in the process.)

Sales training programs have several goals:

- Sales representatives need to know and identify with the company.
- Sales representatives need to know the company's products.
- Sales representatives need to know customers' and competitors' characteristics.
- Sales representatives need to know how to make effective sales presentations.
- Sales representatives need to understand field procedures and responsibilities.

New methods of training are continually emerging, such as role playing and sensitivity training; the use of cassette tapes, videotapes, and CD-ROMs; and programmed learning, distance learning, and films on selling.

IBM   IBM uses a self-study system called Info-Window that combines a personal computer and a laser videodisc. A trainee can practice sales calls with an on-screen actor who portrays a buying executive in a particular industry. The actor-buyer responds differently depending on what the trainee says.

Whirlpool   In order to increase its sales reps' understanding of its appliances, Whirlpool rented an eight-bedroom farmhouse near its headquarters in Benton Harbor, Michigan, and outfitted it with Whirlpool dishwashers, microwaves, washers, dryers, and refrigerators. It sent eight new salespeople to live in the house, to cook and do laundry and household chores. When they emerged, they knew a great deal about Whirlpool appliances and gained more confidence than if they had taken the traditional two-week classroom training course.[18]

supervising sales representatives

Companies vary in how closely they supervise sales reps. Reps paid mostly on commission generally receive less supervision. Those who are salaried and must cover definite accounts are likely to receive substantial supervision.

norms for customer calls

The average salesperson makes about four calls a day, down from five in the previous decade. The downward trend is due to the increased use of the phone, fax machines, and e-mail; the increased reliance on automatic ordering systems; and the drop in cold calls owing to better market research information.

How many calls should a company make on a particular account each year? Magee described an experiment where similar accounts were randomly split into three sets.[19] Sales representatives were asked to spend less than five hours a month with accounts in the first set, five to nine hours a month with those in the second set, and more than nine hours a month with those in the third set. The results demonstrated that additional calls produced more sales, leaving only the question of whether the magnitude of the sales increase justified the additional cost. Some later research has suggested that today's sales reps are spending too much time selling to smaller, less profitable accounts when they should be focusing more of their efforts on selling to larger, more profitable accounts.[20]

NORMS FOR PROSPECT CALLS   Companies often specify how much time reps should spend prospecting for new accounts. Spector Freight wants its sales representatives to spend 25 percent of their time prospecting and to stop calling on a prospect after three unsuccessful calls.

Companies set up prospecting standards for a number of reasons. Left to their own devices, many reps will spend most of their time with current customers, who are known quantities. Reps can depend on them for some business, whereas a prospect might never deliver any business. Some companies rely on a missionary sales force to open new accounts.

USING SALES TIME EFFICIENTLY   Studies have shown that the best sales reps are those who manage their time effectively.[21] One effective planning tool is configurator software, a program that automates the order preparation process. DAA Solutions of Hartford, Connecticut, is a producer of an online version of this time-saving product.

DAA Solutions   DAA Solutions Configurator software is intended especially for companies with highly complex engineered products that require drawings. DAA Solutions software links the customer to all the resources of the seller, but the software operates through the sales reps. On a sales call, reps can present product specifications to experts on a customer's staff without having to develop their own technical expertise. The reps can also access pricing information and production schedules, as well as input customization information on behalf of the customer. The configurator software integrates all this information and writes up a virtual order in a matter of minutes. In addition to saving time, the software builds goodwill by reducing errors. DAA Solutions offers all these features using its online configurator software, Design-To-Order, which enables the customer to write an order without necessitating a visit from a sales rep. The sales rep achieves greater efficiency by monitoring the order over the Internet.[22]

Another tool is *time-and-duty analysis*, which helps reps understand how they spend their time and how they might increase their productivity. Sales reps spend time in the following ways:

- *Preparation:* Getting information and planning call strategy.
- *Travel:* In some jobs, travel time amounts to over 50 percent of total time. Travel time can be cut down by using faster means of transportation—but this will increase costs.

DAA Solutions' home page describes its Design-to-Order™ software application.

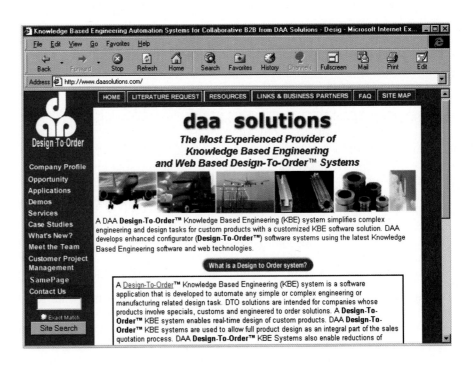

- *Food and breaks:* Some portion of the workday is spent in eating and taking breaks.
- *Waiting:* Time spent in the buyer's outer office, which is dead time unless the representative uses it to plan or to fill out reports.
- *Selling:* Time spent with the buyer in person or on the phone.
- *Administration:* Time spent in report writing and billing, attending sales meetings, and talking to others in the company about production, delivery, billing, sales performance, and other matters.

With so many duties, it is no wonder that actual face-to-face selling time amounts to as little as 29 percent of total working time![23] Companies are constantly seeking ways to improve sales-force productivity. Their methods take the form of training sales representatives in the use of "phone power," simplifying record keeping and administrative time, and using the computer and the Internet to develop call and routing plans and to supply customer and competitive information.

Owens-Corning Owens-Corning recently put its sales force online with FAST—its newly developed Field Automation Sales Team system. FAST gives its salespeople a constant supply of information about the company and the people they are dealing with. Using laptop computers, each salesperson can access three types of programs. First, FAST gives them a set of *generic tools*, everything from word processing to fax and e-mail transmission to creating presentations online. Second, it provides *product information*—tech bulletins, customer specifications, pricing information, and other data that can help close a sale. Finally, it offers up a wealth of *customer information*—buying history, types of products ordered, and preferred payment terms. Salespeople can prime themselves on backgrounds of clients; call up prewritten sales letters; transmit orders and resolve customer service issues on the spot during customer calls; and have samples, pamphlets, brochures, and other materials sent to clients with a few keystrokes.

To reduce time demands on their outside sales force, many companies have increased the size and responsibilities of their inside sales force. In a survey of 135 electronics distributors, Narus and Anderson found that an average of 57 percent of the sales force's members were inside salespeople.[24] As reasons for the growth of the internal sales force, managers cited the escalating cost of outside sales calls and the growing use of computers and innovative telecommunications equipment.

Inside salespeople are of three types. There are *technical support people*, who provide technical information and answers to customers' questions. There are *sales assistants*, who provide clerical backup for the outside salespersons. They call ahead and confirm appointments, carry out credit checks, follow up on deliveries, and answer customers' questions. *Telemarketers* use the phone to find new leads, qualify them, and sell to them. Telemarketers can call up to 50 customers a day compared to the four an outside salesperson can contact. They can cross-sell the company's other products; upgrade orders; introduce new products; open new accounts and reactivate former accounts; give more attention to neglected accounts; and follow up and qualify direct-mail leads.

The inside sales force frees the outside reps to spend more time selling to major accounts, identifying and converting new major prospects, placing electronic ordering systems in customers' facilities, and obtaining more blanket orders and systems contracts. The inside salespeople spend more time checking inventory, following up orders, and phoning smaller accounts. The outside sales reps are paid largely on an incentive-compensation basis, and the inside reps on a salary or salary plus bonus pay.

Another dramatic breakthrough is the new high-tech equipment—desktop and laptop PCs, videocassette recorders, videodiscs, automatic dialers, e-mail, fax machines, and teleconferencing and videophones. The salesperson has truly gone "electronic." Not only is sales and inventory information transferred much faster, but specific computer-based

marketing for the **new economy**

Automation for the Personal Touch

The array of technological resources available to the contemporary sales representative—Web sites, laptop computers, software, printers, modems, fax-copiers, e-mail, cellular phones, and pagers—is giving reps more time for personal interaction with customers. The old paradigm of the sales presentation in which the rep discerns the customer's needs and then offers the product or service that comes closest to meeting them has been replaced by a new model. In **relationship marketing,** a rep sells a long-term partnership in which both parties collaborate on identifying needs and developing, maintaining, and updating products and services customized to fulfill them.

One of the most valuable electronic tools for the sales rep is the company Web site, and one of its most useful applications is as a prospecting tool. Company Web sites can help define the firm's relationships with individual accounts and identify those whose business warrants a personal sales call. The Web site provides an introduction to self-identified potential customers. Depending on the nature of the business, the initial order may even take place online. For more complex transactions, the site provides a way for the buyer to contact the seller. Pall Corporation, a manufacturer of fluid filtration and purification technologies, has all e-mail directed to company headquarters, with leads going directly to the appropriate sales rep.

Not every company has achieved immediate success in using a Web site for sales and sales support. Grainger, an industrial-supply company, had less encouraging results with its initial efforts. Less than 1 percent of its customers registered to open a Web account during its first year in operation, and less than 1 percent of the company's revenue in fiscal 1998 came from Web sales. Still, Grainger anticipated that its Internet customer base would grow, and spent more than $25 million over the next year bringing its full catalog of 220,000 products to the Web. Customers began flocking to Grainger.com, and in 2000 the company's digital businesses contributed

$337 million—or 6 percent—of total sales, growth of 150 percent from the previous year.

Making a Web site an effective selling tool requires experts in both the medium and the content of the site. The site can attract and keep customers only if the information is kept up-to-date and presented in a way that is easily accessible and appealing to visitors, both technically and in terms of communication style. Selling over the Internet supports relationship marketing by solving problems that do not require live intervention and thus allowing more time to be spent on issues that are best addressed face-to-face.

Sources: Charles Waltner, "Pall Corp. Wins Business with Info-Driven Web Site," *Net Marketing* (October 1996); Beth Snyder, "Execs: Traditional Sales Still Key," *Net Marketing* (May 1998); John Evan Frok, "Grainger's Buy-in Plan," *Business Marketing* (November 1998): 1, 48; "Grainger Reports EPS of 51 Cents for the 2000 Fourth Quarter," *Business Wire*, January 30, 2001; "10 Companies That Get It," *Fortune*, November 8, 1999.

Company Web site as a prospecting tool: Pall's site helps customers find solutions and contact the company.

decision support systems on CDs have been created for sales managers and sales representatives. (See "Marketing for the New Economy: Automation for the Personal Touch.")

motivating sales representatives

Some sales representatives will put forth their best effort without any special coaching from management. To them, selling is the most fascinating job in the world; they are ambitious and self-starters. However, the majority require encouragement and special incentives. This is especially true of field selling: Reps usually work alone, their hours are irregular, and they are often away from home. They confront aggressive, competing sales reps; they have an inferior status relative to the buyer; they often do not have the authority to do what is necessary to win an account; and they sometimes lose large orders they have worked hard to obtain.

The problem of motivating sales representatives has been studied by Churchill, Ford, and Walker.[25] Their basic model says that the higher the salesperson's motivation, the greater the effort. Greater effort will lead to greater performance; greater performance will lead to greater rewards; greater rewards will lead to greater satisfaction; and greater satisfaction will reinforce motivation. The model thus implies the following:

- *Sales managers must be able to convince salespeople that they can sell more by working harder or by being trained to work smarter:* But if sales are determined largely by economic conditions or competitive actions, this linkage is undermined.
- *Sales managers must be able to convince salespeople that the rewards for better performance are worth the extra effort:* But if the rewards seem to be set arbitrarily or are too small or of the wrong kind, this linkage is undermined.

The researchers went on to measure the importance of different rewards. The reward with the highest value was pay, followed by promotion, personal growth, and sense of accomplishment. The least-valued rewards were liking and respect, security, and recognition. In other words, salespeople are highly motivated by pay and the chance to get ahead and satisfy their intrinsic needs, and less motivated by compliments and security. However, the researchers also found that the importance of motivators varied with demographic characteristics: Financial rewards were mostly valued by older, longer-tenured people and those who had large families. Higher-order rewards (recognition, liking and respect, sense of accomplishment) were more valued by young salespeople who were unmarried or had small families and usually more formal education.

Motivators also vary across countries. Whereas money is the number-one motivator of 37 percent of U.S. salespeople, only 20 percent of salespeople in Canada feel the same way. Salespeople in Australia and New Zealand were the least motivated by a fat paycheck.[26]

SALES QUOTAS Many companies set annual sales quotas. Quotas can be set on dollar sales, unit volume, margin, selling effort or activity, and product type. Compensation is often tied to degree of quota fulfillment.

Sales quotas are developed from the annual marketing plan. The company first prepares a sales forecast. This forecast becomes the basis for planning production, workforce size, and financial requirements. Management then establishes quotas for regions and territories, which typically add up to more than the sales forecast. Quotas are set higher than the sales forecast to encourage managers and salespeople to perform at their best levels. If they fail to make their quotas, the company nevertheless might reach its sales forecast.

Each area sales manager divides the area's quota among the area's reps. There are three schools of thought on quota setting. The *high-quota school* sets quotas higher than what most sales reps will achieve but that are attainable. Its adherents believe that high quotas spur extra effort. The *modest-quota school* sets quotas that a majority of the sales force can achieve. Its adherents feel that the sales force will accept the quotas as fair, will attain them, and gain confidence. The *variable-quota school* thinks that individual differences among sales reps warrant high quotas for some, modest quotas for others.

One general view is that a salesperson's quota should be at least equal to the person's last year's sales plus some fraction of the difference between territory sales potential and last year's sales. The more the salesperson reacts favorably to pressure, the higher the fraction should be.

Setting sales quotas creates certain problems. If the company underestimates sales potential, and the sales reps easily achieve their quotas, the company has overpaid its reps. If the company overestimates sales potential, the sales people will find it very hard to reach their quotas, and be frustrated or quit.

Another problem: If a sales rep covers 50 products, should he "sell everything in the bag" or should he focus his selling effort on a few of the more important products and not worry about missing quotas on the rest? Should he visit every customer or focus on the more profitable customers? The general wisdom is that profits are maximized by sales reps focusing on the major products and customers.

Reps are not likely to achieve their quotas when the company is launching several new products at the same time. New-product launches demand a sizeable selling effort. Sales reps will have less time for meeting their quotas on the company's established products. The company will need to expand its sales force whenever it is launching major new products.

Some companies are dropping quotas.[27] Quotas drive reps to get as much business as possible—often resulting in the reps ignoring the service side of the business. The company gains short-term results at the cost of long-term customer satisfaction. Companies such as Siebel, Nortel, and AT&T Worldnet prefer to use a larger set of measures for motivating and rewarding sales reps.

Siebel Systems   Siebel, the leading supplier of sales automation software, does not set quotas for its reps. Siebel judges its sales reps using a number of metrics, such as customer satisfaction, repeat business, and profitable revenues. Almost 40 percent of sales reps' incentive compensation is based on their customers' reported satisfaction with service and product. According to Siebel's vice president, Steve Mankoff, "[If reps] close a contract with a customer, continue to follow up with that customer, and make sure that customer is successful, chances are that customer will come back for more." The main point is to set guidelines for sales reps that drive the kind of rep behavior the company wants to see.

Siebel uses its own software to monitor the responsiveness of the sales staff and measure customer satisfaction. Each rep is required to enter into a database all information about a sales call, including conversations with customers and price quotes. The sales call data is compared with sales goals and customer satisfaction, and the rep is evaluated using a scoring system. Bonuses and commissions are scaled according to the score. The company's close scrutiny of the sales process leads to satisfied customers: Over 50 percent of Siebel's revenue comes from repeat business.[28]

SUPPLEMENTARY MOTIVATORS   Companies use additional motivators to stimulate sales-force effort. Periodic *sales meetings* provide a social occasion, a break from routine, a chance to meet and talk with "company brass" and each other, and a chance to air feelings and to identify with a larger group. Sales meetings are an important tool for education, communication, and motivation.

Companies also sponsor *sales contests* to spur the sales force to a special selling effort above what is normally expected. The contest should present a reasonable opportunity for enough salespeople to win. At IBM, about 70 percent of the sales force qualifies for the 100 percent Club. The reward is a holiday trip that includes a recognition dinner and a blue-and-gold pin. The contest period should not be announced in advance. If it is, some salespersons will defer sales and others pad their sales during the period with customer promises to buy that do not materialize after the contest period ends.

Whether a sales contest is focused on selling a specific product or products during a limited time period or is a more general recognition of top revenue earners for the quarter, the reward should be commensurate with the achievement. Reps who are well paid and whose earnings are based in large part on commissions are more likely to be motivated by a trip, a trophy, or merchandise than by a check of equal value. Consider Okidata's program.

Okidata   Okidata Printers of Mt. Laurel, New Jersey, knows that recognition is part of the prize. Merchandise won in a sales contest is a reminder of the rep's success each time the item is used. Its President's Club is another strong incentive. Reps who achieve their annual goal, and their spouses, are rewarded with five-day vacations at world-class tourist destinations. A poll of salespeople taken by *Incentive* magazine suggests that Okidata knows how to motivate its employees. Respondents whose earnings top $100,000 indicate a preference for prizes of group travel with other winners. They value the recognition and companionship of other top sellers.[29]

evaluating sales representatives

We have been describing the *feed-forward* aspects of sales supervision—how management communicates what the sales reps should be doing and motivates them to do it; but good feed-forward requires good *feedback*, which means getting regular information from reps to evaluate performance.

SOURCES OF INFORMATION   The most important source of information about reps is sales reports. Additional information comes through personal observation, customer letters and complaints, customer surveys, and conversations with other sales representatives.

Sales reports are divided between *activity plans* and *write-ups of activity results*. The best example of the former is the salesperson's work plan, which reps submit a week or month in advance. The plan describes intended calls and routing. This report forces sales reps to plan and schedule their activities, informs management of their whereabouts, and provides a basis for comparing their plans and accomplishments. Sales reps can be evaluated on their ability to "plan their work and work their plan."

Many companies require representatives to develop an annual territory marketing plan in which they outline their program for developing new accounts and increasing business from existing accounts. This type of report casts sales reps into the role of market managers and profit centers. Sales managers study these plans, make suggestions, and use them to develop sales quotas. Sales reps write up completed activities on *call reports*. Sales representatives also submit expense reports, new-business reports, lost-business reports, and reports on local business and economic conditions.

These reports provide raw data from which sales managers can extract key indicators of sales performance: (1) average number of sales calls per salesperson per day, (2) average sales call time per contact, (3) average revenue per sales call, (4) average cost per sales call, (5) entertainment cost per sales call, (6) percentage of orders per hundred sales calls, (7) number of new customers per period, (8) number of lost customers per period, and (9) sales-force cost as a percentage of total sales.

FORMAL EVALUATION   The sales force's reports along with other observations supply the raw materials for evaluation. There are several approaches to conducting evaluations. One type of evaluation compares current performance to past performance. An example is shown in Table 21.2

The sales manager can learn many things about a rep from this table. Total sales increased every year (line 3). This does not necessarily mean that the person is doing a better job. The product breakdown shows that he has been able to push the sales of product B further than the sales of product A (lines 1 and 2). According to his quotas for the two products (lines 4 and 5), his success in increasing product B sales could be at the expense of product A sales. According to gross profits (lines 6 and 7), the company earns more selling A than B. The rep might be pushing the higher-volume, lower-margin product at the expense of the more profitable product. Although he increased total sales by $1,100 between 2001 and 2002 (line 3), the gross profits on total sales actually decreased by $580 (line 8).

Sales expense (line 9) shows a steady increase, although total expense as a percentage of total sales seems to be under control (line 10). The upward trend in total dollar expense

table **21.2**

Form for Evaluating
Sales Representative's
Performance

Territory: Midland Sales
Representative: John Smith

	1999	2000	2001	2002
1. Net sales product A	$251,300	$253,200	$270,000	$263,100
2. Net sales product B	423,200	439,200	553,900	561,900
3. Net sales total	674,500	692,400	823,900	825,000
4. Percent of quota product A	95.6	92.0	88.0	84.7
5. Percent of quota product B	120.4	122.3	134.9	130.8
6. Gross profits product A	$50,260	$50,640	$54,000	$52,620
7. Gross profits product B	42,320	43,920	55,390	56,190
8. Gross profits total	92,580	94,560	109,390	108,810
9. Sales expense	$10,200	$11,100	$11,600	$13,200
10. Sales expense to total sales (%)	1.5	1.6	1.4	1.6
11. Number of calls	1,675	1,700	1,680	1,660
12. Cost per call	$6.09	$6.53	$6.90	$7.95
13. Average number of customers	320	24	328	334
14. Number of new customers	13	14	15	20
15. Number of lost customers	8	10	11	14
16. Average sales per customer	$2,108	$2,137	$2,512	$2,470
17. Average gross profit per customer	$289	$292	$334	$326

does not seem to be explained by any increase in the number of calls (line 11), although it might be related to success in acquiring new customers (line 14). There is a possibility that in prospecting for new customers, this rep is neglecting present customers, as indicated by an upward trend in the annual number of lost customers (line 15).

The last two lines show the level and trend in sales and gross profits per customer. These figures become more meaningful when they are compared with overall company averages. If this rep's average gross profit per customer is lower than the company's average, he could be concentrating on the wrong customers or not spending enough time with each customer. A review of annual number of calls (line 11) shows that he might be making fewer annual calls than the average salesperson. If distances in the territory are similar to other territories, this could mean that he is not putting in a full workday, he is poor at sales planning and routing, or he spends too much time with certain accounts.

The rep might be quite effective in producing sales but not rate high with customers. Perhaps he is slightly better than the competitors' salespeople, or his product is better, or he keeps finding new customers to replace others who do not like to deal with him. An increasing number of companies are measuring customer satisfaction not only with their product and customer support service, but also with their salespeople. The customers' opinion of the salesperson, product, and service can be measured by mail questionnaires or telephone calls.

Evaluations can also assess the salesperson's knowledge of the company, products, customers, competitors, territory, and responsibilities. Personality characteristics can be rated, such as general manner, appearance, speech, and temperament. The sales manager can review any problems in motivation or compliance.[30]

The sales manager can also check that the representative knows and observes the law. For example, it is illegal for salespeople to lie to consumers or mislead them about the advantages of buying a product. Under U.S. law, salespeople's statements must match advertising claims. In selling to businesses, salespeople may not offer bribes to purchasing agents or others influencing a sale. They may not obtain or use competitors' technical or trade secrets through bribery or industrial espionage. Finally, salespeople must not disparage competitors or competing products by suggesting things that are not true.[31]

principles of personal selling

Personal selling is an ancient art. It has spawned a large literature and many principles. Effective salespersons have more than instinct; they are trained in methods of analysis and customer management. We will examine three major aspects of personal selling: sales professionalism, negotiation, and relationship marketing.[32] Figure 21.3 shows these aspects in schematic form.

professionalism

Today's companies spend hundreds of millions of dollars each year to train salespeople in the art of selling. Over a million copies of books, cassettes, and videotapes on selling are purchased annually, with such tantalizing titles as *Questions That Make the Sale; Green Light Selling: Your Secret Edge to Winning Sales and Avoiding Dead Ends; You'll Never Get No for an Answer; Secrets of Power Persuasion; What They Don't Teach You in Sales 101; Close! Close! Close! How to Make the Sale; How to Make Money Tomorrow Morning; Samurai Selling;* and *World Class Selling.* One of the most enduring books is Dale Carnegie's *How to Win Friends and Influence People.*

Sales-training approaches try to convert a salesperson from a passive order taker into an active order getter. Order takers operate on the assumption that customers know their own needs, resent attempts to influence them, and prefer courteous and self-effacing salespersons. There are two basic approaches in training salespersons to be order getters, a sales-oriented approach and a customer-oriented approach. The *sales-oriented approach* trains the person in the stereotyped high-pressure techniques used in selling encyclopedias or automobiles. This form of selling assumes that customers are not likely to buy except under pressure, that they are influenced by a slick presentation, and that they will not be sorry after signing the order—or, if they are, that it does not matter.

The *customer-oriented approach* trains salespeople in customer problem solving. The salesperson learns how to listen and question in order to identify customer needs and come up with sound product solutions. Presentation skills are secondary to customer-need analysis skills. This approach assumes that customers have latent needs that constitute opportunities, that they appreciate constructive suggestions, and that they will be loyal to sales reps who have their long-term interests at heart. The problem solver is a much more congruent concept for the salesperson under the marketing concept than the hard seller or order taker.

Two vocal exponents of the customer-oriented approach are Neil Rackham and Sharon Drew Morgen. Neil Rackham has developed a method that he calls *SPIN selling* (Situation, Problem, Implication, Need-Payoff). Gone is the script of the slick salesperson, and in its place is the salesperson who knows how to raise good questions and listen and learn. Neil Rackham trains salespeople to raise four types of questions with the prospect:

1. *Situation questions:* These ask about facts or explore the buyer's present situation. For example, "What system are you using to invoice your customers?"
2. *Problem questions:* These deal with problems, difficulties, and dissatisfactions the buyer is experiencing. For example, "What parts of the system create errors?"
3. *Implication questions:* These ask about the consequences or effects of a buyer's problems, difficulties, or dissatisfactions. For example, "How does this problem affect your people's productivity?"
4. *Need-payoff questions:* These ask about the value or usefulness of a proposed solution. For example, "How much would you save if our company could help reduce the errors by 80 percent?"

figure **21.3**

Managing the Sales Force: Improving Effectiveness

figure **21.4**

Major Steps in Effective
Selling

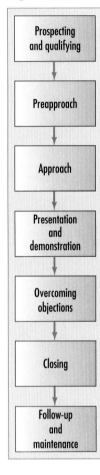

Rackham suggests that companies, especially those selling complex products or services, should have their salesperson move from *preliminaries*, to *investigating* the prospect's problems and needs, to *demonstrating* the supplier's superior capabilities, and then *obtaining* a long-term commitment. This approach reflects the growing interest of many companies in moving from pursuing an immediate sale to developing a long-term customer relationship.[33]

Sharon Drew Morgen takes Rackham's approach a step further with what she calls the Buying Facilitation Method.[34] She holds that the job of a salesperson is to help prospects go through a process to decide first whether their company's performance can be improved, and second whether the seller's offering would provide a solution. Prospects only buy when they realize they have a problem, that they lack resources to solve their problem, and that the seller's offering can add value. The salesperson uses a questioning and listening process to help buyers navigate through their unique decision process. The seller thus becomes a true consultant not only in regard to the seller's product, but in regard to the buyer's need to function more efficiently. The seller willingly terminates the sales call if it is clear that the buyer cannot benefit from the seller's products and services.

No approach works best in all circumstances. Yet most sales-training programs agree on the major steps involved in any effective sales process. These steps are shown in Figure 21.4, and their application to industrial selling is discussed next.[35]

PROSPECTING AND QUALIFYING The first step in selling is to identify and qualify prospects. Historically, most companies have left it to their salespeople to find leads. Now, more companies are taking responsibility for finding and qualifying leads so that the salespeople can use their expensive time doing what they can do best: selling. Companies can generate leads in the following ways:

- Examining data sources (newspapers, directories, CD-ROMs) in search of names. Firms can acquire company and industry information from commercial list vendors such as Dun & Bradstreet, R. L. Polk, and TRW.
- Putting up a booth at trade shows to encourage drop-bys.
- Inviting current customers to suggest the names of prospects.
- Cultivating other referral sources, such as suppliers, dealers, noncompeting sales representatives, bankers, and trade association executives.
- Contacting organizations and associations to which prospects belong.
- Engaging in speaking and writing activities that will draw attention.
- Using the telephone, mail, and the Internet to find leads.
- Dropping in unannounced on various offices (cold canvassing).

Companies can then qualify the leads by contacting them by mail or phone to assess their level of interest and financial capacity. The leads can be categorized as hot prospects, warm prospects, and cool prospects, with the hot prospects turned over to the field sales force and the warm prospects turned over to the telemarketing unit for follow-up. Even then, it usually takes about four calls on a prospect to consummate a business transaction.

Sometimes companies develop original sales prospecting approaches.

John Deere In 1993, the dwindling demand for farm equipment and the aggressive actions of competitors pushed Deere's managers to create a strategy that involved its hourly assembly workers in finding and approaching prospects. Deere sent some of its more experienced and knowledgeable workers to regional trade exhibits across North America to pitch the company's equipment to dealers and farmers. The workers also made unscheduled visits to local farmers to discuss their special problems. Customers perceived these new "reps" as presenting an honest, grassroots view of what goes into making Deere products. Once the new reps had wooed potential customers with their expertise in advanced manufacturing methods and total quality programs, the company could decide how to introduce sales reps to make further presentations or close the sale.[36]

PREAPPROACH   The salesperson needs to learn as much as possible about the prospect company (what it needs, who is involved in the purchase decision) and its buyers (their personal characteristics and buying styles). The salesperson can consult standard sources (Moody's, Standard & Poor's, Dun & Bradstreet), acquaintances, and others to learn about the company. The salesperson should set call objectives: to qualify the prospect, gather information, make an immediate sale. Another task is to decide on the best contact approach, which might be a personal visit, a phone call, or a letter. The best timing should also be considered because many prospects are busy at certain times. Finally, the salesperson should plan an overall sales strategy for the account.

APPROACH   The salesperson should know how to greet the buyer to get the relationship off to a good start. The salesperson might consider wearing clothes similar to what buyers wear (for instance, in California, office clothing is more casual than in Washington, DC); show courtesy and attention to the buyer; and avoid distracting mannerisms, such as staring at the customer. The opening line should be positive; for example, "Mr. Smith, I am Alice Jones from the ABC Company. My company and I appreciate your willingness to see me. I will do my best to make this visit profitable and worthwhile for you and your company." This opening line might be followed by key questions and active listening to understand the buyer's needs. (For new approaches being used to reach doctors, see "Marketing Insight: Drug Salespeople Rely on New Technology to Reach Doctors.")

PRESENTATION AND DEMONSTRATION   The salesperson now tells the product "story" to the buyer, following the AIDA formula of gaining *attention*, holding *interest*, arousing *desire*, and obtaining *action*. The salesperson uses a *features, advantages, benefits*, and *value* approach (FABV). Features describe physical characteristics of a market offering, such as chip processing speeds or memory capacity. Advantages describe why the features provide an advantage to the customer. Benefits describe the economic, technical, service, and social benefits delivered by the offering. Value describes the summative worth (often in monetary terms) of the offering. Too often, salespeople spend too much time dwelling on product features (a product orientation) and not enough stressing the offering's benefits and value (a customer orientation).

Companies have developed three different styles of sales presentation. The oldest is the *canned approach*, which is a memorized sales talk. It is based on stimulus-response thinking; that is, the buyer is passive and can be moved to purchase by the use of the right stimulus words, pictures, terms, and actions. The *formulated approach* is also based on stimulus-response thinking but first identifies the buyer's needs and buying style and then uses a formulated approach to this type of buyer. The *need-satisfaction approach* starts with a search for the customer's real needs by encouraging the customer to do most of the talking. The salesperson takes on the role of a knowledgeable business consultant hoping to help the customer save money or make more money.

Sales presentations can be improved with demonstration aids such as booklets, flip charts, slides, movies, audio- and videocassettes, product samples, and computer-based simulations. Visual aids can show how a product performs and provide other information about it. Booklets and brochures remain useful as "leave behinds" for customer reference. For group presentations, Powerpoint and similar software have replaced the flip chart. These programs enable reps to project professionally prepared visuals on a screen or download them to the laptops of audience members. Johnson & Johnson's Advanced Sterilization Products division uses a visual aid that includes a small video player with five headsets, all easily transported in a briefcase-sized package. Computer animation shows the viewer the inner workings of the Sternad Sterilization System, providing more information in a more engaging way than could be done by displaying the actual machinery—even if the system were portable.[37]

marketing **insight**

Drug Salespeople Rely on New Technology to Reach Doctors

Over 63,000 U.S. sales reps "detail" doctors every day, hoping to get five minutes of a busy doctor's time. Some 40 percent of the calls do not even result in the doctor being available. As a result, pharmaceutical companies are employing new technologies to reach doctors. Among them:

- EPocrates sends brief product information to the handheld devices now used by 130,000 doctors who can e-mail to request more detailed product information.

- RxCentric, an online marketing solutions company, provides doctors with online services that include interactive learning programs like Continuing Medical Education, market research, and promotion presentations. Through these programs, pharmaceutical companies can more effectively detail doctors and gather research information. Doctors can participate whenever they have access to the Internet, 24 hours a day, 7 days a week, not just when a sales rep is available.

- IPhysicianNet has installed free computers, high-speed phone lines, and videoconferencing equipment in the offices of 7,000 high-prescribing doctors in exchange for each doctor agreeing to participate in one video-detailing session per month where nine drug firms will

present their latest products. These drug firms bear the cost of the equipment and videocast time. Doctors can request a video call at a time that is convenient. Video callcenters are typically open 12 hours a day Monday through Friday. A live office visit costs nearly twice as much as a video session, and pilot trials have increased new prescriptions by 14 percent over office visits.

Source: "Rebirth of a Salesman," *The Economist,* April 14, 2001.

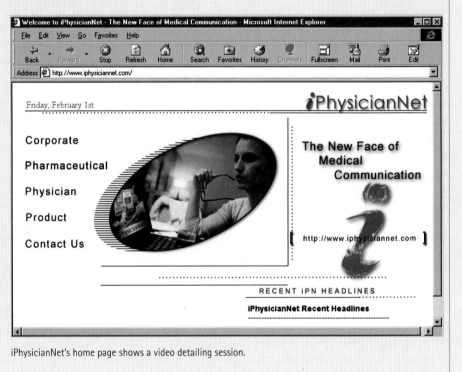

iPhysicianNet's home page shows a video detailing session.

OVERCOMING OBJECTIONS   Customers typically pose objections during the presentation or when asked for the order. *Psychological resistance* includes resistance to interference, preference for established supply sources or brands, apathy, reluctance to giving up something, unpleasant associations created by the sales rep, predetermined ideas, dislike of making decisions, and neurotic attitude toward money. *Logical resistance* might consist of objections to the price, delivery schedule, or certain product or company characteristics. To handle these objections, the salesperson maintains a positive approach, asks the buyer to clarify the objection, questions the buyer in a way that the buyer has to answer his or her own objection, denies the validity of the objection, or turns the objection into a reason for buying. Handling and overcoming objections is a part of the broader skills of negotiation.

CLOSING   Now the salesperson attempts to close the sale. Some salespeople do not get to this stage or do not do it well. They lack confidence or feel uncomfortable about asking for the order or do not recognize the right psychological moment. Salespersons need to know how to recognize closing signs from the buyer, including physical actions, statements or comments, and questions. There are several closing techniques. They can ask for the order, recapitulate the points of agreement, offer to help the secretary write up the order, ask whether the buyer wants A or B, get the buyer to make minor choices such as the color or size, or indicate what the buyer will lose if the order is not placed now. The salesperson might offer the buyer specific inducements to close, such as a special price, an extra quantity, or a token gift.

FOLLOW-UP AND MAINTENANCE Follow-up and maintenance are necessary if the salesperson wants to ensure customer satisfaction and repeat business. Immediately after closing, the salesperson should cement any necessary details on delivery time, purchase terms, and other matters that are important to the customer. The salesperson should schedule a follow-up call when the initial order is received to make sure there is proper installation, instruction, and servicing. This visit or call will detect any problems, assure the buyer of the salesperson's interest, and reduce any cognitive dissonance that might have arisen. The salesperson should also develop a maintenance and growth plan for the account.

negotiation

Much B2B selling involves negotiating skills. The two parties need to reach agreement on the price and the other terms of sale. Salespersons need to win the order without making concessions that will hurt profitability.

Marketing is concerned with exchange activities and the manner in which the terms of exchange are established. In *routinized exchange*, the terms are established by administered programs of pricing and distribution. In *negotiated exchange*, price and other terms are set via bargaining behavior, in which two or more parties negotiate long-term binding agreements. Although price is the most frequently negotiated issue, other issues include contract completion time; quality of goods and services offered; purchase volume; responsibility for financing, risk taking, promotion, and title; and product safety.

Marketers who find themselves in bargaining situations need certain traits and skills to be effective. The most important are preparation and planning skill, knowledge of subject matter being negotiated, ability to think clearly and rapidly under pressure and uncertainty, ability to express thoughts verbally, listening skill, judgment and general intelligence, integrity, ability to persuade others, and patience.[38]

WHEN TO NEGOTIATE Dobler has listed the following circumstances where negotiation is an appropriate procedure for concluding a sale:

1. When many factors bear not only on price, but also on quality and service.
2. When business risks cannot be accurately predetermined.
3. When a long period of time is required to produce the items purchased.
4. When production is interrupted frequently because of numerous change orders.[39]

Negotiation is appropriate whenever a *zone of agreement* exists,[40] when there are simultaneously overlapping acceptable outcomes for the parties. This concept is illustrated in Figure 21.5. Suppose two parties are negotiating a price. The seller has a *reservation prices, s,* which is the minimum he will accept. Any final-contract value, x, that is below s is worse than not reaching an agreement at all. For any $x > s$, the seller receives a surplus. Obviously, the seller desires as large a surplus as possible while maintaining good relations with the buyer. Likewise, the buyer has a reservation price, b, that is the maximum he will pay; any x above b is worse than no agreement. For any $x < b$, the buyer receives a surplus. If the seller's reservation price is below the buyer's— that is, $s < b$—then a zone of agreement exists, and the final price will be determined through bargaining.

There is an obvious advantage in knowing the other party's reservation price and in making one's own reservation price seem higher (for a seller) or lower (for a buyer) than

<table>
<tr><td>

figure **21.5**

The Zone of Agreement

</td><td>

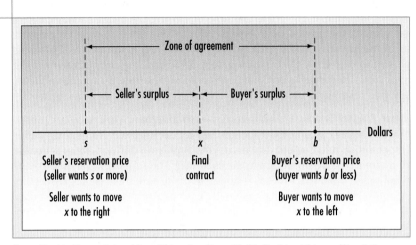

</td></tr>
</table>

Source: Reprinted by permission of the publishers from Howard Raiffa, *The Art and Science of Negotiation,* (Cambridge, MA: The Belknap Press of Harvard University Press, copyright 1982 by the President and Fellows of Harvard College).

it really is. The openness with which buyers and sellers reveal their reservation prices depends on the bargainers' personalities, the negotiation circumstances, and expectations about future relations.

FORMULATING A NEGOTIATION STRATEGY   Negotiation involves preparing a strategic plan before meeting the other party and making good tactical decisions during the negotiation sessions. A **negotiation strategy** is a commitment to an overall approach that has a good chance of achieving the negotiator's objectives.

Some negotiators pursue a "hard" strategy with opponents, whereas others maintain that a "soft" strategy yields more favorable results. Fisher and Ury propose another strategy, that of "principled negotiation," described in "Marketing Memo: The Principled-Negotiation Approach to Bargaining."

Marketing
MEMO

The Principled-Negotiation Approach to Bargaining

In a research program known as the Harvard Negotiation Project, Roger Fisher and William Ury arrived at four points for conducting principled negotiations:

1. *Separate the people from the problem:* Each party must understand the other side's viewpoint and the level of emotion with which they hold it, but the focus should be on the parties' interests rather than their differences. Active listening to opposing arguments and addressing the problem in response improve the chance of reaching a satisfactory conclusion.
2. *Focus on interests, not positions:* The distinction between positions and interests is similar to that between solutions and desired outcome or means and end. By focusing on interests rather than positions, the negotiators are more likely to find a mutually agreeable means of achieving common interests.
3. *Invent options for mutual gain:* Search for a larger pie rather than arguing over the size of each side's slice. Looking for options that offer mutual gain helps identify shared interests.
4. *Insist on objective criteria:* Insist that the agreement reflect fair objective criteria independent of either side's position. This approach avoids a situation in which one side must yield to the position of the other. Instead, both sides are yielding to a fair solution based on criteria they both accept.

Source: Adapted from Roger Fisher and William Ury, *Getting to Yes: Negotiating Agreement without Giving In,* rev. ed. (Boston: Houghton Mifflin, 1992), p. 57.

Negotiators use a variety of tactics when bargaining. Bargaining tactics are maneuvers made at specific points in the bargaining process. Several classic bargaining tactics are listed in Table 21.3. Fisher and Ury have offered tactical advice that is consistent with their strategy of principled negotiation. If the other party is more powerful, the best tactic is to know one's BATNA—Best Alternative to a Negotiated Agreement. By identifying the alternatives if a settlement is not reached, the company sets a standard against which any offer can be measured. Knowing its BATNA protects the company from being pressured into accepting unfavorable terms from a more powerful opponent.

		table **21.3**
Acting Crazy	Put on a good show by visibly demonstrating your emotional commitment to your position. This increases your credibility and may give the opponent a justification to settle on your terms.	Classic Bargaining Tactics
Big Pot	Leave yourself a lot of room to negotiate. Make high demands at the beginning. After making concessions, you will still end up with a larger payoff than if you started too low.	
Get a Prestigious Ally	The ally can be a person or a project that is prestigious. You try to get the opponent to accept less because the person/object he or she will be involved with is prestigious.	
The Well Is Dry	Take a stand and tell the opponent you have no more concessions to make.	
Limited Authority	You negotiate in good faith with the opponent, and when you are ready to sign the deal, you say, "I have to check with my boss."	
Whipsaw/Auction	You let several competitors know you are negotiating with them at the same time. Schedule competitors' appointments with you for the same time and keep them all waiting to see you.	
Divide and Conquer	If you are negotiating with the opponent's team, sell one member of the team on your proposals. That person will help you sell the other members of the team.	
Get Lost/Stall for Time	Leave the negotiation completely for a while. Come back when things are getting better and try to renegotiate then. Time period can be long (say you are going out of town) or short (go to the bathroom to think).	
Wet Noodle	Give no emotional or verbal response to the opponent. Do not respond to his or her force or pressure. Sit there like a wet noodle and keep a "poker face."	
Be Patient	If you can afford to outwait the opponent, you will probably win big.	
Let's Split the Difference	The person who first suggests this has the least to lose.	
Trial Balloon	You release your possible/contemplated decision through a so-called reliable source before the decision is actually made. This enables you to test reactions to your decision.	
Surprises	Keep the opponent off balance by a drastic, dramatic, sudden shift in your tactics. Never be predictable—keep the opponent from anticipating your moves.	

Another set of bargaining tactics are responses intended to deceive, distort, or otherwise influence the bargaining. What tactic should be used when the other side uses a take-it-or-leave-it tactic or seats the other party on the side of the table with the sun in his eyes? A negotiator should recognize the tactic, raise the issue explicitly, and question the tactic's legitimacy and desirability—in other words, negotiate over it. If negotiating fails, the company should resort to its BATNA and terminate the negotiation until the other side ceases to employ these tactics. Meeting such tactics with defending principles is more productive than counterattacking with tricky tactics.

relationship marketing

The principles of personal selling and negotiation thus far described are transaction-oriented because their purpose is to close a specific sale, but in many cases the company is not seeking an immediate sale, but rather to build a long-term supplier–customer relationship. The company wants to demonstrate that it has the capabilities to serve the account's needs in a superior way. Today's customers are large and often global. They prefer suppliers who can sell and deliver a coordinated set of products and services to many locations; who can quickly solve problems that arise in different locations; and who can work closely with customer teams to improve products and processes. Salespeople working with key customers must do more than call when they think customers might be ready to place orders. They should call or visit at other times, take customers to dinner, and make useful suggestions about their business. They should monitor key accounts, know their problems, and be ready to serve them in a number of ways.

When a relationship management program is properly implemented, the organization will begin to focus as much on managing its customers as on managing its products. At the same time, companies should realize that while there is a strong and warranted move toward relationship marketing, it is not effective in all situations. Ultimately, companies must judge which segments and which specific customers will respond profitably to relationship management. (For some guidelines, see "Marketing Memo: When—and How—to Use Relationship Marketing.")

Marketing
MEMO

When—and How—to Use Relationship Marketing

Barbara Jackson argues that relationship marketing is not effective in all situations but is extremely effective in the right situations. She sees transaction marketing as more appropriate with customers who have a short time horizon and low switching costs, such as buyers of commodities. Relationship marketing pays off handsomely with customers who have long time horizons and high switching costs, such as buyers of office automation systems. The customer for a major system carefully researches competing suppliers and chooses one from whom it can expect good long-term service and state-of-the-art technology. Both the customer and the supplier invest a lot of money and time in the relationship.

Anderson and Narus believe that transaction versus relationship marketing is not so much an issue of the type of industry as of the particular customer's wishes. Some customers value a high service bundle and will stay with that supplier for a long time. Other customers want to cut their costs and will switch suppliers for lower costs. In this case, the company can still retain the customer by agreeing to reduce the price, provided the customer is willing to accept fewer services. This customer would be treated on a transaction basis rather than on a relationship-building basis.

Sources: Barbara Bund Jackson, *Winning and Keeping Industrial Customers: The Dynamics of Customer Relationships* (Lexington, MA: D. C. Heath, 1985); James C. Anderson and James A. Narus, "Partnering as a Focused Market Strategy," *California Management Review,* (Spring 1991): 95–113.

summary

1. Sales personnel serve as a company's link to its customers. The sales rep is the company to many of its customers, and it is the rep who brings back to the company much-needed information about the customer.

2. Designing the sales force requires decisions regarding objectives, strategy, structure, size, and compensation. Objectives may include prospecting, targeting, communicating, selling, servicing, information gathering, and allocating. Determining strategy requires choosing the mix of selling approaches that is most effective. Choosing the sales-force structure entails dividing territories by geography, product, or market (or some combination of these). Estimating how large the sales force needs to be involves estimating the total workload and how many sales hours (and hence salespeople) will be needed. Compensating the sales force entails determining what types of salaries, commissions, bonuses, expense accounts, and benefits to give, and how much weight customer satisfaction should have in determining total compensation.

3. There are five steps involved in managing the sales force: (1) recruiting and selecting sales representatives; (2) training the representatives in sales techniques and in the company's products, policies, and customer-satisfaction orientation; (3) supervising the sales force and helping reps to use their time efficiently; (4) motivating the sales force, and balancing quotas, monetary rewards, and supplementary motivators; (5) evaluating individual and group sales performance.

4. Effective salespeople are trained in the methods of analysis and customer management, as well as the art of sales professionalism. No approach works best in all circumstances, but most trainers agree that selling is a seven-step process: prospecting and qualifying customers, preapproach, approach, presentation and demonstration, overcoming objections, closing, and follow-up and maintenance.

5. Another aspect of selling is negotiation, the art of arriving at transaction terms that satisfy both parties. A third aspect is relationship marketing, which focuses on developing long-term, mutually beneficial relationships between two parties.

applications

marketing debate – are great salespeople born that way?

One difference of opinion with respect to sales concerns the potential impact of training versus selection in developing an effective sales force. Some observers maintain that the best salespeople are "born" that way and are effective due to their personalities and all the interpersonal skills they have developed over their lifetimes. Others disagree and contend that application of leading-edge sales techniques can make virtually anyone a sales star.

Take a position: The key to developing an effective sales force is selection versus The key to developing an effective sales force is training.

marketing and advertising

1. Saab uses ads such as the one in Figure 1, which appeared in a national business magazine, to bring prospects into its dealers' showrooms. Note that Sweden-based Saab, owned by General Motors, is promoting GM's OnStar navigation system as a standard feature in this convertible.

   a. What kind of training do you think Saab's dealers' sales reps need to successfully sell to consumers?

   b. How can Saab dealers qualify prospects for this convertible?

   c. Why are good follow-up and maintenance skills important for dealers' sales reps?

2. The Anthro direct-response ad shown in Figure 2 is geared toward businesses that need office furniture for their employees. The headline refers to follow-up calls placed by Anthro reps to check on customer satisfaction, and the fine print invites business buyers to call to discuss needs or request a product catalog.

   a. Which of the six types of sales representatives are prospects likely to speak with when they call Anthro's toll-free phone number?

   b. Which of the specific sales tasks is this sales rep likely to perform?

   c. Why would Anthro's advertising put so much emphasis on its follow-up call policy?

Figure 1

Figure 2

online marketing today

As noted earlier in this chapter, Siebel Systems uses its own sales-management software to monitor its sales reps' activities, manage the sales process, and assess customer satisfaction. In the past, Siebel worked with 20 resellers who sold the company's software, as well as with 760 other "Siebel Partners" who provide support in the form of installation, customization, upgrading, and other services. Now, however, the company has eliminated indirect sales in favor of its direct sales force. "When we analyzed customer feedback from the reseller channel, the results were not living up to the standards that we expected," explains Siebel's vice president and general manager for alliances. "The customers were effectively telling us that they would rather have Siebel involved in the sale." Partners still

have an opportunity to build sales and profits because customers spend at least $7 in implementation, training, hardware, and other items for every $1 spent on Siebel software.[41]

Go to Siebel's Web site (*www.siebel.com*) and review the products, events, and customized views available on the home page. Then follow the link to information for sales professionals (or, if this is unavailable, locate the information about Siebel's sales management software). What benefits does Siebel highlight for its sales management offerings? Why are these benefits important for business customers? How do both Siebel and its prospects gain from the company's online product demonstrations? From attendance at the company's product seminars?

you're the marketer: sonic pda marketing plan

Marketing Plan Pro

Many marketers have to consider sales-force management in their marketing plans. However, because of the high cost of maintaining a direct sales force, some companies are substituting online, mail, and telephone sales for some of their personal sales calls.

In your marketing role at Sonic, you are planning a sales strategy for the company's new personal digital assistant (PDA). After reviewing the data you previously gathered and the deci-

sions you made about other marketing-mix activities, answer these questions about Sonic's use of personal selling:

- Does Sonic need a direct sales force or can it sell through agents and other outside representatives?
- Toward whom should Sonic's sales activities be geared? How can the company's sales activities support the rest of the marketing plan and the goals that have been set?
- What kinds of sales objectives should Sonic set for its sales personnel?

- What kind of training will sales representatives need to sell the new Sonic PDA?

Once you have answered these questions and looked at how your sales management ideas will work with Sonic's goals and objectives, either summarize your programs in a written marketing plan or type them into the Marketing Mix, Marketing Organization, and Sales Forecast sections of the *Marketing Plan Pro* software.

notes

1. Adapted from Robert N. McMurry, "The Mystique of Super-Salesmanship," *Harvard Business Review* (March–April 1961): 114. Also see William C. Moncrief III, "Selling Activity and Sales Position Taxonomies for Industrial Salesforces," *Journal of Marketing Research* (August 1986): 261–70.

2. Lawrence G. Friedman and Timothy R. Furey, *The Channel Advantage: Going to Marketing with Multiple Sales Channels* (Oxford, UK: Butterworth-Heinemann, 1999).

3. Sarah Lorge, "A Priceless Brand," *Sales & Marketing Management* (October 1998): 102–10.

4. Christopher Power, "Smart Selling: How Companies Are Winning Over Today's Tougher Customer," *BusinessWeek*, August 3, 1992, pp. 46–48.

5. "BA Shake-up 'Not Due to New Scheme'," *Travel Trade Gazette UK & Ireland*, May 7, 2001.

6. Philip B. Clark and Sean Callahan, "Sales Staffs: Adapt or Die," *B to B*, April 10, 2000.

7. For estimates of sales reps' salaries, see *Sales & Marketing Management* (October 1998): 98.

8. Luis R. Gomez-Mejia, David B. Balkin, and Robert L. Cardy, *Managing Human Resources* (Upper Saddle River, NJ: Prentice Hall, 1995), pp. 416–18.

9. "What Salespeople Are Paid," *Sales & Marketing Management* (February 1995): 30–31; Power, "Smart Selling," pp. 46–48; William Keenan Jr., ed., *The Sales & Marketing Management Guide to Sales Compensation Planning: Commissions, Bonuses & Beyond* (Chicago: Probus Publishing, 1994).

10. George H. Lucas Jr., A. Parasuraman, Robert A. Davis, and Ben M. Enis, "An Empirical Study of Sales Force Turnover," *Journal of Marketing* (July 1987): 34–59.

11. Charles Garfield, *Peak Performers: The New Heroes of American Business* (New York: Avon Books, 1986); "What Makes a Supersalesperson?" *Sales & Marketing Management* (August 1984): 86; "What Makes a Top Performer?" *Sales & Marketing Management* (May 1989): Timothy J. Trow, "The Secret of a Good Hire: Profiling," *Sales & Marketing Management* (May 1990): 44–55.

12. McMurry, "The Mystique of Super-Salesmanship," p. 117.

13. Ibid., p. 118.

14. David Mayer and Herbert M. Greenberg, "What Makes a Good Salesman?" *Harvard Business Review* (July–August 1964): 119–25.

15. James M. Comer and Alan J. Dubinsky, *Managing the Successful Sales Force* (Lexington, MA: Lexington Books, 1985), pp. 5–25.

16. From an address given by Donald R. Keough at the 27th Annual Conference of the Super-Market Institute, Chicago, April 26–29, 1964. Also see Judy Siguaw, Gene Brown, and Robert Widing II, "The Influence of the Market Orientation of the Firm on Sales Force Behavior and Attitudes," *Journal of Marketing Research* (February 1994): 106–16.

17. Joel E. Urbany, "Justifying Profitable Pricing," Working Paper Series, Marketing Science Institute, Report No. 00-117, 2000, pp. 17–18.

18. "Welcome to the Real Whirled: How Whirlpool Training Forced Salespeople to Live with the Brand," *Sales & Marketing Management* (February 2001): 87–88.

19. John F. Magee, "Determining the Optimum Allocation of Expenditures for Promotional Effort with Operations Research Methods," in *The Frontiers of Marketing Thought and Science*, ed. Frank M. Bass (Chicago: American Marketing Association, 1958), pp. 140–56.

20. Michael R. W. Bommer, Brian F. O'Neil, and Beheruz N. Sethna, "A Methodology for Optimizing Selling Time of Salespersons," *Journal of Marketing Theory and Practice* (Spring 1994): 61–75. See also, Lissan Joseph, "On the Optimality of Delegating Pricing Authority to the Sales Force," *Journal of Marketing* 65 (January 2001): 62–70.

21. Thomas Blackshear and Richard E. Plank, "The Impact of Adaptive Selling on Sales Effectiveness within the Pharmaceutical Industry," *Journal of Marketing Theory and Practice* (Summer 1994): 106–25.

22. Paul Mann, "Success Mode," *Manufacturing Systems* (September 2000).

23. Dartnell Corporation, 30th Sales Force Compensation Survey. Other breakdowns show that 12.7 percent is spent in service calls, 16 percent in administrative tasks, 25.1 percent in telephone selling, and 17.4 percent in waiting/traveling.

24. James A. Narus and James C. Anderson, "Industrial Distributor Selling: The Roles of Outside and Inside Sales," *Industrial Marketing Management* 15 (1986): 55–62.

25. Gilbert A. Churchill Jr., Neil M. Ford, and Orville C. Walker Jr., *Sales Force Management: Planning, Implementation and Control*, 4th ed. (Homewood, IL: Irwin, 1993). Also see Jhinuk Chowdhury, "The Motivational Impact of Sales Quotas on Effort," *Journal of Marketing Research* (February 1993): 28–41; Murali K. Mantrala, Prabhakant Sinha, and Andris A. Zoltners, "Structuring a Multiproduct Sales Quota-Bonus Plan for a Heterogeneous Sales Force: A Practical Model-Based Approach," *Marketing Science* 13, no. 2 (1994): 121–44; Wujin Chu, Eitan Gerstner, and James D. Hess, "Costs and Benefits of Hard-Sell," *Journal of Marketing Research* (February 1995): 97–102; Manfred Krafft, "In Empirical Investigation of the Antecedents of Sales Force Control Systems," *Journal of Marketing* 63 (July 1999): 120–34.

26. "What Motivates U.S. Salespeople?" *American Salesman*, (February 1994): 25, 30.

27. Eilene Zimmerman, "Quota Busters," *Sales & Marketing Management* (January 2001): pp. 59–63.

28. Melanie Warner, "Confessions of a Control Freak," *Fortune*, September 4, 2000, p. 30; Peter Burrows, "The Era of Efficiency," *BusinessWeek*, June 18, 2001, p. 92.

29. Kenneth Heim and Vincent Alonzo, "This Is What We Want!" *Incentive* (October 1998): 40–49.

30. Philip M. Posdakoff and Scott B. MacKenzie, "Organizational Citizenship Behaviors and Sales Unit Effectiveness," *Journal of Marketing Research* (August 1994): 351–63. See also, Andrea L. Dixon, Rosann L. Spiro and Magbul Jamil, "Successful and Unsuccessful Sales Calls: Measuring Salesperson Attributions and Behavioral Intentions," *Journal of Marketing* 65 (July 2001): 64–78. Willem Verbeke and Richard P. Bagozzi, "Sales Call Anxiety: Exploring What It Means When Fear Rules a Sales Encounter," *Journal of Marketing* 64 (July 2000): 88–101.

31. For further reading, see Dorothy Cohen, *Legal Issues in Marketing Decision Making* (Cincinnati, OH: South-Western, 1995).

32. For an excellent summary of the skills needed today by sales representatives and sales managers, see Rolph Anderson and Bert Rosenbloom, "The World Class Sales Manager: Adapting to Global Megatrends," *Journal of Global Marketing* 5, no. 4 (1992): 11–22.

33. Neil Rackham, *SPIN Selling* (New York: McGraw-Hill, 1988). Also see his *The SPIN Selling Fieldbook* (New York: McGraw-Hill, 1996); and his latest book, co-authored with John De Vincentis, *Rethinking the Sales Force* (New York: McGraw-Hill, 1996).

34. Sharon Drew Morgen, *Selling With Integrity: Reinventing Sales Through Collaboration, Respect, and Serving* (New York: Berkeley Books, 1999).

35. Some of the following discussion is based on W. J. E. Crissy, William H. Cunningham, and Isabella C. M. Cunningham, *Selling: The Personal Force in Marketing* (New York: John Wiley, 1977), pp. 119–29.

36. Norton Paley, "Cultivating Customers," *Sales & Marketing Management* (September 1994): 31–32.

37. "Notebook: Briefcase Full of Views: Johnson and Johnson Uses Virtual Reality to Give Prospects an Inside Look at Its Products," *Marketing Tools* (April 1997).

38. For additional reading, see Howard Raiffa, *The Art and Science of Negotiation* (Cambridge, MA: Harvard University Press, 1982); Max H. Bazerman and Margaret A. Neale, *Negotiating Rationally* (New York: The Free Press, 1992); James C. Freund, *Smart Negotiating* (New York: Simon & Schuster, 1992); Frank L. Acuff, *How to Negotiate Anything with Anyone Anywhere Around the World* (New York: American Management Association, 1993); Jehoshua Eliashberg, Gary L. Lilien, and Nam Kim, "Searching for Generalizations in Business Marketing Negotiations," *Marketing Science* 14, no. 3 (pt. 1) (1995): G47–G60.

39. Donald W. Dobler, *Purchasing and Materials Management*, 5th ed. (New York: McGraw-Hill, 1990).

40. This discussion of zone of agreement is fully developed in Raiffa, *Art and Science of Negotiation*.

41. "Siebel Systems Cuts Sales Agents' Network," *Sunday Business*, October 30, 2001, <*www.sundaybusiness.co.uk*>.